Louise H.

1076

A

19. Mon – 2:30 a. IV   Sc 3
        4:00   IV   "   142

Chapel
20. Tue,   2:30   III   Sc 1 epg 41
          3:15   III   Sc 1 beg 41
          3:15   III   " 2 & 3

Chapel
21 Wed   7:06   IV   Sc 5.

22. Thur, 2:30   II   Sc 3
                   I   Sc 1

26 mon   2:30   act I

Roots of Chaucer's language.

Med ment — spiritual & abstract
Ren.   "   — sensuous & concrete

Med - tends to communism
Ren   "   " individualism

age of faith gives way to reason

Age of Chaucer
1. **Politically** — trend to national consciousness
2. Church corrupt — spred to whole social body
3. Intellectual ferment — lit & art breaking
   away from conventional & going to nature
      Gower
      Wycliffe
      Chaucer

This is a time of transition
Age of Chaucer was beginning of Age of Ren.
Old faith & knowledge, proving unsound — role of
practices, religious inst, proving inadequate
Chaucer's time - represents awakening of
intellectual practices. Cha. sums up life
of all middle ages in his work. Also
represents spirit of doubt & curiosity
which Med looked upon institutions. Chau
questioned quite freely.

Chaucer as a man

Many sided —

Personally - a man of the world & affairs,
very practical, All his life attached to
court & govt positions. Knew how to
handle people - & had moral limitations
of a man of that type.

Had enormous intellectual curiosity
Had extraordinary amt. of knowledge.
Knew Latin & Greek pretty well.
His knowledge of antiquity & had great love
for that knowledge.

Wrote under influence of great books of Middle Ages

Work under 3 periods

How he þ queynt was mayden marie
Ans lat his lone floure ans fruitifie

Al þogh his lyfe be queynt þe resemblaunce
Of him hath in me so fressh lyfflynesse
Þat to putte othir men in remembraunce
Of his psone I haue heere his lyknesse
Do make to þis ende in soothfastnesse
Þat þei þt haue of him lest þought & mynde
By þis peynture may ageyn him fynde

The ymages þt in þe chirche been
Maken folk þenke on god & on his seyntes
Whan þe ymages þei biholden & seen
Were oft vnsyre of hem cansith restreyntes
Of þoughtes gode whan a þing depeynt is
Or entailed if men take of it heede
Thoght of þe liknesse it wil in hym brede

Yit conne holden oppynyon and sey
Þat none ymages schuld ymaked be
Þei erren foule & goon out of þe wey
Of trouth haue þei scant sensibilite
Passe ovir þt now blessid trinite
Vpon my maistres soule mercy haue
ffor him lady eke þi mercy I craue

More othir þing wolde I fayne speke & touche
Heere in þis booke but such is my dulnesse
ffor al voyde and empty is my pouche
Þat al my lust is queynt wt heuynesse
Ans heuy spirit comaundeth stilnesse

SELECTIONS FROM
CHAUCER

EDITED BY

WILLIAM ALLAN NEILSON, Ph.D., LL.D.

PRESIDENT OF SMITH COLLEGE, FORMERLY PROFESSOR
OF ENGLISH IN HARVARD UNIVERSITY

AND

HOWARD ROLLIN PATCH, Ph.D.

ASSOCIATE PROFESSOR OF ENGLISH IN SMITH COLLEGE

NEW YORK
HARCOURT, BRACE AND COMPANY

TO G. L. K.

IN GRATITUDE AND AFFECTION

PREFACE

In the making of this book the editors have had in mind both the general reader and the student. The texts have been selected to represent, as fully as a volume of selections may, the many sides of Chaucer's genius and the variety of his poetic forms. The introduction is meant to supply the necessary background of information, and deals with the character of the Medieval period in general and of fourteenth century England in particular, the biography of the poet, the dates and sources of his poems, and his quality as an artist. A concise grammar of Middle English, a guide to pronunciation, and a glossary afford the foundation for a thorough grasp of the language.

Skeat's text, which has been taken as a basis, has been collated with the reprints of the Chaucer Society, and a number of principles applied, which, it is hoped, will simplify the task of the student by a greater degree of normalization without any loss of authenticity. Important changes from Skeat's readings, unless supported by manuscript authority, are recorded in the Variant Readings.

It has been possible to include the large variety of Chaucer's works here presented only by resorting to the omission of certain passages. The editors are well aware of the loss from the point of view of the scholar which is involved in a cutting of the text, however skillfully performed. For the exhaustive study of the poet, the present volume will, of course, not suffice. The problem which the editors faced was the quite different one of selecting as much of Chaucer's work as might be read in a single college course, and of making such a course as rich as possible. To print in full the poems chosen would have meant the inclusion of a smaller number of poems, and they were already painfully conscious of how much of high value had to be omitted in any case. Condensation, then, seemed the lesser evil. As often as possible the passages omitted were those of least interest; but the clarity and continuity of the plot were regarded first in determining what must be retained.

It must be added most emphatically, however, that the editors do not feel that by this method of reducing the text it is in any sense "improved." In the *Troilus*, for example, the loss of the charming scene in the garden (Book II) with Antigone's song of love, and again that of the dialogue with Cassandra (Book V), are losses for which any gain in compactness is no ultimate compensation. No doubt, too, there is a loss in proportion in the poems, especially in the *Hous of Fame*, where Book I is greatly cut down. Eventually every one will want to read all the poems in the full form as they have come down to us. But for facilitating instruction in the ordinary college course, where some abridgment has always been necessary, as well as for making a book of convenient size, what has seemed to count most in the Chaucerian tradition has been gathered together, and it is hoped that even in their present form the poems may be enjoyed for themselves.

For the choice of contents and the treatment of the text, the editors are jointly responsible, as they are for all errors of fact and judgment. But by far the larger share of the labor in the preparation of the volume has fallen to Dr. Patch, to whom thus belongs whatever credit the book may earn. Professor K. S. Woodward has read the proof of the text and the introduction, and Mrs. Helen K. Patch has rendered valuable and laborious service in the preparation of the glossary. To both of these ladies the editors wish to express their warm gratitude.

W. A. NEILSON.

Northampton, June, 1921.

TABLE OF CONTENTS

THE INTRODUCTION

I. CHAUCER'S LIFE AND TIMES

1. THE BACKGROUND

Chaucer lived in the latter part of the period called the Middle Ages, a term which is variously applied, but which may be safely used to cover all the centuries of Christian culture that preceded the Renaissance. In England the full development of the Renaissance does not appear until after 1500; but long before that various signs of its coming were perceptible. Indeed during the late fourteenth century, in the active expression of discontent among the lower classes, which were eager to have their part of the increasing luxuries, in the spreading corruption among the representatives of the Church, in the elaboration of costume regardless of utility or logic, we may find evidences of that disintegration of Medieval manners and morals which marked the closing of the period. In order to comprehend intelligently the traditions which formed the poet's *milieu* it is necessary to attempt some characterization of the Middle Ages as a whole.

This is no easy task; for, in the first place, the decades of the period mark changes, and the centuries have each a distinct individuality of their own, so that a failure to discriminate between different stages in the growth of the epoch is responsible for much misunderstanding of what constituted its life. We cannot bundle together as equally characteristic of Medievalism the ignorance prevalent in the early centuries, the early struggle against barbaric invasions, and the rich artistic fruition of the thirteenth century or the achievements in philosophy and letters. Furthermore, modern prejudice against tradition has led to the assumption that all features of the past which have not endured have necessarily been outworn and may therefore be disre-

garded. The morbid endeavor to glean scandals from accounts of the monasteries and to ignore the virtues, the appreciation of Medieval art purely for its decorative value
apart from its purpose, such modes of approach have not
served the honest desire to understand the Medieval point
of view. It is necessary to lay aside some of our modern
intolerance and dogmatism in order to give due fairness to a
study of what was a quite different period from the one in
which we live. Remembering, then, the difficulty of trying
to summarize all the centuries, a difficulty which is only
partially met by dealing with the thought rather than with
the events, and attempting to view the facts with candor, we
may take up the chief phases of Medieval life according to the
way in which the interests group themselves conveniently,—
those which are predominantly artistic, religious, or social.

Under the heading of ARTISTIC PRODUCTION it is not too
arbitrary to include literature. Like all of the other expres-
sions of the artistic instinct, the literature of that time shows
in general a passion for enlightening mankind which fills it
with a lofty idealism, but which sometimes leads to a sacrifice
of proportion or a too great schematism. The long treatises
on sin, the complicated allegories, the moral poems, illustrate
faults of this kind; and, again, the lyrics which hymn the
various motifs of love are a notable exception to the rule.
On the other hand, there is a great body of Medieval literature intended primarily for entertainment. To such a class
belong the romances of Troy, Thebes, and Rome, and those
of Charlemagne and of Arthur, where the artistic technique is
almost accidental because of the lack of self-consciousness in
the composition. Here the morality is implicit in the structure, where sometimes pagan and Christian ethics collide.
The Medieval artist was more concerned with what he was
doing than with how it was done. It is typical that in the
thirteenth century men were interested in the philosophy of
the Classics, while Renaissance figures like Petrarch cared
more about their literary form. The early painters were
occupied with the sincere delineation of scriptural subjects;
but as the Renaissance draws near, the emphasis on beauty is

more and more apparent. Although there is a lack of technical experience in the early Siennese and Florentine paintings, the Blessed Virgin in some of these works is vastly more acceptable as the mother of Christ than in some of the more realistic representations of later times.

But however much art was busied with its idealism, there was not a complete sacrifice of beauty; rather it was subordinated to convey the spiritual meaning. Possibly the greatest example of this tendency is to be found in that noblest embodiment of all things Medieval, Gothic architecture. Other forms of art, like manuscript illumination, decorated bindings, and the like, may have to give way before some of the modern accomplishments in corresponding fields; the glass of the cathedrals stands perhaps unique in loveliness. But surely the splendor and the dedication of Gothic architecture is unrivaled by anything that later ages have seen produced by their own draftsmen; and here the spiritual yearning, the exaltation, the prayer, of the Middle Ages is carried in the upward sweep of the lines in a structure majestic with beauty and fervent with truth. Even the lack of completion of some of the buildings, the chapels still to be added and the towers yet unraised, expresses the spirit of incompleteness characteristic of the thought, the striving toward infinity compared with the Greek calm and finish.

Medieval art still commends itself to our appreciation; and more or less successful imitations of its works constantly have their vogue. In some respects the PHILOSOPHY of the times is likely to be harder for us to understand. We think of the man of that period as dogmatic and intolerant, as closing his mind to any conception of the changes and varieties that life presents. But however arrogant his position may seem to us, however unintellectual his views, he was fundamentally humble and logically consistent. Man, he thought, was too limited in experience and power, and too open to prejudice and self-deception, to construct in his own life-time a religion on which he could safely depend. Even if he was gifted with righteousness, he was also tainted with weakness rendering him susceptible of evil; and if he were forced to rely on his own observations and principles he might too easily see the universe simply as he wanted to find it. Unaided science could never leave earth; Virgil, the intelligence, cannot guide Dante beyond Purgatory. Therefore it was reasonable to suppose that a definite revelation would come to mankind which would give man the truth sufficient for his spiritual development. Such a revelation must come in a form that would allow no doubt; for otherwise the need of a life-long test of its claims would introduce all the difficulties found in a life without revelation. The united western Church testified that such a revelation had been made, and that its priests were consecrated to the interpretation of its doctrines. When it was tried this revealed religion worked well: it accounted for man's life and gave it significance; it served to control it; and it gave a seemingly valid expression to man's instinctive need for religious experience.

The organized body to which this revelation had been entrusted was necessarily dogmatic in the pronouncements of its truth. In the face of divine authority doubt had no value whatsoever; a heretic was simply an eccentric, and error must not be tolerated. Intellectual stagnation was by no means a concomitant of such a view; for one could build on the basis afforded by the knowledge of the universal scheme, and apply the truth to individual instances. Philosophy, therefore, was chiefly deductive; and science in the modern sense, although its Medieval successes have been often underrated, did not advance very far. The physical inconveniences resulting, like bad roads, poor medical attention, and danger of various kinds, did not seem very important, because life after death was so much more important than the prolongation of life. Medieval philosophy has often been judged by its poorest examples; but its best form, that of scholasticism, gave the world the philosophy of Aristotle applied to Christianity and furnished thereby a more fundamentally humanistic basis for life than is to be found in any of the Renaissance appreciation of the Classics. According to modern opinion, perhaps, the great thirteenth century philosophers like Albertus Magnus and Thomas Aquinas

were not intellectually free inasmuch as they submitted to
ecclesiastical dogma. The man of the Middle Ages would
have answered that the dogma was a mere statement of the
truth; in the words of Boethius (at the beginning of this era):

"For if thou rememberest of what country thou art, it is not governed
as Athens was wont to be, by the multitude, but 'one is its ruler, one its
king,' who desires to have abundance of citizens, and not to have them
driven away. To be governed by whose authority, and to be subject to
her laws, is the greatest freedom that can be." [1]

"But the minds of men must needs be more free when they conserve
themselves in the contemplation of God, and less when they come to
their bodies, and yet less when they are bound with earthly fetters. But
their greatest bondage is when, giving themselves to vices, they lose
possession of their own reason." [2]

Doubt is slavery, and the truth shall make men free. Granting, then, the physical disabilities of the time, and granting
even moral lapses—since the people whom the Middle Ages
originally discovered and educated were pagans at a pretty
low stage of moral enlightenment—it must be recognized
that the religious fervor of the thirteenth century, which inspired the artistic, philosophic, and social life, would be a
glory to any age.

The Church played a most intimate part in the SOCIAL
LIFE of the people, because, in the first place, it was politically
independent of, and sometimes superior to, the state, and,
secondly, because it made its influence felt in the every day
matters of personal activity. The Crusades gave a legitimate
opportunity for the expression of the combative and ambi-
tious instincts in men; the monasteries opened the way for the
fulfillment of the desire for mystical retirement from the
world; the guilds, which were dedicated to their tasks under
the names of patron saints, bound the workmen together in
mutual support and responsibility in a way that called forth
the most conscientious work from each laborer; and the local

[1] Boethius, the Loeb Classical Library, London, 1918, the *Consolation
of Philosophy*, translated by H. F. Stewart and E. K. Rand, p. 159.

[2] *Ibid.*, p. 371.

churches, by their various feast-days and daily ceremonies, kept religious ideals strongly before the minds of the people not merely on Sunday but on all the days of the week. Too much has been made in recent times of the religious and social oppression of the average man. It is true that the lack of printing hampered education; but education was furnished as thoroughly as possible under the circumstances, and the germ of democratic ideals may be seen at least as far back as the Magna Charta. Although the feudal system prevented any realization of the principle of equal opportunity, it served to check inordinate ambitions on the part of the serf to leap into the nobility in a day, and it put the responsibility for government and social power in the hands of people trained for generations to its necessities. At its worst this feature meant the giving of power to decadent families with all the attendant evils; at its best it meant the preservation of the noblest standards in art as well as society.

The educational principle of the Middle Ages was that which to-day underlies and animates the Liberal Arts. In certain aspects it was doubtless impractical, but no more so than the culture of any period. Apart from literature and philosophy and some rudimentary science, the Bible formed the staple of popular knowledge, and its text was widely known in various forms, from scriptural paraphrases in the vernacular and dramatic renderings to the Vulgate itself. Women were often educated, as a line of celebrated ladies from the nun Hrosvitha to the militant Christine de Pisan will testify; an essentially Medieval contribution is the adoration of womanhood in the *dolce stil nuovo* of Italy, the *service des dames* of France, and the cult of the Virgin, which together established the tenets of chivalry towards women.

To the institutions of the Middle Ages the world of to-day owes much. Chivalry contributed much as a civilizing force in ways that are not to be confused with the superficial rites with which it is so often identified. The discipline of the humanistic philosophy, which may prove to be a safeguard against some of the dangers of the modern world, the sincere religious mysticism, which we associate particularly with St. Francis of Assisi, and the use of art to contribute not merely to man's sensuous experience but to his spiritual welfare, are opportunities that are still open to modern life. In the Renaissance, features like these were abandoned only temporarily if at all. Philosophy, having traveled far with deductive logic, naturally turned to inductive research as an alternative, and began to test what had been previously taken as assumptions; the result was, in some quarters a rigorous readjustment in others a greater faith in the assumptions than in the tests applied and the further assumptions that their use involved, and in general people were, perhaps, less confident and more certain. Science gained enormously, and its practical achievements drew the attention and ultimately the respect of the world. Luxuries were afforded thereby which brought ardent support to its undertakings. Through the Middle Ages the commoner may be detected more and more asserting his personality and demanding a recognition of his powers, until finally *Piers Plowman* celebrates his virtue and he serves as a balance to the nobility and a corrective to the priesthood. The influence of the Church was gradually diminished because its representatives gave themselves up to the increasing corruptions of the times which the growth of luxury and the unmoral art induced. The world was occupied with material interests like explorations, inventions, added wealth and comfort. If its spiritual guide failed now it was because men, who had free-will, chose the obvious and abundant delights. But the testimony of the older scheme remained, and its morality at least was called upon when the inevitable reaction came in the period known as the Reformation. And if to-day we can bring ourselves to take counsel with tradition, it is to be hoped that we may look back with candid minds to some of the characteristics of the past, to the discipline, the moral responsibility, and—that finer breath of religion—mysticism, which flourished during the Middle Ages, and that we may find an application of them for our own times. Anything that contributes to a proper understanding of the day when these cardinal virtues flourished seems to have its *raison d'être;* and to such a purpose this volume may well be dedicated.

2. ENGLAND IN THE FOURTEENTH CENTURY

Even with the loss of Scotland at the outset, the political situation of England in the fourteenth century promised to be strong. As part of the Hundred Years' War, Edward III, who laid claim to the crown of France, carried on successful invasions marked by the Battles of Creçy (1346) and Poitiers (1356); and at the Peace of Brétigny (1360), although he gave up his claim to the crown, he was ceded a vast expanse of territory including the Duchy of Aquitaine and a large portion of the country south of the Loire. After his death (1377), however, his successor, Richard II, was more seriously occupied with domestic difficulties in England and failed to retain the inherited power abroad. These difficulties included the results of the bubonic plague which in 1348–49 had devastated English homes, and had left few laborers to satisfy the needs of the country. Because of the losses incurred in various ways during the plagues, the lords of the manors desired to secure labor at its lowest terms; the laborers, on the other hand, being reduced in number, could command higher wages than ever before. The Statute of Laborers of 1351, intended to fix the rates according to the conditions known before the plague, failed to relieve the tension. Revolts of the lower classes were led by John Ball, a socialist who wanted to abolish rank and property, and by Wat Tyler and Jack Straw. Conspiracy of a mild type weakened the power of Richard, who might have had the assistance of his uncle John of Gaunt but for intrigue and misunderstanding. Two long truces (1390–95) kept France from interfering for part of the time, and a peace which lasted twenty-five years was concluded in 1396, when Richard took as his second wife, Isabella, the daughter of Charles VI. But although Richard succeeded in keeping the country out of war for a while, England's possessions in France were diminished to merely Calais and a small strip of

the attempt to overturn the older scheme of life and to
itute a strongly individualistic philosophy. One mani-
tion of this change is to be found in the growing sympa-
the lower classes. Chaucer, it will be seen, introduces
ddle classes to literature because by the latter part of
tury they were inescapable. In the past they had
in hardly more than the *fabliau* or the *exemplum*.
y shows not merely a desire to correct the religious
the times, but to establish what was really a totally
conception of the Church. The clamor of the
risings could not be stilled by temporary measures,
y of anarchy was intermingled. And yet the
ple in general do not appear to have abandoned
yalties. In this respect Chaucer seems to be
ve: he goes as far as the Lollards in religious
t this quality is characteristic of Dante as well)
that he says can be construed as heretical;
om the lower classes take part in the *Caunterbury*
ere is no apparent desire to ignore differences in
. On the whole, Chaucer and the fourteenth
still Medieval.

3. Chaucer's Life

the known facts with regard to Chaucer's career
ient is that his good fortune furnished him with
ent which was supremely well suited to develop
ir kind of genius. He described the life and
all ranks of society, and he was able to do it so
artly because he had the opportunity of knowing
ell. He himself sprang from the middle classes.
ather, Robert, was a collector of the customs on
father, John, was a vintner who early won a posi-
ttendant to the king. Like many another family
s was gradually making its way upward. He was
ut 1340, and by 1357 he was in the service of the
Elizabeth, wife of Lionel Duke of Clarence, as the
ld Accounts show, referring to an expenditure for his

territory along the coast. His rule had been somewh
arbitrary, the turmoil in England was too much for him,
after his abdication, it was left to Henry IV (1399) to
back the lost foreign power.

From the close contact with France during this perio
also from direct negotiations with the continent came s
the changes in social life that appear at this time.
Anne of Bohemia, Richard's first wife, came to Lond
brought startling fashions which immediately p
society. These were ornaments of dress of a kind
familiar on the continent which prepare the way
superfluous puffs and ruffs of the Renaissance.
Boccaccio and Petrarch were evincing an interes
and Latin, not so much for the learning as for th
ment and artistic enjoyment to be derived; and
scripts came into English hands. The culture
universities was spreading abroad. On the oth
England from 1349 on, the education of childre
became more general, superseding the French th
prevalent hitherto; and under Richard, with
independence of the control of French culture,
the English vernacular began markedly to flo
French romances were, many of them, transla
sturdy English idiom appears in works like t
Piers Plowman. As another manifestation of
came the assertion of the middle-class conscious
protestantism of Lollardry.

Wycliffe and the Lollards launched their atta
the Church like the revolt of the peasants against
They denied the authority of the Pope, declare
Scriptures were a complete revelation in themse
set up their own dogmas in place of the old. Wyc
lished his own translation of the Bible, and spread
the country a group of lay preachers to dissemi
views. For a time he was supported by John of Gau
however, did little more than afford him protecti
could not follow him in his subversive opinions.

In many aspects of the period one can detect, as w

territory along the coast. His rule had been somewh at arbitrary, the turmoil in England was too much for him, and after his abdication, it was left to Henry IV (1399) to win back the lost foreign power.

From the close contact with France during this period and also from direct negotiations with the continent came some of the changes in social life that appear at this time. When Anne of Bohemia, Richard's first wife, came to London, she brought startling fashions which immediately pervaded society. These were ornaments of dress of a kind already familiar on the continent which prepare the way for the superfluous puffs and ruffs of the Renaissance. In Italy Boccaccio and Petrarch were evincing an interest in Greek and Latin, not so much for the learning as for the entertainment and artistic enjoyment to be derived; and their manuscripts came into English hands. The culture from new universities was spreading abroad. On the other hand, in England from 1349 on, the education of children in English became more general, superseding the French that had been prevalent hitherto; and under Richard, with the English independence of the control of French culture, literature in the English vernacular began markedly to flourish. The French romances were, many of them, translated, and a sturdy English idiom appears in works like the allegory *Piers Plowman*. As another manifestation of English life came the assertion of the middle-class consciousness in the protestantism of Lollardry.

Wycliffe and the Lollards launched their attack against the Church like the revolt of the peasants against their lords. They denied the authority of the Pope, declared that the Scriptures were a complete revelation in themselves, and set up their own dogmas in place of the old. Wycliffe published his own translation of the Bible, and spread through the country a group of lay preachers to disseminate his views. For a time he was supported by John of Gaunt, who, however, did little more than afford him protection, and could not follow him in his subversive opinions.

In many aspects of the period one can detect, as we have

said, the attempt to overturn the older scheme of life and to substitute a strongly individualistic philosophy. One manifestation of this change is to be found in the growing sympathy for the lower classes. Chaucer, it will be seen, introduces the middle classes to literature because by the latter part of the century they were inescapable. In the past they had figured in hardly more than the *fabliau* or the *exemplum*. Lollardry shows not merely a desire to correct the religious abuses of the times, but to establish what was really a totally different conception of the Church. The clamor of the peasant uprisings could not be stilled by temporary measures, but the cry of anarchy was intermingled. And yet the English people in general do not appear to have abandoned their old loyalties. In this respect Chaucer seems to be representative: he goes as far as the Lollards in religious sincerity (but this quality is characteristic of Dante as well) and nothing that he says can be construed as heretical; characters from the lower classes take part in the *Caunterbury Tales*, but there is no apparent desire to ignore differences in social station. On the whole, Chaucer and the fourteenth century were still Medieval.

3. Chaucer's Life

Among all the known facts with regard to Chaucer's career the most salient is that his good fortune furnished him with an environment which was supremely well suited to develop his particular kind of genius. He described the life and manners of all ranks of society, and he was able to do it so concretely partly because he had the opportunity of knowing them all well. He himself sprang from the middle classes. His grandfather, Robert, was a collector of the customs on wines; his father, John, was a vintner who early won a position as attendant to the king. Like many another family Chaucer's was gradually making its way upward. He was born about 1340, and by 1357 he was in the service of the Countess Elizabeth, wife of Lionel Duke of Clarence, as the Household Accounts show, referring to an expenditure for his clothes. From then on he was in almost constant touch with royalty: in 1359–60 he traveled with an expedition to France under Edward III, and was taken prisoner near Rheims, where the king ransomed him. He earned enough confidence to be later entrusted to carry certain letters from Calais to England. In 1367 he was a "valet of the king's household," and as "*dilectus valettus noster*" was granted an annual salary of twenty marks (a little over £13 in the money of that time). By 1369 he was again in military service in France. The year 1372 found him one of the king's *esquires*, and other royal favors came to him from time to time, such as the daily pitcher of wine granted in 1374 (later changed to an annuity of twenty marks). Through his entire life, in fact, he seems to have had opportunity to know the world at court, and yet his military service, his travels, his duties in London, brought him into contact with all social classes.

How really intimate he was with any of the royal personages it is hard to say. The question is somewhat complicated by the fact that Chaucer was subject in part to the system of literary patronage: for example, the *Book of the Duchesse* was written in memory of Blanche, John of Gaunt's first wife, in 1369 or 1370, though the poem itself suggests genuinely friendly feelings for the man in black. He wrote a late addition to the Monk's Tale in order to include an account of "worthy Petro, glorie of Spayne," the father of John of Gaunt's second wife, Constance. To this gentle lady the saintly Constance of the Man of Lawe's Tale may be a further allusion. Certain words of advice in the Phisicien's Tale to "maistresses" "that lordes doghtres han in governaunce" have been taken to be directed toward Katherine Swynford, who was a governess in the Duke's household and who became his third wife. Very possibly she was Chaucer's sister-in-law; but at any rate the passage implies considerable familiarity. As to what personal allusions should be read into such poems as the *Compleynte of Mars*, the *Hous of Fame*, and the *Parlement of Foules*, we remain practically in ignorance as yet. Various suggestions and interpretations have been made, but none seems to be wholly satisfactory. Possibly here are to be found the results of royal patronage, as also in the *Legende of Good Women*. And Chaucer had some return, not only from the king but also from John of Gaunt, who gave him a pension of ten pounds in 1374, and in 1377 an annuity of twenty marks more. It is a strange fact that John of Gaunt neglected to mention Chaucer in his will, but its importance may be overestimated. We may be sure that the poet was on terms of intimacy with several figures at court; his personality, however reserved, was calculated to win him affectionate regard from high as well as low.

Chaucer's marriage, probably as early as 1366, further connected him with court life. From the position of *domicella* to the Queen, Philippa Chaucer went into the service of the Lancaster household, and received from that source an annual pension of ten pounds in 1372, and in 1373 six silvergilt buttons and a "botoner" (button-hook). Further gifts are recorded up until 1382. Practically nothing is known of Chaucer's wedded life; and although his allusions to his fortunes in love and his experience in wedlock do not suggest felicity, these are often conventional jokes and need not be taken too seriously. After all, the bitterness in the Envoy to Bukton and in the remarks of the Merchant in the *Caunterbury Tales*, even if it is read literally, is offset by the optimism of the Franklin discoursing on the theme of marriage. Philippa died about 1387; and Chaucer was left, perhaps with two sons: Lewis and Thomas. Much of Chaucer's lovepoetry is, of course, based merely on the conventional themes of his time, drawn often from French literature, which may have been brought more vividly to his attention by his interest in the affairs of court, where French influence was still strong even after the days of Edward III, and by his travels.

His standing at court undoubtedly gave him the opportunities to go abroad, which meant so much for the development of his art. His early training was fostered under French influence; but later, diplomatic missions took him also to Italy, where he went just possibly as early as 1368 and certainly in 1372 or 1373. The chance of meeting Petrarch on one of these journeys he may actually have enjoyed, but at any rate he certainly made an extensive acquaintance with Italian literature, bringing back with him, no doubt, plenty of manuscripts of which he later made good use. His traveling reveals a practical ability; for in 1372 he was commissioned with one James Provan and John de Mari to treat with the duke, citizens, and merchants of Genoa for the purpose of choosing an English port which the Genoese might use as a commercial base. In 1377 he went to Flanders on secret negotiations; and in 1378, with various other men, he went abroad to arrange a marriage between Richard II and a daughter of the king of France. In 1378, also, business took him again to Italy, where he visited Barnabo Visconti, Lord of Milan, and became sufficiently interested in that vivid gentleman to give his story later in the Monk's Tale.

Because of this practical ability he had the chance to associate with other classes of his time. In 1374, when he was living in a house over Aldgate (one of the city gates), he was appointed Comptroller of the Customs and Subsidy of wools, skins, and tanned hides in the Port of London. In 1376 he received from the king a grant of over £71, which was the fine imposed on a certain man who shipped wool without paying the duty for it. In 1382 he was also made Comptroller of the Petty Customs in the Port of London, and was allowed to turn over the duties of that office to a deputy. In 1385, when apparently he was living in Greenwich, he was made Justice of the Peace for Kent, and in the next year he sat in Parliament as a Knight of the Shire for the county. Although through a change in the political situation Chaucer lost his Comptrollership of the Customs in 1386, he was again favored in 1389 when he was made Clerk of the King's Works to supervise the royal properties at Westminster, the Tower of London, and various manors, with a salary of two shillings a day or about thirty-six pounds a year. For these tasks he was again allowed a deputy. In 1390 he was selected to be on a commission to repair the banks of the Thames between Woolwich and Greenwich; he managed the erection of the scaffolding for the jousts in Smithfield; he was appointed a forester of North Petherton Park, Somersetshire; and he was ordered to get workmen and materials for the repair of St. George's Chapel, Windsor. Altogether his income from these duties must have been very substantial, and the variety of his work testifies to his efficiency in public employment.

The opportunity of meeting and dealing with all sorts and conditions of men would be appreciated to the full by a man of Chaucer's temperament. Fortunately the names of a few of those who were his friends have come down to us. Perhaps it may be a son of Sir Lewis Clifford that is addressed in the "Lowis" of the *Astrolabe*, instead of a son of Chaucer as has ordinarily been supposed. Sir Lewis's daughter Elizabeth was married to Sir Philip la Vache, to whom is dedicated *Trouthe*. And when the French poet Eustache Deschamps sent his verses asking Chaucer to cull some of the flowers of French rhetoric, Clifford himself brought the poem to England. To this poem, beginning "O Socrates plains de philosophie" and terming Chaucer a "grant translateur," Chaucer perhaps responded by borrowing heavily from Deschamps for the *Legende of Good Women*. There are other names linked with the English poet's in various ways for which we cannot pause: Sir John Clanvowe and Richard Morel. To Ralph Strode, Fellow of Merton College, Oxford, and to John Gower the poet, Chaucer dedicated his *Troilus* in a manner half flippant, half serious. In 1378, when Chaucer was in Italy, Gower acted for him in the capacity of attorney; and perhaps, when he came back, Chaucer brought a fresh manuscript of the *Filostrato*, which aroused many a discussion between the poets as to literary technique, and as to what Criseyde was in Benoit and Boccaccio and what she ought to be. A quarrel between Chaucer and Gower has been read into the supposed disparaging allusion to the *Confessio Amantis* in the introduction to the Man of Lawe's prologue and into the fact that in later versions of the *Confessio* a passage praising Chaucer does not appear. But, at most, this exchange of courtesies reveals in the two poets a difference in sense of humor.

Other items concerning Chaucer's circle of acquaintances we must infer from his activities: In 1375 he received the responsibility of being ward to Edmond Staplegate of Kent (and for his trouble received £104); in 1380 he was somehow concerned with what appears to have been a case of abduction, and in which one Cecilia Chaumpaigne released to him all rights of action against him; in 1386 he testified in the Scrope-Grosvenor suit as to the right of Sir Richard Scrope to bear a certain coat of arms.

In the miscellaneous information of this kind that presents itself in relation to Chaucer, one fact is especially clear. The events of his life are hardly more than those of the average man,—to-day we should say, the average business man. Although he had fair financial success, he went through difficulties that forced him to make appeals for money, as in the hint at the end of the *Parlement*, and, again, in the Envoy to Scogan and the *Compleinte to his Purs*. He was thrice robbed, in Kent, at Westminster, and at Hatcham, in 1390. How far the shifting favor of the men in power in the nineties could affect his fortunes is not entirely clear. Before that time in choosing his guildsmen for the *Prologe* of the *Caunterbury Tales* he was careful not to offend Mayor Brembre by taking any who were out of political favor. The protection of John of Gaunt does not stay by him apparently. In 1393 he was without public employment; in 1394 the king bestowed on him a grant of twenty pounds a year for life; in 1395 he was for some reason forced to make various loans; in 1398 he was sued. The *Compleinte to his Purs* of 1399 seems to have been responsible for the gift of a yearly sum of forty marks, and he was thus enabled to leave Greenwich and its "shrewes" to take a house in the garden of the Chapel of St. Mary, Westminster, near the Abbey. Here on the twenty-fifth of October, 1400, the poet died, and he was buried in the Abbey, where in 1556 a tomb of gray marble was erected in his memory.

All the details of his life show that Chaucer was in many respects a typical figure, occupied with the normal cares and duties of his time. Perhaps many of the official posts came his way as a kind of royal patronage, from the burdens of which he might occasionally be relieved by a deputy. But that he was versatile is evident from the manifold tasks that were imposed on him from which he was not relieved. Doubtless many people knew him simply as an unusually able man of affairs who happened to have a delightful and endearing nature. And all the while, as a spectator, Chaucer had a remarkable opportunity to observe the whole of what constituted the world of his time, giving the subjects of his attention no impression that they were specimens under the glass of an analyst, but nevertheless going about with an active step and an inquiring eye, whether on diplomatic missions or in the bustle of London. The pageant of life that moved about him was necessarily as inclusive as his own pilgrimage: knights and squires, monks and nuns, pardoners and clerks, franklins and merchants, craftsmen and ecclesiasts, men and women of all types, he could know them all, and he was undoubtedly a good "mixer." His "companye" was the company of all mankind.

A word may be added as to his later reputation. Full appreciation of his powers from the general public naturally did not come in his own day, but it followed soon after with the testimonials of Lydgate, Hoccleve, the "Scottish Chaucerians," and others. To these writers Chaucer was a "maister." The early printers brought out editions of his works together with certain spurious productions which were for a long time attributed to him. With the changes in the development of the English language the proper method of pronouncing Middle English was forgotten; small wonder, then, that Dryden found in Chaucer's verse merely the sweetness of a rude Scotch tune! Urry, in his edition (1721), suggested that many of the printed final *e*'s should be pronounced; and this idea was carried further by the scholar Tyrwhitt, whose edition appeared in 1775 with a mass of useful information together with remarkably careful editing. Anything like complete understanding of Chaucer's language, however, did not come until the study of Professor Francis J. Child in 1862, "Observations upon the Language of Chaucer," extended and amplified by many other scholars of to-day.

4. THE CHRONOLOGY OF CHAUCER'S WORKS

The dates assigned to Chaucer's works are only approximate. In most cases the evidence for the date is based on style, source, or assumed allusions to historical events. The following list includes only the more important works:

1369–70. *Book of the Duchesse.*
        Many of the shorter minor poems, such as the *A. B. C.*, the *Compleynte unto Pite*, part of the *Romaunt of the Rose*, and the *Compleynte of Mars*, belong to the early period.
1377–83. The translation of Boethius.
        Fortune, Former Age, etc.
1378. Or possibly 1383–84. *Hous of Fame.*
1381. *Parlement of Foules.*
        Anelida and Arcite.
        Palamon and Arcite.
1381–84. *Troilus and Criseyde.*
        Wordes unto Adam.
1386. Beginning of the *Legende of Good Women.*
1386–90. *Trouthe.*
1387–1400. The *Caunterbury Tales.* Several of the tales were earlier pieces of work: e. g. the Knight's Tale (as *Palamon and Arcite*), parts of the Monk's Tale, possibly the Clerk's Tale, and the Second Nun's Tale.
1391–92. *Treatise on the Astrolabe.*
1394. Reworking of the *Legende of Good Women.*
        Lenvoy a Scogan.
1396. *Lenvoy a Bukton.*
1399. *Compleinte to his Purs.*

Other works of Chaucer now lost are the *Book of the Leoun*, the *Wreched Engendring of Mankinde*, and *Origines upon the Maudeleyne*, of which we know, in part, from the prologue of the *Legende of Good Women* and, in part, from the "retraccioun" at the end of the Parson's Tale.

5. CHAUCER'S LEARNING

From Chaucer's poetry and prose it is clear that he was not only a close observer of life but an omnivorous reader. The choice of his reading was exceedingly catholic, ranging from

the lighter poetry (virelays, roundels, complaints, and bal-
lades) and romance and fabliau to long allegories and philosophical and moral treatises. He himself tells how he continually pored over a book; and his time was not idly spent.
That his interest was sincere can be discovered in the pains-
taking translations like the Tale of Melibeus, a disquisition
as ponderous as it is long, and the *De Consolatione Philosophie* of Boethius, and in his ready use of what he read, as in
the mosaic of borrowed lines in the portrait of the Duchess
(*The Book of the Duchesse*) and again in the prologue of the
Second Nun's Tale. It is because he laid up such a store of
wisdom, from which he was always able to draw, and which
shows how deep an impression the books made on his mind,
that he may be fairly called learned.

The work which had the most profound influence upon him
was undoubtedly the *Consolation of Philosophy* written by
Anicius Manlius Severinus Boethius (c. 480–524 A. D.), who
was a Christian consul under Theodoric the Ostrogoth, and
who on the accusation of treason was put to death. Describing a dialogue between Dame Philosophy and the con-
demned author waiting in prison for his death, the book
presents Aristotelian and Platonic philosophy in order to
justify the ways of God to man. It achieved an almost con-
tinuous popularity down to the Renaissance; allusions to it
and adaptations of it appear everywhere. The problems involved in the discussion aroused Chaucer's keenest interest,
and to them he recurs again and again. Verbal echoes appear
with remarkable frequency in his works, and sometimes he
lifts entire sections of the argument for his purposes. A similarly deep, if not at all so pervasive, influence was that of the
Divine Comedy of Dante, to which Chaucer was indebted in
many superficial ways, but which reached furthest for him
in his solution of the problem of fate. The *Hous of Fame* and
the *Parlement* show that Chaucer enjoyed reading Dante;
lines in the *Troilus*, in the prologue of the Prioress's Tale, and
elsewhere, show that the appeal was something more than
simply to the imagination.

Of a more secular type was the influence of the *Roman de la*

Rose, which he translated, at least in part, and which furnished him with a great deal of material that he put to practical use. This thirteenth century work, originally an allegory of the Court of Love by Guillaume de Lorris, and developed by Jean de Meun as a small compendium of knowledge, served, perhaps, to lead Chaucer's attention to some of the authors whose writings later engrossed him. Here he found story, allegory, and philosophy, and borrowings from Alanus de Insulis, Ovid, and others. Stories of love were especially accessible to him in his "owne book," Ovid's *Metamorphoses;* and he also knew and made use of Ovid's *Heroides*.

These works gave Chaucer most of his material, but there are others to which he owes much. In his early work he reveals that he has gained a thorough knowledge of French writers. Guillaume de Machaut, of the generation before Chaucer's, and Froissart and Eustache Deschamps of his own time, wrote poetry of the Court of Love vision which served as the model of several of his poems. So immersed was he in the literature of this type that this time of his apprenticeship is often called his "French period." With the *Hous of Fame* and the *Parlement of Foules*, however, the results of his Italian journeys begin to appear. The sentimentalism of Boccaccio in the *Teseide* and the *Filostrato* were transmuted into respectively the greatly reduced romance of the Knight's Tale and the greatly extended psychological "tragedie" of the *Troilus*. The Latin *De Casibus Virorum Illustrium* of Boccaccio inspired the Monk's Tale; *De Claris Mulieribus* of the same author contributed probably to the *Legende of Good Women*. From Petrarch came the Latin rendering of Boccaccio's story of Griselda which was the basis of the Clerk's Tale, and a sonnet of Petrarch's appears translated in the *Troilus*.

It is difficult to estimate with any accuracy Chaucer's knowledge of Latin. Presumably a man of his time might have had much. But he often employs a French translation of Latin works, as, in the case of Boethius, he leaned on the version attributed to Jean de Meun. He appears to have had an extensive acquaintance with Virgil's *Æneid*, as well as with Ovid, and with the twelfth century allegorist, Alanus de Insulis, of whose *Anticlaudianus* and *De Planctu Naturæ* he makes considerable use, and with the *Somnium Scipionis* of Cicero in the edition of Macrobius (fl. 400 A. D.) The story of Troy Chaucer knew chiefly from the *Æneid* and the accounts in the twelfth century French of Benoît de Sainte-More and in the thirteenth century Latinization of this by Guido delle Colonne. Apparently he did not know Greek.

In a writer like Chaucer, who has so many undeniable sources for his material, a modern reader will wonder whether any originality is left. It is true that the range of the books with which he had some familiarity was astonishingly wide, and that he not only read but borrowed freely. But plagiarism, in a sense, was the literary fashion of his time; Deschamps sincerely hoped that Chaucer would dignify him by a few borrowings from his verse. The ancients in general were not passionate for novelty; they had some good stories, and loved to have them retold, with perhaps new color, new characterization, or new subtlety. And do we need to be reminded that originality does not consist simply in the matter of plot? If that were the case Shakspere would suffer much at the hands of criticism. The Knight's Tale in plot and in many of the verses is Boccaccio's; but in its form as we have it in the *Caunterbury Tales*, in its changes in characterization, notably in the case of Arcite, and in its new language, it is Chaucer's alone.

Many writers in French and Latin, whom we have not listed, contributed to Chaucer's knowledge. The culture of his time, from the wealth of the patristic writings to the lyrics and folk-tales, was well digested in his reading. Current romances and lays from the popular as well as from literary sources appear in his stories; and information of a scientific or pseudo-scientific character came not only from books, but probably from the common stock of lore of his day. Perhaps the most striking fact in regard to Chaucer's material is that it represents so many of the different literary types of the Middle Ages. In his works the varying forms all appear, such as the Court of Love vision, the shorter lyric forms, the moral exemplum, the lay, the romance (parodied and also several times honestly attempted), the fabliau, the mock-heroic animal epic, the allegory, the sermon, the treatise (moral as well as philosophical), and the tales within a framework. The result shows not only the scope of his reading, but also how thoroughly he was a man of his time. Like Dante he presents a synthesis of Medieval expression. Like Dante, again, he does not reject the conventions of his period, but utilizes them, in word, phrase, and form, for the expression of his unique genius. The Clerk's Tale remains the story of Griselda; but in its setting in relation to the Wife of Bathe's prologue it becomes a delicate and sharp satire. The *Book of the Duchesse* is a love vision; but as an elegy that very fact conveys a fine and caressing sympathy. In the *Troilus* the young hero still suffers the infidelity of Criseyde; but he and Criseyde and Pandarus are not Troilo, Griseida, and Pandaro, and at the end of the poem Troilus suffers a change of view as to his "fate" that is not found in the Italian source. If ever a convention threatened to control Chaucer, as in the *Legende of Good Women*, he dropped the work entirely. What he alters, he does not alter by pressing it into a new mould, but by filling it with a new spirit. By watching Chaucer's intricate and composite borrowings from various sources we learn a great deal about literary art; by observing what he does with his reading we learn still more about genius.

II. CHAUCER'S LITERARY ART

Many of the values of Chaucer's literary work have always been too obvious for discursive criticism. The rich detail drawn from human life, the range of characterization, the clear glimpses of natural scenery, the kindling mellow humor, qualities in Chaucer like these were appreciated long before the American critic, Lowell, wrote his famous essay on the poet and apologized for venturing to add a word to the subject. The pilgrimage to Canterbury has long stirred the imagination of readers. Centuries before the well-known Stothard painting of the group, and before William Blake gave his independent interpretation, a Medieval artist was inspired to try his hand at depicting the pilgrims in the Ellesmere Manuscript. "Modernizations" or translations of some of the tales have appeared from Dryden's day to ours. Indeed it seems likely that, but for the hindrance in the change of language, Chaucer would have remained the poet of the people at large as he has always been a favorite of the few. But much as he has been enjoyed in all periods, the full understanding of his genius has been growing lately with the increased knowledge of his methods. The study of literary sources is sufficiently well justified by the discoveries concerning the fund of material of which he made use. It has become apparent that Chaucer is not merely the student of human-nature or the satirical commentator, but also a narrative and imaginative poet of great skill and a thinker. The growth in the development of his art, and the ripening of his faculties and judgment, have become more and more perceptible.

The problem of chronology is still somewhat a matter of doubt; but certainly one of the earliest works is the *Book of the Duchesse*, which was written in 1369 or shortly thereafter as an elegy for the death of Blanche, the first wife of John of Gaunt. It is probably to this poem that Chaucer refers in the prologue of the Man of Lawe's Tale, where he says, "In youthe he made of Ceys and Alcione." The lack of metrical fluency (if our manuscripts give us anything like a true account), the rather tedious mass of details which fail to contribute a full quota to the total effect, a structural tendency to ramble, show the amateurishness of the work. Yet there are also elements of great talent. In theme the poem follows a strongly conventionalized type, and yet it remains fresh and to the point. Based on the Court of Love vision, especially on the form developed in Machaut's *Jugement dou Roy de Behaingne*, the *Book of the Duchesse* is in some ways like hundreds of poems in Old French literature; but in one point, in particular, it is different,—namely, in the fact that it is an elegy. As in the case of the Middle English *Pearl*, the very conventionality of the form, the associations called up by the machinery so familiar in love poetry, indicate the poet's devotion to the lady who is gone. The poet recounts how he fell into a sleep one day after reading the story of Alcyone and her lament for her husband, and how he dreamed of the knight in black who was mourning the loss of his lady. A slumberous incoherence surrounds the episodes as they are told, which begin with the vision of a hunt, proceed with the aimless wandering led by the little dog, and, for no apparent reason except that which unites the elements of a dream, come to the meeting of the knight in black and the long dialogue in which the dreamer seems not to understand the drift of the knight's discourse so that he may draw him out and ease him of his pain. When the knight at last definitely repeats the fact that his lady is dead, the dreamer's sympathy, emphasized by the suspense, gains in climax: "Is that your los? By God, hit is routhe!" A notable feature in the poem is the description of the Duchess, which is a composition of lines taken from various foreign sources, with few original touches, and yet resulting in a picture in which the lady was presumably recognizable to a contemporary.

The technical advance over this poem in the *Hous of Fame* is, however, striking. The main structure of the latter is based, to be sure, on that of the *Panthère d'Amours* of Nicole de Margival (of the thirteenth century), and from this source come the mountain home which Fame adopts, and many other suggestions. But the plot is much more completely Chaucer's own, and certainly the old idea that the poem reflected the plan of the *Divine Comedy* is completely unfounded. Hints from the Italian begin to appear nevertheless; the account of Dido, the eagle, and other features, owe much to Virgil and Dante and Boccaccio. Other indebtednesses are here: the turning house of Rumor, a magical transformation of the whirling castles of Medieval romance, and reminiscent, perhaps, of certain houses of twigs which Chaucer may have seen in Wales, is in substance a borrowing. And yet the idea of such a factory of rumors is Chaucer's own; the humor of the educative discourse of the eagle, who holds his audience spellbound in his very clutches, the satire of the types that present themselves to Fame for her rewards, the imagination displayed in the conception of such a realm (although here again the suggestion comes from Ovid) whither the speech of earth makes its way like any element seeking its sphere, these qualities show Chaucer himself, a genius at play with material over which he has a perfect mastery. What the chief point of the whole story is we do not know. The man of great authority appears, and we are doubtless just about to learn certain important tidings of love. Perhaps, in fact, in a manuscript which formed the presentation copy, the tidings were told. But for us the poem remains incomplete.

And perhaps, after all, the purpose intended in this poem was better served by what seems to have been the next work, the *Parlement of Foules*. For this the *De Planctu Naturæ* of Alanus de Insulis, lines from Dante describing the gate of the Inferno, possibly a tale concerning a lovers' debate, furnished the chief outlines. The satire on the English parliament of Chaucer's day, the characterization of the birds in a way that recalls certain human traits, and the portraits of the lovers, are original with Chaucer. Here we find a transition from the octosyllabics of the previous poems to the seven-line stanza, an imitation of the Italian *ottava rima*, and later called "rime royal" (because of its use by James I of Scotland in the *Kingis Quhair*), a verse which is more fluent than the rollicking measure of the *Hous of Fame*, and which, as Chaucer uses it, is richer in substance and more quotable. Although this poem may be less of an imaginative achievement than the *Hous of Fame*, it has been universally admired, and is the first which was afterward largely imitated. Many contemporary allusions have been read into its allegory: it has been proposed that the poem was intended to celebrate the match of Richard II and Anne of Bohemia, or again that it dealt with the attempted betrothal of Richard with Philippa Lancaster, John of Gaunt's daughter. But all the suggestions so far are open to serious question.

With the French influence strong hitherto, and with the Italian contributions affecting the *Hous of Fame* and the *Parlement* more and more directly, Chaucer's full maturity arrives with the complete treatment of an Italian theme in the *Troilus*. This poem, consisting of more than eight thousand lines, is a modified translation of Boccaccio's *Il Filostrato*, itself an adaptation of a story familiar in the *Roman de Troye* of Benoît de Sainte-More and in the Latin rendering of Guido delle Colonne. Chaucer's additions, amounting to almost a third of the poem, include philosophy from Boethius and a supply of motivation for the characters. Pandarus is older than his prototype in the original, and Criseyde more complex than hers. In both versions Troilus proceeds as a typical hero of the Court of Love; but the interpretation of his tragedy is different. In Chaucer he blames Fate or Fortune for what occurs, he takes great pains to expound his self-pitying philosophy, but at the end a passage is borrowed from Boccaccio's *Il Teseide* to describe his flight through the spheres to a pitch of enlightenment where he sees that his own folly was the cause of his disaster and that his troubles are not so grave as he had supposed. The story is told in the manner of a drama with climax and catastrophe, and in the end, as a relief and solution, a remarkably detached mood is introduced, original with Chaucer, to give the setting of the story its proper irony, by which it attains a far wider significance. The Court of Love, all the fuming and fussing of lovers, much of human turmoil in general, is the subject of laughter against the background of the universe and eternity. Criseyde, who wished to stay herself at least by fidelity to Diomede, and Diomede himself "making hay while the sun shines," ladies and lovers, fate and Troy, all are trivial; all shall pass. The eternal things are those to which we must hold fast. The poem closes with a moral warning, a dedication (not made too solemnly), and a prayer. It may be maintained that in this poem too little of the atmosphere of Greece and Troy is introduced, that Troilus is a Medieval knight, and that the scenes are those of the fourteenth century. While there is truth in this, the fault is not primarily Chaucer's; for similar anachronisms were allowed in literature until a much later period.

Pandarus, Troilus, and Criseyde are characterizations not of the fourteenth century alone but of all time. In the ripeness of their art they anticipate some of the best figures of the *Caunterbury Tales*. But Chaucer did not wholly sustain this level in the works that followed. Having experimented in a new verse-form, the decasyllabic couplet, in the *Palamon and Arcite* (the Knight's Tale before it was put into the group), he returned after using the seven-line stanza of the *Troilus* to another venture in decasyllabics with the *Legende of Good Women*. Here the Court of Love vision, employed thrice before in different ways in his poems, served as the framework for a collection of stories about ladies who were martyrs in love like saints who were martyrs to the faith of the Church. The parallelism between the conventions of love and of the Church had been the scheme for many secular poems in European literature; the commandments, the ritual, and the relics were familiar as literary formulæ. Now a collection of "Saints' legends of Cupid" was to be made. Theoretically the idea was a good one; it offered pleasant satirical possibilities. Beginning with the light and charming verse of the Prologue (which introduces the *Balade* of fair ladies) some zest for the undertaking is apparent in the initial effort. But either the monotony of the task, which required story after story of the same general type, wearied Chaucer; or else the far greater resources in the scheme of the Canterbury pilgrimage lured his interest away. In any case he let the theme drop (in the form known as Prologue B, with the stories about as we know them); and later (after working on the introduction to the Man of Lawe's Tale) he took it up again (in the form of Prologue A), reminded perhaps of its possibilities, but again he lost interest.

The variety of literary opportunity in the *Caunterbury Tales* is, of course, clear enough. According to the difference in the pilgrims there must be stories for every taste. And the appeal is similarly varied. The power of criticism of life in every rank of society, the sympathy with all that is called human, whether good or bad, the relish for every activity that engages man, this universality is a distinguishing mark of Chaucer's greatness at this point in his career. All types fare equally well in his estimation. The scoundrel is not exonerated, but he may be personally liked, even loved; the virtuous have their faults that make them more approachable; even Chaucer must come down from his high horse and tell another story more suitable to the company (they hope) than his first. The Prioress, gentle Madame Eglantine, as dainty as any heroine of romance, will count her beads, however devotedly, only to reach the brooch inscribed "Amor vincit omnia." As in Medieval romance, too, it is always the best of every class, of every kind, whether knight, ecclesiast, or artisan, that happens, by a miracle of good luck, to be traveling on this pilgrimage. The figures in the *Prologe* are usually typical, except in the case of some of the broader characterizations where the features are picked out with Dürer-like detail; but in the drama of the links between the stories the characters become individual. In the execution of this plan Chaucer exceeds all the framed collections of stories of his time: the *Confessio Amantis*, the *Seven Sages*, the *Decameron*, and even the *Novelle* of Sercambi (where there is a similar pilgrimage and some characterization). The tales with Chaucer become a Human Comedy, in which the Pardoner confesses to the tricks of his trade and, for a change, exalts true piety, and in which the Wife of Bathe takes her fling at the demure Clerk, who, in turn, shows that his philosophy is not without the salt of humor. The gusto with which the tales proceed (we are in them before we know it), the splendor, the riotous joy of living with that company, embody the vitality of "merry England." But much as the poet enters into the delight of the journey, Chaucer the ironist is never absent. We cannot miss the dramatic irony of the long debate between Palamon and Arcite as to their rights in the love-affair which is opposed to their sworn friendship, or that of the knight who mourns his freedom while his brother laments that he is in prison, or that of the solemn and lonely fight in the forest for a lady who is totally unaware of the devotion of either suitor. Boccaccio's *Il Teseide*, here greatly reduced, is no longer the lacrimose tragedy of Arcite. Or, to take another instance, we may remember the three rioters of the Pardoner's Tale who go in search of Death in order to kill him, and when they meet him at last they are only too obsequious about obeying his directions, unconscious who he is.

The tone of the stories varies from earnest to game, from poetry to grim prose. Many themes of vice and virtue are dwelt upon, themes of love and marriage, worldliness and piety. The Wife of Bathe starts the ball rolling down a long course of discussion on the subject of woman's position in the world and of the estate of wedlock. The topic of woman's counsel, whether it is harmful or beneficial, had already been in the air, and it led naturally to this. Now the Wife of Bathe takes her turn to insist on mastery for woman and plenty of wedlock. In varying ways she is answered by the Clerk, who shows that patient Griselda was a somewhat extreme type, by the Squire, who treats of romantic love, by the Merchant, who reveals a bitter disillusionment as to the glamor of love, and by the Franklin, who concludes that man and wife must each have mastery and that wedlock is, after all, a blessed condition.

But great as is the range of appeal in the subject-matter of the tales, they also show a variety in skill. Some of them were obviously written early, like the Man of Lawe's Tale, the Monk's Tale (with later additions), and the Tale of the Second Nun. From the sentimental pathos of the succession of tragedies in the Monk's Tale, appropriate to the luxury-loving Monk with his furred wrists, jingling bells, and genuine concern only for worldly matters, the pilgrims ask to be delivered, led by the only fit spokesman for such a protest, the Knight. These early tales are rather slight in material, compared, say, with the rich mock-heroic of the Nun's Priest's Tale or with the abundant humanity of the Wife of Bathe's Prologue. And their thinness is not due to the fact of their being religious in cast; for Chaucer shows his power in eloquent morality in *Trouthe* and in lyric piety in the Prioress's Tale. There is some indication that the tales were not all originally assigned to the speakers who now have them. Thus it is possible that the Melibeus first belonged to the Man of Lawe, who says that he speaks "in prose" and who might be expected to be somewhat argumentative; at present, however, it is Chaucer's lengthy retort to the pilgrims' dislike of *Sir Thopas*. The best of the stories seem to have been written with their tellers in mind, like those of the Pardoner, the Franklin, and the Canon's Yeoman. The Pardoner's Tale, even apart from its setting as an exemplum in a homily, is a masterpiece of narrative skill. Its simplicity and directness, its swift conclusion, are worthy of admiration. Some of the tales Chaucer never finished, specifically those of the Cook and the Squire. For the Cook he was obviously preparing a *fabliau;* the loss of the rest of the Squire's Tale (which Spenser supplies in the *Faerie Queene*) is regrettable, but the fragment, like *Kubla Khan*, gains in romantic charm by leaving much to the imagination. The grouping of the stories as a whole shows a certain lack of finish. But it was evidently never intended to be managed with any view to climax (except, perhaps, in the Marriage Cycle); climaxes arrive according to the subjects that obviously most engaged the enthusiasm of the poet. The last tale of all is the least impressive, that of the Parson, not in any sense a story but a sombre moral treatise without artistic relief; it has some interest, however, from the fact that it is concluded by a Retraction in which Chaucer apologizes for his worldly poems. The scheme of the *Caunterbury Tales* itself was left unfinished: the pilgrims fail to tell their full number of stories; some of them, in fact, do not have any turn at all. It remained for other poets, like Lydgate in his *Story of Thebes*, to add further contributions. The most remarkable work done in Chaucer's vein, however, has nothing to do with this group; it is the continuation of the *Troilus* by the Scottish poet Henryson in his *Testament of Cresseid*.

Like all Chaucer's works, the *Caunterbury Tales* derive from literary sources. The legend which formed the basis of the Prioress's Tale was well known in various forms; the story of Chaunteclere goes back through different versions to the cycle of animal epics which formed such a great body of literature in Europe; the Pardoner's Tale traces its beginnings to the Orient; and the tale of Patient Griselda, reworked in Latin by Petrarch from the Italian of Boccaccio, was European literary property. But the procession of vividly human beings that makes its way toward the shrine of Becket, the variegated throng of fourteenth century England that forms a part of English literary tradition, in which Harry Bailly still does business at the Tabard, and the Wife of Bathe is worthy to be mentioned along with characters like Falstaff, all this Chaucer created. It may be that some of the traits of the pilgrims were drawn from living people of Chaucer's day; that a contemporary might have laughed to recognize a familiar figure in the Cook or the Summoner. But the spirit of the English people infuses them all, interpreted with warm humor by the poet. And not only the creation of this friendly company is Chaucer's, but also the artistic skill and the poetry of their stories (which is evident in conception if not in figurative ornament of speech), whereby the monotonous and dreary, the pietistic, the sentimental, or qualities even less desirable in the sources, become transformed and gain genuine and wholesome significance.

III. THE PRESENT TEXT

The basis of the text of the present edition is that of the Reverend W. W. Skeat, published by the Clarendon Press, Oxford, 1894–1900, modified by a collation with manuscript readings which are accessible in the Chaucer Society prints. Since it is impossible to discover the exact Chaucerian forms and wording, it has seemed justifiable to normalize the text somewhat with a view to making it easier for the beginner in Middle English. For instance, the common forms **had, did, eek,** and **whan,** are always used except when the final **e** (**hadde, dide, eke, whanne**) is metrically desirable; **evere** and **nevere** are regularly so spelled; the present participle and the gerund in most cases take a final **e** only at the end of a line; some effort has been made to establish normal forms for the imperative singular of the verb; words which are normally entitled to a final **e** by the evidence of rime (unless this is ambiguous) are always so spelled. Of these alterations it was discovered that a large number were supported by manuscript readings, and only the exceptional cases are recorded in the list of variants in the back of the book. Some features of the change may seem arbitrary: as, for instance, the use of the form **out** when it appears as a preposition, and of the form **oute** when it functions as an adverb. But the changes are in general slight, and it is hoped that the gain in consistency will render the text easier for the student and average reader to comprehend. For every modification the standard has always been the accepted Chaucerian grammar.

The choice of the poems for the present edition, and the abridgment of the text have already been discussed in the Preface. The Skeat numbering of the lines is given at the foot of each page so that students may consult the notes of the larger edition.

IV. THE LANGUAGE

1. The dialect used by Chaucer is that of the East Midland district together with some Kentish forms. In general the inflectional system is like that of modern English. But it is complicated somewhat by the survival of certain Anglo-Saxon forms, by some of the Anglo-Saxon endings reduced to final unaccented **e**, by forms taken over from the Old French with final **e**'s, and by a few final **e**'s which do not seem to be historically justifiable. In the preservation of such forms Chaucer keeps to a standard slightly conservative in comparison with the spoken language of his time, probably for the increased facility that it contributed to solving metrical problems and for the liquid quality gained thereby in the verse.

NOUNS

2. The normal declension of the **noun** is as follows:

	Sing.		Plu.	
N. D. A.	**dom**	**nonne**	**domes**	**nonnes**
Gen.	**domes**	**nonnes**	**domes**	**nonnes**

3. The stem of **nonne** has a final **e**, which appears in the nominative singular. This ending is found: in nouns where the Anglo-Saxon nominative singular ended in a vowel, like **nonne** from A. S. **nunne**; in nouns derived from A. S. feminines (of which the oblique cases ended in **e**), like **lore** from A. S. **lār**; and in nouns which had a final **e** in Old French, like **grace, Ioye.** In a few other cases, like **hewe** from A. S. **hēow** (neuter), or like **travaile** from O. Fr. **travail,** an "unhistorical" or "inorganic" final **e** appears for which full explanation is still lacking.

4. A few survivals from an A. S. genitive singular appear which in Middle English have no ending: **fader soule** (**fader** here means "father's," coming from the A. S. r-declension);

lady grace ("lady's," coming from the A. S. weak declension with a genitive in **-an**). Proper nouns ending in **s** appear without the genitive ending: **Epicurus owne sone.** A few Old Fr. words also lack the ending: **your heritage right.**

5. In certain stereotyped phrases a final **e** survives from the A. S. dative, forming in Middle English what is sometimes called the "petrified dative": **on lyve; in toune; in honde.** This dative **e** sometimes appears in other phrases, where it was probably taken over by analogy: **in the fyre** (**on fyre**, petrified dative).

6. The plurals sometimes end in **s** instead of **es**: **naciouns, daungers.** Nouns ending in **s** usually add no plural ending: **caas, paas, vers.** Some nouns take plurals in **-en** from the A. S. weak declension, like **eyen, asshen, been;** and by analogy with these are formed **children, doughtren, sustren.** There are some plurals without ending, like **hors, yeer,** from A. S. neuters; and some nouns form their plurals by umlaut, like **men, feet,** as in A. S.

ADJECTIVES

7. As in modern German there are two declensions for **adjectives,** the strong and the weak. These are declined as follows:

Strong	Sing.	**yong**	swete
	Plu.	**yonge**	swete
Weak	Sing.	**yonge**	swete
	Plu.	**yonge**	swete

8. Some adjectives, like **swete,** have a final **e** in the singular of the strong declension because in A. S. they ended in a vowel (A. S. **swete**), or because they were derived from Old Fr. adjectives with final **e** (like **contraire**). A few adjectives take an **e** in Middle English which (like **longe**) in A. S. or (like **comune**) in O. Fr. ended in a consonant. **Lyte** and **muche** retain the **e** from A. S. **lytel** and **mycel.**

9. The weak declension of the adjective may be used under the following circumstances:

(a) When the adjective is used substantively: **the beste, by weste.**
(b) When it is preceded by the definite article or a demonstrative: **the yonge sonne.**
(c) When it is preceded by a noun or pronoun in the genitive case: **his halve cours.**
(d) When it modifies a noun in the vocative: **O blake nyght.**
(e) When it modifies a proper name: **faire Venus.**

10. Survivals from the A. S. are found in the adjective: in the dative **e** (A. S. **-um**) of the strong declension in certain phrases, like **of evene lengthe, in warme wex;** and in the strong genitive plural form **aller, alder,** or **alther** (A. S. **ealra**). From O. Fr. comes a plural ending in **es: places delitables.**

11. The comparative of the adjective ends in **er(e):** **gretter, ferre** (contracted), from **gret, fer.** The superlative ends in **est** inflected as **este: the frendlyeste.**

12. Occasionally as in A. S. the comparison of adjectives shows umlaut: as in **long, lenger; old, elder.** Irregularity appears in certain comparisons: as **good,** and **better, bettre,** or **bet; muche**(l) and **more** or **mo; lyte**(l) and **lasse** or **lesse.**

Adverbs

13. The **adverb** ends normally in **e:** e. g., **sore, smerte.** Sometimes the **e** is not found in the A. S. original: as **here** (A. S. **hēr**). Some adverbs do not take a final **e:** as **ful, streyght, y-wys.**

14. The comparison of the adverb is like that of the adjective: **more, lengere, ferther.** Also note the irregular forms: **bet, mo, lasse.** The superlative ends in **est,** which after a definite article may take an **e: the moste free.**

Pronouns

15. The Personal **Pronoun** of the First Person has two

forms for the nominative singular: **I** and **ich.** Otherwise the
forms are like those of modern English.

16. The Second Person has the following forms in the
singular: **thou** (nom.), **thy, thyn** (gen.), **thee** (dat., accus.);
and in the plural it has: **ye** (nom.), **your** (gen.), **you** (dat.,
accus.).

17. In the Third Person the declension is as follows:

	Sing.			Plu.
	Masc.	Neut.	Fem.	
N.	he	hit	she	they
G.	his	his	hir(e), her(e)	hir(e), her(e)
D.	him	him	hir(e), her(e)	hem
A.	him	hit	hir(e), her(e)	hem

18. The following forms appear of the Possessive Pronouns:—in the singular: (first person) **my, myn,** (second person) **thy, thyn,** (third person) **his** (m. n.), **hir(e), her(e)**
(fem.); in the plural: (first person) **our(e),** (second person)
your(e), (third person) **hir(e), her(e).** The forms **myn** and
thyn of the first and second persons respectively are usually
employed before vowels. The final **e** of **hire, here, oure,
youre, hire, here** (plural), appears chiefly in the predicate
use.

19. The Demonstrative Pronouns are inflected as follows:

Sing.	**this**	**that**
Plu.	**this(e), thes(e)**	**tho**

A survival from an old dative singular is found in the phrase
for the nonys (A. S. **for þæm ānes**).

20. Of the Interrogative Pronouns, **which** is inflected when
it is used as an adjective: **of whiche two, the whiche day.**
Other pronominal forms show inflection: **al, bothe, self,
swich,** are sometimes declined like adjectives.

Verbs

21. In order to understand the conjugation of **verbs**
properly, a distinction must be recognized between weak
verbs, which form their preterit by adding **d** or **t,** and strong

verbs, which lack a special preterit ending of this kind, but which indicate the change in tense by a shift in the root vowel. Some forms of this vowel-shift show a variety of sound-change known as "ablaut" or "vowel-gradation."

22. The different types of ablaut or vowel-gradation in A. S. may be classified in six principal groups. In the following table it will be seen that there is a tendency in Middle English to drop some of the variations; the preterit singular and plural are often identified (except for the endings). New forms are introduced, however, which complicate the scheme somewhat, and only the chief forms will be indicated here.

Class I

	Infin.	Pret. sing.	Pret. plu.	Past Partic.
A. S.	ī	ā	ĭ	ĭ
M. E.	rīde(n)	rọ̄d	rĭde(n)	rĭden

So agrīse, bīde, bīte, glīde, shīne, shrīve, etc.

Class II

A. S.	ēo	ēa	ŭ	ŏ
M. E.	ẹ̄	ẹ̄	ẹ̄ (from the sing.)	ọ̄
	bẹ̄de(n)	bẹ̄d	bẹ̄de(n)	bọ̄den

So chẹ̄se, crẹ̄pe, clẹ̄ve, etc. Sometimes forms in ī or ou appear in the present from A. S. ēo +g or A. S. ū respectively.

Class III

A. S.	ĕ, ĭ	ă	ŭ	ŭ, ŏ
M. E.	ĕ, ĭ	ă, ŏ	ŏ, ŭ	ŏ, ŭ
	hĕlpe(n)	hălp	hŏlpe(n)	hŏlpen
	bīnde(n)	bond	bounde(n)	bounden
	(ĭ lengthened before nd)		(ŭ lengthened before nd; ou =ū.)	(ŭ lengthened before nd; ou =ū.)
	drĭnke(n)	drănk	dronke(n) (o =ŭ)	dronken (o =ŭ)

So swĕlle, kĕrve, brĕste, wĭnne, spĭnne, begĭnne, etc.

Class IV

A. S.	ĕ	æ	ǣ	ŏ
M. E.	ę̄	ă	ę̄	ǭ
	bę̄re(n)	băr	bę̄re(n)	bǭren
			bāren	

To this class belong **stę̄le, shę̄re, hę̄le, brę̄ke, spę̄ke,** etc. Two verbs
of this class are especially irregular:

come (o = ŭ)	cōm (căm)	cōme(n)	come (o = ŭ)
nĭme	nam (nōm)	nōme(n)	nomen (o = ŭ)

Class V

A. S.	ĕ	æ	ǣ	ĕ
M. E.	ę̄	ă	ă, ę̄	ę̄
	gę̄te	găt		gę̄ten
	yę̄ve	yăf	yāve(n)	yę̄ven
	ę̄te	eet	ę̄te(n)	ę̄ten

To this class belong **wrę̄ke** and (with **i** and a double consonant in the
present) **bĭdde, sĭtte, lĭgge. Sę̄n** is irregular:

sę̄n	saugh		
	saw		
	seigh		
	say, sey	seye(n)	seyn, seye
	sȳ	sȳe(n)	

Class VI

A. S.	ă	ō	ō	ă
M. E.	ā	ǭ	ǭ	ā
	tāke	tǭk	tǭke(n)	tāken

So **wāke, bāke, forsāke, shāke, shāpe,** etc. Irregular verbs belonging
to this class include the following:

stŏnde(n)	stǭd	stǭde(n)	stŏnden
drawe(n)	drough	drowe(n)	drawen
laughe(n	lough		laughen
swę̄re(n)	swōr	swǭre(n)	swǭrn

23. A seventh class of strong verbs is formed from verbs of
which the preterit tense-stems were once reduplicated: in A. S.
these reduplications were lost, apparently by contraction.

Class VII

slẹ̄pe(n)	slẹ̄p	slẹ̄pe(n)	slẹ̄pen
wẹ̄pe(n)	wẹ̄p		wọ̄pen
họ̄lde(n)	hẹld	hẹlde(n)	họ̄lden
fǎlle	fěl (fĭll)	fĭlle	fǎlle
họ̄te	hẹ̄t		họ̄ten

In general the characteristic of this class is the appearance of the same vowel in the present (infin.) and the past participle, and ẹ or ẹw in the preterit.

24. Sometimes verbs which once were strong have become weak or have weak forms in Middle English. For example: lẹ̄se (class II), pret. lŏste; hẹle (class IV), pret. hẹled; fāre (class VI), pret. fērde, p. p. fāred (beside the strong fāren); slẹ̄pe (class VII), pret. slẹ̆pte (also the strong slẹ̄p); họ̄te (class VII), pret. hīghte (also an old strong preterit hīght— A. S. hĭht—which serves as a present).

25. The weak verbs fall into two classes:

	Infin.	Pret.	Past Partic.
Class I	—e(n)	—ed(e)	—ed
	love(n)	loved(e)	loved

So were, herie, dere, clepe, make, etc. Verbs from O. Fr. are usually conjugated according to this class.

Class II	—e(n)	—d(e), —t(e)	—d, —t
	here(n)	herde	herd

So also fede, lede (with pret. ledde or ladde), sette (with pret. sette), etc. To this class also belong verbs which in A. S. had umlaut in the present stem but not in the preterit:

telle	tolde	told
strecche	straughte	straught
reche	raughte	——
seke	soughte	sought

Irregularities are found in this class: dreme and seme have preterit and past participle like those in class I; deme and fele have past participle in —ed.

26. The conjugation in the present indicative and in the present subjunctive is the same for both strong and weak verbs:

Indic. Sing.		Plu.		
1. speke	love	1. 2. 3. speke(n)	love(n)	
2. spekest	lovest			
3. speketh	loveth			
Subj. 1. 2. 3. speke	love	1. 2. 3. speke(n)	love(n)	

In the third person singular the ending is frequently —**th**: and sometimes the form is contracted: e. g., **setteth** > **set; rideth** > **rit**. A third person singular ending in **es** is occasionally found: e. g., **telles**.

27. In the preterit indicative the conjugation of strong verbs differs from that of weak verbs thus:

	Strong		Weak	
Sing. 1.	spak	fond	loved(e)	herde
2.	spak(e)	found(e)	lovedest	herdest
3.	spak	fond	loved(e)	herde
Plu. 1. 2. 3.	spake(n)	founde(n)	lovede(n)	herde(n)

In A. S. the second person singular of the strong verbs has the radical vowel of the plural; but in M. E. it often takes that of the first and third persons singular by analogy.

28. The preterit subjunctive of strong verbs is formed on the stem of the preterit plural indicative; that of weak verbs has the stem of the preterit indicative:

	Strong		Weak	
Sing.	spake	founde	lovede	herde
Plu.	spake(n)	founde(n)	lovede(n)	herde(n)

29. The imperative of strong verbs takes no ending in the singular, and, in the plural, **-e** or **-eth** or no ending; that of weak verbs sometimes takes **-e** in the singular and **-e** or **-eth** or no ending in the plural:

	Strong	Weak	
Sing.	tak	make	werk
Plu.	taketh	maketh	werketh

30. The infinitive ends in **-e** or **-en.** Stems ending in a vowel often simply have **-n:** e. g., **sen, goon.** Some cases of an inflected infinitive or of the survival of the gerund from A. S. appear in such phrases as **to sene, to done.**

31. The present participle ends in **-ing(e).** The final **e** is usually sounded only at the end of a verse.

32. The past participle of strong verbs ends in **-e(n);** of weak verbs, in **-ed, -d,** or **-t.** (see § 25). Frequently the prefix **y** (from the A. S. **ge**) appears: **y-taken, y-sought.**

33. Preterit-present verbs have a somewhat irregular conjugation. These verbs were originally formed from the preterit tense of strong verbs which, in that tense, had come to have a present meaning. Thus A. S. **wāt** (from the strong verb **wītan,** class I, "to pay heed to," "to see") means "I have learned," "I know." For these verbs a new preterit was created on the basis of weak verbs, and a new second person singular (in the present indicative) from the present (former preterit) stem.

34. These verbs may be classified according to the types of strong verbs from which they came:

Class I		A. S. **witan**	M. E. **wite(n)**
		Sing.	Plu.
Pres. indic.	1.	wǫt	1. 2. 3. **wǐte(n), wǫte(n)**
	2.	wǫst	
	3.	wǫt	
Preterit	1.	wǐste	1. 2. 3. **wǐste(n)**
	2.	wǐstest	
	3.	wǐste	
		A. S. **āgan**	M. E. **owe(n)**
Pres. indic.	1.	owe	1. 2. 3. **owe(n)**
	2.	owest	
	3.	owe	
Preterit		oghte	
Class III		A. S. **cunnan**	M. E. **conne(n)**
Pres. indic.	1.	can	1. 2. 3. **conne, can**
	2.	canst	
	3.	can	
Preterit		couthe, coude	

A. S. þurfan
Pres. indic. 3. thar
Preterit thurfte

A. S. **durran** M. E. **durre**
Pres. indic. 1. dar 1. 2. 3. **dar dorr,**
2. darst
3. dar
Preterit dorste

Class IV A. S. sculan
Pres. indic. 1. shal 1. 2. 3. **shul, shulle(n), shal**
2. shalt
3. shal
Preterit sholde, shulde.

Class V A. S. **magan** M. E. **mowe(n)**
Pres. indic. 1. may 1. 2. 3. **mowe, may**
2. mayst
3. may
Preterit myghte

Class VI A. S. mōtan
Pres. indic. 1. mōt 1. 2. 3. **mōte(n)**
2. mōste
3. mōt
Preterit mōste

35. Other irregular verbs include **be, wil, do, go,** and **have,**
which are conjugated as follows:

			Sing.	Plu.
(a)	Pres. indic.	1.	am	1. 2. 3. bę̄(n) bę̄th ārn
		2.	art	
		3.	is	
	subj.	1. 2. 3.	bę̄	1. 2. 3. bę̄n
	imper.		bę̄	bę̄th
	Pret. indic.	1.	was	1. 2. 3. wę̄re(n)
		2.	wę̄re	
		3.	was	
	subj.	1. 2. 3.	wę̄re	1. 2. 3. wę̄re (n)
	Past partic.		been	

(b) Pres. indic. 1. wil, wol   1. 2. 3. wil(e)(n), wol(e)(n)
2. wilt, wolt
3. wil, wol
    subj. 1. 2. 3. wil(e), wol(e) 1. 2. 3. wil(e), wol(e)
Pret. indic. 1. wolde   1. 2. 3. wolde (n)
2. woldest
3. wolde
    subj. wolde
Past partic. wold

(c) Pres. indic. 1. dǫ   1. 2. 3. dǫn
2. dǫst
3. dǫth
    subj. 1. 2. 3. dǫ   1. 2. 3. doon
Pret. indic. 1. dïd(e)   1. 2. 3. dïde(n)
2. dïdest
3. dïd(e)
Imper. dǫ   dǭth

(d) Pres. indic. 1. gǭ   1. 2. 3. gǭ(n)
2. gǭst
3. gǭth
    subj. 1. 2. 3. gǭ   1. 2. 3. gǭn
    imper. gǭ   gǭth
Preterit (wente, yēde)

(e) Pres. indic. 1. have   1. 2. 3. han, have
2. hast
3. hath
    subj. 1. 2. 3. have   1. 2. 3. have
Pret. indic. 1. had(de)   1. 2. 3. hadde(n)
2. haddest
3. had(de)
Imper hav(e)   haveth

36. From this grammatical outline the forms in which final unaccented **e** are justified may be determined. The student must bear in mind, however, that only the more customary forms are cited, and that there are numerous irregularities of which we cannot here take account but which must be studied in relation to their context. Furthermore, it is necessary to remember that not all of the justifiable final

e's are to be pronounced.   Those which occur at the end of a verse are almost always sounded; but within the line the needs of the measure are the determining factor.   For instance, final **e** in adjectives of more than two syllables is usually not sounded.   In general final **e** is usually elided before vowels or "weak **h**" (as in **he, her, hadde, here,** etc., or the French **h** in **honour, humblesse,** etc.).   A table giving the quality of the sounds in Chaucer's language will be found on the page facing the text; and in the text itself the final **e**'s which are printed but which are probably not to be sounded are indicated by a dot beneath the letter.   The dotting of the **e**'s, however, is not intended to impose restrictions on the reader, but is purely advisory.

V. BIBLIOGRAPHICAL SUGGESTIONS

1. Bibliography:

E. P. Hammond, *Chaucer: A Bibliographical Manual*, N. Y., 1908.

J. E. Wells, *A Manual of the Writings in Middle English, 1050–1400*, New Haven, 1916, pp. 599ff., 866ff. Also the *First Supplement*, New Haven, 1919, pp. 994ff., 1027ff.

2. Editions:

Rev. W. W. Skeat, *The Complete Works of Geoffrey Chaucer*, in six volumes, Oxford, 1894–1900.

Rev. W. W. Skeat, *The Student's Chaucer*, in one volume, Oxford University Press.

Pollard, Heath, Liddell, and McCormick, *The Works of Chaucer*, the Globe Edition, in one volume, Macmillan and Co.

3. Criticism:

T. R. Lounsbury, *Studies in Chaucer*, in three volumes, N. Y., 1892.

G. L. Kittredge, *Chaucer and his Poetry*, Cambridge, 1915.

E. Legouis, *Geoffrey Chaucer*, translated by L. Lailavoix, London, 1913.

R. K. Root, *The Poetry of Chaucer*, Boston, 1906.

SELECTIONS FROM CHAUCER

THE SOUNDS OF CHAUCER'S LANGUAGE

The Vowels:

ā like **a** in **father**................e. g., **bathed.**
ă like **a** in German **man**.............. **that.**
ẹ̄ (close) like **a** in **name**.............. **swete.**
ę̄ (open) like **e** in **there**.............. **heeth.**
ĕ like **e** in **met**...................... **hem.**
ī (ȳ) like the **i** in **machine**........... **ride, ryde.**
ĭ (ȳ) like **i** in **pin**................... **his, dyde.**
ọ̄ (close) like **o** in **note**.............. **roote.**
ǭ (open) like **a** in **all**................ **everychon.**
ŏ like **o** in **not, hot**.................. **croppes.**
ū (ou, ow, o) like **oo** in **moon**........ **droghte, fowles, flour.**
ŭ (o) like **u** in **full**.................. **ful, sonne.**
ü like **ü** in French **user**.............. **vertu.**

Final unaccented **e** was pronounced like **a** in **about:** e. g., **sonne.**

The Diphthongs:

ai (ay), ei (ey) like **ay** in **day** or **ei** in **veil**................. **day, wey.**
au (aw) like **ou** in **house**................................ **draughte.**
ẹ̄u (ew) ẹ̄ and **u** sounded together with stress on the ẹ̄...... **knew.**
ę̄u (ew) ę̄ and **u** sounded together with stress on the ę̄....... **fewe.**
oi (oy) like **oy** in **boy**.................................... **coy.**
ōu (ow) **o** and **u** sounded together with stress on **o**.......... **foughten, bowe.**

Note: the vowels of Chaucer's day were probably sounded without the addition of the **i** or **u** glide which we attach today: e. g., ō in modern English **note** is usually pronounced as ō+u; ā in **name** as ā+i.

The Consonants:

The Middle English consonant-sounds were much like those of modern English. There were, however, no silent consonants: medial and final **gh** had the sound of **ch** in modern German **ich** or **nacht; k, l,** and **w** were never silent: e. g., **knyght, palmeres, write; ng** followed by a vowel was pronounced like **ng** in **finger:** cf. **yonge.** Other differences are as follows: **r** was trilled; **s** and **th** when final or next voiceless consonants were unvoiced (like **s** in **this,** and **th** in **thing**); **th** in proper names was probably sounded like **t;** -**cion, -tion, -sion,** were pronounced clearly as in French with the consonants distinct (as **-sion,** not **-shun**); **g** before **e** or **i** was often pronounced as in modern English **gem** or **ginger:** e. g., **age, gipser.**

In the manuscripts a double vowel indicates a long vowel; **u** before **n, m** or **u,** and occasionally after **c** or **w** is written **o:** e. g., **sonne, coppe; u** and **v** are interchangeable, and so are **i** and **y.** These features are retained in the present text.

SELECTIONS FROM CHAUCER

written at age of 29

THE BOOK OF THE DUCHESSE

The Proem

I have gret wonder, by this light,
How that I live; for day ne night
I may nat slepe wel nigh noght. *ne mean*
I have so many an ydel thoght
Purely for defaute of sleep
That, by my trouthe, I take no keep
Of no-thing, how hit cometh or goth,
Ne me nis no-thing leef nor loth.
Al is y-liche good to me—
Ioye or sorowe, wherso hit be—
For I have feling in no-thing,
But, as it were, a mased thing,
Alway in point to falle a-doun:
For sorwful imaginacioun
Is alway hoolly in my minde.

And wel ye woote, agaynes kinde
Hit were to liven in this wyse;
For nature wolde nat suffyse
To noon erthely creature
Not longe tyme to endure
Withoute sleep, and be in sorwe.
And I ne may, ne night ne morwe,
Slepe; and this melancolye
And drede I have for to dye,
Defaute of sleep, and hevinesse
Hath sleyn my spirit of quiknesse
That I have lost al lustihede:
Suche fantasyes ben in myn hede.
So I not what is best to do.

Sk. 1–29

But men mighte axe me, why so
I may not slepe, and what me is,
But natheles, who aske this
Leseth his asking trewely.
My-selven can not telle why
The sooth; but trewly, as I gesse,
I holde hit be a siknesse
That I have suffred this eight yeer.
And yet my bote is nevere the neer;
For ther is phisicien but oon,
That may me hele.　But that is doon.
Passe we over until eft:
That wil not be, moot nede be left;
Our first matere is good to kepe.

So whan I saw I might not slepe
Til now late, this other night,
Upon my bed I sat upright
And bad oon reche me a book,
A romaunce, and he hit me took
To rede and dryve the night away.
For me thoghte it better play
Than play either at chesse or tables.

And in this book were writen fables
That clerkes hadde, in olde tyme,
And other poets, put in ryme
To rede, and for to be in minde
Whyl men loved the lawe of kinde.
This book ne spak but of such thinges,
Of quenes lyves, and of kinges,
And many othere thinges smale.
Among al this I fond a tale
That me thoughte a wonder thing.

This was the tale: Ther was a king
That highte Seys, and had a wyf,
The beste that mighte bere lyf
And this quene highte Alcyone.
So hit befel, therafter sone,
This king wol wenden over see.

To tellen shortly, whan that hè
Was in the see, thus in this wyse,
Soch a tempest gan to ryse
That brak hir mast, and made it falle,
And clefte hir ship, and dreinte hem alle,
That nevere was founden, as it telles,
Bord ne man, ne nothing elles.
Right thus this king Seys loste his lyf.

    Now for to speken of his wyf:—
This lady, that was left at hom,
Hath wonder that the king ne com
Hoom, for hit was a longe terme.
Anon her herte gan to erme.
And for that hir thoughte everemo,
Hit was not wel hir thoughte so.
She longed so after the king
That certes hit were a pitous thing
To telle hir hertely sorwful lyf
That hadde, alas! this noble wyf,
For him she loved alderbest.
Anon she sente bothe eest and west
To seke him, but they founde nought.

    "Alas!" quoth she, "that I was wrought!
And wher my lord, my love, be deed?
Certes, I nil nevere ete breed,
I make a-vow to my god here,
But I mowe of my lord here!"
Such sorwe this lady to her took
That trewely I, which made this book,
Had swich pite and swich rowthe
To rede hir sorwe, that, by my trowthe,
I ferde the worse al the morwe
After, to thenken on her sorwe.

    So when this lady coude here no word
That no man mighte fynde hir lord,
Ful oft she swouned and seide "Alas!"
For sorwe ful nigh wood she was.
Ne she coude no reed but oon;

But doun on knees she sat anoon
And weep, that pite was to here.
   "A! mercy! swete lady dere!"
Quod she to Iuno, hir goddesse.
"Help me out of this distresse,
And yeve me grace my lord to see
Sone, or wite wher-so he be,
Or how he fareth or in what wyse,
And I shal make you sacrifyse,
And hoolly youres become I shal
With good wille, body, herte, and al.
And but thou wilt this, lady swete,
Send me grace to slepe, and mete
In my sleep som certeyn sweven,
Wher-through that I may knowen even
Whether my lord be quik or deed."
With that word she heng doun the heed,
And fil a-swown as cold as ston.
Hir women caughte her up anon,
And broghten hir in bed al naked;
And she, forweped and forwaked,
Was wery, and thus the dede sleep
Fil on her, or she took keep,
Through Iuno, that had herd hir bone,
That made hir to slepe sone.
For as she prayde, right so was don
In dede; for Iuno right anon
Called thus her messager
To do her erand, and he com neer.
Whan he was come, she bad him thus:
"Go bet," quod Iuno, "to Morpheus—
Thou knowest him wel, the god of sleep.
Now understond wel and tak keep.
Sey thus on my half, that he
Go faste into the grete see,
And bid him that on alle thing
He take up Seys' body the king,
That lyth ful pale and no-thing rody.

Bid him crepe into the body
And do it goon to Alcyone
The quene, ther she lyth alone,
And shewe hir shortly, hit is no nay,
How hit was dreynt this other day;
And do the body speke right so,
Right as hit was wont to do
The whyles that hit was on lyve.
Go now faste, and hy thee blyve!"

  This messager took leve and wente
Upon his wey, and nevere ne stente
Til he com to the derke valeye
That stant bytwene roches tweye,
Ther nevere yet grew corn ne gras,
Ne tree, ne nothing that ought was,
Beste, ne man, ne nothing elles,
Save ther were a fewe welles
Came renning fro the cliffes adoun,
That made a deedly sleping soun,
And ronnen doun right by a cave
That was under a rokke y-grave
Amid the valeye wonder depe.
Ther thise goddes laye and slepe,
Morpheus, and Eclympasteyr
(That was the god of slepes heyr),
That slepe and did non other werk,

  This cave was also as derk
As helle pit over-al aboute.
They had good leyser for to route,
To envye who might slepe best.
Some henge hir chin upon hir brest
And slepe upright, hir heed y-hed,
And some laye naked in hir bed,
And slepe whyles the dayes laste.

  This messager com flying faste,
And cryed, "O ho! awak anon!"
Hit was for noght; ther herde him non.
"Awak!" quod he, "who is, lyth there?"

And blew his horn right in hir ere, *host*
And cryed "Awaketh!" wonder hyë.
This god of sleep with his oon yë
Cast up and axed, "Who clepeth ther?"
"Hit am I," quod this messager;
"Iuno bad thou shuldest goon"—
And tolde him what he shulde doon
As I have told yow heer-tofore:
Hit is no need reherse hit more:
And wente his wey, whan he had sayd.

Anon this god of sleep a-brayd
Out of his sleep, and gan to goon
And did as he had bede him doon,
Took up the dreynte body sone
And bar hit forth to Alcyone,
His wyf the quene, ther-as she lay,
Right even a quarter before day,
And stood right at hir beddes feet,
And called hir right as she heet
By name, and seyde, "My swete wyf,
Awak! let be your sorwful lyf!
For in your sorwe ther lyth no reed;
For certes, swete, I am but deed.
Ye shul me nevere on lyve y-see.
But goode swete herte, that ye
Bury my body, for such a tyde
Ye mowe hit finde the see besyde.
And far-wel, swete, my worldes blisse!
I praye God your sorwe lisse.
To litel whyl our blisse lasteth!"

With that hir eyen up she casteth,
And saw noght. "Allas!" quod she for sorwe,
And deyed within the thridde morwe.
But what she sayde more in that swow
I may not telle yow as now;
It were to longe for to dwelle.
My first matere I wil yow telle,
Wherfore I have told this thing

Of Alcione and Seys the king.
   For thus mochę dar I saye wel:
I had be dolven everydel,
And deed, right through defaute of sleep,
If I nad red and taken keep
Of this tale next before.
And I wol telle yow wherfore;
For I ne might, for botę ne bale,
Slepe or I had red this tale
Of this dreynte Seys the king
And of the goddes of sleping.
Whan I had red this tale wel
And over-loked hit everydel,
Me thoughte wonder if hit werę so;
For I had nevere herd speke, or tho,
Of no goddes that coude make
Men to slepe, ne for to wake,
For I ne knew nevere god but oon.
And in my game I sayde anoon
(And yet me list right evel to pleye)
" Rather then that I shulde deye
Through defaute of sleping thus,
I woldę yivę thilke Morpheus,
Or his goddesse, damę Iuno,
Or som wight elles, I ne roghte who—
To makę me slepe and havę som reste—
I wil yive him the alder-beste
Yifte that evęre he abood his lyve,
And here on wardę, right now, as blyve.
If he wol makę me slepe a lyte,
Of downe of pure dowves whyte
I wil yive him a fether-bed,
Rayed with gold, and right wel cled
In fyn blak satin doutremere,
And many a pilow, and every bere
Of cloth of Reynes, to slepe softe;
Him thar not nede to turnen ofte.
And I wol yive him al that falles

To a chambre; and al his halles
I wol do peynte with pure gold
And tapite hem ful many a fold
Of oo sute. This shal he have,
If I wiste wher were his cave,
If he can make me slepe sone
As did the goddesse Alcione.
And thus this ilke god, Morpheus,
May winne of me mo feës thus
Than evere he wan. And to Iuno,
That is his goddesse, I shall so do,
I trow that she shal holde her payd.

I had unnethe that word y-sayd
Right thus as I have told hit yow,
That sodeynly, I niste how,
Swich a lust anoon me took
To slepe, that right upon my book
I fil asleep, and therwith even
Me mette so inly swete a sweven,
So wonderful that nevere yit
I trowe no man hadde the wit
To conne wel my sweven rede:
No, not Ioseph, withoute drede,
Of Egypte, he that redde so
The kinges meting Pharao,
No more than coude the leste of us;
Ne nat scarsly Macrobeus,
(He that wroot al thavisioun
That he mette, King Scipioun,
The noble man, the Affrican—
Swiche mervayles fortuned than)
I trowe, a-rede my dremes even.
Lo, thus hit was, this was my sweven.

The Dream

Me thoughte thus:—that hit was May,
And in the dawning ther I lay,
Me mette thus, in my bed al naked;

And loked forth, for I was waked
With smale foules a gret heep,
That had affrayęd me out of my sleep
Through noyse and swetnesse of hir song.
And, as me mette, they sate among
Upon my chambre-roof withoute,
Upon the tyles over-al a-boute,
And songen, everich in his wyse,
The moste solempne servyse
By note, that evere man, I trowe,
Had herd; for som of hem song lowe,
Som hye, and al of oon acord.
To telle shortly, at oo word,
Was nevere y-herd so swete a stevene
But hit had be a thing of hevene:
So merye a soun, so swete entunes,
That certes, for the toun of Tewnes
I noldę but I had herd hem singe;
For al my chambre gan to ringe
Through singing of hir armonye.
For instrument nor melodye
Was nowher herd yet half so swete,
Nor of acorde half so mete;
For ther was noon of hem that feyned
To singe, for ech of hem him peyned
To finde outę merye crafty notes.
They ne spared not hir throtes.
And sooth to seyn, my chambre was
Ful wel depeynted, and with glas
Were al the windowęs wel y-glased
Ful clere, and nat an hool y-crased,
That to beholde hit was gret Ioye.
For hoolly al the storie of Troye
Was in the glasing y-wroght thus
Of Ector and of King Priamus,
Of Achilles and of King Lamedon,
And eek of Medea and of Iason,
Of Paris, Eleyne, and of Lavyne.

Conventional yet Chaucers sincere appreciation of a May morning

And alle the walles with colours fyne
Were peynted, bothe text and glose,
And al the Romaunce of the Rose.
My windowes weren shet echon,
And through the glas the sunne shon
Upon my bed with brighte bemes,
With many glade gilden stremes.
And eek the welken was so fair,
Blew, bright, clere was the air,
And ful atempre for sothe hit was:
For nother to cold nor hoot hit nas,
Ne in al the welken was a cloude.
    And as I lay thus, wonder loude
Me thoughte I herde an hunte blowe
Tassaye his horn, and for to knowe
Whether hit were cleer or hors of soun.
And I herde going bothe up and doun,
Men, hors, houndes, and other thing,
And al men speken of hunting,
How they wolde slee the hert with strengthe,
And how the hert had, upon lengthe,
So moche embosed, I not now what.
Anon-right whan I herde that,
How that they wolde on hunting goon,
I was right glad, and up anoon
Took my hors, and forth I wente
Out of my chambre. I nevere stente
Til I com to the feld withoute.
Ther overtook I a gret route
Of huntes and eek of foresteres,
With many relayes and lymeres,
And hyed hem to the forest faste
And I with hem. So at the laste
I asked oon, ladde a lymere:
"Say, felowe, who shal hunte here?"
Quod I, and he answerde ageyn:
"Sir, themperour Octovien,"
Quod he, "and is heer faste by."

"A Goddes half, in good tymę!" quod I,
"Go we faste!" and gan to ryde.
Whan we camę to the forest-syde,
Every man did right anoon
As to hunting fil to doon.
The mayster-hunte anoon, fot-hoot,
With a gret horn blew three moot
At the uncoupling of his houndes.
Within a whyl the hert y-founde is,
Y-halowed and rechased faste
Longę tyme; and so at the laste
This hert rused and stal away
Fro alle the houndes a prevy way.
The houndes had overshote hem alle,
And were on a defaute y-falle.
Therwith the hunte wonder faste
Blew a forloyn at the laste.
   I was go walked fro my tree,
And as I wente, ther cam by me
A whelp, that faunęd me as I stood,
That had y-folowed, and coudę no good.
Hit coom and creep to me as lowe,
Right as hit hadde me y-knowe,
Hild doun his heed and Ioyned his eres,
And leyde al smothe doun his heres.
I wolde havę caught hit, and anoon
Hit fledde and was fro me goon.
And I him folwed, and hit forth wente
Doun by a floury grene wente
Ful thikke of gras, ful softe and swete,
With floures fele, faire under fete,
And litel used, hit semed thus:
For bothe Flora and Zephirus,
They two that make floures growe,
Had made hir dwelling ther, I trowe.
For hit was, on to beholde,
As thogh the erthe envye wolde
To be gayer than the hevene

To have mo floures, swiche sevene
As in the welken sterres be.
Hit had forgete the povertee
That winter through his colde morwes
Had mad hit suffren, and his sorwes:
Al was forgeten, and that was sene.
For al the wode was waxen grene,
Swetnesse of dewe had mad it waxe.

Hit is no nede eek for to axe
Wher ther werȩ many grene greves,
Or thikke of trees so ful of leves;
And every tree stood by him-selve
Fro other wel ten foot or twelve:
So grete trees, so huge of strengthe,
Of fourty or fifty fadme lengthe,
Clenȩ withoute bough or stikke,
With croppes brode and eek as thikke—
They were nat an inche a-sonder—
That hit was shadwe over-al under.
And many an hert and many an hinde
Was both beforȩ me and bihinde.
Of founes, soures, bukkes, doës
Was ful the wode, and many roës,
And many squirelles, that sete
Ful hye upon the trees and ete
And in hir maner made festes.
Shortly, hit was so ful of bestes
That thogh Argus, the noble countour,
Sete to rekene in his countour
And rekȩne with his figures ten
(For by tho figures mowe al ken,
If they be crafty, rekene and noumbre
And telle of every thing the noumbre)
Yet shulde he fayle to rekene even
The wondres me mette in my sweven.

But forth they romed right wonder faste
Doun the wode. So at the laste
I was war of a man in blak,

That sat and had y-turned his bak
To an ook, an huge tree.
"Lord!" thoughte I, "who may that be?
What ayleth him to sitten heer?"
Anoon-right I wente neer.
Than fond I sitten even upright
A wonder wel-faringe knight
(By the maner me thoughte so)
Of good mochel and right yong thereto,
Of the age of four and twenty yeer.
Upon his berd but litel heer,
And he was clothed al in blak.
I stalked even unto his bak
And ther I stood as stille as ought
That, sooth to saye, he saw me nought.
He sayde a lay, a maner song,
Withoute note, withoute song,
And hit was this (for wel I can
Reherse hit)—right thus hit began:—

　　"I have of sorwe so gret woon
　　That Ioye gete I nevere noon
　　　　Now that I see my lady bright,
　　　　Which I have loved with al my might,
　　Is fro me deed, and is a-goon.

　　"Allas, O Deeth! what ayleth thee,
　　That thou noldest have taken me
　　　　Whan that thou toke my lady swete?
　　That was so fayr, so freshe, so free,
　　So good, that men may wel see
　　　　Of al goodnesse she had no mete!"—
Whan he had maad thus his complaynte,
His sorowful herte gan faste faynte;
For he had wel nigh lost his minde,
Thogh Pan, that men clepe god of kinde,
Were for his sorwes nevere so wrooth.

　　But at the laste, to sayn right sooth,
He was war of me, how I stood
Before him and did of myn hood

And had y-gret him as I best coude.
Debonairly and no-thing loude
He sayde, "I prey thee, be not wrooth.
I herde thee not, to sayn the sooth,
Ne I saw thee not, sir, trewely."

"A! goode sir, no fors," quod I,
"I am right sory if I have ought
Destroubled yow out of your thought.
For-yive me if I have mis-take."

"Yis, thamendes is light to make,"
Quod he, "for ther lyth noon ther-to.
Ther is no-thing missayd nor do."

Lo! how goodly spak this knight,
As it had been another wight;
He made it nouther tough ne queynte.
And I saw that and gan me aqueynte
With him, and fond him so tretable,
Right wonder skilful and resonable,
As me thoghte, for al his bale.
Anoon-right I gan finde a tale
To him, to loke wher I might ought
Have more knowing of his thought.

"Sire," quod I, "this game is doon.
I holde that this hert be goon:
Thise huntes conne him nowher see."

"I do no fors thereof," quod he,
"My thought is ther-on nevere a del."

"By our Lord," quod I, "I trow yow wel,
Right so me thinketh by your chere.
But, sir, oo thing wol ye here?
Me thinketh in gret sorwe I yow see.
But certes, sire, yif that ye
Wolde ought discure me your wo,
I wolde, as wis God helpe me so,
Amende hit, yif I can or may.
Ye mowe preve hit by assay;
For, by my trouthe, to make yow hool
I wol do al my power hool.

Sk. 517–554

And telleth me of your sorwes smerte:
Paraventure hit may ese your herte,
That semeth ful seek under your syde."
    With that he loked on me asyde,
As who sayth, "Nay, that wol not be."
"Graunt mercy, goode frend," quod he,
"I thanke thee that thou woldest so,
But hit may nevere the rather be do.
No man may my sorwe glade,
That maketh my hewe to falle and fade;
For I am sorwe and sorwe is I.
Allas! and I wol telle the why.
My song is turned to pleyninge
And al my laughter to wepinge,
My glade thoghtes to hevinesse;
In travaile is myn ydelnesse.
My boldnesse is turned to shame,
For false Fortune hath pleyd a game
At the ches with me, allas! the whyle!
The trayteresse false and ful of gyle,
That al behoteth and no-thing halt,
She goth upryght and yet she halt,
That baggeth foule and loketh faire,
The dispitouse debonaire!
Ful many oon hath she thus y-blent.
She is pley of enchauntement,
That semeth oon and is nat so.
The false theef! what hath she do,
Trowest thou? By our Lord, I wol thee seye.
At the ches with me she gan to pleye;
With hir false draughtes divers
She stal on me and took my fers.
And whan I saw my fers aweye,
Alas! I couthe no lenger pleye,
But seyde, 'Farwel, swete, y-wis,
And farwel al that evere ther is!'
Therwith Fortune seyde 'Chek heer!'
And 'Maat!' in the mid point of the chekker

With a poun erraunt, allas!
Ful craftier to pley she was
Than Athalus, that made the game
First of the ches. So was his name.
I have more sorowe than Tantale."

  And whan I herde him telle this tale
Thus pitously, as I yow telle,
Unnethe mighte I lenger dwelle.
Hit did myn herte so moche wo.

  "A! good sir!" quod I, "say not so!
Have som pite on your nature
That formed yow to creature.
Remembre yow of Socrates:
For he ne counted nat three strees
Of noght that Fortune coude do."

  "Why so?" quod he. "Hit is nat so!
Thou wost ful litel what thou menest;
I have lost more than thou wenest."

  "Lo, sir, how that may be," quod I,
"Goode sir, tel me al hoolly;
In what wyse, how, why, and wherfore
That ye have thus your blisse lore."

  "Blythly," quod he. "Com sit adoun.
I telle thee upon a condicioun
That thou shalt hoolly, with al thy wit,
Do thyn entente to herkene hit."

  "Yis, sir." "Swer thy trouthe ther-to."
  "Gladly." "Do than holde her-to."

  "I shal right blythly, so God me save,
Hoolly, with al the wit I have,
Here yow as wel as I can."

  "A Goddes half!" quod he and began:—
"Sire," quod he, "sith first I couthe
Have any maner wit fro youthe,
Or kyndely understonding
To comprehende in any thing
What love was, in myn owne wit,
Dredeles I have evere yit

Be tributary and yeve rente
To Love hoolly with good entente,
And through plesaunce become his thral,
With good wille, body, herte, and al.
Al this I putte in his servage,
As to my lord, and did homage.
Hit happed that I cam on a day
Into a place ther that I say
Trewly the fayrest companyë
Of ladies that evere man with yë
Had seen togedres in oo place.
Shal I clepe hit hap other grace
That broghte me there? Nay, but Fortune,
That is to lyen ful comune,
The false trayteresse, pervers,
God wolde I coude clepe hir wers!
For now she worcheth me ful wo,
And I wol telle sone why so.

"Among thise ladies thus echoon,
Sooth to seyen, I saw oon
That was lyk noon of the route.
For I dar swere, withoute doute,
That as the someres sonne bright
Is fairer, clerer, and hath more light
Than any other planete in hevene,
The mone, or the sterres sevene,
For al the world, so hadde she
Surmounted hem alle of beaute,
That purely tho myn owne thoght
Seyde hit were bettre serve hir for noght
Than with another to be wel.
And hit was sooth, for everydel
I wil anoon-right telle thee why.

"I saw hir daunce so comlily,
Carole and singe so swetely,
Laughe and pleye so womanly,
And loke so debonairly,
So goodly speke and so frendly,

That certes, I trow, that everemor
Nas seyn so blisful a tresor.
For every heer upon hir heed,
Soth to seyn, hit was not reed,
Ne nouther yelowe, ne broun hit nas:
Me thoghte most lyk gold hit was.
And whiche eyen my lady hadde!
Debonaire, goode, glade, and sadde,
Simple, of good mochel, noght to wyde.
Therto hir look nas not a-syde,
Ne overthwert, but beset so wel,
Hit drew and took up everydel
Alle that on hir gan beholde.
Hir eyen semed anoon she wolde
Have mercy.   Fooles wenden so;
But hit was nevere the rather do.
Hit nas no countrefeted thing:
It was hir owne pure loking,
That the goddesse, Dame Nature,
Had made hem opene by mesure
And close.   For were she nevere so glad,
Hir loking was not foly sprad
Ne wildely, thogh that she pleyde;
But evere, me thoghte, hir eyen seyde,
'By God, my wrathe is al for-yive!'
   "Therwith hir liste so wel to live
That dulnesse was of hir a-drad.
She nas to sobre ne to glad.
In alle thinges more mesure
Had nevere, I trowe, creature.
But many oon with hir look she herte;
And that sat hir ful lyte at herte;
For she knew no-thing of hir thoght.
But whether she knew, or knew it noght,
Algate she ne roghte of hem a stree!
To gete hir love no ner nas he
That woned at home, than he in Inde:
The formest was alway behinde.

But goode folk, over al other,
She loved as man may do his brother,
Of which love she was wonder large
In skilful places that bere charge.
  "But which a visage had she ther-to!
Allas! myn herte is wonder wo
That I ne can discryven hit!
Me lakketh bothe English and wit
For to undo hit at the fulle.
And eek my spirits be so dulle
So greet a thing for to devyse.
I have no wit that can suffyse
To comprehenden hir beaute.
But thus moche dar I seyn, that she
Was rody, freshe, and lyvely hewed,
And every day hir beaute newed.
And negh hir face was alder-best,
For certes, Nature had swich lest
To make that faire, that trewly she
Was hir cheef patron of beautee,
And cheef ensample of al hir werk,
And moustre. For be hit nevere so derk
Me thinketh I see hir evere-mo.
And yet more-over, thogh alle tho
That evere lived were now a-lyve,
Ne sholde have founde to discryve
In al hir face a wikked signe,
For hit was sad, simple, and benigne.
  "And which a goodly softe speche
Hadde that swete, my lyves leche!
So frendly, and so wel y-grounded,
Up al resoun so wel y-founded
And so tretable to alle gode,
That I dar swere wel by the rode,
Of eloquence was nevere founde
So swete a sowninge facounde,
Ne trewer tonged, ne scorned lasse,
Ne bet coude hele: that by the masse

I durste swere, thogh the pope hit songe,
That ther was nevere yet through hir tonge
Man ne woman gretly harmed.
As for hire was al harm hid;
Ne lasse flatering in hir word
That purely hir simple record
Was founde as trewe as any bond,
Or trouthe of any mannes hond.
Ne chide she coude nevere a del,
That knoweth al the world ful wel.

    "But swich a fairnesse of a nekke
Had that swete, that boon nor brekke
Nas ther non sene that mis-sat.
Hit was whyt, smothe, streght, and flat,
Withouten hole; or canel-boon
As by scming had she noon.
Hir throte, as I have now memoire,
Semed a round tour of yvoire
Of good gretnesse and noght to greet.

    "And gode faire Whyt she heet,
That was my lady name right.
She was bothe fair and bright,
She hadde not hir name wrong.
Right faire shuldres and body long
She hadde, and armes, every lith
Fattish, flesshly, not greet therwith.
Therto she coude so wel pleye,
Whan that hir liste, that I dar seye
That she was lyk to torche bright,
That every man may take of light
Ynogh, and hit hath nevere the lesse.

    "Of manere and of comlinesse
Right so ferde my lady dere.
For every wight of hir manere
Might cacche ynogh, if that he wolde,
If he had eyen hir to beholde.
For I dar swere wel, if that she
Had among ten thousand be,

She wolde havę be, at the leste,
A cheef mirour of al the feste,
Thogh they had stonden in a rowe
To mennes eyen that coude havę knowe.
For wher-so men had pleyd or waked,
Me thoghte the felawshipe as naked
Withouten hir, that I saw ones,
As a coroune withoute stones.
Trewly she was, to myn yë,
The soleyn fenix of Arabyë,
For ther liveth nevere but oon.
Ne swich as she ne knew I noon.

"To speke of goodnessę, trewly she
Had as moche debonairte
As evere had Hester in the Bible,
And more if more werę possible.
And soth to seyne, therewith-al
She had a wit so general,
So hool enclyned to alle gode,
That al hir wit was set, by the rode,
Withoutę malice upon gladnesse.
And thereto I saw nevere yet a lesse
Harmful than she was in doinge.
I sey nat that she ne had knowinge
What harm was; or elles she
Had coud no gode, so thinketh me.

"And trewly, for to speke of trouthe,
But she had had, hit had be routhe.
Thereof she had so moche hir del—
And I dar seyn and swere hit wel—
That Trouthe him-self, over al and al,
Had chose his maner principal
In hir, that was his resting-place.
Ther-to she hadde the moste grace
To havę stedfast perseveraunce,
And esy, atempre governaunce,
That evere I knew or wiste yit:
So pure suffraunt was hir wit.

And reson gladly she understood;
Hit folowed wel she coude good.
She used gladly to do wel.
These were hir maners every-del.

"Therwith she loved so wel right,
She wrong do wolde to no wight.
No wight might do hir no shame,
She loved so wel hir owne name.
Hir luste to holde no wight in honde:
Ne, be thou siker, she nolde fonde
To holde no wight in balaunce
By halfe word ne by countenaunce,
But-if men wolde upon hir lye;
Ne sende men in-to Walakye,
To Pruyse and in-to Tartarye,
To Alisaundre ne in-to Turkye,
And bidde him faste anoon that he
Go hoodless in-to the drye see
And come hoom by the Carrenar,
And seye, 'Sir, be now right war
That I may of yow here seyn
Worship or that ye come ageyn!'
She ne used no suche knakkes smale.

"But wherfore that I telle my tale?
Right on this same, as I have seyd.
Was hoolly al my love leyd.
For certes, she was, that swete wyf,
My suffisaunce, my lust, my lyf,
Myn hap, myn hele, and al my blisse,
My worldes welfare and my lisse,
And I hirs hoolly, everydel."

"By our lord," quod I, "I trowe yow wel!
Hardely your love was wel beset,
I not how ye mighte have do bet."
"Bet? Ne no wight so wel!" quod he.
"I trowe hit, sir," quod I, "parde!"
"Nay, leve hit wel!" "Sir, so do I.
I leve yow wel, that trewely

Yow thoghte that she was the beste,
And to beholde the alderfaireste,
Who so had loked her with your eyen."

"With myn? Nay, alle that hir seyen
Seyde, and sworen hit was so.
And thogh they ne hadde, I wolde tho
Have loved best my lady fre,
Thogh I had had al the beautee
That ever had Alcipyades,
And al the strengthe of Ercules.
For wonder fayn I wolde hir see:
So mochel hit amended me
That whan I saw hir first a-morwe
I was warished of al my sorwe
Of al day after, til hit were eve.
Me thoghte no-thing mighte me greve,
Were my sorwes nevere so smerte.
And yit she sit so in myn herte
That, by my trouthe, I nolde noght,
For al this world, out of my thoght
Leve my lady—no, trewly!"

"Now, by my trouthe, sir," quod I,
"Me thinketh ye have such a chaunce
As shrift withoute repentaunce."

"Repentaunce! Nay, fy!" quod he.
"Shulde I now repente me
To love? Nay, certes, than were I wel
Wers than was Achitofel,
Or Anthenor, so have I Ioye,
The traytour that betraysed Troye,
Or the false Genelon,
He that purchased the treson
Of Rowland and of Oliver.
Nay, whyl I am a-lyve heer
I nil foryete hir nevere-mo."

"Now, goode sire," quod I tho,
"Ye han wel told me her-before.
It is no nede reherse hit more

How ye sawe hir first and where.
But woldę ye telle me the manere,
To hir which was your firste speche
(Therof I wolde yow be-seche)
And how she knewe first your thoght,
Whether ye loved hir or noght.
And telleth me eek what ye have lore;
I herde yow telle her-before."

    "Ye," seyde he, "thou nost what thou menest.
I havę lost more than thou wenest."

    "What los is that?" quod I tho.
"Nil she not lovę yow? Is it so?
Or have ye oght doon amis
That she hath left yow? Is hit this?
For Goddes love, telle me al."

    "Beforę God," quod he, "and I shal.
I saye right as I have seyd.
On hir was al my love leyd,
And yet she niste hit nevere a del
Noght longe tyme, leve hit wel!
For be right siker, I durste noght
For al this world telle hir my thoght,
Ne I wolde have wratthed hir, trewly.
For wostow why? She was lady
Of the body: she had the herte,
And who hath that, may not asterte.

    "But, for to kepę me fro ydelnesse,
Trewly I did my besinesse
To make songes as I best coude,
And ofte tyme I song hem loude.
I thoughte ones I wolde fonde
To do hir knowe and understonde
My wo; and she wel understood
That I ne wilned thing but good
And worship and to kepe hir name
Over al thing, and drede hir shame.
And was so besy hir to serve,
And pite were I shulde sterve,

Sith that I wilned noon harm, y-wis.
So whan my lady knew al this,
My lady yaf me al hoolly
The noble yifte of hir mercy,
Saving hir worship, by al weyes.
Dredles, I mene noon other weyes.
And therwith she yaf me a ring—
I trowe hit was the firste thing.
But if myn herte was y-waxe
Glad, that is no nede to axe!
As helpe me God, I was as blyve
Reysed as fro dethe to lyve:
Of alle happes the alder-beste,
The gladdest and the most at reste.
For trewely, that swete wight,
Whan I had wrong and she the right,
She wolde alwey so goodely
For-yeve me so debonairly.
In alle my youthe, in alle chaunce,
She took me in hir governaunce.

"Therwith she was alway so trewe,
Our Ioye was ever y-liche newe.
Our hertes wern so even a payre
That nevere nas that oon contrayre
To that other, for no wo.
For sothe, y-liche they suffred tho
Oo blisse and eek oo sorwe bothe.
Y-liche they were bothe gladde and wrothe;
Al was us oon, withoute wer.
And thus we lived ful many a yeer
So wel, I can nat telle how."

"Sire," quod I, "wher is she now?"
"Now!" quod he, and stinte anoon.
Therwith he wex as deed as stoon,
And seyde, "Allas! that I was bore!
That was the los that her-before
I tolde thee that I had lorn.
Bethenk how I seyde her-beforn,

'Thou wost ful litel what thou menest;
I have lost more than thou wenest.'
God wot, allas! right that was she!"

   "Allas! sir, how? What may that be?"
"She is deed!" "Nay!" "Yis, by my trouthe!"
"Is that your los? By God, hit is routhe!"
   And with that word, right anoon,
They gan to strake forth: al was doon,
For that tyme, the hert-hunting.

   With that me thoghte, that this king
Gan quickly hoomward for to ryde
Unto a place, was ther besyde,
Which was from us but a lyte,
A long castel with walles whyte,
By Seynte Iohan! on a riche hil,
As me mette, but thus it fil.

   Right thus me mette, as I yow telle,
That in the castel ther was a belle,
As hit had smiten houres twelve.—
Therwith I awook my-selve,
And fond me lying in my bed.
And the book that I had red,
Of Alcyone and Seys the king
And of the goddes of sleping,
I fond it in myn hond ful even.

   Thoghte I, "This is so queynte a sweven
That I wol, by processe of tyme,
Fonde to putte this sweven in ryme
As I can best, and that anoon."
This was my sweven. Now hit is doon.

Explicit the Book of the Duchesse.

Sk. 1305–1334

a humorous grotesque

THE HOUS OF FAME

Book I

God turne us every dreem to gode!
For hit is wonder, by the rode,
To my wit, what causeth swevenes
Either on morwes or on evenes;
And why the effect folweth of somme,
And of somme hit shal nevere come;
Why that is an avisioun,
And why this a revelacioun;
Why this a dreem, *vision* why that a sweven, *dream*
And nat to every man liche even;
Why this a fantome, why these oracles,
I noot; but who-so of these miracles
The causes knoweth bet than I,
Devyne he; for I certeinly
Ne can hem noght, ne nevere thinke
To besily my wit to swinke
To knowe of hir signifiaunce
The gendres, neither the distaunce
Of tymes of hem, ne the causes
For-why this is more than that cause is—
As if folkes complexiouns
Make hem dreme of reflexiouns,
Or elles thus, as other sayn,
For to greet feblenesse of her brayn,
By abstinence or by seeknesse,
Prison, stewe, or greet distresse,
Or elles by disordinaunce
Of naturel acustomaunce,
That som man is to curious
In studie, or melancolious,
Or thus, so inly ful of drede
That no man may him bote bede;

Or elles, that devocioun
Of somme, and contemplacioun
Causeth swiche dremes ofte;
Or that the cruel lyf unsofte
Which these ilke lovers leden
That hopen over muche or dreden
That purely hir impressiouns
Causeth hem avisiouns;
Or if that spirits have the might
To make folk to dreme a-night,
Or if the soule, of propre kinde,
Be so parfit as men finde
That hit forwot that is to come,
And that hit warneth alle and somme
Of everich of hir aventures
By avisiouns or by figures,
But that our flesh ne hath no might
To understonden hit aright,
For hit is warned to derkly—
But why the cause is, noght wot I.
Wel worthe of this thing grete clerkes,
That trete of this and other werkes;
For I of noon opinioun
Nil as now make mencioun,
But only that the holy rode
Turne us every dreem to gode!
For nevere sith that I was born,
Ne no man elles me biforn
Mette, I trowe stedfastly,
So wonderful a dreem as I
The tenthe day did of Decembre,
The which, as I can now remembre,
I wol yow tellen every del.

The Invocation

But at my ginning, trusteth wel,
I wol make invocacioun
With special devocioun

Unto the god of sleep anoon,
That dwelleth in a cave of stoon
Upon a streem that comth fro Lete,
That is a flood of helle unswete.
Besyde a folk men clepę Cimerie
Ther slepeth ay this god unmerie
With his slepy thousand sones
That alway for to slepe hir wone is,
And to this god that I of rede,
Preye I that he wol me spede
My sweven for to telle aright,
If every dreem stonde in his might.
And He, that mover is of al
That is and was and evere shal,
So yive hem Ioye that hit here
Of alle that they dremę to-yere,
And for to stonden alle in grace
Of hir loves, or in what place
That hem wer levest for to stonde,
And shelde hem fro poverte and shonde;
And fro unhappe and ech disese,
And sende hem al that may hem plese,
That take hit wel and scorne hit noght,
Ne hit misdemen in her thoght
Through malicious entencioun.
And who-so through presumpcioun,
Or hate or scorn or through envye,
Dispyt, or Iape, or vilanye,
Misdeme hit, preye I Iesus God
That—dreme he barfoot, dreme he shod—
That every harm that any man
Hath had sith the world began
Befalle him thereof or he sterve,
And graunte he mote hit ful deserve,
Lo! with swich a conclusioun
As had of his avisioun
Cresus, that was king of Lyde,
That high upon a gebet dyde!

This prayer shal he have of me;
I am no bet in charite!
Now herkneth, as I have you seyd,
What that I mette, or I abreyd.

The Dream

Of Decembre the tenthe day
Whan hit was night to slepe I lay
Right ther as I was wont to done,
And fil on slepe wonder sone
As he that wery was for-go
On pilgrimage myles two
To the corseynt Leonard
To make lythe of that was hard.

　　But as I sleep, me mette I was
Within a temple y-mad of glas,
In which ther were mo images
Of gold, stonding in sondry stages,
And mo riche tabernacles,
And with perre mo pinacles,
And mo curious portreytures,
And queynte maner of figures
Of olde werk then I saw evere.
For certeynly I niste nevere
Wher that I was, but wel wiste I
Hit was of Venus redely
The temple; for in portreyture
I saw anoon-right hir figure
Naked fleting in a see,
And also on hir heed, parde,
Hir rose-garlond whyt and reed,
And hir comb to kembe hir heed,
Hir dowves, and Daun Cupido,
Hir blinde sone, and Vulcano,
That in his face was ful broun.

　　But as I romed up and doun,
I fond that on a wal ther was
Thus writen on a table of bras:

"I wol now singe, if that I can,
The armes and also the man,
That first cam through his destinee,
Fugitif of Troye contree,
In Itaile with moche pyne
Unto the strondes of Lavyne."
And tho began the story anoon,
As I shal telle yow echoon.

First saw I the destruccioun
Of Troye through the Greek Sinoun,
With his false forsweringe,
And his chere and his lesinge,
Made the hors broght into Troye,
Thorgh which Troyens loste al hir Ioye.
And after this was grave, allas!
How Ilioun assailed was
And wonne, and King Priam y-slain,
And Polites his sone, certayn,
Dispitously of Dan Pirrus.

And next that saw I how Venus,
Whan that she saw the castel brende,
Doun fro the hevene gan descende
And bad hir sone Eneas flee;
And how he fledde, and how that he
Escaped was from al the pres,
And took his fader, Anchises,
And bar him on his bak away,
Crying, "Allas, and welaway!"
Ther saw I graven eek how he,
His fader eek and his meynee,
With his shippes gan to sayle
Toward the contree of Itaile.
Ther saw I swich tempest aryse
That every herte mighte agryse
To see hit peynted on the wal.
Ther saw I graven eek withal,
Venus, how ye, my lady dere,
Weping with ful woful chere,

Prayen Iupiter an hye
To save and kepe that navye
Of the Troyan Eneas
Sith that he hir sone was.
Ther saw I Ioves Venus kisse
And graunted of the tempest lisse.
Ther saw I how the tempest stente,
And how with alle pyne he wente
And prevely took arrivage
In the contree of Cartage.
Ther saw I grave how Eneas
Tolde Dido every cas
That him was tid upon the see
And after grave was how she
Made of him, shortly, at oo word,
Hir lyf, hir love, hir lust, hir lord:
Lo, how a woman doth amis
To love him that unknowen is!

But let us speke of Eneas,
How he betrayed hir, allas!
And lefte hir ful unkindely.
So whan she saw al-utterly
That he wolde hir of trouthe faile,
And wende fro hir to Itaile,
She gan to wringe hir hondes two.
"Allas!" quod she, "What me is wo!"

Tho saw I grave al tharivaile
That Eneas had in Itaile,
And with King Latine his tretee,
And alle the batailles that he
Was at himself and eek his knightes
Or he had al y-wonne his rightes,
And how he Turnus refte his lyf
And wan Lavyna to his wyf,
And al the mervelous signals
Of the goddes celestials,
How, maugre Iuno, Eneas,
For al hir sleighte and hir compas,

Acheved al his aventure,
For Iupiter took of him cure
At the prayere of Venus:
The which I preye alway save us,
And us ay of our sorwes lighte!

Whan I had seyen al this sighte
In this noble temple thus,
"A, Lord!" thoughte I, "that madest us,
Yet saw I nevere swich noblesse
Of images ne swich richesse
As I saw graven in this chirche;
But not woot I who did hem wirche,
Ne wher I am, ne in what contree.
But now wol I go oute and see
Right at the wiket if I can
See o-wher stering any man
That may me telle wher I am."

Whan I out at the dores cam,
I faste aboute me beheld.
Then saw I but a large feld
As fer as that I mighte see,
Withoutcn toun, or hous, or tree,
Or bush, or gras, or ered lond;
For al the feld nas but of sond
As smal as man may see yet lye
In the desert of Libye.
Ne I no maner creature
That is y-formed by nature
Ne saw I me to rede or wisse.
"O Crist," thoughte I, "that art in blisse,
Fro fantome and illusioun
Me save!" and with devocioun
Myn yën to the hevene I caste.

Tho was I war, lo! at the laste,
That faste by the sonne, as hyë
As kenne mighte I with myn yë,
Me thoughte I saw an egle sore,
But that hit semed moche more

Then I had any egle seyn.
But this as sooth as deeth, certeyn,
Hit was of gold and shoon so brighte
That nevere sawe men such a sighte
But if the hevene had y-wonne
Al newe of gold another sonne.
So shoon the egles fethres brighte,
And somewhat dounward gan hit lighte.

Explicit liber primus.

Book II

Incipit liber secundus.

Proem

Now herkneth, every maner man
That English understonde can,
And listeth of my dreem to lere:
For now at erste shul ye here
So selly an avisioun
That Isaye ne Scipioun
Ne King Nabugodonosor,
Pharo, Turnus, ne Elcanor,
Ne mette swich a dreem as this!
Now faire blisful, O Cipris,
So be my favour at this tyme!
And ye me to endyte and ryme
Helpeth that on Parnaso dwelle
By Elicon the clere welle.
O Thought, that wroot al that I mette,
And in the tresorie hit shette
Of my brayn! now shal men see
If any vertu in thee be
To tellen al my dreem aright.
Now kyth thyn engyn and might.

The Dream.

This egle, of which I have yow told,
That shoon with fethres as of gold,
Which that so hyë gan to sore,
I gan beholde more and more,
To see hir beautee and the wonder.
But nevere was ther dint of thonder,
Ne that thing that men calle foudre,
That smoot somtyme a tour to poudre
And in his swifte coming brende,
That so swythe gan descende
As this foul whan hit beheld
That I a-roume was in the feld;
And with his grimme pawes stronge
Within his sharpe nayles longe
Me, fleing, at a swap he hente,
And with his sours agayn up wente
Me carying in his clawes starke
As lightly as I were a larke,—
How high, I can not telle yow,
For I cam up, I niste how.
For so astonied and a-sweved
Was every vertu in my heved,
What with his sours and with my drede,
That al my feling gan to dede,
For-why hit was to greet affray.

Thus I longe in his clawes lay
Til at the laste he to me spak
In mannes vois and seyde, "Awak!
And be not so a-gast, for shame!"
And called me tho by my name.
And for I sholde the bet abreyde,
Me mette "Awak!" to me he seyde
Right in the same vois and stevene
That useth oon I coude nevene;
And with that vois, soth for to sayn,

My minde cam to me agayn,
For hit was goodly seyd to me,
So nas hit nevere wont to be.

   And herwithal I gan to stere
And he me in his feet to bere
Til that he felte that I haddę hete
And felte eek tho myn herte bete.
And tho gan he me to disporte
And with wordes to comforte,
And sayde twyes, "Seynte Marie!
Thou are noyous for to carie,
And nothing nedeth hit, parde!
For al-so wis God helpe me
As thou non harm shalt have of this;
And this cas that betid thee is
Is for thy lore and for thy prow.
Let see! darst thou yet loke now?
Be ful assured, boldely,—
I am thy frend." And therwith I
Gan for to wondren in my minde.
"O God," thoughte I, "that madest kinde,
Shal I non other weyes dye?
Wher Ioves wol me stellifye
Or what thing may this signifye?
I neither am Enok, ne Elye,
Ne Romulus, ne Ganymede
That was y-bore up, as men rede,
To hevene with Dan Iupiter
And maad the goddes boteler."

   Lo! this was tho my fantasye!
But he that bar me gan espye
That I so thoghte, and seyde this:
"Thou demest of thy-self amis;
For Ioves is not ther-aboute
(I dar wel puttę thee out of doute)
To make of thee as yet a sterre.
But er I berę thee moche ferre,
I wol thee telle what I am

And whider thou shalt and why I cam
To done this, so that thou take
Good herte and not for fere quake."
"Gladly," quod I. "Now wel," quod he,
"First I that in my feet have thee,
Of which thou hast a fere and wonder,
Am dwelling with the god of thonder,
Which that men callen Iupiter,
That dooth me flee ful ofte fer
To done al his comaundement.
And for this cause he hath me sent
To thee: now herke, by thy trouthe!—
Certeyn, he hath of thee routhe
That thou so longe trewely
Hast served so ententifly
His blinde nevew Cupido,
And faire Venus goddesse also,
Withoute guerdoun ever yit,
And nevertheles hast set thy wit—
Although that in thy heed ful lyte is—
To make bokes, songes, dytees,
In ryme or elles in cadence,
As thou best canst, in reverence
Of Love and of his servants eke
That have his servise soght and seke;
And peynest thee to preyse his art,
Althogh thou haddest nevere part:
Wherfore, also God me blesse,
Ioves halt hit greet humblesse
And vertu eek that thou wolt make
A-night ful ofte thyn heed to ake,
In thy studie so thou wrytest
And evere-mo of love endytest
In honour of him and preysinges,
And in his folkes furtheringes,
And in hir matere al devysest
And noght him nor his folk despysest,
Although thou mayst go in the daunce

Of hem that him list not avaunce.
"Wherfore, as I seyde, y-wis,
Iupiter considereth this
And also, beau sir, other thinges:
That is, that thou hast no tydinges
Of Loves folk, if they be glade,
Ne of noght elles that God made;
And noght only fro fer contree
That ther no tydinge comth to thee,
But of thy verray neyghebores,
That dwellen almost at thy dores,
Thou herest neither that ne this.
For whan thy labour doon al is,
And hast y-maad thy rekeninges,
In stede of reste and newe thinges
Thou gost hoom to thy hous anoon,
And also domb as any stoon
Thou sittest at another book
Til fully daswed is thy look,
And livest thus as an hermyte,
Although thyn abstinence is lyte.

"And therfore Ioves through his grace
Wol that I bere thee to a place
Which that hight THE HOUS OF FAME,
To do thee som disport and game
In som recompensacioun
Of labour and devocioun
That thou hast had, lo! causeles,
To Cupido, the reccheles!
And thus this god thorgh his meryte
Wol with som maner thing thee quyte,
So that thou wolt be of good chere.
For truste wel that thou shalt here,
When we be comen ther I seye,
Mo wonder thinges, dar I leye,
And of Loves folk mo tydinges,
Bothe soth-sawes and lesinges;
And mo loves newe begonne,

And longe y-served loves wonne,
And mo loves casuelly
That ben betid, no man wot why,
But as a blind man stert an hare;
And more Iolytee and fare,
Whyl that they finde love of stele,
As thinketh hem, and over-al wele;
Mo discords and mo Ielousyes,
Mo murmurs and mo novelryes,
And mo dissimulaciouns
And feyned reparaciouns;
And mo berdes in two houres
Withoute rasour or sisoures
Y-maad, then greynes be of sondes;
And eke mo holding in hondes;
And also mo renovelaunces
Of olde forleten aqueyntaunces;
Mo love-dayes and acordes
Then on instruments ben cordes;
And eek of loves mo eschaunges
Than evere cornes were in graunges:—
Unethe maistow trowen this?"
Quod he, "No, helpe me God so wis!"—
Quod I. "No? Why?" quod he. "For hit
Were impossible to my wit,
Though that Fame had al the pyes
In al a realme, and al the spyes,
How that yet she shulde here al this
Or they espye hit." "O yis, yis!"
Quod he to me, "that can I preve
By resoun worthy for to leve,
So that thou yeve thyn advertence
To understonde my sentence.

    "First shalt thou heren wher she dwelleth:
And so thyn owne book hit telleth,
Hir paleys stant, as I shal seye,
Right even in middes of the weye
Betwixen hevene, erthe, and see,

That what-so-evere in al thesẹ three
Is spoken in privee or apert,
The way therto is so overt
And stant eek in so Iuste a place
That every soun mot to hit pace,
Or what so comth fro any tonge,
Be hit rouned, red, or songe,
Or spoke in seurtee or drede,
Certein, hit moste thider nede.

"Now herkne wel, for-why I wil
Tellen thee a propre skil
And worthy demonstracioun
In myn imaginacioun.

"Geffrey, thou wost right wel this,
That every kindly thing that is
Hath a kindly stede ther he
May best in hit conserved be,
Unto which placë every thing,
Through his kindly enclyning,
Moveth for to come to
Whan that hit is awey therfro.
As thus: lo, thou mayst al day see
That any thing that hevy be,
As stoon or leed or thing of wighte,
And ber hit nevere so hye on highte,
Lat go thyn hand, hit falleth doun.
Right so seye I by fyre or soun
Or smoke or other thinges lighte,
Alwey they seke upward on highte;
Whyl ech of hem is at his large,
Light thing up, and dounward charge.

"And for this cause mayst thou see
That every river to the see
Enclyned is to go by kinde,
And by these skilles, as I finde,
Hath fish dwelling in flood and see,
And treës eek in erthe be.
Thus every thing by this resoun

Hath his propre mansioun, *dwelling*
To which hit seketh to repaire
As ther hit shulde not apaire.
Lo, this sentence is knowen couth
Of every philosophres mouth,
As Aristotle and Dan Platon
And other clerkes many oon.
And to confirme my resoun,
Thou wost wel this, that speche is soun,
Or elles no man mighte hit here.
Now herke what I wol thee lere. *teach*

"Soun is noght but air y-broken;
And every speche that is spoken,
Loud or privee, foul or fair,
In his substaunce is but air.
For as flaumbe is but lighted smoke,
Right so soun is air y-broke.
But this may be in many wyse,
Of which I wil thee two devyse, *describe*
As soun that comth of pype or harpe.
For whan a pype is blowen sharpe,
The air is twist with violence
And rent: lo, this is my sentence;
Eek, whan men harpe-stringes smyte,
Whether hit be moche or lyte,
Lo, with the strook the air to-breketh.
Right so hit breketh whan men speketh:
Thus wost thou wel what thing is speche.

"Now hennesforth I wol thee teche
How every speche or noise or soun
Through his multiplicacioun,
Thogh hit were pyped of a mous,
Moot nede come to Fames Hous.
I preve hit thus—tak hede now—
By experience: for if that thou
Throwe on water now a stoon,
Wel wost thou hit wol make anoon
A litel roundel as a cercle,

Paraventure brood as a covercle;
And right anoon thou shalt see weel,
That wheel wol cause another wheel,
And that the thridde and so forth, brother,
And every cercle causing other,
Wyder than himselve was.
And thus, fro roundel to compas,
Ech aboute other goinge,
Caused of othres steringe,
And multiplying evere-mo
Til that hit be so fer y-go
That hit at bothe brinkes be.
Al-thogh thou mowe hit not y-see
Above, hit goth yet alway under,
Although thou thenke hit a gret wonder.
And who-so seith of trouthe I varie,
Bid him proven the contrarie.
And right thus every word, y-wis,
That loude or privee spoken is,
Moveth first an air aboute,
And of this moving, out of doute,
Another air anoon is meved.
As I have of the water preved
That every cercle causeth other,
Right so of air, my leve brother:
Everich air in other stereth
More and more, and speche up bereth,
Or vois or noise or word or soun,
Ay through multiplicacioun,
Til hit be atte Hous of Fame:—
Tak hit in ernest or in game.

    "Now have I told, if thou have minde,
How speche or soun, of pure kinde,
Enclyned is upward to meve.
This, mayst thou fele, wel I preve.
And that same place, y-wis,
That every thing enclyned to is,
Hath his kindeliche stede:

That sheweth hit, withouten drede,
That kindely the mansioun
Of every speche, of every soun,
Be hit either foul or fair,
Hath his kinde place in air.
And sin that every thing that is
Out of his kinde place, y-wis,
Moveth thider for to go
If hit a-weye be therfro,
As I before have preved thee,
Hit seweth, every soun, pardee,
Moveth kindely to pace
Al up into his kindely place.
And this place of which I telle,
Ther as Fame list to dwelle,
Is set amiddes of these three,
Hevene, erthe, and eek the see,
As most conservatif the soun.
Than is this the conclusioun,
That every speche of every man,
As I thee telle first began,
Moveth up on high to pace
Kindely to Fames place.
  "Telle me this feithfully:—
Have I not preved thus simply,
Withouten any subtiltee
Of speche, or gret prolixitee
Of termes of philosophye,
Of figures of poetrye,
Or colours of rethoryke?
Pardee, hit oghte thee to lyke;
For hard langage and hard matere
Is encombrous for to here
At ones. Wost thou not wel this?"
And I answerde, and seyde, "Yis."
  "A ha!" quod he, "lo, so I can,
Lewedly to a lewed man
Speke, and shewe him swiche skiles

That he may shake hem by the biles,
So palpable they shulden be.
But telle me this, now pray I thee,
How thinkth thee my conclusioun?"
Quod he.   "A good persuasioun,"
Quod I, "hit is, and lyk to be
Right so as thou hast preved me."
"By God," quod he, "and as I leve,
Thou shalt have yit, or hit be eve,
Of every word of this sentence
A preve, by experience,
And with thyn eres heren wel
Top and tail and everydel,
That every word that spoken is
Comth into Fames Hous, y-wis,
As I have seyd: what wilt thou more?"
And with this word upper to sore
He gan, and seyde, "By Seynt Iame!
Now wil we speken al of game."—

    "How farest thou?" quod he to me.
"Wel," quod I.   "Now see," quod he,
"By thy trouthe, yond adoun,
Wher that thou knowest any toun
Or hous or any other thing.
And whan thou hast of ought knowing
Loke that thou warne me,
And I anoon shal telle thee
How fer that thou art now therfro."

    And I adoun gan loken tho
And beheld feldes and plaines,
And now hilles and now mountaines,
Now valeys, and now forestes,
And now, unethes, grete bestes,
Now riveres, now citees,
Now tounes, and now grete trees,
Now shippes sailing in the see.

    But thus sone in a whyle he
Was flowen fro the grounde so hyë

That al the world, as to myn yë,
No more semed than a prikke,
Or elles was the air so thikke
That I ne mighte not discerne.
With that he spak to me as yerne,
And seyde, "Seestow any toun
Or ought thou knowest yonder doun?"
　　I seyde, "Nay." "No wonder nis,"
Quod he, "for half so high as this
Nas Alexander Macedo;
Ne the king, Dan Scipio,
That saw in dreem, at point devys,
Helle and erthe and paradys;
Ne eek the wrecche Dedalus,
Ne his child, nyce Icarus,
That fleigh so highe that the hete
His winges malt, and he fel wete
In-mid the see, and ther he dreynte,
For whom was maked mochę compleynte.
　　"Now turn upward," quod he, " thy face,
And behold this large place,
This air.　But loke thou ne be
Adrad of hem that thou shalt see;
For in this regioun, certein,
Dwelleth many a citezein,
Of which that speketh Dan Plato.
These ben the eyrishe bestes, lo!"
And so saw I al that meynee
Bothe goon and also flee.
"Now," quod he tho, " cast up thyn yë!
See yonder, lo, the galaxye,
Which men clepeth the Milky Wey,
For hit is whyt; and sommę, parfey,
Callen hit Watlinge Strete,
That ones was y-brent with hete
Whan the sonnes sone, the rede,
That highte Pheton, wolde lede
Algate his fader carte, and gye.

The carté-hors gonne wel espye
That he ne coudé no governaunce,
And gonne for to lepe and launce,
And beren him now up, now doun,
Til that he saw the Scorpioun,
Which that in hevene a signe is yit.
And he for ferde loste his wit
Of that, and leet the reynes goon
Of his hors; and they anoon
Gonne up to mounte and doun descende
Til bothe the eyr and erthe brende,
Til Iupiter, lo, atte laste,
Him slow and fro the carte caste.
Lo, is it not a greet mischaunce
To lete a fool han governaunce
Of thing that he can not demeine?"

And with this word, soth for to seyne,
He gan alway upper to sore,
And gladded me ay more and more,
So feithfully to me spak he.

Tho gan I loken under me,
And beheld the eyrishe bestes,
Cloudes, mistes, and tempestes,
Snowes, hailes, reines, windes,
And thengendring in hir kindes,
And al the wey through which I cam.
"O God," quod I, "that made Adam,
Moche is thy might and thy noblesse!"

And tho thoughte I upon Boëce,
That writ, "A thought may flee so hyë,
With fetheres of Philosophye,
To passen everich element;
And whan he hath so fer y-went,
Than may be seen, behind his bak,
Cloude and al that I of spak."

Tho gan I wexen in a wer,
And seyde, "I woot wel I am heer;
But wher in body or in gost

I noot, y-wis: but God, thou wost!"
For more cleer entendement
Nad he me nevere yit y-sent.
And than thoughte I on Marcian,
And eek on Anteclaudian,
That sooth was hir descripcioun
Of al the hevenes regioun
As fer as that I saw the preve.
Therfore I can hem now beleve.

    With that this egle gan to crye:
"Lat be," quod he, "thy fantasye!
Wilt thou lere of sterres aught?"
"Nay, certeinly," quod I, "right naught."
"And why?" " For I am now to old."
"Elles I wolde thee have told,"
Quod he, "the sterres names, lo,
And alle the hevenes signes to,
And which they been." "No fors," quod I.
"Yis, pardee," quod he; "wostow why?
For whan thou redest poetrye,
How goddes gonne stellifye
Brid, fish, beest, or him or here,
As the Raven, or either Bere,
Or Ariones harpe fyn,
Castor, Pollux, or Delphyn,
Or Atlantes doughtres sevene,
How alle these arn set in hevene:
For though thou have hem ofte on honde,
Yet nostow not wher that they stonde."
"No fors," quod I, "hit is no nede.
I leve as wel, so God me spede,
Hem that wryte of this matere
As though I knew hir places here.
And eek they shynen here so brighte,
Hit shulde shenden al my sighte
To loke on hem." "That may wel be,"
Quod he. And so forth bar he me
A whyle, and than he gan to crye

That nevere herde I thing so hye,
"Now up the heed, for al is wel;
Seynt Iulian, lo, bon hostel!
See here the Hous of Fame, lo!
Maistow not heren that I do?"
"What?" quod I. "The grete soun,"
Quod he, "that rumbleth up and doun
In Fames Hous, ful of tydinges,
Bothe of faire speche and chydinges,
And of false and sothe compouned.
Herkne wel. Hit is not rouned.
Herestow not the grete swogh?"
"Yis, pardee," quod I, "wel y-nogh."
"And what soun is it lyk?" quod he.
"Peter! lyk beting of the see,"
Quod I, "again the roches holowe
Whan tempest doth the shippes swalowe,
And lat a man stonde, out of doute,
A myle thens and here hit route;
Or elles lyk the last humblinge
After the clappe of a thundringe,
Whan Ioves hath the air y-bete.
But hit doth me for fere swete!"
"Nay, dred thee not therof," quod he,
"Hit is nothing wil byten thee.
Thou shalt non harm have, trewely."
     And with this word bothe he and I
As nigh the place arryved were
As men may casten with a spere.
I niste how, but in a strete
He sette me faire on my fete,
And seyde, "Walke forth a pas,
And tak thyn aventure or cas
That thou shalt finde in Fames place."
     "Now," quod I, "whyl we han space
To speke, or that I go fro thee,
For the love of God, telle me,
In sooth, that wil I of thee lere,

If this noise that I here
Be, as I have herd thee tellen,
Of folk that doun in erthe dwellen,
And comth heer in the same wyse
As I thee herde or this devyse;
And that ther lyves body nis
In al that hous that yonder is,
That maketh al this loude fare?"
"Now," quod he, "by Seynte Clare,
And also wis God rede me!
But o thing I wil warne thee
Of the which thou wolt have wonder.
Lo, to the Hous of Fame yonder
Thou wost how cometh every speche;
Hit nedeth noght thee eft to teche.
But understond now right wel this:
Whan any speche y-comen is
Up to the paleys, anon-right
Hit wexeth lyk the same wight
Which that the word in erthe spak,
Be hit clothed reed or blak,
And hath so verray his lyknesse
That spak the word, that thou wilt gesse
That hit the same body be,
Man or woman, he or she.
And is not this a wonder thing?"
"Yis," quod I tho, "by Hevene-king!"
And with this word, "Farwel," quod he,
"And heer I wol abyden thee.
And God of hevene sende thee grace
Som good to lernen in this place."
And I of him took leve anoon,
And gan forth to the paleys goon.

Explicit liber secundus.

Sk. 1058-1090

Book III

Incipit liber tercius.

Invocation

O god of science and of light,
Apollo, through thy grete might,
This litel laste book thou gye!
Nat that I wilne for maistrye
Heer art poetical be shewed,
But, for the rym is light and lewed,
Yit make hit sumwhat agreable
Though som vers faile in a sillable;
And that I do no diligence
To shewe craft, but o sentence.
And if, divyne vertu, thou
Wilt helpe me to shewe now
That in myn heed y-marked is
(Lo, that is for to menen this,
The Hous of Fame to descryve)
Thou shalt see me go as blyve
Unto the nexte laure I see
And kisse hit, for hit is thy tree.
Now entreth in my brest anoon!—

The Dream

Whan I was fro this egle goon,
I gan beholde upon this place.
And certein, or I ferther pace,
I wol yow al the shap devyse
Of hous and site, and al the wyse
How I gan to this place aproche
That stood upon so high a roche,
Hyer stant ther noon in Spaine.
But up I clomb with alle paine;
And though to climbe hit greved me,

Sk. 1091-1119

Yit I ententif was to see
And for to pouren wonder lowe
If I coude any weyes knowe
What maner stoon this roche was.
For hit was lyk a thing of glas
But that hit shoon ful more clere.
But of what congeled matere
Hit was, I niste redely.

But at the laste espyed I,
And found that hit was every deel
A roche of yse and not of steel.
Thoughte I, "By Seynt Thomas of Kent!
This were a feble foundement
To bilden on a place hyë.
He oughte him litel glorifye
That her-on bilte, God so me save!"

Tho saw I al the half y-grave
With famous folkes names fele,
That had y-been in mochel wele,
And hir fames wyde y-blowe.
But wel unethes coude I knowe
Any lettres for to rede
Hir names by; for out of drede
They were almost of-thowed so
That of the lettres oon or two
Was molte away of every name:
So unfamous was wexe hir fame.
But men seyn, "What may evere laste?"

Tho gan I in myn herte caste
That they were molte awey with hete
And not awey with stormes bete.
For on that other syde I sey
Of this hil that northward lay,
How hit was writen ful of names
Of folk that hadden grete fames
Of olde tyme, and yit they were
As fresshe as men had writen hem there
That selve day right, or that houre

That I upon hem gan to poure.
But wel I wiste what hit made.
Hit was conserved with the shade—
Al this wryting that I sy—
Of a castel, that stood on hy,
And stood eek on so cold a place
That hete mighte hit not deface.

Tho gan I up the hil to goon,
And fond upon the cop a woon,
That alle the men that ben on lyve
Ne han the cunning to descryve
The beautee of that ilke place,
Ne coude casten to compace
Swich another for to make
That mighte of beautee be his make
Ne so wonderliche y-wrought:
That hit astonieth yit my thought
And maketh al my wit to swinke
On this castel to bethinke.
So that the grete beautee,
The cast, the curiositee,
Ne can I not to yow devyse,
My wit ne may me not suffyse.

But natheles al the substance
I have yit in my remembrance.
For-why me thoughte, by Seynt Gyle!
Al was of stone of beryle,
Bothe the castel and the tour,
And eek the halle and every bour,
Withouten peces or Ioininges.
But many subtil compassinges,
Babewinnes and pinacles,
Imageries and tabernacles,
I saw; and ful eek of windowes,
As flakes falle in grete snowes.
And eek in ech of the pinacles
Weren sondry habitacles,
In which stoden, al withoute,

Ful the castel al aboute
Of alle maner of minstrales,
And gestiours, that tellen tales
Bothe of weping and of game,
Of al that longeth unto fame.

Ther herde I pleyen on an harpe,
That souned bothe wel and sharpe,
Orpheus ful craftely,
And on his syde, faste by,
Sat the harper Orion,
And Eacides Chiron,
And other harpers many oon,
And the Bret Glascurion.
And smale harpers with her gleës
Seten under hem in seës,
And gonne on hem upward to gape,
And countrefete hem as an ape,
Or as craft countrefeteth kinde.

Tho saugh I stonden hem behinde,
A-fer fro hem, al by hemselve,
Many thousand tymes twelve,
That maden loude menstralcyes
In cornemusë, and shalmyes,
And many other maner pype,
That craftely begunne pype
Bothe in doucet and in rede,
That ben at festes with the brede;
And many floute and lilting-horn,
And pypes made of grene corn,
As han thise litel herde-gromes
That kepen bestes in the bromes.

Ther saugh I than Atiteris,
And of Athenes Dan Pseustis,
And Marcia that lost her skin *marsyas*
Bothe in face, body, and chin,
For that she wolde envyen, lo!
To pypen bet then Apollo.
Ther saugh I famous, olde and yonge,

Pypers of the Duche tonge
To lerne love-daunces, springes,
Reyes, and these straunge thinges.

Tho saugh I in another place
Stonden in a large space
Of hem that maken blody soun
In trumpe, beme, and clarioun.
For in fight and blood-shedinge
Is used gladly clarioninge.

Ther herde I trumpen Messenus,
Of whom that speketh Virgilius.
Ther herde I Ioab trumpe also,
Theodomas, and other mo,
And alle that used clarion
In Cataloigne and Aragon,
That in hir tyme famous were
To lerne, saugh I trumpe there.

Ther saugh I sitte in other seës,
Pleying upon sondry gleës,
Whiche that I cannot nevene,
Mo then sterres been in hevene,
Of which I nil as now not ryme,
For ese of yow and los of tyme.
For tyme y-lost, this knowen ye,
By no way may recovered be.

Ther saugh I pleyen Iogelours,
Magiciens and tregetours,
And phitonesses, charmeresses,
Olde wicches, sorceresses,
That use exorsisaciouns
And eek thisę fumigaciouns;
And clerkes eke, which conne wel
Al this magyk naturel,
That craftely don hir ententes
To make in certeyn ascendentes
Images, lo! through which magyk
To make a man ben hool or syk!
Ther saugh I thee, Queen Medea,

And Circes eek, and Calipsa.
Ther saugh I Hermes Ballenus,
Lymote, and eek Simon Magus.
Ther saugh I and knew hem by name
That by such art don men han fame.
Ther saugh I Colle tregetour
Upon a table of sicamour
Pleye an uncouth thing to telle:
I saugh him carien a wind-melle
Under a walsh-note shale.

What shuld I make lenger tale
Of al the peple that I say,
Fro hennes in-to domesday?

Whan I had al this folk beholde,
And fond me lous and noght y-holde,
And eft y-mused longe whyle
Upon these walles of beryle,
That shoon ful lighter than a glas,
And made wel more than hit was
To semen every thing, y-wis,
As kinde thing of fames is,
I gan forth romen til I fond
The castel-yate on my right hond,
Which that so wel corven was
That nevere swich another nas,
And yit hit was by aventure
Y-wrought as often as by cure.

Hit nedeth noght yow for to tellen,
To make yow to longe dwellen,
Of this yates florisshinges,
Ne of compasses, ne of kervinges,
Ne how they hatte in masoneries,
As corbets fulle of imageries.
But Lord! so fair hit was to shewe,
For hit was al with gold behewe.
But in I wente and that anoon;
Ther mette I crying many oon:
"A largesse, largesse, hold up wel!

God save the lady of this pel,
Our owne gentil lady Fame,
And hem that wilnen to havę name
Of us!" Thus herde I cryen alle,
And faste comen out of halle
And shoken nobles and sterlinges.
And somme crouned were as kinges
With crounes wrought ful of losenges;
And many riban and many frenges
Were on hir clothes trewely.
    Tho atte laste aspyed I
That pursevauntes and heraudes,
That cryen riche folkes laudes,
Hit weren alle. And every man
Of hem, as I yow tellen can,
Had on him throwen a vesture,
Which that men clepe a cote-armure,
Enbrowded wonderliche riche
Al-though they nere nought y-liche.
But noght nil I, so mote I thryve,
Been aboute to discryve
Al these armes that ther weren,
That they thus on hir cotes beren,
For hit to me were impossible.
Men mighte make of hem a bible
Twenty foot thikke, as I trowe.
For certeyn, who-so coude y-knowe
Mighte ther alle the armes seen
Of famous folk that han y-been
In Auffrike, Europe, and Asye,
Sith first began the chevalrye.
    Lo! how shulde I now telle al this?
Ne of the halle eek what nede is
To tellen yow, that every wal
Of hit, and floor, and roof and al
Was plated half a fote thikke
Of gold, and that nas no-thing wikke,
But, for to prove in alle wyse,

As fyn as ducat in Venyse,
Of which to lyte al in my pouche is?
And they were set as thikke of nouchis
Fulle of the fynest stones faire,
That men rede in the Lapidaire,
As greses growen in a mede.
But hit were al to longę to rede
The names, and therfore I pace.

But in this riche lusty place,
That Fames halle called was,
Ful moche prees of folk ther nas,
Ne crouding for to mochil prees.
But al on hye, above a dees,
Sitte in a see imperial,
That maad was of a rubee al
Which that a carbuncle is y-called,
I saugh, perpetually y-stalled,
A feminyne creature,
That nevere formed by nature
Nas swich another thing y-seye.
For altherfirst, soth for to seye,
Me thoughte that she was so lyte
That the lengthe of a cubyte
Was lenger than she semed be;
But thus sone in a whyle she
Hir tho so wonderliche streighte
That with hir feet she therthe reighte,
And with hir heed she touched hevene,
Ther as shynen sterres sevene.
And ther-to eek, as to my wit,
I saugh a gretter wonder yit,
Upon hir eyen to beholde.
But certeyn I hem nevere tolde;
For as fele eyen hadde she
As fetheres upon foules be,
Or weren on the bestes foure
That Goddes trone gunne honoure
As Iohn writ in thapocalips.

Hir heer, that oundy was and crips,
As burned gold hit shoon to see.
And sooth to tellen, also she
Had also fele up-stonding eres
And tonges as on bestes heres.
And on hir feet wexen saugh I
Partriches winges redely.

But Lord! the perrie and the richesse
I saugh sitting on this goddesse!
And Lord! the hevenish melodye
Of songes, ful of armonye,
I herde aboute her trone y-songe,
That al the paleys-walles ronge!
So song the mighty Muse, she
That cleped is Caliopee,
And hir eighte sustren eke,
That in hir face semen meke.
And everemo, eternally,
They songe of Fame, as tho herde I:
"Heried be thou and thy name,
Goddesse of renoun and of fame!"

Tho was I war, lo! atte laste,
As I myn eyen gan up caste,
That this ilke noble quene
On hir shuldres gan sustene
Bothe tharmes and the name
Of tho that hadde large fame:
Alexander, and Hercules
That with a sherte his lyf lees!
And thus fond I sitting this goddesse
In nobleye, honour, and richesse,
Of which I stinte a whyle now,
Other thing to tellen yow.

Tho saugh I stonde on either syde,
Streight doun to the dores wyde
Fro the dees, many a pileer
Of metal, that shoon not ful cleer.
But though they nere of no richesse,

Yet they werę maad for greet noblesse,
And in hem greet and hy sentence.
And folk of digne reverence,
Of which I wol yow telle fonde,
Upon the piler saugh I stonde.

Alderfirst, lo! ther I sigh,
Upon a piler stonde on high,
That was of leed and yren fyn,
Him of secte Saturnyn,
The Ebrayk Iosephus, the olde,
That of Iewes gestes tolde;
And bar upon his shuldres hye
The fame up of the Iewerye.
And by him stoden other sevene,
Wyse and worthy for to nevene,
To helpen him bere up the charge,
Hit was so hevy and so large.
And for they writen of batailes
As wel as other oldę mervailes,
Therefore was, lo, this pileer,
Of which that I yow telle heer
Of leed and yren bothe, y-wis.
For yren Martes metal is,
Which that god is of bataile;
And the leed, withouten faile,
Is, lo, the metal of Saturne,
That hath ful large wheel to turne.
Tho stoden forth, on every rowe,
Of hem which that I coude knowe,
Thogh I hem noght by ordre telle
To make yow to longę to dwelle.

These, of which I ginne rede,
Ther saugh I stonden, out of drede,
Upon an yren piler strong,
That peynted was al endelong
With tygres blood in every place,
The Tholosan that highte Stace,
That bar of Thebes up the fame

Upon his shuldres, and the name
Also of cruel Achilles.
And by him stood, withouten lees,
Ful wonder hye on a pileer
Of yren, he, the grete Omeer,
And with him Dares and Tytus
Before, and eek he Lollius,
And Guido eek de Columpnis,
And English Gaufride eek, y-wis.
And ech of these, as have I Ioye,
Was besy for to bere up Troye.
So hevy ther-of was the fame
That for to bere hit was no game.
But yit I gan ful wel espye,
Betwix hem was a litel envye.
Oon seyde, Omer made lyes,
Feyning in his poetryes,
And was to Grekes favorable:
Therfore held he hit but fable.

Tho saugh I stonde on a pileer,
That was of tinned yren cleer,
That Latin poete, Virgyle,
That borę hath up a longe whyle
The fame of Pius Eneas.

And next him on a piler was
Of coper, Venus clerk, Ovyde,
That hath y-sowen wonder wyde
The grete god of Loves name.
And ther he bar up wel his fame,
Upon this piler, also hyë
As I might see hit with myn yë:
For-why this halle, of which I rede
Was woxe on highte, lengthe and brede,
Wel more by a thousand del
Than hit was erst, that saugh I wel.

Tho saugh I on a piler by,
Of yren wroght ful sternely,
The grete poete, Daun Lucan,

And on his shuldres bar up than
As highe as that I mighte see
The fame of Iulius and Pompee.
And by him stoden allę these clerkes
That writen of Romes mighty werkes,
That, if I wolde hir names telle,
Al to longe moste I dwelle.

And next him on a piler stood
Of soulfre, lyk as he werę wood,
Dan Claudian, the soth to telle,
That bar up al the fame of helle,
Of Pluto, and of Proserpyne,
That quene is of the derke pyne.

What shulde I more telle of this?
The halle was al ful, y-wis,
Of hem that writen olde gestes,
As ben on treës rokes nestes.
But hit a ful confus matere
Were al the gestes for to here,
That they of write, and how they highte.
But whyl that I beheld this sighte,
I herde a noise aprochen blyve
That ferde as been don in an hyve
Agen her tyme of out-fleyinge.
Right swich a maner murmuringe
For al the world hit semed me.

Tho gan I loke aboute and see
That ther com entring into the halle
A right gret company with-alle,
And that of sondry regiouns,
Of alleskinnęs condiciouns
That dwelle in erthe under the mone,
Pore and ryche. And also sone
As they were come into the halle,
They gonne doun on kneës falle
Before this ilke noble quene
And seyde, "Graunte us, lady shene,
Ech of us, of thy grace, a bone!"

And somme of hem she graunted sone;
And somme she werned wel and faire;
And somme she graunted the contraire
Of hir axing utterly.
But thus I seye yow trewely,
What hir cause was, I niste.
For this folk, ful wel I wiste,
They hadde good fame ech deserved,
Althogh they were diversly served:
Right as hir suster, Dame Fortune,
Is wont to serven in comune.

Now herkne how she gan to paye
That gonne hir of hir grace praye;
And yit, lo, al this companye
Seyden sooth and noght a lye.

"Madame," seyden they, "we be
Folk that heer besechen thee
That thou graunte us now good fame,
And lete our werkes han that name.
In ful recompensacioun
Of good werk, yef us good renoun."

"I werne yow hit," quod she anoon.
"Ye gete of me good fame noon,
By God! and therfore go your wey."

"Alas," quod they, "and welaway!
Telle us what may your cause be?"

"For me list hit noght," quod she.
"No wight shal speke of yow, y-wis,
Good ne harm, ne that ne this."
And with that word she gan to calle
Hir messager, that was in halle,
And bad that he shulde faste goon,
Up peyne to be blind anoon,
For Eolus, the god of winde:—
"In Trace ther ye shul him finde,
And bid him bringe his clarioun,
That is ful dyvers of his soun,
And hit is cleped Clere Laude,

With which he wont is to heraude
Hem that me list y-preised be.
And also bid him how that he
Bringe his other clarioun,
That highte Sclaundre in every toun,
With which he wont is to diffame
Hem that me list, and do hem shame."

This messager gan faste goon,
And found wher in a cave of stoon,
In a contree that highte Trace,
This Eolus (with harde grace!)
Held the windes in distresse,
And gan hem under him to presse,
That they gonne as beres rore,
He bond and pressed hem so sore.

This messager gan faste crye;
"Rys up," quod he, "and faste hye
Til that thou at my lady be.
And tak thy clarions eek with thee
And speed thee forth." And he anon
Took to a man that hight Triton
His clariouns to bere tho,
And leet a certeyn wind to go
That blew so hidously and hye
That hit ne lefte not a skye
In al the welken longe and brood.

This Eolus no-wher abood
Til he was come at Fames feet,
And eek the man that Triton heet;
And ther he stood as still as stoon.

And her-withal ther com anoon
Another huge companye
Of gode folk, and gunne crye,
"Lady, graunte us now good fame,
And lat our werkes han that name
Now, in honour of gentilesse,
And also God your soule blesse!
For we han wel deserved hit,

Therfore is right that we ben quit."
    "As thryve I," quod she, "ye shal faile,
Good werkes shal yow noght availe
To have of me good fame as now.
But wote ye what? I graunte yow
That ye shal have a shrewed fame
And wikked loos and worse name,
Though ye good loos have wel deserved.
Now go your wey, for ye be served.
And thou, Dan Eolus, let see!
Tak forth thy trumpe anon," quod she,
"That is y-cleped Sclaundre light,
And blow hir loos that every wight
Speke of hem harm and shrewednesse
In stede of good and worthinesse.
For thou shalt trumpe al the contraire
Of that they han don wel or faire."
    "Alas," thoughte I, "what aventures
Han these sory creatures!
For they amonges al the pres
Shul thus be shamed gilteles!
But what! hit moste nedes be."
    What did this Eolus, but he
Tok oute his blakke trumpe of bras,
That fouler than the devil was,
And gan this trumpe for to blowe,
As al the world shulde overthrowe,
That through-oute every regioun
Wente this foule trumpes soun
As swift as pelet out of gonne
Whan fyr is in the poudre ronne.
And swich a smoke gan out-wende
Out of his foule trumpes ende,
Blak, blo, grenish, swartish reed,
As doth wher that men melte leed,
Lo, al on high fro the tuel!
And therto oo thing saugh I wel,
That the ferther that hit ran

The gretter wexen hit began,
As doth the river from a welle,
And hit stank as the pit of helle.
Alas, thus was hir shame y-ronge,
And giltelees, on every tonge.

Tho com the thridde companye
And gunne up to the dees to hye,
And doun on knees they fille anon,
And seyde, "We ben everychon
Folk that han ful trewely
Deserved fame rightfully,
And praye yow hit mot be knowe
Right as hit is, and forth y-blowe."
"I graunte," quod she, "for me list
That now your gode werkes be wist.
And yit ye shul han better loos,
Right in dispyt of alle your foos,
Than worthy is, and that anoon.
Lat now," quod she, "thy trumpe goon,
Thou Eolus, that is so blak,
And oute thyn other trumpe tak
That highte Laude, and blow hit so
That through the world hir fame go
Al esely and not to faste,
That hit be knowen atte laste."

"Ful gladly, lady myn," he seyde.
And oute his trumpe of gold he brayde
Anon, and sette hit to his mouth,
And blew hit est, and west, and south,
And north, as loude as any thunder,
That every wight had of hit wonder,
So brode hit ran or than hit stente.
And certes al the breeth that wente
Out of his trumpes mouth hit smelde
As men a pot-ful of bawme helde
Among a basket ful of roses.
This favour did he til hir loses.

And right with this I gan aspye

Ther com the ferthe companye.
But certeyn they were wonder fewe,
And gonne stonden in a rewe,
And seyden, "Certes, lady bright,
We han don wel with al our might,
But we ne kepen have no fame.
Hyd our werkes and our name,
For Goddes love! For certes we
Han certyn doon hit for bountee
And for no maner other thing."
" I graunte yow al your asking,"
Quod she; "let your werkes be deed."

    With that aboute I clew myn heed,
And saugh anoon the fifte route
That to this lady gonne loute
And doun on knees anoon to falle.
And to hir tho besoughten alle
To hyde hir gode werkes eek,
And seyde they yeven noght a leek
For fame ne for swich renoun.
For they, for contemplacioun
And Goddes love, had y-wrought;
Ne of fame wolde they noght.

    "What?" quod she, "and be ye wode?
And wene ye for to do gode
And for to have of that no fame?
Have ye dispyt to have my name?
Nay, ye shul liven everichoon!
Blow thy trumpe and that anoon,"
Quod she, "thou Eolus, I hote,
And ring this folkes werk by note
That al the world may of hit here."
And he gan blowe hir loos so clere
In his golden clarioun
That through the world wente the soun
So kenely and eek so softe,
But atte laste hit was on-lofte.

    Thoo com the sexte companye,

And gonne faste on Fame crye.
Right verraily in this manere
They seyden, "Mercy, lady dere!
To telle certein, as hit is,
We han don neither that ne this,
But ydel al our lyf y-be.
But natheles yit preye we
That we mowe han so good a fame
And greet renoun and knowen name
As they that han don noble gestes
And acheved alle hir lestes,
As wel of love as other thing.
Al was us nevere brooch ne ring,
Ne elles nought, from wimmen sent,
Ne ones in hir herte y-ment
To make us only frendly chere
But mighte temen us on bere,
Yet lat us to the peple seme
Swich as the world may of us deme,
That wimmen loven us for wode.
Hit shal don us as moche gode,
And to our herte as moche availe
To countrepeise ese and travaile,
As we had wonne hit with labour;
For that is dere boght honour
At regard of our grete ese.
And yit thou most us more plese:
Let us be holden eek, therto,
Worthy, wyse, and gode also,
And riche, and happy unto love.
For Goddes love, that sit above,
Though we may not the body have
Of wimmen, yet, so God yow save,
Let men glewe on us the name.
Suffyceth that we han the fame."
    "I graunte," quod she, "by my trouthe!
Now, Eolus, with-outen slouthe,
Tak out thy trumpe of gold," quod she,

" And blow as they han axed me,
That every man wene hem at ese
Though they gon in ful badde lese."
This Eolus gan hit so blowe
That through the world hit was y-knowe.

   Tho com the seventh route anoon,
And fel on kneës everichoon,
And seyde, "Lady, graunte us sone
The same thing. the same bone,
That this nexte folk han doon."
"Fy on yow," quod she, "everichoon!
Ye masty swyn, ye ydel wrecches,
Ful of roten slowe tecchcs!
What? false theves! wher ye wolde
Be famous good, and no-thing nolde
Deserve why, ne nevere roughte?
Men rather yow to-hangen oughte!
For ye be lyk the sweynte cat
That wolde havę fish, but wostow what?
He wolde no-thing wete his clowes.
Yvel thrift come on your Iowes
And eek on myn if I hit graunte
Or do yow favour yow to avaunte!
Thou Eolus, thou king of Trace!
Go, blow this folk a sory grace,"
Quod she, "anoon. And wostow how?
As I shal telle thee right now.
Sey: 'These ben they that wolde honour
Have, and do noskinnes labour,
Ne do no good, and yit han laude,
And that men wendę that bele Isaude
Ne coude hem nought of love werne,
And yit she that grint at a querne
Is al to good to ese hir herte.'"

   This Eolus anon up sterte,
And with his blakke clarioun
He gan to blasen out a soun
As loude as belweth wind in helle.

And eke therwith, sooth to telle,
This soun was so ful of Iapes
As evere mowes were in apes.
And that wente al the world aboute,
That every wight gan on hem shoute
And for to laughe as they were wode:
Such game fondę they in hir hode.

Tho com another companye,
That had y-doon the traiterye,
The harm, the gretest wikkednesse
That any herte couthe gesse,
And preyed hir to han good fame,
And that she nolde hem doon no shame,
But yeve hem loos and good renoun,
And do hit blowe in clarioun.
"Nay, wis," quod she, "hit were a vyce!
Al be ther in me no Iustyce,
Me list not to do hit now,
Ne this nil I not graunte yow."

Tho com ther leping in a route,
And gan choppen al aboute
Every man upon the croune
That al the halle gan to soune,
And seyden: "Lady, lefe and dere,
We ben swich folk as ye mowe here.
To tellen al the tale aright,
We ben shrewes, every wight,
And han delyt in wikkednesse
As gode folk han in goodnesse,
And Ioye to be knowen shrewes
And ful of vyce and wikked thewes.
Wherforę we preyen yow, a-rowe,
That our fame swich be knowe
In alle thing right as hit is."

"I graunte hit yow," quod she, "y-wis.
But what art thou that seyst this tale,
That werest on thy hose a pale,
And on thy tipet swich a belle!"

"Madame," quod he, "sooth to telle,
I am that ilke shrewe, y-wis,
That brendę the temple of Isidis
In Athenes, lo, that citee."
"And wherforę didest thou so?" quod she.
"By my thrift," quod he, "madame,
I wolde fayn han had a fame
As other folk had in the toun,
Al-thogh they were of greet renoun
For hir vertu and for hir thewes.
Thoughte I, as greet a fame han shrewes,
Thogh hit be for shrewednesse,
As gode folk han for goodnesse.
And sith I may not havę that oon,
That other nil I noght for-goon.
And for to gette of Fames hyre,
The temple sette I al a-fyre.
Now do our loos be blowen swythe
As wisly be thou evere blythe."
"Gladly," quod she; "thou Eolus,
Herestow not what they preyen us?"
"Madame, yis, ful wel," quod he,
"And I wil trumpen hit, parde!"
And tok his blakke trumpe faste,
And gan to puffen and to blaste,
Til hit was at the worldes ende.

    With that I gan aboute wende.
For oon that stood right at my bak,
Me thoughte, goodly to me spak
And seyde: "Frend, what is thy name?
Artow come hider to han fame?"
"Nay, for-sothe, frend!" quod I;
"I cam noght hider, graunt mercy!
For no swich cause, by my heed!
Suffyceth me, as I were deed.
That no wight havę my name in honde.
I woot my-self best how I stonde.
For what I drye or what I thinke,

I wol my-selven al hit drinke,
Certeyn, for the more part,
As ferforth as I can myn art."
"But what dost thou here than?" quod he.
Quod I, "That wol I tellen thee—
The cause why I stondë here:
Som newe tydinges for to lere;
Som newe thinges, I not what,
Tydinges, other this or that,
Of love or swiche thinges glade.
For certeynly, he that me made
To comen hider, seyde me
I shulde bothe here and see,
In this place, wonder thinges.
But these be no swiche tydinges
As I mene of." "No?" quod he.
And I answerde, "No, pardee!
For wel I wiste evere yit,
Sith that first I hadde wit,
That som folk han desyred fame
Dyversly, and loos, and name;
But certeynly, I niste how
Ne wher that Fame dwelled er now,
Ne eek of hir descripcioun,
Ne also hir condicioun,
Ne the ordrë of hir doom,
Unto the tyme I hider com."
"Which than be, lo! these tydinges,
That thou now thus hider bringes,
That thou hast herd?" quod he to me;
"But now, no fors. For wel I see
What thou desyrest for to here.
Com forth, and stond no longer here,
And I wol thee, withouten drede,
In swich another place lede,
Ther thou shalt here many oon."
    Tho gan I forth with him to goon
Out of the castel, sooth to seye.

Tho saugh I stonde in a valeye,
Under the castel, faste by,
An hous that *domus Dedali*,
That *Laborintus* cleped is,
Nas maad so wonderliche, y-wis,
Ne half so queynteliche y-wrought.
And everemo, so swift as thought,
This queynte hous aboute wente,
That nevere-mo hit stille stente.
And ther-oute com so greet a noise
That, had hit stonden upon Oise,
Men mighte hit han herd esely
To Rome, I trowe sikerly.
And the noyse which that I herde
For al the world right so hit ferde
As doth the routing of the stoon
That from thengyn is leten goon.
And al this hous, of which I rede,
Was maad of twigges, falwe, rede,
And grene eek, and som weren whyte,
Swich as men to these cages thwyte,
Or maken of these paniers,
Or elles hottes or dossers,
That for the swough and for the twigges
This hous was also ful of gigges,
And also ful eek of chirkinges,
And of many other werkinges.
And eek this hous hath of entrees
As fele as leves been on trees
In somer, whan they grene been.
And on the roof men may yit seen
A thousand holes and wel mo
To leten wel the soun oute go.
    And by day, in every tyde,
Ben al the dores open wyde,
And by night, echoon unshette.
Ne porter ther is noon to lette
No maner tydinges in to pace;

Ne nevere reste is in that place
That hit nis fild ful of tydinges,
Other loude, or of whispringes.
And over alle the houses angles
Is ful of rouninges and of Iangles
Of werres, of pees, of mariages,
Of restes, of labour, of viages,
Of abood, of deeth, of lyf,
Of love, of hate, acord, of stryf,
Of loos, of lore, and of winninges,
Of hele, of sekenesse, of bildinges,
Of faire windes, of tempestes,
Of qualm of folk, and eek of bestes,
Of dyvers transmutaciouns
Of estats, and eek of regiouns,
Of trust, of drede, of Ielousye,
Of wit, of winning, of folye,
Of plentee, and of greet famyne,
Of chepe, of derth, and of ruyne,
Of good or mis governement,
Of fyr, and dyvers accident.
    And lo, this hous, of which I wryte
Siker be ye hit nas not lyte;
For hit was sixty myle of lengthe.
Al was the timber of no strengthe,
Yet hit is founded to endure
Whyl that hit list to Aventure,
That is the moder of tydinges,
As the see of welles and springes.
And hit was shapen lyk a cage.
    "Certes," quod I, "in al myn age
Ne saugh I swich a hous as this!"
And as I wondred me, y-wis,
Upon this hous, tho war was I
How that myn egle faste by
Was perched hye upon a stoon.
And I gan streight to him goon
And seyde thus: "I preye thee

That thou a whyle abyde me
For Goddes love, and let me seen
What wondres in this place been.
For yit, paraunter, I may lere
Som good ther-on, or sumwhat here
That leef me were, or that I wente."

"Peter! that is myn entente,"
Quod he to me. "Therfore I dwelle.
But certein, oon thing I thee telle,
That, but I bringe thee ther-in,
Ne shalt thou nevere cunne gin
To come in-to hit, out of doute.
So faste hit whirleth, lo, aboute.
But sith that Ioves of his grace,
As I have seyd, wol thee solace
Fynally with these thinges:
Uncouthe sightes and tydinges,
To passe with thyn hevinesse,
(Such routhe hath he of thy distresse,—
That thou suffrest debonairly,
And wost thy-selven utterly
Disesperat of alle blis,
Sith that Fortune hath maad a-mis
The fruit of al thyn hertes reste
Languisshe and eek in point to breste,—
That he, through his mighty meryte,
Wol do thee ese, al be hit lyte,
And yaf in expres commaundement,
To which I am obedient,
To furthre thee with al my might,
And wisse and teche thee aright
Wher thou maist most tydinges here)
Shaltow heer anoon many oon lere."

With this word he right anoon
Hente me up bitwene his toon,
And at a windowe in me broghte,
That in this hous was, as me thoghte
(And ther-withal me thoghte hit stente,

And no-thing hit aboute wente)
And me sette in the floor adoun.
But which a congregacioun
Of folk, as I saugh rome aboute
Some within and some withoute,
Nas nevere seen, ne shal ben eft,
That, certes, in this world nis left
So many formed by Nature,
Ne deed so many a creature:
That wel unethe in that place
Had I oon foot-brede of space.
And every wight that I saugh there
Rouned everich in otheres ere
A newe tydinge prevely;
Or elles tolde al openly
Right thus, and seyde: "Nost not thou
That is betid, lo, late or now?"

   "No," quod the other, "telle me what!"
And than he tolde him this or that,
And swoor ther-to that hit was sooth—
"Thus hath he seyd"—and "Thus he dooth"—
And "Thus shal hit be"—and "Thus herde I
          seye"—
"That shal be found"— "That dar I leye"—
That al the folk that is a-lyve
Ne han the cunning to discryve
The thinges that I herde there,
What aloude, and what in ere.
But al the wonder-most was this:—
Whan oon had herd a thing, y-wis,
He com forth to another wight
And gan him tellen anoon-right
The same that to him was told
Or hit a furlong-way was old,
But gan somwhat for to eche
To this tydinge in this speche
More than hit evere was.
And nat so sone departed nas

That he fro him, that he ne mette
With the thridde; and, or he lette
Any stounde, he tolde him als.
Were the tydinge sooth or fals,
Yit wolde he telle hit nathelees,
And everemo with more encrees
Than hit was erst. Thus north and south
Wente every tydingẹ fro mouth to mouth,
And that encresing evere-mo,
As fyr is wont to quikke and go
From a sparke spronge amis
Til al a citee brent up is.

And whan that was ful y-spronge
And woxen more on every tonge
Than evere hit was, hit wente anoon
Up to a windowe outẹ to goon,
Or, but hit mightẹ outẹ ther pace,
Hit gan outẹ crepe at som crevace
And fleigh forth faste for the nones.

And somtymẹ saugh I tho, at ones,
A lesing and a sad soth-sawe,
That gonne of aventure drawe
Outẹ at a windowẹ for to pace;
And when they metten in that place,
They were a-chekked bothe two
And neither of hem moste outẹ go.
For other so they gonne croude
Til ech of hem gan cryen loude,
"Lat me go first!" "Nay, but lat me!
And heer I wol ensuren thee
With the nones that thou wolt do so
That I shal nevere fro thee go
But be thyn owne sworen brother!
We wil medle us ech with other
That no man, be he nevere so wrooth,
Shal han that oon of two but both
At ones, al beside his leve,
Come we a-morwe or on eve,

Sk. 2069–2106

Be we cryed or stille y-rouned."
Thus saugh I fals and sooth compouned
Togeder flee for oo tydinge.

   Thus out at holes gonne wringe
Every tydinge streight to Fame.
And she gan yeven ech his name
After hir disposicioun,
And yaf hem eek duracioun,
Some to wexe and wane sone
As dooth the faire whyte mone,
And leet hem gon.   Ther mighte I seen
Wenged wondres faste fleen,
Twenty thousand in a route,
As Eolus hem blew aboute.

   And Lord! this hous in alle tymes
Was ful of shipmen and pilgrymes,
With scrippes bret-ful of lesinges,
Entremedled with tydinges,
And eek alone by hem-selve.
O, many thousand tymes twelve
Saugh I eek of these pardoneres,
Currours, and eke messageres,
With boistes crammed ful of lyes
As evere vessel was with lyes.
And as I alther-fastest wente
Aboute and did al myn entente
Me for to pleye and for to lere
And eek a tydinge for to here
That I had herd of som contree
That shal not now be told for me—
For hit no nede is, redely:
Folk can singe hit bet than I;
For al mot oute other late or rathe,
Alle the sheves in the lathe—
I herde a gret noise withalle
In a corner of the halle
Ther men of love tydinges tolde,
And I gan thiderward beholde.

For I saugh renning every wight *creature*
As faste as that they hadden might;
And everich cryed, "What thing is that?"
And som seyde, "I not nevere what!"
And whan they were alle on an hepe, *heap*
Tho behinde gonne up lepe,
And clamben up on other faste, *close*
And up the nose on hye caste, *up*
And troden faste on otheres heles
And stampe, as men don after eles.

   Atte laste I saugh a man
Which that I nevene naught ne can, *name*
But he semed for to be
A man of greet auctoritee . . . . .

Sk. 2145–2158

(Unfinished.)

1382 — poem of compliment to Richard & Anne
Shows influences of older lit, 12 cent. nature
poem by Alanus — munk.
Humorous & —

THE PARLEMENT OF FOULES

The lyf so short, the craft so long to lerne,
Thassay so hard, so sharp the conqueringe,
The dredful Ioye, that alwey slit so yerne,
Al this mene I by love, that my felinge
Astonyeth with his wonderful worchinge
So sore y-wis, that whan I on him thinke,
Nat wot I wel wher that I wake or winke.

For al be that I knowe not love in dede,
Ne wot how that he quyteth folk hir hyre,
Yet happeth me ful ofte in bokes rede
Of his miracles and his cruel yre.
Ther rede I wel he wol be lord and syre,—
I dar not seyn his strokes been so sore,
But God save swich a lord! I can no more.

Of usage, what for luste what for lore,
On bokes rede I ofte, as I yow tolde.
But wherfore that I speke al this? not yore
Agon, hit happed me for to beholde
Upon a book, was write with lettres olde;
And ther-upon, a certeyn thing to lerne,
The longe day ful faste I radde and yerne.

For out of olde feldes, as men seith,
Cometh al this newe corn fro yeer to yere;
And out of olde bokes, in good feith,
Cometh al this newe science that men lere.
But now to purpos as of this matere:
To rede forth hit gan me so delyte
That al the day me thoughte but a lyte.

This book of which I make mencioun,
Entitled was al thus as I shal telle,
"Tullius of the dreem of Scipioun."

Sk. 1–31

Chapitres sevene hit hadde, of hevene and helle,
And erthe, and soules that therinne dwelle,
Of which, as shortly as I can hit trete,
Of his sentence I wol yow seyn the grete.

First telleth hit, whan Scipioun was come
In Afrike, how he mette Massinisse,
That him for Ioye in armes hath y-nome.
Than telleth hit hir speche and al the blisse
That was betwix hem til the day gan misse;
And how his auncestre, African so dere,
Gan in his sleep that night to him appere.

Than telleth hit that fro a sterry place
How African hath him Cartage shewed,
And warned him before of al his grace,
And seyde him what man, lered other lewed,
That loveth comune profit, wel y-thewed,
He shal unto a blisful place wende,
Ther as Ioye is that last withouten ende.

Than asked he if folk that heer be dede
Have lyf and dwelling in another place.
And African seyde, "Ye, withoute drede,"
And that our present worldes lyves space
Nis but a maner deth, what wey we trace,
And rightful folk shal go after they dye
To hevene, and shewed him the galaxye.

Than shewed he him the litel erthe that heer is,
At regard of the hevenes quantite;
And after shewed he him the nyne speres,
And after that the melodye herde he
That cometh of thilke speres thryes three,
That welle is of musyke and melodye
In this world heer, and cause of armonye.

Than bad he him, sin erthe was so lyte
And ful of torment and of harde grace,
That he ne shulde him in the world delyte.

Than tolde he him, in certeyn yeres space,
That every sterre shulde come into his place
Ther hit was first, and al shulde out of minde
That in this world is don of al mankinde.

Than prayde him Scipioun to telle him al
The wey to come un-to that hevene blisse.
And he seyde, "Know thy-self first immortal,
And loke ay besily thou werke and wisse
To comune profit, and thou shalt nat misse
To comen swiftly to that place dere,
That ful of blisse is and of soules clere.

"But brekers of the lawe, sooth to seyne,
And lecherous folk, after that they be dede,
Shul alwey whirle aboute therthe in peyne
Til many a world be passed, out of drede,
And than, for-yeven alle hir wikked dede,
Than shul they come unto that blisful place,
To which to comen God thee sende his grace!"

The day gan failen, and the derke night,
That reveth bestes from hir besinesse,
Berafte me my book for lak of light,
And to my bed I gan me for to dresse,
Fulfild of thought and besy hevinesse.
For bothe I hadde thing which that I nolde,
And eek I ne hadde that thing that I wolde.

But fynally my spirit at the laste
For wery of my labour al the day
Took reste, that made me to slepe faste,
And in my sleep I mette, as I lay,
How African, right in that selfe aray
That Scipioun him saw before that tyde,
Was comen and stood right at my beddes syde.

The wery hunter, sleping in his bed,
To wode ayein his minde goth anoon;
The Iuge dremeth how his plees ben sped;

The carter dremeth how his cartes goon;
The riche, of gold; the knight fight with his foon;
The seke met he drinketh of the tonne;
The lover met he hath his lady wonne.

Can I nat seyn if that the cause were
For I had red of African beforn,
That made me to mete that he stood there;
But thus seyde he, "Thou hast thee so wel born
In loking of myn olde book to-torn,
Of which Macrobie roghte nat a lyte,
That somdel of thy labour wolde I quyte!"

Citherea! thou blisful lady swete,
That with thy fyr-brand dauntest whom thee lest,
And madest me this sweven for to mete,
Be thou my help in this for thou mayst best.
As wisly as I saw thee north-north-west
When I began my sweven for to wryte,
So yif me might to ryme hit and endyte!

The Story

This forseid African me hente anoon,
And forth with him unto a gate broghte
Right of a park walled with grene stoon;
And over the gate, with lettres large y-wroghte,
Ther were vers y-writen, as me thoghte,
On eyther halfe, of ful gret difference,
Of which I shal yow seye the pleyn sentence.

"Thorgh me men goon in-to that blisful place
Of hertes hele and dedly woundes cure;
Thorgh me men goon unto the welle of Grace,
Ther grene and lusty May shal evere endure;
This is the wey to al good aventure;
Be glad, thou reder, and thy sorwe of-caste,
Al open am I: passe in, and hy the faste!"

"Thorgh me men goon," than spak that other syde,
"Unto the mortal strokes of the spere,
Of which Disdayn and Daunger is the gyde,
Ther tree shal nevere fruyt ne leves bere.
This streem yow ledeth to the sorwful were
Ther as the fish in prison is al drye;
Theschewing is only the remedye."

Thise vers of gold and blak y-writen were,
The which I gan a-stonyed to beholde;
For with that oon encresed ay my fere,
And with that other gan myn herte bolde.
That oon me hette, that other did me colde:
No wit had I, for errour, for to chese
To entre or flee, or me to save or lese.

Right as betwixen adamauntes two
Of even might a pece of iren y-set
That hath no might to meve to ne fro
(For what that oon may hale, that other let)
Ferde I, that niste whether me was bet
To entre or leve, til African my gyde
Me hente, and shoof in at the gates wyde.

And seyde, "Hit stondeth writen in thy face
Thyn errour, though thou telle it not to me.
But dred thee nat to come in-to this place,
For by this wryting is no-thing ment by thee,
Ne by noon but he Loves servant be.
For thou of love hast lost thy tast, I gesse,
As seek man hath of swete and bitternesse.

"But natheles, al-though that thou be dul,
Yit that thou canst not do, yit mayst thou see.
For many a man that may not stonde a pul
Yit lyketh him at the wrastling for to be,
And demeth yit wher he do bet or he.
And if thou haddest cunning for tendyte,
I shal thee shewen matere of to wryte."

With that my hond in his he took anoon,
Of which I comfort caughte, and wente in faste.
But Lord! so I was glad and wel begoon!
For over-al wher that I myn eyen caste
Werę treës clad with levęs that ay shal laste,
Ech in his kinde, of colour freshe and grene
As emeraude, that Ioye was to sene.

The bilder ook, and eek the hardy asshe;
The piler elm, the cofre unto careyne;
The box-tree piper; holm to whippes lasshe;
The sayling firr; the cipres, deth to pleyne;
The sheter ew, the asp for shaftes pleyne;
The olyve of pees, and eek the drunken vyne;
The victor palm, the laurer to devyne.

A garden saw I, ful of blosmy bowes,
Upon a river, in a grene mede,
Ther as that swetnesse everemore y-now is,
With floures whyte, blewe, yelowe, and rede;
And colde welle-stremes, no-thing dede,
That swommen ful of smale fisshes lighte,
With finnes rede and scales silver-brighte.

On every bough the briddes herde I singe,
With voys of aungel in hir armonye.
Som besyed hem hir briddes forth to bringe.
The litel conyes to hir pley gunne hye,
And further al aboute I gan espye
The dredful roo, the buk, the hert and hinde,
Squerels, and bestes smale of gentil kinde.

Of instruments of strenges in acord
Herde I so pleye a ravisshing swetnesse
That God, that maker is of al and lord,
Ne herde nevere better, as I gesse.
Therwith a wind, unnethe hit might be lesse,
Made in the leves grene a noise softe
Acordant to the foules song on-lofte.

Sk. 169–203

The air of that place so attempre was
That nevere was grevaunce of hoot ne cold.
Ther wex eek every holsom spyce and gras;
Ne no man may ther wexe seek ne old.
Yet was ther Ioye more a thousand fold
Then man can telle; ne nevere wolde it nighte,
But ay cleer day to any mannes sighte.

Under a tree besyde a welle I say
Cupyde our lord his arwes forge and fyle.
And at his feet his bowe al redy lay,
And wel his doghter tempred al the whyle
The hedes in the welle, and with hir wyle
She couched hem after as they shulde serve,
Som for to slee, and som to wounde and kerve.

Tho was I war of Plesaunce anon-right,
And of Aray, and Lust, and Curtesye;
And of the Craft that can and hath the might
To doon by force a wight to do folye—
Disfigurat was she, I nil not lye;
And by him-self under an ook, I gesse,
Sawe I Delyt, that stood with Gentilnesse.

I saw Beautee withouten any atyr,
And Youthe ful of game and Iolytè,
Fool-hardinesse, Flaterye, and Desyr,
Messagerye, and Mede, and other three—
Hir names shul noght heer be told for me—
And upon pilers grete of Iasper longe
I saw a temple of bras y-founded stronge.

Aboute the temple daunceden alway
Wommen y-nowe, of which somme ther were
Faire of hem-self, and somme of hem were gay.
In kirtels, al disshevele, wente they there
(That was hir office alwey, yeer by yere)
And on the temple, of doves whyte and faire
Saw I sitting many a hundred paire.

Before the temple-dore ful soberly
Dame Pees sat with a curteyn in hir hond.
And hir besyde, wonder discretly,
Dame Pacience sitting ther I fond
With face pale, upon an hil of sond;
And alder-next, within and eek with-oute,
Beheste and Art, and of hir folk a route.

Within the temple, of syghes hote as fyr
I herde a swogh that gan aboute renne;
Which syghes were engendred with desyr,
That maden every auter for to brenne
Of newe flaume. And wel aspyed I thenne
That al the cause of sorwes that they drye
Com of the bitter goddesse Ialousye.

The god Priapus saw I as I wente,
Within the temple in soverayn place stonde,
In swich aray as whan the asse him shente
With cry by night and with his ceptre in honde.
Ful besily men gunne assaye and fonde
Upon his heed to sette, of sondry hewe,
Garlondes ful of fresshe floures newe.

And in a privee corner in disport
Fond I Venus and hir porter Richesse,
That was ful noble and hauteyn of hir port.
Derk was that place, but afterward lightnesse
I saw a lyte—unnethe hit might be lesse—
And on a bed of gold she lay to reste
Til that the hote sonne gan to weste.

Hir gilte heres with a golden threed
Y-bounden were, untressed as she lay,
And naked fro the breest unto the heed
Men mighte hir see; and sothly for to say,
The remenant wel kevered to my pay
Right with a subtil kerchef of Valence,
Ther was no thikker cloth of no defence.

Sk. 239-273

The place yaf a thousand savours swote,
And Bachus, god of wyn, sat hir besyde,
And Ceres next, that doth of hunger bote;
And, as I seide, amiddes lay Cipryde,
To whom on knees two yonge folkes cryde
To ben hir help.   But thus I leet hir lye,
And ferther in the temple I gan espye

That in dispyt of Diane the chaste
Ful many a bowe y-broke heng on the wal
Of maydens, such as gunne hir tymes waste
In hir servyse; and peynted over al
Of many a storye, of which I touche shal
A fewe, as of Calixte and Athalaunte,
And many a mayde, of which the name I wante.

Semyramus, Candace, and Ercules,
Biblis, Dido, Tisbe and Piramus,
Tristram, Isoude, Paris, and Achilles,
Eleyne, Cleopatre, and Troilus,
Silla, and eek the moder of Romulus—
Alle these were peynted on that other syde,
And al hir love, and in what plyt they dyde.

Whan I was come ayen into the place
That I of spak, that was so swote and grene,
Forth welk I tho, my-selven to solace.
Tho was I war wher that ther sat a quene
That, as of light the somer-sonne shene
Passeth the sterre, right so over mesure
She fairer was than any creature.

And in this launde, upon an hil of floures,
Was set this noble goddesse Nature.
Of braunches were hir halles and hir boures
Y-wrought after hir craft and hir mesure.
Ne ther nas foul that cometh of engendrure
That they ne were prest in hir presence
To take hir doom and yeve hir audience.

For this was on Seynt Valentynes day,
Whan every foul cometh ther to chese his make,
Of every kinde that men thenke may.
And that so huge a noyse gan they make
That erthe and see, and tree and every lake,
So ful was that unnethe was ther space
For me to stonde: so ful was al the place.

And right as Aleyn in the Pleynte of Kinde
Devyseth Nature of aray and face,
In swich aray men mighten hir ther finde.
This noble emperesse ful of grace
Bad every foul to take his owne place
As they were wont alwey fro yeer to yere
Seynt Valentynes day to stonden there.

That is to sey, the foules of ravyne
Were hyest set; and than the foules smale,
That eten as hem nature wolde enclyne,
As worm or thing of which I telle no tale;
But water-foul sat lowest in the dale;
And foul that liveth by seed sat on the grene,
And that so fele that wonder was to sene.

Ther mighte men the royal egle finde,
That with his sharpe look perceth the sonne;
And other egles of a lower kinde,
Of which that clerkes wel devysen conne.
Ther was the tyraunt with his fethres donne
And greye, I mene the goshauk, that doth pyne
To briddes for his outrageous ravyne.

The gentil faucon, that with his feet distreyneth
The kinges hond; the hardy sperhauk eke,
The quayles foo; the merlion that peyneth
Him-self ful ofte the larke for to seke;
Ther was the douve, with hir eyen meke;
The Ialous swan, ayens his deth that singeth;
The oule eek, that of deth the bode bringeth;

The cran the geaunt, with his trompes soun;
The theef, the chogh; and eek the Iangling pye;
The scorning Iay; the eles foo, the heroun;
The false lapwing, ful of trecherye;
The stare, that the counseyl can bewrye;
The tame ruddok; and the coward kyte;
The cok, that orloge is of thorpes lyte;

The sparwe, Venus sone; the nightingale,
That clepeth forth the fresshe leves newe;
The swalwe, mordrer of the flyës smale
That maken hony of floures fresshe of hewe;
The wedded turtel, with hir herte trewe;
The pekok, with his aungels fethres brighte;
The fesaunt, scorner of the cok by nighte;

The waker goos; the cokkow evere unkinde;
The popiniay, ful of delicasye;
The drake, stroyer of his owne kinde;
The stork, the wreker of avouterye;
The hote cormeraunt of glotonye;
The raven wys, the crowe with vois of care;
The throstel old; the frosty feldefare.

What shulde I seyn? of foules every kinde
That in this world han fethres and stature
Men mighten in that place assembled finde
Before the noble goddesse Nature.
And everich of hem did his besy cure
Benignely to chese or for to take
By hir acord his formel or his make.

But to the poynt:—Nature held on hir hond
A formel egle, of shap the gentileste
That evere she among hir werkes fond,
The most benignë and the goodlieste.
In hir was every vertu at his reste,
So ferforth that Nature hir-self had blisse
To loke on hir and ofte hir bek to kisse.

Nature, the vicair of thalmyghty Lord,
That hoot, cold, hevy, light, and moiste, and dreye
Hath knit by even noumbre of acord,
In esy vois began to speke and seye,
"Foules, tak hede of my sentence, I preye,
And for your ese, in furthering of your nede,
As faste as I may speke I wol me spede.

"Ye know wel how, Seynt Valentynes day,
By my statut and through my governaunce,
Ye come for to chese—and flee your way—
Your makes as I prik yow with plesaunce.
But natheles my rightful ordenaunce
May I not lete, for al this world to winne,
That he that most is worthy shal beginne.

"The tercel egle, as that ye knowen wel,
The foul royal above yow in degree,
The wyse and worthy, secree, trewe as stel,
The which I formed have, as ye may see,
In every part as hit best lyketh me—
Hit nedeth noght his shap yow to devyse—
He shal first chese and speken in his gyse.

"And after him by ordre shul ye chese,
After your kinde, everich as yow lyketh,
And as your hap is shul ye winne or lese.
But which of yow that love most entryketh,
God sende him hir that sorest for him syketh."
And therwith-al the tercel gan she calle,
And seyde, "My sone, the choys is to thee falle.

"But natheles in this condicioun
Mot be the choys of everich that is here:
That she agree to his eleccioun,
Who-so he be that shulde been hir fere.
This is our usage alwey fro yeer to yere.
And who so may at this time have his grace,
In blisful tyme he com in-to this place."

With hed enclynęd and with ful humble chere
This royal tercel spak and taried nought:
"Unto my sovereyn lady, and noght my fere,
I chese, and chesę with wille and herte and thought,
The formel on your hond so wel y-wrought,
Whos I am al and evere wol hir serve,
Do with hir list to do me live or sterve.

"Beseching hir of mercy and of grace,
As she that is my lady sovereyne,
Or let me dye present in this place.
For certes, longe may I not live in peyne;
For in myn herte is corven every veyne.
Having reward only to my trouthe,
My dere herte, have on my wo som routhe.

"And if that I to hir be founde untrewe,
Disobeysaunt, or wilful negligent,
Avauntour, or in proces love a newe,
I pray to yow this be my Iugement,
That with thesę foules I be al to-rent
That ilke day that evere she me finde
To hir untrewe or in my gilt unkinde.

"And sin that noon lovęth hir so wel as I,
Al be she nevere of love me behette,
Than oghte she be myn thourgh hir mercy,
For other bond can I noon on hir knette.
For nevere for no wo ne shal I lette
To serven hir, how fer so that she wende.
Sey what yow list, my tale is at an ende."

Right as the fresshe, rede rose newe
Ayen the somer-sonne coloured is,
Right so for shame al wexen gan the hewe
Of this formel whan she herde al this.
She neyther answerde "wel," ne seyde amis;
So sore abasshęd was she til that Nature
Seydę, "Doghter, drede yow noght, I yow assure!"

Another tercel egle spak anoon
Of lower kinde, and seyde, "That shal not be.
I love hir bet than ye do, by Seynt Iohn!—
Or atte leste I love hir as wel as ye,
And lenger have served hir in my degree.
And if she shulde have loved for long lovinge,
To me allone had been the guerdoninge.

"I dar eek seye, if she me finde fals,
Unkinde, Iangler, or rebel any wyse,
Or Ialous, do me hongen by the hals!
And but I bere me in hir servyse
As wel as that my wit can me suffyse,
Fro poynt to poynt hir honour for to save,
Take she my lyf and al the good I have."

The thridde tercel egle answerde tho:
"Now, sirs, ye seen the litel leyser here!
For every foul cryeth oute to been a-go
Forth with his make or with his lady dere;
And eek Nature hir-self ne wol nought here,
For tarying heer, noght half that I wolde seye.
And but I speke, I mot for sorwe deye.

"Of longe servyse avaunte I me no-thing;
But as possible is me to dye to-day
For wo, as he that hath ben languisshing
Thise twenty winter, and wel happen may
A man may serven bet and more to pay
In half a yeer, al-though hit were no more,
Than som man doth that hath served ful yore.

"I ne say not this by me, for I ne can
Do no servyse that may my lady plese;
But I dar seyn I am hir trewest man
As to my doom, and feynest wolde hir ese.
At shorte wordes, til that deth me sese
I wol ben hires whether I wake or winke
And trewe in al that herte may bethinke."

Of al my lyf sin that day I was born
So gentil plee in love or other thing
Ne herde nevere no man me beforn,
Who that hadde leyser and cunning
For to reherse hir chere and hir speking.
And from the morwe gan this speche laste
Til dounward drow the sonne wonder faste.

The noyse of foules for to ben delivered
So loude rong, "Have doon and let us wende!"
That wel wende I the wodę had al to-shivered.
"Come of!" they cryde, "allas! ye wil us shende!
Whan shal your cursed pleding have an ende?
How shulde a Iugë eyther party leve,
For yee or nay, with-outen any preve?"

The goos, the cokkow, and the doke also
So cryden "Kek, kek!" "Kukkow!" "Quek,
        quek!" hye,
That thorgh myn eręs the noyse wente tho.
The goos seyde, "Al this nis not worth a flye!
But I can shape hereof a remedye,
And I wol sey my verdit faire and swythe
For water-foul, who-so be wrooth or blythe."

"And I for worm-foul," seyde the fool cokkow,
"For I wol of myn owne auctoritè
For comunę speed take the charge now,
For to delivere us is gret charitè."
"Ye may abyde a whyle yet, pardè!"
Seyde the turtel, "if hit be your wille
A wight may speke, him were as good be stille.

"I am a seed-foul, oon the unworthieste,
That wot I wel, and litel of kunninge.
But bet is that a wightes tonge reste
Than entremeten him of such doinge
Of which he neyther rede can nor singe.
And who-so doth, ful foule himself acloyeth,
For office uncommitted ofte anoyeth."

Nature, which that alway had an ere
To murmour of the lewednesse behinde,
With facound voys seide, "Hold your tonges there!
And I shal sone, I hope, a counseyl finde
Yow to delivere and fro this noyse unbinde.
I Iuge, of every folk men shal oon calle
To seyn the verdit for yow foules alle."

Assented were to this conclusioun
The briddes alle. And foules of ravyne
Han chosen first by pleyn eleccioun
The tercelet of the faucon to diffyne
Al hir sentence, and as him list, termyne;
And to Nature him gonnen to presente,
And she accepteth him with glad entente.

The tercelet seide than in this manere:
"Ful hard were hit to preve hit by resoun
Who loveth best this gentil formel here;
For everich hath swich replicacioun
That noon by skilles may be broght a-doun.
I can not seen that arguments avayle:
Than semeth hit ther moste be batayle."

"Al redy!" quod these egles tercels tho.
"Nay, sirs!" quod he, "if that I dorste hit seye,
Ye doon me wrong. My tale is not y-do!
For sirs, ne taketh noght a-gref, I preye:
It may noght gon as ye wolde in this weye.
Our is the voys that han the charge in honde,
And to the Iuges doom ye moten stonde.

"And therfore pees! I seye, as to my wit,
Me wolde thinke how that the worthieste
Of knighthode, and lengest hath used hit,
Moste of estat, of blood the gentileste,
Were sittingest for hir, if that hir leste;
And of these three she wot hir-self, I trowe,
Which that he be, for hit is light to knowe."

Sk. 519-553

The water-foules han her hedes leyd
Togeder, and of short avysement
Whan everich had his large golee seyd,
They seyden sothly al by oon assent
How that "the goos with hir facounde gent
That so desyreth to pronounce our nede
Shal telle our tale," and preyde " God hir spede."

And for these water-foules tho began
The goos to speken, and in hir cakelinge
She seyde, " Pees! now tak keep, every man,
And herkeneth which a reson I shal bringe.
My wit is sharp, I love no taryinge.
I seye, I rede him though he were my brother
But she wol love him lat him love another!"

"Lo heer! a parfit reson of a goos!"
Quod the sperhauk. "'Nevere mot she thee!
Lo, swich hit is to have a tonge loos!
Now parde, fool, yet were hit bet for thee
Have holde thy pees than shewed thy nycete!
Hit lyth not in his wit nor in his wille,
But sooth is seyd, 'A fool can noght be stille.'"

The laughter aroos of gentil foules alle,
And right anoon the seed-foul chosen hadde
The turtel trewe, and gunne hir to hem calle,
And preyden hir to seye the sothe sadde
Of this matere, and asked what she radde.
And she answerde that pleynly hir entente
She wolde shewe and sothly what she mente.

"Nay, God forbede a lover shulde chaunge!"
The turtel seyde, and wex for shame al reed.
"Thogh that his lady evere-more be straunge,
Yet let him serve hir evere til he be deed.
For sothe, I preyse noght the gooses reed;
For thogh she deyed, I wolde non other make,—
I wol ben hires til that the deth me take."

"Wel bourded!" quod the doke, "by my hat!
That men shulde alwey loven causeles,
Who can a reson finde or wit in that?
Daunceth he murye that is mirtheles?
Who shulde recche of that is reccheles?
Ye, quek!" yit quod the doke ful wel and faire,
"Ther been mo sterres, God wot, than a paire!"

"Now fy, cherl!" quod the gentil tercelet.
"Out of the dunghil com that word ful right.
Thou canst noght see which thing is wel be-set.
Thou farest by love as oules doon by light;
The day hem blent, ful wel they see by night.
Thy kinde is of so lowe a wrechednesse
That what love is thou canst nat see ne gesse."

Tho gan the cokkow putte him forth in prees
For foul that eteth worm, and seide blyve,
"So I," quod he, "may have my make in pees,
I recche not how longe that ye stryve.
Lat ech of hem be soleyn al hir lyve,
This is my reed sin they may not acorde.
This shorte lesson nedeth noght recorde."

"Ye! have the glotoun fild ynogh his paunche,
Than are we wel!" seyde the merlioun;
"Thou mordrer of the heysugge on the braunche
That broghte thee forth, thou rewthelees glotoun!
Live thou soleyn, wormes corrupcioun!
For no fors is of lakke of thy nature.
Go, lewed be thou, whyl the world may dure!"

"Now pees," quod Nature, "I comaunde heer!
For I have herd al your opinoun,
And in effect yet be we nevere the neer.
But fynally, this is my conclusioun:
That she hir-self shal han the eleccioun
Of whom hir list, who-so be wrooth or blythe;
Him that she cheest, he shal hir have as swythe.

"For sith hit may not heer discussed be
Who loveth hir best, as seide the tercelet,
Than wol I doon hir this favour, that she
Shal have right him on whom hir herte is set,
And he hir that his herte hath on hir knet.
This Iuge I, Nature, for I may not lyë.
To noon estat I have non other yë.

"But as for counseyl for to chese a make,
If hit were reson, certes, than wolde I
Counseyle yow the royal tercel take,
As seide the tercelet ful skilfully,
As for the gentilest and most worthy
Which I have wroght so wel to my plesaunce.
That to yow oghte been a suffisaunce."

With dredful vois the formel hir answerde,
"My rightful lady, Goddesse of Nature,
Soth is that I am evere under your yerde
Lyk as is everich other creature,
And moot be youres whyl my lyf may dure.
And therfore graunteth me my firste bone,
And myn entente I wol yow sey right sone."

"I graunte hit yow," quod she.   And right anoon
This formel egle spak in this degree:
"Almighty quene, unto this yeer be doon
I aske respit for to avysen me.
And after that to have my choys al free.
This al and som that I wolde speke and seye;
Ye gete no more, al-though ye do me deye.

"I wol noght serven Venus ne Cupyde
For sothe as yet, by no manere weye."
"Now sin hit may non other wyse betyde,"
Quod tho Nature, " heer is no more to seye,
Than wolde I that these foules were aweye
Ech with his make, for tarying lenger here"—
And seyde hem thus as ye shul after here.

"To yow speke I, ye tercelets," quod Nature.
"Beth of good herte and serveth, alle three.
A yeer is not so longe to endure,
And ech of yow peyne him, in his degree,
For to do wel; for, God wot, quit is she
Fro yow this yeer, what after so befalle.
This entremes is dressed for yow alle."

And whan this werk al broght was to an ende,
To every foul Nature yaf his make
By even acord, and on hir wey they wende.
A! Lord! the blisse and Ioye that they make!
For ech of hem gan other in winges take,
And with hir nekkes ech gan other winde,
Thanking alwey the noble goddesse of kinde.

But first were chosen foules for to singe,
As yeer by yere was alwey hir usaunce
To singe a roundel at hir departinge
To do Nature honour and plesaunce.
The note, I trowe, maked was in Fraunce;
The wordes were swich as ye may heer finde,
The nexte vers as I now have in minde.

Qui bien aime a tard oublie.
"Now welcome somer with thy sonne softe,
That hast this wintres weders over-shake,
And driven awey the longe nightes blake!

" Seynt Valentyn, that art ful hy on-lofte:—
Thus sungen smale foules for thy sake—
  Now welcom somer with thy sonne softe,
  That hast this wintres weders over-shake.

"Wel han they cause for to gladen ofte,
Sith ech of hem recovered hath his make;
Ful blisful may they singen whan they wake;
  Now welcom somer with thy sonne softe,
  That hast this wintres weders over-shake,
  And driven awey the longe nightes blake."

And with the showting whan hir song was do
That foules maden at hir flight a-way,
I wook, and other bokes took me to
To rede upon, and yet I rede alway.
I hope, y-wis, to rede so som day
That I shal mete som thing for to fare
The bet, and thus to rede I nil not spare.

Explicit tractatus de congregacione Volucrum
      die sancti Valentini.

Sk. 693–699

TROILUS AND CRISEYDE

Book I

The double sorwe of Troilus to tellen,
That was the King Priamus sone of Troye,
In loving, how his aventures fellen
Fro wo to wele, and after out of Ioye,
My purpos is er that I parte fro ye.
Thesiphone, thou help me for tendyte
Thise woful vers that wepen as I wryte!

To thee clepe I, thou goddesse of torment,
Thou cruel Furie, sorwing evere in peyne:
Help me, that am the sorwful instrument
That helpeth lovers, as I can, to pleyne!
For wel sit it the sothe for to seyne,
A woful wight to han a drery fere,
And to a sorwful tale a sory chere.

It is wel wist how that the Grekes stronge
In armes with a thousand shippes wente
To Troyewardes, and the citee longe
Assegeden neigh ten yeer er they stente;
And in diverse wyse and oon entente
The ravisshing to wreken of Eleyne,
By Paris doon, they wroughten al hir peyne.

Now fil hit so that in the toun ther was
Dwelling a lord of greet auctoritee,
A gret devyn that cleped was Calkas,
That in science so expert was that he
Knew wel that Troye sholde destroyed be,
By answere of his god, that highte thus,
Daun Phebus or Apollo Delphicus.

So whan this Calkas knew by calculinge,
And eek by answere of this Appollo,
That Grekes sholden swich a peple bringe
Thorough which that Troye moste been for-do,
He caste anoon out of the toun to go.
For wel wiste he by sort that Troye sholde
Destroyed been, ye! wolde who-so nolde.

For which for to departen softely
Took purpos ful this forknowinge wyse,
And to the Grekes ost ful prively
He stal anoon; and they in curteys wyse
Him deden bothe worship and servyse
In trust that he hath conning hem to rede
In every peril which that is to drede.

The noyse up roos whan it was first aspyed
Thorough al the toun, and generally was spoken
That Calkas traytor fled was, and allyed
With hem of Grece; and casten to ben wroken
On hem that falsly had his feith so broken;
And seyden he and al his kin at ones
Ben worthy for to brennen, fel and bones.

Now hadde Calkas left in this meschaunce
Al unwist of this fals and wikked dede
His doughter, which that was in gret penaunce,
For of hir lyf she was ful sore in drede,
As she that niste what was best to rede:
For bothe a widowe was she and allone
Of any freend to whom she durste hir mone.

Criseyde was this lady name a-right.
As to my doom, in al Troyes citee
Nas noon so fair; for passing every wight
So aungellyk was hir natyf beautee
That lyk a thing inmortal semed she,
As doth an hevenish parfit creature
That doun were sent in scorning of nature.

Sk., I, 71–105

This lady, which that al-day herde at ere
Hir fadres shame, his falsnesse, and tresoun,
Wel nigh out of hir wit for sorwe and fere,
In widewes habit large of samit broun,
On knees she fil biforn Ector a-doun;
With pitous voys and tendrely wepinge
His mercy bad, hir-selven excusinge.

Now was this Ector pitous of nature,
And saw that she was sorwfully bigoon
And that she was so fair a creature.
Of his goodnesse he gladed hir anoon,
And seyde, "Lat your fadres treson goon
Forth with mischaunce! and ye your-self in Ioye
Dwelleth with us, whyl you good list, in Troye.

"And al thonour that men may doon yow have,
As ferforth as your fader dwelled here,
Ye shul han and your body shal men save
As fer as I may ought enquere or here."
And she him thonked with ful humble chere,
And ofter wolde and it had ben his wille,
And took hir leve, and hoom, and held hir stille.

And so bifel whan comen was the tyme
Of Aperil, whan clothed is the mede
With newe grene, of lusty Ver the pryme,
And swote smellen floures whyte and rede,
In sondry wyses shewed, as I rede,
The folk of Troye hir observaunces olde
Palladiones feste for to holde.

And to the temple in al hir beste wyse
In general ther wente many a wight
To herknen of Palladion the servyse.
And namely so many a lusty knight,
So many a lady freshe and mayden bright,
Ful wel arayed bothe moste and leste,
Ye, bothe for the seson and the feste.

Among thise othere folk was Criseyda
In widewes habit blak; but nathelees
Right as our firste lettre is now an A,
In beautee first so stood she makelees.
Hir godly looking gladede al the prees.
Nas nevere seyn thing to ben preysed derre,
Nor under cloude blak so bright a sterre

As was Criseyde as folk seyde everichoon
That hir bihelden in hir blake wede;
And yet she stood ful lowe and stille alloon
Behinden othere folk in litel brede
And neigh the dore, ay under shames drede,
Simple of atyr and debonaire of chere,
With ful assured loking and manere.

This Troilus, as he was wont to gyde
His yonge knightes, ladde hem up and doun
In thilke large temple on every syde,
Biholding ay the ladyes of the toun,
Now heer, now ther; for no devocioun
Had he to noon to reven him his reste,
But gan to preyse and lakken whom him leste.

And in his walk ful faste he gan to wayten
If knight or squyer of his companye
Gan for to syke, or lete his eyen bayten
On any woman that he coude aspye;
He wolde smyle, and holden it folye,
And seye him thus, "God wot, she slepeth softe
For love of thee whan thou tornest ful ofte!

"I have herd told, pardieux, of your livinge,
Ye lovers, and your lewede observaunces,
And which a labour folk han in winninge
Of love, and in the keping, which doutaunces;
And whan your preye is lost, wo and penaunces.
O verrey foles! nyce and blinde be ye:
Ther nis not oon can war by other be."

And with that word he gan cast up the browe,
Ascaunces, "Lo! is this nought wysly spoken?"
At which the God of Love gan loken rowe
Right for despyt, and shoop for to ben wroken.
He kidde anoon his bowe nas not broken;
For sudeynly he hit him at the fulle.
And yet as proud a pekok can he pulle!

With-in the temple he wente him forth pleyinge,
This Troilus, of every wight aboute,
On this lady and now on that lokinge,
Wher-so she were of toune or of with-oute.
And up-on cas bifel that thorugh a route
His eye perced, and so depe it wente
Til on Criseyde it smoot, and ther it stente.

And sodeynly he wex ther-with astoned,
And gan hire bet biholde in thrifty wyse:
"O mercy, God!" thoughte he, "wher hastow woned,
That art so fair and goodly to devyse?"
Ther-with his herte gan to sprede and ryse,
And softe sighed lest men mighte him here,
And caughte a-yein his firste pleying chere.

She nas not with the leste of hir stature,
But alle hir limes so wel answeringe
Weren to womanhod, that creature
Was nevere lasse mannish in seminge.
And eek the pure wyse of here mevinge
Shewede wel that men mighte in hir gesse
Honour, estat, and wommanly noblesse.

To Troilus right wonder wel with-alle
Gan for to lyke hir meving and hir chere,
Which somdel deynous was, for she leet falle
Hir look a lite a-side in swich manere,
Ascaunces, "What! may I not stonden here?"
And after that hir loking gan she lighte,
That nevere thoughte him seen so good a sighte.

Sk., I, 204–210; 267–294

And of hir look in him ther gan to quiken
So greet desir and swich affeccioun
That in his hertes botme gan to stiken
Of hir his fixe and depe impressioun.
And though he erst had poured up and doun,
He was tho glad his hornes in to shrinke.
Unnethes wiste he how to loke or winke.

Lo, he that leet him-selven so konninge
And scorned hem that Loves peynes dryen,
Was ful unwar that Love had his dwellinge
With-in the subtile stremes of hir yën,
That sodeynly him thoughte he felte dyën,
Right with hir look, the spirit in his herte.
Blessed be Love that thus can folk converte!

She, this in blak, lyking to Troilus,
Over alle thyng he stood for to biholde.
Ne his desir ne wherfore he stood thus
He neither chere made, ne word tolde.
But from a-fer, his manere for to holde,
On other thing his look som-tyme he caste
And eft on hir, whyl that servyse laste.

And after this, not fully al awhaped,
Out of the temple al esiliche he wente,
Repenting him that he had evere y-iaped
Of Loves folk, lest fully the descente
Of scorn fille on him-self; but, what he mente,
Lest it were wist on any maner syde,
His wo he gan dissimulen and hyde.

Whan he was fro the temple thus departed,
He streyght anoon un-to his paleys torneth,
Right with hir look thurgh-shoten and thurgh-darted,
Al feyneth he in lust that he soiorneth.
And al his chere and speche also he borneth;
And ay of Loves servants every whyle,
Him-self to wrye, at hem he gan to smyle.

And seyde, "Lord, so ye live al in lest,
Ye loveres! for the conningest of yow,
That serveth most ententiflich and best,
Him tit as often harm ther-of as prow.
Your hyre is quit ayein, ye! God wot how!
Nought wel for wel, but scorn for good servyse.
In feith your ordre is ruled in good wyse!"

But for al this, whan that he say his tyme,
He held his pees,—non other bote him gayned.
For Love bigan his fetheres so to lyme
That wel unnethe un-to his folk he feyned
That othere besye nedes him destrayned.
For wo was him that what to doon he niste,
But bad his folk to goon wher that hem liste.

And whan that he in chaumbre was allone,
He doun up-on his beddes feet him sette,
And first he gan to syke and eft to grone,
And thoughte ay on hir so withouten lette,
That, as he sat and wook, his spirit mette
That he hir saw a temple, and al the wyse
Right of hir look, and gan it newe avyse.

Thus gan he make a mirour of his minde,
In which he saugh al hoolly hir figure.
And that he wel coude in his herte finde,
It was to him a right good aventure
To love swich oon; and if he did his cure
To serven hir, yet mighte he falle in grace,
Or elles, for oon of hir servaunts pace.

Imagininge that travaille nor grame
Ne mighte for so goodly oon be lorn
As she, ne him for his desir ne shame,
Al were it wist, but in prys and up-born
Of alle lovers wel more than biforn:
Thus argumented he in his ginninge,
Ful unavysed of his wo cominge.

Sk., I, 330-336; 351-378

Thus took he purpos loves craft to suwe,
And thoughte he wolde werken prively,
First, to hyden his desyr in muwe
From every wight y-born, al-outrely,
But he mighte ought recovered be therby;
Remembring him that love to wyde y-blowe
Yelt bittre fruyt, though swete seed be sowe.

And to the God of Love thus seyde he
With pitous voys, "O lord, now youres is
My spirit, which that oughte youres be.
You thanke I, lord, that han me brought to this.
But whether goddesse or womman, y-wis,
She be, I noot, which that ye do me serve;
But as hir man I wol ay live and sterve.

"Ye stonden in hire eyen mightily
As in a place un-to your vertu digne.
Wherfore, lord, if my servyse or I
May lyke yow, so beth to me benigne.
For myn estat royal heer I resigne
In-to hir hond, and with ful humble chere
Bicome hir man as to my lady dere."

In him ne deyned sparen blood royal
The fyr of love, (wher-fro God me blesse!)
Ne him forbar in no degree, for al
His vertu or his excellent prowesse;
But held him as his thral lowe in distresse,
And brende him so in sondry wyse ay newe
That sixty tyme a day he loste his hewe.

The sharpe shoures felle of armes preve
That Ector or his othere bretheren diden
Ne made him only ther-fore ones meve;
And yet was he, wher-so men wente or riden,
Founde oon the best, and lengest tyme abiden
Ther peril was, and did eek such travayle
In armes that to thenke it was mervayle.

Sk., I, 379–385; 421–441; 470–476

But for non hate he to the Grekes hadde,
Ne also for the rescous of the toun,
Ne made him thus in armes for to madde;
But only, lo, for this conclusioun,
To lyken hir the bet for his renoun,
Fro day to day in armes so he spedde
That alle the Grekes as the deeth him dredde.

And fro this forth tho refte him love his sleep,
And made his mete his foo; and eek his sorwe
Gan multiplye that, who-so toke keep,
It shewed in his hewe, bothe eve and morwe.
Therfore a title he gan him for to borwe
Of other syknesse, lest of him men wende
That the hote fyr of love him brende.

And seyde, he had a fevere and ferde amis;
But how it was, certayn, can I not seye,
If that his lady understood not this,
Or feyned hir she niste, oon of the tweye.
But wel I rede that by no maner weye
Ne semed it as that she of him roughte,
Nor of his peyne or what-so-evere he thoughte.

But than fel to this Troilus such wo
That he was wel neigh wood; for ay his drede
Was this, that she som wight had loved so
That nevere of him she wolde have taken hede,
For which him thoughte he felte his herte blede.
Ne of his wo ne dorste he not biginne
To tellen it, for al this world to winne.

But whan he had a space fro his care,
Thus to him-self ful ofte he gan to pleyne.
He sayde, "O fool, now art thou in the snare
That whilom Iapedest at loves peyne!
Now artow hent, now gnaw thyn owene cheyne!
Thou were ay wont ech lover reprehende
Of thing fro which thou canst thee nat defende!"

Sk., I, 477–511

Thise wordes and ful manye an-other to
He spak, and called evere in his compleynte
Hir name for to tellen hir his wo,
Til neigh that he in salte teres dreynte.
Al was for nought; she herde nought his pleynte.
And whan that he bithoughte on that folye,
A thousand fold his wo gan multiplye.

Bi-wayling in his chambre thus allone,
A freend of his that called was Pandare
Com ones in unwar, and herde him grone,
And sey his freend in swich distresse and care.
"Allas!" quod he, "who causeth al this fare?
O mercy, God! what unhap may this mene?
Han now thus sone Grekes maad yow lene?

"Or hastow som remors of conscience,
And art now falle in som devocioun,
And waylest for thy sinne and thyn offence,
And hast for ferde caught attricioun?
God save hem that bi-seged han our toun
And so can leye our Iolyte on presse
And bringe our lusty folk to holinesse!"

These wordes seyde he for the nones alle,
That with swich thing he mighte him angry maken,
And with an angre don his sorwe falle
As for the tyme, and his corage awaken.
But wel he wiste, as fer as tonges spaken,
Ther nas a man of gretter hardinesse
Than he, ne more desired worthinesse.

"What cas," quod Troilus, "or what aventure
Hath gyded thee to sen my languisshinge,
That am refus of every creature?
But for the love of God, at my preyinge,
Go henne a-way, for certes my deyinge
Wol thee disese, and I mot nedes deye.
Therfore go wey, ther is no more to seye.

"But if thou wene I be thus syk for drede,
It is not so, and therforę scorne nought.
Ther is a-nother thing I take of hede
Wel more than ought the Grekes han y-wrought
Which cause is of my deeth for sorwe and thought.
But though that I now telle thee it ne leste,
Be thou nought wrooth: I hyde it for the beste."

This Pandarę, that neigh malt for wo and routhe,
Ful often seyde, "Allas! what may this be?"
"Now freend," quod he, "if evere love or trouthe
Hath been, or is, bi-twixen thee and me,
Ne do thou nevere swich a crueltee
To hyde fro thy freend so greet a care.
Wostow nought wel that it am I, Pandare?

"I wole parten with thee al thy peyne,
If it be so I do thee no comfort,
As it is freendes right, sooth for to seyne,
To entreparten wo as glad desport.
I have, and shal, for trewe or fals report,
In wrong and right y-loved thee al my lyve.
Hyd not thy wo fro me but telle it blyve."

Than gan this sorwful Troilus to syke,
And seyde him thus, "God leve it be my beste
To telle it thee! For sith it may thee lyke,
Yet wole I telle it though myn herte breste.
And yet wot I thou mayst do me no reste.
But lest thow deme I truste not to thee,
Now herke, freend, for thus it stant with me.

"Love, a-yeins the which who-so defendeth
Him-selven most, him alder-lest avayleth,
With desespeir so sorwfully me offendeth
That streyght un-to the deeth myn herte sayleth.
Ther-to desyr so brenningly me assayleth
That to ben slayn it were a gretter Ioye
To me than king of Grece been and Troye!

"Suffiseth this, my fulle freend Pandare,
That I have seyd, for now wostow my wo.
And for the love of God, my colde care
So hyd it wel: I tolde it nevere to mo;
For harmes mighte folwen, mo than two,
If it were wist. But be thou in gladnesse
And lat me sterve, unknowe, of my distresse."

"How hastow thus unkindely and longe
Hid this fro me, thou fool?" quod Pandarus;
"Paraunter thou might after swich oon longe
That myn avys anoon may helpen us."
"This were a wonder thing," quod Troylus,
"Thou coudest nevere in love thy-selven wisse;
How devel maystow bringen me to blisse?"

"Ye, Troilus, now herke," quod Pandare,
"Though I be nyce; it happeth ofte so
That oon that excesse doth ful yvele fare
By good counseyl can kepe his freend ther-fro.
I have my-self eek seyn a blind man go
Ther-as he fel that coude loke wyde.
A fool may eek a wys man ofte gyde.

"A whetston is no kerving instrument
And yet it maketh sharpe kerving-tolis.
And ther thow woost that I have ought miswent,
Eschewe thou that, for swich thing to thee scole is:
Thus ofte wyse men ben war by folis.
If thou do so, thy wit is wel biwared;
By his contrarie is every thing declared.

"The wyse seyth, 'Wo him that is allone,
For, and he falle, he hath noon help to ryse.'
And sith thou hast a felawe, telle thy mone;
For this nis not, certeyn, the nexte wyse
To winnen love, as techen us the wyse,—
To walwe and wepe as Niobe the quene,
Whos teres yet in marbel been y-sene.

"If God wolę thou art not agast of me
Lest I wolde of thy lady thee bigyle,
Thow wost thy-self whom that I love, pardee,
As I best can, gon sithen longe whyle.
And sith thou wost I do it for no wyle,
And sith I am he that thou tristest most,
Tellę me sumwhat, sin al my wo thou wost."

Yet Troilus for al this no word seyde,
But longe he lay as stille as he ded were.
And after this with syking he abreyde,
And to Pandarus voys he lente his ere,
And up his eyen caste he, that in fere
Was Pandarus lest that in frenesye
He sholde falle, or elles sone dye:

And cryde "A-wak!" ful wonderly and sharpe;
"What? slombrestow as in a lytargye?
Or artow lyk an asse to the harpe,
That hereth soun whan men the strenges plye
But in his minde of that no melodye
May sinken, him to glade, for that he
So dul is of his bestialitee?"

And with that Pandare of his wordes stente;
But Troilus yet him no word answerde,
For-why to telle nas not his entente
To nevere no man, for whom that he so ferde.
For it is seyd, "Man maketh ofte a yerde
With which the maker is him-self y-beten
In sondry manere," as thisę wyse treten,

And namely in his counseyl tellinge
That toucheth love that oughte be secree;
For of him-self it wolde y-nough out-springe,
But-if that it the bet governed be.
Eek som-tyme it is craft to seme flee
Fro thing which in effect men hunte faste:
Al this gan Troilus in his herte caste.

But nathelees whan he had herd him crye
"Awak!" he gan to syke wonder sore,
And seyde, "Freend, though that I stille lye,
I am not deef. Now pees, and crye no more!
For I have herd thy wordes and thy lore;
But suffre me my mischef to biwayle,
For thy proverbes may me nought avayle.

"Nor other cure canstow noon for me.
Eek I nil not be cured, I wol deye;
What knowe I of the quene Niobe?
Lat be thyn olde ensaumples, I thee preye!"
"No," quod tho Pandarus, "therfore I seye,
Swich is delyt of foles to biwepe
Hir wo, but seken bote they ne kepe.

"Now knowe I that ther reson in thee fayleth.
But telle me if I wiste what she were
For whom that thee al this misaunter ayleth?
Dorstestow that I tolde hir in hir ere
Thy wo, sith thou darst not thy-self for fere,
And hir bisoughte on thee to han som routhe?"
"Why, nay," quod he, "by God and by my trouthe!"

"What? not as bisily," quod Pandarus,
"As though myn owene lyf lay on this nede?"
"No, certes, brother," quod this Troilus.
"And why?"—"For that thou sholdest nevere spede."
"Wostow that wel?"—"Ye, that is out of drede,"
Quod Troilus, "for al that evere ye conne,
She nil to noon swich wrecche as I be wonne."

Quod Pandarus, "Allas! what may this be,
That thou despeyred art thus causelees?
What? liveth not thy lady? *benediste!*
How wostow so that thou art gracelees?
Swich yvel is not alwey botelees.
Why, put not impossible thus thy cure,
Sin thing to come is ofte in aventure.

"What may she demen other of thy deeth,
If thou thus deye, and she not why it is,
But that for fere is yolden up thy breeth
For Grekes han biseged us, y-wis?
Lord! which a thank than shaltow han of this!
Thus wol she seyn, and al the toun at ones,
'The wrecche is deed, the devel have his bones!'

"Thou mayst allone heer wepe and crye and knele;
But love a woman that she woot it nought
And she wol quyte that thou shalt not fele.
Unknowe, unkist; and lost that is un-sought.
What! many a man hath love ful dere y-bought
Twenty winter that his lady wiste,
That nevere yet his lady mouth he kiste.

"What? shulde he therfore fallen in despeyr,
Or be recreaunt for his owene tene,
Or sleen him-self, al be his lady fair?
Nay, nay, but evere in oon be fresh and grene
To serve and love his dere hertes quene,
And thenke it is a guerdoun hir to serve
A thousand-fold more than he can deserve."

And of that word took hede Troilus,
And thoughte anoon what folye he was inne,
And how that sooth him seyde Pandarus,
That for to sleen him-self mighte he not winne,
But bothe doon unmanhod and a sinne,
And of his deeth his lady nought to wyte;
For of his wo, God woot, she knew ful lyte.

And with that thought he gan ful sore syke,
And seyde, "Allas! what is me best to do?"
To whom Pandare answerde, "If thee lyke,
The best is that thou telle me al thy wo;
And have my trouthe, but thou finde it so
I be thy bote or that it be ful longe,
To peces do me drawe and sithen honge!"

Sk., I, 799-833

"Ye, so thou seyst," quod Troilus tho, "allas!
But, God wot, it is not the rather so.
Ful hard were it to helpen in this cas,
For wel finde I that Fortune is my fo,
Ne alle the men that ryden conne or go
May of hir cruel wheel the harm withstonde;
For as hir list she pleyeth with free and bonde."

Quod Pandarus, "Than blamestow Fortune
For thou art wrooth, ye, now at erst I see.
Wostow nat wel that Fortune is commune
To every maner wight in som degree?
And yet thou hast this comfort, lo, pardee!
That as hir Ioyes moten over-goon,
So mote hir sorwes passen everichoon.

"For if hir wheel stinte any-thing to torne,
Than cessed she Fortune anoon to be:
Now sith hir wheel by no wey may soiorne,
What wostow if hir mutabilitee,
Right as thy-selven list, wol doon by thee,
Or that she be not fer fro thyn helpinge?
Paraunter thou hast cause for to singe!

"And therfore wostow what I thee beseche?
Lat be thy wo and turning to the grounde;
For who-so list have helping of his leche,
To him bihoveth first unwrye his wounde.
To Cerberus in helle ay be I bounde,
Were it for my suster al thy sorwe,
By my wille, she sholde al be thyn to-morwe.

"Loke up, I seye, and telle me what she is
Anoon, that I may goon aboute thy nede.
Knowe ich hir ought? For my love telle me this!
Than wolde I hopen rather for to spede."
Tho gan the veyne of Troilus to blede,
For he was hit, and wex al reed for shame.
"A ha!" quod Pandare, "heer biginneth game!"

And with that word he gan him for to shake,
And seyde, "Theef, thou shalt hir name telle!"
But tho gan sely Troilus for to quake
As though men sholde han lad him in-to helle,
And seyde, "Allas! of al my wo the welle,
Than is my swete fo called Criseyde!"
And wel nigh with the word for fere he deyde.

And whan that Pandare herde hir name nevene,
Lord! he was glad, and seyde, "Freend so dere,
Now far a-right, for Ioves name in hevene!
Love hath biset the wel, be of good chere;
For of good name and wysdom and manere
She hath y-nough, and eek of gentilesse.
If she be fayr thow wost thy-self, I gesse.

"Ne I nevere saw a more bountevous
Of hir estat, ne a gladder, ne of speche
A freendlier, ne a more gracious
For to do wel, ne lasse had nede to seche
What for to doon; and al this bet to eche
In honour, to as fer as she may strecche,
A kinges herte semeth by hires a wrecche.

"And for-thy loke of good comfort thou be.
For certeinly, the firste poynt is this
Of noble corage and wel ordeyne,
A man to have pees with him-self, y-wis.
So oughtest thou, for nought but good it is
To loven wel and in a worthy place.
Thee oughte not to clepe it hap, but grace.

"And also thenk, and ther-with glade thee,
That sith thy lady vertuous is al,
So folweth it that ther is som pitee
Amonges alle thise othere in general;
And for-thy see that thou in special
Requere nought that is ayein hir name:
For vertu streccheth not him-self to shame.

Sk., I, 869-903

"But wel is me that evere I was born
That thou biset art in so good a place.
For, by my trouthe, in love I dorste havę sworn
Thee sholde nevere han tid thus fayr a grace.
And wostow why? for thou werę wont to chace
At Love in scorn, and for despyt him calle
'Seynt Idiot, lord of thisę foles alle.'

"How often hastow maad thy nyce Iapes,
And seyd that Loves servants everichone
Of nycetee ben verray Goddes apes;
And some wolde monche hir mete alone,
Ligging a-bedde, and make hem for to grone;
And som, thou seydest, had a blaunche fevere,
And preydest God he sholde nevere kevere!

"Now beet thy brest, and sey to God of Love,
'Thy grace, lord! For now I me repente
If I mis-spak, for now my-self I love!'—
Thus sey with al thyn herte in good entente."
Quod Troilus, "A! lord! I me consente,
And pray to thee my Iapes thou foryive,
And I shal nevere-more whyl I live."

"Thou seyst wel," quod Pandare, "and now I hope
That thou the goddes wraththe hast al apesed.
And sithen thou hast wepen many a drope,
And seyd swich thing wher-with thy god is plesed,
Now wolde nevere God but thou were esed.
And think wel she of whom rist al thy wo
Heer-after may thy comfort been al-so.

"Wherfore I am, and wol be, ay redy
To peyne me to do yow this servyse.
For bothe yow to plese thus hope I
Her-afterward; for ye beth bothe wyse,
And conne it counseyl kepe in swich a wyse
That no man shal the wyser of it be,
And so may we be gladed alle three."

Sk., I, 904-917; 932-945; 988-994

Whan Troilus had herd Pandare assented
To been his help in loving of Criseyde,
Wex of his wo, as who seyth, untormented,
But hotter wex his love, and thus he seyde
With sobre chere, al-though his herte pleyde:
"Now blisful Venus helpe, er that I sterve,
Of thee, Pandare, I may som thank deserve!

"But dere frend, how shal myn wo ben lesse
Til this be doon? and goode, eek tellẹ me this:
How wiltow seyn of me and my distresse?
Lest she be wrooth, this drede I most, y-wis,
Or nil not here or trowen how it is.
Al this drede I, and eek for the manere
Of thee, hir eem, she nil no swich thing here."

Quod Pandarus, "Thou hast a ful gret care
Lest that the cherl may falle out of the mone!
Why, Lord! I hate of thee thy nyce fare!
Why, entremete of that thou hast to done!
For Goddes love, I bidde thee a bone:
So lat me alone, and it shal be thy beste!"—
"Why freend," quod he, "now do right as thee leste.

"But herke, Pandare, o word, for I nolde
That thou in me wendest so greet folye
That to my lady I desiren sholde
That toucheth harm or any vilenye.
For dredelees, me were lever dye
Than she of me ought elles understode
But that that mighte sounen in-to gode."

Tho lough this Pandare, and anoon answerde,
"And I thy borwẹ? fy! no wight dooth but so!
I roughte nought though that she stode and herde
How that thou seyst; but far-wel, I wol go.
A-dieu! be glad! God spede us bothe two!
Yif me this labour and this besinesse,
And of my speed be thyn al that swetnesse."

Tho Troilus gan doun on knees to falle,
And Pandare in his armes hente faste,
And seyde, "Now fy on the Grekes alle!
Yet, pardee, God shal helpe us at the laste.
And dredelees, if that my lyf may laste,
And God to-forn, lo, some of hem shal smerte.
And yet me athinketh that this avaunt me asterte!

"Now, Pandare, I can no more seye,
But thou wys, thou wost, thou mayst, thou art al!
My lyf, my deeth, hool in thyn hond I leye.
Help now," quod he.   "Yis, by my trouthe, I shal."
"God yelde thee, freend, and this in special,"
Quod Troilus, "that thou me recomaunde
To hir that to the deeth me may comaunde."

This Pandarus tho, desirous to serve
His fulle freend, than seyde in this manere,
"Far-wel, and thenk I wol thy thank deserve.
Have heer my trouthe, and that thou shalt wel here."—
And wente his wey, thenking on this matere,
And how he best mighte hir beseche of grace
And finde a tyme ther-to and a place.

For every wight that hath an hous to founde
Ne renneth nought the werk for to biginne
With rakel hond, but he wol byde a stounde,
And sende his hertes lyne oute fro with-inne
Alderfirst his purpos for to winne.
Al this Pandare in his herte thoughte,
And caste his werk ful wysly or he wroughte.

But Troilus lay tho no lenger doun,
But up anoon up-on his stede bay,
And in the feld he pleyde tho leoun.
Wo was that Greek that with him mette that day;
And in the toun his manere tho forth ay
So goodly was and gat him so in grace
That ech him lovede that loked on his face.

For he bicom the frendlyeste wight,
The gentileste, and eek the moste free,
The thriftieste and oon the beste knight,
That in his tyme was or mighte be.
Dedę were his Iapes and his crueltee,
His heighe port and his manere estraunge,
And ech of tho gan for a vertu chaunge.

Now lat us stinte of Troilus a stounde,
That fareth lyk a man that hurt is sore,
And is somdel of aking of his wounde
Y-lissed wel, but heled no del more;
And, as an esy pacient, the lore
Abit of him that gooth aboute his cure.
And thus he dryveth forth his aventure.

Explicit Liber Primus.

Book II

Incipit Liber Secundus

Out of thesę blake wawes for to sayle,
O wind, O wind, the weder ginneth clere;
For in this see the boot hath swich travayle,
Of my conning that unnethe I it stere:
This see clepe I the tempestous matere
Of desespeyr that Troilus was inne.
But now of hope the calendes biginne.

O lady myn, that called art Cleo,
Thou be my speed fro this forth, and my muse,
To ryme wel this book til I havę do.
Me nedeth heer noon other art to use.
For-why to every lover I me excuse
That of no sentement I this endyte,
But out of Latin in my tonge it wryte.

Sk., I, 1079–1092; II, 1–14

In May, that moder is of monthes glade,
That fresshe floures, blewe, and whyte, and rede,
Ben quike agayn that winter dede made,
And ful of bawme is fleting every mede,
Whan Phebus doth his brighte bemes sprede
Right in the whyte Bole, it so bitidde
As I shal singe, on Mayes day the thridde,

That Pandarus for al his wyse speche
Felte eek his part of loves shottes kene
That, coude he nevere so wel of loving preche,
It made his hewe a-day ful ofte grene.
So shoop it that him fil that day a tene
In love, for which in wo to bedde he wente
And made er it was day ful many a wente.

The swalwe Proignè with a sorwful lay,
Whan morwe com, gan make hir weymentinge
Why she forshapen was; and evere lay
Pandare a-bedde half in a slomeringe
Til she so neigh him made hir chiteringe
How Tereus gan forth hir suster take
That with the noyse of hir he gan a-wake;

And gan to calle, and dresse him up to ryse,
Remembring him his erand was to done
From Troilus, and eek his greet empryse;
And caste and knew in good plyt was the mone
To doon viage, and took his wey ful sone
Un-to his neces paleys ther bi-syde.
Now Ianus, god of entree, thou him gyde!

Whan he was come un-to his neces place,
"Wher is my lady?" to hir folk seyde he.
And they him tolde; and he forth in gan pace,
And fond two othere ladyes sete and she
With-inne a paved parlour; and they three
Herden a mayden reden hem the geste
Of the Sege of Thebes whyl hem leste.

Quod Pandarus, "Ma dame, God yow see,
With al your book and al the companye!"
"Ey, uncle myn, welcome y-wis," quod she,
And up she roos and by the hond in hye
She took him faste, and seyde, "This night thrye,
To goode mote it turne, of yow I mette!"
And with that word she doun on bench him sette.

"Ye, nece, ye shal fare wel the bet,
If God wole, al this yeer," quod Pandarus;
"But I am sory that I have yow let
To herken of your book ye preysen thus.
For Goddes love, what seith it? telle it us!
Is it of love? O, som good ye me lere!"
"Uncle," quod she, "your maistresse is not here!"

With that they gonnen laughe, and tho she seyde,
"This romaunce is of Thebes, that we rede.
And we han herd how that King Laius deyde
Thurgh Edippus his sone, and al that dede.
And heer we stenten at these lettres rede,
How the bisshop, as the book can telle,
Amphiorax, fil thurgh the ground to helle."

Quod Pandarus, "Al this knowe I my-selve,
And al the assege of Thebes and the care,
For her-of been ther maked bokes twelve:—
But lat be this and telle me how ye fare!
Do wey your barbe and shew your face bare!
Do wey your book, rys up, and lat us daunce,
And lat us don to May som observaunce!"

"Ey! God forbede!" quod she, "be ye mad?
Is that a widewes lyf, so God you save?
By God, ye maken me right sore a-drad,
Ye ben so wilde, it semeth as ye rave!
It sate me wel bet ay in a cave
To bidde, and rede on holy seyntes lyves:
Lat maydens gon to daunce, and yonge wyves!"

Sk., II, 85-119

"As evere thryve I," quod this Pandarus,
"Yet coude I telle a thing to doon you pleye."
"Now uncle dere," quod she, "telle it us
For Goddes love! Is than the assege aweye?
I am of Grekes so ferd that I deye."
"Nay, nay," quod he, "as evere mote I thryve!
It is a thing wel bet than swiche fyve."

"Ye, holy God!" quod she, "what thing is that?
What? bet than swiche fyve? ey, nay, y-wis!
For al this world ne can I reden what
It sholde been. Som Iape, I trowe, is this.
And but your-selven telle us what it is,
My wit is for to arede it al to lene.
As helpe me God, I noot nat what ye mene."

"And I your borowe, ne nevere shal, for me,
This thing be told to yow, as mote I thryve!"
"And why so, uncle myn? why so?" quod she.
"By God," quod he, "that wol I telle as blyve;
For prouder womman were ther noon on-lyve
And ye it wiste, in al the toun of Troye.
I Iape nought, as evere have I Ioye!"

Tho gan she wondren more than biforn
A thousand fold, and doun hir eyen caste;
For nevere sith the tyme that she was born
To knowe thing desired she so faste.
And with a syk she seyde him at the laste,
"Now, uncle myn, I nil yow nought displese
Nor axen more that may do yow disese."

So after this with many wordes glade
And freendly tales and with mery chere
Of this and that they pleyde and gunnen wade
In many an uncouth glad and deep matere,—
As freendes doon whan they ben met y-fere,—
Til she gan axen him how Ector ferde,
That was the tounes wal and Grekes yerde.

"Ful wel, I thanke it God," quod Pandarus,
"Save in his arm he hath a litel wounde;
And eek his fresshe brother Troilus,
The wyse worthy Ector the secounde,
In whom that every vertu list abounde,
As alle trouthe and alle gentillesse,
Wysdom, honour, fredom, and worthinesse."

"By God," quod she, "of Ector that is sooth.
Of Troilus the same thing trowe I;
For dredelees, men tellen that he dooth
In armes day by day so worthily,
And bereth him heer at hoom so gentilly
To every wight, that al the prys hath he
Of hem that me werę levest preysed be."

"Ye sey right sooth, y-wis," quod Pandarus;
"For yesterday who-so had with him been,
He might havę wondred up-on Troilus;
For nevere yet so thikke a swarm of been
Ne fleigh as Grekes fro him gonne fleen.
And thorugh the feld in every wightes ere
Ther nas no cry but 'Troilus is there!'

"Therto he is the freendlieste man
Of greet estat that evere I saw my lyve;
And wher him list, best felawshipe can
To such as him thinkęth able for to thryve."
And with that word tho Pandarus as blyve
He took his leve, and seyde, "I wol go henne."
"Nay, blame have I, myn uncle," quod she thenne.

"What eyleth yow to be thus wery sone
And namelich of wommen? Wol ye so?
Nay, sitteth down! By God, I havę to done
With yow, to speke of wisdom er ye go."
And every wight that was a-boute hem tho
That herde that, gan fer a-wey to stonde,
Whyl they two had al that hem liste in honde.

Sk., II, 155–161; 183–196; 204–217

Whan that hir tale al brought was to an ende
Of hire estat and of hir governaunce,
Quod Pandarus, "Now is it tyme I wende.
But yet, I seye, aryseth, lat us daunce,
And cast your widwes habit to mischaunce!
What list yow thus your-self to disfigure,
Sith yow is tid thus fair an aventure?"

"A! wel bithought! for love of God," quod she,
"Shal I not witen what ye mene of this?"
"No, this thing axeth layser," tho quod he,
"And eek me wolde muche greve, y-wis,
If I it tolde, and ye it toke amis.
Yet were it bet my tonge for to stille
Than seye a sooth that were ayeins your wille.

"For, nece, by the Goddesse Minerve,
And Iuppiter, that maketh the thonder ringe,
And by the blisful Venus that I serve,
Ye been the womman in this world livinge,
With-oute paramours, to my witinge,
That I best love and lothest am to greve,
And that ye witen wel your-self, I leve."

"Y-wis, myn uncle," quod she, "grant mercy;
Your freendship have I founden evere yit.
I am to no man holden trewely
So muche as yow, and have so litel quit.
And, with the grace of God, emforth my wit
As in my gilt I shal you nevere offende.
And if I have er this, I wol amende.

"But for the love of God I yow beseche,
As ye ben he that I most love and triste,
Lat be to me your fremde maner speche,
And seye to me, your nece, what yow liste."
And with that word hir uncle anoon hir kiste,
And seyde, "Gladly, leve nece dere.
Tak it for good that I shal seye yow here."

With that she gan hir eyen doun to caste,
And Pandarus to coghe gan a lyte,
And seyde, "Nece, alwey, lo! to the laste,
How-so it be that som men hem delyte
With subtil art hir tales for to endyte,
Yet for al that, in hir entencioun,
Hir tale is al for som conclusioun.

"And sithen thende is every tales strengthe,
And this matere is so bihovely,
What sholde I peynte or drawen it on lengthe
To yow that been my freend so feithfully?"
And with that word he gan right inwardly
Biholden hir and loken on hir face,
And seyde, "On such a mirour goode grace!"

Than thoughte he thus, "If I my tale endyte
Ought hard, or make a proces any whyle,
She shal no savour han ther-in but lyte,
And trowe I wolde hir in my wille bigyle.
For tendre wittes wenen al be wyle
Ther-as they can nat pleynly understonde.
For-thy hir wit to serven wol I fonde."—

And loked on hir in a besy wyse,
And she was war that he byheld her so,
And seyde, "Lord! so faste ye me avyse!
Sey ye me nevere er now? What sey ye, no?"
"Yes, yes," quod he, "and bet wol er I go.
But by my trouthe I thoughte now if ye
Be fortunat, for now men shal it see.

"Good aventure, O bele nece, have ye
Ful lightly founden, and ye conne it take.
And for the love of God and eek of me,
Cacche it anoon lest aventure slake.
What sholde I lenger proces of it make?
Yif me your hand, for in this world is noon,
If that you list, a wight so well begoon.

Sk., II, 253–280; 288–294

" Beth nought agast, ne quaketh nat. Wher-to?
Ne chaungeth nat for fere so your hewe.
For hardely, the werste of this is do;
And though my tale as now be to yow newe,
Yet trist alwey ye shal me finde trewe.
And were it thing that me thoughte unsittinge,
To yow nolde I no swiche tales bringe."

"Now, my good eem, for Goddes love, I preye,"
Quod she, "com of, and tel me what it is.
For bothe I am agast what ye wol seye,
And eek me longeth it to wite, y-wis.
For whether it be wel or be amis,
Sey on, lat me not in this fere dwelle!"
"So wol I doon, now herkneth, I shal telle.

"Now, nece myn, the kinges dere sone,
The goode, wyse, worthy, fresshe, and free,
Which alwey for to do wel is his wone,
The noble Troilus, so loveth thee
That, bot ye helpe, it wol his bane be.
Lo, heer is al, what sholde I more seye?
Doth what yow list to make him live or deye.

"But if ye lete him deyë, I wol sterve—
Have her my trouthe, nece, I nil not lyen!—
Al sholde I with this knyf my throte kerve!"
With that the teres braste out of his yën,
And seyde, "If that ye doon us bothe dyën,
Thus giltelees, than have ye fisshed faire!
What mende ye, though that we bothe apeyre?

"And also thenk wel that this is no gaude;
For me werę lever thou and I and he
Were hanged than I sholde been his baude,
As heyghe, as men mighte on us alle y-see:
I am thyn eem, the shame werę to me
As wel as thee if that I sholde assente,
Thorugh myn abet, that he thyn honour shente.

"Now understond, for I yow nought requere
To binde yow to him thorugh no biheste,
But only that ye make him bettre chere
Than ye han doon er this, and more feste,
So that his lyf be saved at the leste:
This al and som, and playnly our entente.
God helpę me so, I nevere other mente!"

Criseyde, which that herde him in this wyse,
Thoughte, "I shal fele what he meneth, y-wis."
"Now eem," quod she, "what wolde ye devyse?
What is your reed I sholde doon of this?"
"That is wel seyd," quod he, "certayn, best is
That ye him love ayein for his lovinge,
As lovę for love is skilful guerdoninge.

"Thenk eek how elde wasteth every houre
In ech of yow a party of beautee;
And therfore, er that age thee devoure,
Go lovę, for, oldę, ther wol no wight of thee.
Lat this proverbe a lore un-to yow be:
'To late y-war, quod Beautee, whan it paste;'
And 'Elde daunteth Daunger at the laste.'

"The kinges fool is wont to cryen loude
Whan that him thinkęth a womman beręth hir hye
'So longe motę ye live, and alle proude,
Til crowes feet be growe under your yë,
And sendę yow than a mirour in to pryë
In which that ye may see your face a-morwe!'
Nece, I biddę wisshe yow no morę sorwe."

With this he stente, and caste adoun the heed,
And she bigan to breste a-wepe anoon.
And seyde, "Allas, for wo! why nere I deed?
For of this world the feith is al agoon!
Allas! what sholden straunge to me doon
When he that for my beste freend I wende
Ret me to love, and sholde it me defende?

" Allas! I wolde han trusted doutelees
That if that I thurgh my disaventure
Had loved other him or Achilles,
Ector, or any mannes creature,
Ye nolde han had no mercy ne mesure
On me, but alwey had me in repreve.
This false world, allas! who may it leve?"

With that she gan ful sorwfully to syke.
"A! may it be no bet?" quod Pandarus;
"By God, I shal no-morę com heer this wyke,
And God to-forn, that am mistrusted thus;
I see ful wel that ye sette lyte of us
Or of our deeth! Allas! I woful wrecchc!
Mighte he yet live, of me is nought to recche.

"But sith it lyketh yow that I be deed,
By Neptunus, that god is of the see,
Fro this forth shal I nevere eten breed
Til I myn owene herte blood may see;
For certayn I wol deye as sone as he."—
And up he sterte, and on his wey he raughte,
Til she agayn him by the lappe caughte.

Criseyde, which that wel neigh starf for fere,
So as she was the ferfulleste wight
That mighte be, and herde eek with hir ere
And saw the sorwful ernest of the knight,
And in his preyere eek saw noon unright,
And for the harm that mighte eek fallen more
She gan to rewe and dradde hir wonder sore;

And thoughte thus, "Unhappes fallen thikke
Alday for love and in swich maner case,
As men ben cruel in him-self and wikke.
And if this man slee heer him-self, allas!
In my presence it wol be no solas.
What men wolde of hit deme I can nat seye.
It nedeth me ful sleyly for to pleye."

Sk. , II, 414–420; 428–434; 442–462

And with a sorwful syk she seyde thrye,
"A! Lord! what me is tid a sory chaunce!
For myn estat now lyth in Iupartye
And eek myn emes lyf lyth in balaunce;
But nathelees with Goddes governaunce
I shal so doon, myn honour shal I kepe,
And eek his lyf;" and stinte for to wepe.

"Of harmes two the lesse is for to chese.
Yet have I lever maken him good chere
In honour than myn emes lyf to lese.
Ye seyn ye no-thing elles me requere?"
"No, wis," quod he, " myn owene nece dere."
"Now wel," quod she, "and I wol doon my peyne.
I shal myn herte ayeins my lust constreyne,

"But that I nil not holden him in honde
Ne love a man, ne can I not ne may
Ayeins my wille; but elles wol I fonde,
Myn honour sauf, plese him fro day to day.
Ther-to nolde I nought ones have seyd nay,
But that I dredde as in my fantasye.
But cesse cause, ay cesseth maladye.

"And heer I make a protestacioun
That in this proces if ye depper go
That certaynly, for no savacioun
Of yow, though that ye sterve bothe two,
Though al the world on o day be my fo,
Ne shal I nevere on him han other routhe."—
"I graunte wel," quod Pandare, "by my trouthe.

"But may I truste wel ther-to," quod he,
" That of this thing that ye han hight me here
Ye wol it holden trewly un-to me?"
"Ye, doutelees," quod she, "myn uncle dere."
"Ne that I shal han cause in this matere,"
Quod he, "to pleyne, or after yow to preche?"
"Why no, pardee! What nedeth more speche?"

Tho fillen they in othere tales glade
Til at the laste, "O good eem," quod she tho,
"For love of God, which that us bothe made,
Tel me how first ye wisten of his wo:
Wot noon of hit but ye?" He seyde, "No."
"Can he wel speke of love?" quod she, "I preye,
Tel me, for I the bet me shal purveye."

Tho Pandarus a litel gan to smyle
And seyde, "By my trouthe I shal yow telle.
This other day, nought gon ful longe whyle,
In-with the paleys-gardyn by a welle,
Gan he and I wel half a day to dwelle,
Right for to speken of an ordenaunce,
How we the Grekes mighte disavaunce.

"Sone after that bigonne we to lepe,
And casten with our dartes to and fro,
Til at the laste he seyde he wolde slepe,
And on the gres a-doun he leyde him tho.
And I after gan rome to and fro
Til that I herde, as that I welk allone,
How he bigan ful wofully to grone.

"Tho gan I stalke him softely bihinde,
And sikerly the sothe for to seyne,
As I can clepe ayein now to my minde,
Right thus to Love he gan him for to pleyne:
He seyde, 'Lord, have routhe up-on my peyne,
Al have I been rebel in myn entente!
Now *mea culpa*, lord! I me repente.'

"And God wot nevere sith that I was born
Was I so bisy no man for to preche,
Ne nevere was to wight so depe y-sworn
Or he me tolde who mighte been his leche.
But now to yow rehersen al his speche,
Or alle his woful wordes for to soune,
Ne bid me not, but ye wol see me swoune.

Sk., II, 498–525; 568–574

"And right good thrift I pray to God havȩ ye,
That han swich oon y-caught with-oute net.
And be ye wys as ye ben fair to see
Wel in the ring than is the ruby set.
Ther were nevere two so wel y-met,
Whan ye ben his al hool as he is youre:
Ther mighty God yet graunte us see that houre!"

"Nay, therof spak I not, a, ha!" quod she,
"As helpȩ me God, ye shenden every deel!"
"O mercy, dere nece," anoon quod he,
"What-so I spak I mente nought but weel,
By Mars the god that helmed is of steel!
Now beth nought wrooth, my blood, my nece dere!"
"Now wel," quod she, "foryeven be it here!"

With this he took his leve and hoom he wente;
And Lord! how he was glad and wel bigoon!
Criseyde aroos, no lenger she ne stente,
But straught in-to hir closet wente anoon,
And sette herȩ doun as stille as any stoon,
And every word gan up and doun to winde
That he had seyd, as it com hir to minde.

And wex somdel astonied in hir thought
Right for the newe cas. But whan that she
Was ful avysed, tho fond she right nought
Of peril, why she oughte afered be.
For man may love of possibilitee
A womman so his herte may to-breste
And she nought love ayein but-if hir leste.

But as she sat allone and thoughte thus
Thascry aroos at skarmishe al with-oute,
And men cryde in the stretȩ, "See, Troilus
Hath right now put to flightȩ the Grekes route!"
With that gan al hir meynee for to shoute,
"A! go we see, caste up the latis wyde!
For thurgh this strete he moot to palays ryde!

Sk., II, 582–616

"For other wey is fro the yate noon
Of Dardanus, ther open is the cheyne."
With that com he and al his folk anoon
An esy pas ryding, in routes tweyne,
Right as his happy day was, sooth to seyne
For which, men say, may nought disturbed be
That shal bityden of necessitee.

This Troilus sat on his baye stede,
Al armed save his heed ful richely,
And wounded was his hors, and gan to blede,
On which he rood a pas ful softely.
But swich a knightly sighte, trewely,
As was on him, was nought with-outen faile
To loke on Mars, that god is of batayle.

So lyk a man of armes and a knight
He was to seen, fulfild of heigh prowesse;
For bothe he had a body and a might
To doon that thing, as wel as hardinesse.
And eek to seen him in his gere him dresse,
So freshe, so yong, so weldy semed he,
It was an hevene up-on him for to see.

His helm to-hewen was in twenty places,
That by a tissew heng his bak bihinde,
His sheld to-dasshed was with swerdes and maces,
In which men mighte many an arwe finde
That thirled hadde horn and nerf and rinde.
And ay the peple cryde, "Heer cometh our Ioye,
And, next his brother, holder up of Troye!"

For which he wex a litel reed for shame
Whan he the peple up-on him herde cryen,
That to biholde it was a noble game,
How sobreliche he caste doun his yën.
Criseÿda gan al his chere aspyen,
And leet so softe it in hir herte sinke,
That to hir-self she seyde, "Who yaf me drinke?"

For of hir owene thought she wex al reed,
Remembring hir right thus, "Lo, this is he
Which that myn uncle swereth he moot be deed
But I on him have mercy and pitee;"
And with that thought for pure a-shamed she
Gan in hir heed to pulle, and that as faste,
Whyl he and al the peple for-by paste,

And gan to caste and rollen up and doun
With-in hir thought his excellent prowesse,
And his estat, and also his renoun,
His wit, his shap, and eek his gentillesse.
But most hir favour was, for his distresse
Was al for hir, and thoughte it was a routhe
To sleen swich oon if that he mente trouthe.

Now mighte som envyous Iangle thus:
"This was a sodeyn love! How mighte it be
That she so lightly lovede Troilus
Right for the firste sighte; ye, pardee?"
Now who-so seyth so, mote he nevere thee!
For every thing a ginning hath it nede
Er al be wrought, with-outen any drede.

For I sey nought that she so sodeynly
Yaf him hir love, but that she gan enclyne
To lyke him first, and I have told yow why;
And after that, his manhod and his pyne
Made love with-in hir for to myne,
For which by proces and by good servyse
He gat hir love, and in no sodeyn wyse.

And Lord! so she gan in hir thought argue
In this matere of which I have yow told,
And what to doon best were, and what eschue,
That plyted she ful ofte in many fold.
Now was hir herte warm, now was it cold,
And what she thoughte somwhat shal I wryte,
As to myn auctor listeth for to endyte.

Sk., II, 652-679; 694-700

She thoughte wel that Troilus persone
She knew by sighte and eek his gentillesse,
And thus she seyde, "Al were it nought to done
To graunte him love, yet for his worthinesse
It were honour with pley and with gladnesse
In honestee with swich a lord to dele
For myn estat and also for his hele.

"Eek wel wot I my kinges sone is he,
And sith he hath to see me swich delyt,
If I wolde utterly his sighte flee
Paraunter he mighte have me in dispyt,
Thurgh which I mighte stonde in worse plyt.
Now were I wys me hate to purchace
With-outen nede ther I may stonde in grace!

"In every thing, I woot, ther lyth mesure.
For though a man forbede dronkenesse,
He nought for-bet that every creature
Be drinkelees for alwey, as I gesse.
Eek sith I woot for me is his distresse,
I ne oughte not for that thing him despyse,
Sith it is so he meneth in good wyse.

"And eek I knowe of longe tyme agoon
His thewes goode and that he is not nyce.
Ne avauntour, seyth men, certein, is he noon;
To wys is he to do so gret a vyce.
Ne als I nel him nevere so cheryce
That he may make avaunt, by Iuste cause.
He shal me nevere binde in swich a clause.

"Now set a cas, the hardest is, y-wis,
Men mighten deme that he loveth me:
What dishonour were it un-to me this?
May I him lette of that? Why nay, pardee!
I knowe also, and alday here and see,
Men loven wommen al this toun aboute;
Be they the wers? Why, nay, with-outen doute!

"I thenk eek how he able is for to have
Of al this noble toun the thriftieste
To been his love, so she hir honour save;
For out and out he is the worthieste,
Save only Ector, which that is the beste.
And yet his lyf al lyth now in my cure,
But swich is love and eek myn aventure.

"Ne me to love, a wonder is it nought;
For wel wot I my-self, so God me spede,
Al wolde I that noon wistë of this thought,
I am oon the fayreste, out of drede,
And goodlieste, who-so taketh hede;
And so men seyn in al the toun of Troye.
What wonder is it though he of me havę Ioye?

"I am myn owene woman, wel at ese,
I thank it God, as after myn estat;
Right yong, and stonde unteyd in lusty lese,
With-outen Ialousye or swich debat.
Shal noon housbonde seyn to me 'Chekmat!'
For either they ben ful of Ialousye,
Or maisterful, or loven novelrye.

"What shal I doon? to what fyn live I thus?
Shal I nat loven in cas if that me leste?
What, *par dieux!* I am nought religious!
And though that I myn herte sette at reste
Upon this knight, that is the worthieste,
And kepe alwey myn honour and my name,
By alle right it may do me no shame."

But right as whan the sonne shyneth brighte,
In March that chaungeth ofte tyme his face,
And that a cloude is put with wind to flighte
Which over-sprat the sonne as for a space,
A cloudy thought gan thorugh hir soule pace,
That over-spradde hir brighte thoughtes alle,
So that for fere almost she gan to falle.

Sk., II, 736–770

That thought was this: "Allas! sin I am free,
Sholde I now love, and putte in Iupartye
My sikernesse, and thrallen libertee?
Allas! how dorste I thenken that folye?
May I nought wel in other folk aspye
Hir dredful Ioye, hir constreynte, and hir peyne?
Ther loveth noon that she nath why to pleyne."

And after that hir thought bigan to clere,
And seyde, "He which that no-thing under-taketh,
No thing ne acheveth, be him looth or dere."
And with an other thought hir herte quaketh;
Than slepeth hope, and after drede awaketh:
Now hoot, now cold, but thus bi-twixen tweye
She rist hir up and wente hir for to pleye.

The dayes honour and the hevenes yë,
The nightes fo,—al this clepe I the sonne,—
Gan westren faste, and dounward for to wrye,
As he that had his dayes cours y-ronne;
And whyte thinges wexen dimme and donne
For lak of light, and sterres for to appere,
That she and al hir folk in wente y-fere.

So whan it lyked hir to goon to reste,
And voyded weren they that voyden oughte,
She seyde that to slepe wel hir leste.
Hir wommen sone til hir bed hir broughte.
Whan al was hust, than lay she stille and thoughte
Of al this thing the manere and the wyse.
Reherce it nedeth nought, for ye ben wyse.

A nightingale upon a cedre grene
Under the chambre-wal ther as she lay
Ful loude sang ayein the mone shene,
Paraunter, in his briddes wyse, a lay
Of love, that made hir herte fresh and gay.
That herkned she so longe in good entente,
Til at the laste the dede sleep hir hente.

Sk., II, 771–777; 806–812; 904–924

And as she sleep, anoon-right tho hir mette
How that an egle, fethered whyt as boon,
Under hir brest his longe clawes sette,
And oute hir herte he rente, and that a-noon,
And did his herte in-to hir brest to goon,
Of which she nought agroos ne no-thing smerte,
And forth he fleigh with herte left for herte.

Now lat hir slepe, and we our tales holde
Of Troilus, that is to paleys riden
Fro the scarmuche, of the which I tolde,
And in his chambre sit, and hath abiden
Til two or three of his messages yeden
For Pandarus, and soughten him ful faste
Til they him founde and broughte him at the laste.

This Pandarus com leping in at ones
And seide thus, "Who hath ben wel y-bete
To-day with swerdes and with slinge-stones
But Troilus, that hath caught him an hete?"
And gan to Iape, and seyde, "Lord, so ye swete!
But rys and lat us soupe and go to reste."
And he answerde him, "Do we as thee leste."

With al the haste goodly that they mighte
They spedde hem fro the souper un-to bedde;
And every wight oute at the dore him dighte,
And wher him list upon his wey he spedde.
But Troilus, that thoughte his herte bledde
For wo, til that he herde som tydinge,
He seyde, "Freend, shal I now wepe or singe?"

Quod Pandarus, "Ly stille and lat me slepe,
And don thyn hood, thy nedes spedde be.
And chees if thou wolt singe or daunce or lepe:
At shorte wordes, thow shalt trowe me,
Sire, my nece wol do wel by thee
And love thee best, by God and by my trouthe,
But lak of pursuit make it in thy slouthe.

Sk., II, 925-959

" For thus ferforth I have thy work bigonne,
Fro day to day, til this day by the morwe,
Hir love of freendship have I to thee wonne,
And also hath she leyd hir feyth to borwe.
Algate a foot is hameled of thy sorwe."
What sholde I lenger sermon of it holde?
As ye han herd bifore, al he him tolde.

But right as floures, thorugh the colde of night
Y-closed, stoupen on hir stalkes lowe,
Redressen hem a-yein the sonne bright,
And spreden on hir kinde cours by rowe,
Right so gan tho his eyen up to throwe
This Troilus, and seyde, "O Venus dere,
Thy might, thy grace, y-heried be it here!"

And to Pandare he held up bothe his hondes,
And seyde, "Lord, al thyn be that I have.
For I am hool, al brosten been my bondes.
A thousand Troians who-so that me yave,
Ech after other, God so wis me save,
Ne mighte me so gladen. Lo, myn herte,
It spredeth so, for Ioye it wol to-sterte!"

"Al esily, now, for the love of Marte,"
Quod Pandarus, "for every thing hath tyme.
So longe abyd til that the night departe;
For al so siker as thow lyst here by me,
And God toforn, I wol be ther at pryme,
And for-thy werk somwhat as I shal seye,
Or on som other wight this charge leye.

"I woot wel that thow wyser art than I
A thousand fold, but if I were as thou,
God helpe me so, as I wolde outrely
Right of my owene hond wryte hir right now
A lettre, in which I wolde hir tellen how
I ferde amis, and hir beseche of routhe.
Now help thy-self, and leve it not for slouthe.

Sk., II, 960–980; 988–994; 1002–1008

"And I my-self shal ther-with to hir goon;
And whan thou wost that I am with hir there,
Worth thou up-on a courser right anoon,
Ye, hardily, right in thy beste gere,
And ryd forth by the place as nought ne were;
And thou shalt finde us, if I may, sittinge
At som windowe, in-to the strete lokinge.

"And if thee list than maystow us saluwe,
And up-on me make thy contenaunce.
But, by thy lyf, be war and faste eschuwe
To tarien ought; God shilde us fro mischaunce!
Ryd forth thy wey, and hold thy governaunce,
And we shal speke of thee som-what, I trowe,
Whan thou art goon, to do thyn eres glowe!

"Touching thy lettre, thou art wys y-nough,
I woot thow nilt it digneliche endyte;
As make it with thise argumentes tough;
Ne scrivenish or craftily thou it wryte.
Beblotte it with thy teres eek a lyte.
And if thou wryte a goodly word al softe,
Though it be good reherce it not to ofte.

"Ne Iompre eek no discordaunt thing y-fere,
As thus, to usen termes of phisyk.
In loves termes hold of thy matere
The forme alwey, and do that it be lyk;
For if a peyntour wolde peynte a pyk
With asses feet, and hede it as an ape,
It cordeth nought; so nere it but a Iape."

This counseyl lyked wel to Troilus;
But as a dreedful lover he seyde this:
"Allas, my dere brother, Pandarus,
I am ashamed for to wryte, y-wis,
Lest of myn innocence I seyde a-mis,
Or that she nolde it for despyt receyve.
Thanne were I deed, ther mighte it no-thing weyve."

Sk., II, 1009-1029; 1037-1050

To that Pandare answerdë, "If thee lest,
Do that I seye, and lat me therwith goon.
For by that Lord that formed est and west,
I hope of it to bringe answere anoon
Right of hir hond; and if that thou nilt noon,
Lat be, and sory mote he been his lyve,
Ayeins thy lust that helpeth thee to thryve."

Quod Troilus, "*Depardieux*, I assente.
Sin that thee list, I will aryse and wryte,
And blisful God preye ich with good entente
The vyage, and the lettre I shal endyte,
So spede it! And thou Minerva, the whyte,
Yif thou me wit my lettre to devyse!"
And sette him doun, and wroot right in this wyse.—

First he gan hir his righte lady calle,
His hertes lyf, his lust, his sorwes leche,
His blisse, and eek thise othere termes alle
That in swich cas these loverẹs alle seche.
And in ful humble wyse, as in his speche,
He gan him recomaunde un-to hir grace,—
To telle al how, it axeth muchel space.

And after this ful lowly he hir preyde
To be nought wrooth, though he of his folye
So hardy was to hir to wryte, and seyde
That love it made or elles moste he dye,
And pitously gan mercy for to crye;
And after that he seyde, and ley ful loude,
Him-self was litel worth, and lesse he coude;

And that she sholde han his conning excused
That litel was, and eek he dredde hir so,
And his unworthinesse he ay acused;
And after that than gan he telle his wo;
But that was endeles, withouten ho;
And seyde he wolde in trouthe alwey him holde;—
And radde it over, and gan the lettre folde.

And with his salte teres gan he bathe
The ruby in his signet, and it sette
Upon the wex deliverliche and rathe.
Ther-with a thousand tymes er he lette
He kiste tho the lettre that he shette,
And seyde, "Lettre, a blisful destenee
Thee shapen is, my lady shal thee see!"

This Pandarę took the lettre, and that by tyme
A-morwe, and to his neces paleys sterte,
And faste he swoor that it was passed pryme,
And gan to Iape, and seyde, "Y-wis, myn herte,
So fresh it is, al-though it sore smerte,
I may not slepe nevere a Mayes morwe.
I have a Ioly wo, a lusty sorwe."

Criseyde, whan that she hir uncle herde,
With dreedful herte and desirous to here
The cause of his cominge, thus answerde,
"Now by your feyth, myn uncle," quod she, "dere,
What maner windes gydeth yow now here?
Tel us your Ioly wo and your penaunce.
How ferforth be ye put in loves daunce?"

"By God," quod he, "I hoppe alwey bihinde!"
And she to-laugh, it thoughte hir herte breste.
Quod Pandarus, "Loke alwey that ye finde
Game in myn hood, but herkneth if yow leste.
Ther is right now come in-to toune a geste,
A Greek espye, and telleth newe thinges,
For which come I to telle yow tydinges.

"Into the gardin go we, and we shal here
Al prevely of this a long sermoun."
With that they wenten arm in arm y-fere
In-to the gardin from the chaumbre doun.
And whan that he so fer was that the soun
Of that he speke, no man here mighte,
He seyde hir thus, and out the lettre plighte:

"Lo, he that is al hoolly youres free
Him recomaundeth lowly to your grace,
And sent to you this lettre heer by me.
Avyseth you on it whan ye han space,
And of som goodly answere yow purchace,
Or, helpę me God, so pleynly for to seyne,
He may not longe liven for his peyne."

Ful dredfully tho gan she stonde stille,
And took it nought, but al hir humble chere
Gan for to chaunge, and seyde, "Scrit ne bille,
For love of God, that toucheth swich matere,
Ne bring me noon! And also, uncle dere,
To myn estat have more reward I preye
Than to his lust. What sholde I more seye?

"And loketh now if this be resonable,
And letteth nought for favour ne for slouthe
To seyn a sooth: Now were it covenable
To myn estat, by God and by your trouthe,
To taken it, or to han of him routhe,
In harming of my-self or in repreve?
Ber it ayein, for him that ye on leve!"

This Pandarus gan on hir for to stare,
And seyde, "Now is this the grettest wonder
That evere I sey! Lat be this nyce fare!
To deethe mote I smiten be with thonder
If, for the citee which that stondeth yonder,
Wolde I a lettre un-to yow bringe or take
To harm of yow. What list yow thus it make?

" But thus ye faren wel neigh alle and some
That he that most desireth yow to serve,
Of him ye recche leest wher he bicome,
And whether that he live or elles sterve.
But for al that that evere I may deserve,
Refuse it nought," quod he and hente hir faste,
And in hir bosom the lettre doun he thraste.

And seyde hir, "Now cast it away anoon,
That folk may seen and gauren on us tweye."
Quod she, "I can abyde til they be goon,"
And gan to smyle, and seyde him, "Eem, I preye,
Swich answere as yow list your-self purveye,
For trewely I nil no lettre wryte."
"No? Than wol I," quod he, "so ye endyte."

Therwith she lough, and seyde, "Go we dyne."
And he gan at him-self to Iape faste,
And seyde, "Nece, I have so greet a pyne
For love that every other day I faste;"
And gan his beste Iapes forth to caste,
And made hir so laugh at his folye
That she for laughter wende for to dye.

And whan that she was comen in-to halle,
"Now eem," quod she, "we wol go dyne anoon."
And gan some of hir women to hir calle,
And streyght in-to hir chaumbre gan she goon.
But of hir besinesses, this was oon
A-monges othere thinges, out of drede,
Ful prively this lettre for to rede;

Avysed word by word in every lyne,
And fond no lak, she thoughte he coude good;
And up it putte, and wente hir in to dyne.
And Pandarus, that in a studye stood,
Er he was war she took him by the hood
And seyde, "Ye were caught er that ye wiste!"
"I vouche sauf," quod he, "do what yow liste."

Tho wesshen they, and sette hem doun and ete.
And after noon ful sleyly Pandarus
Gan drawe him to the windowe next the strete,
And seyde, "Nece, who hath arayed thus
The yonder hous that stant afor-yeyn us?"
"Which hous?" quod she, and gan for to biholde,
And knew it wel, and whos it was him tolde,

And fillen forth in speche of thinges smale,
And seten in the windowe bothe tweye.
Whan Pandarus saw tyme un-to his tale,
And saw wel that hir folk were alle a-weye,
"Now nece myn, tel on," quod he, "I seye,
How lyketh yow the lettre that ye woot?
Can he ther-on? For by my trouthe I noot."

Therwith al rosy hewed tho wex she,
And gan to humme, and seyde, "So I trowe."
"Acquyte him wel, for Goddes love," quod he;
"My-self to medes wol the lettre sowe,"
And held his hondes up, and sat on knowe,
"Now goode nece, be it nevere so lyte,
Yif me the labour it to sowe and plyte."

"Ye, for I can so wryte," quod she tho;
"And eek I noot what I sholde to him seye."
"Nay, nece," quod Pandare, "sey not so.
Yet at the leste thanketh him, I preye,
Of his good wille, and doth him not to deye.
Now for the love of me, my nece dere,
Refuseth not at this tyme my preyere."

"*Depar-dieux*," quod she, "God leve al be wel!
God helpe me so, this is the firste lettre
That evere I wroot, ye, al or any del."
And in-to a closet, for to avyse hir bettre,
She wente allone, and gan hir herte unfettre
Out of disdaynes prison but a lyte;
And sette hir doun and gan a lettre wryte,

Of which to telle in short is myn entente
Theffect as fer as I can understonde:—
She thonked him of al that he wel mente
Towardes hir, but holden him in honde
She nolde nought, ne make hir-selven bonde
In love, but as hir suster him to plese
She wolde fayn, to doon his herte an ese.

She shette it, and to Pandarus gan goon,
Ther as he sat and loked in-to strete,
And doun she sette hir by him on a stoon
Of Iaspre, up-on a quisshin gold y-bete,
And seyde, "As wisly helpe me God the grete,
I nevere did a thing with more peyne
Than wryte this, to which ye me constreyne;"

And took it him. He thonked hir and seyde:
"God woot, of thing ful ofte looth bigonne
Cometh ende good; and nece myn, Criseyde,
That ye to him of hard now ben y-wonne
Oughte he be glad, by God and yonder sonne!
For-why men seyth, 'Impressiounes lighte
Ful lightly been ay redy to the flighte.'"

And right as they declamed this matere,
Lo, Troilus, right at the stretes ende,
Com ryding with his tenthe som y-fere
Al softely, and thiderward gan bende
Ther-as they sete, as was his wey to wende
To paleys-ward. And Pandare him aspyde,
And seyde, "Nece, y-see who cometh here ryde!

"O flee not in!—he seeth us, I suppose,—
Lest he may thinke that ye him eschuwe."
"Nay, nay," quod she, and wex as reed as rose.
With that he gan hir humbly to saluwe,
With dreedful chere, and ofte his hewes muwe;
And up his look debonairly he caste,
And bekkede on Pandare, and forth he paste.

Pandare, which that stood hir faste by,
Felte iren hoot, and he bigan to smyte,
And seyde, "Nece, I pray yow hertely,
Tel me that I shal axen yow a lyte.
A womman, that were of his deeth to wyte
With-outen gilt but for hir lakkede routhe,
Were it wel doon?" Quod she, "Nay, by my trouthe!"

Sk., II, 1226–1239; 1247–1260; 1275–1281

"God helpę me so," quod he, "ye sey me sooth.
Ye felen wel your-self that I not lye.
Lo, yond he rit!" Quod she, "Ye, so he dooth."
"Wel," quod Pandare, "as I havę told yow thrye,
Lat be your nyce shame and your folye,
And spek with him in esing of his herte.
Lat nycetee not do yow bothe smerte."

But ther-on was to heven and to done:
Considered al thing it may not be;
And why? for shame; and it were eek to sone
To graunten him so greet a libertee.
For playnly hir entente, as seyde she,
Was for to love him unwist if she mighte,
And guerdon him with no-thing but with sighte.

But Pandarus thoughte, "It shal not be so,
If that I may. This nyce opinioun
Shal not be holden fully yeres two."
What sholde I make of this a long sermoun?
He moste assente on that conclusioun
As for the tyme; and whan that it was eve,
And al was wel, he roos and took his leve.

And on his wey ful faste homward he spedde,
And right for Ioye he felte his herte daunce;
And Troilus he fond alone a-bedde,
That lay as dooth thesę loveres, in a traunce,
Bitwixen hope and derk desesperaunce.
But Pandarus right at his in-cominge
He song, as who seyth, "Lo! sumwhat I bringe."

And seyde, "Who is in his bed so sone
Y-buried thus?" "It am I, freend," quod he.
"Who Troilus? Nay, helpę me so the mone,"
Quod Pandarus, "thou shalt aryse and see
A charme that was sent right now to thee,
The which can helen thee of thyn accesse,
If thou do forth-with al thy besinesse."

"Ye, through the might of God!" quod Troilus.
And Pandarus gan him the lettre take,
And seyde, "Pardee, God hath holpen us.
Have heer a light, and loke on al this blake."
But ofte gan the herte glade and quake
Of Troilus, whyl that he gan it rede,
So as the wordes yave him hope or drede.

But fynally, he took al for the beste
That she him wroot, for sumwhat he biheld
On which, him thoughte, he mighte his herte reste,
Al covered she the wordes under sheld.
Thus to the more worthy part he held,
That, what for hope and Pandarus biheste,
His grete wo for-yede he at the leste.

Wherfore I seye alwey that day and night
This Troilus gan to desiren more
Than he did erst, thurgh hope, and did his might
To pressen on, as by Pandarus lore,
And wryten to hir of his sorwes sore
Fro day to day. He leet it not refreyde
That by Pandare he wroot somwhat or seyde.

But to Pandare alwey was his recours,
And pitously gan ay til him to pleyne,
And him bisoughte of rede and som socours.
And Pandarus, that sey his wode peyne,
Wex wel neigh deed for routhe, sooth to seyne,
And bisily with al his herte caste
Som of his wo to sleen, and that as faste.

And seyde, "Lord and freend and brother dere,
God woot that thy disese dooth me wo.
But woltow stinten al this woful chere,
And, by my trouthe, or it be dayes two,
And God to-forn, yet shal I shape it so
That thou shalt come in-to a certayn place,
Ther-as thou mayst thy-self hir preye of grace.

Sk., II, 1317-1330; 1338-1344; 1352-1365

"But Troilus, yet telle me, if thee lest,
A thing now which that I shal axen thee:
Which is thy brother that thou lovest best
As in thy verray hertes privetee?"
"Y-wis, my brother Deiphebus," quod he.
"Now," quod Pandare, "er houres twyes twelve,
He shal thee ese unwist of it him-selve.

"Now lat me allone and werken as I may,"
Quod he; and to Deiphebus wente he tho
Which had his lord and grete freend ben ay.
Save Troilus no man he levede so.
To telle in short, with-outen wordes mo,
Quod Pandarus, "I pray yow that he be
Freend to a cause which that toucheth me."

"Yis, pardee," quod Deiphebus, "wel thow wost,
In al that evere I may, and God to-fore,
Al nere it but for man I love most,
My brother Troilus. But sey wherfore
It is; for sith that day that I was bore,
I nas, ne nevere-mo to been I thinke,
Ayeins a thing that mighte thee for-thinke."

Pandare gan him thonke, and to him seyde,
"Lo, sir, I have a lady in this toun
That is my nece, and called is Criseyde,
Which som men wolden doon oppressioun
And wrongfully have hir possessioun.
Wherfore I of your lordship yow b'seche
To been our freend, with-oute more speche."

Deiphebus him answerde, "O, is not this,
That thow spekest of to me thus straungely,
Criseÿda my freend?" He seyde, "Yis."
"Than nedeth," quod Deiphebus hardely,
"Na-more to speke; for trusteth wel that I
Wol be hir champioun with spore and yerde.
I roughte nought though alle hir foos it herde.

"But telle me, thou that woost al this matere,
How I might best avaylen? Now, lat see."
Quod Pandarus, "If ye, my lord so dere,
Wolden as now don this honour to me,
To prayen hir to-morwe, lo, that she
Com un-to yow hir playntes to devyse,
Hir adversaries wolde of hit agryse.

"And if I more dorste preye as now,
And chargen yow to have so greet travayle,
To han som of your bretheren heer with yow
That mighten to hir cause bet avayle,
That woot I wel she mighte nevere fayle
For to be holpen, what at your instaunce,
What with hir othere freendes governaunce."

Deiphebus, which that comen was of kinde
To al honour and bountee to consente,
Answerde, "It shal be doon. And I can finde
Yet gretter help to this in myn entente.
What wolt thow seyn if I for Eleyne sente
To speke of this? I trowe it be the beste;
For she may leden Paris as hir leste.

"Of Ector, which that is my lord, my brother,
It nedeth nought to preye him freend to be.
For I have herd him o tyme and eek other
Speke of Criseyde swich honour that he
May seyn no bet, swich hap to him hath she.
It nedeth nought his helpes for to crave;
He shal be swich right as we wole him have.

"Spek thou thy-self also to Troilus
On my bihalve, and pray him with us dyne."
"Sir, al this shal be doon," quod Pandarus;
And took his leve, and nevere gan to fyne,
But to his neces hous as streyt as lyne
He com; and fond hir fro the mete aryse;
And sette him doun, and spak right in this wyse.

Sk., II, 1429–1463

He seyde, "O veray God, so have I ronne!
Lo, nece myn, see ye nought how I swete?
I noot whether ye the more thank me conne.
Be ye nought war how that fals Poliphete
Is now aboute eft-sones for to plete
And bringe on yow advocacyës newe?"
"I? No," quod she, and chaunged al hir hewe.

"What is he more aboute? me to drecche
And doon me wrong? What shal I do, allas?
Yet of him-self no-thing ne wolde I recche,
Nere it for Antenor and Eneas,
That been his freendes in swich maner cas.
But for the love of God, myn uncle dere,
No fors of that, lat him have al y-fere;

"Withouten that, I have ynough for us."
"Nay," quod Pandare, "it shal no-thing be so.
For I havȩ been right now at Deiphebus
And Ector and myn othere lordes mo,
And shortly maked ech of hem his fo,
That by my thrift, he shal it nevere winne
For ought he can, whan that so he biginne."

And as they casten what was best to done,
Deiphebus of his owene curtasye
Com hir to preye in his propre persone
To holde him on the morwe companye
At diner, which she nolde not denye,
But goodly gan to his preyere obeye.
He thonked hir, and wente up-on his weye.

Whan this was doon, this Pandare up a-noon,
To telle in short, and forth gan for to wende
To Troilus as stille as any stoon,
And al this thing he tolde him word and ende,
And how that he Deiphebus gan to blende.
And seyde him, "Now is tyme, if that thou conne,
To berȩ thee wel to-morwe and al is wonne.

"Thow shalt gon over night, and that as blyve,
Un-to Deiphebus hous as thee to pleye,
Thy maladye a-wey the bet to dryve,
For-why thou semest syk, soth for to seye.
Sone after that, doun in thy bed thee leye
And sey thow mayst no lenger up endure,
And ly right ther, and byd thyn aventure.

"Sey that thy fevere is wont thee for to take
The same tyme and lasten til a-morwe.
And lat see now how wel thou canst it make;
For par-dee, syk is he that is in sorwe.
Go now, farwel! And, Venus heer to borwe,
I hope, and thou this purpos holde ferme,
Thy grace she shal fully ther conferme."

Quod Troilus, "Y-wis, thou nedelees
Counseylest me that sykliche I me feyne!
For I am syk in ernest, doutelees,
So that wel neigh I sterve for the peyne."
Quod Pandarus, "Thou shalt the bettre pleyne,
And hast the lasse nede to countrefete;
For him men demen hoot that men seen swete.

"Lo, hold thee at thy triste cloos, and I
Shal wel the deer un-to thy bowe dryve."
Therwith he took his leve al softely,
And Troilus to paleys wente blyve.
So glad ne was he nevere in al his lyve;
And to Pandarus reed gan al assente,
And to Deiphebus hous at night he wente.

What nedeth yow to tellen al the chere
That Deiphebus un-to his brother made,
Or his accesse, or his syklych manere,
How men gan him with clothes for to lade
Whan he was leyd, and how men wolde him glade?
But al for nought; he held forth ay the wyse
That ye han herd Pandare er this devyse.

But certayn is, er Troilus him leyde,
Deiphebus had him prayed over night
To been a freend and helping to Criseyde.
God woot that he it grauntede anon-right
To been hir fulle freend with al his might.
But swich a nede was to preye him thenne,
As for to bidde a wood man for to renne.

The morwen com, and neighen gan the tyme
Of meel-tyde, that the faire quene Eleyne
Shoop hir to been, an houre after the pryme,
With Deiphebus, to whom she nolde feyne;
But as his suster, hoomly, sooth to seyne,
She com to diner in hir playn entente.
But God and Pandare wiste al what this mente.

Com eek Criseyde, al innocent of this,
Antigone, hir suster Tarbe also.
But flee we now prolixitee best is,
For love of God, and lat us faste go
Right to the effect with-oute tales mo,
Why al this folk assembled in this place,
And lat us of hir saluinges pace.

Gret honour did hem Deiphebus certeyn,
And fedde hem wel with al that mighte lyke.
But evere-more, "Allas!" was his refreyn,
"My goode brother Troilus, the syke,
Lyth yet"—and therwith-al he gan to syke.
And after that he peyned him to glade
Hem as he mighte, and chere good he made.

Compleyned eek Eleyne of his syknesse
So feithfully that pitee was to here,
And every wight gan waxen for accesse
A leche anoon, and seyde, "In this manere
Men curen folk; this charme I wol yow lere."
But ther sat oon, al list hir nought to teche,
That thoughte, "Best coude I yet been his leche!"

The tyme com fro diner for to ryse,
And, as hem oughte, arisen everychoon,
And gonne a while of this and that devyse.
But Pandarus brak al this speche anoon
And seyde to Deiphebus, "Wole ye goon,
If it your wille be, as I yow preyde,
To speke heer of the nedes of Criseyde?"

Eleyne, which that by the hond hir held,
Took first the tale, and seyde, "Go we blyve!"
And goodly on Criseyde she biheld,
And seyde, "Ioves lat him nevere thryve
That dooth yow harm, and bringe him sone of lyve!
And yeve me sorwe but he shal it rewe
If that I may and alle folk be trewe."

"Telle thou thy neces cas," quod Deiphebus
To Pandarus, "for thou canst best it telle."—
"My lordes and my ladyes, it stant thus:
What sholde I lenger," quod he, "do yow dwelle?"
He rong hem out a proces lyk a belle
Up-on hir fo, that highte Poliphete,
So heynous that men mighte on it spete.

Spak than Eleyne, and seyde, "Pandarus,
Woot ought my lord, my brother, this matere,
I mene Ector? or woot it Troilus?"
He seyde, "Ye, but wole ye now me here?
Me thinketh this, sith Troilus is here
It were good, if that ye wolde assente,
She tolde hir-self him al this er she wente.

"For he wole have the more hir grief at herte
By-cause, lo, that she a lady is.
And by your leve I wol but right in sterte
And do you wite, and that anoon, y-wis,
If that he slepe, or wole ought here of this."
And in he lepte, and seyde him in his ere,
"God have thy soule, y-brought have I thy bere!"

Sk., II, 1597-1617; 1625-1638

To smylen of this gan tho Troilus,
And Pandarus with-oute rekeninge
Oute wente anoon to Eleyne and Deiphebus,
And seyde hem, "So ther be no taryinge,
Ne more pres, he wol wel that ye bringe
Criseÿda, my lady, that is here;
And as he may enduren, he wole here.

"But wel ye woot the chaumbre is but lyte,
And fewe folk may lightly make it warm.
Now loketh ye—for I wol have no wyte
To bringe in prees that mighte doon him harm
Or him disesen, for my bettre arm!—
Wher it be bet she byde til eft-sones,
Now loketh ye that knowen what to doon is.

"I sey for me, best is, as I can knowe,
That no wight in ne wente but ye tweye,
But it were I; for I can in a throwe
Reherce hir cas unlyk that she can seye;
And after this she may him ones preye
To ben good lord, in short, and take hir leve.
This may not muchel of his ese him reve.

"And eek, for she is straunge, he wol forbere
His ese, which that him thar nought for yow.
Eek other thing that toucheth not to here
He wol me telle, I woot it wel right now,
That secret is and for the tounes prow."
And they, that no-thing knewe of this entente,
With-oute more to Troilus in they wente.

Eleyne in al hir goodly softe wyse
Gan him saluwe, and womanly to pleye,
And seyde, "Y-wis, ye moste alweys aryse!
Now fayre brother, beth al hool, I preye!"
And gan hir arm right over his sholder leye,
And him with al hir wit to recomforte.
As she best coude, she gan him to disporte.

So after this quod she, "We yow biseke,
Me dere brother, Deiphebus, and I,
For love of God, and so doth Pandare eke,
To been good lord and freend right hertely
Un-to Criseyde, which that certeinly
Receyveth wrong, as woot wel heer Pandare,
That can hir cas wel bet than I declare."

This Pandarus gan newe his tunge affyle,
And al hir cas reherce, and that anoon.
Whan it was seyd, sone after in a whyle,
Quod Troilus, "As sone as I may goon,
I wol right fayn with al my might ben oon,
Have God my trouthe, hir cause to sustene."
"Good thrift have ye," quod Eleyne the quene.

Quod Pandarus, "And it your wille be
That she may take hir leve er that she go?"
"Or elles God for-bede," tho quod he,
"If that she vouche sauf for to do so."
And with that word quod Troilus, "Ye two,
Deiphebus, and my suster leef and dere,
To yow have I to speke of o matere,

" To been avysed by your reed the bettre:"—
And fond, as hap was, at his beddes heed
The copie of a tretis and a lettre
That Ector had him sent to axen reed.
If swich a man was worthy to ben deed,
Woot I nought who; but in a grisly wyse
He preyede hem anoon on it avyse.

Deiphebus gan this lettre to unfolde
In ernest greet; so did Eleyne the quene.
And roming outward faste it gan biholde,
Downward a steyre in-to an herber grene.
This ilke thing they redden hem bi-twene,
And largely the mountaunce of an houre
They gonne on it to reden and to poure.

Now lat hem rede, and turne we anoon
To Pandarus, that gan ful faste prye
That al was wel, and oute he gan to goon
In-to the grete chambre and that in hye,
And seyde, "God save al this companye!
Com, nece myn; my lady quene Eleyne,
Abydeth yow, and eek my lordes tweyne.

"Rys, take with yow your nece Antigone,
Or whom yow list, or no fors, hardily:
The lasse prees, the bet; com forth with me.
And loke that ye thonke humblely
Hem alle three and, whan ye may goodly
Your tyme y-see, taketh of hem your leve
Lest we to longe his restes him bireve."

Al innocent of Pandarus entente
Quod tho Criseyde, "Go we, uncle dere."
And arm in arm inward with him she wente,
Avysed wel hir wordes and hir chere.
And Pandarus in ernestful manere
Seyde, "Alle folk, for Goddes love I preye,
Stinteth right heer and softely yow pleye.

"Avyseth yow what folk ben heer with-inne,
And in what plyt oon is, God him amende!
And inward thus ful softely biginne.
Nece, I coniure and heighly yow defende,
On his half which that sowle us alle sende,
And in the vertu of corounes tweyne,
Slee nought this man that hath for yow this peyne!

"Fy on the devel! thenk which oon he is
And in what plyt he lyth. Com of anoon!
Thenk al swich taried tyde but lost it nis!
That wol ye bothe seyn whan ye ben oon.
Secoundelich, ther yet devyneth noon
Up-on yow two: com of now if ye conne!
Whyl folk is blent, lo! al the tyme is wonne!"

But now to yow, ye lovers that ben here,
Was Troilus nought in a cankedort,
That lay and mighte whispring of hem here,
And thoughte, "O Lord, right now renneth my sort
Fully to dye or han anoon comfort!"
And was the firste tyme he shulde hir preye
Of love: O mighty God, what shal he seye?

Explicit Secundus Liber.

Book III

Incipit Liber Tercius

O blisful light, of which the bemes clere
Adorneth al the thridde hevene faire!
O sonnes leef, O Ioves doughter dere,
Plesaunce of love, O goodly debonaire,
In gentil hertes ay redy to repaire!
O verray cause of hele and of gladnesse,
Y-heried be thy might and thy goodnesse!

Ye in my naked herte sentement
Inhelde, and do me shewe of thy swetnesse.
Caliope, thy vois be now present,
For now is nede: sestow not my destresse,
How I mot telle anon-right the gladnesse
Of Troilus, to Venus heryinge?
To which gladnesse, who nede hath, God him bringe!

Lay al this mene whyle Troilus
Recording his lessoun in this manere:
"Ma fey!" thoughte he, "thus wol I seye and thus;
Thus wol I pleyne un-to my lady dere;
That word is good, and this shal be my chere;
This nil I not foryeten in no wyse."
God leve him werken as he gan devyse.

Sk., II, 1751-1757; III, 1-7; 43-56

And Lord! so that his herte gan to quappe, *leave*
Hering hir come, and shorte for to syke!
And Pandarus, that ladde hir by the lappe,
Com ner, and gan in at the curtin pyke,
And seyde, "God do bote on alle syke!
See who is heer yow comen to visyte:
Lo, heer is she that is your deeth to wyte!"

Ther-with it semed as he wepte almost.
"A ha!" quod Troilus so rewfully,
"Wher me be wo, O mighty God, thou wost!
Who is al ther? I see nought trewely."
"Sire," quod Criseyde, "it is Pandare and I."
"Ye, swete herte? Allas, I may not ryse
To knele, and do yow honour in som wyse."

And dressede him upward, and she right tho
Gan bothe here hondes softe upon him leye.
"O, for the love of God, do ye not so
To me!" quod she; "Ey! what is this to seye?
Sir, come am I to yow for causes tweye:
First, yow to thonke, and of your lordship eke
Continuaunce I wolde yow biseke." *beseech*

This Troilus, that herde his lady preye
Of lordship him, wex neither quik ne deed, *grow*
Ne mighte a word for shame to it seye,
Al-though men sholde smyten of his heed.
But Lord, so he wex sodeinliche reed!
And sire, his lesson, that he wende conne
To preyen hir, is thurgh his wit y-ronne. *run together*

Cryseyde al this aspyede wel y-nough,
For she was wys and lovede him nevere-the-lasse,
Al nere he malapert or made it tough, *forward*
Or was to bold to singe a fool a masse, *was troublesome*
But whan his shame gan somwhat to passe,
His resons, as I may my rymes holde,
I yow wol telle as techen bokes olde.

In chaunged vois, right for his verray drede,
Which vois eek quook, and ther-to his manere
Goodly abayst, and now his hewes rede, *complexion*
Now pale, un-to Criseyde, his lady dere,
With look doun cast and humble yolden chere,
Lo, the alderfirste word that him <u>asterte</u> *escape*
Was twyes, "Mercy, mercy, swete herte!"

And <u>stinte</u> a whyle, and whan he mighte out-bringe,
The nexte word was, "God wot, for I have,
As feythfully as I have had konninge,
Ben youres, also God my sowle save!
And shal til that I, woful wight, be grave.
And though I dar ne can un-to yow pleyne,
Y-wis, I suffre nought the lasse peyne.

"Thus muche as now, O wommanliche wyf,
I may out-bringe, and if this yow displese,
That shal I wreke upon myn owne lyf
Right sone, I trowe, and doon your herte an ese,
If with my deeth your herte I may apese.
But sin that ye han herd me somwhat seye,
Now recche I nevere how sone that I deye."

Ther-with his manly sorwe to biholde
It mighte han maad an herte of stoon to rewe.
And Pandare weep as he to watre wolde,
And poked evere his nece newe and newe,
And seyde, "Wo bigon ben hertes trewe!
For love of God, make of this thing an ende,
Or slee us bothe at ones er ye wende!"

"I? what?" quod she, "by God and by my trouthe,
I noot nought what ye wilne that I seye."
"I? what?" quod he, "that ye han on him routhe,
For Goddes love, and doth him nought to deye."
"Now thanne thus," quod she, "I wolde him preye
To telle me the fyn of his entente.
Yet wiste I nevere wel what that he mente."

"What that I mene, O swete herte dere?"
Quod Troilus, "O goodly fresshe free!
That with the stremes of your eyen clere
Ye wolde som-tyme freendly on me see,
And thanne agreën that I may ben he,
With-oute braunche of vyce in any wyse,
In trouthe alwey to doon yow my servyse.

"And I to ben your verray humble trewe,
Secret, and in my paynes pacient,
And evere-mo desire freshly newe
To serven and been y-lyke diligent,
And with good herte al hoolly your talent
Receyven wel, how sore that me smerte,—
Lo, this mene I, myn owene swete herte."

Quod Pandarus, "Lo, heer an hard requeste,
And resonable a lady for to werne!
Now nece myn, by natal Ioves feste,
Were I a god, ye sholde sterve as yerne,
That heren wel this man wol no-thing yerne
But your honour, and seen him almost sterve,
And been so looth to suffren him yow serve."

With that she gan hir eyen on him caste
Ful esily and ful debonairly,
Avysing hir, and hyed not to faste
With nevere a word, but seyde him softely,
"Myn honour sauf, I wol wel trewely,
And in swich forme as he can now devyse
Receyven him fully to my servyse,

"Biseching him for Goddes love that he
Wolde in honour of trouthe and gentilesse,
As I wel mene, eek mene wel to me,
And myn honour with wit and besinesse
Ay kepe. And if I may don him gladnesse
From hennes-forth, y-wis, I nil not feyne.
Now beth al hool, no lenger ye ne pleyne.

Sk., III, 127–133; 141–168

"But nathelees, this warne I yow," quod she,
"A kinges sone al-though ye be, y-wis,
Ye shul na-more have soverainetee
Of me in love than right in that cas is.
Ne I nil forbere, if that ye doon a-mis,
To wrathen yow; and whyl that ye me serve,
Cherycen yow right after ye deserve.

"And shortly, dere herte and al my knight,
Beth glad, and draweth yow to lustinesse,
And I shal trewely with al my might
Your bittre tornen al in-to swetnesse.
If I be she that may yow do gladnesse,
For every wo ye shal recovere a blisse."
And him in armes took, and gan him kisse.

Fil Pandarus on knees, and up his yën
To hevene threw, and held his hondes hye.
"Immortal God!" quod he, "that mayst nought dyen,
Cupide I mene, of this mayst glorifye.
And Venus, thou mayst make melodye!
With-outen hond, me semeth that in towne
For this merveyle I here ech belle sowne.

"But, ho! no more as now of this matere,
For-why this folk wol comen up anoon
That han the lettre red. Lo, I hem here.
But I coniure thee, Criseyde, and oon
And two, thou Troilus, whan thow mayst goon,
That at myn hous ye been at my warninge;
For I ful wel shal shape your cominge.

"And eseth ther your hertes right y-nough;
And lat see which of yow shal bere the belle
To speke of love a-right!" Ther-with he lough.
"For ther have ye a layser for to telle."
Quod Troilus, "How longe shal I dwelle
Er this be doon?" Quod he, "Whan thou mayst ryse,
This thing shal be right as I yow devyse."

With that Eleyne and also Deiphebus
Tho comen upward, right at the steyres ende;
And Lord! so than gan grone Troilus,
His brother and his suster for to blende.
Quod Pandarus, "It tyme is that we wende.
Tak, nece myn, your leve at alle three,
And lat hem speke, and cometh forth with me."

She took hir leve at hem ful thriftily,
As she wel coude, and they hir reverence
Un-to the fulle diden hardely,
And speken wonder wel in hir absence
Of hir in preysing of hir excellence,
Hir governaunce, hir wit, and hir manere
Commendeden: it Ioye was to here.

Now lat hir wende un-to hir owne place,
And torne we to Troilus a-yein,
That gan ful lightly of the lettre passe,
That Deiphebus had in the gardin seyn.
And of Eleyne and him he wolde fayn
Delivered been, and seyde that him leste
To slepe and after tales have reste.

Eleyne him kiste and took hir leve blyve,
Deiphebus eek, and hoom wente every wight.
And Pandarus as faste as he may dryve
To Troilus tho com as lyne right.
And on a paillet al that glade night
By Troilus he lay with mery chere
To tale; and wel was hem they were y-fere.

Whan every wight was voided but they two,
And alle the dores were faste y-shette,
To telle in short, with-oute wordes mo,
This Pandarus with-outen any lette
Up roos and on his beddes syde him sette
And gan to speken in a sobre wyse
To Troilus, as I shal yow devyse.

"Myn alderlevest lord and brother dere,
God woot and thou that it sat me ful sore
When I thee saw so languisshing to-yere
For love of which thy wo wex alwey more;
That I with al my might and al my lore
Have evere sithen doon my bisinesse
To bringe thee to Ioye out of distresse;

"And have it brought to swich plyt as thou wost,
So that thorugh me thow stondest now in weye
To fare wel. I seye it for no bost,
And wostow why? For shame it is to seye,
For thee have I bigonne a gamen pleye
Which that I nevere doon shal eft for other
Al-though he were a thousand fold my brother.

"That is to seye, for thee am I bicomen,
Bitwixen game and ernest, swich a mene
As maken wommen un-to men to comen:
Al sey I nought, thou wost wel what I mene.
For thee have I my nece, of vyces clene,
So fully maad thy gentilesse triste
That al shal been right as thy-selve liste.

"But God, that al wot, take I to witnesse
That nevere I this for coveityse wroughte,
But only for to abregge that distresse,
For which wel nygh thou deydest, as me thoughte.
But gode brother, do now as thee oughte,
For Goddes love, and keep hir out of blame,
Sin thou art wys, and save alwey hir name.

"Wherfore, er I wol ferther goon a pas,
Yet eft I thee biseche and fully seye
That privetee go with us in this cas,
That is to seye, that thou us nevere wreye.
And be nought wrooth though I thee ofte preye
To holden secree swich an heigh matere;
For skilful is, thow wost wel, my preyere.

Sk., III, 239-266; 281-287

"For wel I woot thou menest wel, parde:
Therfore I dar this fully undertake.
Thou wost eek what thy lady graunted thee,
And day is set the chartres up to make.
Have now good night, I may no lenger wake;
And bid for me sin thou art now in blisse
That God me sende deeth or sone lisse."

Who mighte telle half the Ioye or feste
Which that the sowle of Troilus tho felte,
Hering theffect of Pandarus biheste?
His olde wo that made his herte swelte
Gan tho for Ioye wasten and to-melte;
And al the richesse of his sykes sore
At ones fledde, he felte of hem no more.

And gan his look on Pandarus up caste
Ful sobrely and frendly for to see,
And seyde, "Freend, in Aperil the laste,
As wel thou wost if it remembre thee,
How neigh the deeth for wo thou founde me;
And how thou didest al thy bisinesse
To knowe of me the cause of my distresse.

"Thou wost how longe I it for-bar to seye
To thee that art the man that I best triste;
And peril was it noon to thee by-wreye,
That wiste I wel. But telle me, if thee liste,
Sith I so looth was that thy-self it wiste
How dorste I mo tellen of this matere,
That quake now and no wight may us here?

"But natheles by that God I thee swere
That as him list may al this world governe,
And, if I lye, Achilles with his spere
Myn herte cleve, al were my lyf eterne
As I am mortal, if I late or yerne
Wolde it biwreye, or dorste, or sholde conne,
For al the good that God made under sonne.

"But heer with al myn herte I thee biseche
That nevere in me thou deme swich folye
As I shal seyn: me thoughte by thy speche
That this, which thou me dost for companye,
I sholde wene it were a bauderye.
I am nought wood, al-if I lewed be;
It is not so, that woot I wel, pardee!

"And that thou knowe I thenke nought ne wene
That this servyse a shame be or Iape,
I have my faire suster Polixene,
Cassandre, Eleyne, or any of the frape.
Be she nevere so faire or wel y-shape,
Telle me which thou wilt of everichone
To han for thyn, and lat me thanne allone."

Thus held him ech with other wel apayed
That al the world ne mighte it bet amende.
And on the morwe whan they were arayed,
Ech to his owene nedes gan entende.
But Troilus, though as the fyr he brende
For sharp desyr of hope and of plesaunce,
He not for-gat his gode governaunce.

But certeyn is, to purpos for to go,
That in this whyle, as writen is in geste,
He say his lady som-tyme; and also
She with him spak whan that she dorste or leste.
And by hir bothe avys as was the beste
Apoynteden ful warly in this nede,
So as they dorste, how they wolde procede.

But it was spoken in so short a wyse,
In swich awayt alwey and in swich fere,
Lest any wyght divynen or devyse
Wolde of hem two, or to it leye an ere,
That al this world so leef to hem ne were
As that Cupido wolde hem grace sende
To maken of hir speche aright an ende.

Sk., III, 393–399; 407–413; 421–427; 449–462

And shortly of this proces for to pace,
So wel his werk and wordes he bisette
That he so ful stood in his lady grace
That twenty thousand tymes or she lette
She thonked God she evere with him mette;
So coude he him governe in swich servyse
That al the world ne mighte it bet devyse.

But now, paraunter, som man wayten wolde
That every word or sonde or look or chere
Of Troilus that I rehersen sholde,
In al this whyle, un-to his lady dere:
I trowe it were a long thing for to here;
Or of what wight that stant in swich disioynte,
His wordes alle, or every look, to poynte.

But to the grete effect: than sey I thus,
That stonding in concord and in quiete
Thise ilke two, Criseyde and Troilus,
As I have told, and in this tyme swete,
Save only often mighte they not mete,
Ne layser have hir speches to fulfelle,
That it befel right as I shal yow telle,

That Pandarus, that evere did his might
Right for the fyn that I shal speke of here,
As for to bringe to his hous som night
His faire nece and Troilus y-fere,
Wher-as at leyser al this heigh matere
Touching hir love were at the fulle up-bounde,
Had out of doute a tyme to it founde.

And Troilus, that al this purveyaunce
Knew at the fulle, and waytede on it ay,
Had heer-up-on eek maad gret ordenaunce
And founde his cause and ther-to his aray,
If that he were missed night or day
Ther-whyl he was aboute this servyse,
That he was goon to doon his sacrifyse.

And moste at swich a temple alone wake,
Answered of Appollo for to be;
And first to seen the holy laurer quake
Er that Apollo spak out of the tree
To telle him next whan Grekes sholden flee,
And forthy lette him no man, God forbede,
But preye Apollo helpen in this nede.

Now is ther litel more for to done,
But Pandare up, and shortly for to seyne,
Right sone upon the chaunging of the mone,
Whan lightles is the world a night or tweyne
And that the welken shoop him for to reyne,
He streight a-morwe un-to his nece wente.
Ye han wel herd the fyn of his entente.

Whan he was come, he gan anoon to pleye
As he was wont, and of him-self to Iape.
And fynally, he swor and gan hir seye,
By this and that, she sholde him not escape,
Ne lenger doon him after hir to gape,
But certeynly she moste, by hir leve,
Come soupen in his hous with him at eve.

At which she lough, and gan hir faste excuse,
And seyde, "It rayneth. Lo, how sholde I goon?"
"Lat be," quod he, "ne stond not thus to muse.
This moot be doon, ye shal be ther anoon."
So at the laste her-of they felle at oon;
Or elles, softe he swor hir in hir ere,
He nolde nevere come ther she were.

Sone after this to him she gan to rowne,
And askede him if Troilus were there.
He swor hir, "Nay, for he was out of towne,"
And seyde, "Nece, I pose that he were,
Yow thurfte nevere have the more fere.
For rather than men mighte him ther aspye,
Me were lever a thousand fold to dye."

Sk., III, 540–574

Nought list myn auctor fully to declare
What that she thoughte whan he seyde so,
That Troilus was out of towne y-fare,
As if he seyde ther-of sooth or no;
But that with-oute awayt with him to go
She graunted him, sith he hir that bisoughte,
And as his nece obeyed as hir oughte.

But nathelees, yet gan she him biseche,
Al-though with him to goon it was no fere,
For to be war of goosish peples speche,
That dremen thinges which that nevere were,
And wel avyse him whom he broughte there.
And seyde him, "Eem, sin I mot on yow triste,
Loke al be wel, and do now as yow liste."

He swor hir, "Yis, by stokkes and by stones,
And by the goddes that in hevene dwelle,
Or elles were him lever, soule and bones,
With Pluto king as depe been in helle
As Tantalus!" What sholde I more telle?
Whan al was wel he roos and tak his leve,
And she to souper com whan it was eve,

With a certayn of hir owene men,
And with hir faire nece Antigone,
And othere of hir wommen, nyne or ten.
But who was glad now, who as trowe ye
But Troilus, that stood and mighte it see
Thurgh-oute a litel windowe in a stewe
Ther he bishet sin midnight was in mewe,

Unwist of every wight but of Pandare?
But to the poynt: Now whan she was y-come
With alle Ioye and alle frendes fare,
Hir eem anoon in armes hath hir nome,
And after to the souper, alle and some,
Whan tyme was, ful softe they hem sette.
God wot, ther was no deyntee for to fette.

And after souper gonnen they to ryse,
At ese wel with hertes fresshe and glade,
And wel was him that coude best devyse
To lyken hir, or that hir laughen made.
He song; she pleyde; he tolde tale of Wade.
But at the laste, as every thing hath ende,
She took hir leve, and nedes wolde wende.

But O Fortune, executrice of wierdes,
O influences of thise hevenes hye!
Soth is that under God ye ben our hierdes,
Though to us bestes been the causes wrye.
This mene I now, for she gan hoomward hye,
But execut was al bisyde hir leve
At the goddes wille; for which she moste bleve.

The bente mone with hir hornes pale,
Saturne and Iove in Cancro ioyned were,
That swich a rayn from hevene gan avale
That every maner womman that was there
Had of that smoky reyn a verray fere;
At which Pandare tho lough and seyde thenne,
"Now were it tyme a lady to go henne!

"But goode nece, if I mighte evere plese
Yow any-thing, than prey I yow," quod he,
"To doon myn herte as now so greet an ese
As for to dwelle heer al this night with me,
For-why this is your owene hous, pardee.
For by my trouthe I sey it nought a-game,
To wende as now it were to me a shame."

Criseyde, which that coude as muche good
As half a world, took hede of his preyere.
And sin it ron and al was on a flood,
She thoughte, "As good chep may I dwellen here,
And graunte it gladly with a freendes chere,
And have a thank, as grucche and than abyde.
For hoom to goon it may nought wel bityde."

Sk., III, 610–644

"I wol," quod she, "myn uncle leef and dere,—
Sin that yow list, it skil is to be so.
I am right glad with yow to dwellen here;
I seyde but agame I wolde go."
"Y-wis, graunt mercy, nece!" quod he tho;
"Were it a game or no, soth for to telle,
Now am I glad, sin that yow list to dwelle."

Thus al is wel; but tho bigan aright
The newe Ioye and al the feste agayn.
But Pandarus, if goodly had he might,
He wolde han hyed hir to bedde fayn,
And seyde, "Lord, this is an huge rayn!
This were a weder for to slepen inne,
And that I rede us sone to biginne.

"And nece, woot ye wher I wol yow leye,
For that we shul not liggen fer asonder,
And for ye neither shullen, dar I seye,
Heren noise of reynes nor of thondre?
By God, right in my lyte closet yonder.
And I wol in that outer hous allone
Be wardeyn of your wommen everichone.

"And in this middel chaumbre that ye see
Shul youre wommen slepen wel and softe;
And ther I seyde shal your-selve be.
And if ye liggen wel to-night com ofte
And careth not what weder is on-lofte.
The wyn anon, and whan so that yow leste,
So go we slepe: I trowe it be the beste."

Tho Pandarus, hir eem, right as him oughte,
With women swiche as were hir most aboute,
Ful glad un-to hir beddes syde hir broughte
And took his leve and gan ful lowe loute
And seyde, "Heer at this closet-dore with-oute,
Right over-thwart, your wommen liggen alle,
That whom yow liste of hem ye may heer calle."

So whan that she was in the closet leyd,
And alle hir wommen forth by ordenaunce
A-bedde weren ther as I havę seyd,
Ther was no morę to skippen nor to traunce,
But boden go to bedde, with mischaunce!
If any wight was stering any-where,
And late hem slepe that a-bedde were.

But Pandarus, that wel coude ech a del
The olde daunce, and every poynt ther-inne,
Whan that he sey that alle thing was wel,
He thoughte he wolde up-on his werk biginne,
And gan the stewe-dore al softe un-pinne,
And stille as stoon with-outen lenger lette,
By Troilus a-doun right he him sette.

And shortly to the poynt right for to gon,
Of al this werk he tolde him word and ende,
And seyde, "Makę thee redy right anon,
For thou shalt in-to hevenę blisse wende."
"Now blisful Venus, thou me grace sende,"
Quod Troilus, "for nevere yet no nede
Had I er now, ne halvendel the drede."

Quod Pandarus, "Thou wrecched mouses herte,
Art thou agast so that she wol thee byte?
Why, don this furred cloke up-on thy sherte,
And folowe me, for I wol han the wyte.
But byd, and lat me go bifore a lyte."
And with that word he gan un-do a trappe,
And Troilus he broughte in by the lappe.

The sterne wind so loude gan to route
That no wight other noyse mighte here;
And they that layen at the dorę with-oute
Ful sykerly they slepten alle y-fere.
And Pandarus with a ful sobre chere
Goth to the dore anon with-outen lette
Ther-as they laye, and softely it shette.

                              Sk., III, 687-707; 736-749

And as he com ayeinward prively,
His nece awook and asked, "Who goth there?"
"My dere nece," quod he, "it am I.
Ne wondreth not ne have of it no fere."
And ner he com, and seyde hir in hir ere,
"No word, for love of God, I yow biseche!
Lat no wight ryse and heren of our speche!"

"What! which wey be ye comen, *bendiste?*"
Quod she, "and how thus unwist of hem alle?"
"Heer at this secre trappe-dore," quod he.
Quod tho Criseyde, "Lat me som wight calle."
"Ey! God forbede that it sholde falle,"
Quod Pandarus, "that ye swich foly wroughte!
They mighte deme thing they nevere er thoughte!

"Now nece myn, ye shul wel understonde,"
Quod he, "so as ye wommen demen alle,
That for to holde in love a man in honde
And him hir 'leef' and 'dere herte' calle,
And maken him an howve above a calle,
I mene as love an other in this whyle,
She doth hir-self a shame and him a gyle.

"Now wherby that I telle yow al this?
Ye woot your-self, as wel as any wight,
How that your love al fully graunted is
To Troilus, the worthieste knight
Oon of this world, and ther-to trouthe plyght
That, but it were on him along, ye nolde
Him nevere falsen whyl ye liven sholde.

"Now stant it thus, that sith I fro yow wente,
This Troilus, right platly for to seyn,
Is thurgh a goter by a privè wente
In-to my chaumbre come in al this reyn,
Unwist of every maner wight, certeyn,
Save of my-self, as wisly have I Ioye,
And by that feith I shal Priam of Troye!

"And he is come in swich peyne and distresse
That, but he be al fully wood by this,
He sodeynly mot falle in-to wodnesse,
But-if God helpe. And cause why this is:
He seyth him told is of a freend of his
How that ye sholde love oon that hatte Horaste,
For sorwe of which this night shal been his laste."

Criseyde, which that al this wonder herde,
Gan sodeynly aboute hir herte colde,
And with a syk she sorwfully answerde,
"Allas! I wende, who-so tales tolde,
My dere herte wolde me not holde
So lightly fals! Allas! conceytes wronge,
What harm they doon, for now live I to longe!

"Horaste? Allas! and falsen Troilus?
I knowe him not, God helpe me so," quod she;
"Allas! what wikked spirit tolde him thus?
Now certes, eem, to-morwe, and I him see,
I shal ther-of as ful excusen me
As evere dide womman, if him lyke."
And with that word she gan ful sore syke.

Quod Pandarus, "Thus fallen is this cas."
"Why, uncle myn," quod she, "who tolde him this?
Why doth my dere herte thus, allas?"
"Ye woot, ye nece myn," quod he, "what is.
I hope al shal be wel that is amis.
For ye may quenche al this if that yow leste,
And doth right so, for I holde it the beste."

"So shal I do to-morwe, y-wis," quod she,
"And God to-forn, so that it shal suffyse."
"To-morwe? Allas, that were a fayr," quod he,
"Nay, nay, it may not stonden in this wyse.
For, nece myn, thus wryten clerkes wyse,
That peril is with drecching in y-drawe:
Nay, swich abodes been nought worth an hawe.

"And nece myn, ne take it not a-greef,—
If that ye suffre him al night in this wo,
God helpę me so, ye had him nevere leef,
That dar I seyn, now ther is but we two.
But wel I woot that ye wol not do so:
Ye been to wys to do so gret folye
To putte his lyf al night in Iupartye."

"Had I him nevere leef? By God, I wene
Ye hadde nevere thing so leef," quod she.
"Now by my thrift," quod he, "that shal be sene.
For sin ye make this ensample of me,
If I al night wolde him in sorwe see
For al the tresour in the toun of Troye,
I bidde God I nevere mote havę Ioye!"

Quod tho Criseyde, "Wolę ye doon o thing,
And ye therwith shal stinte al his disese?
Have heer, and bereth him this blewe ring;
For ther is no-thing mighte him bettre plese
Save I my-self, ne more his herte apese.
And sey my dere herte that his sorwe
Is causeles, that shal be seen to-morwe."

"A ring?" quod he, "ye, hasel-wodes shaken!
Ye, nece myn, that ring moste han a stoon
That mighte dede men alyve maken,
And swich a ring trowe I that ye havę noon.
Discrecioun out of your heed is goon:
That fele I now," quod he, "and that is routhe.
O tyme y-lost, wel maystow cursen slouthe!"

Criseyde answerde, "As wisly God at reste
My sowle bringe as me is for him wo!
And eem, y-wis, fayn wolde I doon the beste
If that I hadde grace to do so.
But whether that ye dwelle or for him go,
I am til God me bettre minde sende
At Dulcarnon, right at my wittes ende."

Quod Pandarus, "Ye, nece, wol ye here?
Dulcarnon called is 'fleming of wrecches:'
It semeth hard, for wrecches wol not lere
For verray slouthe or othere wilful tecches.
This seyd by hem that be not worth two fecches;
But ye ben wys, and that we han on honde
Nis neither hard, ne skilful to withstonde."

"Than, eem," quod she, "doth her-of as yow list.
But er he come I wil up first aryse;
And for the love of God, sin al my trist
Is on yow two and ye ben bothe wyse,
So wircheth now in so discreet a wyse
That I honour may have and he plesaunce.
For I am heer al in your governaunce."

"That is wel seyd," quod he, "my nece dere,
Ther good thrift on that wyse gentil herte!
But liggeth stille, and taketh him right here.
It nedeth not no ferther for him sterte;
And ech of yow ese otheres sorwes smerte
For love of God! And Venus, I thee herie,
For sonę hope I we shullę ben alle merie!"

This Troilus ful sone on knees him sette
Ful sobrely, right by hir beddes heed,
And in his beste wyse his lady grette;
But Lord, so she wex sodeynliche reed!
Ne though men sholden smyten of hir heed,
She coude nought a word a-right out-bringe
So sodeynly for his sodeyn cominge.

But Pandarus, that so wel coude fele
In every thing, to pleye anoon bigan,
And seyde, "Necę, see how this lord can knele!
Now for your trouthe, seeth this gentil man!"
And with that word he for a quisshen ran,
And seyde, "Kneleth now whyl that yow leste,
Ther God your hertes bringe sone at reste!"

Can I not seyn, for she bad him not ryse,
If sorwe it putte out of hir remembraunce,
Or elles if she toke it in the wyse
Of duëtee, as for his observaunce;
But wel finde I she did him this plesaunce
That she him kiste, al-though she syked sore;
And bad him sitte a-doun with-outen more.

Criseyde, that was Troilus lady right,
And clerę stood on a ground of sikernesse,
Al thoughte she, hir servaunt and hir knight
Ne sholde of right non untrouthe in hir gesse,
Yet nathelees, considered his distresse,
And that love is in cause of swich folye,
Thus to him spak she of his Ialousye:

"Lo, herte myn, as wolde the excellence
Of love, ayeins the which that no man may,
Ne oughte eek goodly maken resistence,
And eek bycause I felte wel and say
Your grete trouthe and servyse every day,
And that your herte al myn was, sooth to seyne,
This droof me for to rewe up-on your peyne;

"And your goodnessę have I founde alwey yit,
Of which, my dere herte and al my knight,
I thonke it yow as fer as I havę wit,
Al can I nought as muche as it werę right.
And I, emforth my conning and my might,
Have and ay shal, how sore that me smerte,
Ben to yow trewe and hool with al myn herte!"

With that a fewe brighte teres newe
Out of hir eyen fille, and thus she seyde:
"Now God, thou wost, in thought ne dede untrewe
To Troilus was nevere yet Criseyde!"
With that hir heed doun in the bed she leyde
And with the shete it wreigh, and syghed sore,
And held hir pees: not o word spak she more.

Sk., III, 967–973; 981–1001; 1051–1057

This Troilus, whan he hir wordes herde,
Have ye no care, him liste not to slepe;
For it thoughte him no strokes of a yerde
To here or seen Criseyde his lady wepe.
But wel he felte aboute his herte crepe,
For every tere which that Criseyde asterte,
The crampe of deeth to streyne him by the herte.

And in his minde he gan the tyme acurse
That he cam there, and that he was born;
For now is wikke y-turned in-to worse,
And al that labour he hath doon biforn
He wende it lost, he thoughte he nas but lorn.
"O Pandarus," thoughte he, "allas! thy wyle
Serveth of nought, so welawey the whyle!"

And therwithal he heng a-doun the heed,
And fil on knees, and sorwfully he sighte.
What mighte he seyn? He felte he nas but deed;
For wrooth was she that shulde his sorwes lighte.
But nathelees, whan that he speken mighte,
Than seyde he thus: "God woot that of this game,
Whan al is wist, than am I not to blame!"

Ther-with the sorwe so his herte shette
That from his eyen fil ther not a tere,
And every spirit his vigour in-knette,
So they astoned and oppressed were.
The feling of his sorwe or of his fere
Or of ought elles fled was out of towne,
And doun he fel al sodeynly a-swowne.

Therwith his pous and pawmes of his hondes
They gan to frote, and wete his temples tweyne;
And, to deliveren him from bittre bondes,
She ofte him kiste. And shortly for to seyne,
Him to revoken she did al hir peyne.
And at the laste he gan his breeth to drawe,
And of his swough sone after that adawe,

And gan bet minde and reson to him take,
But wonder sore he was abayst, y-wis.
And with a syk, whan he gan bet a-wake,
He seyde, "O mercy God, what thing is this?"
"Why do ye with your-selven thus amis?"
Quod tho Criseyde, "is this a mannes game?
What Troilus! wol ye do thus, for shame?"

And therwith-al hir arm over him she leyde,
And al foryaf, and ofte tyme him keste.
He thonked hir, and to hir spak, and seyde
As fil to purpos for his herte reste.
And she to that answerde him as hir leste,
And with hir goodly wordes him disporte
She gan, and ofte his sorwes to comforte.

Quod Pandarus, "For ought I can espyen,
This light nor I ne serven heer of nought;
Light is not good for syke folkes yën.
But for the love of God, sin ye be brought
In thus good plyt, lat now no hevy thought
Ben hanging in the hertes of yow tweye:"
And bar the candel to the chimeneye.

Sone after this, though it no nede were,
Whan she swiche othes as hir list devyse
Had of him take, hir thoughte tho no fere
Ne cause eek non to bidde him thennes ryse.
Yet lesse thing than othes may suffyse
In many a cas; for every wight, I gesse,
That loveth wel meneth but gentilesse.

But in effect she wolde wite anoon
Of what man and eek wher and also why
He Ielous was, sin ther was cause noon;
And eek the signe that he took it by
She bad him that to telle hir bisily
Or elles, certeyn, she bar him on honde
That this was doon of malice hir to fonde.

Sk., III, 1121–1155

With-outen more, shortly for to seyne,
He moste obeye un-to his lady heste;
And for the lasse harm he moste feyne
He seyde hir whan she was at swich a feste
She mighte on him han loked at the leste:
Not I not what, al dere y-nough a risshe,
As he that nedes moste a cause fisshe.

And she answerde, "Swete, al were it so,
What harm was that sin I non yvel mene?
For by that God that boughte us bothe two
In alle thing is myn entente clene.
Swiche arguments ne been not worth a bene;
Wol ye the childish Ialous contrefete?
Now were it worthy that ye were y-bete."

Tho Troilus gan sorwfully to syke
Lest she be wrooth, him thoughte his herte deyde;
And seyde, "Allas! upon my sorwes syke
Have mercy, swete herte myn, Criseyde!
And if that in tho wordes that I seyde
Be any wrong, I wol no more trespace.
Do what yow list, I am al in your grace."

And she answerde, "Of gilt misericorde!
That is to seyn that I foryeve al this.
And evere-more on this night yow recorde,
And beth wel war ye do no more amis."
"Nay, dere herte myn," quod he, "y-wis."
"And now," quod she, "that I have do yow smerte,
Foryeve it me, myn owne swete herte."

This Troilus with blisse of that supprysed
Putte al in Goddes hond, as he that mente
No-thing but wel; and sodeynly avysed
He hir in armes faste to him hente.
And Pandarus with a full good entente
Leyde him to slepe, and seyde, "If ye ben wyse,
Swowneth not now lest more folk aryse."

Sk., III, 1156-1190

This Troilus in armes gan hir streyne,
And seyde, "O swete, as evere mote I goon,
Now be ye caught, now is ther but we tweyne:
Now yeldeth yow, for other bote is noon!"
To that Criseyde answerde thus anoon,
"Ne had I er now, my swete herte dere,
Ben yolde, y-wis, I were now not here!"

O! sooth is seyd that heled for to be,
As of a fevre or other gret syknesse,
Men moste drinke, as men may often see,
Ful bittre drinke; and for to han gladnesse
Men drinken often peyne and greet distresse:
I mene it heer, as for this aventure,
That thourgh a peyne hath founden al his cure.

O blisful night, of hem so longe y-sought,
How blithe un-to hem bothe two thou were!
Why ne had I swich on with my soule y-bought,
Ye, or the leeste Ioye that was there?
Awey, thou foule Daunger and thou Fere,
And lat hem in this hevene blisse dwelle,
That is so heygh that al ne can I telle!

Thise ilke two that ben in armes laft,
So looth to hem a-sonder goon it were
That ech from other wende been biraft,
Or elles, lo, this was hir moste fere,
That al this thing but nyce dremes were:
For which ful ofte ech of hem seyde, "O swete,
Clippe ich yow thus, or elles I it mete?"

But whan the cok, comune astrologer,
Gan on his brest to bete and after crowe,
And Lucifer, the dayes messager,
Gan for to ryse and oute hir bemes throwe;
And estward roos, to him that coude it knowe,
Fortuna maior, than anoon Criseyde
With herte sore to Troilus thus seyde:—

Sk., III, 1205-1218; 1317-1323; 1338-1344; 1415-1421

"Myn hertes lyf, my trist, and my plesaunce,
That I was born, allas! what me is wo
That day of us mot makę desseveraunce!
For tyme it is to ryse and hennes go,
Or elles I am lost for everemo!
O night, allas! why niltow over us hove
As longe as whanne Almena lay by Iove?

"Thou dost, allas! to shortly thyn offyce,
Thou rakel night, ther God, maker of kinde,
Thee for thyn haste and thyn unkinde vyce
So faste ay to our hemi-spere binde
That nevere-more under the ground thou winde!
For now, for thou so hyest out of Troye,
Have I forgon thus hastily my Ioye!"

This Troilus, that with tho wordes felte,
As thoughte him tho, for pietous distresse
The blody teres from his herte melte,
As he that nevere yet swich hevinesse
Assayed had out of so greet gladnesse,
Gan therwith-al Criseyde his lady dere
In armes streyne, and seyde in this manere:—

"O cruel day, accusour of the Ioye
That night and love han stole and faste y-wryen,
A-cursed be thy coming in-to Troye,
For every bore hath oon of thy bright yën!
Envyous day, what list thee so to spyen?
What hastow lost? Why sekestow this place,
Ther God thy lyght so quenche, for his grace?

"Allas! what han thisę loveres thee agilt,
Dispitous day? Thyn be the pyne of helle!
For many a lover hastow slayn and wilt;
Thy pouring in wol no-wher lete hem dwelle.
What proferestow thy light heer for to selle?
Go selle it hem that smale seles graven:
We wol thee nought, us nedeth no day haven."

Sk., III, 1422–1428; 1436–1463

Therwith ful sore he sighte, and thus he seyde,
"My lady right, and of my wele or wo
The welle and rote, O goodly myn, Criseyde,
And shal I ryse, allas! and shal I go?
Now fele I that myn herte moot a-two!
For how sholde I my lyf an houre save
Sin that with yow is al the lyf I have?

"But nathelees, myn owene lady bright,
Yit were it so that I wiste outrely
That I, your humble servaunt and your knight,
Were in your herte set so fermely
As ye in myn, the which thing trewely
Me lever were than thise worldes tweyne,
Yet sholde I bet enduren al my peyne."

To that Criseyde answerde right anoon,
And with a syk she seyde, "O herte dere,
The game, y-wis, so forforth now is goon
That first shal Phebus falle fro his spere,
And every egle been the dowves fere,
And every roche out of his place sterte,
Er Troilus out of Criseydes herte!

"Ye be so depe in-with myn herte grave
That, though I wolde it turne out of my thought,
As wisly verray God my soule save,
To dyen in the peyne, I coude nought!
And for the love of God that hath us wrought,
Lat in your brayn non other fantasye
So crepe that it cause me to dye!

"And that ye me wolde han faste in minde
As I have yow, that wolde I yow bi-seche;
And if I wiste soothly that to finde,
God mighte not a poynt my Ioyes eche.
But, herte myn, with-oute more speche,
Beth to me trewe, or elles were it routhe;
For I am thyn, by God and by my trouthe!"

Sk., III, 1471–1477; 1485–1512

Agayns his wille, sin it mot nedes be,
This Troilus up roos, and faste him cledde,
And in his armes took his lady free
An hundred tyme, and on his wey him spedde,
And with swiche wordes as his herte bledde,
He seyde, "Farewel, my dere herte swete,
Ther God us graunte sounde and sone to mete!"

To which no word for sorwe she answerde,
So sore gan his parting hir distreyne;
And Troilus un-to his paleys ferde
As woo bigon as she was, sooth to seyne.
So hard him wrong of sharp desyr the peyne
For to ben eft ther he was in plesaunce
That it may nevere out of his remembraunce.

Retorned to his real palais, sone
He softe in-to his bed gan for to slinke,
To slepe longe as he was wont to done.
But al for nought; he may wel ligge and winke,
But sleep ne may ther in his herte sinke,
Thenking how she, for whom desyr him brende,
A thousand-fold was worth more than he wende.

Criseyde also, right in the same wyse,
Of Troilus gan in hir herte shette
His worthinesse, his lust, his dedes wyse,
His gentilesse, and how she with him mette,
Thonking Love he so wel hir bisette,
Desyring eft to have hir herte dere
In swich a plyt she dorste make him chere.

Pandare, a-morwe, which that comen was
Un-to his nece, and gan hir fayre grete,
Seyde, "Al this night so reyned it, allas!
That al my drede is that ye, nece swete,
Han litel layser had to slepe and mete.
Al night," quod he, "hath reyn so do me wake
That som of us, I trowe, hir hedes ake."

And ner he com and seyde, "How stont it now
This mery morwe, nece,—how can ye fare?"
Criseyde answerde, "Nevere the bet for yow,
Fox that ye been, God yevę your herte care!
God helpę me so, ye caused al this fare.
Trowe I," quod she, "for allę your wordes whyte.
O! who-so seeth yow knoweth yow ful lyte!"

With that she gan hir face for to wrye
With the shete, and wex for shame al reed.
And Pandarus gan under for to prye,
And seyde, "Nece, if that I shal been deed,
Havę heer a swerd and smyteth of myn heed."
With that his arm al sodeynly he thriste
Under hir nekke, and at the laste hir kiste.

I passe al that which chargeth nought to seye,—
What! God foryaf his deeth, and she al-so
Foryaf, and with hir uncle gan to pleye,
For other cause was ther noon than so.
But of this thing right to the effect to go,
Whan tyme was, hom til hir hous she wente,
And Pandarus hath fully his entente.

Now torne we ayein to Troilus,
That resteles ful longe a-bedde lay,
And prevely sente after Pandarus
To him to come in al the haste he may.
He com anoon, nought ones seyde he "Nay,"
And Troilus ful sobrely he grette,
And doun upon his beddes syde him sette.

This Troilus, with al the affeccioun
Of frendes lovę that herte may devyse,
To Pandarus on kneës fil adoun,
And er that he wolde of the place aryse,
He gan him thonken in his beste wyse.
A hondred sythe he gan the tyme blesse
That he was born to bringe him fro distresse.

He seyde, "O frend, of frendes the alderbeste
That evere was, the sothe for to telle,
Thou hast in hevene y-brought my soule at reste
Fro Flegiton, the fery flood of helle,
That though I mighte a thousand tymes selle
Upon a day my lyf in thy servyse,
It mighte nought a mot in that suffyse.

"Thus hastow me no litel thing y-yive,
For which to thee obliged be for ay
My lyf, and why? For thorugh thyn help I live;
For elles deed had I be many a day."
And with that word doun in his bed he lay,
And Pandarus ful sobrely him herde
Til al was seyd, and than he him answerde:

"My dere frend, if I have doon for thee
In any cas, God wot, it is me leef;
And am as glad as man may of it be,
God helpe me so. But tak now not a-greef
That I shal seyn: be war of this mischeef,
That ther-as thou now wrought art in-to blisse
That thou thy-self ne cause it nought to misse.

"For of Fortunes sharp adversitee
The worste kinde of infortune is this:
A man to have ben in prosperitee,
And it remembren whan it passed is.
Thou art wys y-nough, for-thy do nought amis.
Be not to rakel though thou sitte warme,
For if thou be, certeyn it wol thee harme."

Quod Troilus, "I hope, and God to-forn,
My dere frend, that I shal so me bere
That in my gilt ther shal no thing be lorn,
Ne I nil not rakle as for to greven here.
It nedeth not this matere ofte tere;
For wistestow myn herte wel, Pandare,
God woot, of this thou woldest litel care."

Sk., III, 1597-1603; 1611-1631; 1639-1645

Tho gan he telle him of his glade night.
And wher-of first his herte dredde, and how,
And seyde, "Freend, as I am trewe knight,
And by that feyth I shal to God and yow,
I had it nevere half so hote as now;
And ay the more that desyr me byteth
To love hir best, the more it me delyteth.

"I noot my-self not wisly what it is;
But now I fele a newe qualitee,
Ye, al another than I did er this."
Pandare answerde, and seyde thus, that "he
That ones may in hevene blisse be,
He feleth other weyes, dar I leye,
Than thilke tyme he first herde of it seye."

This is o word for al; this Troilus
Was nevere ful to speke of this matere,
And for to preysen un-to Pandarus
The bountee of his righte lady dere,
And Pandarus to thanke and maken chere.
This tale ay was span-newe to biginne
Til that the night departed hem a-twinne.

Sone after this, for that Fortune it wolde,
I-comen was the blisful tyme swete,
That Troilus was warned that he sholde,
Ther he was erst, Criseyde his lady mete;
For which he felte his herte in Ioye flete,
And feythfully gan alle the goddes herie.
And lat see now if that he can be merie.

Nought nedeth it to yow, sin they ben met,
To aske at me if that they blythe were;
For if it erst was wel, tho was it bet
A thousand-fold, this nedeth not enquere.
A-gon was every sorwe and every fere;
And bothe, y-wis, they had, and so they wende,
As muche Ioye as herte may comprende.

Sk., III 1646-1673; 1681-1687

But cruel day, so wel-awey the stounde!
Gan for to aproche, as they by signes knewe,
For which hem thoughte felen dethes wounde.
So wo was hem that changen gan hir hewe,
And day they gonnen to dispyse al newe,
Calling it traytour, envyous, and worse,
And bitterly the dayes light they curse.

Quod Troilus, "Allas! now am I war
That Pirous and tho swifte stedes three,
Which that drawen forth the sonnes char,
Han goon som by-path in despyt of me,
That maketh it so sone day to be.
And for the sonne him hasteth thus to ryse
Ne shal I nevere doon him sacrifyse!"

But nedes day departe moste hem sone;
And whan hir speche doon was and hir chere,
They twinne anoon as they were wont to done,
And setten tyme of meting eft y-fere.
And many a night they wroughte in this manere,
And thus Fortune a tyme ladde in Ioye
Criseyde and eek this kinges sone of Troye.

In suffisaunce, in blisse, and in singinges,
This Troilus gan al his lyf to lede.
He spendeth, Iusteth, maketh festeyinges;
He yeveth frely ofte, and chaungeth wede,
And held aboute him alwey, out of drede,
A world of folk, as cam him wel of kinde,
The fressheste and the beste he coude fynde.

And most of love and vertu was his speche,
And in despyt had alle wrecchednesse;
And doutelees, no nede was him biseche
To honouren hem that hadde worthinesse
And esen hem that weren in distresse.
And glad was he if any wight wel ferde,
That lover was, whan he it wiste or herde.

Sk., III, 1695–1722; 1786–1792

For sooth to seyn, he lost held every wight
But-if he were in Loves heigh servyse,
I mene folk that oughte it been of right.
And over al this, so wel coude he devyse
Of sentement, and in so unkouth wyse
Al his array, that every lover thoughte
That al was wel, what-so he seyde or wroughte.

Thou lady bright, the doughter to Dione,
Thy blinde and winged sone eek, Daun Cupyde;
Ye sustren nyne eek that by Elicone
In hil Parnaso listen for to abyde:
That ye thus fer han deyned me to gyde,
I can no more but—sin that ye wol wende—
Ye heried been for ay, with-outen ende!

Thourgh yow have I seyd fully in my song
Theffect and Ioye of Troilus servyse,
Al be that ther was som disese among,
As to myn auctor listeth to devyse.
My thridde book now ende ich in this wyse;
And Troilus in lust and in quiete
Is with Criseyde, his owne herte swete.

Explicit Liber Tercius.

BOOK IV

Incipit Quartus Liber

But al to litel, weylawey the whyle,
Lasteth swich Ioye, y-thonked be Fortune!
That semeth trewest whan she wol bygyle,
And can to foles so hir song entune
That she hem hent and blent, traytour comune;
And whan a wight is from hir wheel y-throwe,
Than laugheth she and maketh him the mowe.

Sk., III, 1793–1799; 1807–1820; IV, 1–7

O ye Herines, Nightes doughtren three,
That endelees compleynen evere in pyne,
Megera, Alete, and eek Thesiphone;
Thou cruel Mars eek, fader to Quiryne:
This ilke ferthe book me helpeth fyne,
So that the los of lyf and love y-fere
Of Troilus be fully shewed here.

Ligging in ost, as I have seyd er this,
The Grekes stronge aboute Troye toun,
Bifel that whan that Phebus shyning is
Up-on the brest of Hercules Lyoun,
That Ector, with ful many a bold baroun,
Caste on a day with Grekes for to fighte,
As he was wont to greve hem what he mighte.

The longe day, with speres sharpe y-grounde,
With arwes, dartes, swerdes, maces felle,
They fighte and bringen hors and man to grounde,
And with hir axes oute the braynes quelle.
But in the laste shour, sooth for to telle,
The folk of Troye hem-selven so misledden
That with the worse at night homward they fledden.

At whiche day was taken Antenor,
Maugre Polydamas or Monesteo,
Santipee, Sarpedon, Polynestor,
Polyte, or eek the Troian Daun Ripheo,
And othere lasse folk, as Phebuseo.
So that for harm that day the folk of Troye
Dredden to lese a greet part of hir Ioye.

Of Pryamus was yeve at Greek requeste
A tyme of trewe, and tho they gonnen trete
Hir prisoneres to chaungen, moste and leste,
And for the surplus yeven sommes grete.
This thing anoon was couth in every strete,
Bothe in thassege, in toune, and every-where,
And with the firste it cam to Calkas ere.

Whan Calkas knew this tretis sholde holde
In consistorie among the Grekes, sone
He gan in thringe forth with lordes olde,
And sette him ther-as he was wont to done;
And with a chaunged face hem bad a bone,
For love of God, to don that reverence
To stinte noyse and yeve him audience.

Than seyde he thus, "Lo! lordes myne, I was
Troian, as it is knowen out of drede;
And if that yow remembre, I am Calkas;
That alderfirst yaf comfort to your nede,
And tolde wel how that ye sholden spede.
For dredelees thorugh yow shal in a stounde
Ben Troye y-brend and beten doun to grounde.

"Having un-to my tresour ne my rente
Right no resport, to respect of your ese,
Thus al my good I loste and to yow wente,
Wening in this you, lordes, for to plese.
But al that los ne doth me no disese.
I vouche-sauf, as wisly have I Ioye,
For yow to lese al that I have in Troye,

"Save of a doughter that I lafte, allas!
Sleping at hoom, whan out of Troye I sterte.
O sterne, O cruel fader that I was!
How mighte I have in that so hard an herte?
Allas! I ne had y-brought hir in hir sherte!
For sorwe of which I wol not live to morwe,
But-if ye lordes rewe up-on my sorwe.

"Ye have now caught and fetered in prisoun
Troians y-nowe; and if your willes be
My child with oon may have redempcioun,
Now for the love of God and of bountee,
Oon of so fele, allas! so yeve him me!
What nede were it this preyere for to werne
Sin ye shul bothe han folk and toun as yerne?"

Sk., IV, 64–77; 85–98; 106–112

Telling his tale alwey, this olde greye,
Humble in speche and in his loking eke,
The salte teres from his eyen tweye
Ful faste ronnen doun by eyther cheke.
So longe he gan of socour hem by-seke
That for to hele him of his sorwes sore
They yave him Antenor, with-oute more.

But who was glad y-nough but Calkas tho?
And of this thing ful sone his nedes leyde
On hem that sholden for the tretis go,
And hem for Antenor ful ofte preyde
To bringen hoom King Toas and Criseyde.
And whan Pryam his save-garde sente,
Thembassadours to Troye streyght they wente.

The cause y-told of hir coming, the olde
Pryam the king ful sone in general
Let heer-upon his parlement to holde,
Of which the effect rehersen yow I shal.
Thembassadours ben answered for fynal,
Theschaunge of prisoners and al this nede
Hem lyketh wel, and forth in they procede.

This Troilus was present in the place
Whan axed was for Antenor Criseyde,
For which ful sone chaungen gan his face,
As he that with tho wordes wel neigh deyde.
But nathelees, he no word to it seyde
Lest men sholde his affeccioun espye;
With mannes herte he gan his sorwes drye.

And ful of anguish and of grisly drede
Abood what lordes wolde un-to it seye.
And if they wolde graunte, as God forbede,
Theschaunge of hir, than thoughte he thinges tweye:
First, how to save hir honour, and what weye
He mighte best theschaunge of hir withstonde.
Ful faste he caste how al this mighte stonde.

Love him made al prest to doon hir byde,
And rather dye than she sholde go;
But rcsoun seyde him, on that other syde,
"With-oute assent of hir ne do not so,
Lest for thy werk she wolde be thy fo
And seyn that thorugh thy medling is y-blowe
Your bother love, ther it was erst unknowe."

For which he gan deliberen, for the beste,
That though the lordes wolde that she wente,
He wolde late hem graunte what hem leste,
And telle his lady first what that they mente.
And whan that she had seyd him hir entente,
Ther-after wolde he werken also blyve
Though al the world ayein it wolde stryve.

Ector, which that wel the Grekes herde,
For Antenor how they wolde han Criseyde,
Gan it withstonde, and sobrely answerde:
"Sires, she nis no prisoner," he seyde;
"I noot on yow who hath this charge leyde,
But on my part ye may eft-sone him telle
We usen heer no wommen for to selle."

The noyse of peple up-stirte than at ones,
As breme as blase of straw y-set on fyre;
For infortune it wolde, for the nones,
They sholden hir confusioun desyre.
"Ector," quod they, "what goost may yow enspyre
This womman thus to shilde and doon us lese
Daun Antenor? A wrong wey now ye chese,

"That is so wys and eek so bold baroun,
And we han nede of folk, as men may see.
He is eek oon the grettest of this toun.
O Ector, lat tho fantasyës be!
O King Pryam," quod they, "thus seggen we,
That al our voys is to for-gon Criseyde;"
And to deliveren Antenor they preyde.

O Iuvenal, lord! trewe is thy sentence
That litel witen folk what is to yerne
That they ne finde in hir desyr offence;
For cloude of errour lat hem not descerne
What best is: and lo, heer ensample as yerne.
This folk desiren now deliveraunce
Of Antenor, that broughte hem to mischaunce!

For he was after traytour to the toun
Of Troye; allas! they quitte him out to rathe!
O nyce world, lo, thy discrecioun!
Criseyde, which that nevere did hem skathe,
Shal now no lenger in hir blisse bathe;
But Antenor, he shal come hoom to toune,
And she shal oute: thus seyden here and howne.

For which delibered was by parlement
For Antenor to yelden up Criseyde,
And it pronounced by the president,
Al-theigh that Ector "Nay" ful ofte preyde.
And fynaly what wight that it with-seyde,
It was for nought, it moste been, and sholde;
For substaunce of the parlement it wolde.

Departed out of parlement echone,
This Troilus, with-oute wordes mo,
Un-to his chaumbre spedde him faste allone,
But-if it were a man of his or two,
The which he bad oute faste for to go
By-cause he wolde slepen, as he seyde,
And hastely up-on his bed him leyde.

He rist him up, and every dore he shette
And windowe eek, and tho this sorweful man
Up-on his beddes syde a-doun him sette,
Ful lyk a deed image pale and wan.
And in his brest the heped wo bigan
Out-breste, and he to werken in this wyse
In his woodnesse, as I shal yow devyse.

Sk., IV, 197-224; 232-238

Right as the wilde bolę biginneth springe
Now heer, now ther, y-darted to the herte,
And of his deeth roreth in compleyninge,
Right so gan he aboutę the chaumbre sterte,
Smyting his brest ay with his festes smerte.
His head ay to the wal, his body to the grounde,
Ful ofte he swapte, him-selven to confounde.

But after whan the furie and the rage
Which that his herte twiste and faste threste,
By lengthe of tyme somwhat gan asswage,
Up-on his bed he leyde him doun to reste.
But tho bigonne his teres more out-breste
That wonder is the body may suffyse
To half this wo which that I yow devyse.

Than seyde he thus, "Fortune! allas, the whyle!
What have I doon, what have I thus a-gilt?
How mightestow for reuthe me bigyle?
Is ther no grace, and shal I thus be spilt?
Shal thus Criseyde awey for that thou wilt?
Allas! how maystow in thyn herte finde
To been to me thus cruel and unkinde?

"O olde, unholsom, and mislyved man!
Calkas I mene, allas! what eyleth thee
To been a Greek, sin thou art born Troian?
O Calkas, which that wilt my bane be,
In cursed tyme was thou born for me!
As wolde blisful Iove, for his Ioye,
That I thee hadde wher I wolde in Troye!"

A thousand sykes hotter than the glede
Out of his brest ech after other wente,
Medled with pleyntes newe, his wo to fede,
For which his woful teres nevere stente.
And shortly, so his peynes him to-rente
And wex so mat that Ioye nor penaunce
He feleth noon, but lyth forth in a traunce.

Sk., IV, 239-245; 253-266; 330-343

Pandare, which that in the parlement
Had herd what every lord and burgeys seyde,
And how ful graunted was by oon assent
For Antenor to yelden so Criseyde,
Gan wel neigh wood out of his wit to breyde,
So that for wo he niste what he mente;
But in a rees to Troilus he wente.

A certeyn knight, that for the tyme kepte
The chaumbre-dore, un-did it him anoon.
And Pandarę, that ful tendreliche wepte,
In-to the derke chaumbre, as stille as stoon,
Toward the bed gan softely to goon,
So confus that he niste what to seye.
For verray wo his wit was neigh aweye.

And with his chere and loking al to-torn
For sorwe of this, and with his armes folden,
He stood this woful Troilus biforn
And on his pitous face he gan biholden.
But Lord, so often gan his herte colden,
Seing his frend in wo, whos hevinesse
His herte slow, as thoughte him, for distresse!

But at the lastę this woful Troilus,
Ney ded for smert, gan bresten outę to rore,
And with a sorwful noyse he seyde thus
Among his sobbes and his sykes sore:
"Lo! Pandare, I am deed, with-outen more.
Hastow nought herd at parlement," he seyde,
"For Antenor how lost is my Criseyde?"

This Pandarus, ful deed and pale of hewe,
Ful pitously answerde and seyde, "Yis!
As wisly were it fals as it is trewe
That I have herd and wot al how it is!
O mercy, God, who wolde havę trowed this?
Who wolde havę wend that in so litel a throwe
Fortune our Ioye wolde han over-throwe?

"But telle me this, why thou art now so mad
To sorwen thus? why lystow in this wyse,
Sin thy desyr al holly hastow had,
So that by right it oughte y-now suffyse?
But I, that nevere felte in my servyse
A frendly chere or loking of an yë,
Lat me thus wepe and wayle, til I dye.

"And over al this, as thou wel wost thy-selve,
This town is ful of ladies al aboute;
And to my doom, fairer than swiche twelve
As evere she was, shal I finde in som route,
Ye, oon or two, with-outen any doute.
For-thy be glad, myn owene dere brother,
If she be lost, we shul recovere another."

Thise wordes seyde he for the nones alle
To helpe his freend lest he for sorwe deyde.
For doutelees, to doon his wo to falle,
He roughte not what unthrift that he seyde.
But Troilus, that neigh for sorwe deyde,
Tok litel hede of al that evere he mente:
Oon ere it herde, at the other oute it wente.

But at the laste answerde and seyde, "Freend,
This lechecraft, or heled thus to be,
Were wel sitting if that I were a feend,
To traysen hir that trewe is unto me!
I pray God lat this consayl nevere y-thee;
But do me rather sterve anon-right here
Er I thus do as thou me woldest lere.

"She that I serve, y-wis, what so thou seye,
To whom myn herte enhabit is by right,
Shal han me holly hires til that I deye.
For Pandarus, sin I have trouthe hir hight,
I wol not been untrewe for no wight;
But as hir man I wol ay live and sterve
And nevere other creature serve.

"And ther thou seyst thou shalt as faire finde
As she, lat be, makę no comparisoun
To creature y-formed heer by kinde.
O leve Pandare, in conclusioun,
I wol not be of thyn opinioun,
Touching al this. For which I thee biseche
So hold thy pees; thou sleest me with thy speche!"

This Troilus in teres gan distille
As licour out of alambyk ful faste;
And Pandarus gan holde his tunge stille,
And to the grounde his eyen doun he caste.
But nathelees, thus thoughte he at the laste,
"What, parde, rather than my felawę deye,
Yet shal I som-what more un-to him seye."

And seyde "Freend, sin thou hast swich distresse,
And sin thee list myn arguments to blame,
Why nilt thy-selven helpen doon redresse,
And with thy manhod letten al this grame?
Go ravisshe hir ne canstow not? For shame!
And outher lat hir out of toune fare,
Or hold hir stille and levę thy nyce fare!

"Artow in Troye, and hast non hardiment
To take a womman which that loveth thee,
And wolde hir-selven been of thyn assent?
Now is not this a nyce vanitee?
Rys up anoon, and lat this weping be,
And kyth thou art a man; for in this houre
I wil be deed, or she shal bleven oure."

To this answerde him Troilus ful softe
And seyde, "Parde, leve brother dere,
Al this have I my-self yet thought ful ofte,
And more thing than thou devysest here.
But why this thing is laft, thou shalt wel here;
And whan thou me hast yeve an audience,
Ther-after mayst thou telle al thy sentence.

"First, sin thou wost this toun hath al this werre
For ravisshing of wommen so by might,
It sholde not be suffred me to erre,
As it stant now, ne doon so gret unright.
I sholde han also blame of every wight,
My fadres graunt if that I so withstode,
Sin she is chaunged for the tounes goode.

"I have eek thought, so were it hir assent,
To aske hir at my fader of his grace;
Than thenke I this were hir accusement,
Sin wel I woot I may hir not purchace.
For sin my fader in so heigh a place
As parlement hath hir eschaunge enseled,
He nil for me his lettre be repeled.

"Yet drede I most hir herte to pertourbe
With violence, if I do swich a game;
For if I wolde it openly distourbe,
It moste been disclaundre to hir name.
And me were lever deed than hir defame,
As nolde God but-if I sholde have
Hir honour lever than my lyf to save!

"Thus am I lost for ought that I can see;
For certeyn is sin that I am hir knight,
I moste hir honour lever han than me
In every cas, as lover oughte of right.
Thus am I with desyr and reson twight:
Desyr for to distourben hir me redeth,
And reson nil not, so myn herte dredeth."

Thus weping that he coude nevere cesse,
He seyde, "Allas! how shal I, wrecche, fare?
For wel fele I alwey my love encresse,
And hope is lasse and lasse alwey, Pandare!
Encressen eek the causes of my care;
So wel-a-wey, why nil myn herte breste?
For as in love ther is but litel reste."

Pandare answerde, "Freend, thou mayst, for me,
Don as thee list. But had ich it so hote,
And thyn estat, she sholde go with me.
Though al this toun cryęde on this thing by note,
I nolde sette at al that noyse a grote.
For when men han wel cryęd, than wol they roune:
A wonder last but nynę night nevere in toune.

"Devyne not in reson ay so depe
Ne curteysly, but help thy-self anoon.
Bet is that othere than thy-selven wepe,
And namely, sin ye two been al oon.
Rys up, for by myn heed, she shal not goon!
And rather be in blame a lyte y-founde
Than sterve heer as a gnat with-oute wounde!"

This Troilus gan with tho wordes quiken,
And seyde, "Freend, graunt mercy, ich assente.
But certaynly thou mayst not me so priken,
Ne peyne anoon ne may me so tormente,
That for no cas it is not myn entente,
At shorte wordes, though I dyen sholde,
To ravisshe hir, but-if hir-self it wolde."

"Why, so mene I," quod Pandarus, "al this day.
But tellę me than, hastow hir wel assayed,
That sorwest thus?" And he answerde, "Nay."
"Wher-of artow," quod Pandarę, "than a-mayed,
That nost not that she wol ben yvel apayed
To ravisshe hir, sin thou hast not ben there,
But-if that Iove tolde it in thyn ere?

"For-thy rys up, as nought ne were, anoon,
And wash thy face, and to the king thou wende,
Or he may wondren whider thou art goon.
Thou most with wisdom him and othere blende;
Or up-on cas he may after thee sende
Er thou be war. And shortly, brother dere,
Be glad and lat me werke in this matere.

Sk., IV, 582–595; 631–651

"For I shal shape it so that sikerly
Thou shalt this night som tyme in som manere
Com speke with thy lady prevely,
And by hir wordes eek and by hir chere
Thou shalt ful sone aparceyve and wel here
Al hir entente, and in this cas the beste.
And far now wel, for in this poynt I reste."

The swifte Fame, which that false thinges
Egal reporteth lyk the thinges trewe,
Was thorugh-oute Troye y-fled with preste winges
Fro man to man, and made this tale al newe,
How Calkas doughter with hir brighte hewe,
At parlement, with-oute wordes more,
I-graunted was in chaunge of Antenore.

The whiche tale anoon-right as Criseyde
Had herd, she which that of hir fader roughte,
As in this cas, right nought, ne whan he deyde,
Ful bisily to Iuppiter bisoughte
Yeve him mischaunce that this tretis broughte.
But shortly, lest thise tales sothe were,
She dorste at no wight asken it for fere.

As she that had hir herte and al hir minde
On Troilus y-set so wonder faste
That al this world ne mighte hir love unbinde
Ne Troilus out of hir herte caste,
She wol ben his, whyl that hir lyf may laste.
And thus she brenneth bothe in love and drede,
So that she niste what was best to rede.

But as men seen in toune and al aboute
That wommen usen frendes to visyte,
So to Criseyde of wommen com a route
For pitous Ioye, and wenden hir delyte.
And with hir tales dere y-nough a myte,
These wommen, which that in the cite dwelle,
They sette hem doun and seyde as I shal telle.

Quod first that oon, "I am glad trewely
By-cause of yow that shal your fader see."
A-nother seyde, "Y-wis, so nam not I;
For al to litel hath she with us be."
Quod tho the thridde, "I hope, y-wis, that she
Shal bringen us the pees on every syde,
That whan she gooth, almighty God hir gyde!"

Tho wordes and tho wommanisshe thinges
She herde hem right as though she thennes were;
For, God it wot, hir herte on other thing is,
Although the body sat among hem there.
Hir advertence is alwey elles-where;
For Troilus ful faste hir soule soughte,
With-outen word alwey on him she thoughte.

For which no lenger mighte she restreyne
Hir teres, so they gonnen up to welle,
That yeven signes of the bittre peyne
In which hir spirit was and moste dwelle,
Remembring hir, fro hevene unto which helle
She fallen was sith she forgoth the sighte
Of Troilus; and sorowfully she sighte.

And thilke foles sitting hir aboute
Wenden that she wepte and sykcd sore
By-cause that she sholde out of that route
Departe and nevere pleye with hem more.
And they that had y-knowen hir of yore
Seye hir so wepe, and thoughte it kindenesse,
And ech of hem wepte eek for hir distresse.

But after al this nyce vanitee
They toke hir leve, and hoom they wenten alle.
Criseyde ful of sorweful pitee,
In-to hir chaumbre up wente out of the halle,
And on hir bed she gan for deed to falle,
In purpos nevere thennes for to ryse.
And thus she wroughte as I shal yow devyse.

Sk., IV, 687-700; 708-721; 729-735

Hir ounded heer that sonnish was of hewe,
She rente, and eek hir fingres longe and smale
She wrong ful ofte, and bad God on hir rewe
And with the deeth to doon bote on hir bale.
Hir hewe, whylom bright, that tho was pale,
Bar witnesse of hir wo and hir constreynte.
And thus she spak, sobbing in hir compleynte:

"Alas!" quod she, "out of this regioun
I, woful wrecche and infortuned wight,
And born in corsed constellacioun,
Mot goon, and thus departen fro my knight.
Wo worth, allas! that ilke dayes light
On which I saw him first with eyen tweyne,
That causeth me, and I him, al this peyne!"

Therwith the teres from hir eyen two
Doun fille as shour in Aperill ful swythe.
Hir whyte brest she bet, and for the wo
After the deeth she cryed a thousand sythe,
Sin he that wont hir wo was for to lythe
She mot for-goon; for which disaventure
She held hir-self a forlost creature.

How mighte it evere y-red ben or y-songe,
The pleynte that she made in hir distresse?
I noot; but as for me, my litel tonge,
If I discreven wolde hir hevinesse,
It sholde make hir sorwe seme lesse
Than that it was, and childishly deface
Hir heigh compleynte, and therfore ich it pace.

Pandare, which that sent from Troilus
Was to Criseyde, as ye han herd devyse.
That for the beste it was accorded thus,
And he ful glad to doon him that servyse,
Un-to Criseyde in a ful secree wyse,
Ther-as she lay in torment and in rage,
Com hir to telle al hoolly his message.

Sk., IV, 736-756; 799-812

And fond that she hir-selven gan to trete
Ful pitously; for with hir salte teres
Hir brest, hir face, y-bathed was ful wete;
The mighty tresses of hir sonnish heres
Unbroyden hangen al aboute hir eres,
Which yaf him verray signal of martyre
Of deeth, which that hir herte gan desyre.

Whan she him saw, she gan for sorwe anoon
Hir tery face a-twixe hir armes hyde,
For which this Pandare is so wo bi-goon
That in the hous he mighte unnethe abyde,
As he that pitee felte on every syde.
For if Criseyde had erst compleyned sore,
Tho gan she pleyne a thousand tymes more.

And in hir aspre pleynte than she seyde,
"Pandare first of Ioyes mo than two
Was cause causing un-to me Criseyde,
That now transmuwed been in cruel wo.
Wher shal I seye to yow 'welcome' or no,
That alderfirst me broughte in-to servyse
Of love, allas! that endeth in swich wyse?"

"And thou, my suster, ful of discomfort,"
Quod Pandarus, "what thenkestow to do?
Why ne hastow to thy-selven som resport,
Why woltow thus thy-selve, allas! for-do?
Leef al this werk and tak now hede to
That I shal seyn, and herkne of good entente
This, which by me thy Troilus thee sente."

Tornede hir tho Criseyde, a wo makinge
So greet that it a deeth was for to see:—
"Allas!" quod she, "what wordes may ye bringe?
What wol my dere herte seyn to me,
Which that I drede nevere-mo to see?
Wol he have pleynte or teres er I wende?
I have y-nowe, if he ther-after sende!"

Sk., IV, 813-833; 848-861

She was right swich to seen in hir visage
As is that wight that men on bere binde:
Hir face, lyk of Paradys the image,
Was al y-chaunged in another kinde.
The pley, the laughtre men was wont to finde
In hir, and eek hir Ioyes everychone,
Ben fled, and thus lyth now Criseyde allone.

Aboute hir eyen two a purpre ring
Bi-trent in sothfast tokning of hir peyne,
That to biholde it was a dedly thing,
For which Pandare mighte not restreyne
The teres from his eyen for to reyne.
But nathelees, as he best mighte, he seyde
From Troilus thise wordes to Criseyde:—

"Lo, nece, I trowe ye han herd al how
The king with othere lordes for the beste
Hath mad eschaunge of Antenor and yow,
That cause is of this sorwe and this unreste.
But how this cas doth Troilus moleste,
That may non erthely mannes tonge seye;
For verray wo his wit is al aweye.

"For which we han so sorwed, he and I,
That in-to litel bothe it had us slawe;
But thurgh my conseil this day fynally
He somwhat is fro weping now with-drawe.
And semeth me that he desyreth fawe
With yow to been al night for to devyse
Remede in this, if ther were any wyse."

"Gret is my wo," quod she, and sighte sore
As she that feleth dedly sharp distresse;
"But yet to me his sorwe is muchel more,
That love him bet than he him-self, I gesse.
Allas! for me hath he swiche hevinesse?
Can he for me so pitously compleyne?
Y-wis, this sorwe doubleth al my peyne.

Sk., IV, 862-889; 897-903

Grevous to me, God wot, is for to twinne,"
Quod she, "but yet it harder is to me
To seen that sorwe which that he is inne;
For wel wot I it wol my bane be,
And deye I wol in certayn," tho quod she.
"But bidde him come, er deeth, that thus me threteth,
Dryve oute that goost which in myn herte beteth."

Thise wordes seyd, she on hir armes two
Fil gruf, and gan to wepe pitously.
Quod Pandarus, "Allas! why do ye so,
Syn wel ye wot the tyme is faste by
That he shal come? Arys up hastely
That he yow nat biwopen thus ne finde,
But ye wol han him wood out of his minde!

"For wiste he that ye ferde in this manere,
He wolde him-selve slee; and if I wende
To han this fare, he sholde not come here
For al the good that Pryam may dispende.
For to what fyn he wolde anoon pretende,
That knowe I wel; and for-thy yet I seye,
So leef this sorwe or platly he wol deye."

"Go," quod Criseyde, "and uncle, trewely,
I shal don al my might me to restreyne
From weping in his sighte, and bisily,
Him for to glade, I shal don al my peyne,
And in myn herte seken every veyne.
If to this soore ther may be founden salve
It shal not lakken, certain, on myn halve."

Goth Pandarus, and Troilus he soughte
Til in a temple he fond him al allone,
As he that of his lyf no lenger roughte.
But to the pitouse goddes everichone
Ful tendrely he preyde and made his mone
To doon him sone out of this world to pace;
For wel he thoughte ther was non other grace.

And shortly, al the sothe for to seye,
He was so fallen in despeyr that day
That outrely he shoop him for to deye.
For right thus was his argument alwey:
He seyde he nas but loren, waylawey!
"For al that comth, comth by necessitee;
Thus to be lorn, it is my destinee.

"For certaynly this wot I wel," he seyde,
"That for-sighte of divyne purveyaunce
Hath seyn alwey me to for-gon Criseyde,
Sin God seeth every thing, out of doutaunce,
And hem desponeth thourgh his ordenaunce
In hir merytes sothly for to be
As they shul comen by predestinee.

"But nathelees, allas! whom shal I leve?
For ther ben grete clerkes many oon
That destinee thorugh argumentes preve;
And som men seyn that nedely ther is noon,
But that free chois is yeven us everichoon.
O, welaway! so sleye arn clerkes olde
That I not whos opinion I may holde.

"For som men seyn, if God seth al biforn,
Ne God may not deceyved ben, pardee,
Than moot it fallen, though men had it sworn,
That purveyaunce hath seyn biforę to be.
Wherfore I seyę that from eterne if he
Hath wist biforn our thought eek as our dede,
We havę no free chois, as thesę clerkes rede."

Than seyde he thus, "Almighty Iove in trone
That wost of al this thing the soothfastnesse,
Rewe on my sorwe or do me deye sone,
Or bring Criseyde and me fro this distresse."
And whyl he was in al this hevinesse
Disputing with him-self in this matere,
Com Pandare in and seyde as ye may here.

Sk., IV, 953–980; 1079-1085

"O mighty God," quod Pandarus, "in trone,
Ey! who seigh evere a wys man faren so?
Why, Troilus, what thenkestow to done?
Hastow swich lust to been thyn owene fo?
What, parde, yet is not Criseyde a-go!
Why lust thee so thy-self for-doon for drede
That in thyn heed thyn eyen semen dede?

"Hastow not lived many a yeer biforn
With-outen hir, and ferd ful wel at ese?
Artow for hir and for non other born?
Hath kinde thee wroughte al-only hir to plese?
Lat be, and thenk right thus in thy disese,
That, in the dees right as ther fallen chaunces,
Right so in love ther come and goon plesaunces.

"And yet this is a wonder most of alle,
Why thou thus sorwest, sin thou nost not yit,
Touching hir going, how that it shal falle,
Ne if she can hir-self distorben it.
Thou hast not yet assayed al hir wit.
A man may al by tyme his nekke bede
Whan it shal of, and sorwen at the nede.

"For-thy tak hede of that that I shal seye:
I have with hir y-spoke and longe y-be,
So as accorded was bitwixe us tweye.
And evere-mo me thinketh thus, that she
Hath som-what in hir hertes prevetee
Wher-with she can, if I shal right arede,
Distorbe al this of which thou art in drede.

"For which my counseil is, whan it is night,
Thou to hir go and make of this an ende;
And blisful Iuno thourgh hir grete might
Shal, as I hope, hir grace un-to us sende.
Myn herte seyth, 'Certeyn she shal not wende;'
And for-thy put thyn herte a whyle in reste,
And hold this purpos, for it is the beste."

Sk., IV, 1086-1120

This Troilus answerde, and sighte sore,
"Thou seyst right wel, and I wil do right so;"
And what him liste, he seyde un-to it more.
And whan that it was tyme for to go,
Ful prevely him-self, with-outen mo,
Un-to hir com as he was wont to done.
And how they wroughte, I shal yow telle sone.

Soth is that whan they gonne first to mete,
So gan the peyne hir hertes for to twiste
That neither of hem other mighte grete,
But hem in armes toke and after, kiste.
The lasse woful of hem bothe niste
Wher that he was, ne mighte o word out-bringe,
As I seyde erst, for wo and for sobbinge.

Tho woful teres that they leten falle
As bittre weren, out of teres kinde,
For peyne as is ligne aloës or galle.
So bittre teres weep nought, as I finde,
The woful Myrra through the bark and rinde.
That in this world ther nis so hard an herte
That nolde han rewed on hir peynes smerte.

But whan hir woful wery gostes tweyne
Retorned been ther-as hem oughte dwelle,
And that som-what to wayken gan the peyne
By lengthe of pleynte, and ebben gan the welle
Of hir teres, and the herte unswelle,
With broken voys al hoors for shright, Criseyde
To Troilus thise ilke wordes seyde:

"O Iove, I deye, and mercy I beseche!
Help, Troilus!" and ther-with-al hir face
Upon his brest she leyde, and loste speche;
Hir woful spirit from his propre place
Right with the word alwey up poynt to pace.
And thus she lyth with hewes pale and grene,
That whylom freshe and fairest was to sene.

This Troilus, that on hir gan biholde,
Cleping hir name—and she lay as for deed
With-oute answere, and felte hir limes colde,
Hir eyen throwen upward to hir heed—
This sorwful man can now noon other reed,
But ofte tyme hir colde mouth he kiste.
Wher him was wo, God and him-self it wiste!

He rist him up and longe streight he hir leyde;
For signe of lyf, for ought he can or may,
Can he noon finde in no-thing on Criseyde,
For which his song ful ofte is "Weylaway!"
But whan he saugh that specheles she lay,
With sorwful voys and herte of blisse al bare
He seyde how she was fro this world y-fare!

So after that he longe had hir complayned,
His hondes wrong, and seyde that was to seye,
And with his teres salte hir brest bireyned,
He gan tho teris wypen of ful dreye,
And pitously gan for the soule preye,
And seyde, "O Lord, that set art in thy trone,
Rewe eek on me, for I shal folwe hir sone!"

And after this, with sterne and cruel herte,
His swerd a-noon out of his shethe he twighte
Him-self to sleen, how sore that him smerte,
So that his sowle hir sowle folwen mighte
Ther-as the doom of Mynos wolde it dighte,
Sin Love and cruel Fortune it ne wolde
That in this world he lenger liven sholde.

Than seyde he thus, fulfild of heigh desdayn,
"O cruel Iove, and thou, Fortune adverse,
This al and som, that falsly have ye slayn
Criseyde, and sin ye may do me no werse,
Fy on your might and werkes so diverse!
Thus cowardly ye shul me nevere winne.
Ther shal no deeth me fro my lady twinne.

Sk., IV, 1156-1176; 1184-1197

"And thou, citee, which that I leve in wo,
And thou, Pryam, and bretheren al y-fere,
And thou, my moder, farewel! for I go!
And Attropos, make redy thou my bere!
And thou, Criseyde, O swete herte dere,
Receyve now my spirit!" wolde he seye,
With swerd at herte al redy for to deye.

But as God wolde, of swough ther-with she abreyde
And gan to syke and "Troilus" she cryde.
And he answerde, "Lady myn Criseyde,
Live ye yet?" and leet his swerd doun glyde.
"Ye, herte myn, that thanked be Cupyde!"
Quod she, and ther-with-al she sore sighte,
And he bigan to glade hir as he mighte.

Took hir in armes two, and kiste hir ofte,
And hir to glade he did al his entente,
For which hir goost, that flikered ay on-lofte,
In-to hir woful herte ayein it wente.
But at the laste, as that hir eyen glente
A-syde, anoon she gan his swerd aspye
As it lay bare, and gan for fere crye,

And asked him why he it had out-drawe.
And Troilus anoon the cause hir tolde,
And how himself ther-with he wolde have slawe,
For which Criseyde up-on him gan biholde,
And gan him in hir armes faste folde,
And seyde, "O mercy, God, lo, which a dede!
Allas! how neigh we were bothe dede!

"Than if I ne hadde spoken, as grace was,
Ye wolde han slayn your-self anoon?" quod she.
"Ye, douteless;" and she answerde, "Allas!
For by that ilke Lord that made me,
I nolde a forlong wey on-lyve han be
After your deeth, to han be crowned quene
Of al the lond the sonne on shyneth shene."

Whan they were in hir bedde in armes folde,
Nought was it lyk tho nightes heer-biforn;
For pitously ech other gan biholde
As they that hadden al hir blisse y-lorn,
Biwayling ay the day that they were born.
Til at the last this sorwful wight Criseyde
To Troilus these ilke wordes seyde:—

"Lo, herte myn, wel wot ye this," quod she,
"That if a wight alwey his wo compleyne,
And seketh nought how holpen for to be,
It nis but folye and encrees of peyne.
And sin that heer assembled be we tweyne,
To finde bote of wo that we ben inne
It were al tyme sone to biginne.

"I am a womman, as ful wel ye woot,
And as I am avysed sodeynly,
So wol I telle yow whyl it is hoot.
Me thinketh thus, that neither ye nor I
Oughte half this wo to make skilfully.
For ther is art y-now for to redresse
That yet is mis, and sleen this hevinesse.

"Sooth is, the wo, the which that we ben inne,
For ought I woot, for no-thing elles is
But for the cause that we sholden twinne.
Considered al, ther nis no-more amis.
But what is than a remede un-to this
But that we shape us sone for to mete?
This al and som, my dere herte swete.

"Now that I shal wel bringen it aboute
To come ayein, sone after that I go,
Ther-of am I no maner thing in doute.
For dredeles, with-in a wouke or two
I shal ben heer. And that it may be so
By alle right, and in a wordes fewe,
I shal yow wel an heep of weyes shewe.

Sk., IV, 1247–1281

"Now herkneth this, ye han wel understonde
My going graunted is by parlement,
So ferforth that it may not be with-stonde
For al this world, as by my Iugement.
And sin ther helpeth noon avysement
To letten it, lat it passe out of minde,
And lat us shape a bettre wey to finde.

"The sothe is that the twinning of us tweyne
Wol us disese and cruelliche anoye.
But him bihoveth som-tyme han a peyne
That serveth Love, if that he wol have Ioye.
And sin I shal no ferther out of Troye
Than I may ryde ayein on half a morwe,
It oughte lasse causen us to sorwe.

"So as I shal not so ben hid in muwe
That day by day, myn owene herte dere,
Sin wel ye woot that it is now a truwe,
Ye shul ful wel al myn estat y-here.
And er that truwe is doon, I shal ben here,
And than have ye bothe Antenor y-wonne
And me also: beth glad now, if ye connc!

"I see that ofte ther-as we ben now
That for the beste, our conseil for to hyde,
Ye spekc not with me nor I with yow
In fourtenight, ne see yow go ne ryde.
May ye not ten dayes than abyde
For myn honour in swich an aventure?
Y-wis, ye mowen elles lite endure!

"Ye knowe eek how that al my kin is here,
But-if that onliche it my fader be;
And eek myn othere thinges alle y-fere,
And nameliche, my dere herte, ye,
Whom that I nolde leven for to see
For al this world as wyd as it hath space;
Or elles see ich nevere Ioves face!

Sk., IV, 1296–1316; 1324–1337

"Why trowe ye my fader in this wyse
Coveiteth so to see me, but for drede
Lest in this toun that folkes me dispyse
By-cause of him for his unhappy dede?
What woot my fader what lyf that I lede?
For if he wiste in Troyę how wel I fare,
Us nedeth for my wending nought to care.

"Ye seen that every day eek, more and more,
Men trete of pees. And it supposed is
That men the quene Eleyne shal restore,
And Grekes us restore that is mis.
So though ther nere comfort noon but this,
That men purposen pees on every syde,
Ye may the bettre at ese of herte abyde.

"And though so be that pees ther may be noon,
Yet hider, though ther nevere pees ne were,
I moste comę; for whider sholde I goon,
Or how mischaunce sholde I dwelle there
Among tho men of armes evere in fere?
For which, as wisly God my soule rede,
I can not seen wher-of ye sholden drede.

"Have heer another wey, if it so be
That al this thing ne may yow not suffyse.
My fader, as ye knowen wel, pardee,
Is old, and elde is ful of coveityse.
And I right now havę founden al the gyse,
With-oute net, wher-with I shal him hente.
And herkneth how, if that ye wole assente.

"The moeble which that I have in this toun
Un-to my fader shal I take, and seye
That right for trust and for savacioun
It sent is from a freend of his or tweye,
The whiche freendes ferventliche him preye
To senden after more, and that in hye,
Whyl that this toun stant thus in Iupartye.

Sk., IV, 1338-1351; 1359-1372; 1380-1386

"And that shal been an huge quantitee,
Thus shal I seyn, but, lest it folk aspyde,
This may be sent by no wight but by me.
I shal eek shewen him if pees bityde
What frendes that ich have on every syde
Toward the court, to doon the wrathe pace
Of Priamus, and doon him stonde in grace.

"So what for o thing and for other, swete,
I shal him so enchaunten with my sawes
That right in hevene his sowle is, shal he mete!
For al Appollo or his clerkes lawes
Or calculing avayleth nought three hawes;
Desyr of gold shal so his sowle blende
That as me lyst I shal wel make an ende.

"And if he wolde ought by his sort it preve
If that I lye, in certayn I shal fonde
Distorben him and plukke him by the sleve,
Making his sort, and beren him on honde,
He hath not wel the goddes understonde.
For goddes speken in amphibologyes,
And for oo sooth they tellen twenty lyes.

"Eek drede fond first goddes, I suppose:
Thus shal I seyn, and that his cowarde herte
Made him amis the goddes text to glose
Whan he for ferde out of his Delphos sterte.
And but I make him sone to converte
And doon my reed with-in a day or tweye
I wol to yow oblige me to deye."

And treweliche, as writen wel I finde,
That al this thing was seyd of good entente;
And that hir herte trewe was and kinde
Towardes him, and spak right as she mente,
And that she starf for wo neigh, whan she wente,
And was in purpos evere to be trewe.
Thus writen they that of hir werkes knewe.

This Troilus with herte and eres spradde
Herde al this thing devysen to and fro;
And verraylich him semed that he hadde
The selve wit, but yet to lete hir go
His herte misforyaf him evere-mo.
But fynally he gan his herte wreste
To trusten hir, and took it for the beste.

But natheles the wending of Criseyde,
For al this world, may nought out of his minde;
For which ful ofte he pitously hir preyde
That of hir heste he mighte hir trewe finde.
And seyde hir, "Certes, if ye be unkinde,
And but ye come at day set in-to Troye,
Ne shal I nevere have hele, honour, ne Ioye.

"For al-so sooth as sonne up-rist on morwe,
And God! so wisly thou me, woful wrecche,
To reste bringe out of this cruel sorwe,
I wol my-selven slee if that ye drecche.
But of my deeth though litel be to recche,
Yet, er that ye me cause so to smerte,
Dwel rather heer, myn owene swete herte!

"For trewely, myn owene lady dere,
Tho sleightes yet that I have herd yow stere
Ful shaply been to failen alle y-fere.
For thus men seyn, 'That oon thenketh the bere,
But al another thenketh his ledere.'
Your sire is wys, and seyd is, out of drede,
'Men may the wyse at-renne, and not at-rede.'

"It is ful hard to halten unespyed
Bifore a crepul, for he can the craft.
Your fader is in sleighte as Argus yëd;
For al be that his moeble is him biraft,
His olde sleighte is yet so with him laft
Ye shal not blende him for your woman hede,
Ne feyne a-right, and that is al my drede.

Sk., IV, 1422-1428; 1436-1463

"I noot if pees shal evere-mo bityde;
But pees or no, for ernest ne for game,
I woot sin Calkas on the Grekes syde
Hath ones been and loste so foule his name,
He dar no more come heer ayein for shame,
For which that wey for ought I can espye
To trusten on nis but a fantasye.

"Ye shal eek seen your fader shal yow glose
To been a wyf; and as he can wel preche
He shal som Grek so preyse and wel alose
That ravisshen he shal yow with his speche,
Or do yow doon by force as he shal teche.
And Troilus, of whom ye nil han routhe,
Shal causeles so sterven in his trouthe!

"And over al this, your fader shal despyse
Us alle, and seyn this citee nis but lorn;
And that thassege nevere shal aryse
For-why the Grekes han it alle sworn
Til we be slayn and doun our walles torn.
And thus he shal you with his wordes fere
That ay drede I that ye wol bleve there.

"Ye shul eek seen so many a lusty knight
A-mong the Grekes ful of worthinesse,
And ech of hem with herte, wit, and might,
To plesen yow don al his besinesse,
That ye shul dullen of the rudenesse
Of us sely Troians, but-if routhe
Remorde yow, or vertu of your trouthe.

"And this to me so grevous is to thinke
That fro my brest it wol my soule rende.
Ne dredeles in me ther may not sinke
A good opinoun if that ye wende,
For-why your faderes sleighte wol us shende.
And if ye goon, as I have told yow yore,
So thenk I nam but deed, with-oute more.

Sk., IV, 1464–1498

"For which with humble, trewe, and pitous herte
A thousand tymes mercy I yow preye.
So reweth on myn aspre peynes smerte,
And doth somwhat as that I shal yow seye
And lat us stele away betwixe us tweye.
And thenk that folye is, whan man may chese,
For accident his substaunce ay to lese.

"I mene this, that sin we mowe er day
Wel stele away and been to-gider so,
What wit were it to putten in assay,
In cas ye sholden to your fader go,
If that ye mighte come ayein or no?
Thus mene I, that it were a gret folye
To putte that sikernesse in Iupartye.

"And vulgarly to speken of substaunce
Of tresour, may we bothe with us lede
Y-nough to live in honour and plesaunce
Til in-to tyme that we shul ben dede.
And thus we may eschewen al this drede;
For everich other wey ye can recorde,
Myn herte, y-wis, may not ther-with acorde.

"And hardily, ne dredeth no poverte,
For I have kin and freendes elles-where
That, though we comen in our bare sherte,
Us sholde neither lakke gold ne gere
But been honoured whyl we dwelten there.
And go we anoon, for, as in myn entente,
This is the beste, if that ye wole assente."

Criseyde, with a syk, right in this wyse
Answerde, "Y-wis, my dere herte trewe,
We may wel stele away as ye devyse,
And finde swiche unthrifty weyes newe,
But afterward ful sore it wol us rewe.
And helpe me God so at my moste nede
As causeles ye suffren al this drede!

Sk., IV, 1499-1533

"For thilke day that I for cherisshinge
Or drede of fader, or of other wight,
Or for estat, delyt, or for weddinge
Be fals to yow, my Troilus, my knight,
Saturnes doughter, Iuno, thorugh hir might,
As wood as Athamante do me dwelle
Eternaly in Stix, the put of helle!

"But that ye speke awey thus for to go
And leten alle your freendes, God for-bede
For any womman that ye sholden so,
And namely sin Troye hath now swich nede
Of help. And eek of o thing taketh hede,
If this were wist, my lyf laye in balaunce
And your honour: God shilde us fro mischaunce!

"And if so be that pees her-after take,
As alday happeth, after anger, game,
Why, Lord! the sorwe and wo ye wolden make
That ye ne dorste come ayein for shame!
And er that ye Iuparten so your name,
Beth nought to hasty in this hote fare;
For hasty man ne wanteth nevere care.

"What trowe ye the peple eek al aboute
Wolde of it seye? It is ful light to arede.
They wolden seye, and swere it, out of doute,
That love ne droof yow nought to doon this dede,
But lust voluptuous and coward drede.
Thus were al lost, y-wis, myn herte dere,
Your honour, which that now shyneth so clere.

"And also thenketh on myn honestee,
That floureth yet, how foule I sholde it shende,
And with what filthe it spotted sholde be,
If in this forme I sholde with yow wende.
Ne though I livede un-to the worldes ende,
My name sholde I nevere ayeinward winne.
Thus were I lost, and that were routhe and sinne.

"And trusteth this, that certes, herte swete,
Er Phebus suster, Lucina the shene,
The Leoun passe out of this Ariete,
I wol ben heer, with-outen any wene.
I mene, as helpe me Iuno, hevenes quene,
The tenthe day, but-if that deeth me assayle,
I wol yow seen, with-outen any fayle."

"And now, so this be sooth," quod Troilus,
"I shal wel suffre un-to the tenthe day,
Sin that I see that nede it moot be thus.
But for the love of God, if it be may,
So lat us stele prively away!
For evere in oon, as for to live in reste,—
Myn herte seyth that it wol been the beste."

"O mercy, God, what lyf is this?" quod she;
"Allas, ye slee me thus for verray tene!
I see wel now that ye mistrusten me;
For by your wordes it is wel y-sene.
Now for the love of Cynthia, the shene,
Mistrust me not thus causeles, for routhe,
Sin to be trewe I have yow plight my trouthe.

"And thenketh wel that som tyme it is wit
To spende a tyme a tyme for to winne;
Ne, pardee, lorn am I nought fro yow yit,
Though that we been a day or two a-twinne.
Dryf out the fantasyes yow with-inne,
And trusteth me, and leveth eek your sorwe,
Or heer my trouthe, I wol not live til morwe.

"For if ye wiste how sore it doth me smerte,
Ye wolde cesse of this; for God, thou wost
The pure spirit wepeth in myn herte
To see yow wepen that I love most,
And that I moot gon to the Grekes ost.
Ye, nere it that I wiste remedye
To come ayein, right heer I wolde dye!

"And over al this, I pray yow," quod she tho,
"Myn owene hertes soothfast suffisaunce,
Sin I am thyn al hool, with-outen mo,
That whyl that I am absent, no plesaunce
Of othere do me fro your remembraunce.
For I am evere a-gast, for-why men rede
That 'Love is thing ay ful of bisy drede.' "

To this answerde Troilus and seyde,
"Now God, to whom ther nis no cause y-wrye,
Me glade, as wis I nevere un-to Criseyde,
Sin thilke day I saw hir first with yë,
Was fals ne nevere shal til that I dyë.
At shorte wordes, wel ye may me leve:
I can no more, it shal be founde at preve."

"Graunt mercy, goode myn, y-wis," quod she,
"And blisful Venus lat me nevere sterve
Er I may stonde of plesaunce in degree
To quyte him wel that so wel can deserve.
And whyl that God my wit wol me conserve,
I shal so doon, so trewe I have yow founde,
That ay honour to me-ward shal rebounde.

"For trusteth wel that your estat royal
Ne veyn delyt, nor only worthinesse
Of yow in werre, or torney marcial,
Ne pompe, array, nobleye, or eek richesse,
Ne made me to rewe on your distresse;
But moral vertu, grounded upon trouthe,
That was the cause I first had on yow routhe!

"And this may lengthe of yeres not for-do,
Ne remuable Fortune deface.
But Iuppiter, that of his might may do
The sorwful to be glad, so yeve us grace
Er nightes ten to meten in this place,
So that it may your herte and myn suffyse.
And fareth now wel, for tyme is that ye ryse."

And after that they longe y-pleyned hadde,
And ofte y-kist and streit in armes folde,
The day gan ryse, and Troilus him cladde,
And rewfulliche his lady gan biholde
As he that felte dethes cares colde.
And to hir grace he gan him recomaunde:
Wher him was wo, this holde I no demaunde.

For mannes heed imaginen ne can,
Ne entendement considere, ne tonge telle,
The cruel peynes of this sorwful man,
That passen every torment doun in helle.
For whan he saugh that she ne mighte dwelle,
Which that his soule out of his herte rente,
With-outen more, out of the chaumbre he wente.

Explicit Liber Quartus.

Book V

Incipit Liber Quintus

Aprochen gan the fatal destinee
That Ioves hath in disposicioun,
And to yow, angry Parcas, sustren three,
Committeth to don execucioun;
For which Criseyde moste out of the toun,
And Troilus shal dwelle forth in pyne
Til Lachesis his threed no lenger twyne.—

Ful redy was at pryme Dyomede,
Criseyde un-to the Grekes ost to lede,
For sorwe of which she felte hir herte blede
As she that niste what was best to rede.
And trewely, as men in bokes rede,
Men wiste nevere womman han the care
Ne was so looth out of a toun to fare.

This Troilus, with-outen reed or lore,
As man that hath his Ioyes eek forlore,
Was wayting on his lady evere-more
As she that was the soothfast crop and more
Of al his lust or Ioyes heer-tofore.
But Troilus, now farwel al thy Ioye,
For shaltow nevere seen hir eft in Troye!

Soth is that whyl he bood in this manere,
He gan his wo ful manly for to hyde,
That wel unnethe it seen was in his chere.
But at the yate ther she sholde oute ryde
With certeyn folk, he hoved hir tabyde
So wo bigoon, al wolde he nought him pleyne,
That on his hors unnethe he sat for peyne.

For ire he quook, so gan his herte gnawe,
Whan Diomede on horse gan him dresse,
And seyde un-to him-self this ilke sawe,
"Allas," quod he, "thus foul wrecchednesse
Why suffre ich it, why nil ich it redresse?
Were it not bet at ones for to dye
Than evere-more in langour thus to drye?

"Why nil I make at ones riche and pore
To have y-nough to done er that she go?
Why nil I bringe al Troye upon a rore?
Why nil I sleen this Diomede also?
Why nil I rather with a man or two
Stele hir a-way? Why wol I this endure?
Why nil I helpen to myn owene cure?"

But why he nolde doon so fel a dede,
That shal I seyn, and why him liste it spare:
He had in herte alwey a maner drede
Lest that Criseyde in rumour of this fare
Sholde han ben slayn; lo, this was al his care.
And elles, certeyn, as I seyde yore,
He had it doon, with-outen wordes more.

Criseyde, whan she redy was to ryde,
Ful sorwfully she sighte, and seyde, "Allas!"
But forth she moot for ought that may bityde,
And forth she rit ful sorwfully a pas.
Ther nis non other remedie in this cas.
What wonder is though that hir sore smerte,
Whan she forgoth hir owene swete herte?

This Troilus in wyse of curteisye,
With hauk on honde, and with an huge route
Of knightes, rood and did hir companye,
Passing al the valeye fer with-oute.
And ferther wolde han riden, out of doute,
Ful fayn, and wo was him to goon so sone,
But torne he moste, and it was eek to done.

And right with that was Antenor y-come
Out of the Grekes ost, and every wight
Was of it glad, and seyde he was wel-come.
And Troilus, al nere his herte light,
He peyned him with al his fulle might
Him to with-holde of weping at the leste,
And Antenor he kiste, and made feste.

And ther-with-al he moste his leve take,
And caste his eye upon hir pitously,
And neer he rood his cause for to make,
To take hir by the hond al sobrely.
And he ful softe and sleighly gan hir seye,
"Now hold your day, and dooth me not to deye!"

With that his courser torned he a-boute
With face pale, and un-to Diomede
No word he spak, ne noon of al his route;
Of which the sone of Tydeus took hede,
As he that coude more than the crede
In swich a craft, and by the reyne hir hente.
And Troilus to Troye homward he wente.

This Diomede, that ladde hir by the brydel,
Whan that he saw the folk of Troye aweye,
Thoughte, "Al my labour shal not been on ydel
If that I may, for somwhat shal I seye.
For at the worste it may yet shorte our weye.
I have herd seyd eek tymes twyës twelve,
'He is a fool that wol for-yete him-selve.'"

But natheles this thoughte he wel ynough,
"That certaynly I am aboute nought
If that I speke of love, or make it tough;
For douteles, if she have in hir thought
Him that I gesse, he may not been y-brought
So sone awey; but I shal finde a mene
That she not wite as yet shal what I mene."

This Diomede, as he that coude his good,
Whan this was doon gan fallen forth in speche
Of this and that, and asked why she stood
In swich disese, and gan hir eek biseche
That if that he encrese mighte or eche
With any thing hir ese, that she sholde
Comaunde it him, and seyde he doon it wolde.

For trewely he swoor hir as a knight
That ther nas thing with which he might hir plese,
That he nolde doon his peyne and al his might
To doon it for to doon hir herte an ese.
And preyede hir she wolde hir sorwe apese,
And seyde, "Y-wis, we Grekes con have Ioye
To honouren yow, as wel as folk of Troye."

He seyde eek thus, "I woot yow thinketh straunge—
No wonder is, for it is to yow newe—
Thaqueintaunce of these Troianes to chaunge
For folk of Grece that ye nevere knewe.
But wolde nevere God but-if as trewe
A Greek ye shulde among us alle finde
As any Troian is, and eek as kinde.

"And by the cause I swoor yow right, lo, now,
To been your freend, and helply, to my might,
And for that more acqueintaunce eek of yow
Have ich had than another straunger wight,
So fro this forth I pray yow, day and night,
Comaundeth me, how sore that me smerte,
To doon al that may lyke un-to your herte;

"And that ye me wolde as your brother trete,
And taketh not my frendship in despyt;
And though your sorwes be for thinges grete,
Noot I not why, but out of more respyt
Myn herte hath for to amende it greet delyt.
And if I may your harmes not redresse
I am right sory for your hevinesse.

"And nere it that we been so neigh the tente
Of Calkas, which that seen us bothe may,
I wolde of this yow telle al myn entente;
But this enseled til another day.
Yeve me your hond, I am and shal ben ay,
God helpe me so, whyl that my lyf may dure,
Your owene aboven every creature.

"Thus seyde I nevere er now to womman born;
For, God myn herte as wisly glade so,
I lovede nevere womman heer-biforn
As paramours, ne nevere shal no mo.
And, for the love of God, beth not my fo:
Al can I not to yow, my lady dere,
Compleyne aright, for I am yet to lere.

"And wondreth not, myn owene lady bright,
Though that I speke of love to you thus blyve;
For I have herd or this of many a wight
Hath loved thing he nevere saugh his lyve.
Eek I am not of power for to stryve
Ayens the God of Love, but him obeye
I wol alwey, and mercy I yow preye.

Sk., V, 127–140; 148–168

"Ther been so worthy knightes in this place,
And ye so fair, that everich of hem alle
Wol peynen him to stonden in your grace.
But mighte me so fair a grace falle
That ye me for your servaunt wolde calle,
So lowly ne so trewely you serve
Nil noon of hem as I shal til I sterve."

Criseyde un-to that purpos lyte answerde,
As she that was with sorwe oppressed so
That in effect she nought his tales herde
But heer and ther, now heer a word or two.
Hir thoughte hir sorwful herte brast a-two.
For whan she gan hir fader fer aspye,
Wel neigh doun of hir hors she gan to sye.

But natheles she thonked Diomede
Of al his travaile, and his goode chere,
And that him liste his friendship hir to bede;
And she accepteth it in good manere,
And wolde do fayn that is him leef and dere;
And trusten him she wolde, and wel she mighte,
As seyde she, and from hir hors she alighte.

Hir fader hath hir in his armes nome,
And twenty tyme he kiste his doughter swete,
And seyde, "O dere doughter myn, wel-come!"
She seyde eek she was fayn with him to mete,
And stood forth mewet, milde, and mansuete.
But heer I leve hir with hir fader dwelle,
And forth I wol of Troilus yow telle.

To Troie is come this woful Troilus,
In sorwe aboven alle sorwes smerte,
With felon look and face dispitous.
Tho sodeinly doun fro his hors he sterte,
And thorugh his paleys with a swollen herte
To chambre he wente. Of no-thing took he hede,
Ne noon to him dar speke a word for drede.

And ther his sorwes that he spared hadde
He yaf an issu large, and "Deeth!" he cryde;
And in his throwes frenetyk and madde
He cursedę Iove, Appollo, and eek Cupyde,
He cursedę Ceres, Bacus, and Cipryde,
His burthe, him-self, his fate, and eek nature,
And save his lady every creature.

And rewen on him-self so pitously
That wonder was to here his fantasye.
Another tyme he sholde mightily
Conforte him-self, and seyn it was folye
So causeles swich drede for to drye.
And eft biginne his aspre sorwes newe
That every man mighte on his sorwes rewe.

On hevene yet the sterres were sene,
Al-though ful pale y-waxen was the mone,
And whyten gan the orisonte shene
Al estward as it wonted is to done,
And Phebus with his rosy carte sone
Gan after that to dresse him up to fare,
Whan Troilus hath sent after Pandare.

This Pandarę, that of al the day biforn
Ne mighte have comen Troilus to see,
Al-though he on his heed it had y-sworn,
For with the King Pryam alday was he
So that it lay not in his libertee
No-wher to gon, but on the morwe he wente
To Troilus whan that he for him sente.

"My Pandarus," quod Troilus, "the sorwe
Which that I drye, I may not longe endure.
I trowe I shal not liven til to-morwe,
For which I wolde alwey, on aventure,
To thee devysen of my sepulture
The forme, and of my moeble thou dispone
Right as thee semeth best is for to done.

Sk., V, 204–210; 260–266; 274–287; 295–301

"But of the fyr and flaumbe funeral
In which my body brenne shal to glede,
And of the feste and pleyes palestral
At my vigile, I praye thee take good hede
That al be wel; and offre Mars my stede,
My swerd, myn helm, and, leve brother dere,
My sheld to Pallas yef, that shyneth clere.

"The poudre in which myn herte y-brend shal torne,
That preye I thee thou take and it conserve
In a vessel that men clepe an urne
Of gold, and to my lady that I serve,
For love of whom thus pitously I sterve,
So yef it hir, and do me this plesaunce
To preye hir kepe it for a remembraunce."

Pandare answerde, and seyde, "Troilus,
My dere freend, as I have told thee yore
That it is folye for to sorwen thus
And causeles, for which I can no-more.
But who-so wol not trowen reed ne lore,
I can not seen in him no remedye,
But lat him worthen with his fantasye.

"But Troilus, I pray thee, telle me now
If that thou trowe er this that any wight
Hath loved paramours as wel as thou?
Ye, God wot, and fro many a worthy knight
Hath his lady goon a fourtenight
And he not yet made halvendel the fare.
What nede is thee to maken al this care?

"For which with al myn herte I thee biseche
Un-to thy-self that al this thou foryive;
And rys up now with-oute more speche,
And lat us caste how forth may best be drive
This tyme, and eek how freshly we may live
Whan that she cometh, the which shal be right sone:
God helpe me so, the beste is thus to done."

Sk., V, 302–315; 323–336; 386–392

This Troilus answerde, "O brother dere,
This knowen folk that han y-suffred peyne,
That though he wepe and make sorwful chere,
That feleth harm and smert in every veyne,
No wonder is; and though I evere pleyne
Or alwey wepe, I am no-thing to blame,
Sin I have lost the cause of al my game.

"But sin of fyne force I moot aryse,
I shal aryse as sone as evere I may;
And God, to whom myn herte I sacrifyse,
So sende us hastely the tenthe day!
For was ther nevere fowl so fayn of May
As I shal been whan that she cometh in Troye
That cause is of my torment and my Ioye.

"But whider is thy reed," quod Troilus,
"That we may pleye us best in al this toun?"
"By God, my conseil is," quod Pandarus,
"To ryde and pleye us with King Sarpedoun."
So longe of this they speken up and doun,
Til Troilus gan at the laste assente
To ryse, and forth to Sarpedoun they wente.

Thus Pandarus with alle peyne and wo
Made him to dwelle, and at the woukes ende
Of Sarpedoun they toke hir leve tho,
And on hir wey they spedden hem to wende.
Quod Troilus, "Now God me grace sende
That I may finden at myn hom-cominge
Criseyde comen!" and ther-with gan he singe.

"Ye, hasel-wode!" thoughte this Pandare,
And to him-self ful softely he seyde,
"God woot, refreyden may this hote fare
Er Calkas sende Troilus Criseyde!"
But natheles he Iaped thus and seyde
And swor, y-wis, his herte him wel bihighte
She wolde come as sone as evere she mighte.

Sk., V, 414-434; 498-511

Whan they un-to the paleys were y-comen
Of Troilus, they doun of hors alighte,
And to the chambre hir wey than han they nomen.
And in-to tyme that it gan to nighte,
They spaken of Criseÿde the brighte.
And after this, whan that hem bothe leste,
They spedde hem fro the soper un-to reste.

On morwe, as sone as day bigan to clere,
This Troilus gan of his sleep tabreyde,
And to Pandare, his owene brother dere,
"For love of God," ful pitously he seyde,
"As go we seen the paleys of Criseyde;
For sin we yet may have namore feste,
So lat us seen hir paleys at the leste."

And ther-with-al, his meyne for to blende,
A cause he fond in toune for to go,
And to Criseydes hous they gonnen wende.
But Lord! this sely Troilus was wo!
Him thoughte his sorweful herte braste a-two;
For whan he saugh hir dores sperred alle,
Wel neigh for sorwe a-doun he gan to falle.

Therwith whan he was war and gan biholde
How shet was every windowe of the place,
As frost, him thoughte, his herte gan to colde;
For which with chaunged deedlich pale face,
With-outen word, he forth bigan to pace.
And as God wolde, he gan so faste ryde
That no wight of his contenaunce aspyde.

Than seyde he thus, "O paleys desolat,
O hous of houses whylom best y-hight,
O paleys empty and disconsolat,
O thou lanterne of which queynt is the light,
O paleys whylom day that now art night,
Wel oughtestow to falle and I to dye,
Sin she is went that wont was us to gye!"

Ther-with he caste on Pandarus his yë
With chaunged face, and pitous to biholde.
And whan he mighte his tyme aright aspye,
Ay as he rood to Pandarus he tolde
His newe sorwe, and eek his Ioyes olde,
So pitously and with so dede an hewe,
That every wight mighte on his sorwe rewe.

Fro thennesforth he rydeth up and doun,
And every thing com him to remembraunce
As he rood forth by places of the toun
In which he whylom had al his plesaunce.
"Lo, yond saugh I myn owene lady daunce,
And in that temple with hir eyen clere
Me caughte first my righte lady dere.

"And yonder have I herd ful lustily
My dere herte laughe, and yonder pleye
Saugh I hir ones eek ful blisfully.
And yonder ones to me gan she seye,
'Now goode swete, love me wel, I preye!'
And yond so goodly gan she me biholde
That to the deeth myn herte is to hir holde."

Than thoughte he thus, "O blisful lord Cupyde,
Whan I the proces have in my memorie
How thou me hast werreyed on every syde,
Men mighte a book make of it, lyk a storie.
What nede is thee to seke on me victorie,
Sin I am thyn, and hoolly at thy wille?
What Ioye hastow thyn owene folk to spille?

"Wel hastow, lord, y-wroke on me thyn ire,
Thou mighty god, and dredful for to greve!
Now mercy, lord, thou wost wel I desire
Thy grace most, of alle lustes leve.
And live and deye I wol in thy bileve,
For which I naxe in guerdon but a bone,
That thou Criseyde ayein me sende sone."

Sk., V, 554-574; 582-595

And after this he to the yates wente
Ther-as Criseyde out-rood a ful good paas,
And up and doun ther made he many a wente,
And to him-self ful ofte he seyde "Allas!
From hennes rood my blisse and my solas!
As wolde blisful God now for his Ioye
I mighte hir seen ayein come in-to Troye."

Upon the walles faste eek wolde he walke,
And on the Grekes ost he wolde see,
And to him-self right thus he wolde talke,
"Lo, yonder is myn owene lady free,
Or elles yonder ther tho tentes be!
And thennes comth this eyr that is so sote
That in my soule I fele it doth me bote."

This longe tyme he dryveth forth right thus,
Til fully passed was the nynthe night;
And ay bi-syde him was this Pandarus,
That bisily did al his fulle might
Him to comforte and make his herte light,
Yeving him hope alwey, the tenthe morwe
That she shal come and stinten al his sorwe.

Up-on that other syde eek was Criseyde
With wommen fewe among the Grekes stronge,
For which ful ofte a day "Allas!" she seyde,
"That I was born! Wel may myn herte longe
After my deeth; for now live I to longe!
Allas! and I ne may it not amende,
For now is wors than evere yet I wende.

"My fader nil for no-thing do me grace
To goon ayein, for nought I can him queme;
And if so be that I my terme passe,
My Troilus shal in his herte deme
That I am fals, and so it may wel seme.
Thus shal I have unthank on every syde.
That I was born, so welawey the tyde!

Sk., V, 603–609; 666–672; 680–700

"And if that I me putte in Iupartye
To stele awey by night, and it bifalle
That I be caught, I shal be holde a spye;
Or elles,—lo, this drede I most of alle,—
If in the hondes of som wrecche I falle,
I am but lost, al be myn herte trewe.
Now mighty God, thou on my sorwe rewe!"

Ful pale y-waxen was hir brighte face,
Hir limes lene, as she that al the day
Stood whan she dorste and loked on the place
Ther she was born and ther she dwelte had ay.
And al the night weping, allas! she lay.
And thus despeired, out of alle cure,
She ladde hir lyf, this woful creature.

Ful ofte a day she sighte eek for destresse,
And in hir-self she wente ay portrayinge
Of Troilus the grete worthinesse,
And alle his goodly wordes recordinge
Sin first that day hir love bigan to springe.
And thus she sette hir woful herte a-fyre
Thorugh remembraunce of that she gan desyre.

Ful rewfully she loked up-on Troye,
Biheld the toures heighe and eek the halles.
"Allas!" quod she, "the plesaunce and the Ioye,
The which that now al torned in-to galle is,
Have I had ofte with-inne yonder walles!
O Troilus, what dostow now?" she seyde.
"Lord! whether yet thou thenke up-on Criseyde?

"Allas! I ne hadde trowed on your lore
And went with yow, as ye me radde er this!
Than hadde I now not syked half so sore.
Who mighte have seyd that I had doon a-mis
To stele awey with swich on as he is?
But al to late cometh the letuarie
Whan men the cors un-to the grave carie.

Sk., V, 701-721; 729-742

"But natheles, bityde what bityde,
I shal to-morwe at night, by est or west,
Out of this ost stele on som maner syde,
And go with Troilus wher-as him lest.
This purpos wol I holde, and this is best.
No fors of wikked tonges Ianglerye,
For evere on love han wrecches had envye.

"For which, with-outen any wordes mo,
To Troye I wol, as for conclusioun."
But God it wot, er fully monthes two,
She was ful fer fro that entencioun.
For bothe Troilus and Troye toun
Shal knotteles through-oute hir herte slyde;
For she wol take a purpos for tabyde.

This Diomede, of whom yow telle I gan,
Goth now with-in him-self ay arguinge
With al the sleighte and al that evere he can
How he may best with shortest taryinge
In-to his net Criseydes herte bringe.
To this entente he coude nevere fyne;
To fisshen hir he leyde out hook and lyne.

But natheles wel in his herte he thoughte
That she nas nat with-oute a love in Troye.
For nevere sithen he hir thennes broughte
Ne coude he seen her laughe or make Ioye.
He niste how best hir herte for tacoye.
"But for to assaye," he seyde, "it nought ne greveth;
For he that nought assayeth nought nacheveth."

Yet seide he to him-self upon a night,
"Now am I not a fool, that woot wel how
Hir wo for love is of another wight,
And heer-up-on to goon assaye hir now?
I may wel wite, it nil not been my prow.
For wyse folk in bokes it expresse,
'Men shal not wowe a wight in hevinesse.'

Sk., V, 750–756; 764–791

"But who-so mighte winnen swich a flour
From him for whom she morneth night and day,
He mighte seyn he were a conquerour."
And right anoon, as he that bold was ay,
Thoughte in his herte, "Happe how happe may,
Al sholde I deye, I wol hir herte seche.
I shal no more lesen but my speche."

This Diomede, as bokes us declare,
Was in his nedes prest and corageous;
With sterne voys and mighty limes square,
Hardy, testif, strong, and chevalrous
Of dedes, lyk his fader Tideus,
And som men seyn he was of tunge large;
And heir he was of Calidoine and Arge.

Criseyde mene was of hir stature,
Ther-to of shap, of face, and eek of chere,
Ther mighte been no fairer creature.
And ofte tyme this was hir manere,
To gon y-tressed with hir heres clere
Doun by hir coler at hir bak bihinde,
Which with a threed of gold she wolde binde.

And save hir browes Ioyneden y-fere,
Ther nas no lak in ought I can espyen.
But for to speken of hir eyen clere,
Lo, trewely, they writen that hir syën
That Paradys stood formed in hir yën.
And with hir riche beautee evere-more
Strof love in hir ay which of hem was more.

She sobre was, eek simple and wys with-al,
The best y-norisshed eek that mighte be,
And goodly of hir speche in general,
Charitable, estatlich, lusty, and free;
Ne nevere-mo ne lakkede hir pitee;
Tendre-herted, slyding of corage; *of a drifting nature*
But trewely I can not telle hir age.

Sk., V, 792–826

Tendency to please

always rubbing people the right way

But for to tellen forth of Diomede:—
It fil that after on the tenthe day
Sin that Criseyde out of the citee yede,
This Diomede, as fresshe as braunche in May,
Com to the tente ther-as Calkas lay,
And feyned him with Calkas han to done;
But what he mente I shal yow telle sone.

Criseyde, at shorte wordes for to telle,
Welcomed him, and doun by hir him sette;
And he was ethe y-nough to maken dwelle.
And after this with-outen longe lette
The spyces and the wyn men forth hem fette;
And forth they speke of this and that y-fere,
As freendes doon, of which som ye shal here.

He gan first fallen of the werre in speche
Bitwixe hem and the folk of Troye toun;
And of thassege he gan hir eek byseche
To telle him what was hir opinoun.
Fro that demaunde he so descendeth doun
To asken hir if that hir straunge thoughte
The Grekes gyse, and werkes that they wroughte;

And why hir fader tarieth so longe
To wedden hir un-to som worthy wight.
Criseyde, that was in hir peynes stronge
For love of Troilus, hir owene knight,
As ferforth as she conning had or might,
Answerde him tho; but as of his entente,
It semed not she wiste what he mente.

But natheles, this ilke Diomede
Gan in him-self assure, and thus he seyde:
"If ich aright have taken of yow hede,
Me thinketh thus, O lady myn, Criseyde,
That sin I first hond on your brydel leyde,
Whan ye oute come of Troye by the morwe,
Ne coude I nevere seen yow but in sorwe.

"Can I not seyn what may the cause be
But-if for love of som Troyan it were,
The which right sore wolde athinken me
That ye for any wight that dwelleth there
Sholden spille a quarter of a tere,
Or pitously your-selven so bigyle.
For dredelees, it is nought worth the whyle.

"The folk of Troye, as who seyth, alle and some
In preson been, as ye your-selven see;
For thennes shal not oon on-lyve come
For al the gold bitwixen sonne and see.
For trusteth wel, and understondeth me,
Ther shal not oon to mercy goon on-lyve,
Al were he lord of worldes twyës fyve!

"Swich wreche on hem for fecching of Eleyne
Ther shal be take, er that we hennes wende,
That Manes, which that goddes ben of peyne,
Shal been agast that Grekes wol hem shende.
And men shul drede, un-to the worldes ende,
From hennes-forth to ravisshe any quene,
So cruel shal our wreche on hem be sene.

"And but-if Calkas lede us with ambages,
That is to seyn, with double wordes slye,
Swich as men clepe a 'word with two visages,'
Ye shul wel knowen that I nought ne lye,
And al this thing right seen it with your yë,
And that anoon, ye nil not trowe how sone.
Now taketh hede, for it is for to done.

"What wene ye your wyse fader wolde
Han yeven Antenor for yow anoon,
If he ne wiste that the citee sholde
Destroyed been? Why nay, so mote I goon!
He knew ful wel ther shal not scapen oon
That Troyan is; and for the grete fere
He dorste not ye dwelte lenger there.

Sk., V, 876-910

"What wolę ye more, lufsom lady dere?
Lat Troye and Troyan fro your herte pace!
Dryf oute that bittre hope and make good chere,
And clepe ayein the beautee of your face
That ye with salte teres so deface.
For Troye is brought in swich a Iupartye
That, it to save, is now no remedye.

"And thenketh wel, ye shal in Grekes finde
A more parfit love er it be night
Than any Troyan is, and more kinde,
And bet to serven yow wol doon his might.
And if ye vouche sauf, my lady bright,
I wol ben he to serven yow my-selve,
Ye, lever than be lord of Greces twelve!"

And with that word he gan to waxen reed,
And in his speche a litel wight he quook,
And caste a-syde a litel wight his heed,
And stinte a whyle; and afterward awook,
And sobreliche on hir he threw his look,
And seyde, "I am, al be it yow no Ioye,
As gentil man as any wight in Troye.

"For if my fader Tydeus," he seyde,
"Y-lived had, I hadde been er this
Of Calidoine and Arge a king, Criseyde!
And so hope I that I shal yet, y-wis.
But he was slayn, allas! the more harm is,
Unhappily at Thebes al to rathe,
Polymites and many a man to scathe.

"But herte myn, sin that I am your man,
And been the ferste of whom I seche grace
To serven you as hertely as I can
And evere shal, whyl I to livę havę space,
So, er that I departe out of this place,
Ye wol me graunte that I may to-morwe
At bettre leyser telle yow my sorwe."

What sholde I telle his wordes that he seyde?
He spak y-now for o day at the meste.
It preveth wel he spak so that Criseyde
Graunted, on the morwe, at his requeste
For to speken with him at the leste,
So that he nolde speke of swich matere;
And thus to him she seyde, as ye may here,

As she that had hir herte on Troilus
So faste that ther may it noon arace;
And straungely she spak, and seyde thus:
"O Diomede, I love that ilke place
Ther I was born; and Ioves, for his grace,
Delivere it sone of al that doth it care!
God, for thy might, so leve it wel to fare!

"That Grekes wolde hir wraththe on Troye wreke,
If that they mighte, I knowe it wel, y-wis;
But it shal not bifallen as ye speke.
And God to-forn, and ferther over this,
I wot my fader wys and redy is;
And that he me hath bought, as ye me tolde,
So dere, I am the more un-to him holde.

"That Grekes been of heigh condicioun,
I woot eek wel. But certein, men shal finde
As worthy folk with-inne Troye toun,
As conning, and as parfit, and as kinde,
As been bitwixen Orcades and Inde.
And that ye coude wel your lady serve,
I trowe eek wel, hir thank for to deserve.

"But as to speke of love, y-wis," she seyde,
"I had a lord to whom I wedded was,
The whos myn herte al was til that he deyde.
And other love, as helpe me now Pallas,
Ther in myn herte nis, ne nevere was.
And that ye been of noble and heigh kinrede,
I have wel herd it tellen, out of drede.

"And that doth me to han so gret a wonder,
That ye wol scornen any womman so.
Eek, God wot, love and I be fer a-sonder;
I am disposed bet, so mote I go,
Un-to my deeth, to pleyne and maken wo.
What I shal after doon, I can not seye,
But trewely as yet me list not pleye.

"To-morwe eek wol I speke with yow fayn,
So that ye touchen nought of this matere.
And whan yow list, ye may come heer ayein.
And er ye gon, thus muche I seye yow here:
As helpe me Pallas with hir heres clere,
If that I sholde of any Greek han routhe,
It sholde be your-selven, by my trouthe!

"I sey not therfore that I wol yow love,
Ne I sey not nay, but in conclusioun,
I mene wel, by God that sit above!"
And ther-with-al she caste hir eyen doun,
And gan to syke, and seyde, "O Troye toun,
Yet bidde I God, in quiete and in reste
I may yow seen, or do myn herte breste."

But in effect, and shortly for to seye,
This Diomede al freshly newe ayeyn
Gan pressen on, and faste hir mercy preye;
And after this, the sothe for to seyn,
Hir glove he took, of which he was ful fayn.
And fynally whan it was waxen eve
And al was wel, he roos and took his leve.

The brighte Venus folwede and ay taughte
The wey ther brode Phebus doun alighte;
And Cynthea hir char-hors over-raughte
To whirle out of the Lyon, if she mighte;
And Signifer his candeles shewed brighte
Whan that Criseyde un-to hir bedde wente
In-with hir fadres faire brighte tente.

Sk., V, 981-987; 995-1022

Retorning in hir soule ay up and doun
The wordes of this sodein Diomede,
His greet estat, and peril of the toun,
And that she was allone and hadde nede
Of freendes help; and thus bigan to brede
The cause why, the sothe for to telle,
That she tok fully purpos for to dwelle.

The morwe com, and goostly for to speke,
This Diomede is come un-to Criseyde,
And shortly, lest that ye my tale breke,
So wel he for him-selve spak and seyde,
That alle hir sykes sore adoun he leyde.
And fynally, the sothe for to seyne,
He refte hir of the grete of al hir peyne.

And after this, the storye telleth us
That she him yaf the faire baye stede,
The which she ones wan of Troilus;
And eek a brooch (and that was litel nede)
That Troilus was, she yaf this Diomede.
And eek the bet from sorwe him to releve,
She made him were a pencel of hir sleve.

I finde eek in the stories elles-where,
Whan through the body hurt was Diomede
Of Troilus, tho weep she many a tere
Whan that she saugh his wyde woundes blede;
And that she took to kepen him good hede,
And for to hele him of his sorwes smerte.
Men seyn—I not—that she yaf him hir herte.

But trewely the storye telleth us
Ther made nevere womman more wo
Than she whan that she falsed Troilus.
She seyde, "Allas! for now is clene a-go
My name of trouthe in love for evere-mo!
For I have falsed oon the gentileste
That evere was, and oon the worthieste!

"Allas! of me un-to the worldes ende
Shal neither been y-writen nor y-songe
No good word, for thisę bokes wol me shende.
O, rolled shal I been on many a tonge,
Through-outę the world my belle shal be ronge,
And wommen most wol hate me of alle!
Allas, that swich a cas me sholde falle!

"They wol seyn, in as muche as in me is,
I have hem don dishonour, weylawey!
Al be I not the firstę that did amis,
What helpeth that to do my blame awey?
But sin I see ther is no bettre way,
And that to late is now for me to rewe,
To Diomede algate I wol be trewe.

"But Troilus, sin I no bettre may,
And sin that thus departen ye and I,
Yet preyę I God so yevę yow right good day
As for the gentileste, trewely,
That evere I say to serven feithfully,
And best can ay his lady honour kepe:"
And with that word she braste anon to wepe.

But trewely, how longe it was bitwene
That she for-sook him for this Diomede,
Ther is non auctor telleth it, I wene.
Take every man now to his bokes hede;
He shal no terme finden, out of drede.
For though that he bigan to wowe hir sone,
Er he hir wan yet was ther morę to done.

Ne me ne list this sely womman chyde
Ferther than the storyę wol devyse.
Hir name, allas! is publisshed so wyde
That for hir gilt it oughte y-now suffyse.
And if I mighte excuse hir any wyse,
For she so sory was for hir untrouthe,
Y-wis, I wolde excuse hir yet for routhe.

This Troilus, as I biforn have told,
Thus dryveth forth as wel as he hath might.
But often was his herte hoot and cold,
And namely that ilke nynthe night
Which on the morwe she hadde him byhight
To come ayein. God wot, ful litel reste
Had he that night; no-thing to slepe him leste.

The laurer-crouned Phebus with his hete
Gan in his cours ay upward as he wente
To warmen of the est see the wawes wete;
And Nisus doughter song with freshe entente,
Whan Troilus his Pandare after sente,
And on the walles of the toun they pleyde
To loke if they can seen ought of Criseyde.

Til it was noon they stoden for to see
Who that ther come; and every maner wight
That cam fro fer, they seyden it was she
Til that they coude knowen him a-right.
Now was his herte dul, now was it light.
And thus by-iaped stonden for to stare
Aboute nought, this Troilus and Pandare.

To Pandarus this Troilus tho seyde,
"For ought I wot, bi-fore noon sikerly
In-to this toun ne comth nought heer Criseyde.
She hath y-now to done, hardily,
To winnen from hir fader, so trowe I.
Hir olde fader wol yet make hir dyne
Er that she go, God yeve his herte pyne!"

Pandare answerde, "It may wel be, certeyn,
And for-thy lat us dyne, I thee biseche,
And after noon than mayst thou come ayeyn."
And hoom they go, with-oute more speche;
And comen ayein, but longe may they seche
Er that they finde that they after cape.
Fortune hem bothe thenketh for to Iape.

Sk., V, 1100-1134

Quod Troilus, "I see wel now that she
Is taried with hir olde fader so
That er she come it wol neigh even be.
Com forth, I wol un-to the yate go.
Thise portours been unkonning evere-mo;
And I wol doon hem holden up the yate
As nought ne were, al-though she come late."

The day goth faste, and after that comth eve,
And yet com nought to Troilus Criseyde.
He loketh forth by hegge, by tree, by greve,
And fer his heed over the wal he leyde.
And at the laste he torned him and seyde,
"By God, I woot hir mening now, Pandare!
Almost, y-wis, al newe was my care.

"Now douteles, this lady can hir good;
I woot she meneth ryden prively.
I comende hir wysdom, by myn hood!
She wol not maken peple nycely
Gaure on hir whan she comth; but softely
By night in-to the toun she thenketh ryde.
And, dere brother, thenk not longe to abyde.

"We han nought elles for to don, y-wis.
And Pandarus, now woltow trowen me?
Have heer thy trouthe, I see hir! Yond she is!
Heve up thyn eyen, man! Maystow not see?"
Pandare answerde, "Nay, so mote I thee!
Al wrong, by God! What seystow, man, wher arte?
That I see yond nis but a fare-carte."

The wardein of the yates gan to calle
The folk which that with-oute the yates were,
And bad hem dryven in hir bestes alle,
Or al the night they moste blyven there.
And fer with-in the night, with many a tere
This Troilus gan hoomward for to ryde;
For wel he seeth it helpeth nought tabyde.

But natheles, he gladded him in this:
He thoughte he misacounted had his day.
And seyde, "I understonde have al a-mis;
For thilke night I last Criseyde say,
She seyde, 'I shal ben heer, if that I may,
Er that the mone, O dere herte swete,
The Lyon passe, out of this Ariete;'

"For which she may yet holde al hir biheste."
And on the morwe un-to the yate he wente,
And up and down, by west and eek by este,
Up-on the walles made he many a wente.
But al for nought; his hope alwey him blente,
For which at night, in sorwe and sykes sore,
He wente him hoom, with-outen any more.

The thridde, ferthe, fifte, sixte day
After tho dayes ten, of which I tolde,
Bitwixen hope and drede his herte lay,
Yet som-what trusting on hir hestes olde.
But whan he saugh she nolde hir terme holde,
He can now seen non other remedye
But for to shape him sone for to dye.

Ther-with the wikked spirit, God us blesse,
Which that men clepeth the wode Ialousye,
Gan in him crepe in al this hevinesse;
For which, by-cause he wolde sone dye,
He ne eet ne dronk, for his malencolye,
And eek from every companye he fledde.
This was the lyf that al the tyme he ledde.

He so defet was that no maner man
Unnethe mighte him knowe ther he wente;
So was he lene, and ther-to pale and wan
And feble that he walketh by potente.
And with his ire he thus him-selven shente;
And who-so axed him wher-of him smerte,
He seyde, his harm was al aboute his herte.

Sk., V, 1184-1197; 1205-1225

Pryam ful ofte, and eek his moder dere,
His bretheren and his sustren gonne him freyne
Why he so sorwful was in al his chere,
And what thing was the cause of al his peyne.
But al for nought; he nolde his cause pleyne,
But seyde he felte a grevous maladye
A-boute his herte and fayn he wolde dye.

So on a day he leyde him doun to slepe,
And so bifel that in his sleep him thoughte
That in a forest faste he welk to wepe
For love of hir that him these peynes wroughte.
And up and doun as he the forest soughte,
He mette he saugh a boor with tuskes grete
That sleep ayein the brighte sonnes hete.

And by this boor, faste in his armes folde,
Lay kissing ay his lady bright Criseyde;
For sorwe of which, whan he it gan biholde,
And for despyt, out of his sleep he breyde,
And loude he cryde on Pandarus, and seyde,
"O Pandarus, now knowe I crop and rote!
I nam but deed, ther nis non other bote!

"My lady bright Criseyde hath me bitrayed,
In whom I trusted most of any wight;
She elles-wher hath now hir herte apayed.
The blisful goddes through hir grete might
Han in my dreem y-shewed it ful right.
Thus in my dreem Criseyde I have biholde:"—
And al this thing to Pandarus he tolde.

Pandare answerde and seyde, "Allas the whyle
That I was born! Have I not seyd er this
That dremes many a maner man bigyle?
And why? for folk expounden hem a-mis.
How darstow seyn that fals thy lady is
For any dreem, right for thyn owene drede?
Lat be this thought, thou canst no dremes rede.

Sk., V, 1226-1253; 1275-1281

"Paraunter, ther thou dremest of this boor,
It may so be that it may signifye
Hir fader, which that old is and eek hoor,
Ayein the sonne lyth on poynt to dye,
And she for sorwe ginneth wepe and crye,
And kisseth him ther he lyth on the grounde:
Thus shuldestow thy dreem a-right expounde."

"How mighte I thanne do?" quod Troilus,
"To knowe of this, ye, were it nevere so lyte?"
"Now seystow wysly," quod this Pandarus;
"My reed is this, sin thou canst wel endyte,
That hastely a lettre thou hir wryte,
Thorugh which thou shalt wel bringen it aboute
To knowe a sooth of that thou art in doute.

"And see now why: for this I dar wel seyn,
That if so is that she untrewe be,
I can not trowe that she wol wryte ayeyn.
And if she wryte, thou shalt ful sone see
As whether she hath any libertee
To come ayein, or elles in som clause,
If she be let, she wol assigne a cause."

Acorded been to this conclusioun,
And that anoon, these ilke lordes two;
And hastely sit Troilus adoun
And rolleth in his herte to and fro
How he may best discryven hir his wo.
And to Criseyde, his owene lady dere,
He wroot right thus, and seyde as ye may here:

"Right fresshe flour, whos I have been and shal,
With-outen part of elles-wher servyse,
With herte, body, lyf, lust, thought, and al:
I, woful wight, in every humble wyse
That tonge telle or herte may devyse,
As ofte as matere occupyeth place,
Me recomaunde un-to your noble grace.

"Lyketh it yow to witen, swete herte,
As ye wel knowe how longe tyme agoon
That ye me lafte in aspre peynes smerte
Whan that ye wente, of which yet bote noon
Have I noon had, but evere wers bigoon
Fro day to day am I, and so mot dwelle
Whyl it yow list, of wele and wo my welle!

"And if so be my gilt hath deeth deserved,
Or if you list no more up-on me see,
In guerdon yet of that I have yow served,
Biseche I yow, myn hertes lady free,
That heer-upon ye wolden wryte me,
For love of God, my righte lode-sterre,
Ther deeth may make an ende of al my werre;

"If other cause aught doth yow for to dwelle,
That with your lettre ye me recomforte.
For though to me your absence is an helle,
With pacience I wol my wo comporte.
And with your lettre of hope I wol desporte.
Now wryteth, swete, and lat me thus not pleyne:
With hope or deeth delivereth me fro peyne.

"Y-wis, myn owene dere herte trewe,
I woot that whan ye next up-on me see,
So lost have I myn hele and eek myn hewe,
Criseyde shal nought conne knowe me!
Y-wis, myn hertes day, my lady free,
So thursteth ay myn herte to biholde
Your beautee that my lyf unnethe I holde.
                              Le vostre T."

This lettre forth was sent un-to Criseyde,
Of which hir answere in effect was this:
Ful pitously she wroot ayein, and seyde
That al-so sone as that she mighte, y-wis,
She wolde come, and mende al that was mis.
And fynally she wroot and seyde him thanne
She wolde come, ye, but she niste whanne.

Sk., V, 1324-1330; 1387-1407; 1422-1428

But in hir lettre made she swich festes
That wonder was, and swereth she loveth him best,
Of which he fond but botmelees bihestes.
But Troilus, thou mayst now est or west
Pype in an ivy leef, if that thee lest:
Thus gooth the world! God shilde us fro mischaunce,
And every wight that meneth trouthe avaunce!

Fortune, which that permutacioun
Of thinges hath as it is hir committed
Through purveyaunce and disposicioun
Of heighe Iove, as regnes shal ben flitted
Fro folk in folk, or whan they shal ben smitted,
Gan pulle awey the fetheres brighte of Troye
Fro day to day, til they ben bare of Ioye.

Among al this, the fyn of the parodie
Of Ector gan approchen wonder blyve;
The fate wolde his soule sholde unbodie,
And shapen had a mene it oute to dryve,
Ayeins which fate him helpeth not to stryve.
But on a day to fighten gan he wende,
At which, allas! he caughte his lyves ende.

For whom, as olde bokes tellen us,
Was mad swich wo that tonge it may not telle;
And namely the sorwe of Troilus,
That next him was of worthinesse welle.
And in this wo gan Troilus to dwelle,
That, what for sorwe and love and for unreste,
Ful ofte a day he bad his herte breste.

But natheles, though he gan him dispeyre,
And dradde ay that his lady was untrewe,
Yet ay on hir his herte gan repeyre.
And as these loveres doon, he soughte ay newe
To gete ayein Criseyde, bright of hewe.
And in his herte he wente hir excusinge
That Calkas causede al hir taryinge.

Sk., V, 1429-1435; 1541-1554; 1562-1575

And ofte tyme he was in purpos grete
Him-selven lyk a pilgrim to disgyse
To seen hir; but he may not contrefete
To been unknowen of folk that weren wyse,
Ne finde excuse aright that may suffyse,
If he among the Grekes knowen were;
For which he weep ful ofte many a tere.

To hir he wroot yet ofte tyme al newe
Ful pitously, he lefte it nought for slouthe,
Biseching hir that sin that he was trewe
That she wolde come ayein and holde hir trouthe.
For which Criseyde up-on a day for routhe,
I take it so, touching al this matere,
Wrot him ayein, and seyde as ye may here:

"Cupydes sone, ensample of goodlihede,
O swerd of knighthod, sours of gentilesse!
How mighte a wight in torment and in drede
And helelees, yow sende as yet gladnesse?
I hertelees, I syk, I in distresse,
Sin ye with me nor I with yow may dele,
Yow neither sende ich herte may, nor hele.

"Your lettres ful, the papir al y-pleynted,
Conseyved hath myn hertes piëtee;
I have eek seyn with teres al depeynted
Your lettre, and how that ye requeren me
To come ayein, which yet ne may not be.
But why, lest that this lettre founden were,
No mencioun ne make I now for fere.

"For I have herd wel more than I wende,
Touching us two, how thinges han y-stonde,
Which I shal with dissimuling amende.
And—beth nought wrooth—I have eek understonde
How ye ne doon but holden me in honde.
But now no fors, I can not in yow gesse
But alle trouthe and alle gentilesse.

Sk., V, 1576–1603; 1611–1617

"Comen I wol, but yet in swich disioynte
I stonde as now, that what yeer or what day
That this shal be, that can I not apoynte.
But in effect, I prey yow, as I may,
Of your good word and of your frendship ay.
For trewely, whyl that my lyf may dure,
As for a freend ye may in me assure.
                     La vostre C."

This Troilus this lettre thoughte al straunge
Whan he it saugh, and sorwefully he sighte.
Him thoughte it lyk a kalendes of chaunge;
But fynally he ful ne trowen mighte
That she ne wolde him holden that she highte.
For with ful yvel wille list him to leve
That loveth wel, in swich cas, though him greve.

Stood on a day in his malencolye
This Troilus, and in suspecioun
Of hir for whom he wende for to dye.
And so bifel that through-oute Troye toun,
As was the gyse, y-bore was up and doun
A maner cote-armure, as seyth the storie,
Biforn Deiphebe in signe of his victorie,

The whiche cote, as telleth Lollius,
Deiphebe it had y-rent from Diomede
The same day. And whan this Troilus
It saugh, he gan to taken of it hede,
Avysing of the lengthe and of the brede,
And al the werk. But as he gan biholde,
Ful sodeinly his herte gan to colde,

As he that on the coler fond with-inne
A brooch, that he Criseyde yaf that morwe
That she from Troye moste nedes twinne,
In remembraunce of him and of his sorwe;
And she him leyde ayein hir feyth to borwe
To kepe it ay. But now ful wel he wiste
His lady nas no lenger on to triste.

Sk., V, 1618–1624; 1632–1638; 1646–1666

He gooth him hoom, and gan ful sone sende
For Pandarus; and al this newe chaunce
And of this brooch he tolde him word and ende,
Compleyning of hir hertes variaunce,
His longe love, his trouthe, and his penaunce.
And after deeth, with-outen wordes more,
Ful faste he cryde his reste him to restore.

Than spak he thus: "O lady myn Criseyde,
Wher is your feyth, and wher is your biheste?
Wher is your love, wher is your trouthe?" he seyde.
"Of Diomede have ye now al this feste!
Allas! I wolde have trowed at the leste
That, sin ye nolde in trouthe to me stonde,
That ye thus nolde han holden me in honde!

"O Pandare, that in dremes for to triste
Me blamed hast, and wont art ofte up-breyde,
Now maystow see thy-selve, if that thee liste,
How trewe is now thy nece, bright Criseyde!
In sondry formes, God it woot," he seyde,
"The goddes shewen bothe Ioye and tene
In sleep, and by my dreem it is now sene.

"And certaynly, with-oute more speche,
From hennesforth, as ferforth as I may,
Myn owene deeth in armes wol I seche.
I recche not how sone be the day!
But trewely, Criseyde, swete may,
Whom I have ay with al my might y-served,
That ye thus doon I have it nought deserved."

This Pandarus that alle these thinges herde,
And wiste wel he seyde a sooth of this,
He nought a word ayein to him answerde;
For sory of his frendes sorwe he is,
And shamed, for his nece hath doon a-mis.
And stant astoned of these causes tweye
As stille as stoon: a word ne coude he seye.

But at the laste thus he spak, and seyde,
"My brother dere, I may thee do no-more.
What shulde I seyn? I hate, y-wis, Criseyde!
And God wot, I wol hate hir everemore!
And that thou me bisoughtest doon of yore,
Having un-to myn honour ne my reste
Right no reward I did al that thee leste.

"If I did ought that mighte lyken thee,
It is me leef. And of this treson now,
God woot that it a sorwe is un-to me!
And dredelees, for hertes ese of yow,
Right fayn wolde I amende it, wiste I how.
And fro this world, almighty God I preye
Delivere hir sone: I can no-more seye!"

Gret was the sorwe and pleynte of Troilus;
But forth hir cours Fortune ay gan to holde.
Criseyde loveth the sone of Tydeus,
And Troilus mot wepe in cares colde.
Swich is this world; who-so it can biholde,
In ech estat is litel hertes reste.
God leve us for to take it for the beste!

In many cruel batayle, out of drede,
Of Troilus, this ilke worthy knight,
As men may in these olde bokes rede,
Was sene his knighthod and his grete might.
And dredelees, his ire day and night
Ful cruelly the Grekes ay aboughte;
And alwey most this Diomede he soughte.

And ofte tyme I finde that they mette
With blody strokes and with wordes grete,
Assaying how hir speres weren whette;
And God it woot, with many a cruel hete
Gan Troilus upon his helm to-bete.
But natheles, Fortune it nought ne wolde,
Of otheres hond that either deyen sholde.

The wraththe, as I began yow for to seye,
Of Troilus, the Grekes boughten dere;
For thousandes his hondes maden deye,
As he that was with-outen any pere,
Save Ector in his tyme, as I can here.
But weylaway, save only Goddes wille,
Dispitously him slough the fiers Achille.

And whan that he was slayn in this manere,
His lighte goost ful blisfully is went
Up to the holownesse of the seventh spere,
In convers leting every element;
And ther he saugh with ful avysement
The erratik sterres, herkening armonye
With sounes fulle of hevenish melodye.

And doun from thennes faste he gan avyse
This litel spot of erthe, that with the see
Embraced is, and fully gan despyse
This wrecched world, and held al vanitee
To respect of the pleyn felicitee
That is in hevene above; and at the laste,
Ther he was slayn, his loking doun he caste.

And in him-self he lough right at the wo
Of hem that wepten for his deeth so faste;
And dampned al our werk that folweth so
The blinde lust, the which that may not laste,
And sholden al our herte on hevene caste,
And forth he wente, shortly for to telle,
Ther as Mercurie sorted him to dwelle.—

Swich fyn hath, lo, this Troilus for love,
Swich fyn hath al his grete worthinesse,
Swich fyn hath his estat real above,
Swich fyn his lust, swich fyn hath his noblesse,
Swich fyn hath false worldes brotelnesse.
And thus bigan his loving of Criseyde,
As I have told, and in this wyse he deyde.

Sk., V, 1800-1834

O yonge fresshe folkes, he or she,
In which that love up groweth with your age,
Repeyreth hoom from worldly vanitee,
And of your herte up-casteth the visage
To thilke God that after his image
Yow made, and thinketh al nis but a fayre
This world, that passeth sone as floures fayre.

And loveth him, the which that right for love
Upon a cros, our soules for to beye,
First starf, and roos, and sit in hevene a-bove;
For he nil falsen no wight, dar I seye,
That wol his herte al hoolly on him leye.
And sin he best to love is, and most meke,
What nedeth feyned loves for to seke?

Lo heer, of Payens corsed olde rytes,
Lo heer, what alle hir goddes may availle,
Lo heer, these wrecched worldes appetytes,
Lo heer, the fyn and guerdon for travaille
Of Iove, Appollo, of Mars, of swich rascaille!
Lo heer, the forme of olde clerkes speche
In poetrye, if ye hir bokes seche!—

O moral Gower, this book I directe
To thee, and to the philosophical Strode,
To vouchen sauf, ther nede is, to corecte,
Of your benignitees and zeles gode.
And to that sothfast Crist, that starf on rode,
With al myn herte of mercy evere I preye;
And to the Lord right thus I speke and seye:

Thou oon, and two, and three, eterne on-lyve,
That regnest ay in three and two and oon,
Uncircumscript, and al mayst circumscryve,
Us from visible and invisible foon
Defende. And to thy mercy, everichoon,
So make us, Iesus, for thy grace digne,
For love of mayde and moder thyn benigne! Amen.

     Explicit Liber Troili et Criseydis.

[handwritten marginal note, left margin:] A kind of discrepancy between worldly mood in which story moves & the religion heavenly spirit with which it ends. thorsmood is given. Chaucer must have put a conventional end to the story. or was he more spiritually?

[handwritten note, bottom:] Da

CHAUCER'S WORDES UNTO ADAM, HIS OWNE SCRIVEYN

Adam scriveyn, if evere it thee bifalle
Boece or Troilus to wryten newe,
Under thy longę lokkęs thou most havę the scalle
But after my making thou wryte trewe.
So ofte a daye I mot thy werk renewe,
Hit to correcte and eek to rubbe and scrape:
And al is through thy negligence and rape.

Sources for Troy Story

Ephemeris Belli Trojani of Dictys the Cretan
De Excidio Historia of Dares dePhrygian
Roman de Troie of Benoit de Sainte-More
Historia Trojana – Guido delle Colonne
Filostrato of Boccacio

1. Shak makes love story subservient / to war story. Treachery not mentioned. Pandar / less crafty than Chaucer make him

Tiff humor – more horseplay between P & C

Cres indifferent to Troi – not the noble ?? / of Chaucer. Doesn't say much of Cr. beauty –

more about Ajax & achilles & warriors / Pand not as sly & cunning as Chaucer make ?

In the love scenes – Cr is the bold one / – not the romantic love scenes of Chaucer. / Doesn't give ? the fear that Cr. will / not be faithful. attachment not a secret one / Play ends on bitter note – Troi still ??

BALADE FROM THE LEGENDE OF GOOD WOMEN

Hyd, Absolon, thy gilte tresses clere;
Ester, leye thou thy meknesse al a-doun;
Hyd, Ionathas, al thy frendly manere;
Penalopee, and Marcia Catoun,
Make of your wyfhod no comparisoun;
Hyde ye your beautes, Isoude and Eleyne,
My lady cometh, that al this may disteyne.

Thy faire body, lat hit nat appere,
Lavyne; and thou, Lucresse of Rome toun,
And Polixene, that boghten love so dere,
And Cleopatre, with al thy passioun,
Hyde ye your trouthe of love and your renoun;
And thou, Tisbe, that hast of love swich peyne;
My lady cometh, that al this may disteyne.

Herro, Dido, Laudomia, alle y-fere,
And Phyllis, hanging for thy Demophoun,
And Canace, espyed by thy chere,
Ysiphile, betraysed with Iasoun,
Maketh of your trouthe nayther boost ne soun;
Nor Ypermistre or Adriane, ye tweyne;
My lady cometh, that al this may disteyne.

Sk., L. G. W., Pro. B, 249–269

TROUTHE

Balade de bon conseyl

Flee fro the prees, and dwell with sothfastnesse,
Suffyce unto thy good, though hit be smal;
For hord hath hate, and climbing tikelnesse,
Prees hath envye, and welę blent overal.
Savour no more than thee bihove shal;
Werk wel thy-self, that other folk canst rede;
And trouthe shal delivere, hit is no drede.

Tempeste thee noght al croked to redresse,
In trust of hir that turneth as a bal:
Gret reste stant in litel besinesse;
And eek be war to sporne ageyn an al;
Stryve noght as doth the crokke with the wal.
Daunte thy-self, that dauntest otheres dede;
And trouthe shal delivere, hit is no drede.

That thee is sent, receyve in buxumnesse,
The wrastling for this world axeth a fal.
Her nis non hoom, her nis but wildernesse:
Forth, pilgrim, forth!   Forth, beste, out of thy stal!
Know thy contree, loke up, thank God of al;
Hold the hye wey, and lat thy gost thee lede:
And trouthe shal delivere, hit is no drede.

Envoy

Therforę, thou Vachę, levę thyn old wrecchednesse
Unto the world; leve now to be thral;
Crye him mercy, that of his hy goodnesse
Made thee of noght, and in especial
Draw unto him, and praye in general
For thee, and eek for other, hevenlich mede;
And trouthe shal delivere, hit is no drede.

LENVOY DE CHAUCER A SCOGAN

To-broken been the statuts hye in hevene
That creat were eternally to dure,
Sith that I see the brighte goddes sevene
Mow wepe and wayle, and passioun endure,
As may in erthe a mortal creature.
Allas, fro whennes may this thing procede?
Of which errour I deye almost for drede.

By word eterne whylom was hit shape
That fro the fifte cercle in no manere
Ne mighte a drope of teres doun escape.
But now so wepeth Venus in hir spere
That with hir teres she wol drenche us here.
Allas, Scogan! this is for thyn offence!
Thou causest this deluge of pestilence.

Hast thou not seyd in blaspheme of this goddes,
Through pryde, or through thy grete rakelnesse,
Swich thing as in the lawe of love forbode is?
That, for thy lady saw nat thy distresse,
Therfore thou yave hir up at Michelmesse!
Allas, Scogan! of olde folk ne yonge
Was nevere erst Scogan blamed for his tonge!

Thou drowe in scorn Cupyde eek to record
Of thilke rebel word that thou hast spoken,
For which he wol no lenger be thy lord.
And, Scogan, thogh his bowe be nat broken,
He wol nat with his arwes been y-wroken
On thee, ne me, ne noon of our figure;
We shul of him have neyther hurt ne cure.

Now certes, frend, I drede of thyn unhappe,
Lest for thy gilt the wreche of Love procede
On alle hem that ben hore and rounde of shape
That ben so lykly folk in love to spede.

Than shul we for our labour han no mede.
But wel I wot thou wilt answere and seye:
"Lo! olde Grisel list to ryme and pleye!"

Nay, Scogan, sey not so, for I mexcuse,
God helpe me so! in no rym, doutelees,
Ne thinke I nevere of sleep to wake my muse,
That rusteth in my shethe stille in pees.
Whyl I was yong, I putte hir forth in prees,
But al shal passe that men prose or ryme:
Take every man his turn as for his tyme.

Envoy

Scogan, that knelest at the stremes heed
Of grace, of alle honour and worthinesse,
In thende of which streem I am dul as deed,
Forgete in solitarie wildernesse:
Yet Scogan, thenk on Tullius kindenesse;
Minne thy frend ther it may fructifye!
Far-wel, and loke thou nevere eft Love defye!

LENVOY DE CHAUCER A BUKTON

The counseil of Chaucer touching Mariage, which was
  sent to Bukton.

My maister Bukton, whan of Crist our kinge
Was axed what is trouthe or sothfastnesse,
He nat a word answerde to that axinge,
As who saith, "No man is al trewe," I gesse.
And therfore, thogh I highte to expresse
The sorwe and wo that is in mariage,
I dar not wryte of hit no wikkednesse
Lest I my-self falle eft in swich dotage.

I wol nat seyn how that hit is the cheyne
Of Sathanas, on which he gnaweth evere,
But I dar seyn, were he out of his peyne,
As by his wille, he wolde be bounde nevere.
But thilke doted fool that eft hath levere
Y-cheyned be than out of prison crepe,
God lete him nevere fro his wo dissevere,
Ne no man him bewayle though he wepe.

But yit, lest thou do worse, tak a wyf:
Bet is to wedde than brenne in worse wyse.
But thou shalt have sorwe on thy flesh thy lyf,
And been thy wyves thral, as seyn these wyse,
And if that holy writ may nat suffyse,
Experience shal thee teche, so may happe,
That thee were lever to be take in Fryse
Than eft to falle of wedding in the trappe.

Envoy

This litel writ, proverbes, or figure,
I sende you, tak keep of hit, I rede.
Unwys is he that can no wele endure;
If thou be siker, put thee nat in drede.
The Wyf of Bathe I pray you that ye rede
Of this matere that we have on honde.
God graunte you your lyf frely to lede
In fredom; for ful hard is to be bonde.

THE COMPLEINTE OF CHAUCER TO HIS EMPTY PURS

To you, my purs, and to non other wight
Compleyne I, for ye be my lady dere!
I am so sory now that ye be light;
For certes, but ye make me hevy chere,
Me were as leef be leyd up-on my bere,
For which un-to you mercy thus I crye:
Beth hevy ageyn, or elles mot I dye!

Now voucheth sauf this day or hit be night
That I of you the blisful soun may here,
Or see your colour lyk the sonne bright
That of yelownesse hadde nevere pere.
Ye be my lyf, ye be myn hertes stere,
Quene of comfort and of good companye:
Beth hevy ageyn, or elles mot I dye!

Now purs, that be to me my lyves light,
And saveour, as doun in this world here,
Out of this toune help me through your might,
Sin that ye wole nat been my tresorere;
For I am shave as nye as any frere.
But yit I pray un-to your curtesye:
Beth hevy ageyn, or elles mot I dye.

Lenvoy de Chaucer

O conquerour of Brutes Albioun!
Which that by lyne and free eleccioun
Ben verray king, this song to you I sende;
And ye, that mowen al our harm amende,
Have minde up-on my supplicacioun!

THE CAUNTERBURY TALES

THE PROLOGE

Here biginneth the Book of the Tales of Caunterbury

Whan that Aprille with his shoures sote
The droghte of March hath perced to the rote,
And bathed every veyne in swich licour
Of which vertu engendred is the flour;
Whan Zephirus eek with his swete breeth
Inspired hath in every holt and heeth
The tendre croppes, and the yonge sonne
Hath in the Ram his halfe cours y-ronne,
And smale fowles maken melodye
That slepen al the night with open yë
(So priketh hem nature in hir corages):
Than longen folk to goon on pilgrimages,
And palmers for to seken straunge strondes,
To ferne halwes couthe in sondry londes.
And specially, from every shires ende
Of Engelond, to Caunterbury they wende
The holy blisful martir for to seke
That hem hath holpen whan that they were seke.
  Bifel that in that seson on a day
In Southwerk at the Tabard as I lay
Redy to wenden on my pilgrimage
To Caunterbury with ful devout corage,
At night was come in-to that hostelrye
Wel nyne and twenty in a companye
Of sondry folk, by aventure y-falle
In felawshipe, and pilgrims werę they alle
That toward Caunterbury wolden ryde;
The chambres and the stables weren wyde,
And wel we weren esed atte beste.
And shortly, whan the sonne was to reste,

So had I spoken with hem everichon
That I was of hir felawshipe anon,
And made forward erly for to ryse
To take our wey ther as I yow devyse.

    But natheles, whyl I have tyme and space,
Er that I ferther in this tale pace,
Me thinketh it acordaunt to resoun
To telle yow al the condicioun
Of ech of hem, so as it semed me,
And which they weren and of what degree,
And eek in what array that they were inne;
And at a knight than wol I first biginne:

    A KNIGHT ther was, and that a worthy man,
That fro the tyme that he first bigan
To ryden oute, he loved chivalrye,
Trouthe and honour, fredom and curteisye.
Ful worthy was he in his lordes werre,
And therto had he riden—no man ferre—
As wel in Cristendom as hethenesse,
And evere honoured for his worthinesse.

    At Alisaundre he was whan it was wonne.
Ful ofte tyme he had the bord bigonne
Aboven alle naciouns in Pruce.
In Lettow had he reysed and in Ruce:
No Cristen man so ofte of his degree.
In Gernade at the sege eek had he be
Of Algezir, and riden in Belmarye.
At Lyeys was he, and at Satalye,
Whan they were wonne; and in the Grete See
At many a noblë armee had he be.
At mortal batailles had he been fiftene,
And foughten for our feith at Tramissene
In listes thryes, and ay slayn his foo.
This ilke worthy knight had been also
Somtyme with the lord of Palatye
Ageyn another hethen in Turkye,
And everemore he had a sovereyn prys.
And though that he were worthy, he was wys,

And of his port as meke as is a mayde.
He nevere yet no vileinye ne sayde
In al his lyf un-to no maner wight.
He was a verray parfit, gentil knight.
    But for to tellen yow of his array,
His hors were gode, but he was nat gay.
Of fustian he wered a gipoun
Al bismotered with his habergeoun;
For he was late y-come from his viage,
And wente for to doon his pilgrimage.
    With him ther was his sone, a young SQUYER,
A lovyer and a lusty bacheler,
With lokkes crulle as they were leyd in presse.
Of twenty yeer of age he was, I gesse.
Of his stature he was of evene lengthe,
And wonderly deliver, and of greet strengthe.
And he had ben somtyme in chivachye
In Flaundres, in Artoys, and Picardye,
And born him wel as of so litel space
In hope to stonden in his lady grace.
Embrouded was he, as it were a mede
Al ful of fresshe floures whyte and rede.
Singing he was, or floyting, al the day:
He was as freshe as is the month of May.
Short was his goune, with sleves longe and wyde.
Wel coude he sitte on hors, and faire ryde.
He coude songes make and wel endyte,
Iuste and eek daunce, and wel purtreye and wryte.
So hote he lovede that by nightertale
He sleep namore than dooth a nightingale.
Curteys he was, lowly, and servisable,
And carf biforn his fader at the table.
    A YEMAN had he, and servaunts namo
At that tyme, for him liste ryde so;
And he was clad in cote and hood of grene.
A sheef of pecok-arwes brighte and kene
Under his belt he bar ful thriftily
(Wel coude he dresse his takel yemanly,

His arwes drouped noght with fetheres lowe);
And in his hand he bar a mighty bowe.
A not-heed had he, with a broun visage.
Of wode-craft wel coude he al the usage.
Upon his arm he bar a gay bracer,
And by his syde a swerd and a bokeler;
And on that other syde a gay daggere,
Harneised wel, and sharp as point of spere;
A Cristofre on his brest of silver shene.
An horn he bar, the bawdrik was of grene;
A forster was he, soothly, as I gesse.

Ther was also a Nonne, a PRIORESSE,
That of hir smyling was ful simple and coy;
Hir gretteste ooth was but "By Seinte Loy!"
And she was cleped Madame Eglentyne.
Ful wel she song the service divyne,
Entuned in hir nose ful semely;
And Frensh she spak ful faire and fetisly
After the scole of Stratford atte Bowe
(For Frensh of Paris was to hir unknowe.)
At mete wel y-taught was she with-alle:
She leet no morsel from hir lippes fall,
Ne wette hir fingres in hir sauce depe;
Wel coude she carie a morsel, and wel kepe
That no drope ne fille up-on hir brest.
In curteisye was set ful muche hir lest.
Hir over lippe wyped she so clene
That in hir coppe ther was no ferthing sene
Of grece whan she dronken had hir draughte;
Ful semely after hir mete she raughte.
And sikerly she was of greet disport,
And ful plesaunt, and amiable of port,
And peyned hir to countrefete chere
Of court, and been estatlich of manere,
And to ben holden digne of reverence.
But for to speken of hir conscience,
She was so charitable and so pitous
She wolde wepe if that she sawe a mous

Caught in a trappe, if it werę deed or bledde.
Of smale houndes had she that she fedde
With rosted flesh, or milk and wastel-breed.
But sore weep she if oon of hem werę deed,
Or if men smoot it with a yerde smerte:
And al was conscience and tendre herte.
Ful semely hir wimpel pinched was;
Hir nose tretys; hir eyen greye as glas;
Hir mouth ful smal, and ther-to softe and reed;
But sikerly she had a fair forheed:
It was almost a spanne brood, I trowe;
For hardily she was not undergrowe.
Ful fetis was hir cloke, as I was war.
Of smal coral aboute hir arm she bar
A peire of bedes gauded al with grene,
And ther-on heng a brooch of gold ful shene,
On which ther was first write a crowned "A,"
And after, "*Amor vincit omnia.*"

   Another NONNE with hir hadde she
That was hir chapeleyn, and PREESTES three.

   A MONK ther was, a fair for the maistrye,
An out-ryder, that lovedę venerye;
A manly man, to been an abbot able.
Ful many a deyntee hors had he in stable:
And whan he rood, men mighte his brydel here
Ginglen in a whistling wind as clere
And eek as loude as dooth the chapel-belle
Ther as this lord was keper of the celle.
The reule of Seint Maure or of Seint Beneit,
By-causę that it was old and som-del streit,
This ilkę monk leet olde thinges pace,
And held after the newe world the space.
He yaf nat of that text a pulled hen
That seith that hunters been nat holy men;
Ne that a monk, whan he is cloisterlees,
Is lykned til a fish that is waterlees:
This is to seyn, a monk out of his cloistre.
But thilke text held he nat worth an oistre,

And I seyde his opinioun was good.
What sholde he studie, and make him-selven wood,
Upon a book in cloistre alwey to poure,
Or swinken with his handes and laboure
As Austin bit?   How shal the world be served?
Lat Austin have his swink to him reserved.
Therfore he was a pricasour aright:
Grehoundes he had, as swift as fowel in flight;
Of priking and of hunting for the hare
Was al his lust, for no cost wolde he spare.
I seigh his sleves purfiled at the hond
With grys, and that the fyneste of a lond;
And for to festne his hood under his chin,
He had of gold y-wroght a ful curious pin:
A love-knotte in the gretter ende ther was.
His heed was balled, that shoon as any glas,
And eek his face as he had been anoint.
He was a lord ful fat and in good point:
His eyen stepe, and rolling in his heed,
That stemed as a forneys of a leed;
His botes souple, his hors in greet estat.
Now certeinly he was a fair prelat;
He was nat pale as a for-pyned goost.
A fat swan loved he best of any roost.
His palfrey was as broun as is a berye.

    A FRERE ther was, a wantown and a merye,
A limitour, a ful solempne man.
In alle the ordres foure is noon that can
So muche of daliaunce and fair langage.
He hadde maad ful many a mariage
Of yonge wommen, at his owne cost.
Un-to his ordre he was a noble post.
Ful wel biloved and famulier was he
With frankeleyns over-al in his contree,
And eek with worthy wommen of the toun.
For he had power of confessioun,
As seyde him-self, more than a curat,
For of his ordre he was licentiat.

Ful swetely herde he confessioun,
And plesaunt was his absolucioun.
He was an esy man to yeve penaunce
Ther as he wiste to han a good pitaunce;
For unto a povre ordre for to yive
Is signe that a man is wel y-shrive.
For if he yaf, he dorste make avaunt,
He wiste that a man was repentaunt.
For many a man so hard is of his herte,
He may nat wepe al-thogh him sore smerte.
Therfore in stede of weping and preyeres,
Men mote yeve silver to the povre freres.
His tipet was ay farsed ful of knyves
And pinnes for to yeven faire wyves.
And certeinly he had a mery note;
Wel coude he singe and pleyen on a rote;
Of yeddinges he bar utterly the prys.
His nekke whyt was as the flour-de-lys;
Ther-to he strong was as a champioun.
He knew the tavernes wel in every toun,
And everich hostiler and tappestere
Bet than a lazar or a beggestere;
For un-to swich a worthy man as he
Acorded nat, as by his facultee,
To have with seke lazars aqueyntaunce.
It is nat honest, it may nat avaunce,
For to delen with no swich poraille,
But al with riche and sellers of vitaille.
And over-al, ther as profit sholde aryse
Curteys he was and lowly of servyse.
Ther nas no man no-wher so vertuous.
He was the beste begger in his hous;
For thogh a widwe hadde noght a sho,
So plesaunt was his *"In principio"*
Yet wolde he have a ferthing er he wente.
His purchas was wel bettre than his rente.
And rage he coude as it were right a whelp.
In love-dayes ther coude he muchel help:

For ther he was nat lyk a cloisterer
With a thredbar cope, as is a povre scoler,
But he was lyk a maister or a pope.
Of double worsted was his semi-cope,
That rounded as a belle out of the presse.
Somwhat he lipsed for his wantownesse,
To make his English swete up-on his tonge.
And in his harping, whan that he had songe,
His eyen twinkled in his heed aright
As doon the sterres in the frosty night.
This worthy limitour was cleped Huberd.

A MARCHANT was ther with a forked berd,
In mottelee, and hye on horse he sat,
Up-on his heed a Flaundrish bever hat;
His botes clasped faire and fetisly.
His resons he spak ful solempnely,
Sowning alway thencrees of his winning.
He wolde the see were kept for anything
Bitwixe Middelburgh and Orewelle.
Wel coude he in eschaunge sheeldes selle.
This worthy man ful wel his wit bisette;
Ther wiste no wight that he was in dette,
So estatly was he of his governaunce,
With his bargaynes, and with his chevisaunce.
For sothe he was a worthy man with-alle,
But sooth to seyn, I noot how men him calle.

A CLERK ther was of Oxenford also
That un-to logik hadde longe y-go.
As lene was his hors as is a rake,
And he nas nat right fat, I undertake,
But loked holwe, and ther-to soberly.
Ful thredbar was his overest courtepy;
For he had geten him yet no benefyce,
Ne was so worldly for to have offyce.
For him was lever have at his beddes heed
Twenty bokes clad in blak or reed
Of Aristotle and his philosophye
Than robes riche or fithele or gay sautrye.

But al be that he was a philosophre,
Yet haddë he but litel gold in cofre;
But al that he mighte of his frendes hente,
On bokes and on lerning he it spente,
And bisily gan for the soules preye
Of hem that yaf him wher-with to scoleye.
Of studie took he most cure and most hede.
Noght o word spak he more than was nede,
And that was seyd in forme and reverence,
And short and quik, and ful of hy sentence.
Souning in moral vertu was his speche,
And gladly wolde he lerne, and gladly teche.

A SERGEANT OF THE LAWE, war and wys,
That often hadde been at the parvys,
Ther was also, ful riche of excellence.
Discreet he was, and of greet reverence:
He semed swich, his wordes werę so wyse.
Iustyce he was ful often in assyse,
By patente, and by pleyn commissioun;
For his science, and for his heigh renoun,
Of fees and robes had he many oon.
So greet a purchasour was no-wher noon.
Al was fee simple to him in effect,
His purchasing mighte nat been infect.
No-wher so bisy a man as he ther nas;
And yet he semed bisier than he was.
In termes had he cas and domes alle,
That from the tyme of King William were falle.
Therto he coude endyte and make a thing,
Ther coude no wight pinche at his wryting;
And every statut coude he pleyn by rote.
He rood but hoomly in a medlee cote.
Girt with a ceint of silk with barres smale;
Of his array telle I no lenger tale.

A FRANKELEYN was in his companye;
Whyt was his berd as is the dayesye.
Of his complexioun he was sangwyn.
Wel loved he by the morwe a sop in wyn.

To liven in delyt was evere his wone,
For he was Epicurus owne sone
That heeld opinioun that pleyn delyt
Was verraily felicitee parfyt.
An housholder, and that a greet, was he;
Seint Iulian he was in his contree.
His breed, his ale, was alwey after oon;
A bettre envyned man was no-wher noon.
With-oute bake mete was nevere his hous,
Of fish and flesh, and that so plentevous
It snewed in his hous of mete and drinke,
Of alle deyntees that men coude thinke.
After the sondry sesons of the yeer
So chaunged he his mete and his soper.
Ful many a fat partrich had he in mewe,
And many a breem and many a luce in stewe.
Wo was his cook but-if his sauce were
Poynaunt and sharp, and redy al his gere.
His table dormant in his halle alway
Stood redy covered al the longe day.
At sessiouns ther was he lord and sire;
Ful ofte tyme he was knight of the shire.
An anlas and a gipser al of silk
Heng at his girdel, whyt as morne milk.
A shirreve had he been, and a countour;
Was no-wher such a worthy vavasour.

An HABERDASSHER and a CARPENTER,
A WEBBE, a DYER, and a TAPICER,—
And they were clothed alle in o lyveree
Of a solempne and a greet fraternitee.
Ful freshe and newe hir gere apyked was;
Hir knyves were y-chaped noght with bras
But al with silver, wroght ful clene and weel,
Hir girdles and hir pouches every-deel.
Wel semed ech of hem a fair burgeys
To sitten in a yeldhalle on a deys.
Everich for the wisdom that he can
Was shaply for to been an alderman.

For catel hadde they y-nogh and rente,
And eek hir wyves wolde it wel assente:
And elles certein were they to blame.
It is ful fair to been y-clept "*Madame*,"
And goon to vigilyës al bifore,
And have a mantel royalliche y-bore.

 A COOK they hadde with hem for the nones,
To boille the chiknes with the mary-bones,
And poudre-marchant tart, and galingale.
Wel coude he knowe a draughte of London ale.
He coude roste, and sethe, and broille, and frye,
Maken mortreux, and wel bake a pye.
But greet harm was it, as it thoughte me,
That on his shine a mormal haddë he;
For blankmanger, that made he with the beste.

 A SHIPMAN was ther, woning fer by weste:
For aught I woot, he was of Dertemouthe.
He rood up-on a rouncy as he couthe,
In a gowne of falding to the knee.
A daggere hanging on a laas had he
Aboute his nekke under his arm adoun.
The hote somer had maad his hewe al broun;
And certeinly he was a good felawe.
Ful many a draughte of wyn had he y-drawe
From Burdeux-ward, whyl that the chapman sleep.
Of nyce conscience took he no keep.
If that he faught, and had the hyer hond,
By water he sente hem hoom to every lond.
But of his craft to rekene wel his tydes,
His stremes and his daungers him bisydes,
His herberwe and his mone, his lodemenage,
Ther nas noon swich from Hulle to Cartage.
Hardy he was, and wys to undertake;
With many a tempest had his berd been shake.
He knew wel alle the havenes as they were
From Gootland to the cape of Finistere,
And every cryke in Britayne and in Spayne.
His barge y-cleped was the Maudelayne.

With us ther was a DOCTOUR OF PHISYK,
In al this world ne was ther noon him lyk
To speke of phisik and of surgerye;
For he was grounded in astronomye.
He kepte his pacient a ful greet del
In houres by his magik naturel.
Wel coude he fortunen the ascendent
Of his images for his pacient.
He knew the cause of everich maladye,
Were it of hoot or cold, or moiste or drye,
And wher engendred and of what humour;
He was a verrey parfit practisour.
The cause y-knowe, and of his harm the rote,
Anon he yaf the seke man his bote.
Ful redy had he his apothecaries
To sende him his drogges and his letuaries;
For ech of hem made other for to winne:
Hir frendschip nas nat newe to biginne.
Wel knew he the olde Esculapius,
And Deiscorides, and eek Rufus,
Old Ypocras, Haly, and Galien;
Serapion, Razis, and Avicen;
Averrois, Damascien, and Constantyn;
Bernard, and Gatesden, and Gilbertyn.
Of his diete mesurable was he;
For it was of no superfluitee,
But of greet norissing and digestible.
His studie was but litel on the Bible.
In sangwin and in pers he clad was al,
Lyned with taffata and with sendal;
And yet he was but esy of dispence:
He kepte that he wan in pestilence.
For gold in phisik is a cordial,
Therfore he lovede gold in special.
    A good WYF was ther of bisyde BATHE,
But she was som-del deef, and that was scathe.
Of clooth-making she hadde swich an haunt
She passed hem of Ypres and of Gaunt.

In al the parisshe wyf ne was ther noon
That to the offring bifore hir sholde goon;
And if ther did, certeyn, so wrooth was she
That she was out of alle charitee.
Hir coverchiefs ful fyne were of ground:
I dorste swere they weyeden ten pound
That on a Sonday were upon hir heed.
Hir hosen weren of fyn scarlet reed,
Ful streit y-teyd, and shoos ful moiste and newe.
Bold was hir face, and fair, and reed of hewe.
She was a worthy womman al hir lyve,
Houshondes at chirche-dore she hadde fyve
Withouten other companye in youthe;
But therof nedeth nat to speke as nouthe.
And thryes had she been at Ierusalem;
She hadde passed many a straunge streem;
At Rome she hadde been, and at Boloigne,
In Galice at Seint Iame, and at Coloigne;
She coude muche of wandring by the weye.
Gat-tothed was she, soothly for to seye.
Up-on an ambler esily she sat,
Y-wimpled wel, and on hir heed an hat
As brood as is a bokeler or a targe;
A foot-mantel aboute hir hipes large,
And on hir feet a paire of spores sharpe.
In felawschipe wel coude she laughe and carpe.
Of remedyes of love she knew per-chaunce,
For she coude of that art the olde daunce.

　A good man was ther of religioun,
And was a povre PERSOUNE of a toun;
But riche he was of holy thoght and werk.
He was also a lerned man, a clerk,
That Cristes Gospel trewely wolde preche;
His parisshens devoutly wolde he teche.
Benigne he was, and wonder diligent,
And in adversitee ful pacient,
And swich he was y-preved ofte sythes.
Ful looth were him to cursen for his tythes,

But rather wolde he yeven, out of doute,
Un-to his povre parisshens aboute
Of his offring, and eek of his substaunce.
He coude in litel thing han suffisaunce.
Wyd was his parisshe, and houses fer a-sonder,
But he ne lafte nat, for reyn ne thonder,
In siknesse nor in meschief, to visyte
The ferreste in his parisshe, muche and lyte,
Up-on his feet, and in his hand a staf.
This noble ensample to his sheep he yaf,
That first he wroghte and afterward he taughte.
Out of the Gospel he tho wordes caughte;
And this figure he added eek ther-to,
That if gold ruste, what shal iren do?
For if a preest be foul, on whom we truste,
No wonder is a lewed man to ruste;
Wel oghte a preest ensample for to yive
By his clennesse how that his sheep shold live.
He sette nat his benefice to hyre,
And leet his sheep encombred in the myre,
And ran to London, un-to Seynte Poules,
To seken him a chaunterie for soules,
Or with a bretherhede to been withholde;
But dwelte at hoom, and kepte wel his folde,
So that the wolf ne made it nat miscarie;
He was a shepherde and no mercenarie.
And though he holy were and vertuous,
He was to sinful man nat despitous,
Ne of his speche daungerous ne digne,
But in his teching discreet and benigne.
To drawen folk to hevene by fairnesse
By good ensample was his bisinesse:
But it were any persone obstinat,
What-so he were, of heigh or lowe estat,
Him wolde he snibben sharply for the nones.
A bettre preest, I trowe that nowher noon is.
He wayted after no pompe and reverence,
Ne maked him a spyced conscience;

But Cristes lore, and his apostles twelve,
He taughte, and first he folwed it him-selve.
  With him ther was a PLOWMAN, was his brother,
That had y-lad of dong ful many a fother.
A trewe swinker and a good was he,
Living in pees and parfit charitee.
God loved he best with al his hole herte
At alle tymes, thogh him gamed or smerte,
And than his neighebour right as him-selve.
He wolde thresshe, and ther-to dyke and delve,
For Cristes sake, for every povre wight,
Withouten hyre, if it lay in his might.
His tythes payed he ful faire and wel,
Bothe of his propre swink and his catel.
In a tabard he rood upon a mere.
  Ther was also a Reve and a Millere,
A Somnour and a Pardoner also,
A Maunciple and my-self; ther were namo.
  The MILLER was a stout carl for the nones:
Ful big he was of braun and eek of bones;
That proved wel, for over-al ther he cam,
At wrastling he wolde have alwey the ram.
He was short-sholdred, brood, a thikke knarre,
Ther nas no dore that he nolde heve of harre
Or breke it at a renning with his heed,
His berd as any sowe or fox was reed,
And ther-to brood as though it were a spade.
Up-on the cop right of his nose he hadde
A werte, and ther-on stood a tuft of heres
Reed as the bristles of a sowes eres;
His nose-thirles blake were and wyde.
A swerd and bokeler bar he by his syde.
His mouth as greet was as a greet forneys;
He was a Iangler and a goliardeys,
And that was most of sinne and harlotryes.
Wel coude he stelen corn, and tollen thryes;
And yet he had a thombe of gold, pardee.
A whyt cote and a blew hood wered he.

A baggepypę wel coude he blowe and sowne,
And ther-with-al he broghte us out of towne.

A gentil MAUNCIPLE was ther of a temple,
Of which achatours mighte take exemple
For to be wyse in bying of vitaille.
For whether that he payde or took by taille,
Algate he wayted so in his achat
That he was ay biforn and in good stat.
Now is nat that of God a ful fair grace,
That swich a lewed mannes wit shal pace
The wisdom of an heep of lerned men?
Of maistres had he mo than thryes ten
That were of lawe expert and curious,
Of which ther were a doseyn in that hous,
Worthy to ben stiwardęs of rente and lond
Of any lord that is in Engelond,
To make him live by his propre good,
In honour dettelees but he werę wood,
Or live as scarsly as him list desire;
And able for to helpen al a shire
In any cas that mighte falle or happe;
And yit this maunciple sette hir aller cappe.

The REVE was a sclendre colerik man;
His berd was shave as ny as evere he can;
His heer was by his eres rounde y-shorn;
His top was dokked lyk a preest biforn;
Ful longe were his legges and ful lene,
Y-lyk a staf, ther was no calf y-sene.
Wel coude he kepe a gerner and a binne;
Ther was noon auditour coude on him winne.
Wel wiste he by the droghte and by the reyn
The yelding of his seed and of his greyn.
His lordes sheep, his neet, his dayerye,
His swyn, his hors, his stoor, and his pultrye
Was hoolly in this reves governinge,
And by his covenaunt yaf the rekeninge,
Sin that his lord was twenty yeer of age.
Ther coudę no man bringe him in arrerage.

Ther nas baillif, ne herde, në other hyne,
That he ne knew his sleighte and his covyne;
They were adrad of him as of the deeth.
His woning was ful fair up-on an heeth,
With grene treës shadwed was his place.
He coude bettre than his lord purchase.
Ful riche he was astored prively;
His lord wel coude he plesen subtilly,
To yeve and lene him of his owne good
And have a thank and yet a cote and hood.
In youthe he lerned had a good mister:
He was a wel good wrighte, a carpenter.
This reve sat up-on a ful good stot,
That was al pomely grey and highte Scot.
A long surcote of pers up-on he hadde,
And by his syde he bar a rusty blade.
Of Northfolk was this reve of which I telle,
Bisyde a toun men clepen Baldeswelle.
Tukked he was, as is a frere, aboute,
And evere he rood the hindreste of our route.

A SOMNOUR was ther with us in that place
That had a fyr-reed cherubinnes face;
For sawcefleem he was with eyen narwe.
As hoot he was and lecherous as a sparwe,
With scalled browes blake, and piled berd:
Of his visage children were aferd.
Ther nas quik-silver, litarge, ne brimstoon,
Boras, ceruce, ne oille of tartre noon,
Ne oynement that wolde clense and byte,
That him mighte helpen of his whelkes whyte,
Nor of the knobbes sitting on his chekes.
Wel loved he garleek, oynons, and eek lekes,
And for to drinken strong wyn, reed as blood.
Than wolde he speke, and crye as he werę wood.
And whan that he wel dronken had the wyn,
Than wolde he speke no word but Latyn.
A fewe termes had he, two or three,
That he had lerned out of som decree:

No wonder is, he herde it al the day,
And eek ye knowen wel how that a Iay
Can clepen "Watte" as wel as can the pope.
But who-so coude in other thing him grope,
Than had he spent al his philosophye:
Ay "*Questio quid Iuris*" wolde he crye.
He was a gentil harlot and a kinde;
A bettre felawe sholde men noght finde.
And if he fond o-wher a good felawe,
He wolde techen him to have non awe,
In swich cas, of the erchedeknes curs,
But-if a mannes soule were in his purs,
For in his purs he sholde y-punisshed be.
"Purs is the erchedeknes helle," seyde he.
But wel I woot he lyed right in dede:
Of cursing oghte ech gilty man him drede,
For curs wol slee, right as assoiling saveth;
And also war him of a *significavit*.
In daunger had he at his owne gyse
The yonge girles of the diocyse,
And knew hir counseil, and was al hir reed.
A gerland had he set up-on his heed
As greet as it were for an ale-stake;
A bokeler had he maad him of a cake.

　　With him ther rood a gentil PARDONER
Of Rouncival, his freend and his compeer,
That streight was comen fro the court of Rome.
Ful loude he song, "Com hider, love, to me."
This somnour bar to him a stif burdoun,
Was nevere trompe of half so greet a sound.
This pardoner had heer as yelow as wex,
But smothe it heng as dooth a strike of flex;
By ounces henge his lokkes that he hadde,
And ther-with he his shuldres overspradde,
But thinne it lay, by colpons oon and oon.
But hood, for Iolitee, ne wered he noon,
For it was trussed up in his walet.
Him thoughte he rood al of the newe Iet:

Dischevele, save his cappe, he rood al bare.
Swiche glaring eyen had he as an hare.
A vernicle had he sowed on his cappe.
His walet lay biforn him in his lappe
Bretful of pardoun come from Rome al hoot.
A voys he had as smal as hath a goot.
No berd had he, ne nevere sholde have;
As smothe it was as it were late y-shave.
Ne was ther swich another pardoner:
For in his male he had a pilwe-beer
Which that, he seyde, was our lady veyl;
He seyde he had a gobet of the seyl
That Seynte Peter had, whan that he wente
Up-on the see, til Iesu Crist him hente;
He had a croys of latoun, ful of stones,
And in a glas he hadde pigges bones.
But with these relikes, whan that he fond
A povre persone, dwelling up-on lond,
Up-on a day he gat him more moneye
Than that the persone gat in monthes tweye.
And thus with feyned flaterye and Iapes
He made the persone and the peple his apes.
But trewely to tellen, atte laste,
He was in chirche a noble ecclesiaste.
Wel coude he rede a lessoun or a storie,
But alderbest he song an offertorie;
For wel he wiste, whan that song was songe,
He moste preche, and wel affyle his tonge
To winne silver, as he ful wel coude;
Therfore he song so merily and loude.

Now have I told you shortly, in a clause,
Thestat, tharray, the nombre, and eek the cause
Why that assembled was this companye
In Southwerk at this gentil hostelrye
That highte the Tabard, faste by the Belle.
But now is tyme to yow for to telle
How that we baren us that ilke night,
Whan we were in that hostelrye alight.

Sk., A, 683-690; 693-722

And after wol I telle of our viage,
And al the remenaunt of our pilgrimage.
But first I pray yow, of your curteisye,
That ye narette it nat my vileinye,
Thogh that I pleynly speke in this matere,
To telle yow hir wordes and hir chere;
Ne thogh I speke hir wordes properly.
For this ye knowen al-so wel as I,
Who-so shal telle a tale after a man,
He moot reherce as ny as evere he can
Everich a word if it be in his charge,
Al speke he nevere so rudeliche and large;
Or elles he moot telle his tale untrewe,
Or feyne thing, or finde wordes newe.
He may nat spare, al-thogh he were his brother;
He moot as wel seye o word as another.
Crist spak him-self ful brode in holy writ,
And wel ye wot no vileinye is it.
Eek Plato seith, who-so that can him rede,
The wordes mote be cosin to the dede.
Also I prey yow to foryeve it me,
Al have I nat set folk in hir degree
Heer in this tale, as that they sholde stonde:
My wit is short, ye may wel understonde.
    Greet chere made our host us everichon,
And to the soper sette he us anon;
And served us with vitaille at the beste.
Strong was the wyn, and wel to drinke us leste.
A semely man our hoste was with-alle
For to han been a marshal in an halle;
A large man he was with eyen stepe,
A fairer burgeys is ther noon in Chepe:
Bold of his speche, and wys, and wel y-taught,
And of manhod him lakkede right naught.
Eek therto he was right a mery man,
And after soper pleyen he bigan,
And spak of mirthe amonges othere thinges,
Whan that we had maad our rekeninges;

Sk., A, 723–760

And seyde thus: "Now lordinges, trewely,
Ye been to me right welcome hertely:
For by my trouthe, if that I shal nat lye,
I ne saugh this yeer so mery a companye
At ones in this herberwe as is now.
Fayn wolde I doon yow mirthe, wiste I how.
And of a mirthe I am right now bithoght,
To doon yow ese, and it shal coste noght.

"Ye goon to Caunterbury: God yow spede,
The blisful martir quyte yow your mede!
And wel I woot, as ye goon by the weye,
Ye shapen yow to talen and to pleye;
For trewely, confort ne mirthe is noon
To ryde by the weye doumb as a stoon.
And therfore wol I maken yow disport,
As I seyd erst, and doon yow som confort.
And if yow lyketh alle, by oon assent,
Now for to stonden at my Iugement,
And for to werken as I shal yow seye,
To-morwe, whan ye ryden by the weye,
Now, by my fader soule, that is deed,
But ye be merye, I wol yeve yow myn heed.
Hold up your hond, withouten more speche."

Our counseil was nat longe for to seche.
Us thoughte it was noght worth to make it wys,
And graunted him withouten more avys,
And bad him seye his verdit, as him leste.

"Lordinges," quod he, "now herkneth for the beste,
But tak it not, I prey yow, in desdeyn!
This is the poynt, to speken short and pleyn,
That ech of yow to shorte with your weye
In this viage shal telle tales tweye
To Caunterbury-ward, I mene it so,
And hom-ward he shal tellen othere two,
Of aventures that whylom han bifalle.
And which of yow that bereth him best of alle,
That is to seyn, that telleth in this cas
Tales of best sentence and most solas,

Shal have a soper at our aller cost
Heer in this place, sitting by this post,
Whan that we come agayn fro Caunterbury.
And for to make yow the more mery,
I wol my-selven gladly with yow ryde,
Right at myn owne cost, and be your gyde.
And who-so wol my Iugement withseye
Shal paye al that we spenden by the weye.
And if ye vouche-sauf that it be so,
Tel me anon, with-outen wordes mo,
And I wol erly shape me therfore."

This thing was graunted, and our othes swore
With ful glad herte, and preyden him also
That he wold vouche-sauf for to do so,
And that he wolde been our governour,
And of our tales Iuge and reportour,
And sette a soper at a certeyn prys,
And we wold reuled been at his devys
In heigh and lowe; and thus by oon assent
We been acorded to his Iugement.
And ther-up-on the wyn was fet anon:
We dronken, and to reste wente echon
With-outen any lenger taryinge.

A-morwe, whan that day bigan to springe,
Up roos our host and was our aller cok,
And gadred us togidre, alle in a flok,
And forth we riden, a litel more than pas,
Un-to the watering of Seint Thomas.
And ther our host bigan his hors areste,
And seyde, "Lordinges, herkneth, if yow leste.
Ye woot our forward, and I it yow recorde.
If even-song and morwe-song acorde,
Lat se now who shal telle the firste tale.
As evere mote I drinke wyn or ale,
Who-so be rebel to my Iugement
Shal paye for al that by the weye is spent.
Now draweth cut, er that we ferrer twinne;
He which that hath the shortest shal biginne.

Sirę knight," quod he, "my maister and my lord,
Now draweth cut, for that is myn acord.
Cometh neer," quod he, "my lady prioresse;
And ye, sirę clerk, lat be your shamfastnesse:
Ne studieth noght; ley hond to, every man."
     Anon to drawen every wight bigan,
And shortly for to tellen as it was,
Were it by aventure or sort or cas,
The sothe is this, the cut fil to the knight,
Of which ful blythe and glad was every wight;
And telle he moste his tale, as was resoun,
By forward and by composicioun
As ye han herd. What nedeth wordes mo?
And whan this godę man saugh that it was so,
As he that wys was and obedient
To kepe his forward by his free assent,
He seyde, "Sin I shal biginnę the game,
What, welcomę be the cut, a Goddes name!
Now lat us ryde, and herkneth what I seye."
     And with that word we riden forth our weye,
And he bigan with right a mery chere
His tale anon, and seyde in this manere.

Here endeth the prologe of this book; and here biginneth the
     first tale, which is the Knightes Tale.

THE KNIGHTES TALE

Whylom, as olde stories tellen us,
Ther was a duk that highte Theseus:
Of Athenęs he was lord and governour,
And in his tyme swich a conquerour
That gretter was ther noon under the sonne.
Ful many a riche contree had he wonne;
What with his wisdom and his chivalrye,
He conquered al the regne of Femenye,

That whylom was y-cleped Scithia;
And weddede the quene Ipolita,
And broghte hir hoom with him in his contree
With muchel glorie and greet solempnitee,
And eek hir yonge suster Emelye.
And thus with victorie and with melodye,
This duk, of whom I make mencioun,
When he was come almost unto the toun,
In al his wele and in his moste pryde,
He was war, as he caste his eye asyde,
Wher that ther kneled in the hye weye
A companye of ladies, tweye and tweye,
Ech after other, clad in clothes blake.
But swich a cry and swich a wo they make
That in this world nis creature livinge
That herde swich another weymentinge;
And of this cry they nolde nevere stenten
Til they the reynes of his brydel henten.

"What folk ben ye, that at myn hoom-cominge
Perturben so my feste with cryinge?"
Quod Theseus. "Have ye so greet envye
Of myn honour, that thus compleyne and crye?
Or who hath yow misboden or offended?
And telleth me if it may been amended,
And why that ye ben clothed thus in blak!"

The eldest lady of hem alle spak,
When she had swouned with a deedly chere,
That it was routhe for to seen and here,
And seyde, "Lord, to whom Fortune hath yiven
Victorie, and as a conquerour to liven,
Noght greveth us your glorie and your honour;
But we biseken mercy and socour.
Have mercy on our wo and our distresse.
Som drope of pitee, thurgh thy gentillesse,
Up-on us wrecched wommen lat thou falle.
For certes, lord, ther nis noon of us alle,
That she nath been a duchesse or a quene.
Now be we caitifs, as it is wel sene!

Sk., A, 867–872; 893–924

"I wrecche, which that wepe and waille thus,
Was whylom wyf to King Capaneus,
That starf at Thebes, cursed be that day!
And alle we that been in this array
And maken al this lamentacioun,
We losten alle our housbondęs at that toun
Whyl that the sege ther-aboute lay.
And yet now the olde Creon, weylaway!
That lord is now of Thebes the citee,
Fulfild of ire and of iniquitee,
He for despyt and for his tirannye,
To do the dede bodyes vileinye
Of alle our lordes, which that ben y-slawe,
Hath allę the bodyes on an heep y-drawe,
And wol nat suffren hem by noon assent
Neither to been y-buried nor y-brent,
But maketh houndes ete hem in despyt."
And with that word, with-outen more respyt,
They fillen gruf, and cryden pitously,
"Have on us wrecched wommen som mercy,
And lat our sorwe sinken in thyn herte!"
    This gentil duk doun from his courser sterte
With herte pitous, whan he herde hem speke.
Him thoughte that his herte wolde breke
Whan he saugh hem so pitous and so mat
That whylom weren of so greet estat.
And in his armes he hem alle up hente,
And hem conforteth in ful good entente;
And swoor his ooth, as he was trewe knight
He wolde doon so ferforthly his might
Up-on the tyraunt Creon hem to wreke,
That al the peple of Grece sholde speke
How Creon was of Theseus y-served,
As he that had his deeth ful wel deserved.
And right anoon, with-outen more abood,
His baner he desplayeth and forth rood
To Thebes-ward, and al his host bisyde:
No neer Athenes wolde he go ne ryde.

Sk., A, 931–968

The rede statue of Mars with spere and targe
So shyneth in his whyte baner large
That alle the feeldes gliteren up and doun;
And by his baner born is his penoun
Of gold ful riche, in which ther was y-bete
The Minotaur, which that he slough in Crete.
But shortly for to speken of this thing,
With Creon, which that was of Thebes king,
He faught, and slough him manly as a knight
In pleyn bataille, and putte the folk to flight.
And by assaut he wan the citee after,
And rente adoun bothe wal and sparre and rafter;
And to the ladyes he restored agayn
The bones of hir housbondes that were slayn,
To doon obsequies as was tho the gyse.
But it were al to longe for to devyse
The grete clamour and the waymentinge
That the ladyes made at the brenninge
Of the bodyes, and the grete honour
That Theseus, the noble conquerour,
Doth to the ladyes whan they from him wente;
But shortly for to telle is myn entente.
Whan that this worthy duk, this Theseus,
Hath Creon slayn, and wonne Thebes thus,
Stille in that feeld he took al night his reste,
And did with al the contree as him leste.

To ransake in the tas of bodyes dede,
Hem for to strepe of harneys and of wede,
The pilours diden bisinesse and cure
After the bataille and disconfiture.
And so bifel that in the tas they founde,
Thurgh-girt with many a grevous blody wounde,
Two yonge knightes ligging by and by,
Bothe in oon armes wroght ful richely,
Of whiche two, Arcita hight that oon,
And that other knight hight Palamon.
Nat fully quike, ne fully dede they were;
But by hir cote-armures and by hir gere

The heraudęs knewe hem best in special
As they that weren of the blood royal
Of Thebes, and of sustren two y-born.
Out of the tas the pilours han hem torn,
And han hem caried softe un-to the tente
Of Theseus, and he ful sone hem sente
To Athenes, to dwellen in prisoun
Perpetuelly, he nolde no raunsoun.
And whan this worthy duk hath thus y-don,
He took his host, and hoom he rood anon
With laurer crowned as a conquerour.
And ther he livęth in Ioye and in honour
Terme of his lyf: what nedeth wordes mo?
And in a tour in angwish and in wo
Dwellen this Palamoun and eek Arcite
For everemorę; ther may no gold hem quyte.

   This passeth yeer by yeer, and day by day,
Til it fel ones, in a morwe of May,
That Emelye, that fairer was to sene
Than is the lilie upon his stalke grene,
And fressher than the May with floures newe—
For with the rose colour stroof hir hewe,
I noot which was the fairer of hem two—
Er it werę day, as was hir wonę to do,
She was arisen and al redy dight;
For May wol havę no slogardye a-night.
The sesoun priketh every gentil herte,
And maketh him out of his sleep to sterte,
And seith, "Arys, and do thyn observaunce!"
This maked Emelye havę remembraunce
To doon honour to May, and for to ryse.
Y-clothed was she freshę, for to devyse;
Hir yelow heer was broyded in a tresse
Bihinde hir bak a yerde long, I gesse.
And in the gardin at the sonne up-rist
She walketh up and doun, and as hir list
She gadereth floures, party whyte and rede,
To make a sotil gerland for hir hede,

And as an aungel hevenly she song.
The grete tour, that was so thikke and strong,
Which of the castel was the chief dongeoun
(Ther-as the knightes weren in prisoun,
Of which I tolde yow, and tellen shal),
Was evene Ioynant to the gardin-wal,
Ther-as this Emelye had hir pleyinge.
Bright was the sonne, and cleer that morweninge,
And Palamon, this woful prisoner,
As was his wone, by leve of his gayler,
Was risen, and romed in a chambre on heigh,
In which he al the noble citee seigh
And eek the gardin ful of braunches grene,
Ther-as this fresshe Emelye the shene
Was in hir walk, and romed up and doun.
This sorweful prisoner, this Palamoun,
Goth in the chambre roming to and fro,
And to him-self compleyning of his wo.
That he was born, ful ofte he seyde, "Alas!"
And so bifel by aventure or cas
That thurgh a windowe thikke of many a barre
Of yren greet, and squar as any sparre,
He caste his eye upon Emelya,
And ther-with-al he bleynte, and crydë "A!"
As though he stongen were un-to the herte.
And with that cry Arcite anon up-sterte,
And seyde, "Cosin myn, what eyleth thee,
That art so pale and deedly on to see?
Why crydestow? Who hath thee doon offence?
For Goddes love, tak al in pacience
Our prisoun, for it may non other be:
Fortune hath yeven us this adversitee.
Som wikke aspect or disposicioun
Of Saturne, by sum constellacioun,
Hath yeven us this, al-though we had it sworn.
So stood the hevene whan that we were born.
We moste endure it: this is the short and pleyn."
    This Palamon answerde, and seyde ageyn,

"Cosyn, for sothe, of this opinioun
Thou hast a veyn imaginacioun.
This prison caused me nat for to crye.
But I was hurt right now thurgh-outę myn yë
In-to myn hertę, that wol my bane be.
The fairnesse of that lady that I see
Yond in the gardin romen to and fro
Is cause of al my crying and my wo.
I noot wher she be womman or goddesse,
But Venus is it soothly as I gesse."
And ther-with-al on kneës doun he fil,
And seyde, "Venus, if it be thy wil
Yow in this gardin thus to transfigure
Biforę me, sorweful wrecche creature,
Out of this prisoun help that we may scapen.
And if so be my destinee be shapen
By eterne word to dyen in prisoun,
Of our linage havę som compassioun,
That is so lowe y-brought by tirannye."
And with that word Arcite gan espye
Wher-as this lady romed to and fro.
And with that sighte hir beautee hurte him so
That, if that Palamon was wounded sore,
Arcite is hurt as muche as he, or more.
And with a sigh he seyde pitously,
"The fresshe beautee sleeth me sodeynly
Of hir that rometh in the yonder place;
And but I have hir mercy and hir grace
That I may seen hir atte leeste weye,
I nam but deed; ther nis namorę to seye."
    This Palamon, whan he tho wordes herde,
Dispitously he loked, and answerde,
"Whether seistow this in ernest or in pley?"
    "Nay," quod Arcite, "in ernest, by my fey!
God helpę me so, me list ful yvele pleye."
    This Palamon gan knitte his browes tweye.
"It nerę," quod he, "to thee no greet honour
For to be fals, ne for to be traytour

To me that am thy cosin and thy brother
Y-sworn ful depe, and ech of us til other,
That nevere, for to dyen in the peyne,
Til that the deeth departe shal us tweyne,
Neither of us in love to hindren other,
Ne in non other cas, my leve brother;
But that thou sholdest trewely forthren me
In every cas, and I shal forthren thee.
This was thyn ooth and myn also, certeyn;
I wot right wel, thou darst it nat withseyn.
Thus artow of my counseil, out of doute,
And now thou woldest falsely been aboute
To love my lady, whom I love and serve,
And evere shal til that myn herte sterve.
Now certes, fals Arcite, thou shalt nat so!
I loved hir first, and tolde thee my wo
As to my counseil and my brother sworn
To forthre me, as I have told biforn,
For which thou art y-bounden as a knight
To helpen me, if it lay in thy might,
Or elles artow fals, I dar wel seyn."
    This Arcitë ful proudly spak ageyn:
"Thou shalt," quod he, "be rather fals than I.
But thou art fals, I telle thee utterly;
For *par amour* I loved hir first er thow.
What wiltow seyn? Thou wistest nat yet now
Whether she be a womman or goddesse!
Thyn is affeccioun of holinesse,
And myn is love as to a creature,
For which I tolde thee myn aventure
As to my cosin and my brother sworn.
I pose that thou lovedest hir biforn;
Wostow nat wel the olde clerkes sawe,
That 'Who shal yeve a lover any lawe?'
Love is a gretter lawe, by my pan,
Than may be yeve to any erthly man.
And therfore positif lawe and swich decree
Is broke al-day for love, in ech degree."

Greet was the stryf and long bitwixe hem tweye,
If that I hadde leyser for to seye;
But to theffect. It happed on a day—
To telle it yow as shortly as I may—
A worthy duk that highte Perotheus,
That felawe was un-to Duk Theseus
Sin thilke day that they were children lyte,
Was come to Athenes, his felawe to visyte,
And for to pleye, as he was wont to do,
For in this world he loved no man so,
And he loved him as tendrely ageyn.
So wel they loved, as olde bokes seyn,
That whan that oon was deed, sothly to telle,
His felawe wente and soghte him doun in helle;
But of that storye list me nat to wryte.
Duk Perotheus loved wel Arcite,
And had him knowe at Thebes yeer by yere.
And fynally at requeste and preyere
Of Perotheus, with-oute any raunsoun,
Duk Theseus him leet out of prisoun
Freely to goon wher that him liste over-al,
In swich a gyse as I you tellen shal.

This was the forward, pleynly for tendyte,
Bitwixen Theseus and him Arcite:
That if so were that Arcite were y-founde
Evere in his lyf, by day or night or stounde
In any contree of this Theseus,
And he were caught, it was acorded thus,
That with a swerd he sholde lese his heed;
Ther nas non other remedye ne reed,
But taketh his leve, and homward he him spedde.
Let him be war, his nekke lyth to wedde!

How greet a sorwe suffreth now Arcite!
The deeth he feleth thurgh his herte smyte;
He wepeth, wayleth, cryeth pitously;
To sleen him-self he wayteth prively.
He seyde, "Allas that day that I was born!
Now is my prison worse than biforn;

Now is me shape eternally to dwelle
Noght in purgatorie but in helle.
Allas that evere knew I Perotheus!
For elles had I dwelled with Theseus
Y-fetered in his prisoun evere-mo.
Than had I been in blisse and not in wo.
Only the sighte of hir whom that I serve,
Though that I nevere hir grace may deserve,
Wolde han suffised right y-nough for me.
O dere cosin Palamon," quod he,
"Thyn is the victorie of this aventure,
Ful blisfully in prison maistow dure!

"Allas, why pleynen folk so in commune
Of purveyaunce of God or of Fortune,
That yeveth hem ful ofte in many a gyse
Wel bettre than they can hem-self devyse?
Som man desyreth for to han richesse,
That cause is of his mordre or greet siknesse.
And som man wolde out of his prison fayn,
That in his hous is of his meynee slayn.
Infinite harmes been in this matere;
We witen nat what thing we preyen here.
Sin that I may nat seen yow, Emelye,
I nam but deed: ther nis no remedye."

Up-on that other syde Palamon,
Whan that he wiste Arcite was agon,
Swich sorwe he maketh that the grete tour
Resouneth of his youling and clamour.
The pure fettres on his shines grete
Weren of his bittre salte teres wete.
"Allas!" quod he, "Arcita, cosin myn,
Of al our stryf, God woot, the fruyt is thyn.
Thow walkest now in Thebes at thy large,
And of my wo thou yevest litel charge.
Thou mayst, sin thou hast wisdom and manhede,
Assemblen alle the folk of our kinrede,
And make a werre so sharp on this citee
That by som aventure or som tretee

Sk., A, 1225-1236; 1251-1260; 1273-1288

Thou mayst have hir to lady and to wyf,
For whom that I mostę nedes lesę my lyf.
For, as by wey of possibilitee,
Sith thou art at thy large, of prison free,
And art a lord, greet is thyn avauntage,
Morę than is myn that sterve heer in a cage.
For I mot wepe and wayle whyl I live,
With al the wo that prison may me yive,
And eek with peynę that lovę me yivęth also
That doubleth al my torment and my wo."
Ther-with the fyr of Ielousye up-sterte
With-in his brest, and hente him by the herte
So woodly that he lyk was to biholde
The box-tree, or the asshen dede and colde.
Tho seyde he, "O cruel goddes that governe
This world with binding of your word eterne,
And wryten in the table of athamaunt
Your parlement and your eterne graunt,
What is mankinde more un-to yow holde
Than is the sheep that rouketh in the folde?
For slayn is man right as another beest,
And dwelleth eek in prison and arest,
And hath siknesse and greet adversitee,
And ofte tymes giltelees, pardee!

    "What governaunce is in this prescience
That giltelees tormenteth innocence?
Allas, I see a serpent or a theef,
That many a trewe man hath doon mescheef,
Goon at his large and wher him list may turne;
But I mot been in prison thurgh Saturne!"

    The somer passeth, and the nightes longe
Encresen double wyse the peynes stronge
Bothe of the lover and the prisoner.
I noot which hath the wofuller mester.
Yow loveres axe I now this questioun:
Who hath the worse, Arcite or Palamoun?
That oon may see his lady day by day,
But in a prison he moot dwelle alway;

That other wher him list may ryde or go,
But seen his lady shal he nevere-mo.
Now demeth as yow liste, ye that can,
For I wol telle forth as I bigan.

Explicit prima pars. Sequitur pars secunda.

Whan that Arcite to Thebes comen was,
Ful ofte a day he swelte and seyde "Allas!"
For seen his lady shal he nevere-mo.
And shortly to concluden al his wo,
So muche sorwe had nevere creature
That is, or shal, whyl that the world may dure.
His sleep, his mete, his drinke, is him biraft,
That lene he wex and drye as is a shaft.
His eyen holwe, and grisly to biholde;
His hewe falwe, and pale as asshen colde,
And solitarie he was, and evere allone,
And wailling al the night making his mone.
And if he herde song or instrument,
Then wolde he wepe, he mighte nat be stent.
So feble eek were his spirits and so lowe,
And chaunged so, that no man coude knowe
His speche nor his vois though men it herde.
And in his gere for al the world he ferde
Nat oonly lyk the loveres maladye
Of hereos, but rather lyk manye
Engendred of humour malencolyk,
Biforen in his celle fantastyk.
And shortly, turned was al up-so-doun
Bothe habit and eek disposicioun
Of him, this woful lover Daun Arcite.
     What sholde I al-day of his wo endyte?
Whan he endured had a yeer or two
This cruel torment and this peyne and wo
At Thebes in his contree as I seyde,
Up-on a night in sleep as he him leyde

Him thoughte how that the winged god Mercurie
Biforn him stood, and bad him to be murye.
His slepy yerde in hond he bar uprighte;
An hat he werede up-on his heres brighte.
Arrayed was this god, as he took keep,
As he was whan that Argus took his sleep;
And seyde him thus: "To Athenęs shaltou wende.
Ther is thee shapen of thy wo an ende."
And with that word Arcite wook and sterte.
"Now trewely, how sore that me smerte,"
Quod he, "to Athenęs right now wol I fare;
Ne for the drede of deeth shal I nat spare
To see my lady that I love and serve.
In hir presence I recche nat to sterve."

    And with that word he caughte a greet mirour,
And saugh that chaunged was al his colour,
And saugh his visage al in another kinde.
And right anoon it ran him in his minde
That sith his face was so disfigured,
Of maladye, the which he had endured,
He mighte wel, if that he bar him lowe,
Live in Athenes evere-more unknowe
And seen his lady wel ny day by day.
And right anon he chaunged his array,
And cladde him as a povre laborer,
And al allonę, save oonly a squyer.
That knew his privetee and al his cas,
Which was disgysed povrely as he was,
To Athenes is he goon the nexte way.
And to the court he wente up-on a day,
And at the gate he profreth his servyse
To drugge and drawę what so men wol devyse.
And shortly of this materę for to seyn,
He fil in officę with a chamberleyn,
The which that dwelling was with Emelye.
For he was wys, and coude soon aspye
Of every servaunt which that serveth here.
Wel coude he hewen wode, and water bere;

For he was yong and mighty for the nones,
And ther-to he was strong and big of bones
To doon that any wight can him devyse.
A yeer or two he was in this servyse,
Page of the chambre of Emelye the brighte,
And "Philostrate" he seide that he highte.
But half so wel biloved a man as he
Ne was ther nevere in court of his degree;
He was so gentil of condicioun
That thurghoute al the court was his renoun.
They seyden that it were a charitee
That Theseus wolde enhauncen his degree,
And putten him in worshipful servyse
Ther as he mighte his vertu exercyse.
And thus, with-in a whyle, his name is spronge
Bothe of his dedes and his goode tonge,
That Theseus hath taken him so neer
That of his chambre he made him a squyer,
And yaf him gold to mayntene his degree.
And eek men broghte him out of his contree
From yeer to yeer ful prively his rente;
But honestly and slyly he it spente
That no man wondred how that he it hadde.
And three yeer in this wyse his lyf he ladde,
And bar him so in pees and eek in werre,
Ther nas no man that Theseus hath derre.
And in this blisse lete I now Arcite,
And speke I wol of Palamon a lyte.

In derknesse and horrible and strong prisoun
This seven yeer hath seten Palamoun,
Forpyned what for wo and for distresse.
Who feleth double sore and hevinesse
But Palamon, that love destreyneth so
That wood out of his wit he gooth for wo?
And eek therto he is a prisoner
Perpetually, noght oonly for a yeer.
Who coude ryme in English proprely
His martirdom? For sothe, it am nat I;

Sk., A, 1423-1460

Therfore I passe as lightly as I may.

It fel that in the seventhe yeer, in May,
The thridde night (as olde bokes seyn
That al this storie tellen more pleyn),
Were it by aventure or destinee—
As whan a thing is shapen it shal be—
That, sone after the midnight, Palamoun
By helping of a freend brak his prisoun
And fleeth the citee faste as he may go.
For he had yive his gayler drinke so
Of a clarree, maad of a certeyn wyn
With nercotikes and opie of Thebes fyn,
That al that night, thogh that men wolde him shake,
The gayler sleep, he mighte nat awake.
And thus he fleeth as faste as evere he may.
The night was short, and faste by the day,
That nedes-cost he moste him-selven hyde,
And til a grove faste ther besyde
With dredful foot than stalketh Palamoun.
For shortly this was his opinioun,
That in that grove he wolde him hyde al day,
And in the night than wolde he take his way
To Thebes-ward, his freendes for to preye
On Theseus to helpe him to werreye.
And shortly, outher he wolde lese his lyf,
Or winnen Emelye un-to his wyf.
This is theffect and his entente pleyn.

Now wol I torne un-to Arcite ageyn,
That litel wiste how ny that was his care,
Til that Fortune had broght him in the snare.

The bisy larke, messager of day,
Salueth in hir song the morwe gray;
And fyry Phebus ryseth up so bright
That al the orient laugheth of the light,
And with his stremes dryeth in the greves
The silver dropes hanging on the leves.
And Arcite, that is in the court royal
With Theseus, his squyer principal,

Is risen and loketh on the myrie day.
And for to doon his observaunce to May,
Remembring on the poynt of his desyr,
He on a courser startling as the fyr
Is riden in-to the feeldes him to pleye
Out of the court, were it a myle or tweye.
And to the grove, of which that I yow tolde,
By aventure his wey he gan to holde
To maken him a gerland of the greves,
Were it of wodebinde or hawethorn-leves,
And loude he song ageyn the sonne shene:
"May, with alle thy floures and thy grene,
Wel-come be thou, faire fresshe May,
In hope that I som grene gete may."
And from his courser with a lusty herte
In-to the grove ful hastily he sterte,
And in a path he rometh up and doun,
Ther-as by aventure this Palamoun
Was in a bush that no man mighte him see,
For sore afered of his deeth was he.
No-thing ne knew he that it was Arcite:
God wot he wolde have trowed it ful lyte.
But sooth is seyd, gon sithen many yeres,
That "Feeld hath eyen, and the wode hath eres."
It is ful fair a man to bere him evene,
For al-day meteth men at unset stevene.
Ful litel woot Arcite of his felawe,
That was so ny to herknen al his sawe,
For in the bush he sitteth now ful stille.

   Whan that Arcite had romed al his fille,
And songen al the roundel lustily,
In-to a studie he fil sodeynly
As doon thise loveres in hir queynte geres,
Now in the croppe, now doun in the breres,
Now up, now doun, as boket in a welle.
Right as the Friday, soothly for to telle,
Now it shyneth, now it reyneth faste,
Right so can gery Venus overcaste

The hertes of hir folk; right as hir day
Is gerful, right so chaungeth she array.
Selde is the Friday al the wyke y-lyke.
Whan that Arcite had songe, he gan to syke,
And sette him doun with-outen any more.
"Alas!" quod he, "that day that I was bore!
How longe, Iuno, thurgh thy crueltee,
Woltow werreyen Thebes the citee?
Allas! y-broght is to confusioun
The blood royal of Cadme and Amphioun.
And yet doth Iuno me wel more shame,
For I dar noght biknowe myn owne name;
But ther-as I was wont to highte Arcite,
Now highte I Philostrate, noght worth a myte.
And over al this, to sleen me utterly,
Love hath his fyry darte so brenningly
Y-stiked thurgh my trewe careful herte,
That shapen was my deeth erst than my sherte.
Ye sleen me with your eyen, Emelye:
Ye been the cause wherfore that I dye.
Of al the remenaunt of myn other care
Ne sette I nat the mountaunce of a tare,
So that I coude don aught to your plesaunce!"
And with that word he fil doun in a traunce
A longe tyme; and after he up-sterte.
     This Palamoun, that thoughte that thurgh his herte
He felte a cold swerd sodeynliche glyde,
For ire he quook, no lenger wolde he byde.
And whan that he had herd Arcites tale,
As he were wood, with face deed and pale,
He sterte him up out of the buskes thikke,
And seyde, "Arcite, false traitour wikke,
Now artow hent, that lovest my lady so,
For whom that I have al this peyne and wo,
And art my blood, and to my counseil sworn,
As I ful ofte have told thee heer-biforn,
And hast by-iaped heer Duk Theseus,
And falsly chaunged hast thy name thus:

I wol be deed or elles thou shalt dye.
Thou shalt nat love my lady Emelye,
But I wol love hir only, and namo;
For I am Palamoun, thy mortal fo.
And though that I no wepne have in this place,
But out of prison am astert by grace,
I drede noght that outher thou shalt dye,
Or thou ne shalt nat loven Emelye.
Chees which thou wilt, for thou shalt nat asterte."
   This Arcite, with ful despitous herte,
Whan he him knew, and had his tale herd,
As fiers as leoun pulled oute a swerd,
And seyde thus: "By God that sit above,
Nere it that thou art sik and wood for love,
And eek that thou no wepne hast in this place,
Thou sholdest nevere out of this grove pace,
That thou ne sholdest dyen of myn hond.
For I defye the seurtee and the bond
Which that thou seyst that I have maad to thee.
What, verray fool, think wel that love is free,
And I wol love hir maugre al thy might!
But for as muche as thou art a worthy knight,
And wilnest to darreyne hir by batayle,
Have heer my trouthe, to-morwe I wol nat fayle,
With-outen witing of any other wight,
That heer I wol be founden as a knight,
And bringen harneys right y-nough for thee;
And chees the beste, and leve the worste for me.
And mete and drinke this night wol I bringe
Y-nough for thee, and clothes for thy beddinge.
And if so be that thou my lady winne,
And slee me in this wode ther I am inne,
Thou mayst wel have thy lady, as for me."
This Palamon answerde, "I graunte thee."
And thus they been departed til a-morwe,
When ech of hem had leyd his feith to borwe.
   O Cupide, out of alle charitee!
   O regne, that wolt no felawe have with thee!

Ful sooth is seyd, that love ne lordshipe
Wol noght, his thankes, have no felaweshipe;
Wel finden that Arcite and Palamoun.
Arcite is riden anon un-to the toun,
And on the morwe er it werę dayes light,
Ful prively two harneys hath he dight,
Bothę suffisaunt and mete to darreyne
The bataille in the feeld bitwix hem tweyne,
And on his hors, allone as he was born,
He carieth al this harneys him biforn;
And in the grove, at tyme and place y-set,
This Arcite and this Palamon ben met.

    The destinee, ministre general,
That executeth in the world over-al
The purveyauncę that God hath seyn biforn,
So strong it is that though the world had sworn
The contrarie of a thing by ye or nay,
Yet somtyme it shal fallen on a day
That falleth nat eft with-in a thousand yeer.
For certeinly, our appetytes heer,
Be it of werre or pees or hate or love,
Al this is reuled by the sighte above.
This mene I now by mighty Theseus,
That for to hunten is so desirous,
And namely at the grete hert in May,
That in his bed ther daweth him no day
That he nis clad and redy for to ryde
With hunte and horn, and houndes him bisyde.
For in his hunting hath he swich delyt
That it is al his Ioye and appetyt
To been him-self the grete hertes bane;
For after Mars he serveth now Diane.

    Cleer was the day, as I havę told er this,
And Theseus with alle Ioye and blis
With his Ipolita, the faire quene,
And Emelye, clothed al in grene,
On hunting be they riden royally.
And to the grovę that stood ful faste by,

In which ther was an hert, as men him tolde,
Duk Theseus the streighte wey hath holde.
And to the launde he rydeth him ful right;
For thider was the hert wont have his flight,
And over a brook, and so forth on his weye.
This duk wol han a cours at him or tweye,
With houndes swiche as that him list comaunde.

And whan this duk was come un-to the launde,
Under the sonne he loketh, and anon
He was war of Arcite and Palamon,
That foughten breme as it werę bores two.
The brighte swerdes wenten to and fro
So hidously that with the leeste strook
It semed as it wolde felle an ook;
But what they were, no-thing he ne woot.
This duk his courser with his spores smoot,
And at a stert he was bitwix hem two,
And pulled oute a swerd and cryed, "Ho!
Namore, up peyne of lesing of your heed.
By mighty Mars, he shal anon be deed
That smyteth any strook that I may seen!
But telleth me what mister men ye been,
That been so hardy for to fighten heer
With-outen Iuge or other officer,
As it were in a listes royally?"

This Palamon answerde hastily,
And seyde, "Sir, what nedeth wordes mo?
We havę the deeth deserved bothe two.
Two woful wrecches been we, two caytyves,
That been encombred of our owne lyves;
And as thou art a rightful lord and Iuge,
Ne yif us neither mercy ne refuge,
But slee me first, for seynte charitee;
But slee my felawe eek as wel as me.
Or slee him first; for though thou knowe it lyte,
This is thy mortal fo, this is Arcite,
That fro thy lond is banishęd on his heed,
For which he hath deserved to be deed.

Sk., A, 1689–1726

For this is he that cam un-to thy gate,
And seyde that he highte Philostrate.
Thus hath he Iaped thee ful many a yeer,
And thou hast maked him thy chief squyer;
And this is he that loveth Emelye.
For sith the day is come that I shal dye,
I make pleynly my confessioun
That I am thilke woful Palamoun
That hath thy prison broken wikkedly.
I am thy mortal fo, and it am I
That loveth so hote Emelye the brighte
That I wol dye present in hir sighte.
Therfore I axe deeth and my Iuwyse;
But slee my felawe in the same wyse,
For bothe han we deserved to be slayn."

This worthy duk answerde anon agayn,
And seyde, "This is a short conclusioun:
Your owne mouth by your confessioun
Hath dampned you, and I wol it recorde.
It nedeth noght to pyne yow with the corde.
Ye shul be deed, by mighty Mars the rede!"

The quene anon, for verray wommanhede,
Gan for to wepe, and so did Emelye,
And alle the ladies in the companye.
Gret pitee was it, as it thoughte hem alle,
That evere swich a chaunce sholde falle;
For gentil men they were, of greet estat,
And no-thing but for love was this debat.
And sawe hir blody woundes wyde and sore,
And alle cryden, bothe lasse and more,
"Have mercy, lord, up-on us wommen alle!"
And on hir bare knees adoun they falle,
And wolde have kist his feet ther-as he stood,
Til at the laste aslaked was his mood;
For pitee renneth sone in gentil herte.
And though he first for ire quook and sterte,
He hath considered shortly in a clause
The trespas of hem bothe, and eek the cause.

And al-though that his ire hir gilt accused,
Yet in his reson he hem bothe excused;
As thus: he thoghte wel that every man
Wol helpe him-self in love if that he can,
And eek delivere him-self out of prisoun;
And eek his herte had compassioun
Of wommen, for they wepen evere in oon;
And in his gentil herte he thoghte anoon,
And softe un-to him-self he seyde, "Fy
Up-on a lord that wol have no mercy!
But been a leoun bothe in word and dede
To hem that been in repentaunce and drede
As wel as to a proud despitous man
That wol maynteyne that he first bigan!
That lord hath litel of discrecioun
That in swich cas can no divisioun
But weyeth pryde and humblesse after oon."
And shortly whan his ire is thus agoon,
He gan to loken up with eyen lighte,
And spak thise same wordes al on highte:
"The God of Love, a! *benedicite!*
How mighty and how greet a lord is he!
Lo heer, this Arcite and this Palamoun,
That quitly weren out of my prisoun,
And mighte han lived in Thebes royally,
And witen I am hir mortal enemy,
And that hir deeth lyth in my might also,
And yet hath Love, maugree hir eyen two,
Y-broght hem hider bothe for to dye!
Now loketh, is nat that an heigh folye?
Who may been a fool but-if he love?
Bihold, for Goddes sake that sit above,
Se how they blede! Be they noght wel arrayed?
Thus hath hir lord, the God of Love, y-payed
Hir wages and hir fees for hir servyse!
And yet they wenen for to been ful wyse
That serven Love, for aught that may bifalle!
But this is yet the beste game of alle,

That she, for whom they han this Iolitee,
Can hem ther-fore as muche thank as me;
She woot namore of al this hote fare,
By God, than woot a cokkow or an hare!
But al mot been assayed, hoot or cold;
A man mot been a fool, or yong or old:
I woot it by my-self ful yore agoon;
For in my tyme a servant was I oon.
And therfore sin I knowe of Loves peyne,
And woot how sore it can a man distreyne,
As he that hath ben caught ofte in his las,
I yow foryeve al hoolly this trespas
At requeste of the quene that kneleth here,
And eek of Emelye, my suster dere.
And ye shul bothe anon un-to me swere
That nevere-mo ye shul my contree dere,
Ne make werre up-on me night ne day,
But been my freendes in al that ye may;
I yow foryeve this trespas every del."
And they him swore his axing fayre and wel,
And him of lordshipe and of mercy preyde,
And he hem graunteth grace, and thus he seyde:

    "To speke of royal linage and richesse,
Though that she were a quene or a princesse,
Ech of yow bothe is worthy, doutelees,
To wedden whan tyme is, but nathelees
I speke as for my suster Emelye,
For whom ye have this stryf and Ielousye.
Ye woot your-self she may not wedden two
At ones, though ye fighten evere-mo;
That oon of yow, al be him looth or leef,
He moot go pypen in an ivy-leef.
And for-thy I yow putte in this degree,
That ech of yow shal have his destinee
As him is shape; and herkneth in what wyse.
Lo, heer your ende of that I shal devyse.

    "My wille is this, for plat conclusioun,
With-outen any replicacioun,—

If that yow lyketh, tak it for the beste—
That everich of yow shal gon wher him leste
Frely, with-outen raunsoun or daunger,
And this day fifty wykes, fer ne ner,
Everich of yow shal bringe an hundred knightes,
Armed for listes up at alle rightes,
Al redy to darreyne hir by bataille.
And this bihote I yow with-outen faille
Up-on my trouthe and as I am a knight,
That whether of yow bothe that hath might,
This is to seyn, that whether he or thou
May with his hundred, as I spak of now,
Sleen his contrarie or out of listes dryve,
Him shal I yeve Emelya to wyve.
This is your ende and your conclusioun."
  Who loketh lightly now but Palamoun?
Who springeth up for Ioye but Arcite?
Who couthe telle, or who couthe it endyte,
The Ioye that is maked in the place
Whan Theseus hath doon so fair a grace?
But doun on knees wente every maner wight,
And thanked him with al her herte and might,
And namely the Thebans ofte sythe.
And thus with good hope and with herte blythe
They take hir leve, and hom-ward gonne they ryde
To Thebes, with his olde walles wyde.

  Explicit secunda pars.   Sequitur pars tercia.

  I trowe men wolde deme it necligence,
If I foryete to tellen the dispence
Of Theseus, that goth so bisily
To maken up the listes royally,
That swich a noble theatre as it was
I dar wel seyn that in this world ther nas.
The circuït a myle was aboute,
Walled of stoon, and diched al with-oute.

Round was the shap in manere of compas,
Ful of degrees the heighte of sixty pas,
That whan a man was set on o degree
He lette nat his felawę for to see.
　　Est-ward ther stood a gate of marbel whyt,
West-ward right swich another in the opposit.
And shortly to concluden, swich a place
Was noon in erthe as in so litel space;
For in the lond ther nas no crafty man,
That geometrie or ars-metrik can,
Ne purtreyour ne kerver of images,
That Theseus ne yaf him mete and wages
The theatre for to maken and devyse.
And for to doon his ryte and sacrifyse,
He est-ward hath up-on the gate above
In worship of Venus, goddesse of love,
Don make an auter and an oratorie;
And west-ward, in the minde and in memorie
Of Mars, he maked hath right swich another,
That coste largely of gold a fother.
And north-ward in a touret on the wal,
Of alabastre whyt and reed coral
An oratorie riche for to see
In worship of Dyane of chastitee
Hath Theseus don wroght in noble wyse.
　　But yet had I foryeten to devyse
The noble kerving and the portreitures,
The shap, the countenaunce, and the figures,
That weren in thise oratories three.
　　First in the temple of Venus maystow see
Wroght on the wal, ful pitous to biholde,
The broken slepes and the sykes colde,
The sacred teres and the waymentinge,
The fyry strokes of the desiringe
That Loves servaunts in this lyf enduren,
The othes that hir covenants assuren,
Plesaunce and Hope, Desyr, Fool-hardinesse,
Beautee and Youthe, Bauderie, Richesse,

Charmes and Forcȩ, Lesinges, Flaterye,
Dispense, Disynesse, and Ielousye
That wered of yelwe goldes a gerland,
And a cokkow sitting on hir hand,
Festes, instruments, caroles, daunces,
Lust and Array, and allȩ the circumstaunces
Of lovȩ which that I rekne and rekne shal,
By ordre weren peynted on the wal,
And mo than I can make of mencioun.
For soothly al the mount of Citheroun,
Ther Venus hath hir principal dwellinge,
Was shewed on the wal in portreyinge,
With al the gardin and the lustinesse.
Nat was foryeten the porter Ydelnesse,
Ne Narcisus the faire of yore agon,
Ne yet the folyȩ of King Salamon.

The statue of Venus, glorious for to see,
Was naked fleting in the large see,
And fro the navele doun al covered was
With wawes grene, and brighte as any glas.
A citole in hir right hand hadde she,
And on hir heed, ful semely for to see,
A rose gerland, fresh and wel smellinge;
Above hir heed hir dowves flikeringe.
Biforn hir stood hir sone Cupido,
Up-on his shuldres winges had he two;
And blind he was as it is ofte sene;
A bowe he bar and arwes brighte and kene.

Why sholde I noght as wel eek tellȩ yow al
The portreiturȩ that was up-on the wal
With-in the temple of mighty Mars the rede?
Al peynted was the wal in lengthe and brede
Lyk to the estres of the grisly place
That highte the grete temple of Mars in Trace,
In thilke colde frosty regioun
Ther-as Mars hath his sovereyn mansioun.

First on the wal was peynted a forest
In which ther dwelleth neither man ne beest,

With knotty, knarry, bareyn treës olde
Of stubbes sharpe and hidous to biholde,
In which ther ran a rumbel and a swough
As though a storm sholdę bresten every bough.
And downward from an hil, under a bente,
Ther stood the temple of Mars armipotente,
Wroght al of burned steel, of which thentree
Was long and streit, and gastly for to see.
And ther-oute cam a rage and such a vese
That it made al the gates for to rese.
The northren light in at the dores shoon;
For windowe on the wal ne was ther noon
Thurgh which men mighten any light discerne.
The dorę were alle of adamant eterne,
Y-clenched overthwart and endelong
With iren tough; and for to make it strong,
Every piler the temple to sustene
Was tonne-greet of iren bright and shene.
  Ther saugh I first the derke imagininge
Of Felonye, and al the compassinge;
The cruel Ire reed as any glede;
The pykepurs, and eek the pale Drede;
The smyler with the knyf under the cloke;
The shepne brenning with the blake smoke;
The treson of the mordring in the bed;
The open Werre with woundes al bi-bled;
Contek, with blody knyf and sharp manace;
Al ful of chirking was that sory place.
The sleër of him-self yet saugh I ther,
His herte-blood hath bathed al his heer;
The nayl y-driven in the shode a-night;
The colde Deeth with mouth gaping up-right.
Amiddes of the temple sat Meschaunce
With Disconfort and Sory Contenaunce.
Yet saugh I Woodnessę laughing in his rage;
Armed Compleinte, Out-hees, and fiers Outrage.
The careyne in the bush with throte y-corve;
A thousand slayn, and nat of qualm y-storve;

The tiraunt with the preyȩ by force y-raft;
The toun destroyed, ther was no-thing laft.

The statue of Mars up-on a carte stood,
Armed, and loked grim as he werȩ wood.
And over his heed ther shynen two figures
Of sterres, that been cleped in scriptures
That oon Puella, that other Rubeus.
This god of armes was arrayed thus:
A wolf ther stood biforn him at his feet
With eyen rede, and of a man he eet;
With sotil pencel was depeynt this storie
In redouting of Mars and of his glorie.

Now to the temple of Diane the chaste
As shortly as I can I wol me haste
To telle yow al the descripcioun.
Depeynted been the walles up and doun
Of hunting and of shamfast chastitee.
Ther saugh I how woful Calistopee,
Whan that Diane agreved was with here,
Was turned from a womman til a bere,
And after was she maad the lode-sterre;
Thus was it peynted, I can say yow no ferre.
Hir sone is eek a sterre, as men may see.
Ther saugh I Dane, y-turned til a tree:
I mene nat the goddesse Diane,
But Penneus doughter which that highte Dane.
Ther saugh I Attheon an hert y-maked,
For vengeauncȩ that he saugh Diane al naked;
I saugh how that his houndes have him caught
And freten him, for that they knewe him naught.
Yet peynted was a litel forther-moor,
How Atthalante hunted the wilde boor,
And Meleagre and many another mo,
For which Diane wroghte him care and wo.
Ther saugh I many another wonder storie,
The which me list nat drawen to memorie.

This goddesse on an hert ful hyȩ seet,
With smale houndes al aboute hir feet;

And undernethe hir feet she had a mone,
Wexing it was and sholde wanie sone.
In gaude grene hir statue clothed was,
With bowe in honde, and arwes in a cas.
Hir eyen caste she ful lowe adoun,
Ther Pluto hath his derke regioun.
A womman travailing was hir biforn,
But for hir child so longe was unborn
Ful pitously Lucyna gan she calle,
And seyde, "Help, for thou mayst best of alle!"
Wel couthe he peynten lyfly that it wroghte,
With many a florin he the hewes boghte.

  Now been thise listes maad, and Theseus,
That at his grete cost arrayed thus
The temples and the theatre every del,
Whan it was doon, him lyked wonder wel.
But stinte I wol of Theseus a lyte,
And speke of Palamon and of Arcite.

  The day approcheth of hir retorninge,
That everich sholde an hundred knightes bringe
The bataille to darreyne, as I yow tolde;
And til Athenes, hir covenant to holde,
Hath everich of hem broght an hundred knightes
Wel armed for the werre at alle rightes,
Everich after his opinioun.

  Ther maistow seen coming with Palamoun
Ligurge him-self, the grete king of Trace.
Blak was his berd, and manly was his face;
The cercles of his eyen in his heed,
They gloweden bitwixe yelow and reed;
And lyk a griffon loked he aboute
With kempe heres on his browes stoute;
His limes grete, his braunes harde and stronge,
His shuldres brode, his armes rounde and longe.
And as the gyse was in his contree,
Ful hye up-on a char of gold stood he,
With foure whyte boles in the trays.
In-stede of cote-armure over his harnays,

With nayles yelwe and brighte as any gold
He had a beres skin, col-blak for old.
His longe heer was kembd bihinde his bak,
As any ravenes fether it shoon for blak;
A wreeth of gold arm-greet, of huge wighte,
Upon his heed, set ful of stones brighte,
Of fyne rubies and of dyamaunts.
Aboute his char ther wenten whyte alaunts,
Twenty and mo, as grete as any steer,
To hunten at the leoun or the deer,
And folwed him with mosel faste y-bounde,
Colers of gold, and torets fyled rounde.
An hundred lordes had he in his route
Armed ful wel, with hertes sterne and stoute.

With Arcita, in stories as men finde,
The grete Emetreus, the king of Inde,
Up-on a stede bay, trapped in steel,
Covered in cloth of gold diapred weel,
Cam ryding lyk the god of armes, Mars.
His cote-armure was of cloth of Tars,
Couched with perles whyte and rounde and grete.
His sadel was of brend gold newe y-bete;
A mantelet upon his shuldre hanginge
Bret-ful of rubies rede, as fyr sparklinge.
His crispe heer lyk ringes was y-ronne,
And that was yelow, and glitered as the sonne.
His nose was heigh, his eyen bright citryn,
His lippes rounde, his colour was sangwyn,
A fewe fraknes in his face y-spreynd,
Betwixen yelow and somdel blak y-meynd,
And as a leoun he his loking caste.
Of fyve and twenty yeer his age I caste.
His berd was wel bigonne for to springe;
His voys was as a trompe thunderinge.
Up-on his heed he wered of laurer grene
A gerland freshe and lusty for to sene.
Up-on his hand he bar for his deduyt
An egle tame, as any lilie whyt.

An hundred lordes had he with him there,
Al armed, sauf hir heddęs, in al hir gere
Ful richely in alle maner thinges.
For trusteth wel that dukes, erles, kinges,
Were gadered in this noble companye
For love and for encrees of chivalrye.
Aboutę this king ther ran on every part
Ful many a tame leoun and lepart.
And in this wysę thisę lordes alle and some
Ben on the Sonday to the citee come
Aboute pryme, and in the toun alight.

This Theseus, this duk, this worthy knight,
Whan he had broght hem in-to his citee,
And inned hem, everich in his degree,
He festeth hem and dooth so greet labour
To esen hem, and doon hem al honour,
That yet men weneth that no mannes wit
Of noon estat ne coude amenden it.

The Sonday night, er day bigan to springe,
When Palamon the larke herde singe—
Although it nerę nat day by houres two,
Yet song the larke and Palamon also—
With holy herte and with an heigh corage
He roos to wenden on his pilgrimage
Un-to the blisful Citherea benigne,
I mene Venus, honurable and digne.
And in hir houre he walketh forth a pas
Un-to the listes ther hir temple was,
And doun he kneleth, and with humble chere
And herte soor he seyde as ye shul here.

"Fairest of faire, O lady myn, Venus,
Doughter to Iove and spouse of Vulcanus,
Thou glader of the mount of Citheroun,
For thilke lovę thou haddest to Adoun,
Have pitee of my bittre teres smerte,
And tak myn humble preyere at thyn herte.
Allas! I ne have no langagę to telle
Theffectes ne the torments of myn helle.

Sk., A, 2179–2196; 2209–2228

Myn herte may myne harmes nat biwreye;
I am so confus that I can noght seye.
But mercy, lady bright, that knowest weel
My thought, and seest what harmes that I feel,
Considere al this, and rewe up-on my sore,
As wisly as I shal for everemore
Emforth my might thy trewe servant be,
And holden werre alwey with chastitee.
That make I myn avow, so ye me helpe.
I kepe noght of armes for to yelpe,
Në I ne axe nat to-morwe to have victorie
Ne renoun in this cas, ne veyne glorie
Of pris of armes blowen up and doun,
But I wolde have fully possessioun
Of Emelye and dye in thy servyse.
Find thou the manere how and in what wyse.
I recche nat, but it may bettre be,
To have victorie of hem or they of me,
So that I have my lady in myne armes.
For though so be that Mars is god of armes,
Your vertu is so greet in hevene above
That if yow list I shal wel have my love.
Thy temple wol I worshipe evermo,
And on thyn auter, wher I ryde or go,
I wol don sacrifice and fyres bete.
And if ye wol nat so, my lady swete,
Than preye I thee, to-morwe with a spere
That Arcita me thurgh the herte bere.
Than rekke I noght, whan I have lost my lyf,
Though that Arcita winne hir to his wyf.
This is theffect and ende of my preyere,
Yif me my love, thou blisful lady dere."

Whan thorisoun was doon of Palamon,
His sacrifice he did, and that anon,
Ful pitously with alle circunstaunces,
Al telle I noght as now his observaunces.
But atte laste the statue of Venus shook,
And made a signe, wher-by that he took

That his preyere accepted was that day.
For thogh the signe shewed a delay,
Yet wiste he wel that graunted was his bone;
And with glad herte he wente him hoom ful sone.

The thridde houre inequal that Palamon
Bigan to Venus temple for to goon,
Up roos the sonne and up roos Emelye,
And to the temple of Diane gan hye.
Hir maydens, that she thider with hir ladde,
Ful redily with hem the fyr they hadde,
Thencens, the clothes, and the remenant al
That to the sacrifyce longen shal;
The hornes ful of meth as was the gyse;
Ther lakked noght to doon hir sacrifyse.
Hir brighte heer was kempt, untressed al;
A coroune of a grene ook cerial
Up-on hir heed was set ful fair and mete.
Two fyres on the auter gan she bete,
And did hir thinges, as men may biholde
In Stace of Thebes, and thise bokes olde.
Whan kindled was the fyr, with pitous chere
Un-to Diane she spak as ye may here.

"O chaste goddesse of the wodes grene,
To whom bothe hevene and erthe and see is sene,
Quene of the regne of Pluto derk and lowe,
Goddesse of maydens, that myn herte hast knowe:
I am, thou woost, yet of thy companye,
A mayde, and love hunting and venerye,
And for to walken in the wodes wilde,
And noght to been a wyf and be with childe.
Noght wol I knowe companye of man.
Now help me, lady, sith ye may and can,
For tho thre formes that thou hast in thee.
And Palamon, that hath swich love to me,
And eek Arcite, that loveth me so sore,
This grace I preye thee with-oute more,
As sende hem love and pees bitwixe hem two;
And fro me turne awey hir hertes so

Sk., A, 2267-2280; 2289-2300; 2307-2318

That al hir hote love and hir desyr,
And al hir bisy torment and hir fyr,
Be queynt, or turned in another place.
And if so be thou wolt not do me grace,
Or if my destinee be shapen so
That I shal nedes have oon of hem two,
As sende me him that most desireth me.
Bihold, goddesse of clene chastitee,
The bittre teres that on my chekes falle.
Sin thou art mayde, and keper of us alle,
My maydenhede thou keep and wel conserve,
And whyl I live a mayde, I wol thee serve."
      The fyres brenne up-on the auter clere,
Whyl Emelye was thus in hir preyere;
But sodeinly she saugh a sighte queynte,
For right anon oon of the fyres queynte
And quiked agayn, and after that anon
That other fyr was queynt and al agon.
And as it queynte, it made a whistelinge,
As doon thise wete brondes in hir brenninge,
And at the brondes ende out-ran anoon
As it were blody dropes many oon;
For which so sore agast was Emelye
That she was wel ny mad, and gan to crye,
For she ne wiste what it signifyed,
But only for the fere thus hath she cryed
And weep that it was pitee for to here.
And ther-with-al Diane gan appere
With bowe in hond, right as an hunteresse,
And seyde, " Doghter, stint thyn hevinesse.
Among the goddes hye it is affermed,
And by eterne word write and confermed,
Thou shalt ben wedded un-to oon of tho
That han for thee so muchel care and wo;
But un-to which of hem I may nat telle.
Farwel, for I ne may no lenger dwelle.
The fyres which that on myn auter brenne
Shul thee declaren, er that thou go henne,

Thyn aventure of love, as in this cas."
And with that word the arwes in the cas
Of the goddesse clateren faste and ringe,
And forth she wente and made a vanisshinge;
For which this Emelye astoned was,
And seyde, "What amounteth this, allas!
I putte me in thy proteccioun,
Diane, and in thy disposicioun."
And hoom she gooth anon the nexte weye.
This is theffect, ther is namore to seye.

The nexte houre of Mars folwinge this,
Arcite un-to the temple walked is
Of fierse Mars, to doon his sacrifyse
With alle the rytes of his payen wyse.
With pitous herte and heigh devocioun,
Right thus to Mars he seyde his orisoun;
"O stronge god, that in the regnes colde,
Of Trace honoured art, and lord y-holde,
And hast in every regne and every lond
Of armes al the brydel in thyn hond,
And hem fortunest as thee list devyse,
Accept of me my pitous sacrifyse.
For thilke peyne and thilke hote fyr
In which thou whylom brendest for desyr,
Whan that thou usedest the grete beautee
Of fayre yonge fresshe Venus free,
And haddest hir in armes at thy wille,
Al-though thee ones on a tyme misfille
Whan Vulcanus had caught thee in his las,
And fond thee ligging by his wyf, allas!
For thilke sorwe that was in thyn herte,
Have routhe as wel up-on my peynes smerte.
I am yong and unkonning as thou wost,
And, as I trowe, with love offended most,
That evere was any lyves creature;
For she that dooth me al this wo endure
Ne reccheth nevere wher I sinke or flete.
And wel I woot, er she me mercy hete,

Sk., A, 2357-2378; 2383-2398

I moot with strengthe winne hir in the place;
And wel I woot, withouten help or grace
Of thee, ne may my strengthe noght availle.
Than help me, lord, to-morwe in my bataille.
Thy soverein temple wol I most honouren
Of any place, and alwey most labouren
In thy plesaunce and in thy craftes stronge,
And in thy temple I wol my baner honge,
And alle the armes of my companye;
And evere-mo un-to that day I dye,
Eterne fyr I wol biforn thee finde.
And eek to this avow I wol me binde:
My berd, myn heer that hongeth long adoun,
That nevere yet ne felte offensioun
Of rasour nor of shere, I wol thee yive,
And ben thy trewe servant whyl I live.
Now lord, have routhe up-on my sorwes sore;
Yif me victorie, I aske thee namore."

The preyere stinte of Arcita the stronge,
The ringes on the temple-dore that honge,
And eek the dores, clatereden ful faste,
Of which Arcita som-what him agaste.
The fyres brende up-on the auter brighte,
That it gan al the temple for to lighte;
And swete smel the ground anon up-yaf,
And Arcita anon his hand up-haf,
And more encens in-to the fyr he caste,
With othere rytes mo; and atte laste
The statue of Mars bigan his hauberk ringe.
And with that soun he herde a murmuringe
Ful lowe and dim, that sayde thus: "Victorie!"
For which he yaf to Mars honour and glorie.
And thus with Ioye, and hope wel to fare,
Arcite anon un-to his in is fare,
As fayn as fowel is of the brighte sonne.

And right anon swich stryf ther is bigonne
For thilke graunting in the hevene above
Bitwixe Venus, the goddesse of love,

And Mars, the sterne god armipotente,
That Iupiter was bisy it to stente,
Til that the pale Saturnus the colde,
That knew so manye of aventures olde,
Fond in his olde experience an art
That he ful sone hath plesed every part.
As sooth is sayd, elde hath greet avantage;
In elde is bothe wisdom and usage.

Explicit tercia pars. Sequitur pars quarta.

Greet was the feste in Athenes that day,
And eek the lusty seson of that May
Made every wight to been in swich plesaunce
That al that Monday Iusten they and daunce,
And spenden it in Venus heigh servyse.
But by the cause that they sholde ryse
Erly for to seen the grete fight,
Unto hir reste wente they at night.
And on the morwe whan that day gan springe,
Of hors and harneys, noyse and clateringe
Ther was in hostelryes al aboute;
And to the paleys rood ther many a route.
Ther as nede is, they weren no-thing ydel;
The fomy stedes on the golden brydel
Gnawing, and faste the armurers also
With fyle and hamer priking to and fro;
Yemen on fote, and communes many oon
With shorte staves, thikke as they may goon;
Pypes, trompes, nakers, clariounes
That in the bataille blowen blody sounes;
The paleys ful of peples up and doun,
Heer three, ther ten, holding hir questioun,
Divyning of thise Thebane knightes two.
Somme seyden thus, somme seyde it shal be so;
Somme helden with him with the blake berd,
Somme with the balled, somme with the thikke herd;

Sk., A, 2441-2448; 2483-2494; 2505-2518

Somme sayde he loked grim and he woldę fighte;
He hath a sparth of twenty pound of wighte.
Thus was the halle ful of divyninge
Longe after that the sonne gan to springe.

The grete Theseus, that of his sleep awaked
With minstralcye and noyse that was maked,
Held yet the chambrë of his paleys riche
Til that the Thebanę knightes, bothe y-liche
Honoured, were into the paleys fet.
Duk Theseus was at a windowe set,
Arrayęd right as he were a god in trone.
The peple preesseth thider-ward ful sone
Him for to seen and doon heigh reverence,
And eek to herkne his heste and his sentence.

An heraud on a scaffold made an " ho,"
Til al the noyse of peple was y-do;
And whan he saugh the peple of noyse al stille,
Tho shewed he the mighty dukes wille.

"The lord hath of his heigh discrecioun
Considered that it werę destruccioun
To gentil blood to fighten in the gyse
Of mortal bataillę now in this empryse.
Wherforę to shapen that they shul not dye,
He wol his firste purpos modifye.
No man therfore, up peyne of los of lyf,
No maner shot ne pollax ne short knyf
Into the listes sende or thider bringe;
Ne short swerd for to stokę, with poynt bytinge,
No man ne drawę ne bere it by his syde.
Ne no man shal un-to his felawę ryde
But o cours, with a sharp y-grounde spere;
Foyne, if him list, on fote, him-self to were.
And he that is at meschief shal be take,
And noght slayn, but be brought un-to the stake
That shal ben ordeyned on either syde;
But thider he shal by force, and ther abyde.
And if so falle the chieftayn be take
On either syde, or elles slee his make,

No lenger shal the turneyinge laste.
God spede yow; go forth and ley on faste.
With longę swerd and with maces fight your fille.
Goth now your wey; this is the lordes wille."

  The voys of peple touchede the hevene,
So loude cryden they with merye stevene:
"God save swich a lord that is so good,
He wilneth no destruccioun of blood!"
Up goon the trompes and the melodye.
And to the listes rit the companye
By ordinaunce, thurgh-outę the citee large,
Hanged with cloth of gold and nat with sarge.
Ful lyk a lord this noble duk gan rydc,
Thisę two Thebanes up-on either syde,
And after rood the quene and Emelye,
And after that another companye
Of oon and other, after hir degree.
And thus they passen thurgh-outę the citee,
And to the listes come they by tyme.
It nas not of the day yet fully pryme,
Whan set was Theseus ful riche and hye,
Ipolita the quene and Emelye,
And other ladies in degrees aboute.
Un-to the seetes preesseth al the route.
And west-ward thurgh the gates under Marte,
Arcite and eek the hundred of his parte
With baner reed is entred right anon;
And in that selve moment Palamon
Is under Venus, est-ward in the place,
With baner whyt, and hardy chere and face.
In al the world, to seken up and doun,
So even with-outen variacioun,
Ther nere swiche companyes tweye.
For ther nas noon so wys that coude seye
That any had of other avauntage
Of worthinesse, ne of estaat, në age,
So even werę they chosen, for to gesse.
And in two renges faire they hem dresse.

Sk., A, 2557–2594

Whan that hir names rad were everichoon,
That in hir nombre gyle werę ther noon,
Tho werę the gates shet, and cryed was loude,
"Do now your devoir, yonge knightes proude!"
    The heraudes lefte hir priking up and doun;
Now ringen trompes loude and clarioun;
Ther is namorę to seyn, but west and est
In goon the speręs ful sadly in arest;
In goth the sharpe spore in-to the syde.
Ther seen men who can Iuste and who can ryde;
Ther shiveren shaftes up-on sheeldes thikke;
He feleth thurgh the herte-spoon the prikke.
Up springen speres twenty foot on highte;
Outę goon the swerdes as the silver brighte.
The helmes they to-hewen and to-shrede;
Outę brest the blood with sterne stremes rede.
With mighty maces the bones they to-breste.
He thurgh the thikkeste of the throng gan threste.
Ther stomblen stedes stronge, and doun goth al.
He rolleth under foot as dooth a bal.
He foyneth on his feet with his tronchoun,
And he him hurtleth with his hors adoun.
He thurgh the body is hurt and sithen y-take,
Maugree his heed, and broght un-to the stake,
As forward was, right ther he moste abyde;
Another lad is on that other syde.
And som tymę dooth hem Theseus to reste,
Hem to refresshe and drinken if hem leste.
Ful ofte a-day han thise Thebanes two
Togidre y-met, and wroght his felawę wo;
Unhorsed hath ech other of hem tweye.
Ther nas no tygre in the vale of Galgopheye,
Whan that hir whelp is stolę whan it is lyte,
So cruel on the hunte, as is Arcite
For Ielous herte upon this Palamoun.
Ne in Belmarye ther nis so fel leoun,
That hunted is or for his hunger wood,
Ne of his prayę desireth so the blood,

As Palamon to sleen his fo Arcite.
The Ielous strokes on hir helmes byte;
Oute renneth blood on bothe hir sydes rede.

Som tyme an ende ther is of every dede;
For er the sonne un-to the reste wente,
The stronge King Emetreus gan hente
This Palamon as he faught with Arcite,
And made his swerd depe in his flesh to byte;
And by the force of twenty is he take
Unyolden, and y-drawe unto the stake.
And in the rescous of this Palamoun
The stronge King Ligurge is born adoun;
And King Emetreus, for al his strengthe,
Is born out of his sadel a swerdes lengthe,
So hitte him Palamon er he were take:
But al for noght, he was broght to the stake.
His hardy herte mighte him helpe naught;
He moste abyde whan that he was caught
By force and eek by composicioun.

Who sorweth now but woful Palamoun,
That moot namore goon agayn to fighte?
And whan that Theseus had seyn this sighte.
Un-to the folk that foghten thus echoon
He cryde, "Ho! namore, for it is doon!
I wol be trewe Iuge, and no partye.
Arcite of Thebes shal have Emelye,
That by his fortune hath hir faire y-wonne."
Anon ther is a noyse of peple bigonne
For Ioye of this, so loude and heigh with-alle
It semed that the listes sholde falle.

What can now faire Venus doon above?
What seith she now? What dooth this quene of love?
But wepeth so for wanting of hir wille
Til that hir teres in the listes fille;
She seyde, "I am ashamed, doutelees."
Saturnus seyde, "Doghter, hold thy pees.
Mars hath his wille, his knight hath al his bone,
And by myn heed thou shalt ben esed sone."

Sk., A, 2633-2670

The trompes with the loude minstralcye,
The heraudes, that ful loude yolle and crye,
Been in hir welę for Ioye of Daun Arcite.
But herkneth me, and stinteth now a lyte,
Which a miracle ther bifel anon.

This fierse Arcite hath of his helm y-don,
And on a courser, for to shewe his face,
He priketh endelong the large place,
Loking upward up-on this Emelye;
And she agayn him caste a freendlich yë,
And she was al his chere, as in his herte.
Out of the ground a furie infernal sterte,
From Pluto sent, at requeste of Saturne,
For which his hors for fere gan to turne,
And leep asyde, and foundred as he leep;
And er that Arcite may taken keep,
He pighte him on the pomel of his heed
That in the place he lay as he werę deed,
His brest to-brosten with his sadel-bowe.
As blak he lay as any col or crowe,
So was the blood y-ronnen in his face.
Anon he was y-born out of the place,
With herte sore, to Theseus paleys.
Tho was he corven out of his harneys,
And in a bed y-brought ful faire and blyve,
For he was yet in memorie and alyve,
And alway crying after Emelye.

Duk Theseus with al his companye
Is comen hoom to Athenes his citee
With alle blisse and greet solempnitee.
Al be it that this aventurę was falle,
He nolde noght disconforten hem alle.
Men seyde eek that Arcitę shal nat dye;
He shal ben heled of his maladye.
And of another thing they were as fayn,
That of hem alle was ther noon y-slayn,
Al werę they sore y-hurt, and namely oon
That with a sperę was thirled his brest-boon.

Sk., A, 2671–2680; 2683–2710

For which anon Duk Theseus leet crye,
To stinten alle rancour and envye,
The gree as wel of o syde as of other,
And either syde y-lyk, as otheres brother;
And yaf hem yiftes after hir degree,
And fully heeld a feste dayes three;
And conveyed the kinges worthily
Out of his toun a Iournee largely.
And hoom wente every man the righte way.
Ther was namore, but " Far wel, have good day!"
Of this bataille I wol namore endyte,
But speke of Palamon and of Arcite.

　　Swelleth the brest of Arcite, and the sore
Encreesseth at his herte more and more.
The clothered blood, for any lechecraft,
Corrupteth and is in his bouk y-laft.
And certeinly, ther nature wol nat wirche,
Far-wel, phisyk! go ber the man to chirche!
This al and som, that Arcita mot dye,
For which he sendeth after Emelye,
And Palamon that was his cosin dere.
Than seyde he thus, as ye shul after here:

　　"Naught may the woful spirit in myn herte
Declare o poynt of alle my sorwes smerte
To yow, my lady, that I love most;
But I biquethe the service of my gost
To yow aboven every creature,
Sin that my lyf ne may no lenger dure.
Allas, the wo! allas, the peynes stronge,
That I for yow have suffred, and so longe!
Allas, the deeth! allas, myn Emelye!
Allas, departing of our companye!
Allas, myn hertes quene! allas, my wyf!
Myn hertes lady, ender of my lyf!
What is this world? What asketh men to have?
Now with his love, now in his colde grave
Allone, with-outen any companye.
Far-wel, my swete fo! myn Emelye!

Sk., A, 2731-2746; 2759-2780

And softe tak me in your armes tweye,
For love of God, and herkneth what I seye.
  "I have heer with my cosin Palamon
Had stryf and rancour, many a day a-gon,
For love of yow and for my Ielousye.
And Iupiter so wis my soule gye,
To speken of a servant proprely,
With alle circumstaunces trewely,
That is to seyn, trouthe, honour, and knighthede,
Wisdom, humblesse, estaat, and heigh kinrede,
Fredom, and al that longeth to that art,
So Iupiter have of my soule part,
As in this world right now ne knowe I non
So worthy to ben loved as Palamon,
That serveth yow and wol don al his lyf.
And if that evere ye shul been a wyf,
Foryet nat Palamon, the gentil man."
And with that word his speche faille gan,
For from his feet up to his brest was come
The cold of deeth, that had him overcome.
And yet more-over in his armes two
The vital strengthe is lost and al ago.
Only the intellect, with-outen more,
That dwelled in his herte syk and sore,
Gan faillen when the herte felte deeth,
Dusked his eyen two and failled breeth.
But on his lady yet caste he his yë;
His laste word was, "Mercy, Emelye!"
His spirit chaunged hous, and wente ther,
As I cam nevere, I can nat tellen wher.
Therfore I stinte, I nam no divinistre;
Of soules finde I nat in this registre,
Ne me ne list thilke opiniouns to telle
Of hem though that they wryten wher they dwelle.
Arcite is cold, ther Mars his soule gye;
Now wol I speken forth of Emelye.
  Shrighte Emelye and howleth Palamon,
And Theseus his suster took anon

Swowning, and bar hir fro the corps away.
What helpeth it to tarien forth the day
To tellen how she weep bothe eve and morwe?
For in swich cas wommen have swich sorwe,
Whan that hir housbonds been from hem ago,
That for the more part they sorwen so,
Or elles fallen in swich maladye,
That at the laste certeinly they dye.

Infinite been the sorwes and the teres
Of olde folk, and folk of tendre yeres,
In al the toun for deeth of this Theban.
For him ther wepeth bothe child and man;
So greet a weping was ther noon, certayn,
Whan Ector was y-broght al freshe y-slayn
To Troye; allas! the pitee that was ther,
Cracching of chekes, rending eek of heer.
"Why woldestow be deed," thise wommen crye,
"And haddest gold y-nough, and Emelye?"
No man mighte gladen Theseus,
Saving his olde fader Egeus,
That knew this worldes transmutacioun,
As he had seyn it chaungen up and doun,
Ioye after wo, and wo after gladnesse,
And shewed hem ensamples and lyknesse.

"Right as ther deyed nevere man," quod he,
"That he ne livede in erthe in some degree,
Right so ther livede nevere man," he seyde,
"In al this world that som tyme he ne deyde.
This world nis but a thurghfare ful of wo,
And we ben pilgrimes passing to and fro;
Deeth is an ende of every worldly sore."
And over al this yet seyde he muchel more
To this effect, ful wysly to enhorte
The peple that they sholde hem reconforte.

Duk Theseus with al his bisy cure
Caste now wher that the sepulture
Of good Arcite may best y-maked be,
And eek most honurable in his degree.

And at the laste he took conclusioun
That ther as first Arcite and Palamoun
Hadden for love the bataille hem bitwene,
That in that selve grove swete and grene,
Ther as he had his amorous desires,
His compleynte, and for love his hote fires,
He wolde make a fyr in which thoffice
Funeral he mighte al accomplice;
And leet comaunde anon to hakke and hewe
The okes olde, and leye hem on a rewe
In colpons wel arrayed for to brenne;
His officers with swifte feet they renne
And ryde anon at his comaundement.
And after this, Theseus hath y-sent
After a bere, and it al over-spradde
With cloth of gold, the richest that he hadde.
And of the same suyte he cladde Arcite;
Upon his hondes had he gloves whyte;
Eek on his heed a croune of laurer grene
And in his hond a swerd ful bright and kene.
He leyde him bare the visage on the bere,
Therwith he weep that pitee was to here.
And for the peple sholde seen him alle,
Whan it was day he broghte him to the halle.

Heigh labour and ful greet apparaillinge
Was at the service and the fyr-makinge,
That with his grene top the hevene raughte,
And twenty fadme of brede the armes straughte;
This is to seyn, the bowes were so brode.
Of stree first ther was leyd ful many a lode.
But how the fyr was maked up-on highte,
And eek the names how the treës highte,
As ook, firr, birch, asp, alder, holm, popler,
Wilow, elm, plane, ashe, box, chasteyn, lind, laurer,
Mapul, thorn, beech, hasel, ew, whippeltree,
How they weren feld, shal nat be told for me;
Ne how the goddes ronnen up and doun,
Disherited of hir habitacioun,

Sk., A, 2857-2880; 2913-2926

In which they woneden in reste and pees,
Nymphes, faunes, and amadrides;
Ne how the bestes and the briddes alle
Fledden for fere whan the wode was falle;
Ne how the ground agast was of the light,
That was nat wont to seen the sonne bright;
Ne how the fyr was couched first with stree,
And than with drye stokkes cloven a three,
And than with grene wode and spycerye,
And than with cloth of gold and with perrye,
And gerlandes hanging with ful many a flour,
The mirre, thencens, with al so greet odour;
Ne how Arcite lay among al this,
Ne what richesse aboute his body is;
Ne how that Emelye, as was the gyse,
Putte in the fyr of funeral servyse;
Ne how she swowned whan men made the fyr,
Ne what she spak, ne what was hir desyr;
Ne what Ieweles men in the fyr tho caste,
Whan that the fyr was greet and brente faste;
Ne how som caste hir sheeld, and som hir spere,
And of hir vestiments, which that they were,
And cuppes ful of wyn, and milk, and blood,
Into the fyr, that brente as it were wood;
Ne how the Grekes with an huge route
Thryes riden al the fyr aboute
Up-on the left hand with a loud shoutinge,
And thryes with hir speres clateringe;
And thryes how the ladies gonne crye;
Ne how that lad was hom-ward Emelye;
Ne how Arcite is brent to asshen colde;
Ne how that liche-wake was y-holde
Al thilke night, ne how the Grekes pleye
The wake-pleyes, ne kepe I nat to seye;
Who wrastleth best naked with oille enoynt,
Ne who that bar him best, in no disioynt.
I wol nat tellen eek how that they goon
Hoom til Athenes, whan the pley is doon;

Sk., A, 2927-2964

But shortly to the poynt than wol I wende,
And maken of my longe tale an ende.

By processe and by lengthe of certeyn yeres
Al stinted is the moorning and the teres
Of Grekes, by oon general assent.
Than semed me ther was a parlement
At Athenȩs, up-on certeyn poynts and cas;
Among the whiche poynts y-spoken was
To havȩ with certeyn contrees alliaunce,
And have fully of Thebans obeisaunce.
For which this noble Theseus anon
Leet senden after gentil Palamon,
Unwist of him what was the cause and why;
But in his blake clothes sorwefully
He cam at his comaundement in hye.
Tho sente Theseus for Emelye.
Whan they werȩ set, and hust was al the place,
And Theseus abiden had a space
Er any word cam fro his wyse brest,
His eyen sette he ther as was his lest,
And with a sad visage he syked stille,
And after that right thus he seyde his wille.

"The firste moever of the cause above,
Whan he first madȩ the faire cheyne of love,
Greet was theffect, and heigh was his entente.
Wel wiste he why, and what ther-of he mente;
For with that faire cheyne of love he bond
The fyr, the eyr, the water, and the lond,
In certeyn boundes that they may nat flee.
That same prince and that moever," quod he,
"Hath stablissȩd in this wrecched world adoun
Certeyn dayes and duracioun
To al that is engendred in this place,
Over the whiche day they may nat pace,
Al mowe they yet tho dayes wel abregge.
Ther needeth non auctoritee allegge,
For it is preved by experience,
But that me list declaren my sentence.

Than may men by this ordre wel discerne
That thilke moever stable is and eterne.
Wel may men knowe, but it be a fool,
That every part deryveth from his hool.
For nature hath nat take his beginning
Of no partye ne cantel of a thing,
But of a thing that parfit is and stable,
Descending so til it be corrumpable.
And therfore of his wyse purveyaunce,
He hath so wel biset his ordinaunce
That speces of thinges and progressiouns
Shullen enduren by successiouns,
And nat eterne be, with-oute lye:
This maistow understonde and seen at yë.
Ther helpeth noght, al goth that ilke weye.
Than may I seyn that al this thing moot deye.
What maketh this but Iupiter the king?
The which is prince and cause of alle thing,
Converting al un-to his propre welle,
From which it is deryved, sooth to telle.
And heer-agayns no creature on lyve
Of no degree availleth for to stryve.
　　"Than is it wisdom, as it thinketh me,
To maken vertu of necessitee,
And take it wel that we may nat eschue,
And namely that to us alle is due.
And who-so gruccheth ought, he dooth folye,
And rebel is to him that al may gye.
And certeynly a man hath most honour
To dyen in his excellence and flour,
Whan he is siker of his gode name;
Than hath he doon his freend, ne him, no shame.
And gladder oghte his freend ben of his deeth,
Whan with honour up-yolden is his breeth,
Than whan his name apalled is for age;
For al forgeten is his vasselage.
The contrarie of al this is wilfulnesse.
Why grucchen we? why have we hevinesse

Sk., A, 3003-3016; 3033-3054; 3057-3058

That good Arcite, of chivalrye flour,
Departed is with duetee and honour
Out of this foule prison of this lyf?
Why grucchen heer his cosin and his wyf
Of his wel-farę that loved hem so weel?
Can he hem thank? Nay, God wot, nevere a deel,
That bothe his soule and eek hem-self offende,
And yet they mowe hir lustes nat amende.
    "Suster," quod he, "this is my fulle assent,
With al thavys heer of my parlement,
That gentil Palamon, your owne knight,
That serveth yow with wille, herte, and might,
And evere hath doon, sin that ye first him knewe,
That ye shul, of your grace, up-on him rewe
And taken him for housbonde and for lord:
Leen my your hond, for this is our acord.
Lat see now of your wommanly pitee.
He is a kinges brother sone, pardee;
And though he were a povre bacheler,
Sin he hath served yow so many a yeer,
And had for yow so greet adversitee,
It moste been considered, leveth me;
For gentil mercy oghtę to passen right."
    Than seyde he thus to Palamon ful right:
"I trowe ther nedeth litel sermoning
To make yow assente to this thing.
Com neer, and tak your lady by the hond."
Bitwixen hem was maad anon the bond
That highte matrimoine or mariage,
By al the counseil and the baronage.
And thus with alle blisse and melodye
Hath Palamon y-wedded Emelye.
And God, that al this wyde world hath wroght,
Sende him his lovę, that hath it dere a-boght.
For now is Palamon in alle wele,
Living in blisse, in richesse, and in hele;
And Emelye him loveth so tendrely,
And he hir serveth al-so gentilly,

Sk., A, 3059-3066; 3075-3104

That nevere was ther no word hem bitwene
Of Ielousye or any other tene.
Thus endeth Palamon and Emelye;
And God save al this faire companye!—Amen.

Here is ended the Knightes Tale.

Bihoold the murie wordes of the Hoost to the lady Prioresse.

Whan that the Knight had thus his tale y-told,
In al the route nas ther yong ne old
That he ne seyde it was a noble storie,
And worthy for to drawen to memorie;
And namely for gentils everichoon.
Our Hoste lough and swoor, "So moot I goon,
This goth aright; unbokeled is the male;
Lat see now who shal telle another tale:

. . . .

My lady Prioresse, by your leve,
So that I wiste I sholde yow nat greve,
I wolde demen that ye tellen sholde
A tale next, if so were that ye wolde.
Now wol ye vouche-sauf, my lady dere?"
"Gladly," quod she, and seyde as ye shal here.

The Prologe of the Prioresses Tale

O Lord, our Lord, thy name how merveillous
Is in this large world y-sprad! —quod she:—
For noght only thy laude precious
Parfourned is by men of dignitee,
But by the mouth of children thy bountee
Parfourned is, for on the brest soukinge
Som tyme shewen they thyn heryinge.

Wherfore in laude, as I best can or may,
Of thee, and of the whyte lilie flour
Which that thee bar and is a mayde alway,
To telle a storie I wol do my labour;
Not that I may encresen hir honour,

For she hir-self is honour, and the rote
Of bountee, next hir sone, and soules bote.

O moder mayde! O mayde moder free!
O bush unbrent, brenning in Moyses sighte,
That ravisedest doun fro the deitee
Thurgh thyn humblesse the goost that in thalighte,
Of whos vertu, whan he thyn herte lighte,
Conceived was the fadres sapience,
Help me to telle it in thy reverence!

Lady! thy bountee, thy magnificence,
Thy vertu, and thy grete humilitee,
Ther may no tonge expresse in no science;
For som-tyme, lady, er men praye to thee,
Thou goost biforn of thy benignitee,
And getest us the light thurgh thy preyere
To gyden us un-to thy sone so dere.

My conning is so wayk, O blisful quene,
For to declare thy grete worthinesse,
That I ne may the weighte nat sustene;
But as a child of twelf month old, or lesse,
That can unnethes any word expresse,
Right so fare I, and therfore I yow preye,
Gydeth my song that I shal of yow seye.

THE PRIORESSES TALE

Here biginneth the Prioresses Tale

Ther was in Asie in a greet citee,
Amonges Cristen-folk a Iewerye,
Sustened by a lord of that contree
For foul usure and lucre of vilanye,
Hateful to Crist and to his companye;
And thurgh the strete men mighte ryde or wende,
For it was free, and open at either ende.

Sk., B, 1655–1684

A litel scole of Cristen folk ther stood
Doun at the ferther ende, in which ther were
Children an heep, y-comen of Cristen blood,
That lerned in that scole yeer by yere
Swich maner doctrine as men used there,
This is to seyn, to singen and to rede,
As smale children doon in hir childhede.

Among thise children was a widwes sone,
A litel clergeon, sevene yeer of age,
That day by day to scole was his wone,
And eek also, wher-as he saugh thimage
Of Cristes moder, had he in usage,
As him was taught, to knele adoun and seye
His *Ave Marie* as he goth by the weye.

Thus hath this widwe hir litel sone y-taught
Our blisful lady, Cristes moder dere,
To worshipe ay, and he forgat it naught,
For sely child wol alday sone lere.
But ay whan I remembre on this matere,
Seint Nicholas stant evere in my presence,
For he so yong to Crist did reverence.

This litel child, his litel book lerninge
As he sat in the scole at his prymer,
He *Alma redemptoris* herde singe,
As children lerned hir antiphoner;
And, as he dorste, he drough him ner and ner,
And herkned ay the wordes and the note,
Til he the firste vers coude al by rote.

Noght wiste he what this Latin was to seye,
For he so yong and tendre was of age;
But on a day his felawe gan he preye
Texpounden him this song in his langage,
Or telle him why this song was in usage.
This preyde he him to construe and declare
Ful ofte tyme upon his knowes bare.

                                        Sk., B, 1685-1719

His felawę, which that elder was than he,
Answerde him thus: "This song I have herd seye
Was maked of our blisful lady free,
Hir to salue, and eek hir for to preye
To been our help and socour whan we deye.
I can no more expounde in this matere;
I lerne song, I can but smal grammere."

"And is this song maked in reverence
Of Cristes moder?" seydę this innocent;
"Now certes, I wol do my diligence
To conne it al er Cristemasse is went.
Though that I for my prymer shal be shent,
And shal be beten thryes in an houre,
I wol it conne, our lady for to honoure."

His felawę taughte him homward prively,
Fro day to day til he coude it by rote,
And than he song it wel and boldely
Fro word to word, acording with the note;
Twyes a day it passed thurgh his throte,
To scoleward and homward whan he wente:
On Cristes moder set was his ententę.

As I havę seyd, thurgh-out the Iewerye
This litel child, as he cam to and fro,
Ful merily than wolde he singe and crye
O Alma redemptoris evere-mo.
The swetnessę hath his herte perced so
Of Cristes moder that to hir to preye
He can nat stinte of singing by the weye.

Our firste fo, the serpent Sathanas,
That hath in Iewes herte his waspes nest,
Up swal, and seide, "O Hebraik peple, allas!
Is this to yow a thing that is honest,
That swich a boy shal walken as him lest
In your despyt, and singe of swich sentence,
Which is agayn your lawes reverence?"

Fro thennes forth the Iewes han conspyred
This innocent out of this world to chace.
An homicyde ther-to han they hyred
That in an aley had a privee place;
And as the child gan for-by for to pace,
This cursed Iew him hente and heeld him faste,
And kitte his throte, and in a pit him caste.

O martir, souded to virginitee,
Now maystou singen, folwing evere in oon
The whyte lamb celestial—quod she:—
Of which the grete evangelist, Seint Iohn,
In Pathmos wroot, which seith that they that goon
Biforn this lamb, and singe a song al newe,
That nevere, fleshly, wommen they ne knewe.

This povre widwe awaiteth al that night
After hir litel child, but he cam noght;
For which as sone as it was dayes light,
With face pale of drede and bisy thoght,
She hath at scole and elles-wher him soght,
Til finally she gan so fer espye
That he last seyn was in the Iewerye.

With modres pitee in hir brest enclosed,
She goth as she were half out of hir minde
To every place wher she hath supposed
By lyklihede hir litel child to finde;
And evere on Cristes moder meke and kinde
She cryde, and atte laste thus she wroghte,
Among the cursed Iewes she him soghte.

She frayneth and she preyeth pitously
To every Iew that dwelte in thilke place
To telle hir if hir child wente oght for-by.
They seyde, "Nay;" but Iesu of his grace
Yaf in hir thought, inwith a litel space,
That in that place after hir sone she cryde
Wher he was casten in a pit bisyde.

O grete God, that parfournest thy laude
By mouth of innocents, lo heer thy might!
This gemme of chastitee, this emeraude,
And eek of martirdom the ruby bright,
Ther he with throte y-corven lay upright
He *Alma redemptoris* gan to singe
So loude that al the place gan to ringe.

The Cristen folk that thurgh the strete wente,
In coomen for to wondre up-on this thing;
And hastily they for the provost sente.
He cam anon with-outen tarying,
And herieth Crist, that is of hevene king,
And eek his moder, honour of mankinde,
And after that, the Iewes leet he binde.

This child with pitous lamentacioun
Up-taken was, singing his song alway;
And with honour of greet procession
They carien him un-to the nexte abbay.
His moder swowning by the bere lay;
Unnethe might the peple that was there
This newe Rachel bringe fro his bere.

With torment and with shamful deth echon
This provost dooth thise Iewes for to sterve
That of this mordre wiste, and that anon;
He nolde no swich cursednesse observe.
Yvel shal have that yvel wol deserve.
Therfore with wilde hors he did hem drawe,
And after that he heng hem by the lawe.

Up-on his bere ay lyth this innocent
Biforn the chief auter whyl the masse laste,
And after that, the abbot with his covent
Han sped hem for to burien him ful faste;
And whan they holy water on him caste,
Yet spak this child, whan spreynd was holy water,
And song, "*O Alma redemptoris mater!*"

This abbot, which that was an holy man
As monkes been, or elles oghten be,
This yonge child to coniure he bigan,
And seyde, "O dere child, I halse thee,
In vertu of the holy Trinitee,
Telle me what is thy cause for to singe,
Sith that thy throte is cut, to my seminge?"

"My throte is cut un-to my nekke-boon,"
Seyde this child, "and as by wey of kinde,
I sholde have deyed, ye, longe tyme agoon,
But Iesu Crist, as ye in bokes finde,
Wil that his glorie laste and be in minde,
And for the worship of his moder dere
Yet may I singe 'O Alma' loude and clere.

"This welle of mercy, Cristes moder swete,
I lovede alwey as after my conninge;
And whan that I my lyf sholde forlete,
To me she cam, and bad me for to singe
This antem verraily in my deyinge,
As ye han herd, and whan that I had songe,
Me thoughte she leyde a greyn up-on my tonge.

"Wherfore I singe, and singe I moot certeyn
In honour of that blisful mayden free,
Til fro my tonge of-taken is the greyn.
And afterward thus seyde she to me:
'My litel child, now wol I fecche thee
Whan that the greyn is fro thy tonge y-take;
Be nat agast, I wol thee nat forsake.' "

This holy monk, this abbot, him mene I,
His tonge oute-caughte, and took a-wey the greyn,
And he yaf up the goost ful softely.
And whan this abbot had this wonder seyn,
His salte teres trikled doun as reyn,
And gruf he fil al plat up-on the grounde,
And stille he lay as he had been y-bounde.

Sk., B, 1832–1866

The covent eek lay on the pavement
Weping, and herien Cristes moder dere,
And after that they ryse, and forth ben went,
And toke awey this martir fro his bere,
And in a tombe of marbul-stones clere
Enclosen they his litel body swete;
Ther he is now, God leve us for to mete.

O yonge Hugh of Lincoln, slayn also
With cursed Iewes, as it is notable,
For it nis but a litel whyle ago;
Preye eek for us, we sinful folk unstable,
That of his mercy God so merciable
On us his grete mercy multiplye,
For reverence of his moder Marye.   Amen.

Here is ended the Prioresses Tale.

Bihoold the murye wordes of the Hoost to Chaucer

Whan seyd was al this miracle, every man
As sobre was that wonder was to se,
Til that our hoste Iapen tho bigan,
And than at erst he loked up-on me,
And seyde thus, "What man artow?" quod he;
"Thou lokest as thou woldest finde an hare,
For evere up-on the ground I see thee stare.

"Approche neer, and loke up merily.
Now war yow, sirs, and lat this man have place.
He in the waast is shape as wel as I;
This were a popet in an arm tenbrace
For any womman, smal and fair of face!
He semeth elvish by his contenaunce,
For un-to no wight dooth he daliaunce.

"Sey now somwhat, sin other folk han sayd.
Telle us a tale of mirthe, and that anoon!"
"Hoste," quod I, "ne beth nat yvel apayd,

For other tales certes can I noon,
But of a rym I lerned longe agoon."
"Ye, that is good," quod he; "now shul we here
Som deyntee thing, me thinketh by his chere."

a clever satire on the metrical romance

(*Here follows the Tale of Sir Thopas.*)

.   .   .   .

.   .   .   .

The Prologe of the Nonne Preestes Tale.

Than spak our host with rude speche and bold,
And seyde un-to the Nonnes Preest anon,
"Com neer, thou preest, com hider, thou Sir Iohn,
Telle us swich thing as may our hertes glade,
Be blythe, though thou ryde up-on a Iade.
What though thyn hors be bothe foul and lene,
If he wol serve thee, rekke nat a bene;
Loke that thyn herte be merye everemo."
"Yis, sir," quod he, "yis, host, so mote I go,
But I be merye, y-wis, I wol be blamed!"—
And right anon his tale he hath attamed,
And thus he seyde un-to us everichon,
This swete preest, this goodly man, Sir Iohn.

satire on domesticity

THE NONNE PREESTES TALE
Nuns

Here biginneth the Nonne Preestes Tale of the Cok and Hen,
Chauntecleer and Pertelote

A povre widwe, somdel stape in age,
advanced *one*
Was whylom dwelling in a narwe cotage
Bisyde a grove stonding in a dale.
This widwe of which I telle yow my tale,
Sin thilke day that she was last a wyf
In pacience ladde a ful simple lyf,
For litel was hir catel and hir rente.
property *income*
By housbondrye of such as God hir sente
economy

Least dramatic: one of most successful beast stories in literature

Sk., B, 1898–1901; 3998–4018

She fond hir-self and eek hir doghtren two.
Three large sowes had she and namo,
Three kyn, and eek a sheep that highte Malle.
Ful sooty was hir bour and eek hir halle,
In which she eet ful many a sclendre meel.
Of poynaunt sauce hir neded nevere a deel.
No deyntee morsel passed thurgh hir throte;
Hir dyete was accordant to hir cote.
Repleccioun ne made hir nevere syk;
Attempree dyete was al hir phisyk,
And exercyse and hertes suffisaunce.
The goute lette hir no-thing for to daunce,
Napoplexye shente nat hir heed.
No wyn ne drank she, neither whyt ne reed;
Hir bord was served most with whyt and blak,
Milk and broun breed, in which she fond no lak,
Seynd bacoun, and somtyme an ey or tweye,
For she was as it were a maner deye.

A yerd she had, enclosed al aboute
With stikkes and a drye dich with-oute,
In which she had a cok heet Chauntecleer.
In al the land of crowing nas his peer.
His vois was merier than the mery orgon
On messe-dayes that in the chirche gon;
Wel sikerer was his crowing in his logge
Than is a clokke, or an abbey orlogge.
By nature knew he ech ascencioun
Of equinoxial in thilke toun;
For whan degrees fiftene were ascended,
Than crew he that it mighte nat ben amended.
His comb was redder than the fyn coral,
And batailed as it were a castel-wal.
His bile was blak, and as the Ieet it shoon;
Lyk asur were his legges and his toon;
His nayles whytter than the lilie flour,
And lyk the burned gold was his colour.
This gentil cok had in his governaunce
Sevene hennes for to doon al his plesaunce,

Which were his sustres and his paramours,
And wonder lyk to him as of colours.
Of which the faireste hewed on hir throte
Was cleped faire damoyselę Pertelote.
Curteys she was, discreet, and debonaire,
And compaignable, and bar hir-self so faire
Sin thilke day that she was sevenę night old
That trewely she hath the herte in hold
Of Chauntecleer loken in every lith;
He loved hir so that wel was him therwith.
But such a Ioyę was it to here hem singe,
Whan that the brighte sonne gan to springe,
In swete accord, "My lief is farcn in londe."
For thilke tyme, as I have understonde,
Bestes and briddes coude speke and singe.

And so bifel that in a daweninge,
As Chauntecleer among his wyves alle
Sat on his perche, that was in the halle,
And next him sat this faire Pertelote,
This Chauntecleer gan gronen in his throte,
As man that in his dreem is drecched sore.
And whan that Pertelotę thus herde him rore,
She was agast, and seyde, "O herte dere,
What eyleth yow to grone in this manere?
Ye ben a verray sleper, fy for shame!"
And he answerde and seyde thus: "Madame,
I pray yow that ye take it nat a-grief:
By God, me mette I was in swich meschief
Right now that yet myn herte is sore afright.
Now God," quod he, " my swevenę recche aright,
And keep my body out of foul prisoun!
Me mette how that I romed up and doun
With-in our yerd, wher-as I saugh a beest,
Was lyk an hound, and wolde han maad arest
Upon my body, and wolde han had me deed.
His colour was bitwixe yelwe and reed;
And tipped was his tail and bothe his eres
With blak, unlyk the remenant of his heres;

His snowte smal, with glowing eyen tweye.
Yet of his look for fere almost I deye:
This caused me my groning doutelees."

"Avoy!" quod she, "fy on yow, hertelees!
Allas!" quod she, "for by that God above,
Now han ye lost myn herte and al my love.
I can nat love a coward, by my feith.
For certes, what so any womman seith,
We alle desyren, if it mighte be,
To han housbondes hardy, wyse, and free,
And secree, and no nigard, ne no fool,
Ne him that is agast of every tool,
Ne noon avauntour, by that God above!
How dorste ye seyn for shame unto your love
That any thing mighte make yow aferd?
Have ye no mannes herte, and han a berd?
Allas! and conne ye been agast of swevenis?
No-thing, God wot, but vanitee in swevene is.
Swevenes engendren of replecciouns,
And ofte of fume and of complecciouns,
Whan humours been to habundant in a wight.
Certes this dreem, which ye han met to-night,
Cometh of the grete superfluitee
Of your rede *colera*, pardee,
Which causeth folk to dreden in here dremes
Of arwes, and of fyr with rede lemes,
Of grete bestes, that they wol hem byte,
Of contek, and of whelpes grete and lyte;
Right as the humour of malencolye
Causeth ful many a man in sleep to crye
For fere of blake beres or boles blake,
Or elles blake develes wole hem take.
Of othere humours coude I telle also
That werken many a man in sleep ful wo;
But I wol passe as lightly as I can.

"Lo, Catoun, which that was so wys a man,
Seyde he nat thus, ne do no fors of dremes?
Now sir," quod she, "whan we flee fro the bemes,

For Goddes love, as tak som laxatyf.
Up peril of my soule, and of my lyf,
I counseille yow the beste, I wol nat lye,
That bothe of colere and of malencolye
Ye purge yow; and for ye shul nat tarie,
Though in this toun is noon apotecarie,
I shal my-self to herbes techen yow
That shul ben for your hele and for your prow.
Ye been ful colerik of compleccioun.
Ware the sonne in his ascencioun
Ne fynde yow nat repleet of humours hote;
And if it do, I dar wel leye a grote
That ye shul have a fevere terciane
Or an agu that may be your bane.
A day or two ye shul have digestyves
Of wormes, er ye take your laxatyves,
Of lauriol, centaure, and fumetere,
Or elles of ellebor, that groweth there,
Of catapuce, or of gaytres beryis,
Of erbe yve, growing in our yerd, that merye is:
Pekke hem up right as they growe and ete hem in.
Be merye, housbonde, for your fader kin!
Dredeth no dreem; I can say yow na-more."

    "Madame," quod he, "*graunt mercy* of your lore.
But nathelees, as touching Daun Catoun,
That hath of wisdom such a greet renoun,
Though that he bad no dremes for to drede,
By God, men may in olde bokes rede
Of many a man, more of auctoritee
Than evere Catoun was, so mote I thee,
That al the revers seyn of his sentence,
And han wel founden by experience
That dremes ben significaciouns
As wel of Ioye as tribulaciouns
That folk enduren in this lyf present.
Ther nedeth make of this noon argument;
The verray preve sheweth it in dede.

    "Oon of the gretteste auctours that men rede

Seith thus, that whylom two felawes wente
On pilgrimage in a ful good entente;
And happed so they come into a toun
Wher-as ther was swich congregacioun
Of peple, and eek so streit of herbergage,
That they ne founde as muche as o cotage
In which they bothe mighte y-logged be.
Wherfore they mosten, of necessitee,
As for that night departen companye;
And ech of hem goth to his hostelrye,
And took his logging as it wolde falle.
That oon of hem was logged in a stalle
Fer in a yerd with oxen of the plough;
That other man was logged wel y-nough,
As was his aventure or his fortune,
That us governeth alle as in commune.

"And so bifel that longe er it were day
This man mette in his bed, ther-as he lay,
How that his felawe gan up-on him calle,
And seyde, 'Allas, for in an oxes stalle
This night I shal be mordred ther I lye.
Now help me, dere brother, er I dye;
In alle haste com to me,' he sayde.
This man out of his sleep for fere abrayde;
But whan that he was wakned of his sleep,
He turned him and took of this no keep;
Him thoughte his dreem nas but a vanitee.
Thus twyes in his sleping dremed he.
And atte thridde tyme yet his felawe
Cam, as him thoughte, and seide, 'I am now slawe;
Bihold my blody woundes depe and wyde!
Arys up erly in the morwe-tyde,
And at the west gate of the toun,' quod he,
'A carte ful of donge ther shaltow see
In which my body is hid ful prively;
Do thilke carte aresten boldely.
My gold caused my mordre, sooth to sayn;'
And tolde him every poynt how he was slayn,

With a ful pitous face, pale of hewe.
And truste wel his dreem he fond ful trewe;
For on the morwe, as sone as it was day,
To his felawes in he took the way.
And whan that he cam to this oxes stalle,
After his felawe he bigan to calle.

　　"The hostiler answerdë him anon,
And seyde, 'Sir, your felawe is agon;
As sone as day he wente out of the toun.'
This man gan fallen in suspecioun,
Remembring on his dremes that he mette,
And forth he goth, no lenger wolde he lette,
Unto the west gate of the toun and fond
A dong-carte, as it werẹ to donge lond,
That was arrayed in the same wyse
As ye han herd the dede man devyse;
And with an hardy herte he gan to crye
Vengeaunce and Iustice of this felonye:
'My felawẹ mordred is this same night,
And in this carte he lyth gaping upright.
I crye oute on the ministres,' quod he,
'That sholden kepe and reulen this citee.
Harrow! allas! her lyth my felawẹ slayn!'
What sholde I more un-to this tale sayn?
The peple out-sterte, and caste the cartẹ to grounde,
And in the middel of the dong they founde
The dede man, that mordred was al newe.

　　"O blisful God, that art so Iust and trewe!
Lo, how that thou biwreyest mordre alway!
Mordre wol outẹ, that see we day by day.
Mordre is so wlatsom and abhominable
To God, that is so Iust and resonable,
That he ne wol nat suffre it heled be;
Though it abyde a yeer or two or three,
Mordre wol outẹ, this my conclusioun.
And right anoon, ministres of that toun
Han hent the carter and so sore him pyned,
And eek the hostiler so sore engyned,

That they biknewe hir wikkednesse anoon,
And were an-hanged by the nekke-boon.
　"Heer may men seen that dremes been to drede.
And certes, in the same book I rede
Right in the nexte chapitre after this
(I gabbe nat, so have I Ioye or blis)
Two men that wolde han passed over see
For certeyn cause in-to a fer contree,
If that the wind ne hadde been contrarie,
That made hem in a citee for to tarie,
That stood ful merye upon an haven-syde.
But on a day, agayn the even-tyde,
The wind gan chaunge, and blew right as hem leste.
Iolif and glad they wente un-to hir reste,
And casten hem ful erly for to saille;
But to that oo man fil a greet mervaille.
That oon of hem in sleping as he lay
Him mette a wonder dreem agayn the day.
Him thoughte a man stood by his beddes syde,
And him comaunded that he sholde abyde,
And seyde him thus: 'If thou to-morwe wende,
Thou shalt be dreynt; my tale is at an ende.'
He wook, and tolde his felawe what he mette,
And preyde him his viage for to lette;
As for that day he preyde him to abyde.
His felawe, that lay by his beddes syde,
Gan for to laughe, and scorned him ful faste.
'No dreem,' quod he, 'may so myn herte agaste
That I wol lette for to do my thinges,
I sette not a straw by thy dreminges;
For swevenes been but vanitees and Iapes.
Men dreme al-day of owles or of apes,
And eek of many a mase therwithal;
Men dreme of thing that nevere was ne shal.
But sith I see that thou wolt heer abyde,
And thus for-sleuthen wilfully thy tyde,
God wot it reweth me; and have good day.'
And thus he took his leve, and wente his way.

Sk., B, 4251–4288

But er that he had half his cours y-seyled,
Noot I nat why, ne what mischaunce it eyled,
But casuelly the shippes botme rente,
And ship and man under the water wente
In sighte of othere shippes it byside,
That with hem seyled at the same tyde.
And therfore, faire Pertelote so dere,
By swiche ensamples olde maistow lere,
That no man sholde been to recchelees
Of dremes, for I sey thee, doutelees,
That many a dreem ful sore is for to drede.

"Lo, in the lyf of Seint Kenelm, I rede,
That was Kenulphus sone, the noble king
Of Mercenrike, how Kenelm mette a thing;
A lyte er he was mordred on a day,
His mordre in his avisioun he say.
His norice him expouned every del
His sweven, and bad him for to kepe him wel
For traisoun; but he nas but sevene yeer old,
And therfore litel talë hath he told
Of any dreem, so holy was his herte.
By God, I hadde lever than my sherte
That ye had red his legende as have I.
Dame Pertelote, I sey yow trewely,
Macrobeus, that writ the avisioun
In Affrike of the worthy Cipioun,
Affermeth dremes, and seith that they been
Warning of thinges that men after seen.

And forther-more, I pray yow loketh wel
In the Olde Testament of Daniel
If he held dremes any vanitee.
Reed eek of Ioseph, and ther shul ye see
Wher dremes ben somtyme (I sey nat alle)
Warning of thinges that shul after falle.
Loke of Egipt the king, Daun Pharao,
His baker and his boteler also,
Wher they ne felte noon effect in dremes.
Who-so wol seken actes of sondry remes,

May rede of dremes many a wonder thing.
"Lo Cresus, which that was of Lyde king,
Mette he nat that he sat upon a tree,
Which signified he sholde anhanged be?
Lo heer Andromacha, Ectores wyf,
That day that Ector sholde lese his lyf,
She dremed on the same night biforn
How that the lyf of Ector sholde be lorn
If thilke day he wente in-to bataille;
She warned him, but it mighte nat availle;
He wente for to fighte nathelees,
But he was slayn anoon of Achilles.
But thilke tale is al to long to telle;
And eek it is ny day, I may nat dwelle.
Shortly I seye, as for conclusioun,
That I shal han of this avisioun
Adversitee; and I seye forther-moor
That I ne telle of laxatyves no stoor,
For they ben venimous, I woot it wel;
I hem defye, I love hem nevere a del.
    "Now let us speke of mirthe, and stinte al this.
Madame Pertelote, so have I blis,
Of o thing God hath sent me large grace;
For whan I see the beautee of your face,
Ye ben so scarlet-reed aboute your yën,
It maketh al my drede for to dyen.
For also siker as ' In principio,'
' Mulier est hominis confusio;'
Madame, the sentence of this Latin is
'Woman is mannes Ioye and al his blis.'
For whan I fele a-night your softe syde,
Al-be-it that I may nat on you ryde,
For that our perche is maad so narwe, alas!
I am so ful of Ioye and of solas
That I defye bothe sweven and dreem."
And with that word he fley doun fro the beem,
For it was day, and eek his hennes alle;
And with a chuk he gan hem for to calle,

For he had founde a corn, lay in the yerd.
Royal he was, he was namore aferd;
He loketh as it were a grim leoun,
And on his toes he rometh up and doun,—
Him deyned not to sette his foot to grounde.
He chukketh whan he hath a corn y-founde,
And to him renneth than his wyves alle.
Thus royal as a prince is in his halle
Leve I this Chauntecleer in his pasture;
And after wol I telle his aventure.

Whan that the month in which the world bigan,
That highte March, whan God first maked man,
Was complet, and y-passed were also,
Sin March bigan, thritty dayes and two,
Bifel that Chauntecleer in al his pryde,
His sevene wyves walking by his syde,
Caste up his eyen to the brighte sonne,
That in the signe of Taurus had y-ronne
Twenty degrees and oon and somwhat more;
And knew by kinde and by noon other lore
That it was pryme, and crew with blisful stevene.
"The sonne," he sayde, "is clomben up on hevene
Fourty degrees and oon and more, y-wis.
Madame Pertelote, my worldes blis,
Herkneth thise blisful briddes how they singe,
And see the fresshe floures how they springe.
Ful is myn herte of revel and solas!"
But sodeinly him fil a sorweful cas;
For evere the latter ende of Ioye is wo.
God woot that worldly Ioye is sone ago;
And if a rethor coude faire endyte,
He in a cronique saufly mighte it wryte
As for a sovereyn notabilitee.
Now every wys man, lat him herkne me:
This storie is al-so trewe, I undertake,
As is the book of Launcelot de Lake,
That wommen holde in ful gret reverence.
Now wol I torne agayn to my sentence.

Sk., B, 4365-4366; 4369-4404

A col-fox ful of sly iniquitee,
That in the grove had woned yeres three,
By heigh imaginacioun forn-cast
The same night thurgh-outę the hegges brast
Into the yerd ther Chauntecleer the faire
Was wont, and eek his wyves, to repaire;
And in a bed of wortes stille he lay
Til it was passed undern of the day,
Wayting his tyme on Chauntecleer to falle,
As gladly doon thise homicydes alle
That in awayt liggen to mordre men.
O false mordrer lurking in thy den!
O newe Scariot, newe Genilon!
False dissimilour, O Greek Sinon,
That broghtest Troye al outrely to sorwe!
O Chauntecleer, acursed be that morwe
That thou into that yerd flough fro the bemes!
Thou werę ful wel y-warned by thy dremes
That thilke day was perilous to thee.
But what that God forwoot mot nedes be,
After the opinioun of certeyn clerkis.
Witnesse on him that any perfit clerk is,
That in scole is gret altercacioun
In this matere, and greet disputisoun,
And hath ben of an hundred thousand men.
But I ne can not bulte it to the bren
As can the holy doctour Augustyn,
Or Boece, or the bishop Bradwardyn,
Whether that Goddes worthy forwiting
Streyneth me nedęly for to doon a thing
(Nedely clepe I simple necessitee);
Or ellęs, if that free choys be graunted me
To do that same thing or do it noght,
Though God forwoot it er that it was wroght;
Or if his witing streyneth nevere a del
But by necessitee condicionel.
I wol not han to do of swich matere;
My tale is of a cok, as ye may here,

That took his counseil of his wyf, with sorwe,
To walken in the yerd upon that morwe
That he had met the dreem that I yow tolde.
Wommennes counseils been ful ofte colde;
Wommannes counseil broghte us first to wo,
And made Adam fro Paradys to go,
Ther-as he was ful merye and wel at ese.
But for I noot to whom it mighte displese
If I counseil of wommen wolde blame,
Passe over, for I seyde it in my game.
Rede auctours, wher they trete of swich matere,
And what they seyn of wommen ye may here.
Thise been the cokkes wordes and nat myne;
I can noon harm of no womman divyne.

Faire in the sond, to bathe hir merily,
Lyth Pertelote, and alle hir sustres by,
Agayn the sonne; and Chauntecleer so free
Song merier than the mermayde in the see:
For Phisiologus seith sikerly
How that they singen wel and merily.
And so bifel that as he caste his yë
Among the wortes on a boterflye,
He was war of this fox that lay ful lowe.
No-thing ne liste him thanne for to crowe,
But cryde anon "Cok, cok," and up he sterte
As man that was affrayed in his herte.
For naturelly a beest desyreth flee
Fro his contrarie if he may it see,
Though he nevere erst had seyn it with his yë.

This Chauntecleer, whan he gan him espye,
He wolde han fled, but that the fox anon
Seyde, "Gentil sir, allas! wher wol ye gon?
Be ye affrayed of me that am your freend?
Now certes, I were worse than a feend
If I to yow wolde harm or vileinye.
I am not come your counseil for tespye;
But trewely, the cause of my cominge
Was only for to herkne how that ye singe.

Sk., B, 4443-4480

For trewely ye have as merye a stevene
As eny aungel hath that is in hevene;
Therwith ye han in musik more felinge
Than had Boece or any that can singe.
My lord your fader (God his soule blesse!)
And eek your moder, of hir gentilesse,
Han in myn hous y-been, to my gret ese.
And certes, sir, ful fayn wolde I yow plese.
But for men speke of singing, I wol saye,
So mote I brouke wel myn eyen tweye,
Save yow I herde nevere man so singe
As did your fader in the morweninge;
Certes, it was of herte al that he song.
And for to make his voys the more strong,
He wolde so peyne him that with bothe his yën
He moste winke, so loude he wolde cryen,
And stonden on his tiptoon ther-with-al,
And strecche forth his nekke long and smal.
And eek he was of swich discrecioun
That ther nas no man in no regioun
That him in song or wisdom mighte passe.
I have wel rad in Daun Burnel the Asse,
Among his vers, how that ther was a cok,
For that a preestes sone yaf him a knok
Upon his leg whyl he was yong and nyce,
He made him for to lese his benefyce.
But certeyn, ther nis no comparisoun
Bitwix the wisdom and discrecioun
Of youre fader, and of his subtiltee.
Now singeth, sir, for seinte charitee,
Lat see, conne ye your fader countrefete?"
This Chauntecleer his winges gan to bete
As man that coude his tresoun nat espye,
So was he ravisshed with his flaterye.

Allas! ye lordes, many a fals flatour
Is in your courtes, and many a losengour,
That plesen yow wel more, by my feith,
Than he that soothfastnesse unto yow seith.

Redeth Ecclesiaste of flaterye;
Beth war, ye lordes, of hir trecherye.

This Chauntecleer stood hye up-on his toos,
Strecching his nekke, and heeld his eyen cloos,
And gan to crowe loude for the nones;
And Daun Russel the fox sterte up at ones,
And by the gargat hente Chauntecleer,
And on his bak toward the wode him beer,
For yet ne was ther no man that him sewed.
O destinee, that mayst nat been eschewed!
Allas, that Chauntecleer fleigh fro the bemes!
Allas, his wyf ne roghte nat of dremes!
And on a Friday fil al this meschaunce.
O Venus, that art goddesse of plesaunce,
Sin that thy servant was this Chauntecleer,
And in thy servicȩ did al his poweer,
Morȩ for delyt than world to multiplye,
Why woldestow suffre him on thy day to dye?
O Gaufred, dere mayster soverayn,
That, whan thy worthy King Richard was slayn
With shot, compleynedest his deth so sore,
Why ne had I now thy sentence and thy lore
The Friday for to chide as diden ye?
(For on a Friday soothly slayn was he.)
Than wolde I shewȩ yow how that I coudȩ pleyne
For Chauntecleres drede and for his peyne.

Certes, swich cry ne lamentacioun
Was nevere of ladies maad whan Ilioun
Was wonne, and Pirrus with his streite swerd,
Whan he had hent King Priam by the berd
And slain him—as saith us *Eneydos*—
As maden alle the hennes in the clos
Whan they had seyn of Chauntecleer the sighte.
But sovereynly Dame Pertelote shrighte
Ful louder than did Hasdrubales wyf
Whan that hir housbonde hadde lost his lyf,
And that the Romayns hadde brend Cartage;
She was so ful of torment and of rage

That wilfully into the fyr she sterte
And brende hir-selven with a stedfast herte.
O woful hennes, right so cryden ye
As, whan that Nero brende the citee
Of Rome, cryden senatoures wyves
For that hir housbondes losten alle hir lyves:
With-outen gilt this Nero hath hem slayn.
Now wol I torne to my tale agayn.

This sely widwe and eek hir doghtres two
Herden thise hennes crye and maken wo,
And oute at dores sterten they anoon,
And syen the fox toward the grove goon,
And bar upon his bak the cok away;
And cryden, "Oute! harrow! and weylaway!
Ha, ha, the fox!" and after him they ran,
And eek with staves many another man;
Ran Colle our dogge, and Talbot, and Gerland,
And Malkin with a distaf in hir hand;
Ran cow and calf, and eek the verray hogges
So were they fered for berking of the dogges
And shouting of the men and wimmen eke,
They ronne so, hem thoughte hir herte breke.
They yelleden as feendes doon in helle;
The dokes cryden as men wolde hem quelle;
The gees for fere flowen over the trees;
Out of the hyve cam the swarm of bees.
So hidous was the noyse, a! *benedicite!*
Certes, he Iakke Straw and his meynee
Ne made nevere shoutes half so shrille
Whan that they wolden any Fleming kille
As thilke day was maad upon the fox.
Of bras they broghten bemes, and of box,
Of horn, of boon, in which they blewe and pouped,
And therwithal they shryked and they houped;
It semed as that hevene sholde falle.
Now, gode men, I pray yow herkneth alle!

Lo, how Fortune turneth sodeinly
The hope and pryde eek of hir enemy!

This cok, that lay upon the foxes bak
In al his drede, un-to the fox he spak
And seyde, "Sir, if that I were as ye,
Yet sholde I seyn—as wis God helpe me!—
' Turneth agayn, ye proude cherles alle!
A verray pestilence up-on yow falle!
Now am I come un-to this wodes syde,
Maugree your heed the cok shal heer abyde;
I wol him ete in feith and that anon!' "
The fox answerde, "In feith, it shal be don;"—
And as he spak that word, al sodeinly
This cok brak from his mouth deliverly,
And heighe up-on a tree he fleigh anon.
And whan the fox saugh that he was y-gon,
"Allas!" quod he, "O Chauntecleer, allas!
I have to yow," quod he, "y-doon trespas,
In-as-muche as I maked yow aferd
Whan I yow hente and broghte out of the yerd.
But, sir, I did it in no wikke entente;
Com doun, and I shal telle yow what I mente.
I shal seye sooth to yow, God helpe me so!"
"Nay than," quod he, "I shrewe us bothe two,
And first I shrewe my-self, bothe blood and bones,
If thou bigyle me ofter than ones.
Thou shalt na-more thurgh thy flaterye
Do me to singe and winke with myn yë.
For he that winketh whan he sholde see,
Al wilfully, God lat him nevere thee!"
"Nay," quod the fox, "but God yeve him meschaunce
That is so undiscreet of governaunce
That Iangleth whan he sholde holde his pees."

    Lo, swich it is for to be recchelees,
And necligent, and truste on flaterye.
But ye that holden this tale a folye,
As of a fox or of a cok and hen,
Taketh the moralitee, good men.
For Seint Paul seith that al that writen is,
To our doctryne it is y-write, y-wis.

Taketh the fruyt, and lat the chaf be stille.
  Now, gode God, if that it be thy wille,
As seith my lord, so make us allę good men;
And bringe us to his heighe blisse. Amen.

Here is ended the Nonne Preestes Tale.

The wordes of the Host to the Pardoner.

"Thou bel amy, thou Pardoner," he seyde,
"Telle us som mirthe or Iapes right anon."
"It shal be doon," quod he, "by Seint Ronyon!
But first," quod he, "heer at this ale-stake
I wol bothę drinke, and eten of a cake."
  But right anon thisę gentils gonnę to crye,
"Nay! lat him telle us of no ribaudye;
Tel us som moral thing that we may lere
Som wit, and thanne wol we gladly here."
"I graunte, y-wis," quod he, "but I mot thinke
Up-on som honest thing whyl that I drinke."

Here folweth the Prologe of the Pardoners Tale.

Lordings,—quod he:—in chirches whan I preche,
I peyne me to han an hauteyn speche,
And ringe it oute as rounde as gooth a belle,
For I can al by rote that I telle.
My theme is alwey oon, and evere was—
"*Radix malorum est Cupiditas*."
  First I pronounce whennes that I come,
And than my bulles shewe I, alle and somme.
Our lige lordes seel on my patente,
That shewe I first, my body to warente,
That no man be so bold, ne preest, ne clerk,
Me to destourbe of Cristes holy werk;
And after that than telle I forth my tales,—
Bulles of popes and of cardinales,
Of patriarkes and bishoppes I shewe;
And in Latyn I speke a wordes fewe

To saffron with my predicacioun,
And for to stirę men to devocioun.
Than shewe I forth my longe cristal stones,
Y-crammed ful of cloutes and of bones;
Reliks been they, as wenen they echoon.
Than have I in latoun a sholder-boon
Which that was of an holy Iewes sheep.
"Good men," seye I, "tak of my wordes keep.
If that this boon be wasshe in any welle,
If cow or calf or sheep or oxe swelle
That any worm hath ete, or worm y-stonge,
Tak water of that welle and wash his tonge,
And it is hool anon; and forthermore,
Of pokkes and of scabbe, and every sore
Shal every sheep be hool that of this welle
Drinketh a draughtę: tak keep eek what I telle.
If that the good man that the bestes oweth
Wol every wike, er that the cok him croweth,
Fasting drinken of this welle a draughte,
As thilke holy Iew our eldres taughte,
His bestes and his stoor shal multiplye.
And, sirs, also it heleth Ialousye;
For though a man be falle in Ialous rage,
Let maken with this water his potage
And nevere shal he more his wyf mistriste,
Though he the sooth of hir defaute wiste,
Al had she taken preestes two or three.
    "Heer is a miteyn eek that ye may see.
He that his hond wol putte in this miteyn,
He shal have multiplying of his greyn,
Whan he hath sowen, be it whete or otes,
So that he offre pens or elles grotes.
    "Good men and wommen, o thing warne I yow,
If any wight be in this chirche now
That hath doon sinne horrible, that he
Dar nat, for shame, of it y-shriven be,
Or any womman, be she yong or old,
That hath y-maad hir housbond cokewold, *cukold*

Swich folk shul have no power ne no grace
To offren to my reliks in this place.
And who-so findeth him out of swich blame,
He wol come up and offre in Goddes name,
And I assoille him by the auctoritee
Which that by bulle y-graunted was to me."
By this gaude have I wonne, yeer by yeer,
An hundred mark sith I was Pardoner.
I stonde lyk a clerk in my pulpet,
And whan the lewed peple is doun y-set,
I preche, so as ye han herd bifore,
And telle an hundred false Iapes more.
Than peyne I me to strecche forth the nekke,
And est and west upon the peple I bekke,
As doth a dowve sitting on a berne.
Myn hondes and my tonge goon so yerne
That it is Ioye to see my bisinesse.
Of avaryce and of swich cursednesse
Is al my preching, for to make hem free
To yeve her pens, and namely un-to me.
For my entente is nat but for to winne,
And no-thing for correccioun of sinne.
I rekke nevere, whan that they ben beried,
Though that her soules goon a-blakeberied!
For certes, many a predicacioun
Comth ofte tyme of yvel entencioun;
Som for plesaunce of folk and flaterye,
To been avaunced by ipocrisye,
And som for veyne glorie and som for hate.
For whan I dar non other weyes debate,
Than wol I stinge him with my tonge smerte
In preching so that he shal nat asterte
To been defamed falsly, if that he
Hath trespased to my brethren or to me.
For, though I telle noght his propre name,
Men shal wel knowe that it is the same
By signes and by othere circumstances.
Thus quyte I folk that doon us displesances;

Thus spitte I oute my venim under hewe
Of holynesse, to seme holy and trewe.

But shortly myn entente I wol devyse;
I preche no-thing but for coveityse.
Therfore my theme is yet, and evere was—
"*Radix malorum est cupiditas.*"
Thus can I preche agayn the same vyce
Which that I use, and that is avaryce.
But, though my-self be gilty in that sinne,
Yet can I maken other folk to twinne
From avaryce, and sore to repente.
But that is nat my principal entente.
I preche no-thing but for coveityse;
Of this matere it oughte y-nogh suffyse.

Than telle I hem ensamples many oon
Of olde stories longe tyme agoon:
For lewed peple loven tales olde;
Swich thinges can they wel reporte and holde.
What? trowe ye, the whyles I may preche
And winne gold and silver for I teche,
That I wol live in poverte wilfully?
Nay, nay, I thoghte it nevere trewely!
For I wol preche and begge in sondry londes,
I wol not do no labour with my hondes,
Ne make baskettes, and live therby,
Because I wol nat beggen ydelly.
I wol non of the apostles counterfete;
I wol have moneye, wolle, chese, and whete,
Al were it yeven of the povrest page,
Or of the povrest widwe in a village,
Al sholde hir children sterve for famyne.
Nay! I wol drinke licour of the vyne,
And have a Ioly wenche in every toun.
But herkneth, lordings, in conclusioun;
Your lyking is that I shal telle a tale.
Now have I dronke a draughte of corny ale,
By God, I hope I shal yow telle a thing
That shal by resoun been at your lyking.

Sk., C, 421–458

For though myself be a ful vicious man,
A moral tale yet I yow telle can,
Which I am wont to preche for to winne.
Now hold your pees, my tale I wol beginne.

THE PARDONERS TALE

Here biginneth the Pardoners Tale.

In Flaundres whylom was a companye
Of yonge folk that haunteden folye,
As ryot, hasard, stewes, and tavernes,
Wher-as with harpes, lutes, and giternes,
They daunce and pleye at dees bothe day and night,
And ete also and drinken over hir might,
Thurgh which they doon the devel sacrifyse
With-in that develes temple in cursed wyse
By superfluitee abhominable.
Hir othes been so grete and so dampnable
That it is grisly for to here hem swere:
Our blissed lordes body they to-tere,
Hem thoughte Iewes rente him noght y-nough;
And ech of hem at otheres sinne lough.
And right anon than comen tombesteres
Fetys and smale, and yonge fruytesteres,
Singers with harpes, baudes, wafereres,
Which been the verray develes officeres
To kindle and blowe the fyr of lecherye,
That is annexed un-to glotonye.
The holy writ take I to my witnesse
That luxurie is in wyn and dronkenesse.
Lo, how that dronken Loth unkindely
Lay by his doghtres two unwitingly;
So dronke he was, he niste what he wroghte.
Herodes (who-so wel the stories soghte),
Whan he of wyn was replet at his feste,
Right at his owene table he yaf his heste

To sleen the Baptist Iohn ful giltelees.
  Senek seith eek a good word doutelees.
He seith he can no difference finde
Bitwix a man that is out of his minde
And a man which that is dronkelewe,
But that woodnesse y-fallen in a shrewe
Persevereth lenger than doth dronkenesse.
O glotonye, ful of cursednesse,
O cause first of our confusioun,
O original of our dampnacioun,
Til Crist had boght us with his blood agayn!
Lo, how dere, shortly for to sayn,
Aboght was thilke cursed vileinye;
Corrupt was al this world for glotonye!
  Adam our fader and his wyf also
From Paradys to labour and to wo
Were driven for that vyce, it is no drede;
For whyl that Adam fasted, as I rede,
He was in Paradys, and whan that he
Eet of the fruyt defended on the tree,
Anon he was out-cast to wo and peyne.
O glotonye, on thee wel oghte us pleyne!
O, wiste a man how many maladyes
Folwen of excesse and of glotonyes,
He wolde been the more mesurable
Of his diete, sitting at his table.
Allas! the shorte throtę, the tendre mouth,
Maketh that est and west and north and south,
In erthe, in eir, in water, men to-swinke
To gete a glotoun deyntee mete and drinke!
Of this matere, O Paul, wel canstow trete:
"Mete un-to wombe, and wombe eek un-to mete,
Shal God destroyen bothe," as Paulus seith.
Allas! a foul thing is it, by my feith,
To seye this word, and fouler is the dede,
Whan man so drinketh of the whyte and rede
That of his throte he maketh his privee,
Thurgh thilke cursed superfluitee.

Sk., C, 491–528

The apostel weping seith ful pitously,
"Ther walken many of which yow told have I,
I seye it now weping with pitous voys,
That they been enemys of Cristes croys,
Of which the ende is deeth, wombe is her god."
O wombe! O bely! O stinking cod!
How greet labour and cost is thee to finde!
Thise cokes, how they stampe, and streyne, and grinde,
And turnen substaunce in-to accident
To fulfille al thy likerous talent!
Out of the harde bones knokke they
The mary, for they caste noght a-wey
That may go thurgh the golet softe and swote;
Of spicerye, of leef, and bark, and rote
Shal been his sauce y-maked by delyt
To make him yet a newer appetyt.
But certes, he that haunteth swich delyces
Is deed whyl that he liveth in tho vyces.

A lecherous thing is wyn, and dronkenesse
Is ful of stryving and of wrecchednesse.
O dronke man, disfigured is thy face,
Sour is thy breeth, foul artow to embrace,
And thurgh thy dronke nose semeth the soun
As though thou seydest ay "Sampsoun, Sampsoun;"
And yet, God wot, Sampsoun drank nevere no wyn.
Thou fallest as it were a stiked swyn;
Thy tonge is lost, and al thyn honest cure;
For dronkenesse is verray sepulture
Of mannes wit and his discrecioun.
In whom that drinke hath dominacioun,
He can no conseil kepe, it is no drede.
Now kepe yow fro the whyte and fro the rede,
And namely fro the whyte wyn of Lepe,
That is to selle in Fish-strete or in Chepe.
This wyn of Spayne crepeth subtilly
In othere wynes, growing faste by,
Of which ther ryseth swich fumositee
That whan a man hath dronken draughtes three,

And weneth that he be at hoom in Chepe,
He is in Spaynę, right at the toun of Lepe,
Nat at the Rochel, ne at Burdeux toun;
And thanne wol he seyę, "Sampsoun, Sampsoun."

But herkneth, lordings, o word, I yow preye,
That allę the sovereyn actes, dar I seye,
Of victories in the Olde Testament,
Thurgh verray God that is omnipotent,
Werę doon in abstinence and in preyere;
Loketh the Bible and ther ye may it lere.

Loke, Attila, the grete conquerour,
Deyde in his sleep with shame and dishonour
Bleding ay at his nose in dronkenesse.
A capitayn sholde live in sobrenesse
And over al this, avyseth yow right wel
What was comaunded un-to Lamuel—
Nat Samuel, but Lamuel, seye I—
Redeth the Bible, and finde it expresly
Of wyn-yeving to hem that han Iustyse.
Na-more of this, for it may wel suffyse.

And now that I havę spoke of glotonye,
Now wol I yow defenden hasardrye.
Hasard is verray moder of lesinges,
And of deceit, and cursed forsweringes,
Blaspheme of Crist, manslaughtre, and wast also
Of catel and of tyme; and forthermo,
It is repreve and contrarie of honour
For to ben holde a commune hasardour.
And evere the hyer he is of estaat,
The morë is he holden desolaat.
If that a princë useth hasardrye,
In alle governaunce and policye
He is, as by commune opinioun,
Y-holdę the lasse in reputacioun.

Stilbon, that was a wys embassadour,
Was sent to Corinthe in ful greet honour
Fro Lacidomie to make hir alliaunce.
And whan he cam, him happede par chaunce

That allę the grettest that were of that lond,
Pleying atte hasard he hem fond.
For which, as sonë as it mighte be,
He stal him hoom agayn to his contree,
And seyde, "Ther wol I nat lesę my name;
Ne I wol nat take on me so greet defame
Yow for to allye un-to none hasardours.
Sendeth othere wyse embassadours;
For, by my trouthe, me werę lever dye
Than I yow sholdę to hasardours allye.
For ye that been so glorious in honours
Shul nat allyen yow with hasardours
As by my wille, ne as by my tretee."
This wyse philosophre, thus seyde he.

Loke eek that, to the king Demetrius
The king of Parthes, as the book seith us,
Sente him a paire of dees of gold in scorn,
For he had used hasard ther-biforn;
For which he heeld his glorie or his renoun
At no value or reputacioun.
Lordes may finden other maner pley
Honest y-nough to dryvę the day awey.

Now wol I speke of othes false and grete
A word or two, as olde bokes trete.
Gret swering is a thing abhominable,
And falsę swering is yet morę reprevable.
The heighe God forbad swering at al,
Witnesse on Mathew; but in special
Of swering seith the holy Ieremye,
"Thou shalt seyę sooth thyn othes, and nat lye,
And swere in doom and eek in rightwisnesse;"
But ydel swering is a cursednesse.
Bihold and see that in the firste table
Of heighe Goddes hestes honurable
How that the second heste of him is this—
"Tak nat my name in ydel or amis."
Lo, rather he forbedeth swich swering,
Than homicyde or many a cursed thing;

I seye that as by ordre thus it stondeth;
This knowen, that his hestes understondeth,
How that the second heste of God is that.
And forther over, I wol thee telle al plat
That vengeance shal nat parten from his hous
That of his othes is to outrageous.
"By Goddes precious herte, and by his nayles,
And by the blood of Crist, that it is in Hayles,
Sevene is my chaunce, and thyn is cink and treye;
By Goddes armes, if thou falsly pleye,
This daggere shal thurgh-oute thyn herte go"—
This fruyt cometh of the bicched bones two:
Forswering, ire, falsnesse, homicyde.
Now, for the love of Crist that for us dyde,
Leveth your othes, bothe grete and smale;
But, sirs, now wol I telle forth my tale.

    Thise ryotoures three, of which I telle,
Longe erst er pryme rong of any belle,
Were set hem in a taverne for to drinke;
And as they satte, they herde a belle clinke
Biforn a cors, was caried to his grave.
That oon of hem gan callen to his knave,
"Go bet," quod he, "and axe redily
What cors is this that passeth heer forby;
And loke that thou reporte his name wel."

    "Sir," quod this boy, "it nedeth nevere-a-del.
It was me told, er ye cam heer, two houres.
He was, pardee, an old felawe of youres;
And sodeinly he was y-slayn to-night,
For-dronke, as he sat on his bench upright;
Ther cam a privee theef men clepeth Deeth,
That in this contree al the peple sleeth,
And with his spere he smoot his herte a-two
And wente his wey with-outen wordes mo.
He hath a thousand slayn this pestilence:
And, maister, er ye come in his presence,
Me thinketh that it were a necessarie
For to be war of swich an adversarie.

Beth redy for to mete him everemore.
Thus taughte me my dame, I sey na-more."
"By Seinte Marie," seydę this taverner,
"The child seith sooth, for he hath slayn this yeer,
Henne over a myle, with-in a greet village,
Bothę man and womman, child and hyne and page.
I trowe his habitacioun be there;
To been avysed greet wisdom it were,
Er that he did a man a dishonour."
"Ye, Goddes armes," quod this ryotour,
"Is it swich peril with him for to mete?
I shal him sekę by wey and eek by strete,
I make avow to Goddes digne bones!
Herkneth, felawes, we three been al ones;
Lat ech of us holde up his hond til other,
And ech of us bicomen otheres brother,
And we wol sleen this false traytour Deeth.
He shal be slayn, which that so many sleeth,
By Goddes dignitee, er it be night."

Togidres han thisę three her trouthes plight
To live and dyen ech of hem for other
As though he were his owene y-boren brother.
And up they sterte al dronken in this rage,
And forth they goon towardes that village
Of which the taverner had spokę biforn;
And many a grisly ooth than han they sworn,
And Cristes blessed body they to-rente,—
Deeth shal be deed, if that they may him hente!

Whan they han goon nat fully half a myle,
Right as they wolde han troden over a style,
An old man and a povre with hem mette.
This olde man ful mekely hem grette,
And seyde thus, "Now, lordes, God yow see!"

The proudest of thisę ryotoures three
Answerde agayn, "What? carl, with sory grace,
Why artow al forwrapped save thy face?
Why livestow so longe in so greet age?"

This olde man gan loke in his visage,

And seyde thus, "For I ne can nat finde
A man, though that I walked in-to Inde,
Neither in citee nor in no village,
That wolde chaunge his youthe for myn age;
And therfore moot I han myn age stille
As longe tyme as it is Goddes wille.
Ne deeth, allas! ne wol nat han my lyf.
Thus walke I lyk a restelees caityf,
And on the ground, which is my modres gate,
I knokke with my staf bothe erly and late,
And seye, 'Leve moder, leet me in!
Lo, how I vanish, flesh and blood and skin!
Allas! whan shul my bones been at reste?
Moder, with yow wolde I chaunge my cheste
That in my chambre longe tyme hath be,
Ye, for an heyre clout to wrappe me!'
But yet to me she wol nat do that grace,
For which ful pale and welked is my face.

"But, sirs, to yow it is no curteisye
To speken to an old man vileinye,
But he trespasse in word or elles in dede.
In holy writ ye may your-self wel rede,
'Agayns an old man, hoor upon his heed,
Ye sholde aryse;' wherfore I yeve yow reed,
Ne dooth un-to an old man noon harm now,
Na-more than ye wolde men did to yow
In age, if that ye so longe abyde.
And God be with yow wher ye go or ryde:
I moot go thider as I have to go."

"Nay, olde cherl, by God, thou shalt nat so,"
Seyde this other hasardour anon;
"Thou partest nat so lightly, by Seint Iohn!
Thou spak right now of thilke traitour Deeth,
That in this contree alle our frendes sleeth.
Have heer my trouthe, as thou art his aspye,
Telle wher he is or thou shalt it abye,
By God and by the holy sacrement!
For soothly thou art oon of his assent,

Sk., C, 721-758

To sleen us yonge folk, thou false theef!"

"Now, sirs," quod he, "if that yow be so leef
To finde Deeth, turne up this croked wey,
For in that grove I lafte him, by my fey,
Under a tree, and ther he wol abyde.
Nat for your boost he wol him no-thing hyde.
See ye that ook? Right ther ye shul him finde.
God save yow, that boghte agayn mankinde,
And yow amende!"—Thus seyde this olde man.
And everich of thise ryotoures ran
Til he cam to that tree, and ther they founde
Of florins fyne of gold y-coyned rounde
Wel ny an eighte busshels, as hem thoughte.
No lenger thannë after Deeth they soughte,
But ech of hem so glad was of that sighte,
For that the florins been so faire and brighte,
That doun they sette hem by this precious hord.
The worste of hem he spak the firste word:—

"Brethren," quod he, "tak keep what I seye;
My wit is greet, though that I bourde and pleye.
This tresour hath Fortune un-to us yiven,
In mirthe and Iolitee our lyf to liven,
And lightly as it comth, so wol we spende.
Ey! Goddes precious dignitee! who wende
To-day that we sholde han so fair a grace?
But mightë this gold be caried fro this place
Hoom to myn hous, or elles un-to youres—
For wel ye woot that al this gold is oures—
Than were we in heigh felicitee.
But trewely, by day it may nat be:
Men wolde seyn that we werë theves stronge,
And for our owene tresour doon us honge.
This tresor moste y-caried be by nighte
As wysly and as slyly as it mighte.
Wherfore I redë that cut among us alle
Be drawe, and lat see wher the cut wol falle;
And he that hath the cut with herte blythe
Shal renne to the toun, and that ful swythe,

And bringe us breed and wyn ful prively.
And two of us shal kepen subtilly
This tresor wel; and if he wol nat tarie,
Whan it is night we wol this tresor carie
By oon assent, wher-as us thinketh best."
That oon of hem the cut broughte in his fest,
And bad hem drawe, and lokę wher it wol falle;
And it fil on the yongeste of hem alle;
And forth toward the toun he wente anon.
And al-so sonë as that he was gon,
That oon of hem spak thus un-to that other:
"Thou knowest wel thou art my sworne brother,
Thy profit wol I telle thee anon.
Thou woost wel that our felawe is agon;
And heer is gold, and that ful greet plentee,
That shal departed been among us three.
But natheles, if I can shape it so
That it departed were among us two,
Had I nat doon a freendes torn to thee?"
   That other answerde, "I noot how that may be.
He woot how that the gold is with us tweye;
What shal we doon, what shal we to him seye?"
   "Shal it be conseil?" seydę the firste shrewe,
"And I shal tellen thee in wordes fewe
What we shal doon and bringe it wel aboute."
   "I graunte," quod that other, "out of doute,
That, by my trouthe, I wol thee nat biwreye."
   "Now," quod the firstę, "thou woost wel we be tweye,
And two of us shal strenger be than oon.
Lokę whan that he is set, and right anoon
Arys as though thou woldest with him pleye,
And I shal ryve him thurgh the sydes tweye
Whyl that thou strogelest with him as in game,
And with thy daggerę lokę thou do the same.
And than shal al this gold departed be,
My dere freend, bitwixen me and thee.
Than may we bothe our lustes al fulfille,
And pleye at dees right at our owene wille."

And thus acorded been thisę shrewes tweye
To sleen the thridde, as ye han herd me seye.

This yongest, which that wente un-to the toun,
Ful ofte in herte he rolleth up and doun
The beautee of thisę florins newe and brighte.

"O Lord!" quod he, "if so werę that I mighte
Have al this tresor to my-self allone,
Ther is no man that liveth under the trone
Of God that sholde livę so merye as I!"
And atte lastę, the feend, our enemy,
Putte in his thought that he sholdę poyson beye,
With which he mighte sleen his felawęs tweye;
For-why the feend fond him in swich lyvinge
That he had leve him to sorwe bringe,
For this was outrely his fulle entente
To sleen hem bothe, and nevere to repente.
And forth he gooth, no lenger wolde he tarie,
Into the toun, un-to a pothecarie,
And preyed him that he him wolde selle
Som poyson that he mighte his rattes quelle;
And eek ther was a polcat in his hawe,
That, as he seyde, his capouns had y-slawe;
And fayn he wolde wreke him, if he mighte,
On verminę that destroyed him by nighte.

The pothecarie answerde, "And thou shalt have
A thing that, al-so God my soule save,
In al this world ther nis no creature,
That ete or dronke hath of this confiture
Noght but the mountance of a corn of whete,
That he ne shal his lyf anon forlete;
Ye, sterve he shal, and that in lasse whyle
Than thou wolt goon a-paas nat but a myle:
This poyson is so strong and violent."

This cursed man hath in his hond y-hent
This poyson in a box, and sith he ran
In-to the nexte strete un-to a man,
And borwed of him large botels three;
And in the two his poyson poured he;

The thridde he kepte clene for his drinke.
For al the night he shoop him for to swinke
In carying of the gold out of that place.
And whan this ryotour, with sory grace!
Had filld with wyn his grete botels three,
To his felawes agayn repaireth he.

What nedeth it to sermone of it more?
For right as they had cast his deeth bifore,
Right so they han him slayn, and that anon.
And whan that this was doon, thus spak that oon,
"Now lat us sitte and drinke, and make us merie,
And afterward we wol his body berie."
And with that word it happed him, par cas,
To take the botel ther the poyson was,
And drank, and yaf his felawe drinke also,
For which anon they storven bothe two.

But certes, I suppose that Avicen
Wroot nevere in no canon, ne in no fen,
Mo wonder signes of empoisoning
Than had thise wrecches two er hir ending.
Thus ended been thise homicydes two,
And eek the false empoysoner also.

O cursed sinne, ful of cursednesse!
O traytours homicyde, O wikkednesse!
O glotonye, luxurie, and hasardrye!
Thou blasphemour of Crist with vileinye
And othes grete, of usage and of pryde!
Allas! mankindë, how may it bityde
That to thy creatour which that thee wroghte,
And with his precious herte-blood thee boghte,
Thou art so false and so unkinde, allas!
Now, goode men, God foryeve yow your trespas,
And ware yow fro the sinne of avaryce.
Myn holy pardoun may yow alle waryce,
So that ye offre nobles or sterlinges,
Or elles silver broches, spones, ringes.
Boweth your heed under this holy bulle!

Comęth up, ye wyves, offreth of your wolle!
Your name I entre heer in my rolle anon;
In-to the blisse of hevenę shul ye gon;
I yow assoile, by myn heigh power,
Yow that wol offre, as clene and eek as cleer
As ye were born:—And, lo, sirs, thus I preche.
And Iesu Crist, that is our soules leche,
So graunte yow his pardon to receyve;
For that is best: I wol yow nat deceyve.
　　But sirs, o word forgat I in my tale,
I have relikes and pardon in my male,
As faire as any man in Engelond,
Which werę me yeven by the popes hond.
If any of yow wol, of devocioun,
Offren, and han myn absolucioun,
Cometh forth anon, and kneleth heer adoun,
And mekely receyveth my pardoun:
Or elles, taketh pardon as ye wende,
Al newe and freshe, at every tounes ende,
So that ye offren alwey newe and newe
Nobles and pens which that be gode and trewe.
It is an honour to everich that is heer
That ye mowe have a suffisant pardoneer
Tassoille yow in contree as ye ryde
For aventures which that may bityde.
Peraventurę ther may falle oon or two
Doun of his hors, and breke his nekke atwo.
Look which a seuretee is it to yow alle
That I am in your felaweshipe y-falle,
That may assoillę yow, bothe more and lasse,
Whan that the soulę shal fro the body passe.
I rede that our host heer shal biginne,
For he is most envoluped in sinne.
Com forth, sir host, and offre first anon,
And thou shalt kissę the reliks everichon,
Ye, for a grote! Unbokele anon thy purs!

Here is ended the Pardoners Tale.

The Prologe of the Wyves Tale of Bathe

Experience, though noon auctoritee
Were in this world, were right y-nough to me
To speke of wo that is in mariage;
For, lordings, sith I twelf yeer was of age,
Thonked be God that is eterne on lyve,
Housbondes at chirche-dore I have had fyve.
For I so ofte have y-wedded be;
And alle were worthy men in hir degree.
Welcome the sixte, whan that evere he shal.
For sothe, I wol nat kepe me chast in al;
Whan myn housbonde is fro the world y-gon,
Som Cristen man shal wedde me anon.
For than thapostle seith that I am free
To wedde, a Goddes half, wher it lyketh me.
He seith that to be wedded is no sinne;
Bet is to be wedded than to brinne.
What rekketh me thogh folk seye vileinye
Of shrewed Lameth and his bigamye?
I woot wel Abraham was an holy man,
And Iacob eek, as ferforth as I can;
And ech of hem had wyves mo than two,
And many another holy man also.
Whan saugh ye evere in any maner age
That hye God defended mariage
By expres word? I pray you tellen me;
Or wher comanded he virginitee?
I woot as wel as ye, it is no drede,
Thapostel, whan he speketh of maydenhede;
He seyde that precept ther-of had he noon.
Men may conseille a womman to been oon,
But conseilling is no comandement;
He putte it in our owene Iugement.
For hadde God comanded maydenhede,
Than had he dampned wedding with the dede;
And certes, if ther were no seed y-sowe,
Virginitee, wher-of than sholde it growe?

Sk., D, 1–8; 45–72

Poul dorste nat comanden atte leste
A thing of which his maister yaf noon heste.
The darte is set up for virginitee;
Cacche who so may, who renneth best lat see.

But this word is nat take of every wight,
But ther as God list give it of his might.
I woot wel that thapostel was a mayde;
But natheless, thogh that he wroot and sayde
He wolde that every wight were swich as he,
Al nis but conseil to virginitee.
And for to been a wyf he yaf me leve
Of indulgence; so it is no repreve
To wedde me if that my make dye,
With-oute excepcioun of bigamye.

My fourthe housbonde was a revelour,—
This is to seyn he had a paramour;
And I was yong and ful of ragerye,
Stiborn and strong, and Ioly as a pye.
Wel coude I daunce to an harpe smale,
And singe, y-wis, as any nightingale.
But, Lord Crist! whan that it remembreth me
Up-on my youthe and on my Iolitee
It tikleth me aboute myn herte rote.
Unto this day it dooth myn herte bote
That I have had my world as in my tyme.
But age, allas! that al wol envenyme,
Hath me biraft my beautee and my pith:
Lat go, fare-wel, the devel go therwith!
The flour is goon, ther is na-more to telle,
The bren, as I best can, now moste I selle;
But yet to be right merye wol I fonde.
Now wol I tellen of my fourthe housbonde.

I seye I had in herte greet despyt
That he of any other had delyt.
But he was quit, by God and by Seint Ioce!
I made him of the same wode a croce;
Nat of my body in no foul manere,
But certeinly, I made folk swich chere

That in his owene grece I made him frye
For angrë and for verray Ialousye.
By God, in erthe I was his purgatorie,
For which I hope his soule be in glorie.
For God it woot, he sat ful ofte and song
Whan that his shoo ful bitterly him wrong.
Ther was no wight, savę God and he, that wiste,
In many wysë, how sore I him twiste.

He deyde whan I cam fro Ierusalem,
And lyth y-grave under the rode-beem,
Al is his tombe noght so curious
As was the sepulcre of him Darius,
Which that Appelles wroghte subtilly;
It nis but wast to burie him preciously.
Lat him farę-wel, God yeve his soule reste,
He is now in his grave and in his cheste.

My fifthe housbonde, God his soule blesse!
Which that I took for love, and no richesse,
He som-tymę was a clerk of Oxenford,
And had left scole, and went at hoom to bord
With my gossib, dwelling in oure toun,
God have hir soule! hir name was Alisoun.
She knew myn herte and eek my privetee
Bet than our parisshę-preest, so moot I thee!

And so bifel that ones in a Lentc
(So often tymęs I to my gossib wente,
For evere yet I lovede to be gay
And for to walke, in March, Averil, and May,
Fro hous to hous to here sondry talis)
That Iankin clerk, and my gossib Dame Alis,
And I my-self, in-to the feldes wente.
Myn housbondę was at London al that Lente;
I had the bettre leyser for to pleye,
And for to see and eek for to be seye
Of lusty folk; what wiste I wher my grace
Was shapen for to be, or in what place?
Therfore I madę my visitaciouns
To vigilies and to processiouns,

To preching eek and to thise pilgrimages,
To pleyes of miracles and mariages,
And wered upon my gaye scarlet gytes.
Thise wormes, ne thise motthes, ne thise mytes,
Upon my peril, frete hem nevere a deel;
And wostow why?   For they were used weel.
　　Now wol I tellen forth what happed me.
I seye that in the feeldes walked we
Til trewely we had swich daliance,
This clerk and I, that of my purveyance
I spak to him, and seyde him how that he,
If I were widwe, sholde wedde me.
For certeinly, I sey for no bobance,
Yet was I nevere with-outen purveyance
Of mariage, nof othere thinges eek.
I holde a mouses herte nat worth a leek
That hath but oon hool for to sterte to,
And if that faille, than is al y-do.
　　I bar him on honde he had enchanted me;
My dame taughte me that soutiltee.
And eek I seyde I mette of him al night:
He wolde han slayn me as I lay upright,
And al my bed was ful of verray blood,
But yet I hope that he shal do me good;
For blood bitokeneth gold, as me was taught.
And al was fals, I dremed it right naught,
But as I folwed ay my dames lore,
As wel of this as of other thinges more.
　　But now, sir, lat me see, what shal I seyn?
A! ha! by God, I have my tale ageyn.
　　Whan that my fourthe housbonde was on bere,
I weep algate, and made a sory chere,
As wyves moten, for it is usage,
And with my coverchief covered my visage;
But for that I was purveyed of a make,
I weep but smal, and that I undertake.
　　To chirche was myn housbonde born a-morwe
With neighebores, that for him maden sorwe;

And Iankin oure clerk was oon of tho.
As helpe me God, whan that I saugh him go
After the bere, me thoughte he had a paire
Of legges and of feet so clene and faire
That al myn herte I yaf un-to his hold.
He was, I trowe, a twenty winter old,
And I was fourty, if I shal seye sooth;
But yet I had alwey a coltes tooth.
Gat-tothed I was, and that bicam me weel;
I had the prente of Seynte Venus seel.
As helpe me God, I was a lusty oon,
And faire and riche, and yong and wel bigoon.

What sholde I seye, but at the monthes ende
This Ioly clerk Iankin, that was so hende,
Hath wedded me with greet solempnitee,
And to him yaf I al the lond and fee
That evere was me yeven ther-bifore;
But afterward repented me ful sore.
He nolde suffre nothing of my list.
By God, he smoot me ones on the list,
For that I rente out of his book a leef,
That of the strook myn ere wex al deef.
Stiborn I was as is a leonesse,
And of my tonge a verray Iangleresse,
And walke I wolde, as I had doon biforn,
From hous to hous, al-though he had it sworn.
For which he often tymes wolde preche,
And me of olde Romayn gestes teche
How he Simplicius Gallus lefte his wyf,
And hir forsook for terme of al his lyf,
Noght but for open-heeded he hir say
Loking out at his dore upon a day.

He had a book that gladly night and day
For his desport he wolde rede alway.
He cleped it Valerie and Theofraste,
At whiche book he lough alwey ful faste.
And eek ther was som-tyme a clerk at Rome,
A cardinal that highte Seint Ierome,

Sk., D, 594–606; 627–646; 669–674

That made a book agayn Iovinian,
In whiche book eek ther was Tertulan,
Crisippus, Trotula, and Helowys,
That was abbesse nat fer fro Parys;
And eek the Parables of Salomon,
Ovydes Art, and bokes many on,
And alle thise were bounden in o volume.
And every night and day was his custume,
Whan he had leyser and vacacioun
From other worldly occupacioun,
To reden on this book of wikked wyves.
He knew of hem mo legendes and lyves
Than been of gode wyves in the Bible.
For trusteth wel, it is an impossible
That any clerk wol speke good of wyves,
But-if it be of holy seintes lyves,
Ne of noon other womman nevere the mo.
Who peyntede the leoun, tel me who?
By God, if wommen hadde writen stories,
As clerkes han with-in hir oratories,
They wolde han writen of men more wikkednesse
Than all the mark of Adam may redresse.

   Of Lyma tolde he me, and of Lucye,
They bothe made hir housbondes for to dye:
That oon for love, that other was for hate
Lyma hir housbonde on an even late
Empoysoned hath, for that she was his fo.
Lucya, likerous, loved hir housbonde so
That, for he sholde alwey up-on hir thinke,
She yaf him swich a maner love-drinke
That he was deed er it were by the morwe;
And thus algates housbondes han sorwe.

   Than tolde he me how oon Latumius
Compleyned to his felawe Arrius
That in his gardin growed swich a tree
On which, he seyde, how that his wyves three
Hanged hem-self for herte despitous.
   "O leve brother," quod this Arrius,

"Yif me a plante of thilke blissed tree,
And in my gardin planted shal it be!"
Of latter date, of wyves hath he red,
That somme han slayn hir housbondęs in hir bed;
Somme han hem yeve poysoun in hir drinke.
He spak more harm than herte may bithinke.
And ther-with-al he knew of mo proverbes
Than in this world ther growen gras or herbes.

"Bet is," quod he, "thyn habitacioun
Be with a leoun or a foul dragoun
Than with a womman using for to chyde.
Bet is," quod he, "hye in the roof abyde
Than with an angry wyf doun in the hous:
They been so wikked and contrarious;
They haten that hir housbondęs loveth ay."
He seyde, "A womman cast hir shame away
Whan she cast of hir smok;" and forther-mo,
"A fair womman, but she be chaast also,
Is lyk a gold ring in a sowes nose."
Who wolde wenen, or who woldę suppose
The wo that in myn herte was, and pyne?

And whan I saugh he wolde nevere fyne
To reden on this cursed book al night,
Al sodeynly three leves have I plight
Out of the book, right as he radde, and eke
I with my fist so took him on the cheke
That in our fyr he fil bakward adoun.
And he up-stirte as dooth a wood leoun,
And with his fist he smoot me on the heed
That in the floor I lay as I werę deed.
And when he saugh how stille that I lay,
He was agast, and wolde han fled his way
Til atte laste out of my swogh I breyde:
"O! hastow slayn me, false theef?" I seyde,
"And for my land thus hastow mordred me?
Er I be deed yet wol I kisse thee."

And neer he cam, and kneled faire adoun,
And seyde, "Dere suster Alisoun,

As helpę me God, I shal thee nevere smyte;
That I havę doon, it is thy-self to wyte.
Foryef it me, and that I thee biseke"—
And yet eft-sonęs I hitte him on the cheke,
And seyde, "Theef, thus muchel am I wreke;
Now wol I dye, I may no lenger speke."
But atte lastę, with muchel care and wo,
We fillę acorded by us selven two.
He yaf me al the brydel in myn hond
To han the governance of hous and lond,
And of his tonge and of his hond also,
And made him brenne his book anon right tho.
And whan that I had geten un-to me,
By maistrie, al the soveraynetee,
And that he seyde, "Myn owene trewe wyf,
Do as thee lust the terme of al thy lyf,
Keep thyn honour, and keep eek myn estaat"—
After that day we hadden nevere debaat.
God helpę me so, I was to him as kinde
As any wyf from Denmark un-to Inde,
And also trewe, and so was he to me.
I prey to God that sit in magestee,
So blesse his soule for his mercy dere!
Now wol I seyę my tale, if ye wol here.

(*Here follow the words between the Somnour and the Frere, and the Tale of the Wyf of Bathe*)

Here folweth the Prologe of the Clerkes Tale of Oxenford.

"Sir clerk of Oxenford," our hoste sayde,
"Ye ryde as coy and stille as dooth a mayde,
Werę newe spoused, sitting at the bord.
This day ne herde I of your tonge a word.
I trowe ye studie aboute som sophyme,
But Salomon seith, 'Every thing hath tyme.'
For Goddes sake, as beth of bettre chere,
It is no tyme for to studien here.

Sk., D, 805–828; E, 1–8

Telle us som mery tale, by your fey;
For what man that is entred in a pley,
He nedes moot unto the pley assente.
But precheth nat, as freres doon in Lente,
To make us for our olde sinnes wepe,
Ne that thy tale make us nat to slepe.
Telle us som mery thing of aventures.
Your termes, your colours, and your figures,
Kepe hem in stoor til so be ye endyte
Heigh style, as whan that men to kinges wryte.
Speketh so pleyn at this tyme, I yow preye,
That we may understonde what ye seye."

This worthy clerk benignely answerde,
"Hoste," quod he, "I am under your yerde;
Ye han of us as now the governaunce,
And therfore wol I do yow obeisaunce
As fer as reson axeth, hardily.
I wol yow telle a tale which that I
Lerned at Padowe of a worthy clerk,
As preved by his wordes and his werk.
He is now deed and nayled in his cheste,
I prey to God so yeve his soule reste!

"Fraunceys Petrark, the laureat poete,
Highte this clerk, whos rethoryke sweete
Enlumined al Itaille of poetrye,
As Linian dide of philosophye
Or lawe or other art particuler;
But Deeth, that wol nat suffre us dwellen heer
But as it were a twinkling of an yë,
Hem bothe han slayn, and alle shul we dye.

"But forth to tellen of this worthy man,
That taughte me this tale as I bigan,
I seye that first with heigh style he endyteth,
Er he the body of his tale wryteth,
A proheme, in the which discryveth he
Pemond, and of Saluces the contree,
And speketh of Apennyn, the hilles hye,
That been the boundes of West Lumbardye,

And of Mount Vesulus in special,
Wher as the Poo out of a welle smal
Taketh his firste springing and his sours,
That estward ay encresseth in his cours
To Emelward, to Ferrare, and Venyse:
The which a long thing were to devyse.
But trewely, as to my Iugement,
Me thinketh it a thing impertinent,
Save that he wol conveyen his matere;
But this his tale, which that ye may here."

THE CLERKES TALE

Here biginneth the Tale of the Clerk of Oxenford.

Ther is at the west syde of Itaille,
Doun at the rote of Vesulus the colde,
A lusty playn, habundant of vitaille,
Wher many a tour and toun thou mayst biholde
That founded were in tyme of fadres olde,
And many another delitable sighte,
And Saluces this noble contree highte.

A markis whylom lord was of that lond,
As were his worthy eldres him bifore;
And obeisant and redy to his hond
Were alle his liges, bothe lasse and more.
Thus in delyt he liveth, and hath don yore,
Biloved and drad, thurgh favour of Fortune,
Bothe of his lordes and of his commune.

Therwith he was, to speke as of linage,
The gentilleste y-born of Lumbardye,
A fair persone, and strong, and yong of age,
And ful of honour and of curteisye;
Discreet y-nogh his contree for to gye,
Save in somme thinges that he was to blame,
And Walter was this yonge lordes name.

I blame him thus, that he considered noght
In tyme coming what mighte him bityde,
But on his lust present was al his thoght,
As for to hauke and hunte on every syde;
Wel ny alle othere cures leet he slyde,
And eek he nolde—and that was worst of alle—
Wedde no wyf, for noght that may bifalle.

Only that point his peple bar so sore
That flokmele on a day they to him wente,
And oon of hem, that wysest was of lore,
Or elles that the lord best wolde assente
That he sholde telle him what his peple mente,
Or elles coude he shewe wel swich matere,
He to the markis seyde as ye shul here.

"O noble markis, your humanitee
Assureth us and yeveth us hardinesse,
As ofte as tyme is of necessitee,
That we to yow mowe telle our hevinesse;
Accepteth, lord, now for your gentilesse,
That we with pitous herte un-to yow pleyne,
And lete your eres nat my voys disdeyne.

"For certes, lord, so wel us lyketh yow
And al your werk, and evere han doon, that we
Ne coude nat us self devysen how
We mighte liven in more felicitee,
Save o thing, lord, if it your wille be,
That for to been a wedded man yow leste,
Than were your peple in sovereyn hertes reste.

"Boweth your nekke under that blisful yok
Of soveraynetee, noght of servyse,
Which that men clepeth spousaille or wedlok;
And thenketh, lord, among your thoghtes wyse,
How that our dayes passe in sondry wyse.
For though we slepe or wake, or rome or ryde,
Ay fleeth the tyme, it nil no man abyde.

"Accepteth than of us the trewe entente,
That nevere yet refuseden your heste,
And we wol, lord, if that ye wol assente,
Chese yow a wyf in short tyme, atte leste,
Born of the gentilleste and of the meste
Of al this lond, so that it oghte seme
Honour to God and yow, as we can deme.

"Deliver us out of al this bisy drede,
And tak a wyf, for hye Goddes sake;
For if it so bifelle, as God forbede,
That thurgh your deeth your linage sholde slake,
And that a straunge successour sholde take
Your heritage, O! wo were us alyve!
Wherfore we pray you hastily to wyve."

Hir meke preyere and hir pitous chere
Made the markis herte han pitee.
"Ye wol," quod he, "myn owene peple dere,
To that I nevere erst thoghte streyne me.
I me reioysed of my libertee
That selde tyme is founde in mariage:
Ther I was free, I moot been in servage.

"But nathelees I see your trewe entente,
And truste upon your wit, and have don ay;
Wherfore of my free wille I wol assente
To wedde me as sone as evere I may.
But ther-as ye han profred me to-day
To chese me a wyf, I yow relesse
That choys, and prey yow of that profre cesse.

"And forthermore, this shul ye swere, that ye
Agayn my choys shul neither grucche ne stryve;
For sith I shal forgoon my libertee
At your requeste, as evere moot I thryve,
Ther-as myn herte is set, ther wol I wyve.
And but ye wole assente in swich manere,
I prey yow, speketh na-more of this matere."

With hertly wille they sworen and assenten
To al this thing, ther seyde no wight nay;
Biseking him of grace, er that they wenten,
That he wolde graunten hem a certein day
Of his spousaille, as sone as evere he may.
For yet alwey the peple som-what dredde
Lest that this markis no wyf wolde wedde.

He graunted hem a day swich as hem leste,
On which he wolde be wedded sikerly,
And seyde he did al this at hir requeste;
And they, with humble entente, buxomly,
Kneling up-on hir knees ful reverently
Him thanken alle, and thus they han an ende
Of hir entente, and hoom agayn they wende.

Explicit prima pars. Incipit secunda pars

Noght fer fro thilke paleys honurable
Ther-as this markis shoop his mariage,
Ther stood a throp of site delitable
In which that povre folk of that village
Hadden hir bestes and hir herbergage,
And of hir labour took hir sustenance
After that the erthe yaf hem habundance.

Amonges thise povre folk ther dwelte a man
Which that was holden povrest of hem alle;
But hye God som tyme senden can
His grace in-to a litel oxes stalle:
Ianicula men of that throp him calle.
A doghter had he, fair y-nogh to sighte,
And Grisildis this yonge mayden highte.

But for to speke of vertuous beautee,
Than was she oon the faireste under sonne;
For povreliche y-fostred up was she,

No likerous lust was thurgh hir herte y-ronne.
Wel ofter of the welle than of the tonne
She drank, and for she wolde vertu plese,
She knew wel labour but non ydel ese.

But thogh this mayde tendre were of age,
Yet in the brest of hir virginitee
Ther was enclosed rype and sad corage;
And in greet reverence and charitee
Hir olde povre fader fostred she.
A fewe sheep spinning on feeld she kepte,
She wolde noght been ydel til she slepte.

Up-on Grisilde, this povre creature,
Ful ofte sythe this markis sette his yë
As he on hunting rood paraventure;
And whan it fil that he mighte hir espye,
He noght with wantoun loking of folye
His yën caste on hir, but in sad wyse
Up-on hir chere he wolde him ofte avyse,

Commending in his herte hir wommanhede,
And eek hir vertu, passing any wight
Of so yong age, as wel in chere as dede.
For thogh the peple have no greet insight
In vertu, he considered ful right
Hir bountee, and disposed that he wolde
Wedde hir only, if evere he wedde sholde.

The day of wedding cam, but no wight can
Telle what womman that it sholde be;
For which merveille wondred many a man,
And seyden, whan they were in privetee,
"Wol nat our lord yet leve his vanitee?
Wol he nat wedde? Allas, allas, the whyle!
Why wol he thus him-self and us bigyle?"

Sk., E. 214–224; 232–252

But natheles this markis hath don make
Of gemmes set in gold and in asure
Broches and ringes for Grisildis sake,
And of hir clothing took he the mesure
By a mayde lyk to hir stature,
And eek of othere ornamentes alle
That un-to swich a wedding sholde falle.

The tyme of undern of the same day
Approcheth, that this wedding sholde be;
And al the paleys put was in array,
Bothe halle and chambres, ech in his degree:
Houses of office stuffed with plentee
Ther maystow seen of deyntevous vitaille
That may be founde as fer as last Itaille.

This royal markis, richely arrayed,
Lordes and ladyes in his companye,
The which unto the feste were y-prayed,
And of his retenue the bachelrye,
With many a soun of sondry melodye,
Un-to the village, of the which I tolde,
In this array the righte wey han holde.

Grisilde of this, God woot, ful innocent
That for hir shapen was al this array,
To fecchen water at a welle is went,
And cometh hoom as sone as evere she may.
For wel she had herd seyd that thilke day
The markis sholde wedde, and, if she mighte,
She wolde fayn han seyn som of that sighte.

She thoghte, "I wol with othere maydens stonde,
That been my felawes, in my dore and see
The markisesse; and therfore wol I fonde
To doon at hoom, as sone as it may be,
The labour which that longeth un-to me,
And than I may at leyser hir biholde,
If she this wey un-to the castel holde."

And as she wolde over hir threshfold goon,
The markis cam and gan hir for to calle;
And she sette doun hir water-pot anoon
Besyde the threshfold, in an oxes stalle,
And doun up-on hir knees she gan to falle,
And with sad contenance kneleth stille
Til she had herd what was the lordes wille.

This thoghtful markis spak un-to this mayde
Ful sobrely, and seyde in this manere,
"Wher is your fader, O Grisildis?" he sayde,
And she with reverence, in humble chere,
Answerde, "Lord, he is al redy here."
And in she gooth with-outen lenger lette,
And to the markis she hir fader fette.

He by the hond than took this olde man,
And seyde thus, whan he him had asyde:
"Ianicula, I neither may ne can
Lenger the plesance of myn herte hyde.
If that thou vouche-sauf, what-so bityde,
Thy doghter wol I take, er that I wende,
As for my wyf, un-to hir lyves ende.

"Thou lovest me, I woot it wel, certeyn,
And art my feithful lige man y-bore;
And al that lyketh me, I dar wel seyn
It lyketh thee, and specially therfore
Telle me that poynt that I have seyd bifore,
If that thou wolt un-to that purpos drawe,
To take me as for thy sone-in-lawe."

This sodeyn cas this man astoned so
That reed he wex, abayst, and al quakinge
He stood; unnethes seyde he wordes mo,
But only thus: "Lord," quod he, "my willinge
Is as ye wole, ne ayeins your lykinge
I wol no-thing. Ye be my lord so dere;
Right as yow lust governeth this matere."

Sk., E, 288–322

"Yet wol I," quod this markis softely,
"That in thy chambre I and thou and she
Have a collacion, and wostow why?
For I wol axe if it hir wille be
To be my wyf, and reule hir after me;
And al this shal be doon in thy presence,
I wol noght speke out of thyn audience."

And in the chambre whyl they were aboute
Hir tretis, which as ye shal after here,
The peple cam un-to the hous with-oute,
And wondred hem in how honest manere
And tentifly she kepte hir fader dere.
But outerly Grisildis wondre mighte,
For nevere erst ne saugh she swich a sighte.

No wonder is thogh that she were astoned
To seen so greet a gest come in that place;
She nevere was to swiche gestes woned,
For which she loked with ful pale a face.
But shortly forth this tale for to chace,
Thise arn the wordes that the markis sayde
To this benigne verray feithful mayde.

"Grisilde," he seyde, "ye shul wel understonde
It lyketh to your fader and to me
That I yow wedde, and eek it may so stonde,
As I suppose, ye wol that it so be.
But thise demandes axe I first," quod he,
"That, sith it shal be doon in hastif wyse,
Wol ye assente, or elles yow avyse?

"I seye this, be ye redy with good herte
To al my lust, and that I frely may,
As me best thinketh, do yow laughe or smerte,
And nevere ye to grucche it, night ne day.
And eek whan I sey 'Ye,' ne sey nat 'Nay,'
Neither by word ne frowning contenance;
Swer this, and heer I swer our alliance."

Wondring upon this word, quaking for drede,
She seyde, "Lord, undigne and unworthy
Am I to thilke honour that ye me bede;
But as ye wol your-self, right so wol I.
And heer I swerę that nevere willingly
In werk ne thoght I nil yow disobeye,
For to be deed, though me werę looth to deye."

"This is y-nogh, Grisilde myn!" quod he.
And forth he goth with a ful sobre chere
Out at the dore, and after that cam she,
And to the peple he seyde in this manere:
"This is my wyf," quod he, "that stondeth here.
Honoureth hir, and loveth hir, I preye,
Who-so me loveth. Ther is na-morę to seye."

And for that no-thing of hir olde gere
She sholde bringe in-to his hous, he bad
That wommen sholde dispoilen hir right there;
Of which thisę ladyes were nat right glad
To handle hir clothes wher-in she was clad.
But natheles this mayde bright of hewe
Fro foot to heed they clothed han al newe.

Hir heres han they kembd, that lay untressed
Ful rudely, and with hir fingres smale
A corone on hir heed they han y-dressed,
And sette hir ful of nowches grete and smale:
Of hir array sholde I make a tale?
Unnethe the peple hir knew for hir fairnesse,
Whan she translated was in swich richesse.

This markis hath hir spoused with a ring
Broght for the same cause, and than hir sette
Up-on an hors, snow-whyt and wel ambling;
And to his paleys er he lenger lette,
With Ioyful peple that hir ladde and mette,
Conveyed hir, and thus the day they spende
In revel, til the sonne gan descende.

And shortly forth this tale for to chace,
I seye that to this newe markisesse
God hath swich favour sent hir of his grace
That it ne semed nat by lyklinesse
That she was born and fed in rudenesse,
As in a cote or in an oxe-stalle,
But norished in an emperoures halle.

To every wight she woxen is so dere
And worshipful that folk ther she was bore,
And from hir birthe knewe hir yeer by yere,
Unnethe trowed they, but dorste han swore
That to Ianicle of which I spak bifore,
She doghter nas, for, as by coniecture,
Hem thoughte she was another creature.

Nat longe tyme after that this Grisild
Was wedded, she a doughter hath y-bore,
Al had hir lever have born a knave child.
Glad was this markis and the folk therfore;
For though a mayde child come al bifore,
She may unto a knave child atteyne
By lyklihede, sin she nis nat bareyne.

Explicit secunda pars. Incipit tercia pars

Ther fil, as it bifalleth tymes mo,
Whan that this child had souked but a throwe,
This markis in his herte longeth so
To tempte his wyf, hir sadnesse for to knowe,
That he ne mighte out of his herte throwe
This merveillous desyr, his wyf tassaye,
Nedeless, God woot, he thoughte hir for taffraye.

He had assayed hir y-nogh bifore,
And fond hir evere good: what neded it
Hir for to tempte and alwey more and more?

Sk., E, 393-406; 442-458

Though som men preise it for a subtil wit,
But as for me, I seyę that yvel it sit
Tassaye a wyf whan that it is no nede,
And putten her in anguish and in drede.

For which this markis wroghte in this manere:
He cam alone a-night, ther as she lay,
With sterne face and with ful trouble chere,
And seyde thus: "Grisild," quod he, "that day
That I yow took out of your povre array,
And puttę yow in estaat of heigh noblesse,
Ye havę nat that forgeten, as I gesse.

"Ye woot your-self wel how that ye cam here
In-to this hous, it is nat longe ago,
And though to me that ye be lief and dere,
Un-to my gentils ye be no-thing so;
They seyn to hem it is greet shame and wo
For to be subgets and ben in servage
To thee that born art of a smal village.

"And namęly, sith thy doghter was y-bore,
Thisę wordes han they spoken doutelees;
But I desyre, as I havę doon bifore,
To live my lyf with hem in reste and pees.
I may nat in this caas be recchelees.
I moot don with thy doghter for the beste,
Nat as I woldę, but as my peple leste.

"And yet, God wot, this is ful looth to me;
But nathelees with-oute your witing
I wol nat doon, but this wol I," quod he,
"That ye to me assente as in this thing.
Shewę now your pacience in your werking
That ye me highte and swore in your village
That day that maked was our mariage."

Whan she had herd al this, she noght ameved
Neither in word, or chere, or countenaunce;
For as it semed, she was nat agreved.
She seyde, "Lord, al lyth in your plesaunce,
My child and I with hertly obeisaunce
Ben youres al, and ye mowe save or spille
Your owene thing. Werketh after your wille.

"Ther may no-thing, God so my soule save,
Lyken to yow that may displese me;
Ne I desyre no-thing for to have,
Ne drede for to lese, save only ye.
This wille is in my herte and ay shal be.
No lengthe of tyme or deeth may this deface,
Ne chaunge my corage to another place."

Glad was this markis of hir answeringe,
But yet he feyned as he were nat so;
Al drery was his chere and his lokinge
Whan that he sholde out of the chambre go.
Sone after this, a furlong wey or two,
He prively hath told al his entente
Un-to a man, and to his wyf him sente.

A maner sergeant was this privee man,
The which that feithful ofte he founden hadde
In thinges grete, and eek swich folk wel can
Don execucioun on thinges badde.
The lord knew wel that he him loved and dradde;
And whan this sergeant wiste his lordes wille,
In-to the chambre he stalked him ful stille.

"Madame," he seyde, "ye mote foryeve it me,
Thogh I do thing to which I am constreyned.
Ye ben so wys that ful wel knowe ye
That lordes hestes mowe nat been y-feyned;
They mowe wel been biwailled or compleyned,
But men mot nede un-to her lust obeye,
And so wol I; ther is na-more to seye.

"This child I am comanded for to take"—
And spak na-morę, but outę the child he hente
Despitously, and gan a chere make
As though he wolde han slayn it er he wente.
Grisildis mot al suffren and consente;
And as a lamb she sitteth meke and stille,
And leet this cruel sergeant doon his wille.

But atte laste speken she bigan,
And mekely she to the sergeant preyde,
So as he was a worthy gentil man,
That she mostę kisse hir child er that it deyde;
And in her barm this litel child she leyde
With ful sad face, and gan the child to kisse
And lulled it, and after gan it blisse.

And thus she seyde in hir benigne voys:
"Far weel, my child! I shal thee nevere see;
But sith I the havę marked with the croys,
Of thilke Fader blessed motę thou be
That for us deyde up-on a croys of tree.
Thy soule, litel child, I him bitake,
For this night shaltow dyen for my sake."

I trowę that to a norice in this cas
It had ben hard this rewthe for to se;
Wel mighte a mooder than han cryed "Allas!"
But nathelees so sad stedfast was she
That she endured all adversitee,
And to the sergeant mekely she sayde,
"Have heer agayn your litel yonge mayde.

"Goth now," quod she, "and dooth my lordes heste,
But o thing wol I preyę yow of your grace,
That, but my lord forbad yow, atte leste
Burieth this litel body in som place
That bestes ne no briddes it to-race."
But he no word wol to that purpos seye,
But took the child and wente upon his weye.

Sk., E, 533–539; 547–574

This sergeant cam un-to his lord ageyn,
And of Grisildis wordes and hir chere
He tolde him point for point, in short and playn,
And him presenteth with his doghter dere.
Somwhat this lord hath rewthe in his manere;
But nathelees his purpos heeld he stille,
As lordes doon whan they wol han hir wille.

And bad his sergeant that he prively
Sholde this child ful softe winde and wrappe
With alle circumstances tendrely,
And carie it in a cofre or in a lappe;
But, up-on peyne his heed of for to swappe,
That no man sholde knowe of his entente,
Ne whenne he cam, ne whider that he wente;

But at Boloigne to his suster dere,
That thilke tyme of Panik was countesse,
He sholde it take, and shewe hir this matere,
Biseking hir to don hir bisinesse
This child to fostre in alle gentilesse,
And whos child that it was he bad hir hyde
From every wight, for oght that may bityde.

The sergeant gooth, and hath fulfild this thing;
But to this markis now retourne we.
For now goth he ful faste imagining
If by his wyves chere he mighte see,
Or by hir word aperceyve that she
Were chaunged; but he nevere hir coude finde
But evere in oon y-lyke sad and kinde.

As glad, as humble, as bisy in servyse,
And eek in love as she was wont to be,
Was she to him in every maner wyse;
Ne of hir doghter noght a word spak she.
Non accident for noon adversitee
Was seyn in hir, ne nevere hir doghter name
Ne nempned she, in ernest nor in game.

Explicit tercia pars. Sequitur pars quarta

In this estaat ther passed been foure yeer
Er she with childe was; but as God wolde,
A knave child she bar by this Walter,
Ful gracious and fair for to biholde.
And whan that folk it to his fader tolde,
Nat only he, but al his contree, merie
Was for this child, and God they thanke and herie.

Whan it was two yeer old, and fro the brest
Departed of his norice, on a day
This markis caughte yet another lest
To tempte his wyf yet ofter if he may.
O nedeles was she tempted in assay!
But wedded men ne knowe no mesure,
Whan that they finde a pacient creature.

"Wyf," quod this markis, "ye han herd er this,
My peple sikly berth our mariage;
And namely sith my sone y-boren is,
Now is it worse than evere in al our age.
The murmur sleeth myn herte and my corage;
For to myne eres comth the voys so smerte
That it wel ny destroyed hath myn herte.

"Now sey they thus: 'Whan Walter is agoon,
Then shal the blood of Ianicle succede
And been our lord, for other have we noon;'
Swich wordes seith my peple, out of drede.
Wel oughte I of swich murmur taken hede;
For certeinly I drede swich sentence,
Though they nat pleyn speke in myn audience.

"I wolde live in pees, if that I mighte;
Wherfore I am disposed outerly,
As I his suster servede by nighte,
Right so thenke I to serve him prively.
This warne I yow, that ye nat sodeynly
Out of your-self for no wo sholde outraye:
Beth pacient, and ther-of I yow preye."

"I have," quod she, "seyd thus, and evere shal,
I wol no thing, ne nil no thing, certayn,
But as yow list.　Noght greveth me at al,
Thogh that my doghter and my sone be slayn,—
At your comandement, this is to sayn.
I have noght had no part of children tweyne
But first siknesse and after wo and peyne.

"Ye been our lord, doth with your owene thing
Right as yow list; axeth no reed at me.
For as I lefte at hoom al my clothing,
Whan I first cam to yow, right so," quod she,
"Left I my wille and al my libertee,
And took your clothing: wherfore I yow preye,
Doth your plesaunce, I wol your lust obeye.

"And certes, if I hadde prescience
Your wille to knowe er ye your lust me tolde,
I wolde it doon with-outen necligence;
But now I woot your lust and what ye wolde,
Al your plesaunce ferme and stable I holde.
For wiste I that my deeth wolde do yow ese,
Right gladly wolde I dyen, yow to plese.

"Deth may noght make no comparisoun
Un-to your love:" and whan this markis sey
The constance of his wyf, he caste adoun
His yën two, and wondreth that she may
In pacience suffre al this array.
And forth he gooth with drery contenaunce,
But to his herte it was ful greet plesaunce.

This ugly sergeant in the same wyse
That he hir doghter caughte, right so he,
Or worsë if men worse can devyse,
Hath hent hir sone, that ful was of beautee.
And evere in oon so pacient was she
That she no chere made of hevinesse,
But kiste hir sone, and after gan it blesse;

Sk., E, 645–679

Savę this: she preyed him that, if he mighte,
Her litel sone he wolde in erthe grave,
His tendre limes, delicat to sighte,
Fro foules and fro bestes for to save.
But she non answere of him mighte have.
He wente his wey, as him no-thing ne roghte;
But to Boloigne he tendrely it broghte.

This markis wondreth evere lenger the more
Up-on hir pacience, and if that he
Ne hadde soothly knowen ther-bifore
That parfitly hir children lovede she,
He wolde havę wend that of som subtiltee,
And of malice or for cruel corage,
That she had suffred this with sad visage.

But wel he knew that next him-self, certayn,
She loved hir children best in every wyse.
But now of wommen wolde I axen fayn
If thise assayes mighte nat suffyse?
What coude a sturdy housbonde more devyse
To preve hir wyfhod and hir stedfastensse,
And he continuing evere in sturdinesse?

The sclaundre of Walter ofte and wyde spradde,
That of a cruel herte he wikkedly,
For he a povre womman wedded hadde,
Hath mordred bothe his children prively.
Swich murmur was among hem comunly.
No wonder is, for to the peples ere
Ther cam no word but that they mordred were.

For which, wher-as his peple ther-bifore
Had loved him wel, the sclaundre of his diffame
Made hem that they him hatede therfore;
To been a mordrer is an hatęful name.
But natheles, for ernest ne for game
He of his cruel purpos nolde stente;
To tempte his wyf was set al his entente.

Whan that his doghter twelf yeer was of age,
He to the court of Rome in subtil wyse,
Enformed of his wille, sente his message,
Comaunding hem swiche bulles to devyse
As to his cruel purpos may suffyse,
How that the pope, as for his peples reste,
Bad him to wedde another, if him leste.

I seye, he bad they sholde countrefete
The popes bulles, making mencioun
That he hath leve his firste wyf to lete
As by the popes dispensacioun,
To stinte rancour and dissencioun
Bitwixe his peple and him: thus seyde the bulle,
The which they han publiced atte fulle.

The rude peple, as it no wonder is,
Wenden ful wel that it had been right so;
But whan thise tydinges cam to Grisildis,
I deme that hir herte was ful wo.
But she, y-lyke sad for everemo,
Disposed was, this humble creature,
Thadversitee of fortune al tendure,

Abyding evere his lust and his plesaunce,
To whom that she was yeven, herte and al,
As to hir verray worldly suffisaunce.
But shortly if this storie I tellen shal,
This markis writen hath in special
A lettre in which he sheweth his entente,
And secretly he to Boloigne it sente.

To the erl of Panik, which that hadde tho
Wedded his suster, preyde he specially
To bringen hoom agayn his children two
In honurable estaat al openly.
But o thing he him preyede outerly,
That he to no wight, though men wolde enquere,
Sholde nat telle whos children that they were,

But seyę the mayden sholde y-wedded be
Un-to the markis of Saluce anon.
And as this erl was preyed, so did he;
For at day set he on his wey is goon
Toward Saluce, and lordes many oon,
In riche array, this mayden for to gyde,
Hir yonge brother ryding hir bisyde.

Arrayed was toward hir mariage
This fresshe mayde, ful of gemmes clere;
Hir brother, which that sevenę yeer was of age,
Arrayed eek ful freshe in his manere.
And thus in greet noblesse and with glad chere,
Toward Saluces shaping hir Iourney,
Fro day to day they ryden in hir wey.

Explicit quarta pars.　Sequitur quinta pars.

Among al this, after his wikke usage,
This markis yet his wyf to tempte more
To the uttereste preve of hir corage,
Fully to han experience and lore
If that she were as stedfast as bifore,
He on a day in open audience
Ful boistously hath seyd hir this sentence:

"Certes, Grisilde, I had y-nough plesaunce
To han yow to my wyf for your goodnesse,
As for your trouthe and for your obeisaunce,
Nought for your linage ne for your richesse;
But now knowe I in verray soothfastnesse
That in gret lordshipe, if I wel avyse,
Ther is gret servitute in sondry wyse.

"I may nat don as every plowman may;
My peple me constreyneth for to take
Another wyf, and cryen day by day;
And eek the pope, rancour for to slake,
Consenteth it, that dar I undertake.

And trewelichę thus muche I wol yow seye,
My newe wyf is coming by the weye.

"Be strong of herte, and voyde anon hir place,
And thilke dowerę that ye broghten me
Tak it agayn, I graunte it of my grace;
Retourneth to your fadres hous," quod he.
"No man may alwey han prosperitee;
With evene herte I rede yow tendure
The strook of fortune or of aventure."

And she answerde agayn in pacience,
"My lord," quod she, "I woot, and wiste alway
How that bitwixen your magnificence
And my poverte no wight can ne may
Maken comparison; it is no nay.
I ne heeld me nevere digne in no manere
To be your wyf, no, ne your chamberere.

"And of your newe wyf, God of his grace
So graunte yow wele and prosperitee;
For I wol gladly yelden hir my place,
In which that I was blisful wont to be.
For sith it lyketh yow, my lord," quod she,
"That whylom weren al myn hertes reste,
That I shal goon, I wol gon whan yow leste.

"But ther-as ye me profre swich dowaire
As I first broghte, it is wel in my minde
It werę my wrecched clothes, no-thing faire,
The which to me werę hard now for to finde.
O gode God! how gentil and how kinde
Ye semed by your speche and your visage
The day that maked was our mariage!

"My lord, ye woot that in my fadres place
Ye did me strepe out of my povre wede,
And richely me cladden, of your grace.

Sk., E, 804–819; 841–854; 862–864

To yow broghte I noght elles, out of drede,
But feyth and nakednesse and maydenhede.
And heer agayn my clothing I restore,
And eek my wedding-ring for everemore.

"The remenant of your Iewels redy be
In-with your chambre, dar I saufly sayn;
Naked out of my fadres hous," quod she,
"I cam, and naked moot I turne agayn.
Al your plesaunce wol I folwen fayn;
But yet I hope it be nat your entente
That I smoklees out of your paleys wente."

"The smok," quod he, "that thou hast on thy bak,
Lat it be stille, and ber it forth with thee."
But wel unnethes thilke word he spak,
But wente his wey for rewthe and for pitee.
Biforn the folk hir-selven strepeth she,
And in hir smok, with heed and foot al bare,
Toward hir fader hous forth is she fare.

The folk hir folwe weping in hir weye,
And fortune ay they cursen as they goon;
But she fro weping kepte hir yën dreye,
Ne in this tyme word ne spak she noon.
Hir fader, that this tydinge herde annoon,
Curseth the day and tyme that nature
Shoop him to been a lyves creature.

For out of doute this olde povre man
Was evere in suspect of hir mariage;
For evere he demed sith that it bigan
That whan the lord fulfild had his corage
Him wolde thinke it were a disparage
To his estaat so lowe for talighte,
And voyden hir as sone as evere he mighte.

Agayns his doghter hastilich goth he,
For he by noyse of folk knew hir cominge,
And with hir olde cote, as it mighte be,

He covered hir, ful sorwefully wepinge;
But on hir body mighte he it nat bringe.
For rude was the cloth, and more of age
By dayes felę than at hir mariage.

Thus with hir fader, for a certeyn space,
Dwelleth this flour of wyfly pacience,
That neither by hir wordes ne hir face
Biforn the folk, ne eek in hir absence,
Ne shewed she that hir was doon offence;
Ne of hir heigh estaat no remembraunce
Ne hadde she, as by hir countenaunce.

Men speke of Iob and most for his humblesse,
As clerkes, whan hem list, can wel endyte,
Namely of men; but as in soothfastnesse,
Thogh clerkes preyse wommen but a lyte,
Ther can no man in humblesse him acquyte
As womman can, ne can ben half so trewe
As wommen been, but it be falle of-newe.

Explicit quinta pars. Sequitur pars sexta.

Fro Boloigne is this erl of Panik come,
Of which the fame up-sprang to more and lesse,
And in the peples eres alle and some
Was couth eek that a newe markisesse
He with him broghte, in swich pompe and richesse
That nevere was ther seyn with mannes yë
So noble array in al West Lumbardye.

The markis, which that shoop and knew al this,
Er that this erl was comę sente his message
For thilke sely povre Grisildis;
And she with humble herte and glad visage,
Nat with no swollen thoght in hir corage,
Cam at his heste, and on hir knees hir sette,
And reverently and wysly she him grette.

"Grisild," quod he, "my wille is outerly,
This mayden, that shal wedded been to me,
Receyved be to-morwe as royally
As it possible is in myn hous to be.
And eek that every wight in his degree
Have his estaat in sitting and servyse
And heigh plesaunce, as I can best devyse.

"I have no wommen suffisaunt certayn
The chambres for tarraye in ordinaunce
After my lust, and therfore wolde I fayn
That thyn were al swich maner governaunce;
Thou knowest eek of old al my plesaunce.
Though thyn array be badde and yvel biseye,
Do thou thy devoir at the leeste weye."

"Nat only, lord, that I am glad," quod she,
"To doon your lust, but I desyre also
Yow for to serve and plese in my degree
With-outen feynting, and shal everemo.
Ne nevere, for no wele ne no wo,
Ne shal the gost with-in myn herte stente
To love yow best with al my trewe entente."

And with that word she gan the hous to dighte,
And tables for to sette and beddes make;
And peyned hir to doon al that she mighte,
Preying the chambereres, for Goddes sake,
To hasten hem, and faste swepe and shake.
And she, the moste servisable of alle,
Hath every chambre arrayed and his halle.

Abouten undern gan this erl alighte,
That with him broghte thise noble children tweye,
For which the peple ran to seen the sighte
Of hir array so richely biseye;
And than at erst amonges hem they seye
That Walter was no fool, thogh that him leste
To chaunge his wyf, for it was for the beste.

For she is fairer, as they demen alle,
Than is Grisild, and more tendre of age,
And fairer fruit bitwene hem sholde falle,
And more plesant, for hir heigh linage.
Hir brother eek so fair was of visage
That hem to seen the peple hath caught plesaunce,
Commending now the markis gouernaunce.

"O stormy peple! unsad and evere untrewe!
Ay undiscreet and chaunging as a vane,
Delyting evere in rumbel that is newe,
For lyk the mone ay wexe ye and wane;
Ay ful of clapping, dere y-nogh a Iane;
Your doom is fals, your constance yvel preveth,
A ful greet fool is he that on yow leveth!"—

Thus seyden sadde folk in that citee,
Whan that the peple gazed up and doun,
For they were glad, right for the noveltee,
To han a newe lady of hir toun.
Na-more of this make I now mencioun;
But to Grisilde agayn wol I me dresse,
And telle hir constance and hir bisinesse.

Ful bisy was Grisilde in every thing
That to the feste was apertinent;
Right noght was she abayst of hir clothing,
Though it were rude and somdel eek to-rent.
But with glad chere to the yate is went
With other folk to grete the markisesse,
And after that doth forth hir bisinesse.

In al this mene whyle she ne stente
This mayde and eek hir brother to commende
With al hir herte in ful benigne entente,
So wel that no man coude hir prys amende.
But atte laste, whan thise lordes wende
To sitten doun to mete, he gan to calle
Grisilde as she was bisy in his halle.

Sk., E, 988-1015; 1023-1029

"Grisildę," quod he, as it were in his pley,
"How lyketh thee my wyf and hir beautee?"
"Right wel," quod she, "my lord. For in good fey,
A fairer say I nevere noon than she.
I prey to God yeve hir prosperitee;
And so hope I that he wol to yow sende
Plesance y-nogh un-to your lyves ende.

"O thing biseke I yow and warne also,
That ye ne prikke with no tormentinge
This tendre mayden, as ye han don mo;
For she is fostred in hir norishinge
More tendrely, and to my supposinge
She coude nat adversitee endure
As coude a povre fostred creature."

And whan this Walter say hir pacience,
Hir glade chere and no malice at al,
And he so ofte had doon to hir offence,
And she ay sad and constant as a wal,
Continuing evere hir innocence overal,
This sturdy markis gan his herte dresse
To rewen up-on hir wyfly stedfastnesse.

"This is y-nogh, Grisilde myn," quod he,
"Be now na-more agast ne yvel apayed.
I havę thy feith and thy benignitee,
As wel as evere womman was, assayed,
In greet estaat, and povreliche arrayed.
Now knowe I, dere wyf, thy stedfastnesse,"—
And hir in armes took and gan hir kesse.

And she for wonder took of it no keep;
She herde nat what thing he to hir seyde;
She ferde as she had stert out of a sleep,
Til she out of hir masednesse abreyde.
"Grisildę," quod he, "by God that for us deyde,
Thou art my wyf, ne noon other I have,
Ne nevere had, as God my soule save!

"This is thy doghter which thou hast supposed
To be my wyf; that other feithfully
Shal be myn heir, as I have ay purposed:
Thou bare him in thy body trewely.
At Boloigne have I kept hem prively;
Tak hem agayn, for now maystow nat seye
That thou hast lorn non of thy children tweye.

"And folk that otherweyęs han seyd of me,
I warne hem wel that I havę doon this dede
For no malicę ne for no crueltee,
But for tassaye in thee thy wommanhede,
And nat to sleen thy children, God forbede!
But for to kepe hem prively and stille
Til I thy purpos knewe and al thy wille."

Whan she this herde, aswowne doun she falleth
For pitous Ioye, and after hir swowninge
She bothe hir yonge children un-to hir calleth,
And in hir armes, pitously wepinge,
Embraceth hem, and tendrely kissinge
Ful lyk a mooder, with hir salte teres
She batheth bothe hir visage and hir heres.

O, which a pitous thing it was to see
Hir swowning, and hir humble voys to here!
"Grauntmercy, lord, that thanke I yow," quod she,
"That ye han saved me my children dere!
Now rekke I nevere to ben deed right here;
Sith I stonde in your love and in your grace,
No fors of deeth, ne whan my spirit pace!

"O tendre, O dere, O yonge children myne,
Your woful mooder wende stedfastly
That cruel houndes or som foul vermyne
Had eten yow; but God of his mercy,
And your benigne fader tendrely
Hath doon yow kept;" and in that same stounde
Al sodeynly she swapte adoun to grounde.

Sk., E, 1065–1099

And in her swough so sadly holdeth she
Hir children two, whan she gan hem tembrace,
That with greet sleighte and greet difficultee
The children from hir arm they gonne arace.
O many a tere on many a pitous face
Doun ran of hem that stoden hir bisyde;
Unnethe abouten hir mighte they abyde.

Walter hir gladeth, and hir sorwe slaketh;
She ryseth up abaysed from hir traunce,
And every wight hir Ioye and feste maketh
Til she hath caught agayn hir contenaunce.
Walter hir dooth so feithfully plesaunce
That it was deyntee for to seen the chere
Bitwixe hem two, now they ben met y-fere.

Thise ladyes, whan that they hir tyme say,
Han taken hir and in-to chambre goon,
And strepen hir out of hir rude array,
And in a cloth of gold that brighte shoon,
With a coroune of many a riche stoon
Up-on hir heed, they in-to halle hir broghte,
And ther she was honoured as hir oghte.

Thus hath this pitous day a blisful ende,
For every man and womman dooth his might
This day in murthe and revel to dispende
Til on the welkne shoon the sterres light.
For more solempne in every mannes sight
This feste was, and gretter of costage,
Than was the revel of hir mariage.

Ful many a yeer in heigh prosperitee
Liven thise two in concord and in reste,
And richely his doghter maried he
Un-to a lord, oon of the worthieste
Of al Itaille; and than in pees and reste
His wyves fader in his court he kepeth
Til that the soule out of his body crepeth.

His sonę succedeth in his heritage
In reste and pees, after his fader day;
And fortunat was eek in mariage,
Al putte he not his wyf in greet assay.
This world is nat so strong, it is no nay,
As it hath been in olde tymes yore,
And herkneth what this auctour seith therfore.

This storie is seyd, nat for that wyves sholde
Folwen Grisilde as in humilitee,
For it were importable though they wolde;
But for that every wight, in his degree,
Sholde be constant in adversitee
As was Grisilde: therforę Petrark wryteth
This storie, which with heigh style he endyteth.

For sith a womman was so pacient
Un-to a mortal man, wel more us oghte
Receyven al in gree that God us sent;
For greet skil is he preve that he wroghte.
But he ne tempteth no man that he boghte,
As seith Seint Iame, if ye his pistel rede;
He preveth folk al day, it is no drede.

But o word, lordingęs, herkneth er I go:—
It werę ful hard to finde now a dayes
In al a toun Grisildes three or two;
For if that they werę put to swiche assayes,
The gold of hem hath now so badde alayes
With bras that, thogh the coyn be fair at yë,
It wolde rather breste a-two than plye.

For which heer, for the wyves love of Bathe,
Whos lyf and al hir secte God mayntene
In heigh maistrye, and elles were it scathe,
I wol with lusty herte fresshe and grene
Seyn yow a song to glade yow, I wene,

And lat us stinte of ernestful matere.
Herkneth my song, that seith in this manere:—

Grisilde is deed, and eek hir pacience,
And bothe atones buried in Itaille;
For which I crye in open audience
No wedded man so hardy be tassaille
His wyves pacience, in hope to finde
Grisildes, for in certein he shal faille!

O noble wyves, ful of heigh prudence,
Lat noon humilitee your tonge naille,
Ne lat no clerk have cause or diligence
To wryte of yow a storie of swich mervaille
As of Grisildis, pacient and kinde,
Lest Chichevache yow swelwe in hir entraille!

Folweth Ekko, that holdeth no silence,
But evere answereth at the countretaille;
Beth nat bidaffed for your innocence,
But sharply tak on yow the governaille.
Emprinteth wel this lesson in your minde
For commune profit, sith it may availle.

Ye archewyves, stondeth at defence,
Sin ye be stronge as is a greet camaille;
Ne suffreth nat that men yow doon offence.
And slendre wyves, feble as in bataille,
Beth egre as is a tygre yond in Inde,
Ay clappeth as a mille, I yow consaille.

Ne dreed hem nat, do hem no reverence;
For though thyn housbonde armed be in maille,
The arwes of thy crabbed eloquence
Shal perce his brest, and eek his aventaille.
In Ialousye I rede eek thou him binde,
And thou shalt make him couche as dooth a quaille.

If thou be fair, ther folk ben in presence
Shew thou thy visage and thyn apparaille;
If thou be foul, be free of thy dispence,
To gete thee freendes ay do thy travaille.
Be ay of chere as light as leef on linde,
And lat him care, and wepe, and wringe, and waille!

Here endeth the Clerk of Oxenford his Tale.

Sk., E, 1207–1212

VARIANT READINGS

The following list includes only the important modifications of the Skeat text, either where there is no manuscript support for the change, or where special problems of grammar, rime, or meter are involved. It has seemed hardly worth while to note all the instances of variation from the norm which we have established for any particular word; the general principles which have been followed in the preparation of the text are discussed in the Introduction. The manuscript readings are taken from the Chaucer Society prints, and minor differences in spelling will not be quoted. For the sake of ease in comparison the line-numbering is based on Skeat.

The Book of the Duchesse. *Manuscripts: B.=Bodley 638; F.=Fairfax 16; T.=Tanner 346. Th.=Thynne's edition.* 5. Sleep; *Skeat and MSS.* slepe. 6. Take no keep; *MSS.* take no kepe; *Sk.* take kepe. 14. Sorwful; *so MSS.; Sk.* [sory]. 16. Woote; *so MSS.; Sk.* wite. 23. This; *so B., T., Th.; Sk.* thus. 37–8. Yeer, neer; *Sk. and MSS.* yere, nere. 46. Bed; *Sk. and MSS.* bedde. 51. Play; *so MSS.; Sk.* playen. 52. Book; *Sk. and MSS.* boke. 60. Among; *Sk. and MSS.* amonge. 67. Wol; *so F., Th.; Sk.* wolde. 77–8. Hom, com; *Sk. and MSS.* home, come. 82. Hir thoughte; *MSS.* her thought; *Sk.* [he dwelte]. 93. A-vow; *Sk. and MSS.* a-vowe. 101. This lady; *so MSS.; Sk.* [she]. 119. Sleep; *Sk. and MSS.* slepe. 128. Took; *Sk. and MSS.* toke. 130. Hir to slepe; *so MSS.; Sk.* hir [for] to slepe. 131. Right so; *so MSS.; Sk.* so. 133. Messager; *Sk. and MSS.* messagere. 134. Neer; *so T.; Sk.* nere. 173–4. Best, brest; *so T., Th.; Sk.* beste, breste. 184. Sleep; *Sk. and MSS.* slepe. 185. Up, and axed; *so MSS.; Sk.* up, axed. 185. Ther; *so B.; Sk.* there. 192. Sleep; *Sk. and MSS.* slepe. 193. Sleep; *Sk. and MSS.* slepe. 199–200. Feet, heet; *Sk. and MSS.* fete, hete. 204. Am; *so MSS.; Sk.* nam. 206. Goode; *Sk. and MSS.* good. 206. That; *Sk.* [look] that. 207. For such a tyde; *so MSS.; Sk.* [at which] a tyde. 213. Allas; *so MSS.; Sk.* A! 236. To slepe; *so MSS.; Sk.* [for] to slepe. 259–60. Gold, fold; *so T.; Sk.* golde, folde. 264. Quene Alcione; *so MSS.; Sk.* Alcione. 294. And; *so MSS.; Sk.* I. 295–6. Heep, sleep; *MSS.* hepe, slepe; *Sk.* hepe, slepe. 300. Overal; *so MSS.; Sk.* al. 307–8. Stevene, hevene; *Sk. and MSS.* steven, heven. 328. And of; *so MSS.; Sk.* of. 329. And of King; *so MSS.; Sk.* and. 330. And eek of; *so MSS. Sk.* of. 331. And of; *so MSS.; Sk.* and. 334. And; *so MSS.; Sk.* [of]. 347. Cleer; *Sk. and MSS.; clere. 348 And I; *so MSS.; Sk.* I. 348. Bothe up; *so MSS.; Sk.* up. 347–8. Soun. doun; *Sk. and MSS.* soune, doune. 357. Took; *so MSS.; Sk.* [I] took, 376. Horn; *Sk. and MSS.* horne. 380. And so; *so MSS.; Sk.* and. 395. Have; *so MSS.; Sk.* han. 407–8. Hevene, sevene; *Sk. and MSS.* heven, seven. 437. Rekene; *so MSS.; Sk.* rekened. 443. Right wonder; *so MSS.; Sk.* wonder. 447. Ook; *Sk. and MSS.* oke. 449–50. Heer, neer; *Sk. and MSS.* here, nere. 451. Sitten; *Sk. and MSS.* sitte.

485. See; *so MSS.; Sk.* y-see. 517. Had y-gret; *so MSS.; Sk.* [grette]. 548. Sire; *MSS.* sir; *Sk.* [good] sir. 659–60. Heer, chekker; *B.* her, chekere; *Sk.* here, chekkere. 660. Maat in the; *MSS.* mate in the; *Sk.* mate in. 745. That may; *so MSS.; Sk.* may that 750. Upon a; *so T., Th.; Sk.* up. 753. Swer; *Sk. and MSS.* swere. 765. Yeve; *so B., Th.; Sk.* yiven. 770. Lord; *Sk. and MSS.* lorde. 806. Ther that; *so MSS.; Sk.* ther. 818. Seyen; *B., F.,* seyn; *T.* sey; *Th.* sayne; *Sk.* seyn. 818. Saw; *so MSS.; Sk.* saw [ther]. 819. Of; *so MSS.; Sk.* of al. 823. Other planete; *so MSS.; Sk.* planete is. 825. World; *Sk. and MSS.* worlde. 844. Bettre; *so MSS.; Sk.* bet. 853–4. Everemor, tresor; *Sk. and MSS.* evermore, tresore. 883. Look; *Sk. and MSS.* loke. 895. But which; *so MSS., Sk.* which. 911–12. Werk, derk; *Sk. and MSS.* werke, derke. 916. Ne; *so MSS.; Sk.* [they] ne. 926. Wel by; *so MSS.; Sk.* by. 930. Yet through; *so MSS.; Sk.* through. 932. Hire; *MSS.* hir; *Sk.* hir [ther]. 934. Record; *Sk. and MSS.* recorde. 935–6. Bond, hond; *Sk. and MSS.* bonde, honde. 948. Heet; *Sk. and MSS.* hete. 971. Swere wel; *so MSS.; Sk.* sweren. 994. And therto; *so MSS.; Sk.* therto. 997. Harm was; *so MSS.; Sk.* was harm. 998. Gode; *so T.; Sk.* good. 1028. In-to; *so MSS.; Sk.* to. 1029–30. Carrenar, war; *Sk. and MSS.* Carrenare, ware. 1051. Her with; *so MSS.; Sk.* with. 1123–4. Oliver, heer; *Sk. and Mss.* Olivere, here. 1126. Sire; *Sk. and MSS.* sir. 1126. Tho; *so MSS.; Sk.* [right] tho. 1139. That; *so MSS.; Sk.* that [sir]. 1141. Doon; *so MSS.; Sk.* [y]-doon. 1150. World; *Sk. and MSS.* worlde. 1295–6. Wer, yeer; *B.* were, yer; *Sk.* were, yere. 1311. Word; *Sk. and MSS.* worde. 1316. Was ther; *so MSS.; Sk.* ther. 1322. Ther was; *so MSS.; Sk.* was. 1329. Hond; *Sk. and MSS.* honde. 1333. *Skeat excludes* "And that anoon" *from the quotation.*

The Hous of Fame. *B.=Bodley 638; F.=Fairfax 16; P.=Pepys 2006. Cx.=Caxton's edition; Th.=Thynne's edition.* 8. Why this; *so MSS.; Sk.* this. 11. Why these; *so MSS.; Sk.* these. 20. This is; *so MSS.; Sk.* this. 95. Scorn; *Sk. and MSS.* scorne. 100. Sith; *so MSS.; Sk.* sith that. 127. Werk; *Sk. and MSS.* werke. 153. With; *so MSS.; Sk.* [that] with. 491. Saw I me to; *so P., Cx., Th.; Sk.* saw me [for] to. 611. Done; *Sk. and MSS.* do. 675. And of; *so P., Cx., Th.; Sk.* of. 757–8. Couth, mouth; *so B.; P.* kowth, mowthe; *Sk.* couthe, mouthe. 764. Herke; *so MSS.; Sk.* herkne. 827. That same place; *B.* that som styde; *F.* sum place styde; *Th.* that some stede; *Sk.* that [the mansioun]. 924. Moche; *B.* much; *F. and Sk.* moch. 979–80. Wer, heer; *Sk. and MSS.* were, here. 995. "And why"? *Sk. includes in the following quotation.* 1056. Telle; *so F., Cx.; Sk.* tel. 1135. Bilte; *so B., Th.; Sk.* bilt. 1173. Ne; *so MSS.; Sk.* ne [be]. 1177. Grete; *so MSS., Sk.* grete craft. 1185. Bothe the; *so MSS.; Sk.* bothe. 1415. And thus; *so MSS.; Sk.* thus. 1483. Poete, Virgyle; *so MSS.; Sk.* poete, [dan] Virgyle. 1527. Into; *so MSS.; Sk.* in. 1558. Yef; *so P.; Sk.* give. 1568. Messager; *so Cx.; B.* messagere; *Sk.* messanger. 1618. Wote: *so P., Cx., Th.; Sk.* wite. 1625.

Sclaundre; *so B., F., P., Th.; Sk.* Sclaunder. 1666. Werkes; *so MSS.; Sk.* werk. 1679–80. Mouth, south; *so B., P., Cx.; Sk.* mouthe, southe. 1685. Mouth hit; *P.* mouth it; *Cx.* trompe it; *Sk.* mouthe. 1686. Pot-ful of; *so MSS.; Sk.* pot-ful. 1693–4. Bright, might; *so MSS.; Sk.* brighte, mighte. 1701. Werkes; *so MSS.; Sk.* werk. 1713–4. Wode, gode; *so F., P.; B., Th.*, woode, good; *Sk.* wood, good. 1747–8. Wode, gode; *so F., P., Cx.; B., Th.*, woode, good; *Sk.* wood, good. 1765. Quod she; *so P., Cx., Th.; Sk.* let see. 1775. That; *so MSS.; Sk.* That [ye]. 1804. Sooth; *so MSS.; Sk.* [the] sooth. 1805. So; *so MSS.; Sk.* [al] so. 1821. List; *so F., P., Cx., Th.; B.* liste; *Sk.* listeth. 1823. Com; *so P., Cx.; Sk.* come. 1824. Gan; *so B., P., Cx., Th.; Sk.* gonne. 1853. Be; *so B., Cx.; Sk.* be [but]. 1902. Dwelled; *so B., F., Th.; Sk.* dwelte. 1905–6. Doom, com; *Sk. and MSS.* dome, come. 1936. Maad, *Sk. and MSS.* made. 1961. Werres, *so MSS.; Sk.* werre. 1962. Restes; *so MSS.; Sk.* reste. 1963–4. Lyf, stryf; *so Cx.; Sk.* lyfe, stryve. 1976. And; *MSS.* and of; *Sk.* of. 1997. Paraunter; *so Th.; Sk.* paraventure. 2003–4. Ther-in, gin; *so Th.; B.* theryn, gynne; *Sk.* ther-inne, ginne; *cf. Leg. G. W.*, ll. 1784–5. 2009. These; *so MSS.; Sk.* [swiche]. 2021. Yaf in; *so MSS.; Sk.* yaf. 2026. Heer anoon; *so B., F.; Sk.* anoon-heer. 2044. Everich; *so Cx., Th.; Sk.* [ech]. 2053. And thus, and thus; *so MSS.; Sk.* thus, thus. 2075–6. South, mouth; *so Cx. B.; Sk.* southe, mouthe. 2076. Tydinge; *so Cx., Th.; Sk.* [word]. 2103–4. Wrooth, both; *so B.; Sk.* wrothe, bothe. 2151. Other; *so MSS.; Sk.* othere. 2153. Otheres; *Th.* others; *Sk.* othere.

The Parlement of Foules. *Arch. = Arch. Seld. B. 24, Bodleian Library; B. = Bodley 638; D. = Digby 181, Bodleian Library; F. = Fairfax 16; Ff. = Ff. 1.6, Cambridge Univ. Library; Gg. = Gg 4.27, Camb. Univ. Library; H. = Harl 7333; Hh. = MS. Hh. 4. 12, Camb. Univ. Library; J. = LVII, St. John's College, Oxford; L. = Longleat 258; Laud = Laud MS. 416, Bodleian Library; P. = Pepys 2006; T. = Tanner 346; Trin. = R. 3. 19, Trinity Coll. Cx.—Caxton's edition.* 37. Afrike; *so B., F., Ff., H., Hh., J., L., P., Trin., Cx.; Sk.* Afrik. 124. Were; *so MSS.; Sk.* weren. 142. A—stonyed; *so Arch., Gg., H., Hh., J., Laud, P., Trin.; Sk.* a stounde. 162–4. Dul, pul; *so Arch., D., Gg., J., T., Trin., Cx.; H., Hh.,* dulle, pull; *P.* dul, pulle; *Sk.* dulle, pulle. 351. Sparwe; *so B., Gg., J., T.; Sk.* sparow. 353. Swalwe; *so Gg., J., T.; Sk.* swalow. 462. Take; *so all but Gg.; Sk.* tak. 550. Blood; *so Arch., Gg. T., Cx.; Sk.* blode. 653–5–6. Weye, seye, aweye; *so Ff., Gg.; D.* weye, seye, awey; *Sk.* wey, sey, awey.

Troilus and Criseyde. *Cl. = Campsall MS.; Cp. = Corpus Christi, Cambridge, 61; Gg. = Gg. 4. 27, Cambridge Univ. Library; H¹. = Harleian 2280; H². = Harleian 3943; H³. = Harleian 1239; J. = L 1, St. John's College, Cambridge.*

Book I. 285. Mevinge (289, meving); *so Cp., H²., H³., J.; Cl.* meuynge (menyng); *Sk.* meninge (mening). 312. Word; *so. Cl., Gg.*,

H^2., J.; Sk. worde. 569. Sen; *so* Cp., J., H^1., H^3.; Sk. see. 613. Tolde; *so* Cp., Gg., H^1., H^2., H^3., J.; Sk. telle. 721. Telle; *so* Cp., H^3.; Sk. tel. 729. A-wak; Sk. *and MSS.* awake. 751. Awak; *so* H^1.; Sk. awake. 753. Crye; *so* Cp., Gg., H^1., H^2., H^3., J.; Sk. cry. 780. Bendiste; *so* Cp., H^1., J.; Sk. benedicite. 878. Far; Sk. *and MSS.* fare.

Book II. Incipit Liber Secundus *moved from before line 50;* Incipit Prohemium *etc. omitted.* 95. Herken; *so* Cl., Cp., Gg., H^2., H^3., J.; Sk. herknen. 113. Ey; *so all but* Cl.; Sk. A. 133. Helpe; *so* H^1., H^3.; J.; Sk. help. 137. Wol; *so* Cp., J.; Sk. wole. 400. Wont; *so* Cp., H^1., H^2., H^3., J.; Sk. woned. 405. Which; *so* Cl., Cp., Gg., H^3., J.; Sk. whiche. 955. Chees; *so* Gg. (sches); Sk. chese. 1519. Ly; *so* Gg.; Sk. lye.

Book III. Incipit Liber Tercius *moved from before line 50;* Incipit Prohemium *etc. omitted.* 52–3. Wol (wol); *so* Cp. (wole), H^1., H^2. (wole), (J. wol); Sk. wole (wole). 144. Y-lyke; *so* Gg., H^2., H^3.; Sk. y-lyke ay. 148–50. Requeste, feste; *so* Cp., H^1., H^2., J.; Cl. request, feste; Sk. request, fest. 360. Apcril; *so* Cl., Cp., H^1., H^2., H^3., J.; Sk. Aprille. 535, Maad; *so* Gg., J.; Sk. made. 683. Took; *so* Cp., Gg., H^1., J.; Sk. toke. 798. Shal; *so all but* Cl.; Sk. shalt. 982. Clere; *so* Cp., H^1., H^2., H^3., J.; Sk. cleer. 1141. Candel; *so* H^2., H^3., J.; Sk. candele. 1459. Slayn; *so* Cp., Gg., H^1., H^2., H^3., J.; Sk. shent. 1604. Mot; *so* Cl.; Sk. mote. 1626. Worste; *so* Cl., Cp., Gg., H^1., J.; Sk. worst.

Book IV. Incipit Quartus Liber *moved from before line 29;* Prohemium *etc. omitted.* 108. Sk. *puts a period at the end of this line.* 337. Hotter; *so* Cp., H^2., H^3., J.; Sk. hottere. 658. Far; *so* Gg.; Sk. fare. 730. Toke; *so* Cp., Gg., H^2., H^3. token; Sk. took. 805. Ich; *so* Cp. H^1., H^3., J.; Sk. I. 947. Al allone; *so* Cp., H^3., J.; Sk. allone. 1132. Woful; *so all but* Cl.; Sk. wofulle. 1407. Oo; *so* H^3.; Sk. a. 1490. Troians; *so MSS.* except H^2 (Troian); Sk. Troianes.

Book V. 81. Hond; *so* Cl., Gg.; Sk. honde. 205. Issu; Sk. *and MSS.* (Gg. isseu) issue. 277. Wonted; *so* Cl.; Sk. woned. 314. Yef; Sk. *and MSS.* yeve. 329. Lat; *so* Cp., H^1., J.; Gg., H^2., H^3. let; Sk. lete. 751–3–4. West, lest, best; *so* Cl., Cp., Gg.; H^2., H^3., J. west, lyste (leste), beste; Sk. weste, leste, beste. 797. Wol; *so* Cp., H^1., J.; H^2., will; Sk. wole. 1040. Broch; *so* H^1.; Sk. broche. 1161–2. Arte,-carte; *so MSS.* except H^2. (art, carte); Sk. art,-cart. 1213. The wode; *so* Cl., Cp., H^3.; Sk wode. 1586. That she; *so MSS.;* Sk. she. 1594. Syk; *so* Cp., Gg., H^1.; Sk. syke.

Chaucer's Wordes Unto Adam. *T.*=R. *3. 20, Trinity Coll. Library;* $S.$=*Stowe's edition.* 3. Thy longe; *so* S.; T. thy long; Sk. thy.

Balade from the Legende. *Add.*[1]=*Add. 12524, British Museum;* *Add.*[2]=*Add. 9832; Arch.*=*Arch. Seld. B. 24;* $B.$=*Bodley 638;* $F.$= *Fairfax 16; Gg.*=*Gg. 4. 27, Camb. Univ. Library; P.*=*Pepys 2006; T.*= *Tanner 346; Trin.*=*R. 3. 19, Trinity College. Th.*=*Thynne's edition.* 250. Leye; Sk. *and MSS.* ley. 253. Make; *so MSS. except* Gg.; Sk. mak.

Trouthe. *Add.*[1]=*Add. 10340; Add.*[2]=*Add. 22139; Arch.*[1]=*Arch. Seld. B. 24; Arch.*[2]=*Arch. Seld. B. 10; Cl.=Cleopatra D. VII; Cp.=Corpus Christi 203; E.=Ellesmere; F.*[1]=*Fairfax 16; F.*[2]=*Fairfax 16 (second copy) Gg.=Gg. 4. 27; H.=Harleian 7333; Hatton=Hatton MS. 73; L.=Lansdowne 699; P.=Phillipps 8299; Trin.*[1]=*Trin. R. 3. 20; Trin.*[2]=*Trin. R. 3. 20 (second copy). Cx.=Caxton's edition.* 1. Dwell; *so Add.*[2]*, Arch.*[2]*, Cl., Cp., E., H., L., P.; Sk.* dwelle. 8. Tempeste; *Sk. and MSS.* tempest. 26. Praye; *Sk. and Add.*[1] pray.

Lenvoy de Chaucer a Scogan. *F.=Fairfax 16; Gg.=Gg. 4. 27, Camb. Univ. Library; P.=Pepys 2006. Th.=Thynne's edition.* 8. Word; *so Gg., P.; Sk.* worde. 38. Sleep to wake; *so Gg.; F.* slepe to wake; *Sk.* slepe wak. 45. Streem; *so Gg.; Sk.* streme.

Lenvoy de Chaucer a Bukton. *F.=Fairfax 16. N.=Julian Notary's edition; Th.=Thynne's edition.* 10-12-13-15. Evere, nevere, levere, dissevere; *so F.; Sk.* ever, never, lever, dissever. 26. Keep; *Sk. and MSS.* kepe.

Compleynte of Chaucer to his Empty Purs. *Add.=Add. 22139; F.=Fairfax 16; Ff.=Ff 1. 6, Camb. Univ. Library; H*[1]*=Harleian 2251; H*[2]*=Harleian 7333; P.=Pepys 2006; Ph.=Phillipps MS. 9053. Cx.= Caxton's edition.* 1. Purs; *so Ff., P., Cx.; Sk.* purse.

The Caunterbury Tales. *Cp.=Corpus Christi; E.=Ellesmore; Gg.= Gg. 4. 27, Camb. Univ. Library; Hn.=Hengwrt; L.=Lansdowne 851; P.=Petworth:—all taken from the Six-text Print.*

The Prologe. 2. March; *so E., Hn.; Sk.* Marche. 60. Armee; *so all except Gg.; Sk.* aryve. 120. Seinte; *so P.; Sk.* seÿnt. 134. Ther was; *so MSS.; Sk.* was. 164. Chapeleyn; *so Gg., P.; Sk.* chapeleyne. 196. A ful; *so MSS.; Sk.* a. 232. Mote; *so MSS.; Sk.* moot. 257-8. Whelp, help; *so Gg.; Sk.* whelpe, helpe. 313. Were; *so Cp., Gg.; Sk* weren. 363. And they were clothed alle; *so MSS. ; Sk.* were with us eek, clothed. 509. Seynte; *so Cp.; Sk.* seÿnt. 697. Seynte; *Sk. and MSS.* seynt. 747. Host; *so Cp., E., Gg., Hn.; Sk.* hoste. 850. That it; *so MSS.; Sk.* it.

Knightes Tale. 942. Which; *so Gg., P.; Sk.* whiche. 942. Y-slawe; *Sk. and MSS.* slawe. 1051-2. Up-rist, list; *so P.; Gg.* upriste, lyst; *Sk.* upriste, liste. 1076. Squar; *Sk. and MSS.* square. 1290. Moste; *so MSS.; Sk.* mot. 1493-4. Bright, light; *so Cp., Gg.; L., P.,* bright, sight; *Sk.* brighte, lighte. 1502. Stertling; *so E., Gg., Hn.; Sk.* sterting (*cf. LGW.* 1204). 1512. In; *so E., Gg., Hn.; Sk.* I. 1669-70. Yeer, heer; *so Hn.; Sk.* yere, here. 1720. Yif; *so Gg., Hn., L.; Sk.* yeve. 1892. Lette; *so E.; Sk.* letted. 1975-6 Forest beest; *so E., Hn.; Gg., L.,* forest beste; *Sk.* foreste, beste. 2001-2. Bed, bibled; *so Gg., Hn.; Sk.* bedde, bibledde. 2060. Peynted; *so MSS.; Sk.* peynt. 2145. Wreeth; *Sk. and MSS.* wrethe. 2329. Keep; *Sk. and MSS.* kepe. 2436. In; *so E., Gg., H.; Sk.* inne. 2534. Of; *so E.; Sk* of the.

Bihoold the murie wordes of the Hoost to the lady Prioresse *is taken from before B 1625;* "to the Shipman and" *is omitted from between* Hoost *and* to.

The Prologe of the Prioresses Tale.   1651. Lilie; *so E., Hn., L.; Sk.* lily.   1674. Month; *so Gg., Hn.; Sk.* monthe.

The Prioresses Tale. 1826. The Masse; *so E., Gg., Hn.; Sk.* masse.

The Nonne Preestes Tale.   4011. Stape; *so E., Hn.; Sk.* stope.   4039. Heet; *so E., Hn.; Sk.* hight.   4343–4. -Moor, stoor; *so E., Hn.; Sk.* -more, store.

The Prologe of the Pardoners Tale. 351–2. Sheep, keep; *so Cp.; Sk.* shepe, kepe.   364. Iew; *so E., Hn.; Sk.* Iewe.   441. Poverte; *so E., Gg., Hn.; Sk.* povert.   448. Moneye; *so E., Gg., Hn.; Sk.* money.   592. Deceit; *Cp.* disceipt; *Gg.* disseyd; *Sk.* deceite.   776. Spak; *so MSS.; Sk.* spake.

The Prologe of the Wyves Tale of Bathe.   604. Seynte; *Sk. and MSS.* seynt.

The Clerkes Tale. 59. Playn; *so P.; Sk.* playne.   64–6. Lond, hond; *so E., Hn., P.; Sk.* londe, honde.   *Before* 939, "Explicit quinta pars. Sequitur pars sexta;" *Sk.*, "Pars Sexta."   1168. Coyn; *so Gg.; Sk.* coyne.   "Lenvoy de Chaucer" *is omitted from before 1177.*

GLOSSARY

GLOSSARY

In general only such words are included in this glossary as differ in form or meaning from the corresponding words in modern English, together with proper names and a few notes. Etymologies are supplied to facilitate the study of the language; but where the sources of the words are doubtful, or where special complications arise, this material is omitted. If the source is identical in form with the Middle English word, the form is not repeated, but is merely indicated by the reference to the language from which it comes.

The following abbreviations are used:

A. F., Anglo-French
A. S., Anglo-Saxon
F., French
L., Latin
L. L., Low Latin

M. E., Middle English
O. F., Old French
O. Du., Old Dutch
O. N., Old Norse

A

A, *prep.*, on, in.

Abasshed, Abaysed, Abayst, *p. p.*, abashed, disconcerted. *O. F.* esbahir.

Abbay, *n.*, abbey. *O. F.* **abbaïe.**

Abet, *n.*, abetting, instigation. *O. F.*

Abhominable, *adj.*, abominable, hateful. *F.* abominable.

Abit, *v., third pers. sing., pres. indic., see* **Abyde.**

Able, *adj.*, able, capable, fit, suitable. *O. F.*

Aboghte, *v., pret., see* **Abye.**

Abood, *n.*, delay.

Abood, *v., pret. sing., see* **Abyde.**

Aboughte, *v., pret., see* **Abye.**

Aboute, *adv., prep.,* about, around. *A. S.* abūtan.

Aboven, *prep.*, above. *A. S.* abufon.

Abrayde, *v.*, awake. *A. S.* ābregdan.

Abregge, *v.*, abridge, shorten. *O. F.* abregier.

Abreyde, *v., see* **Abrayde.**

Absolucioun, *n.*, absolution. *F.* absolution.

Abusioun, *n.*, abuse, deceit, scandal. *O. F.* **abusion.**

Abyde, *v.*, abide, wait for. *A. S.* ābīdan.

Abye, *v.*, pay for, suffer for. *A. S.* ābycgan.

Accesse, *n.*, attack of fever. *O. F.* aces.

Accident, *n.*, the outward changing attribute (as opposed to the substance). *F. Cf.* **Substaunce.**

Accordaunt, *adj.*, agreeable to. *O. F.* acordant.

Accorde, *v.*, agree. *O. F.* acorder.

Accusement, *n.*, accusation. *O. F.* acusement.

Accusour, *n.*, accuser, revealer. *O. F.* acuseor.

Achat, *n.*, buying. *O. F.*

Achatour, *n.*, buyer. *O. F.* achateor.

A-chekked, *p. p.*, checked, hindered.

Acheve, *v.*, achieve. *O. F.* achever.

Achitofel, Ahithophel: *see II Samuel, xvi ff.*

Acloyeth, *v., third pers. sing., pres. indic.,* overburdens. *O. F.* encloer.

Acord, *n.*, agreement, harmony. *O. F.* acort, acorde.

Acordaunt, *adj., see* **Accordaunt.**

425

Acorde, v., see **Accorde.**

Acorse, v., see **Acurse.**

Acoye, v., quiet, allure, decoy. O. F. acoier.

Acquyte, v., acquit. O. F. aquiter.

Acurse, v., curse.

Acuse, v., accuse, blame. O. F. acuser.

Acustomaunce, n., habit. O. F. accustumance.

Adamant, Adamaunt, n., adamant, loadstone. O. F.

Adawe, v., awake.

Adoun, Adonis.

A-doun, adv., down, downwards. A. S. of—dūne.

Adrad, p. p., afraid. See **Drede.** A. S. ofdrǣdan.

Adriane, Ariadne.

Adversarie, n., adversary. L. adversarius.

Adversitee, n., adversity. F. adversité.

Advertence, n., attention. O. F.

Advocacyes, n., pleas. O. F. avocacie.

Afer, adv., afar.

A-fere, on fire. See **Fyre.**

A-fered, Aferd, p. p., afraid. From **Afere,** A. S. afǣran.

Affeccioun, n., affection. F. affection.

Affect, n., desire. L.

Afferme, v., affirm. O. F. afermer.

Affiance, n., trust. O. F. afiance.

Affray, n., fright, terror. O. F. esfrei.

Affraye, v., frighten. O. F. esfreer.

Affyle, v., smooth, polish. O. F. afiler.

Afor-yeyn, prep., over against.

African: Scipio Africanus Major. See **Macrobie.**

Afrighte, v., frighten. A. S. āfyrhtan.

Afrike, Africa.

After, adv., afterwards, next. A. S. æfter.

After, prep., according to, later than. A. S. æfter.

A-fyre, on fire. See **Fyr.**

Agame, adv., in play, in jest.

Agaste, v., terrify. A. S. ā—— gæstan.

Agayn, adv., again. A. S. ongēan.

Agayn, Agaynes, prep., against, before. A. S. ongēan, ongēanes.

Agilte, v., do wrong, offend.

Agon, p. p., gone away, departed. From **Agon.** A. S. āgān.

Agreable, adj., agreeable. F.

A-greef, Agref, Agrief, adv., sadly, ill.

Agreve, v., aggrieve, vex. O. F. agrever.

Agroos, v., pret. sing., see **Agryse.**

Agryse, v., shudder, feel terror. A. S. āgrīsan.

Agu, n., ague. O. F. ague.

Ake, v., ache. A. S. acan.

Al, adj., all. A. S. eall.

Al, n., awl. A. S.

Alabastre, n., alabaster. L. alabaster.

Alambyk, n., alembic: a kind of retort for distilling. O. F. alambic.

Alaunts, n., plu., large hunting dogs. O. F. alan.

Alayes, n., plu., alloys. O. F. alei.

Alceste, Alcestis.

Alcipyades, Alcibiades.

Alcyone, Halcyone.

Alday, adv., all day, continually.

Alderbest, adj., adv., superl., best of all. See **Aller.**

Alderfaireste, adj., superl., fairest of all. See **Aller.**

Alderfirst, adj., adv., superl., first of all. See **Aller.**

Alder-lest, adv., superl., least of all. See **Aller.**

Alderlevest, adv., superl., dearest of all. See **Aller.**

Aldermost, adv., superl., most of all. See **Aller.**

Alder-next, adv., superl., nearest of all. See **Aller.**

Alderwysest, adj., superl., wisest of all. See **Aller.**

Alestake, *n.,* a stake or pole projecting from an alehouse to support a sign or "bush." *A. S.* ealu—staca.

Alete, Alecto: *one of the Furies.*

Aley, *n.,* alley. *O. F.* alée.

Aleyn, Alanus de Insulis *or* **Alain de L'Isle:** *a Cistercian monk of the twelfth century, author of* De Planctu Naturæ *and the* Anticlaudianus.

Algate, Algates, *adv.,* always, in any case, at any rate. *O. N.* alla gotu.

Algezir, Algeciras: *a city in Spain.*

Alighte, *v.,* alight. *A. S.* ālīhtan.

Alisaundre, Alexander.

Alisaundre, Alexandria.

Alle, *adj., dat. sing.; plu.; see* **Al.**

Allegge, *v.,* adduce, cite. *O. F.* esligier.

Aller, *adj., gen. plu., see* **Al.** *A. S.* ealra. *See* **Alder—, Alther—.**

Alliaunce, *n.,* alliance, espousal. *O. F.* aliance.

Allone, *adj.,* alone. *A. S.* eal—ān.

Alma redemptoris, *first words of a Latin hymn:* Alma redemptoris mater. *There are several hymns with this beginning.*

Almena, Alcmena.

Almes-dede, *n.,* alms-deed. *A. S.* ælmysse—dǣd *f.*

Along on, *prep.,* owing to.

Alose, *v.,* praise, commend. *O. F.* aloser.

Al-outerly, *adv.,* entirely, absolutely.

Also, *adv., conj.,* also, so, as. *A. S.* ealswā.

Altercacioun, *n.,* altercation, dispute. *F.* altercation.

Altheigh, *conj.,* although. *A. S.* eal—þēah.

Altherfastest, *adv.,* as fast as possible. *See* **Aller.**

Altherfirst, *adj., adv., superl.,* first of all. *See* **Aller.**

Althogh, *conj., see* **Altheigh.**

Alwey, *adv.,* always. *A. S.* eal—weg.

A-lyve, alive. *See* **On-lyve.**

Amadrides, *n., plu.,* hamadryads.

Amayed, *p. p.,* dismayed. *O. F.* amaier.

Amazones, Amazons.

Ambages, *n., plu.,* ambiguous words. *L.*

Ambler, *n.,* an ambling nag.

Amende, *v.,* amend, make amends, improve. *F.* amender.

Ameved, *v., pret. indic.; p. p.;* moved, changed. *O. F.* esmovoir.

Amiddes, *adv.,* in the midst; *prep.,* in the midst of. *A. S.* on middan.

Amis, *adv.,* amiss.

Among, *adv.,* all the while. *A. S.* onmang.

Amonges, *prep.,* amongst.

Amorwe, on the morrow, in the morning. *See* **Morwe.**

Amphibologyes, *n., plu.,* ambiguities. *O. F.* amphibologie.

Amphiorax, Amphiaraus.

Amphioun, Amphion.

Amy, *n.,* friend. *O. F.*

An, *prep.,* on. *A. S.*

Ancle, *n.,* ankle. *A. S.* anclēow.

Angre, *n.,* anger, trouble. *O. N.* angr.

Anguisshous, *adj.,* anxious.

Angwish, *n.,* anguish. *F.* angoisse.

Anhange, *v.,* hang. *A. S.* onhangian.

Anlas, *n.,* short, two-edged knife or dagger.

Anon, *adv.,* immediately, straightway, anon. *A. S.* on—ān.

Anon-right, *adv.,* immediately, straightway.

Anoy, *n.,* vexation, trouble. *O. F.* anoi.

Anoye, *v.,* annoy, vex, injure. *O. F.* anoier.

Answere, *n.,* answer. *A. S.* andswaru.

Anteclaudian, *the* Anticlaudianus. *See* **Aleyn.**

Antem, *n.,* anthem. *A. S.* antefn; *L.* antiphona.

Anthenor, Antenor: *who, accord-*

ing to Guido's Historia, *betrayed Troy by sending the Palladium to Ulysses.*

Antiphoner, *n.,* anthem-book.

Apaas, *adv.,* at a footpace. *See* **Pas.**

Apaire, *v.,* impair, deteriorate. *O. F.* empeirer.

Apalled, *p. p.,* rendered pale or feeble. *O. F.* apalir.

Aparaile, *n.,* apparel. *O. F.* apareil.

Aparceyve, *v., see* **Aperceyve.**

Apayed, *p. p.,* pleased, satisfied. *O. F.* apaier.

Apeire, *v., see* **Apaire.**

Apeise, *v., see* **Apese.**

Aperceyve, *v.,* perceive, discern. *F.* apercevoir.

Aperill, April. *See* **Aprille.**

Apert, *adj.,* open, manifest; *adv.,* openly, manifestly. *O. F.*

Apertenant, *adj.,* belonging to. *O. F.* apartenir.

Apese, *v.,* appease, pacify. *O. F.* apaisier.

Apeyre, *v., see* **Apaire.**

Apotecarie, *n.,* apothecary. *O. F.*

Apoynte, *v.,* appoint. *O. F.* apointier.

Appalled, *p. p., see* **Apalled.**

Apparaille, *n., see* **Aparaile.**

Apparence, *n.,* appearance, seeming, apparition. *O. F.* aparence.

Appelles: *a Grecian painter; but, according to Gaultier de Chatillon (in the sixth book of the Alexandreid), a Jewish sculptor who erected the tombs of Darius and his wife.*

Appetyt, *n.,* appetite, desire. *F.* appétit.

Appollo, Apollo.

Aprille, April. *See* **Aperill.**

Aproche, *v.,* approach. *O. F.* aprochier.

Apyked, *p. p.,* adorned.

Aqueyntaunce, *n.,* acquaintance. *O. F.* acointance.

Aqueynte, *v.,* acquaint. *O. F.* acointier.

Aquyte, *v., see* **Acquyte.**

Arace, *v.,* eradicate, tear away. *A. F.* aracer.

Aragon, Arragon.

Aray, *n.,* array, dress. *O. F.* arrei.

Arayed, *p. p.,* arrayed, dressed, equipped. *O. F.* arraier.

Archeer, *n.,* archer. *O. F.* archier.

Archewyves, *n., plu.,* arch-wives, ruling wives. *A. S.* arce—wíf.

Arede, *v.,* explain, interpret. *A. S.* arǽdan.

Arest, *n.,* arrest; the rest for a lance. *O. F.*

Areste, *v.,* arrest, stop. *O. F.* arester.

Arette, *v.,* ascribe, impute. *O. F.* areter.

Arge, Argos.

Argumente, *v.,* argue. *L.* argumentari.

Argus: *confused with Algus, the O. F. name for the Arabian mathematician through whose book Arabic numerals became known in Europe.*

Arguwe, *v.,* argue. *F.* arguer.

Ariete, Aries: *the Ram, the zodiacal sign for the latter part of March and the first part of April.*

Ariones harpe, Arion's harp: *the constellation Lyra.*

Arivaile, *n.,* arrival, landing. *O. F.* arrivaille.

Armee, *n.,* expedition. *O. F.*

Arm-greet, *adj.,* as large as an arm. *A. S.* arm—grēat.

Armipotente, *adj.,* powerful in arms. *L.* armipotens.

Armonye, *n.,* harmony. *O. F.* armonie.

Armurers, *n., plu.,* armorers. *F.* armurier.

Arn, *v., pres. plu.,* are. *See* **Ben.**

Aroos, *v., pret. sing., see* **Aryse.**

A-roume, *adv.,* at large. *A. S.* on—rūm.

A-rowe, *adv.,* in a row. *See* **Rewe.**

Arrayed, *p. p., see* **Arayed.**

Arrerage, *n.*, arrears. *F.*

Arrette, *v.*, *see* **Arette**.

Arrivage, *n.*, cunning to shore. *F.*

Ars metrik, *n.*, arithmetic.

Art, *n.*, art, cunning, kind, sort. *F.*

Arte, *v.*, *pron.*, *second pers. sing.*, *pres. indic.*, art thou. *See* **Ben.**

Arte, *v.*, constrain, urge. *L.* artare.

Artow, *v.*, *pron.*, *second pers. sing.*, *pres. indic.*, art thou. *See* **Ben.**

Artoys, Artois,

Arwe, *n.*, arrow. *A. S.* arewe.

Aryse, *v.*, arise, be raised. *A. S.* ārīsan.

As, *adv.*, *conj.*, as, so (*in asseverations*). *A. S.* ealswā.

Ascaunce, *adv.*, as if to say. *M. E.* as—*O. F.* quanses.

Ascencioun of the equinoxial, ascension of the equinoctial: *fifteen degrees of the equinoctial, which make an hour.* *F.* ascension.

Ascendent, *n.*, the degree of thee cliptic rising above the horizon at a given moment. *O.F.*

Ascry, *n.*, alarm. *O. F.* escri.

Ashame, *v.*, shame, put to shame. *A. S.* on—scamian.

Ashe, *n.*, ash-tree. *A. S.* æsc.

Asonder, *adv.*, asunder.

Asp, *n.*, aspen tree. *A. S.* æsp.

Aspect, *n.*, (astrological) planetary relation: *the situation of two planets with respect to each other.*

Aspre, *adj.*, sharp, bitter. *O. F.*

Aspye, *n.*, spy, *O. F.* espie.

Aspye, *v.*, spy, see. *O. F.* espier.

Assaut, *n.*, assault. *O. F.*

Assay, *n.*, trial. *O. F.* asai.

Assaye, *v.*, test, prove, try. *O. F.* asaier.

Asse, *n.*, ass. *A. S.* assa.

Assege, *n.*, siege, besieging force.

Assege, *v.*, besiege, lay siege to. *O. F.* asegier.

Asshen, *n.*, *plu.*, ashes. *A. S.* æsce.

Assoille, *v.*, absolve, pardon. *O. F.* assoudre.

Assure, *v.*, feel secure, take or give confidence. *O. F.* asseurer.

Asswage, *v.*, assuage, mitigate. *O. F.* asuagier.

Assyse, *n.*, assize, session. *O. F.* assise.

Asterte, *v.*, escape.

Astoned, *p. p.*, *see* **Astonie**.

Astonie, *v.*, astonish. *O. F.* estoner.

Astored, *p. p.*, stored, provided.

Astronomye, *n.*, astronomy. *F.* astronomie.

Asure, *n.*, azure. *F.* azur.

Asweved, *p. p.*, dazed. *A. S.* āswebban.

Aswowne, *adv. from p. p.*, in a swoon.

Asyde, *adv.*, aside. *See* **Syde**.

Asye, Asia.

Atempre, *adj.*, temperate, moderate. *O. F.*

Athalaunte, Atalanta.

Athalus, Attalus: *the fabled inventor of chess.*

Athamaunt, *n.*, *see* **Adamant**.

Athamente, Athamas: *Juno caused Athamas, the husband of Ino, to run mad. See Ovid,* Metam. *iv, 416 ff.*

Athenes, Athenis, Athens.

Athinke, *v.*, displease. *A. S.* ofþyncan.

Atiteris: *perhaps* **Tyrtæus** *or* **Tityrus.**

Atlantes doughtres, the daughters of Atlas: *the constellation of the Pleiades.*

At ones, *adv.*, at once.

Atoon, *adv.*, at one.

At-rede, *v.*, surpass in counsel. *A. S.* æt—rǣdan.

At-renne, *v.*, surpass in running. *A. S.* æt—rinnan.

Attamed, *p. p.*, broached. *O. F.* atamer.

Attempre, *adj.*, *see* **Atempre**.

Attendaunce, *n.*, attendance. *O. F.* atendance.

Atteyne, *v.*, attain. *O. F.* ataindre.

Atthalaunte, **Atalanta**.

Attheon, **Actæon**.

Attricioun, *n.*, attrition, grief for sin arising from fear of punishment. *L.* **attritio**.

Attropos, **Atropos**.

Atwinne, *adv.*, apart. *A. S.* on—**getwinne**.

Atwixen, *prep.*, between.

Atwo, *adv.*, in twain. *A. S.* on—**twā**.

Atyr, *n.*, attire, dress. *O. F.* **atir**.

Auctor, *n.*, *see* **Auctour**.

Auctoritee, *n.*, authority. *O. F.* **autorité**.

Auctour, *n.*, author. *O. F.* **autor**.

Audience, *n.*, hearing. *O. F.*

Auditour, *n.*, auditor. *O. F.*

Auffrike, **Africa**. *Cf.* **Afrike**.

Auncestre, *n.*, ancestor. *O. F.* **ancestre**.

Aungel, *n.*, angel. *O. F.* **angele**.

Aungellyk, *adj.*, angelic.

Austin, Saint **Augustine** (*354–430*): *Bishop of Hippo, from whose writings the Augustinian rule was compiled.*

Auter, *n.*, altar. *O. F.*

Avale, *v.*, fall, sink. *O. F.* **avaler**.

Avantage, *n.*, advantage. *O. F.*

Avaunce, *v.*, advance, promote. *O. F.* **avancer**.

Avaunt, *n.*, vaunt, boast. *O. F.*

Avauntage, *n.*, *see* **Avantage**.

Avaunte, *v.*, boast. *O. F.* **avanter**.

Avauntour, *n.*, boaster. *O. F.* **avanteur**.

Avayle, *v.*, avail.

Aventaille, *n.*, the moveable mouthpiece of a helmet. *O. F.* **avantaille**.

Aventure, *n.*, chance, fortune. *O. F.*

Averrois, **Averroes**: *a Moorish scholar of the twelfth century.*

Avicen, **Avicenna**: *an Arabian philosopher and physician of the eleventh century.*

Avisioun, *n.*, vision. *O. F.* **avision**.

Avouterye, *n.*, adultery. *O. F.* **avouterie**.

Avow, *n.*, vow, avowal.

Avoy, *interj.*, fie! *O. F.* **avoi**.

Avys, *n.*, advice, consideration, opinion. *O. F.* **avis**.

Avyse, *v.*, consider, deliberate. *O. F.* **aviser**.

Avysement, *n.*, consideration, counsel. *O. F.* **avisement**.

Awayt, *n.*, watch, waiting. *O. F.* **await**.

Awey, **Aweye**, *adv.*, away, astray, out of the way. *A. S.* on—**weg**.

Awhaped, *p. p.*, amazed, confounded.

Ay, *adv.*, aye, ever. *O. N.* **ei**.

Ayein, **Ayeins**, *adv.*, *prep.*, *see* **Agayn**, **Agaynes**.

Ayeinward, *adv.*, again, on the other hand.

Ayel, *n.*, grandfather. *F.* **aïeul**.

Ayle, *v.*, ail. *A. S.* **eglan**.

B

Babewinnes, *n.*, *plu.*, grotesque figures.

Babiloyne, **Babylon**.

Bacheler, *n.*, a youth, aspirant to knighthood. *O. F.*

Bachelrye, *n.*, company of young men. *O. F.* **bachelerie**.

Bacoun, *n.*, bacon. *O. F.* **bacon**.

Badde, *adj.*, bad. *A. S.* **bæddel?**

Baggepype, *n.*, bagpipe.

Baggeth, *v.*, *third pers. sing.*, looks askant.

Baillif, *n.*, bailiff. *O. F.*

Bak, *n.*, back. *A. S.* **bæc**.

Bake, *p. p.*, baked. *From* **Bake**. *A. S.* **bacan**.

Bal, *n.*, ball.

Balaunce, *n.*, balance, suspense. *O. F.* **balance**.

Baldeswelle, **Baldeswell** *in Norfolk*.

Bale, *n.*, bale, harm. *A. S.* **bealu**, **balu**.

Balled, *adj.*, bald.

Ballenus: *see* **Hermes**.

Bane, *n.*, bane, destruction, death. *A. S.* **bana**.

Baner, *n.*, banner. *O. F.* **baniere**.

Bar, *v.*, *pret. sing.*, *see* **Bere**.

Barbe, *n.*, barb: *a part of a woman's head-dress, consisting of a piece of white plaited linen passed over or under the chin and reaching midway to the waist. O. F.*

Barbour, *n.,* barber, *O. F.* barbeor.

Bareyn, *adj.,* barren. *O. F.* brehaing.

Bargaynes, *n., plu.,* bargains. *O. F.* bargagne.

Barm, *n.,* bosom, lap. *A. S.* bearm.

Baroun, *n.,* baron. *O. F.* baron.

Barre, *n.,* bar, stripe across a girdle. *O. F.*

Bataille, *n.,* battle, fight, troop. *O. F.*

Batailled, *p. p.,* embattled. *O. F.* bateillier.

Baude, *n.,* bawd.

Bauderye, *n.,* bawdry. *O. F.* bauderie.

Bawdrik, *n.,* baldric, belt worn transversely over one shoulder. *O. F.* (*cf.* baldrei).

Bawme, *n.,* balm. *O. F.* bausme.

Bayte, *v.,* bait, feed. *O. N.* beita.

Beblotte, *v.,* blot.

Bede, *v.,* offer, proffer, command. *A. S.* beodan.

Bede, *v., pret. plu.; p. p.; see* Bidde.

Bedes, *n., plu.,* beads. *A. S.* bed.

Beem, *n.,* beam. *A. S.* beam.

Been, *n., plu.,* bees. *A. S.* beo.

Beer, *v., pret., sing., see* Bere.

Beest, *n.,* beast. *O. F.* beste.

Beeth, *v., imper. plu.,* be. *See* Ben.

Begge, *v.,* beg.

Begger, *n.,* beggar.

Beggestere, *n.,* female beggar, beggar. —(*A. S. suffix*) estre.

Begyle, *v., see* Bigyle.

Beheste, *n.,* promise, command. *A. S.* behaes *f.*

Behette, *v., pret. sing., see* Behote.

Behewe, *p. p.,* hewn, carved.

Behote, *v.,* promise. *A. S.* behatan.

Bek, *n.,* beak. *F.* bec.

Bekke, *v.,* nod. (*M. E.* bekenen, *A. S.* beacnian, bycnian.)

Bel amy, good friend, fair friend. *O. F.* bel ami. **Bele,** *adj.,* fair, beautiful. *O. F.* bel.

Belle, *n,* bell. *A. S.* belle. Bere the belle, be the first.

Belmarye, Benamarin: *a Moorish kingdom in Africa.*

Belwe, *v.,* bellow. *A. S.* bylgean.

Bemes, *n., plu., see* Beem.

Ben, *v.,* be. *A. S.* beon.

Bene, *n.,* bean. *A. S.* bean *f.*

Benediste, Benedicite: *bless ye (the Lord).*

Benefyce, *n.,* benefice. *F.* bénéfice.

Beneit, Benedict.

Benigne, *adj.,* benign, kind, gracious. *O. F.*

Benignitee, *n.,* benignity, goodness. *O. F.* benignete.

Bent, *n.,* grassy slope. *A. S.* beonet.

Berd, *n.,* beard. Make a berd, deceive. *A. S.* beard.

Bere, *n.,* bear. *A. S.* bera.

Bere, *n.,* bier. *A. S.* bær *f.*

Bere, *n.,* pillow covering. *Cf.* pilwebeer.

Bere, *v.,* bear. *A. S.* beran. Bere on honde, accuse, make (a person) believe.

Berie, *v.,* bury. *A. S.* byrgan.

Berking, *s.,* barking. *A. S.* beorcan.

Bern, *n.,* barn. *A. S.* bern.

Bernard, Bernardus Gordonius: *a contemporary of Chaucer and professor of medicine at Montpellier.*

Berwik, Berwick: *a town in Northumberland on the Tweed.*

Berye, *n.,* berry. *A. S.* berie.

Beseye, *p. p., see* Biseye.

Bestialitee, *n.,* bestiality, animal condition. *F.* bestialité.

Besy, *adj.,* busy. *A. S.* bysig.

Besyed, *p. p.,* busied. *A. S.* bysgian.

Bet, *adj., adv., compar.,* better. *A. S.* bet. *See* Bettre.

Bete, *v.*, mend, kindle. *A. S.* bētan.

Bete, *v.*, beat. *A. S.* bēatan.

Bettre, *adj.*, *compar.*, better. *A. S.* betera. *See* Bet.

Bever, *n.*, beaver. *A. S.* beofor.

Bewrye, *v. See* Biwreye.

Beye, *v.*, buy. *A. S.* bycgan.

Bibled, *p. p.*, bloodied.

Biblis, Byblis: *changed to a fountain on being repulsed in love. See Ovid,* Metam., *ix, ll. 452.*

Bicched, *adj.*, cursed. Bicched bones, dice.

Bidde, *v.*, pray; (*confused with* Bede) command. *A.S.* biddan.

Bidaffed, *p. p.*, befooled.

Bifalle,*v.*, befall. *A.S.* befeallan.

Biforen, *prep.*, before. *A. S.* beforan.

Biforen, *adv.*, in the front part. *A. S.* beforan.

Biginne, *v.*, begin. *A. S.* beginnan.

Bigon, *p. p.*, situated, beset, attired. *A. S.* bigān.

Bigyle, *v.*, beguile, deceive. Be—*O. F.* guiler.

Bihalve, *n.*, behalf. *A. S.* be—healf.

Biheste, *n., see* Beheste.

Bihete, *v.*, promise. *See* Behote.

Bihighte, *v., pret., see* Behote.

Bihinde, *adv.*, *prep.*, behind. *A. S.* behindan.

Biholde, *v.*, behold. *A. S.* be—healdan.

Bihote, *v., see* Behote.

Bihovely, *adj.*, helpful, needful.

Bi-iape, *v.*, fool, trick.

Biknowe, *v.*, acknowledge, confess. *A. S.* becnāwan.

Bilde, *v.*, build. *A. S.* byldan.

Bilder, *n. as adj.*, builder.

Bile, *n.*, bill. *A. S.* bile.

Bille, *n.*, bill, petition. *A. F.*

Biloved, *p. p.*, beloved. *A. S.* be—lufian.

Binne, *n.*, bin, hutch, chest. *A. S.* binn *f.*

Biquethe, *v.*, bequeath. *A. S.* becweðan.

Bireyned, *p. p.*, rained upon. *A. S.* be—rignan.

Bireve, *v.*, bereave, rob. *A. S.* berēafian.

Birthe, *n.*, birth.

Bischeche, *v.*, beseech. *A. S.* be—sēcan.

Bisege, *v.*, besiege.

Biseke, *v., see* Bischeche.

Bisette, *v.*, bestow, employ. *A. S.* besettan.

Biseye, *p. p.*, beseen, decked, clad. *A. S.* besēon. Goodly beseyn, fair to see. Wel beseyn, good looking.

Bishet, *p. p.*, shut up. *A. S.* be—scyttan.

Bisily, *adv.*, busily.

Bisinesse, *n.*, business, activity.

Bismotered, *p. p.*, besmutted, dirtied.

Bisoghte, Bisoughte, *v., pret., see* Bischeche.

Bisy, *adj., see* Besy.

Bisyde, Bisydes, *prep.*, beside. *See* Syde.

Bit, *v., third pers. sing., pres. indic., see* Bede, Bidde.

Bitake, *v.*, commend, entrust. *A. S.* be—tacan.

Bithinke, *v.*, bethink, imagine, consider. *A. S.* beþencan.

Bitraise, *v.*, betray. Be—*O. F.* traïr.

Bitrende, *v.*, encircle. Bitrent, *third pers., sing., pres. indic.*, encircles. *A. S.* be—trendan.

Bitwixen, *prep.*, between.

Bityde, *v.*, happen. *A. S.* be—tidan.

Biwaile, *v.*, bewail.

Biwared, *p. p.*, expended, laid out (as on wares).

Biwopen, *p. p.*, bathed in tears. *From* Biwepe. *A. S.* bewēpan.

Biwreye, *v.*, reveal. *A. S.* be—wrēgan.

Blak, *adj.*, black. *A. S.* blæc.

Blakebaried, a, a-blackberrying.

Blankmanger, *n.*, minced capon with rice, milk, sugar, and almonds: *named from its white color. O. F.* blanc-manger.

Blase, *n.,* blaze. *A. S.* **blæse.**

Blase, *v.,* blow. *O. N.* **blāsa.**

Blasphemour, *n.,* blasphemer.

Blaste, *v.,* blow.

Blaunche fevere, fever that turns men white: *said jocosely because love makes its victims pale. See* **Fevere.**

Blede, *v.,* bleed. *A. S.* **blēdan.**

Blende, *v.,* blind. **Blent,** *third pers. sing., pres. indic.,* blinds *A. S.* **blendan.**

Bleve, *v.,* remain. *A. S.* **be-læfan.**

Blew, *adj.,* blue. *F.* **bleu.**

Bleynte, *v., pret.* blenched, turned aside. *From* **Blenche.** *A. S.* **blencan.**

Blis, *n., see* **Blisse.**

Blisful, *adj.,* happy, blessed.

Blisse, *n.,* bliss, felicity. *A. S.* **blis** *f.*

Blisse, *v.,* bless. *A. S.* **blētsian.**

Blo, *adj.,* smoke-colored. *O. N.* **blār.**

Blody, *adj.,* bloody. *A. S.* **blōdig.**

Blosmy, *adj.,* blossoming, full of blossoms.

Blythe, *adj.,* blithe, glad. *A. S.* **blīþe.**

Blyve, *adv.,* quickly, soon.

Bobance, *n.,* presumption, boast. *O. F.*

Bocher, *n.,* butcher. *O. F.* **bochier.**

Bode, *n.,* foreboding, omen. *A. S.* **bod.**

Boece, Boethius: *an early scholastic, c. 480–524 A. D., Roman consul, author of theological treatises, treatises on learning and music, and of the famous* De Consolatione Philosophiæ, *put to death on a false charge of treason in the reign of Theodoric the Goth. The* De Consolatione *was one of the most popular books of the Middle Ages and even of later times; it was translated into English by Chaucer and by several others, including King Alfred and Queen Elizabeth,* and among the French translations was one (which Chaucer used) by Jean de Meun.

Boght, *p. p.;* **Boghte,** *v., pret.; see* **Bye.**

Boille, *v.,* boil. *O. F.* **boillir**

Boistes, *n., plu.,* boxes. *O. F.* **boiste.**

Boistously, *adv.,* loudly, boisterously.

Bokeler, *n.,* buckler: *a small round shield usually carried by a handle at the back. O. F.* **bocler.**

Boket, *n.,* bucket.

Bolde, *v.,* grow bold. *A. S.* **bealdian.**

Bole, *n.,* bull. **Bole, Taurus:** *the zodiacal sign.*

Boloigne, Boulogne *or* **Bologna.**

Bonde, *p. p.,* bound. *From* **Binde.** *A. S.* **bindan.**

Bonde, *n.,* bondman. *A. S.* **bonda.**

Bone, *n.,* boon, prayer. *O. N.* **bōn.**

Boon, *n.,* bone. *A. S.* **bān.**

Boor, *n.,* boar. *A. S.* **bār.**

Boost, *n.,* boast. *A. F.* **bost.**

Boot, *n.,* boat. *A. S.* **bāt.**

Boras, *n.,* borax. *F.* **borras.**

Bord, *n.,* table, board. *A. S.* **Had the bord bigonne,** had led the feast, sat at the head of the table.

Bore, *n.,* bore, hole. *O. N.* **bora.**

Bore, *p. p.,* born. *See* **Bere.**

Borne, *v.,* burnish, smooth. *O. F.* **burnir.** *See* **Burne.**

Borowe, Borwe, *n.,* pledge. *A. S.* **borh.**

Bote, *n.,* help, remedy, good. *A. S.* **bōt** *f.*

Botelees, *adj.,* without remedy.

Boteler, *n.,* butler. *O. F.* **bouteillier.**

Boterflye, *n.,* butterfly. *A. S.* **buter-flēge.**

Botes, *n., plu.,* boots. *O. F.* **bote.**

Bothe, *adj., pron.,* both. *O. N.* **bāþir.**

Bother, *adj., pron., gen. plu.,*

of both. *O. N.* **bāþir. Your bother,** of you both.

Botme, *n.,* bottom. *A. S.* **botm.**

Botmelees, *adj.,* bottomless, hollow, unreal.

Bouk, *n.,* body, trunk. *A. S.* **būc.**

Boundes, *n., plu.,* bounds. *O. F.* **bonde.**

Bountee, *n.,* goodness, kindness. *O. F.* **bonté.**

Bountevous, *adj.,* bounteous.

Bour, *n.,* bed-chamber, bower. *A. S.* **būr.**

Bourde, *v.,* jest. *O. F.* **bourder.**

Bowe, *n.,* bow. *A. S.* **boga.**

Bowes, *n., plu.,* boughs. *A. S.* **boh.**

Bracer, *n.,* guard for the arm. *O. F.* **brasseure.**

Bradwardyn, Bradwardine: *proctor at Oxford in 1325, later Chancellor, Archbishop of Canterbury just before his death in 1349, author of a theological treatise* De Causa Dei.

Brak, *v., pret. sing., see* **Breke.**

Braste, *v., pret., see* **Breste.**

Braun, *n.,* brawn, muscle. *O. F.* **braon.**

Braunche, *n.,* branch. *O. F.* **branche.**

Brayde, *v., see* **Breyde.**

Brede, *n.,* breadth. *A. S.* **brǣdu.**

Brede, *n.,* roast. *A. S.* **brǣde.**

Brede, *v.,* breed. *A. S.* **brēdan.**

Breed, *n.,* bread. *A. S.* **brēad.**

Breem, *n.,* bream: *a fish. O. F.* **bresme.**

Breeth, *n.,* breath. *A. S.* **brǣþ.**

Breke, *v.,* break. *A. S.* **brecan.**

Brekers, *n., plu.,* breakers.

Brekke, *n.,* break, defect.

Breme, *adj.,* fierce; *adv.,* fiercely.

Bren, *n.,* bran. *O. F.*

Brenne, *v.,* burn. *O. N.* **brenna.**

Brenningly, *adv.,* burningly, ardently.

Brere, *n.,* brier, underwood. *A. S.* **brēr.**

Brest, *n.,* breast. *A. S.* **brēost.**

Brest-boon, *n.,* breast-bone. *A. S.* **brēost—bān.**

Breste, *v.,* burst. *A. S.* **berstan.**

Brest-plat, *n.,* breast-plate. *A. S.* **brēost—***O. F.* **plate.**

Bret, Briton.

Bretful, *adj.,* brimful. *A. S.* **brerd—ful.**

Bretherhed, *n.,* brotherhood, religious order.

Breyde, *v.,* start, awake, draw. *A. S.* **bregdan.**

Brid, *n.,* bird. *A. S.* **bridd.**

Brinne, *v., see* **Brenne.**

Britayne, Brittany.

Brode, *adv.,* broadly.

Broght, *p. p.,* brought. *From* **Bringe.** *A. S.* **bringan.**

Bromes, *n., plu.,* brooms, the broom (*bushes so-called*). *A. S.* **brōm.**

Brond, *n.,* brand, torch. *A. S.*

Brooch, *n.,* brooch. *O. F.* **broche.**

Brood, *adj.,* broad, thick, large. *A. S.* **brād.**

Broste, *v., pret.;* **Brosten,** *p. p.,* burst. *See* **Breste.**

Brotel, *adj.,* brittle.

Brotelnesse, *n.,* frailty.

Brouke, *v.,* enjoy, use. *A. S.* **brūcan.**

Broun, *adj.,* brown. *A. S.* **brūn.**

Browe, *n.,* brow, eyebrow. *A. S.* **brū** *f.*

Broyded, *p. p.,* braided. *A. S.* **bregdan.** *See* **Breyde.**

Brydel, *n.,* bridle. *A. S.* **brīdel.**

Buk, *n.,* buck. *A. S.* **bucc.**

Bukkes, *n., pl.,* bucks. *A. S.* **bucca.**

Bukton: *either Peter de Buketon, the King's escheator for the county of York in 1397 (Tyrwhitt), or Robert Bukton, esquire to the Queen in 1391, 1393, and 1394 (Tatlock). See* Expeditions by Henry Earl of Derby, Camden soc., 1894, p. 300.

Bulde, *v., see* **Bilde.**

Bulle, *n.,* papal bull. *L.* **bulla.**

Bulte, *v.,* bolt, sift. *O. F.* **buleter.**

Burdeux, Bourdeaux.

Burdoun, *n.,* burden of a song, bass accompaniment. *O. F.* **bourdon.**

Burgeys, *n.,* burgess, citizen. *O. F.* burgeis.

Burned, *p. p.,* burnished, polished. *O. F.* **burnir.** *See* **Borne.**

Burnel, Brunellus: *the ass thus nicknamed in the* Speculum Stultorum *of Nigellus Wireker (fl. the latter part of the twelfth century).* One Gundulf, *according to the story, broke the leg of a cock, who took his revenge by neglecting to crow and waken Gundulf in time to be consecrated for his father's benefice.*

Burthe, *n.,* birth.

Buskes, *n., plu.,* bushes.

But-if, *conj.,* unless.

Buxom, *adj.,* yielding, obedient.

Buxomly, *adv.,* obediently.

By, *adv., prep.,* as regards, with respect to, besides. *A. S.* **bī.**

Bycause, *adv., conj.,* because. Be—*F.* cause.

Byde, *v.,* wait. *A. S.* **bīdan.**

Bye, *v.,* buy. *A. S.* **bycgan.** *See* **Beye.**

By-iape, *v., see* **Bi-iape.**

Byte, *v.,* bite, cut. *A. S.* **bītan.**

Bywreye, *v., see* **Biwreye.**

C

Caas, *n., plu.,* cases of law. *See* **Cas.**

Cacche, *v.,* catch, lay hold of. *O. F.* cachier.

Cadence, *n.,* rhythm, (*Skeat* suggests) stanzaic form. *LL.* cadentia.

Cadme, Cadmus.

Caitif, *adj.,* captive, wretched, miserable.

Caitif, *n.,* captive, wretch. *O. F.*

Cake, *n.,* round and rather flat loaf of bread.

Cakelinge, *n.,* cackling.

Calculinge, *s.,* calculation. F. calculer.

Calendes, *n., plu. See* **Kalendes.**

Calidoine, Calydon: *ancient city of Greece.*

Caliopee, Calliope: *the muse of epic poetry.*

Calipsa, Calypso.

Calistopee, Calixte, Callisto.

Calle, *n.,* caul: *net used to confine women's hair.* **Maken an howve above a calle,** make a hood above a caul: to make a fool of.

Cam, *v., pret. sing.,* came. *From* **Come.** *A. S.* **cuman.**

Camaille, *n.,* camel. *O. F.* **camel.**

Can, *v., pres. indic., see* **Conne.**

Canace: *daughter of Æolus, who was beloved by Poseidon, and who committed incest with her brother.*

Candace: *queen of India, beloved of Alexander, according to medieval romance.*

Candel, *n.,* candle. *A. S.*

Canel-boon, *n.,* collar-bone. *O. F.* canel—*A. S.* **bān.**

Cankedort, *n.,* state of suspense.

Canon: *the title of a book by* Avicenna.

Cantel, *n.,* cantle, portion. *O. F.*

Cape, *v.,* gape.

Capoun, *n.,* capon. *A. S.* **capūn.**

Cappe, *m.,* cap. *A. S.* **cæppe.** **Sette hir aller cappe,** deceived them all, made fools of them all.

Careyne, *n.,* corpse, carrion. *O. F.* caroigne.

Carie, *v.,* carry. *O. F.* **carier.**

Carl, *n.,* fellow, rustic. *O. N.* karl; *A. S.* ceorl.

Carole, *v.,* dance around singing. *O. F.* caroler.

Carpe, *v.,* talk, chatter.

Carrenar: *perhaps the* **Gulf of Carnaro** *or* **Quarnaro** *in the Adriatic (Skeat); or the* **Kara Nor**—*black lake—which is near the* Lop Nor—*sand lake or Desert of Gobi, and therefore the "dry sea"—in Asia (Lowes).*

Cartage, Carthage.

Carte, *n.,* cart, chariot. *A. S.* cræt.

Cas, *n.,* chance, accident, circumstance. *O. F.*

Cas, *n.*, quiver (for arrows). *O. F.* **casse.**

Cast, *n.*, occasion, contrivance, plan. *O. N.* **kast.**

Caste, *v.*, throw, conjecture, consider, plan, contrive. *O. N.* **kasta.**

Castel, *n.*, castle. *A. S.* The "longe castel with walles whyte" *puns on the names* Lancaster *and* Blanche.

Castel-yate, *n.*, castle-gate. *A. S.* **castel—geat.**

Casuel, *adj.*, casual. *F.*

Casuelly, *adv.*, casually.

Cataloigne, Catalonia *in southern France.*

Catapucc, *n.*, caper spurge: *the seeds are purgative.*

Catel, *n.*, property, wealth. *O. F.*

Catoun, Dionysius Cato: *reputed author of the* Disticha de Moribus *assigned to the third or fourth century A. D. and famous throughout the Middle Ages.*

Caughte, *v., pret.*, caught, conceived. *See* **Cacche.**

Caunterbury, Canterbury.

Causeles, *adj.*, without cause.

Ceint, *n.*, cincture, girdle. *O. F.*

Celle, *n.*, cell. *O. F.*

Centaure, *n.*, centaury: *a medicinal herb.*

Cercle, *n.*, circle. *F.*

Cercle, *v.*, encircle. *F.* **cercler.**

Cerial, *adj.*, cerrial: *belonging to a species of oak.*

Certes, *adv.*, certainly. *F.*

Certeyn, *adj.*, certain; *adv.*, certainly. *F.* **certain.**

Ceruce, *n.*, white lead: *used as the basis for a cosmetic.*

Cesse, *v.*, cease. *F.* **cesser.**

Chace, *v.*, chase, hunt, pursue. *O. F.* **chacier.**

Chamberere, *n.*, chambermaid, maidservant.

Chamberleyn, *n.*, chamberlain. *O. F.* **chamberlenc.**

Chambre, *n.*, chamber. *O. F.*

Champioun, *n.*, champion. *F.* **champion.**

Chapitre, *n.*, chapter. *F.*

Chapman, *n.*, trader, merchant. *A. S.* **ceapman.**

Char, *n.*, chariot. *O. F.*

Charge, *n.*, load, burden, importance, responsibility. *O. F.*

Charitable, *adj.*, loving, kind. *F.*

Charitee, *n.*, charity, love. *O. F.* **carité.**

Charme, *n.*, charm. *F.*

Charmeresses, *n., plu.*, workers with charms.

Chast, *adj.*, chaste. *F.* **chaste.**

Chasteyn, *n.*, chestnut. *O. F.* **chastaigne.**

Chaunce, *n.*, chance. *O. F.* **cheance.**

Chaungc, *v.*, change. *O. F.* **changier.**

Chaungeable, *adj.*, changeable. *F.* **changeable.**

Chaunterie, *n.*, chantry: *an endowment for a priest to sing masses for the soul of the giver of the endowment, or of some one designated by him.* *O. F.* **chanterie.**

Cheef, *adj.*, chief. *O. F.* **chief.**

Chek, *n.*, check (at chess). *O. F.* **eschec.**

Cheke, *n.*, cheek, cheek-bone. *A. S.* **ceace.**

Chekker, *n.*, chess-board. *O. F.* **eschequier.**

Chekmat, *n.*, checkmate. *F.* **échec et mat.**

Chep, *n.*, market, price. *A. S.* **ceap.** As good chep, as cheaply. Chepe, *dat.*, time of cheapness.

Chepe, Cheapside *in London.*

Chere, *n.*, face, countenance, cheer. *O. F.* **chiere.**

Cherisse, *v., see* **Cheryce.**

Cherl, *n.*, churl, boor, fellow. *A. S.* **ceorl.**

Cherubinnes, *n., gen.*, cherub's.

Cheryce, *v.*, cherish. *O. F.* **cherir.**

Ches, *n.*, chess. *O. F.* **eschès.** **Chesse,** *dat.*

Chese, *v.*, choose. *A. S.* **ceosan.**

Cheste, *n.*, chest. *A. S.* **cest** *f.*

Chevalrye, *n., see* **Chivalrye.**

Chevisaunce, *n.,* borrowing money, dealing for profit. *O. F.* chevisance.

Cheyne, *n.,* chain. *O. F.* chæne.

Chichevache: the lean cow that fed on patient wives.

Chide, *v.,* chide, rebuke, scold. *A. S.* cīdan. *See* Chyde.

Chiknes, *n., plu.,* chickens. *A. S.* cīcen.

Child, *n.,* child. *A. S.* cild.

Chimeneye, *n.,* fireplace, *F.* cheminée.

Chirche, *n.,* church. *A. S.* cirice.

Chirche-dore, *n.,* church-door. *A. S.* cirice—duru.

Chirking, *n.,* creaking, grating, shriek.

Chiron, Chiron *the centaur: tutor of Achilles.*

Chiteringe, *s.,* chattering, chirping.

Chivachye, *n.,* military expedition. *O. F.* chevauchie.

Chivalrye, *n.,* chivalry, knighthood, valor, knightly deeds. *O. F.* chevalerie.

Chogh, *n.,* chough, crow.

Chois, *n.,* choice. *O. F.*

Choppe, *v.,* strike downwards. knock.

Choys, *n., see* Chois.

Chyde, *v.,* chide, complain. *A. S.* cīdan. *See* Chide.

Cimerie, Cimmerii: *a mythical people described by Homer as dwelling in a remote realm of mist and gloom.*

Cink, *cinque,* five. *O. F.* cinc.

Cipioun, Scipio Africanus the younger: *see* Macrobie.

Cipres, *n.,* cypress. *O. F.*

Cipryde, native of Cyprus: Venus.

Circes, Circe.

Circumscryve, *v.,* bound, enclose. *F.* circonscrire.

Circumstaunces, *n., plu.,* circumstances. *O. F.* circumstance.

Citee, *n.,* city. *O. F.* cité.

Citezein, *n.,* citizen. *O. F.* citeain.

Citherea, of the island of Cythera: Venus.

Citheroun, Cithæron.

Citole, *n.,* stringed musical instrument. *O. F.*

Cladde, *v., pret.,* clad. *From* Clothe. *A. S.* clāðian. *See* Cled.

Clamben, *v., pret. plu., see* Clomb.

Clamour, *n.,* clamor, outcry. *O. F.*

Clappe, *n.,* thunderclap.

Clappe, *v.,* clap, chatter, prattle, *A. S.* clappan.

Clapping, *s.,* chatter, idle talk. *A. S.* clappan.

Clarioninge, *s.,* the music of the clarion.

Clarioun, *n.,* clarion, trumpet. *O. F.* clarion.

Clarree, *n.,* clarified wine, mixed with honey and spices and strained until clear. *O. F.* claré.

Clatere, *v.,* clatter.

Claudian, Claudius Claudianus: *author of* De Raptu Proserpinæ (*c. 400 A. D.*)

Clause, *n.,* clause, sentence, agreement, stipulation. *O. F.*

Clawes, *n., plu.,* claws. *A. S.* clawu.

Clayme, *v.,* claim. *O. F.* clamer.

Cled, *p. p.,* clad. *From* Clothe. *A. S.* clāðian. *See* Cladde.

Cledde, *v., pret.,* clad. *From* Clothe. *A. S.* clāðian. *See* Cled.

Cleer, *adj.,* clear, fine, bright. *O. F.* cler.

Clefte, *v., pret., see* Cleve.

Clene, *adj.,* clean, pure; *adv.,* entirely, wholly. *A. S.* clæne.

Clennesse, *n.,* purity. *A. S.* clænness *f.*

Cleo, Clio: *the muse of history.*

Cleopatre, Cleopatra.

Clepe, *v.,* call, name. *A. S.* clipian, cleopian.

Clere, *adv.,* clearly.

Clere, *v.,* grow clear, grow bright.

Clerer, *adj., compar., see* Cleer.

Clergeon, *n.,* chorister, choir-boy. *O. F.*

Clerk, *n.*, clerk, student, scholar. *A. S.* clerc; *O. F.* clerc.

Cleve, *v.*, adhere to, cling to. *A. S.* cleofian.

Cleve, *v.*, cleave, cut, split. *A. S.* clēofan.

Clew, *v.*, *pret. sing.*, rubbed, clawed. *From* Clawe. *A. S.* clawan.

Clippe, *v.*, embrace. *A. S.* clyppan.

Clippe, *v.*, cut, clip. *O. N.* klippa.

Cloisterer, *n.*, resident in a cloister.

Cloisterlees, *adj.*, cloisterless, outside of a cloister.

Cloistre, *n.*, cloister. *O. F.*

Clokc, *n.*, cloak. *O. F.* cloche.

Clokke, *n.*, clock. *O. F.* cloque.

Clomb, *v.*, *pret. sing.*; Clomben, *v.*, *pret. plu.*; Clomben, *p. p.*; climbed. *From* Climbe. *A. S.* climban.

Cloos, *adj.*, close, hidden, secret; *adv.*, secretly. *O. F.* clos.

Clooth-making, *s.*, making of cloth.

Closet, *n.*, small room. *O. F.*

Clothered, *p. p.*, clotted, coagulated.

Cloude, *n.*, cloud. *A. S.* clūd.

Clout, *n.*, piece of cloth. *A. S.* clūt.

Clowes, *n.*, *plu.*, *see* Clawes.

Cod, *n.*, bag, belly. *A. S.* codd.

Cofre, *n.*, coffer, chest, coffin. *O. F.*

Coghe, *v.*, cough.

Cok, *n.*, cock. *A. S.* coc.

Cokes, *n.*, *plu.*, cooks. *A. S.* cōc.

Cokewold, *n.*, cuckold. *O. F.* coucuol, cucuaut.

Cokkow, *n.*, cuckoo.

Col, *n.*, coal. *A. S.* col.

Cold, *adj.*, cold, baneful. *A. S.* ceald.

Colde, *v.*, grow cold. *A. S.* cealdian.

Coler, *n.*, collar. *O. F.* colier.

Colera, *n.*, choler: *one of the four "humors" of the body according to the old physiology. The*

other three were blood, phlegm, and black bile or melancholy. The relative proportions of these fluids in the body were supposed to determine a person's health and disposition. L. cholera.

Colere, *n.*, choler. *F.* colére *See* Colera.

Colerik, *adj.*, choleric. *L.* cholericus. *See* Colera.

Col-fox, *n.*, coal fox, black fox. Col—*A. S.* fox.

Collacion, *n.*, comparison, conference. *O. F.*

Coloigne, Cologne.

Colour, *n.*, color, rhetorical ornament. *O. F.*

Colpons, *n.*, *plu.*, shreds, bundles.

Com, *v.*, *pret. sing.*, came. *From* Come. *A. S.* cuman.

Comaunde, *v.*, command. *O. F.* comander.

Comaundement, *n.*, commandment, command, order. *O. F.* comandement.

Comende, *v.*, commend. *L.* commendare.

Comlily, *adv.*, in a comely way.

Comlinesse, *n.*, comeliness.

Commaundement, *n.*, *see* Comaundement.

Commissioun, *n.*, commission. *F.*

Commune, *adj.*, general, common. *O. F.* comun.

Commune, *n.*, commons.

Compaignable, *adj.*, companionable. *O. F.*

Compaignye, Companye, *n.*, company. *O. F.* compaignie.

Comparisoun, *n.*, comparison. *F.* comparaison.

Compas, *n.*, compass, circuit, plan, contriving. *O. F.*

Compasse, *v.*, contrive. *F.* compasser.

Compassioun, *n.*, compassion. *F.* compassion.

Compeer, *n.*, gossip, close friend. *O. F.* compair.

Complexioun, *n.*, complexion, temperament of the body (*see*

Colera), make-up, characteristics. *O. F.* **complexion.**

Compleyne, v., complain. *F.* complaindre.

Compleynte, n., complaint, lament. *O. F.* complainte.

Composicioun, n., agreement. *O. F.*

Compoune, v., compose, form. *L.* componere.

Comprende, v., comprehend. *F.* comprendre.

Comune, adj., n., see Commune.

Comunly, adv., commonly.

Conceit, n., conception, thought, notion.

Conclusioun, n., decision, judgment, result, end. *F.* conclusion.

Concubyn, n., concubine.

Condicioun, n., condition, state. *O. F.* condicion.

Conferme, v., confirm, decree. *O. F.* confermer.

Confessioun, n., confession. *F.* confession.

Confiture, n., composition.

Confort, n., comfort, pleasure. *O. F.*

Conforte, v., comfort, strengthen, support. *O. F.* conforter.

Confus, adj., confused, confounded.

Congeled, p. p., congealed, frozen. *O. F.* congeler.

Congregacioun, n., congregation, assemblage. *F.* congrégation.

Conne, v., know, be able, can. *A. S.* cunnan. Conne a thank, owe thanks.

Conning, n., cunning, skill, knowledge.

Conningly, adv., skillfully.

Conquerour, n., conqueror. *O. F.* conquereor.

Conscience, n., feeling, pity, sympathy. *O. F.*

Conseil, n., secret counsel, secret, counsellor. *O. F.*

Conservatif, adj., preserving. *F.*

Conserve, v., preserve. *O. F.* conserver.

Constance, n., constancy. *F.*

Constantyn, Constantius Afer: *an eleventh century monk, one of the founders of the school of Salerno.*

Constellacioun, n., constellation, cluster of stars. *O. F.* constellacion.

Constreyne, v., constrain, restrain, comprise. *O. F.* constreindre.

Constreynte, n., constraint, distress. *O. F.* constrainte.

Contek, n., strife, contest. *O. F.* contec.

Contemplacioun, n., contemplation. *F.* contemplation.

Contenaunce, n., appearance, demeanour. *O. F.* contenance.

Contene, v., contain. *F.* contenir.

Continuacioun, n., continuance. *F.* continuation.

Contraire, adj., contrary, adverse. *O. F.*

Contrarie, n., contrary, opponent. *O. F.* contraire.

Contrarie, v., oppose, go contrary to. *O. F.* contrarier.

Contree, n., country, fatherland. *O. F.*

Contrefete, v., see Countrefete.

Convers, n., opposite, that which is turned about. In convers leting, leaving behind, on the other side.

Conveye, v., convey, introduce. *O. F.* conveier.

Convoye, v., see Conveye.

Cop, n., top, summit. *A. S.* cop.

Cope, n., cope, cloak. *L. L.* capa.

Coper, n., copper.

Coppe, n., cup. *A. S.* cuppe.

Corage, n., heart, spirit, disposition. *O. F.*

Corageous, adj., bold, courageous. *O. F.* corajus.

Corbet, n., corbel: *a projection from the face of a wall to afford support to a structure above. O. F.*

Corde, n., cord. *O. F.*

Corde, *v.,* accord, agree. *See* **Accorde.**

Cordial, *n.,* cordial, something that cheers the heart.

Corecte, *v.,* correct.

Cormeraunt, *n.,* cormorant. *O. F.* cormoran.

Corn, *n.,* corn, grain. *A. S.*

Cornemuse, *n.,* bagpipe.

Corny, *adj.,* strong of the corn or malt.

Corone, Coroune, *n.,* crown, garland. *O. F.* corone.

Corps, *n.,* corpse. *O. F. See* **Cors.**

Corrumpable, *adj.,* corruptible. *O. F.* corrompable.

Corrupcioun, *n.,* destroyer, corruption. *O. F.* corruption.

Cors, *n.,* body, corpse. *O. F. See* **Corps.**

Corse, *v.,* curse. *A. S.* cursian.

Corseynt, *n.,* saint (*literally* holy body), shrine. *O. F.* cors saint.

Corven, *p. p., see* **Kerve.**

Cosin, Cosyn, *n.,* cousin. *As adj.,* akin to, suitable to. *O. F.* cosin.

Costage, *n.,* cost, expense. *O. F.*

Coste, *n.,* coast. *O. F.*

Cote, *n.,* cot, hut; *so* dungeon. *A. S.* cot *f.*

Cote, *n.,* coat, jacket. *O. F.*

Cote-armure, *n.,* coat showing the heraldic arms, coat of arms. *O. F.* cote a armure.

Couche, *v.* lay down, place, set. *O. F.* couchier.

Coude, *v., pret., see* **Conne.**

Counseil, Counseyl, *n., see* **Conseil.**

Counseyle, *v.,* counsel. *F.* conseiller.

Counte, *v.,* account. *O. F.* conter.

Countenance, *n., see* **Contenaunce.**

Countesse, *n.,* countess. *F.* comtesse.

Countour, *n.,* arithmetician; (*perhaps*) auditor. *O. F.* conteor.

Countour, *n.,* counting-board. *O. F.* contouer. .

Countrefete, *v.,* counterfeit, imitate. *O. F.* contrefaire (*p. p.,* contrefait).

Countrepeise, *v.,* counterpoise, render equivalent. *O. F.* contrepeser.

Countretaille, *n.,* correspondence, counter-stroke. *O. F.* contre—taille. At the countretaille, correspondence (*of sound*), in reply.

Cours, *n.,* course. *O. F.*

Courtepy, *n.,* short coat or cloak of coarse cloth.

Couthe, *v., pret., see* **Conne.**

Coveityse, *n.,* covetousness. *O. F.* coveitise.

Covenable, *adj.,* proper, fitting. *O. F.*

Covenaunt, *n.,* covenant, agreement. *O. F.* covenant.

Covent, *n.,* convent, conventual body. *O. F.*

Coverchief, *n.,* kerchief worn on the head. *O. F.* cuevrechief.

Covercle, *n.,* cover, lid. *O. F.*

Covyne, *n.,* deceitfulness, plot. *O. F.* covine.

Cowardye, *n.,* cowardice. *O. F.* couardie.

Cowardyse, *n.,* cowardice. *F.* couardise.

Coy, *adj.,* quiet. *O. F.* coi.

Coyn, *n.,* coin. *O. F.* coin.

Cracching, *s.,* scratching.

Cradel, *n.,* cradle. *A. S.*

Craft, *n.,* cunning, trade, secret. *A. S.* cræft.

Craftily, *adv.,* artfully, skillfully.

Crafty, *adj.,* skillful, clever. *A. S.* cræftig.

Crampe, *n.,* cramp. *F.*

Cran, *n.,* crane. *A. S.* cran.

Crave, *v.,* beg, ask. *A. S.* crafian.

Creat, *p. p.,* created. *L.* creatus.

Creatour, *n.,* creator. *L.* creator.

Crede, *n.,* creed, belief. *A. S.* creda.

Creep, *v., pret. sing., see* **Crepe.**

Crepe, *v.,* creep. *A. S.* crēopan.

Crepul, *n.,* cripple. *A. S.* crypel.

Cresus, Crœsus.

Crevace, *n.*, crevice, crack. *O. F.*

Crips, *adj.*, crisp, curly. *A. S.* crisp.

Crisippus, Chrysippus: *the name of a Greek philosopher mentioned in Jerome's treatise against Jovinian.*

Crist, Christ.

Cristal, *adj.*, crystal. *F.*

Cristemasse, Christmas.

Cristofre, Saint Christopher, (*on a brooch*).

Croce, *n.*, crutch, staff. *O. F.*

Croked, *adj.*, crooked.

Crokke, *n.*, crock, earthenware pot. *A. S.* crocca.

Cronique, *n.*, chronicle. *O. F.*

Crop, *n.*, top, sprout, new twig. *A. S.* crop.

Cropen, *p. p.*, see Crepe.

Cros, *n.*, cross. *A. S.*

Croude, *v.*, push. *A. S.* crēodan.

Croune, *n.*, see Coroune.

Crouned, *p. p.*, crowned. *O. F.* coroner.

Crowe, *n.*, crow. *A. S.* crawe.

Croys, *n.*, cross. *O. F.* crois.

Cruelliche, *adv.*, cruelly.

Crueltee, *n.*, cruelty. *O. F.* cruelté.

Crul, *adj.*, curly.

Crydestow, *v.*, *pron.*, *second pers. sing.*, *pres. indic.*, didst thou cry out. *From* Crye. *F.* crier.

Cryke, *n.*, creek. *O. F.* crique.

Cubyte, *n.*, cubit. *L.* cubitus.

Cukkow, *n.*, see Cokkow.

Cunne, *v.*, see Conne.

Cupido, Cupid.

Curat, *n.*, parish-priest, vicar. *L. L.* curatus.

Cure, *n.*, cure, remedy, heed, care, endeavour. *O. F.*

Curiositee, *n.*, curiosity. *O. F.* curiosité.

Curious, *adj.*, careful, attentive, skillfully made, ornate. *O. F.* curios.

Currours, *n.*, couriers, runners. *Cf. O. F.* courier.

Curs, *n.*, curse. *A. S.*

Cursednesse, *n.*, cursedness, wickedness.

Curteis, *adj.*, courteous. *O. F.*

Curteisye, *n.*, courtesy. *O. F.* curteisie.

Curteyn, Curtin, *n.*, curtain. *O. F.* curtine.

Cut, *n.*, lot.

Cypris, Venus.

D

Daggere, *n.*, dagger. *O. F.* dague.

Dale, *n.*, dale, valley. *A. S.* dæl.

Daliaunce, *n.*, dalliance, gossip, playful demeanour.

Damascien, Johannes Damascenus: *an Arabian physician, probably of the ninth century.*

Damoysele, *n.*, damsel. *O. F.* damoisele.

Dampnable, *adj.*, damnable. *O. F.* damnable.

Dampnacioun, *n.*, damnation, condemnation. *O. F.* damnation.

Dampne, *v.*, condemn. *O. F.* dampner.

Dan, *n.*, lord, sir (*a title of respect*). *O. F.* dan (*L.* dominus).

Dane, Daphne.

Dar, *v.*, dare. *From* Durre. *A. S.* durran.

Dares, Dares Phrygius: *supposed author of a Greek history of the destruction of Troy, the original form of the De Excidio Trojæ Historia. Dares was supposed to have lived before Homer. The De Excidio, in Latin, is a clumsy and meager narrative, probably of the fifth century A. D.*

Darreyne, *v.*, vindicate one's right to, decide one's claim to. *O. F.* deraisnier.

Darte, *n.*, dart. *O. F.* dart.

Daswed, *p. p.*, dazed, confused. *Cf. O. F.* daser; *O. N.* dasa.

Daun, see Dan.

Daunce, *n.*, dance. *O. F.* dance.

Daunce, *v.*, dance. *O. F.* dancer.

Daunger, *n.*, disdain, offishness,

imperiousness. *O. F.* **dangier.**
In daunger, in jurisdiction, in
control.

Daungerous, *adj.*, forbidding,
grudging.

Daunse, *v.*, *see* **Daunce.**

Daunte, *v.*, daunt, tame, subdue.
O. F. **danter.**

Dawe, *v.*, dawn. *A. S.* **dagian.**

Dayerye, *n.*, dairy. *A. S.* **dæge**
—*F.* **erie.**

Dayesye, *n.*, daisy. *A. S.*
dæges—**ēage.**

Debaat, *n.*, strife. *O. F.* **debat.**

Debate, *v.*, fight, quarrel. *O.
F.* **debatre.**

Debonaire, *adj.*, gracious, cour-
tcous, calm, gentle. *O. F.*

Debonairly, *adv.*, debonairly,
gently, graciously.

Debonairte, *n.*, gentleness, gra-
ciousness. *O. F.* **debonaireté.**

Declame, *v.*, declaim, discuss.
L. **declamare.**

Dedalus, Dædalus.

Dede, *n.*, deed, act. *A. S.*
dæd *f.*

Deduyt, *n.*, pleasure. *F.* **déduit.**

Deed, *adj.*, dead. *A. S.* **dēad.**

Deedly, *adj.*, deathlike, mortal.
A. S. **dēadlīc.**

Deef, *adj.*, deaf. *A. S.* **dēaf.**

Deel, *n.*, part, bit. *A. S.* **dǣl.**

Deer, *n.*, animal. *A. S.* **dēor.**

Dees, *n.*, *plu.*, dice. *O. F.* **dé.**

Dees, *n.*, dais. *O. F.* **deis.**

Deeth, *n.*, death. *A. S.* **dēaþ.**
The deeth, death, the plague.

Defaute, *n.*, fault, want. *O. F.*
On a defaute y-falle, had a
check (*hunting*).

Defence, *n.*, defense, interfer-
ence, hindrance, concealment.
O. F. **defense.**

Defende, *v.*, defend, forbid.
O. F. **defendre.**

Defet, *p. p.*, overcome, exhausted.
O. F. **desfait.**

Defyne, *v.*, define, depict. *O. F.*
definer.

Degree, *n.*, rank, step. *O. F.*
degré.

Deiscorides, Dioscorides: *a*

*Greek physician of the second
century A. D.*

Del, *n.*, *see* **Deel.**

Dele, *v.*, to have dealings with,
argue. *A. S.* **dǣlan.**

Deliberacioun, *n.*, deliberation.
L. **deliberatio.**

Delibere, *v.*, deliberate, consider.
L. **deliberare.**

Delicacye, Delicasye, *n.*, amusement, wantonness.

Delicat, *adj.*, delicate, tender,
dainty. *L.* **delicatus.**

Delitable, *adj.*, delightful, pleas-
ing. *O. F.*

Deliver, *adj.*, quick, active. *O.
F.* **delivre.**

Deliverly, *adv.*, nimbly, quickly.

Delphos, Delphi.

Delphyn, Delphinus: *the name
of a constellation.*

Delve, *v.*, dig. *A. S.* **delfan.**

Delyces, *n.*, *plu.*, delights, pleas-
ures. *O. F.* **delice.**

Delyt, *n.*, delight, joy. *O. F.*
delit.

Delyte, *v.*, delight, please. *O. F.*
deleitier.

Demaunde, *n.*, question. *O. F.*
demande.

Deme, *v.*, deem, judge, decide,
suppose. *A. S.* **dēman.**

Demeine, *v.*, manage. *O. F.*
demener.

Demonstracioun, *n.*, demonstra-
tion, *L.* **demonstratio.**

Demophon, Demophoön.

Depardieux, on the part of God,
by God's help.

Departe, *v.*, separate, part. *F.*
départir.

Departinge, *s.*, departure, separation. *F.* **départir.**

Depe, *adv.*, deeply. *A. S.* **dēope.**

Depeynted, *p. p.*, depicted,
painted. *O. F.* **depeindre.**

Depper, *adv.*, *compar.*, *see* **Depe.**

Dere, *adj.*, dear; *adv.*, dearly.
A. S. **dēore.**

Dere, *v.*, injure, harm. *A. S.*
derian.

Derk, *adj.*, dark. *A. S.* **deorc.**

Derkly, *adv.*, darkly, obscurely.

Derre, *adv., compar., see* **Dere.**

Dertemouthe, Dartmouth.

Derth, *n.*, dearth.

Descente, *n.*, descent. *F.*

Descerne, *v.*, discern. *F.* **discerner.**

Descripcioun, *n.*, description. *O. F.* description.

Descryve, *v.*, describe. *O. F.* **descrivre.** *See* **Discryve.**

Desdeyn, *n.*, disdain. *O. F.* **desdein.**

Desert, *n.*, deserted spot, wilderness. *F.*

Desespaired, *p. p.*, in despair. *O. F.* **desesperer.**

Desespeir, *n.*, despair. *O. F.*

Desesperaunce, *n.*, despair. *O. F.* **desesperance.**

Desolat, *adj.*, desolate, forsaken. *L.* **desolatus.**

Despeyred, *p. p.*, sunk in despair. *O. F.* **desperer.** *See* **Dispeyre.**

Despitous, *adj.*, spiteful, angry, scornful. *O. F.*

Despitously, *adv.*, spitefully, maliciously, cruelly.

Desplaye, *v.*, display. *O. F.* **despleier.**

Despone, *v., see* **Dispone.**

Desporte, *v.*, rejoice, amuse. *O. F.* **desporter.**

Despyt, *n.*, malice, spite. *O. F.* **despit.**

Desseveraunce, *n.*, separation. *O. F.* **dessevrance.**

Destinee, *n.*, destiny. *O. F.*

Destourbe, *v.*, disturb, prevent. *O. F.* **destourber.**

Destresse, *n.*, distress. *O. F.* **destrece.**

Destreyne, *v.*, distress, constrain, force. *O. F.* **destreindre.**

Destroubled, *p. p.*, disturbed, troubled. *O. F.* **destroubler.**

Destruccioun, *n.*, destruction. *F.* destruction.

Desyr, *n.*, desire. *F.* **désir.**

Desyre, *v.*, desire. *F.* **désirer.**

Dette, *n.*, debt. *O. F.*

Dettelees, *adj.*, debtless.

Devocioun, *n.*, devotion. *O. F.* **devocion.**

Devoir, *n.*, duty. *O. F.*

Devyn, *n.*, diviner, soothsayer. *O. F.* **devin.**

Devyne, *v.*, divine, guess. *O. F.* **deviner.**

Devys, *v.*, device, contrivance, arrangement. *O. F.* **devis.**

Devyse, *v.*, describe, tell, plan. *O. F.* **deviser.**

Dew, *n.*, dew. *A. S.* **dēaw.**

Deyde, *v., pret., see* **Deye.**

Deye, *n.*, dairy-woman. *O. N.* **deigja.**

Deye, *v.*, die. *O. N.* **deyja.** *See* **Dye.**

Deyed, *v., pret., see* **Deye.**

Deyinge, *s.*, death. *O. N.* **deyja.**

Deyne, *v.*, deign. *O. F.* **deignier.**

Deynous, *adj.*, disdainful, scornful. *O. F.* **(des)deignos.**

Deyntee, *n.*, worth, value, pleasure. *O. F.* **deintié.**

Deyntee, *adj.*, dainty, pleasant, rare.

Deyntevous, *adj.*, dainty.

Deys, *n., see* **Dees.**

Diane, Diana.

Diapred, *p. p.*, variegated, diversified with figures. *O. F.* **diasprer.**

Dich, *n.*, ditch.

Diched, *p. p.*, provided with a ditch or moat. *A. S.* **dīcian.**

Diete, *n.*, diet. *F.* **diète.**

Diffame, *n.*, evil name, ill report. *O. F.*

Diffame, *v.*, defame, dishonor. *O. F.* **diffamer.**

Diffyne, *v., see* **Defyne.**

Digestyves, *n., plu.*, digestives. *F.* **digestif.**

Dighte, *v.*, prepare, array, serve. *A. S.* **dihtan.**

Digne, *adj.*, worthy, honorable, suitable, proud. *O. F.*

Digneliche, *adv.*, worthily, fittingly, scornfully.

Dignitee, *n.*, worth, dignity. *O. F.* **dignité.**

Diner, *n.*, dinner. *F.*

Dint, *n.,* stroke, blow. *A. S.* dynt.

Diocyse, *n.,* diocese. *O. F.* diocise.

Dione: *a female Titan, mother of Venus (Aphrodite).*

Disavaunce, *v.,* check, defeat. *O. F.* desavancier.

Disaventure, *n.,* misfortune. *O. F.* desaventure.

Dischevele, *adj., see* **Disshevele.**

Disclaundre, *v.,* reproach, slander.

Disconfiture, *n.,* defeat, discomfiture. *O. F.* desconfiture.

Disconfort, *n.,* discomfort, discouragement. *O. F.* desconfort.

Disconforte, *v.,* discourage. *O. F.* desconforter.

Disconsolat, *adj.,* disconsolate. *L.* disconsolatus.

Discordaunt, *adj.,* discordant. *O. F.* descordant.

Discrecioun, *n.,* discretion. *F.* discretion.

Discreve, Discryve, *v.,* describe. *O. F.* descrivre. *See* **Descryve.**

Discure, *v.,* discover, reveal. *O. F.* descouvrir.

Disdeyn, *n., see* **Desdeyn.**

Disdeyne, *v.,* disdain. *O. F.* desdeignier.

Disese, *n.,* discomfort, grief, distress, disease. *O. F.* desaise.

Disese, *v.,* trouble, distress, incommode. *O. F.* desaaisier.

Disesperat, *adj.,* hopeless.

Disfigurat, *adj.,* disguised.

Disgyse, *v.,* disguise. *O. F.* desguiser.

Disherited, *p. p.,* disinherited. *F.* déshériter.

Disioynt, *n.,* failure, peril. *O. F.* desjointe.

Disobeysaunt, *adj.,* disobedient.

Disordinaunce, *n.,* disorder, violation of the rules. *O. F.* desordenance.

Disparage, *n.,* disparagement, disgrace. *O. F.* desparage.

Dispence, *n.,* expenditure, expense. *O. F.* despense.

Dispeyre, *v.,* despair. *O. F.* desperer. *See* **Despeyred.**

Dispitous, *adj., see* **Despitous.**

Displesaunce, *n.,* displeasure, offense. *O. F.* desplaisance.

Displese, *v.,* displease. *O. F.* desplaisir.

Dispoile, *v.,* despoil. *O. F.* despoillier.

Dispone, *v.,* dispose, order. *L.* disponere; *O. F.* disponer.

Disport, *n.,* play, sport. *O. F.* desport.

Disporte, *v., see* **Desporte.**

Disposicioun, *n.,* disposition, disposal. *O. F.* disposicion.

Disputisoun, *n.,* disputation, argument. *A. F.* desputeison.

Dispyt, *n., see* **Despyt.**

Disshevele, *adj.,* with hair flowing down. *O. F.* deschevelé.

Dissimulacioun, *n.,* dissimulation. *F.* dissimulation.

Dissimule, *v.,* dissimulate. *O. F.* dissimuler.

Disteyne, *v.,* stain, bedim. *O. F.* desteindre.

Distourbe, *v., see* **Destourbe.**

Distresse, *n., see* **Destresse.**

Distreyne, *v., see* **Destreyne.**

Divers, *adj.,* diverse, different. *F.*

Diversitee, *n.,* diversity, variety. *F.* diversité.

Divinistre, *n.,* divine, theologian.

Divisioun, *n.,* division, distinction. *O. F.* division.

Divyn, *adj.,* divine. *O. F.* divin.

Divyne, *v.,* guess. *O. F.* deviner.

Divynis, *n., plu., see* **Devyn.**

Do, *v.,* do, execute; cause to be. *A. S.* dōn. **Doon make,** cause to be made.

Doctour, *n.,* doctor, teacher. *O. F.* doctur.

Doctryne, *n.,* instruction. *F.* doctrine.

Dogge, *n.,* dog. *A. S.* docga.

Doghter, *n.,* daughter. *A. S.* dohtor. **Doghtren, Doughtren,** *plu.*

Doke, *n.,* duck. *A. S.* dūce.

Dokked, *p. p.,* docked, cut short.

Dolven, *p. p.*, buried. *See* Delve.

Domb, *adj.*, dumb. *A. S.* dumb.

Domesday, *n.*, doom's day. *A. S.* dōmes—dæg.

Dominacioun, *n.*, dominion, power. *L.* dominatio.

Don, *v.*, *see* Do.

Don, do—on, put on. *See* Do.

Dong, *n.*, dung, manure. *A. S.* dung.

Donge, *v.*, dung, manure.

Dongeoun, *n.*, keep-tower. *F.* donjon.

Donne, *adj.*, *plu.*, dun-coloured, dusky. *A. S.* dunn.

Doom, *n.*, judgment, opinion, decision. *A. S.* dōm.

Doon, *v.*, *see* Do.

Dore, *n.*, door. *A. S.* duru.

Dormant, *adj.*, *see* Table.

Dorste, *v.*, *pret.*, *see* Dar.

Doseyn, *n.*, dozen. *O. F.* doseine.

Dossers, *n.*, *plu.*, baskets to carry on the back. *O. F.* dossier.

Doucet, *adj.*, dulcet (*pipe*), sweet-sounding (*pipe*). *F.*

Doughter, *n.*, *see* Doghter.

Doumb, *adj.*, *see* Domb.

Doun, *n.*, down, soft feathers. *O. N.* dūnn.

Doutaunce, *n.*, doubt, perplexity. *O. F.* doutance.

Doute, *n.*, doubt, fear. *O. F.*

Doute, *v.*, doubt, fear. *O. F.* douter.

Doutelees, *adv.*, doubtless.

Doutremere, *adj.*, from beyond the sea, foreign, imported.

Douve, *n.*, dove. (*A. S.* dūfe.)

Dowaire, Dowere, *n.*, dower. *O. F.* douaire.

Dowve, *n.*, *see* Douve.

Drad, *p. p.;* Dradde, *v.*, *pret.;* *see* Drede.

Dragoun, *n.*, dragon. *O. F.* dragon.

Draughte, *n.*, draft, drink.

Drecche, *v.*, be tedious, vex, delay. *A. S.* dreccan.

Drede, *n.*, dread, fear, doubt.

Drede, *v.*, dread, fear. *A. S.* drǣdan.

Dredeles, *adv.*, without doubt, certainly.

Dredful, *adj.*, fearful, timid.

Dredfully, *adv.*, timidly.

Dreem, *n.*, dream.

Dreinte, *v.*, *pret.*, *see* Drenche.

Dreme, *v.*, dream.

Drenche, *v.*, drown. *A. S.* drencan.

Drerinesse, *n.*, dreariness.

Drery, *adj.*, dreary, sad. *A. S.* drēorig.

Dresse, *v.*, direct, prepare. *O. F.* drecier.

Dreye, *adj.*, dry. *A. S.* drȳge.

Dreynt, *p. p.;* Dreynte, *v.*, *pret.;* *see* Drenche.

Drinke, *n.*, drink. *A. S.* drinca.

Drinkelees, *adj.*, without drink.

Drogges, *n.*, *plu.*, drugs. *F.* drogue.

Droghte, *n.*, drought. *A. S.* drūgaðf.

Dronk, *v.*, *pret. sing.*, drank. *From* Drinke. *A. S.* drincan.

Dronkelewe, *adj.*, addicted to drink, drunken. Dronken— *A. S.* lǣwe.

Dronkenesse, *n.*, drunkenness.

Droof, *v.*, *pret. sing.*, *see* Dryve.

Drope, *n.*, drop. *A. S.* dropa.

Droupe, *v.*, droop. *O. N.* drūpa.

Drow, *v.*, *pret. sing.*, drew. *From* Drawe. *A. S.* dragan.

Drugge, *v.*, drudge.

Drye, *adj.*, *see* Dreye.

Drye, *v.*, endure, suffer. *A. S.* drēogan.

Dryve, *v.*, drive, hasten, pass. *A. S.* drīfan.

Duche, German.

Duchesse, *n.*, duchess. *F.*

Duëtee, *n.*, duty, debt. *A. F.* dueté.

Duk, *n.*, duke. *F.* duc.

Dul, *adj.*, dull, sad, stupid. *A. S.* dol.

Dulcarnon, *n.*, an inexplicable dilemma. *Arabic* dhū al-qarnain.

Dulle, *v.*, feel dull, grow tired.

Duracioun, *n.*, duration, term. *O. F.* duration.

Dure, v., endure, last, remain. O. F. **durer.**

Durste v., pret., see **Dar.**

Duske, v., grow dim.

Dwelle, v., remain, tarry, delay. A. S. **dwellan.**

Dyamaunt, n., diamond. O. F. **diamant.**

Dyane, Diana.

Dyde, v., pret., see **Do** or **Dye.**

Dye, v., see **Deye.**

Dyke, v., make dikes or ditches. A. S. **dīcian.** See **Diched.**

Dys, n., plu., see **Dees.**

Dytees, n., plu., ditties. O. F. **ditiê.**

Dyverse, v., vary. O. F. **diverser.**

Dyversitee, n., see **Diversitee.**

E

Eacides, Æacides: Achilles, grandson of Æacus.

Ebrayk, Hebrew. See **Hebraik.**

Ecclesiaste, n., minister.

Ecclesiaste, Ecclesiasticus: one of the books of the Apocrypha.

Ech, adj., each. A. S. **ǣlc.**

Eche, v., increase, augment. A. S. **ēcan.**

Echoon, Echon, pron., each one, every one.

Eclympasteyr: son of Morpheus, named Icelon and Phobetora in Ovid. Chaucer found the present name in Froissart.

Ector, Hector.

Eek, adv., also, eke, moreover. A. S. **ēac.**

Eem, n., uncle. A. S. **ēam.**

Eest, n., adv., east. See **Est.**

Eet, v., pret. sing., see **Ete.**

Eft, adv., again. A. S. **eft.**

Eft-sone, Eft-sones, adv., immediately afterward, soon after, once again. A. S. **eft—sōna.**

Egal, adv., equally. F.

Egipte, Egypt.

Egle, n., eagle. O. F.

Egre, adj., sharp, fierce, bitter. F. **aigre.**

Eighte, n., eight. A. S. **eahta.**

Eir, n., see **Eyr.**

Eke, adv., see **Eek.**

Ekko, n., echo. L. **echo.**

Elcanor: perhaps **Helcanor** of the thirteenth century prose romance Cassidorus (see Tatlock, Mod. Lang. Notes, xxxvi, 95 ff.)

Elde, n., old age. A. S. **eldo.**

Eleccioun, n., choice, election. O. F. **election.**

Eles, n., gen. sing., eel's; plu., eels. A. S. **ǣl.**

Eleyne, Helen.

Elicon, Helicon.

Ellebor, n., hellebore.

Elles, adv., else, otherwise. A. S.

Elvish, adj., elf-like, reserved, shy.

Elye, Elijah.

Embassadour, n., ambassador. F. **ambassadeur.**

Embosed, p. p., plunged into a thicket.

Embrouded, p. p., embroidered.

Emelward, toward Emilia: a region in Italy.

Emeraude, n., emerald. O. F. **esmeraude.**

Emes, n., gen., see **Eem.**

Emforth, prep., to the extent of.

Emperesse, n., empress. O. F.

Empoisoner, n., poisoner.

Empoisoning, s., poisoning. F. **empoisonner.**

Emprente, v., imprint, impress. O. F. **empreindre.**

Empryse, n., enterprise, undertaking, emprise. O. F. **emprise.**

Enbrace, v., embrace, surround. O. F. **embracier.**

Enbrouded, p. p., embroidered. See **Embrouded.**

Encens, n., incense. O. F.

Enchaunte, v., enchant. O. F. **enchanter.**

Enchauntement, n., enchantment. O. F. **enchantement.**

Enchesoun, n., occasion, reason. O. F. **encheson.**

Enclyne, v., induce, incline. O. F. **encliner.**

Encombre, v., encumber, hamper. O. F. **encombrer.**

Encombrous, *adj.*, cumbersome.

Encrees, *n.*, increase.

Encrese, *v.*, increase. *O. F.* encreistre.

Ende, *n.*, end, boundary. *A. S.*

Endelong, *adv.*, *prep.*, all along, lengthways.

Endyte, *v.*, write, compose, relate, dictate. *O. F.* enditer.

Eneydos, Æneid (*Æneidos liber*).

Enforme, *v.*, inform. *O. F.* enformer.

Engelond, England.

Engendrure, *n.*, procreation, begetting. *O. F.* engendreure.

Engyn, *n.*, device, machine. ingenuity. *O. F.* engin.

Engyned, *p. p.*, tortured. *O. F.* engignier.

Enhabit, *p. p.*, devoted. *O. F.* enhabiter.

Enhaunce, *v.*, enhance, raise, exalt. *A. F.* enhauncer.

Enhorte, *v.*, exhort. *O. F.* enhorter.

Enlumine, *v.*, illumine. *F.* enluminer.

Enok, Enoch.

Enoynt, *p. p.*, anointed. *O. F.* enoindre.

Enquere, *v.*, inquire. *O. F.* enquerre.

Ensample, Ensaumple, *n.*, example, pattern. *O. F.* ensample.

Enseled, *p. p.*, sealed up, completed. *O. F.* enseeler.

Enspyre, *v.*, inspire. *O. F.* enspirer.

Ensure, *v.*, promise, certify.

Entencioun, *n.*, intention, attention, design. *O. F.* entencion.

Entende, *v.*, attend, intend, perceive. *O. F.* entendre.

Entendement, *n.*, perception. *O. F.*

Entente, *n.*, intention, meaning, attention. *O. F.* entente.

Ententif, *adj.*, attentive, careful. *O. F.*

Ententifly, *adv.*, attentively.

Entraille, *n.*, entrails, inside. *O. F.*

Entree, *n.*, entry, entrance. *O. F.* entré.

Entremedled, *p. p.*, intermingled. *O. F.* entremedler.

Entremes, *n.*, intervening course, a dish served between courses. *O. F.*

Entremete, *v.*, interfere, meddle with. *O. F.* entremetre.

Entreparte, *v.*, share. *O. F.* entrepartir.

Entryke, *v.*, ensnare, entrap. *O. F.* entriquier.

Entune, *v.*, intone, tune. *O. F.* entoner.

Entunes, *n.*, *plu.*, tunes.

Envoluped, *p. p.*, enveloped. *O. F.* envoluper.

Envye, *n.*, malice, spite, envy. *F.* envie.

Envye, *v.*, vie, strive. *O. F.* envier.

Envyned, *p. p.*, provided with a store of wine. *O. F.* enviné.

Envyous, *adj.*, envious, spiteful, malicious.

Eolus, Æolus.

Equitee, *n.*, equity, justice. *F.* équité.

Er, *adv.*, *conj.*, *prep.*, before. *A. S.* ǽr. *See* Or.

Erand, *n.*, errand. *A. S.* ǽrende.

Erbe Yve, *n.*, herb eve, ground ivy.

Erchedeken, *n.*, archdeacon. *A. S.* arcediacon.

Ercules, Hercules.

Ere, *n.*, ear. *A. S.* éare.

Ere, *v.*, plough. *A. S.* erian.

Erl, *n.*, earl. *A. S.* eorl.

Erly, *adv.*, early. *A. S.* ǽrlíce.

Erme, *v.*, feel sad, grieve. *A. S.* earmian.

Ernest, *n.*, earnest, seriousness. *A. S.* eornost.

Ernestful, *adj.*, serious.

Erratik, *adj.*, wandering. *L.* erraticus.

Erraunt, *adj.*, errant, stray. *O. F.* errant.

Errour, *n.*, error. *O. F.* error.

Erst, *adv.*, first, at first. *A. S.* ærest.

Erthe, *n.*, earth. *A. S.* eorðe.

Erthely, *adj.*, earthly, mortal. *A. S.* eorþlic.

Eschaunge, *n.*, exchange. *O. F.* eschange.

Eschewe, *v.*, eschew, avoid, shun. *O. F.* eschiwer.

Ese, *n.*, ease, pleasure. *O. F.* aise.

Ese, *v.*, give ease, make at home, entertain. *O. F.* aisier.

Esiliche, Esily, *adv.*, easily.

Espye, *n.*, spy. *O. F.* espie.

Espye, *v.*, espy, observe, perceive. *O. F.* espier.

Est, *n.*, *adj.*, east. *A. S.* ēast. *See* Eest.

Estaat, Estat, *n.*, state, rank, condition. *O. F.* estat.

Estatlich, Estatly, *adj.*, stately, dignified.

Estraunge, *adj.*, strange. *O. F.* estrange.

Estre, *n.*, inner part of a building, recess. *O. F.*

Estward, *adv.*, eastward, in the east.

Esy, *adj.*, easy. *O. F.* aisié.

Ete, *v.*, eat. *A. S.* etan.

Eterne, *adj.*, eternal. *O. F.*

Ethe, *adj.*, easy. *A. S.* ēaðe.

Evangelist, *n.*, writer of the Gospel. *F.* évangeliste.

Evel, *adv.*, ill. *A. S.* yfela.

Even, *n.*, evening. *A. S.* æfen.

Even, *adv.*, exactly, evenly. *A. S.* efne.

Eventyde, *n.*, evening. *A. S.* æfentīd *f.*

Evere, *adv.*, ever. *A. S.* æfre.

Everemo, *adv.*, for ever more, always. *A. S.* æfre—mā.

Everich, *adj.*, each, every one. *A. S.* æfre—ælc.

Everichoon, Everychoon, *pron.*, every one, each one. Everich —*A. S.* ān.

Everydel, *adv.*, every bit, altogether. Every—*A. S.* dæl.

Ew, *n.*, yew-tree. *A. S.* ēow.

Excercyse, *n.*, exercise. *F.* exercice.

Excesse, *n.*, excess, excess of feeling. *L.* excessus.

Execucioun, *n.*, execution. *F.* exécution.

Executrice, *n.*, (female) performer, causer. *A. F.*

Exemple, *n.*, example. *O. F.* example.

Exercyse, *n.*, *see* Excercyse.

Exorsisaciouns, *n.*, exorcisms.

Expoune, *v.*, explain, expound. *O. F.* espondre; *L.* exponere.

Expres, *adv.*, expressly. *F.*

Exyle, *v.*, exile. *O. F.* exillier.

Ey, *n.*, egg. *A. S.* æg.

Ey, *interj.*, eh! alas!

Eye, *n.*, eye. *A. S.* ēage. *See* Yë.

Eyen, *n.*, *plu.*, *see* Eye.

Eyle, *v.*, ail. *A. S.* eglan.

Eyr, *n.*, air. *O. F.* air.

Eyrish, *adj.*, of the air, aërial.

Eyther, *adj.*, either. *A. S.* ægðer.

F

Facound, *adj.*, eloquent, fluent. *O. F.* facond.

Facounde, *n.*, eloquence. *O. F.* faconde.

Facultee, *n.*, faculty, power. *F.* faculté.

Fader, *n.*, father. *A. S.* fæder.

Fadme, *n.*, *plu.*, fathoms. *A. S.* fæðm *f.*

Faille, *v.*, fail. *F.* faillir.

Faire, *adv.*, fairly, well, honestly. *A. S.* fægere.

Fairnesse, *n.*, beauty, honesty. *A. S.* fægernes *f.*

Fal, *n.*, fall.

Falding, *n.*, a sort of coarse cloth.

Falle, *v.*, befall, happen, become. *A. S.* feallan.

False, *adj.*, false, cheating. *O. F.* fals.

False, *v.*, deceive, betray, falsify. *L.* falsare.

Falwe, *adj.*, fallow, yellowish. *A. S.* fealo.

Fame, *n.*, notoriety, rumor, renown. *O. F.*

Famulier, *adj.*, familiar, intimate. *F.*

Fantastyk, *adj.*, belonging to the fancy. *F.* **fantastique.**

Fantasye, *n.*, fancy, imagination, desire, pleasure. *O. F.* **fantasie.**

Fantosme, *n.*, phantom, illusion. *O. F.*

Far, *v.*, *imper. sing.*, see **Fare.**

Fare, *n.*, behavior, conduct, condition, goings-on, bustle, proceeding. *A. S.* **faru.**

Fare, *v.*, go, travel, act, behave. *A. S.* **faran.**

Fare-carte, *n.*, travelling cart. See **Carte.**

Farsed, *p. p.*, stuffed. *O. F.* **farsir.**

Faste, *adv.*, closely, close, near. *A. S.* **fæste.**

Faucon, *n.*, falcon. *O. F.*

Faught, *v.*, *pret.*, fought. From **Fighte.** *A. S.* **feohtan.**

Fauned, *v.*, *pret.*, fawned on. *A. S.* **fagnian.**

Faunes, *n.*, *plu.*, fawns. *L.* **faunus.** See **Founes.**

Fawe, *adv.*, fain, anxiously. *A. S.* **fægen.**

Fayn, *adj.*, glad; *adv.*, gladly. *A. S.* **fægen.**

Faynte, *v.*, faint.

Fayre, *n.*, fair, market. *O. F.* **feire.**

Feble, *adj.*, feeble. *O. F.* **feible.**

Feblenesse, *n.*, feebleness.

Fecches, *n.*, *plu.*, vetches. *O. F.* **veche.**

Fecche, *v.*, fetch, get. *A. S.* **feccan.**

Fedde, *v.*, *pret.*, fed. From **Fede.** *A. S.* **fēdan.**

Feeld, *n.*, field. *A. S.* **feld.**

Feend, *n.*, fiend, devil. *A. S.* **fēond.**

Fees, *n. plu.*, fees, payments. *O. F.* **fié.**

Feith, *n.*, faith. *O. F.* **feit.**

Feithful, *adj.*, faithful.

Fel, *n.*, fell, skin. *A. S.* **fell.**

Fel, *adj.*, cruel, fell. *O. F.* **fel.**

Fel, *v.*, *pret. sing.*, see **Falle.**

Felawe, *n.*, fellow, companion. *O. N.* **fēlagi.**

Felaweshipe, *n.*, partnership, companionship. **Felawe—** *A. S.***-scipe.**

Feld, *n.*, see **Feeld.**

Feld, *p. p.*, felled. From **Felle.** *A. S.* **fellan.**

Felde-fare, *n.*, field-fare. *A. S.* **feldefare.**

Fele, *adj.*, many. *A. S.* **feola.**

Fele, *v.*, feel, experience, try to find out. *A. S.* **fēlan.**

Felicitee, *n.*, felicity, happiness. *F.* **félicité.**

Felinge, *s.*, feeling. *A. S.* **fēlan.**

Felingly, *adv.*, feelingly.

Felon, *adj.*, sullen, angry. *O. F.*

Felonye, *n.*, felony, crime. *O. F.* **felonie.**

Femenye: *the country of the Amazons.*

Feminyne, *adj.*, feminine. *L.* **femininus.**

Fen, *n.*, a chapter or subdivision in Avicenna's book called the *Canon. Arabic* **fann.**

Fenix, *n.*, phœnix.

Fer, *adj.*, *adv.*, far. *A. S.* **feor.**

Ferd, *n.*, fear. For ferde, on account of fear.

Ferd, *p. p.;* **Ferde,** *v.*, *pret.; see* **Fare.**

Ferd, Fered, *p. p.*, see **Fere.**

Fere, *n.*, fear. *A. S.* **fǽr.**

Fere, *v.*, frighten. *A. S.* **fǽran.**

Fere, *n.*, companion. *A. S.* **gefēra.**

Fere, *n.*, *dat.*, see **Fyr.**

Ferforth, *adv.*, far.

Ferforthly, *adv.*, thoroughly.

Ferfulleste, *adj.*, *superl.*, most fearful, most timid.

Ferme, *adj.*, firm. *O. F.*

Fermely, *adv.*, firmly.

Ferne, *adj.*, *plu.*, distant, remote. *From* **Ferren.** *A. S.* **feorran.**

Ferrare, Ferrara.

Ferre, *adj.*, *compar.*, see **Fer.**

Ferreste, *adj.*, *superl.*, see **Fer.**

Fers, *n.*, the queen in chess. *O. F.* **fierce.**

Ferthe, *adj.*, fourth. *A. S.* **fēorða.**

Ferther, *adj., adv.,* further. *A. S.* furðra.

Ferthing, *n.,* farthing, small portion. *A. S.* fēorðung.

Ferventliche, *adv.,* fervently.

Fery, *adj.,* see **Fyry.**

Fesaunt, *n.,* pheasant. *O. F.* faisant.

Fest, *n.,* fist. *A. S.* fȳst.

Feste, *n.,* feast, festival, merriment. *O. F.*

Feste, *v.,* feast. *O. F.* fester.

Festeyinge, *s.,* festivity. *O. F.* festeier.

Festne, *v.,* fasten. *A. S.* fæstnian.

Fet, *p. p.,* see **Fecche.**

Fete, *n., dat. plu.,* feet. *A. S.* fōt.

Fether, *n.,* feather. *A. S.* feðer.

Fetherbed, *n.,* feather-bed. *A. S.* feðer-bedd.

Fethered, *adj.,* provided with feathers.

Fetis, *adj.,* neat, well-made, graceful. *O. F.* feitis.

Fetisly, *adv.,* neatly, elegantly.

Fette, *v., pret.,* see **Fecche.**

Fettres, *n., plu.,* fetters. *A. S.* feter.

Fetys, *adj.,* see **Fetis.**

Fevere, *n.,* fever. *A. S.* fēfor; *cf. O. F.* fievre.

Fewe, *adj.,* few. *A. S.* fēawe.

Fey, *n.,* faith. *A. F.* fei.

Feyne, *v.,* feign, pretend. *O. F.* feindre.

Feynest, *adv., superl.,* most gladly. *A. S.* fægen.

Feynte, *v.,* see **Faynte.**

Fiers, *adj.,* fierce. *O. F.* fier (*nom.* fiers).

Fifte, *ord. num.* fifth. *A. S.* fifta.

Fiftene, *adj.,* fifteen. *A. S.* fiftēne.

Fil, *v., pret. sing.,* see **Falle.**

Fille, *n.,* fill. *A. S.* fyllo.

Fille, *v., pret. plu.,* see **Falle.**

Finch, *n.,* finch (*bird*). *A. S.* finc. **Pulle a finch,** pluck a dupe.

Finnes, *n., plu.,* fins. *A. S.* finn.

Firr, *n.,* fir (tree). *Danish* fyrr.

Fisshe, *v.,* fish. *A. S.* fiscian.

Fithele, *n.,* fiddle. *A. S.* fiðele.

Fixe, *adj.,* fixed. *O. F.* fixe.

Flatering, *adj.,* flattering.

Flateringe, *s.,* flattery.

Flatour, *n.,* flatterer. *O. F.* flateor.

Flaumbe, Flaume, *n.,* flame. *O. F.* flame.

Flaundres, Flanders.

Flaundrish, Flemish.

Flawme, *n.,* see **Flaumbe.**

Flee, *v.,* fly. *A. S.* flēogan.

Flee, *v.,* flee. *A. S.* flēon.

Flegiton, Phlegethon.

Fleigh, *v., pret. sing.,* flew, fled. See **Flee.**

Fleming, *s.,* banishment, flight. *A. S.* flȳman.

Flen, *v., pres. plu.,* see **Flee.**

Fleshly, *adv.,* carnally.

Flete, *v.,* float, bathe, flow. *A. S.* flēotan.

Flex, *n.,* flax. *A. S.* fleax.

Fley, *v., pret. sing.,* flew. *From* **Flee,** fly. See **Fleigh.**

Flight, *n.,* flight.

Flikere, *v.,* flicker, flutter. *A. S.* flicerian.

Flitte, *v.,* flit, pass away. *O. N.* flytja.

Flok, *n.,* flock.

Flokmele, *adv.,* in a flock. *A. S.* floc—mǣlum (*dative plu.*).

Flood, *n.,* flood, river. *A. S.* flōd.

Flotery, *adj.,* fluttering, wavy.

Flough, *v., pret. sing.,* see **Flee.**

Flour, *n.,* flower, choice part. *O. F.*

Flour-de-lys, *n.,* fleur-de-lis. *F.*

Floure, *v.,* flower, flourish. *Cf. O. F.* florir.

Floury, *adj.,* flowery.

Floute, *n.,* flute. *O. F.* flehute.

Flowen, *v., pret. plu.; p. p.; see* **Flee.**

Floyting, *pres. partic.,* playing on the flute. *O. F.* fleüter.

Flye, *n.,* fly. *A. S.* flȳge.

Flyen, *v., pret. plu.,* see **Flee.**

Fo, *n.,* see **Foo.**

Folde, *n.,* fold, sheepfold. *A. S.* falod.

Folis, *n., plu., see* **Fool.**
Folwe, *v.,* follow. *A. S.* **folgian.**
Foly, *adv.,* foolishly.
Folye, *n.,* folly. *O. F.* **folie.**
Fomy, *adj.,* foamy. *A. S.* **fāmig.**
Fond, *v., pret. sing.,* found. *From* **Finde.** *A. S.* **findan.**
Fonde, *v.,* endeavour. *A. S.* **fandian.**
Fonde, *v., pret. sing. subj.,* would find. *From* **Finde.** *A. S.* **findan.**
Foo, *n.,* foe. *A. S.* **fāh.**
Fool, *n.,* fool. *O. F.* **fol.**
Foom, *n.,* foam. *A. S.* **fām.**
Foon, *n., plu., see* **Foo.**
Foot-brede, *n.,* foot-breadth. *See* **Brede.**
Foot-mantel, *n.,* foot-cloth, covering to protect the skirt. *A. S.* **fōt**—*O. F.* **mantel.**
Forbar, *v., pret. sing., see* **Forbere.**
Forbede, *v.,* forbid. *A. S.* **forbēodan.**
Forbere, *v.,* forbear. *A. S.* **forberan.**
Forbode, *p. p., see* **Forbede.**
Forby, *adv.,* by, past. *A. S.* **for—bī.**
For-do, *v.,* destroy, overcome. *A. S.* **fordōn.**
For-dronken, *p. p.,* extremely drunk. *A. S. p. p.,* **fordruncen.**
Forest, *n.,* forest. *O. F.*
Foresteres, *n., plu. See* **Forster.**
Forgat, *v., pret. sing.,* forgot. *From* **Forgete.** *A. S.* **forgietan.** *See* **Foryete.**
Forgete, *p. p.,* forgotten. *From* **Forgete.** *A. S.* **forgietan.** *See* **Foryete.**
For-go, *p. p.,* exhausted with walking. *A. S.* **forgān.**
Forgo, *v.,* forgo, give up, lose. *A. S.* **forgān.**
Forheed, *n.,* forehead. *A. S.* **forhēafod.**
Forknowinge, *pres. partic.,* foreknowing. *A. S.* **for—cnāwan.**
Forlete, *v.,* leave, forsake, abandon. *A. S.* **forlǣtan.**
Forlong, *n.,* furlong. *A. S.* **furlang.** A forlong **wey,** a short time.

Forlost, *p. p.,* utterly lost. *A. S.* **for—lēosan.**
Forloyn, *n.,* note on a horn for recall. *Cf. O. F. v.* **forsloignier.**
Forme, *n.,* form. *O. F.*
Formel, *n.,* female of the eagle, female bird in general.
Formest, *adj., superl.,* foremost. *A. S.*
Forn-cast, *p. p.,* premeditated. *A. S.* **foran**—*O. N.* **kasta.**
Forneys, *n.,* furnace. *O. F.* **fornais.**
For-pyned, *p. p.,* wasted away by torment.
Fors, *n.,* force, significance. *O. F.* **force. No fors,** no matter. no consequence. **Do no fors,** take no account of.
Forseid, *p. p. adj.,* aforesaid.
Forshapen, *p. p.,* metamorphosed. *A. S.* **forscieppan.**
Forsleuthe, *v.,* waste in sloth.
Forster, *n.,* forester. *F.* **forestier.**
Forsweringe, *s.,* perjury. *A. S.* **forswerian.**
Forthere, *v.,* further. *A. S.* **fyrðran.**
Forther-moor, *adv.,* further on, moreover. *A. S.* **furðra—māra.**
Forther-over, *adv.,* moreover. *A. S.* **furðra—ofer.**
For-thinke, *v.,* seem amiss, displease, seem serious. *A. S.* **for—þyncan.**
Forthre, *v., see* **Forthere.**
For-thy, *adv.,* therefore. *A. S.* **forðy.**
Fortuna maior: *a name for the planet Jupiter, the influence of which was supposed to be beneficent. Venus was also supposed to have favorable influence, and was called "Fortuna minor."*
Fortune, *v.,* give (good *or* bad) fortune to, happen. *O. F.* **fortuner. Fortunen the ascendent of his images,** choose a fortunate ascendant for treating the images: *in order to effect a cure by magic or planetary influence an image of the*

patient could be made, which was submitted to the proper treatment, and by which the influence was transferred to the patient. The images, of course, had to be made and treated at exactly the right time. See Ascendent.

Forwaked, *p. p.,* exhausted with watching. *A. S.* for—wacian.

Forward, *n.,* agreement, covenant. *A. S.* foreweard.

Forweped, *p. p.,* exhausted through weeping. *A. S.* for—wēpan.

For-why, *conj.,* wherefore, why, because.

Forwiting, *s.,* foreknowledge. *A. S.* forewitan.

Forwot, *v., pres. sing.,* foreknows, foresees. *From* Forewite. *A. S.* forewitan.

Forwrapped, *p. p.,* wrapped up, concealed.

Foryaf, *v., pret. sing., see* Foryive.

Foryede, *v., pret. sing.,* gave up. *See* Forgo.

Foryete, *v.,* forget. *A. S.* forgietan.

Foryetful, *adj.,* forgetful.

Foryeve, Foryive, *v.,* forgive, remit. *A. S.* forgiefan.

Fostre, *v.,* foster. *A. S. n.* fōstor.

Fother, *n.,* load, great quantity. *A. S.* fōðer.

Fot-hoot, *adv.,* instantly, immediately. *A. S.* fōt—hāt.

Foudre, *n.,* thunderbolt. *O. F.* foldre.

Foul, *n.,* bird, fowl. *A. S.* fugol.

Foul, *adj.,* foul. *A. S.* fūl.

Foule, *adv.,* foully, vilely.

Foundement, *n.,* foundation. *O. F.* fundement.

Foundre, *v.,* founder, stumble. *O. F.* fondrer.

Founes, *n., plu.,* fawns. *O. F.* faon. *See* Faunes.

Foure, *adj.,* four. *A. S.* fēower.

Fourtenight, *n.,* fortnight.

Fourty, *adj.,* forty. *A. S.* fēowertig.

Fowel, *n., see* Foul.

Foyne, *v.,* thrust. *O. F. n.* foine.

Fraknes, *n., plu.,* freckles. *O. N.* freknur *(plu.)*

Frankeleyn, *n.,* franklin, *a landowner ranking next below the gentry. A. F.* fraunclein.

Frape, *n.,* company, throng. *O.F.*

Fraternitee, *n.,* fraternity, brotherhood, *O. F.* fraternité.

Fraunce, France.

Frayne, *v.,* pray, beseech, ask, question. *A. S.* frignan.

Fre, *adj., see* Free.

Fredom, *n.,* freedom, liberality. *A. S.* frēodōm.

Free, *adj.,* free, liberal, bounteous, noble. *A. S.* frēo.

Freend, *n.,* friend. *A. S.* frēond.

Freendlich, *adj.,* friendly. *A. S.* frēondlīc.

Freendschipe, *n.,* friendship. *A. S.* frēond—scipe.

Freletee, *n.,* frailty. *O. F.* fraileté.

Frely, *adv.,* freely.

Fremde, Fremede, *adj.,* foreign, strange, wild. *A. S.* fremede.

Frendly, *adv.,* friendly.

Frendlyeste, *adj., superl., see* Freendlich.

Frendschipe, *n., see* Freendschipe.

Frenesye, *n.,* frenzy, madness. *O. F.* frenesie.

Frenetyk, *adj.,* frantic. *O. F.* frenetique.

Frenges, *n., plu.,* fringes. *O. F.* frenge.

Frensh, French.

Frere, *n.,* friar. *O. F.* frére.

Freshe, Fresshe, *adj.,* fresh, bright. *A. S.* fersc; *O. F.* fres.

Fresshe, *adv.,* freshly.

Frete, *v.,* eat, devour. *A. S.* fretan.

Freyne, *v., see* Frayne.

Fro, *adv., prep.,* from.

Frote, *v.,* rub. *O. F.* froter.

Fruyt, *n.,* fruit. *F.* fruit.

Fruytesteres, *n., plu.,* female fruit-sellers, fruit-sellers.

Fryse, Friesland.

Fugitif, *adj.,* fugitive, fleeing from. *F.*

Fulfille, *v.*, fulfill, fill full. *A. S.* fulfyllan.

Fulliche, *adv.*, fully. *A. S.* fullīce.

Fume, *n.*, vapor. *O. F.*

Fumetere, *n.*, fumitory: *an herb.* *O. F.* fumeterre.

Fumigaciouns, *n.*, *plu.*, fumigations. *L.* fumigatio.

Fumositee, *n.*, fumes arising from drink. *O. F.* fumositê.

Fundement, *n.*, *see* Foundement.

Funeral, *adj.*, funereal.

Furie, *n.*, rage, fury, one of the Furies. *F.*

Furlong, *n.*, *see* Forlong.

Fustian, *n.*, fustian: *a kind of coarse cloth.*

Fy, *interj.*, fie!

Fyle, *n.*, file. *A. S.* fēol *f.*

Fyle, *v.*, file, sharpen.

Fyn, *n.*, end, aim, object. *O. F.* fin.

Fyn, *adj.*, fine, good. *O. F.* fin.

Fynal, *adj.*, final. *F.* final.

Fynally, *adv.*, finally.

Fyne, *v.*, finish. *O. F.* finer.

Fyneste, *adj.*, *superl.*, *see* Fyn.

Fyr, *n.*, fire. *A. S.* fȳr.

Fyrbrand, *n.*, fire-brand, torch. *A. S.* fȳr-brand.

Fyr-makinge, *n.*, making of the fire. *A. S.* fȳr—macian.

Fyr-reed, *adj.*, red as fire. *See* Reed.

Fyry, *adj.*, fiery.

Fyve, *adj.*, five. *A. S.* fífe.

G

Gabbe, *v.*, boast, speak idly. *O. N.* gabba.

Gadere, *v.*, gather. *A. S.* gaderian.

Galaxye, *n.*, the Galaxy: *the Milky Way.*

Galgopheye, Gargaphia: *where Actæon was changed into a stag.*

Galice, Gallicia *in Spain.*

Galien, Galen: *a Greek physician, c. 130–200 A. D., famous in the Middle Ages.*

Galingale, *n.*, sweet cyperus: *used as a spice.*

Galle, *n.*, gall. *A. S.* gealla.

Game, *n.*, game, sport. *A. S.* gamen.

Game, *v.*, rejoice, please. *A. S.* gamenian.

Gamen, *n.*, *see* Game.

Gan, *v.*, *pret. sing.*, *see* Ginne.

Gappe, *n.*, gap.

Gardin-wal, *n.*, garden wall. *O. F.* gardin—*A. S.* weall.

Gargat, *n.*, throat. *O. F.* gargate.

Garleek, *n.*, garlic. *A. S.* gārlēac.

Garlondes, *n.*, *plu.*, *see* Gerland.

Gastly, *adv.*, ghastly, terrible.

Gat, *v.*, *pret. sing.*, *see* Gete.

Gatesden, John Gatisden of Oxford: *a distinguished physician of the earlier half of the fourteenth century.*

Gat-tothed, *adj.*, having the teeth far apart: *a sign of an amorous temperament.*

Gaude, *n.*, gaud, toy, trick.

Gaude, *adj.*, dyed with weld.

Gauded, *p. p.*, furnished with beads (*called gauds*).

Gaufred, Geoffrey de Vinsauf: *an Anglo-Norman trouvère of the end of the twelfth century and the beginning of the thirteenth, author of the Nova Poetria.*

Gaufride, Geoffrey of Monmouth.

Gaunt, Ghent.

Gaure, *v.*, stare, gaze.

Gay, *adj.*, gay, finely dressed. *F.* gai.

Gayler, *n.*, jailer. *O. F.* jaiolier.

Gayne, *v.*, avail, profit. *O. N.* gegna.

Gaytres beryis, *n.*, *plu.*, berries of the gait-tree (*according to Skeat*): *the " gait-tree " or goat-tree is the buckthorn.*

Geaunt, *n.*, giant. *O. F.* geant.

Gebet, *n.*, gibbet, gallows. *O. F.* gibet.

Gemme, *n.*, gem. *F.*

Gendres, *n.*, *plu.*, kinds. *O. F.* gendre.

Genelon, Ganelon: *one of the*

twelve peers of Charlemagne. He betrayed Roland and his men at Roncesvalles, and became known through the romances as one of the great traitors.

General, *adj.,* liberal, general, universal. *O. F.*

Genilon, *see* **Genelon.**

Gent, *adj.,* noble, refined, exquisite. *O. F.*

Gentil, *adj.,* gentle, noble, refined, mild. *O. F.*

Gentillesse, *n.,* gentleness, nobility, courtesy, good breeding. *F.* **gentilesse.**

Gentilleste, *adj., superl., see* **Gentil.**

Gentils, *n., plu.,* gentlefolk. *See* **Gentil.**

Geometrie, *n.,* geometry. *F.* **géométrie.**

Gere, *n.,* gear, armor, equipment.

Gere, *n.,* changeful manner, fit of passion.

Gerful, *adj.,* changeable.

Gerland, *n.,* garland. *O. F.* **garlande.**

Gernade, Granada.

Gerner, *n.,* garner. *O. F.* **gernier.**

Gery, *adj.,* changeable.

Gesse, *v.,* suppose, imagine.

Gest, *n.,* guest. *A. S.* **gæst.**

Geste, *n.,* romance, tale, story, exploit, deed. *O. F.*

Gestiours, *n., plu.,* story-tellers.

Gete, *v.,* get, obtain. *O. N.* **geta.**

Gigges, *n., plu.,* rapid movements.

Gilbertyn, *possibly* **Gilbertus Anglicus:** *celebrated writer on medicine, fl. c. 1250.*

Gilden, *adj.,* of gold. *A. S.* **gylden.**

Gilt, *n.,* guilt, offence. *A. S.* **gylt.**

Giltelees, *adj.,* guiltless.

Gilty, *adj.,* guilty. *A. S.* **gyltig.**

Gin, *n.,* contrivance, snare. *O. F.* **engin.**

Gingle, *v.,* jingle.

Ginne, *v.,* begin, attempt. *A. S.*

beginnan. Gan *(as auxiliary verb),* did.

Ginning, *s.,* beginning.

Gipoun, *n.,* tunic, long sleeveless coat worn over armor. *O. F.* **gipon.**

Gipser, *n.,* pouch or purse worn at the girdle. *F.* **gibecière.**

Girdel, *n.,* girdle. *A. S.* **gyrdel.**

Girles, *n., plu.,* young people (male or female).

Giternes, *n., plu., from* **Giterne:** *a wire-strung instrument like a guitar. O. F.* **guiterne.**

Glade, *v.,* gladden, cheer. *A. S.* **gladian.**

Glare, *v.,* glare, shine.

Glas, *n.,* glass. *A. S.* **glæs.**

Glascurion, Glasgerion: *the harper in the ballad of that name. See Child,* English and Scottish Popular Ballads, *no. 67.*

Glasing, *n.,* glazing, glass-work.

Glede, *n.,* burning coal. *A. S.* **glēd** *f.*

Glee, *n.,* music, musical instrument. *A. S.* **glēo.**

Glente, *v., pret. plu.,* glanced. *From* **Glente.**

Glewe, *v.,* glue, fasten. *O. F.* **gluer.**

Glitere, *v.,* glitter.

Glose, *n.,* gloss, comment, marginal comment. *O. F.*

Glose, *v.,* interpret, explain. *O. F.* **gloser.**

Glotonye, *n.,* gluttony. *O. F.* **glotonie.**

Glotoun, *n.,* glutton. *O. F.* **gluton.**

Glyde, *v.,* glide, slip, pass quickly. *A. S.* **glīdan.**

Gobet, *n.,* piece, morsel. *O. F.*

Goddesse, *n.,* goddess.

Godhede, *n.,* godhead, divinity.

Godly, *adj.,* goodly. *A. S.* **gōdlic.**

Goldes, *n., plu.,* marigolds. *A. S.* **golde.**

Golee, *n.,* mouthful (of words), gabble. *O. F.*

Golet, *n.,* gullet. *O. F.* **goulet.**

Goliardeys, *n.,* buffoon, scurrious talker. *O. F.* **goliardois.**

Gonne, *n.,* gun, cannon.

Gonne, *v., pret. plu., see* **Ginne.**

Goodlihede, *n.,* goodliness, seemliness, beauty.

Good-man, *n.,* master of the house. *A. S.* **gōd—man.**

Goon, *v., infin.,* go; *p. p.,* gone; *from* **Go.** *A. S.* **gān.**

Goos, *n.,* goose. *A. S.* **gōs.**

Goosish, *adj.,* goose-like, foolish.

Goostly, *adv.,* spiritually, devoutly, truly. *A. S.* **gāstlīc.**

Goot, *n.,* goat. *A. S.* **gāt.**

Gootland, Gottland: *an island in the Baltic.*

Goshauk, *n.,* goshawk. *A. S.* **gōshafuc.**

Gossib, *n.,* female companion, sponsor. *A. S.* **godsibb.**

Gost, *n.,* ghost, spirit. *A. S.* **gāst.**

Goter, *n.,* gutter. *O. F.* **goutière.**

Goth, *v., pres. sing.,* goes. *From* **Go.** *See* **Goon.**

Goune, *n.,* gown. *O. F.* **gone.**

Goute, *n.,* gout. *F.*

Governaille, *n.,* mastery. *O. F.* **governail.**

Governaunce, *n.,* management, control, demeanor. *O. F.* **gouvernance.**

Governement, *n.,* government. *F.* **gouvernement.**

Governing, *n.,* government, control.

Governour, *n.,* governor, ruler, umpire. *O. F.* **governeor.**

Gowne, *n., see* **Goune.**

Grace, *n.,* favor, grace, honor. *O. F.* **With harde grace,** with ill favor, with displeasure.

Gracelees, *adj.,* void of grace, without favor.

Grame, *n.,* anger, grief, harm. *A. S.* **grama.**

Grammere, *n.,* grammar. *O. F.* **gramaire.**

Gras, *n.,* grass. *A. S.* **græs.**

Graunges, *n., plu.,* barns. *A. F.* **graunge.**

Graunt mercy, *interj.,* thanks,

thank you. *O. F.* **grant merci.**

Graunte, *v.,* grant, agree to. *O. F.* **graanter.**

Grave, *v.,* engrave, cut, impress, dig, bury. *A. S.* **grafan.**

Grece, Greece.

Grece, *n.,* grease. *O. F.* **graisse.**

Gree, *n.,* favor, good part. *O. F.* **gré.**

Greet, *adj.,* great, abundant. *A. S.* **grēat.**

Grehoundes, *n., plu.,* greyhounds. *A. S.* **grīghund.**

Grek, Greek.

Grene, *adj.,* green. *A. S.* **grēne.**

Grenewich, Greenwich.

Grenish, *adj.,* greenish.

Gres, *n., see* **Gras.**

Gret, *adj., see* **Greet.**

Grete, *v.,* greet. *A. S.* **grētan.**

Gretter, *adj., compar., see* **Greet.**

Gretteste, *adj., superl., see* **Greet.**

Grevaunce, *n.,* grievance, trouble, hardship. *O. F.* **grevance.**

Greve, *n.,* grove. *A. S.* **grāf.**

Greve, *v.,* grieve, harm, trouble. *O. F.* **grever.**

Greyn, *n.,* grain, corn. *O. F.* **grein.**

Greyn, *n.,* dye, fast color. *O. F.* **graine.**

Griffon, *n.,* griffin. *O. F.* **grifoun.**

Grint, *v., third pers. sing., pres. indic.,* grinds. *From* **Grinde.** *A. S.* **grindan.**

Grisel, "gray hair": *name given to a gray horse. O. F.*

Grisly, *adj.,* horrible, terrible. *A. S.* **grislic.**

Grone, *v.,* groan. *A. S.* **grānian.**

Grope, *v.,* try, test, examine. *A. S.* **grāpian.**

Grote, *n.,* groat: *a coin. The English groat coined in 1351-2 was equal to four pence. O. Du.* **groot.**

Grove, *n.,* grove. *A. S.* **grāf.** *See* **Greve.**

Grucche, *v.,* murmur, grumble. *O. F.* **grochier.**

Grucching, *s.,* murmuring, grumbling. *O. F.* **grochier.**

Gruf, *adv.*, groveling, on one's face. *O. N.* grūfa.

Grys, *n.*, a gray fur. *O. F.* gris.

Guerdoning, *s.*, reward.

Guerdoun, *n.*, reward, recompense. *O. F.* guerdon.

Guido de Columpnis, Guido delle Colonne: *who in 1270–1287 wrote a Latin redaction (called the* Historia Trojana) *of the* Roman de Troye *of Benôit de Sainte-More.*

Gunne, *v.*, *pret. plu.*, *see* **Ginne**.

Gyde, *n.*, guide. *F.* guide.

Gyde, *v.*, guide, direct, lead. *F.* guider.

Gye, *v.*, guide, instruct, govern. *O. F.* guier.

Gyle, *n.*, deceit, guile. *O. F.* guile.

Gyse, *n.*, guise, manner, way. *O. F.* guise.

Gytes, *n.*, *plu.*, dresses. *Cf. O. F.* guite.

H

Habergeon, *n.*, coat of mail shorter than the hauberk; hauberk. *O. F.* hauberjon (*diminutive of* hauberc).

Habitacioun, *n.*, habitation. *O. F.* habitation.

Habitacles, *n.*, *plu.*, habitable spaces, niches. *O. F.*

Habundant, *adj.*, abundant. *F.* abondant.

Habundaunce, *n.*, abundance. *F.* abondance.

Hadde, *v.*, *pret.*, had. *See* **Han**.

Hailes, *n.*, *plu.*, hail-storms. *A. S.* hægel.

Hakke, *v.*, hack. *A. S.* (tō)-haccian.

Hale, *v.*, draw, haul, attract. *O. F.* haler.

Half, *adj.*, half. *A. S.* healf.

Half, *n.*, side. *A. S.* healf.

Halle, *n.*, hall. *A. S.* heall *f.*

Halp, *v.*, *pret. sing.*, *see* **Helpe**.

Hals, *n.*, neck. *A. S.* heals.

Halse, *v.*, conjure, beseech. *A. S.* healsian.

Halt, *v.*, *third pers. sing.*, *pres. indic.*, *see* **Halte**.

Halt, *v.*, *third pers. sing.*, *pres. indic.*, *see* **Holde**.

Halte, *v.*, go halt, limp. *A. S.* healtian.

Halvendel, *n.*, the half part, half. *See* **Deel**.

Halwes, *n.*, *plu.*, saints. *A. S.* hālig.

Haly: *an Arabian physician of the eleventh century.*

Hameled, *p. p.*, mutilated, cut off. *A. S.* hamelian.

Hamer, *n.*, hammer. *A. S.*

Han, *v.*, *infin.*; *pres. plu.*; have. *A. S.* hæbban.

Hap, *n.*, chance, luck. *O. N.* happ.

Happe, *v.*, happen.

Hardely, *adv.*, hardly, scarcely; boldly, unhesitatingly, certainly. *A. S.* heardlice.

Hardiment, *n.*, boldness. *O. F.* hardement.

Hardinesse, *n.*, boldness.

Hardy, *adj.*, bold, sturdy. *F.* hardi.

Harlot, *n.*, person of low birth, ribald, rogue. *O. F.*

Harlotrye, *n.*, ribaldry, wickedness, ribald jest.

Harneised, *p. p.*, equipped. *Cf. O. F.* harneschier.

Harneys, *n.*, armor, gear. *O. F.* harneis.

Harpe, *n.*, harp. *A. S.* hearpe.

Harpestringes, *n.*, *plu.*, harpstrings. *A. S.* hearpe—streng.

Harpour, *n.*, harper. *A. S.* hearpere.

Harre, *n.*, hinge. *A. S.* heorra.

Harrow, *interj.*, help! alas! *O. F.* haro.

Hasard, *n.*, dice-play, hazard: *the name of a game played with dice. O. F.*

Hasardour, *n.*, gamester. *A. F.*

Hasardrye, *n.*, gaming, playing hazard.

Hasdrubales, **Hasdrubal's**.

Hasel, *n.*, hazel-tree. *A. S.* hæsel.

Hasel-wode, *n.,* hazel-wood: *i. e.,* no news, *a popular saying expressive of incredulity. A. S.* hæsel—wudu.

Haste, *n.,* haste. *O. F.*

Haste, *v.,* hasten. *O. F.* **haster.**

Hastif, *adj.,* hasty. *O. F.*

Hastilich, *adv.,* hastily.

Hastow, *v., pron., second pers. sing., pres. indic.,* hast thou. *See* **Han.**

Hatte, *v., pret.; pret. as pres.; see* Hote.

Hauberk, *n.,* coat of mail. *O. F.* **hauberc.**

Hauk, *n.,* hawk. *A. S.* **hafoc.**

Hauke, *v.,* hunt with a hawk.

Haunt, *n.,* use, practice, skill.

Haunte, *v.,* use, practice, resort to. *O. F.* **hanter.**

Hauteyn, *adj.,* proud, stately. *O. F.* **haltain.**

Hawe, *n.,* yard, enclosure; fruit of the dog-rose, haw. *A. S.* **haga.**

Hawethorn-leves, *n., plu.,* hawthorn-leaves. *A. S.* **hagaþorn—lēaf.**

Hayles, the Abbey of Hailes, *Gloucestershire.*

Hebraik, Hebrew. *See* **Ebrayk.**

Hed, *n., see* **Heed.**

Hede, *n.,* heed.

Hede, *v.,* head, provide with a head.

Heed, *n.,* head. *A. S.* **hēafod.**

Heep, *n.,* heap, crowd, throng. *A. S.* **hēap.**

Heer, *n.,* hair. *A. S.* **hǣr.**

Heer, *adv.,* here. *A. S.* **hēr.**

Heer-agayns, *adv.,* against this, in reply to this. *A. S.* **hēr—ongēanes.**

Heer-tofore, *adv.,* hitherto. *A. S.* **hēr-tō-fore.**

Heet, *v., pret. sing., see* Hote.

Heeth, *n.,* heath. *A. S.* **hǣð.**

Hegge, *n.,* hedge. *A. S.* **hecg.**

Heigh, *adj.,* high, lofty. *A. S.* **hēah.** *See* **Heye, Hy.**

Heighe, *adv.,* high.

Heighly, *adv.,* strongly. *A. S.* **hēalīce.**

Helde, *v.,* bend, incline, pour. *A. S.* **heldan.** **Helde,** *pret.* bent, inclined, poured.

Hele, *n.,* health. *A. S.* **hǣlu.**

Hele, *v.,* conceal. *A. S.* **helan.**

Hele, *v.,* heal. *A. S.* **hǣlan.**

Heled, *p. p.,* concealed. *See* **Hele.**

Helelees, *adj.,* out of health.

Helle, *n.,* hell. *A. S.* **hell** *f.*

Helmed, *p. p.,* furnished with a helm. *A. S.* **helmian.**

Helowys, Heloïse.

Helpe, *v.,* help. *A. S.* **helpan.**

Helply, *adj.,* helpful.

Hem, *pron., dat. plu.,* them.

Hemi-spere, *n.,* hemisphere.

Hem-self, *pron., plu.,* themselves.

Hende, *adj.,* courteous, polite. *A. S.* **gehende.**

Heng, *v., pret. sing.,* hung. *From* **Hange.** *A. S.* **hōn; hangian.**

Henne, *adv.,* hence. *A. S.* **heonan.**

Hennes, *n., plu.,* hens. *A. S.* **henn** *f.*

Hennes, *adv.,* hence.

Hennes-forth, *adv.,* henceforth.

Hente, *v.,* catch, seize, take. *A. S.* **hentan.**

Hepe, *v.,* heap, augment, accumulate. *A. S.* **hēapian.**

Her, *pron., gen. plu.,* their.

Heraud, *n.,* herald. *O. F.* **heraut.**

Heraude, *v.,* herald, proclaim. *O. F.* **herauder.**

Herbe, *n.,* herb. *O. F.*

Her-beforn, *adv.,* before this. *A. S.* **hēr—beforan.**

Herber, *n.,* garden, arbor. *O. F.* **erbier.**

Herbergage, *n.,* lodging, abode. *O. F.*

Herberwe, *n.,* harbor, lodging, shelter. *O. N.* **herbergi.**

Her-by, *adv.,* with respect to this matter, hence. *A. S.* **hēr—bī.**

Herd, *p. p., see* **Here.**

Herde, *n.,* shepherd, herd, keeper of cattle. *A. S.* **heorde.**

Herde, *v., pret. see* **Here.**

Herde-gromes, *n., plu.,* herdsmen.

Here, *pron.*, her. *A. S.* hiere, hire.

Here, *v.*, hear. *A. S.* hīeran.

Here, *adv.*, *see* Heer.

Here and howne, *perhaps* gentle and savage: *i. e.*, one and all.

Hereos, *n.*: *according to Medieval science, the specific name for a malady of love.*

Herie, *v.*, praise, worship. *A. S.* herian.

Herines, Erinyes: *the Furies.*

Herke, *v.*, hearken.

Herkne, *v.*, hearken, listen. *A. S.* hercnian.

Hermes Ballenus: Hermes' Belinous—*Hermes Trismegistus was the fabled founder of alchemy, from whom a certain Belinous professed to have learned the art of talismans. Belinous so far has not been satisfactorily indentified.*

Hermyte, *n.*, hermit. *O. F.* hermite.

Herneys, *n.*, *see* Harneys.

Herodes, Herod.

Heroun, *n.*, heron. *O. F.* hairon.

Hert, *n.*, hart. *A. S.* heort.

Herte, *n.*, heart. *A. S.* heorte.

Herte, *v.*, *pret.*, hurt. *From* Hurte. *O. F.* hurter.

Herte-blood, *n.*, heart's blood. *A. S.* heorte—blōd.

Hertelees, *adj.*, heartless, lacking in courage.

Hertely, *adv.*, heartily, thoroughly.

Herte-spoon, *n.*, the concave part of the breast, the breast bone. *A. S.* heorte—spōn.

Hertly, *adj.*, hearty, honest.

Heryinge, *s.*, praising, glory. *See* Herie.

Heste, *n.*, behest, commandment. *A. S.* hæs *f.*

Hester, Esther.

Hete, *n.*, heat. *A. S.* hæto.

Hete, *v.*, promise, vow. *A. S.* hātan. *See* Hote.

Hethen, *adj.*, heathen. *A. S.* hæðen.

Hethenesse, *n.*, heathen lands. *A. S.* hæðennes *f.*

Hette, *v.*, *pret. sing.*, heated, inflamed. *From* Hete. *A. S.* hætan.

Heve, *v.*, heave, lift. *A. S.* hebban.

Heved, *n.*, *see* Heed.

Hevene, *n.*, heaven. *A. S.* heofon.

Hevenish, *adj.*, heavenly.

Hevenly, *adj.*, heavenly. *A. S.* heofonlic.

Hevinesse, *n.*, sorrow, sadness. *A. S.* hefignes *f.*

Hevy, *adj.*, heavy. *A. S.* hefig.

Hewe, *n.*, hue, color, complexion. *A. S.* hēow.

Hewed, *adj.*, colored, hued.

Heye, *adj.*, *see* Heigh.

Heyghe, *adv.*, *see* Heighe.

Heynous, *adj.*, heinous, hateful. *O. F.* heïnos.

Heyr, *n.*, heir. *O. F.* heir.

Heyre, *adj.*, made of hair. *Cf. O. F.* haire; *A. S.* hær.

Heysugge, *n.*, hedge-sparrow. *A. S.* heges-sugge.

Hider, *adv.*, hither. *A. S.*

Hidous, *adj.*, hideous. *O. F.*

Hidously, *adv.*, hideously, terribly.

Hierdes, *n.*, shepherdess, female guardian.

Hight, *p. p.*; Highte, *v.*, *pret.*; *see* Hote.

Highte, *n.*, height. *A. S.* hēahðu.

Hil, *n.*, hill. *A. S.* hyll.

Hild, *v.*, *pret. sing.*, *see* Helde.

Hinde, *n.*, hind. *A. S.* hind *f.*

Hindreste, *adj.*, *superl.*, hindmost.

Hipes, *n.*, *plu.*, hips. *A. S.* hype.

Hir, *pron.*, her (*A. S.* hiere, hire); their (*A. S.* hiera, hira).

Hires, *pron.*, hers.

His, *pron.*, his; its. *A. S.*

Hit, *pron.*, it. *A. S.*

Ho, *n.*, ho: *exclamation commanding silence;* stop, cessation.

Hogges, *n.*, *gen. sing.*, hog's; *plu.*, hogs. *A. S.* hogga.

Holde, *v.,* hold, keep, preserve, esteem, consider. *A. S.* **healdan. Holde in honde,** delude with false hopes, cajole.

Holm, *n.,* holm-oak.

Holowe, *adj., see* **Holwe.**

Holownesse, *n.,* hollowness, concavity.

Holsom, *adj.,* wholesome, healing. *A. S.* **hāl—sum.**

Holt, *n.,* wood. *A. S.* **holt.**

Holwe, *adj., adv.,* hollow. *A. S.* **holh.**

Hom, *n., see* **Hoom.**

Homicyde, *n.,* murderer; murder. *F.*

Hond, *n.,* hand. *A. S.* **Bere on honde,** *see* **Bere. Holde in honde,** *see* **Holde.**

Honest, *adj.,* creditable, honorable, worthy. *O. F.* **honeste.**

Honestee, *n.,* honor, goodness. *O. F.* **honesté.**

Honge, *v.,* hang, vacillate, depend. *A. S.* **hōn; hangian.**

Honurable, *adj.,* honorable. *F.* **honorable.**

Hony, *n.,* honey. *A. S.* **hunig.**

Hood, *n.,* hood. *A. S.* **hōd. Such game fonde they in hir hode,** such sport they found in their hoods: *i. e.,* such fun they made of them.

Hoodless, *adj.,* without a hood.

Hool, *n.,* hole, *A. S.* **hol.**

Hool, *adj.,* whole, sound, perfect. *A. S.* **hāl.**

Hoolly, *adv.,* wholly.

Hoom, *n.,* home. *A. S.* **hām.**

Hoomlinesse, *n.,* homeliness, domesticity.

Hoomward, *adv.,* homeward. *A. S.* **hāmweard.**

Hoor, *adj.,* hoary, white-haired. *A. S.* **hār.**

Hoost, *n.,* army. *O. F.* **host.**

Hoot, *adj.,* hot. *A. S.* **hāt.**

Hope, *n.,* hope. *A. S.* **hopa.**

Hoppe, *v.,* hop, dance. *A. S.* **hoppian.**

Hord, *n.,* hoard, treasure. *A. S.*

Hors, *n.,* horse. *A. S.*

Hors, *adj.,* hoarse. *A. S.* **hās.**

Hose, *n.,* hose, covering for the feet and legs. *A. S.* **hose.**

Host, Hoste, *n.,* host (*of an inn*), keeper of lodgings. *O. F.* **oste.**

Hostel, *n.,* hostelry. *O. F.*

Hostelrye, *n.,* hostelry, inn. *O. F.* **hostelerie.**

Hostiler, *n.,* hostler, innkeeper. *O. F.* **hostelier.**

Hote, *adv.,* hotly. *A. S.* **hāte.**

Hote, *v.,* command, promise, be called, be named. *A.S.***hātan.**

Hottes, *n., plu.,* baskets carried on the back. *O. F.* **hotte.**

Hound, *n.,* dog. *A. S.* **hund.**

Houpe, *v.,* whoop. *O. F.* **houper.**

Houre, *n.,* hour. *O. F.* **hore. Houre inequal,** unequal hour: *according to astrology an hour formed by dividing the duration of the daylight by twelve.*

Hous, *n.,* house. *A. S.* **hūs.** *In astronomy and astrology a "hous" was either a division (a twelfth) of the whole celestial sphere, or any of the zodiacal signs regarded as the domain of a particular planet.*

Housbonde, *n.,* husband. *A. S.* **hūsbonda.**

Housbondrye, *n.,* husbandry, economy.

Hove, *v.,* hover, dwell, wait.

Howne, *see* **Here and howne.**

Howve, *n.,* hood. *A. S.* **hūfe.**

Huberd, Hubert.

Hugh of Lincoln: *a boy supposed to have been murdered by the Jews at Lincoln in 1255.*

Humanitee, *n.,* humanity, kindness. *F.* **humanité.**

Humblely, *adv.,* humbly.

Humblesse, *n.,* humility, meekness. *O. F.*

Humbling, *n.,* rumbling, low growl.

Humilitee, *n.,* humility. *O. F.* **humilité.**

Humme, *v.,* hum.

Humour, *n.,* humor. *A. F.*

Hunte, *n.,* hunter, huntsman. *A. S.* **hunta.**

Hunteresse, *n.,* female hunter.

Hurtle, *v.*, push, attack.
Hust, *p. p.*, hushed.
Hy, *adj.*, *see* **Heigh, Heye.**
Hyde, *v.*, hide. *A. S.* **hȳdan.**
Hye, *n.*, haste.
Hye, *adv.*, high, aloft.
Hye, *v.*, hie, hasten. *A. S.* **higian.**
Hyer, *adj.*, *compar.*, higher. *See* **Hy.**
Hyest, *adj.*, *superl.*, highest. *See* **Hy.**
Hyne, *n.*, hind, servant, peasant. *A. S.* **hīna.**
Hyre, *n.*, hire, meed, payment. *A. S.* **hȳr** *f.*
Hyre, *v.*, hire. *A. S.* **hȳrian.**
Hyve, *n.*, hive. *A. S.* **hȳf** *f.*

I (*the vowel*)

Ich, *pron.*, I.
I-comen, *p. p.*, come.
Ignoraunce, *n.*, ignorance. *F.* ignorance.
I-graunted, *p. p.*, granted. *See* **Graunte.**
Ilioun, Ilion: *the Greek name for Troy, but occasionally used by Medieval writers to refer to the citadel alone.*
Ilke, *adj.*, same, very. *A. S.* ilca.
Illusioun, *n.*, illusion. *O. F.* illusion.
Imaginacioun, *n.*, imagination, fancy. *O. F.* imaginacion.
Importable, *adj.*, unendurable. *O. F.*
Impressioun, *n.*, impression, notion. *F.* impression.
In, *n.*, inn, lodging, dwelling. *A. S.*
In principio: *the text* "In principio erat verbum" (*John i, 1*), *which the begging friars frequently used.*
Inche, *n.*, inch. *A. S.* **ynce.**
Inde, India.
Inequal, *adj.*, unequal. *L.* inæqualis. **Houre inequal,** *see* **Houre.**
Infect, *adj.*, invalid, of no effect. *L.* infectus.

Infinit, *adj.*, infinite. *O. F.*
Infortune, *n.*, misfortune. *F.*
Infortuned, *p. p.*, ill-starred. *O. F.* infortuner.
Inhelde, *v.*, pour in, infuse. *See* **Helde.**
Iniquitee, *n.*, iniquity, injustice. *O. F.* iniquité.
In-knette, *v.*, *pret. sing.*, knit up, drew in. *A. S.* **in—cnyttan.** *See* **Knitte.**
Inly, *adv.*, inwardly, extremely, wholly. *A. S.* **inlice.**
Inmid, *prep.*, into, amid.
Inmortal, *adj.*, immortal. *L.* immortalis.
Inne, *adv.*, in, within. *A. S.*
Inned, *p. p.*, housed, lodged. *A. S.* innian.
Intellect, *n.*, intelligence. *L.* intellectus.
Invocacioun, *n.*, invocation. *O. F.* invocacion.
In-with, *adv.*, within, in.
Ipocrisye, *n.*, hyprocrisy. *O. F.* ypocrisie.
Iren, *n.*, iron. *A. S.*
Isaude, Iseult.
Isaye, Isaiah.
Isidis, Isis.
Isoude, *see* **Isaude.**
Itaile, Itaille, Italy.
Ivy-leef, *n.*, ivy leaf. *A. S.* **īfig—lēaf.**

I (*for* J).

Iade, *n.*, jade, worn-out horse.
Iakke Straw, Jack Straw: *leader of the London uprisings in 1381.*
Ialous, *adj.*, jealous. *O. F.*
Ialousye, *n.*, jealousy. *O. F.* jalousie.
Iane, *n.*, a small coin of Genoa used in England. *O. F.* janne.
Iangle, *v.*, chatter, prate. *O. F.* jangler.
Iangler, *n.*, story-teller, jester, babbler. *O. F.* jangleor.
Iangleresse, *n.*, (female) prattler, chatterbox. *O. F.*
Ianglerye, *n.*, chatter, gossip. *O. F.* janglerie.

Iangles, *n., plu.,* idle pratings, disputes. *O. F.* jangle.

Iape, *n.,* jest, trick.

Iape, *v.,* jest.

Iaspre, *n.,* jasper. *O. F.*

Ieet, *n.,* jet. *O. F.* jet.

Ieremye, Jeremiah.

Iet, *n.,* fashion, mode. *O. F.* get.

Iewerye, Jewish kingdom, Jewish quarter.

Iogelour, *n.,* juggler. *O. F.* jogeler.

Iolif, *adj.,* jovial, joyful, merry. *O. F.*

Iolitee, *n.,* jollity, sport, merriment. *O. F.* jolité.

Ioly, *adj.,* jolly, joyous, merry. *O. F.* joli.

Iompre, *v.,* jumble.

Ionathas, Jonathan.

Iournee, *n.,* day's work, day's march, journey. *O. F.* jornée.

Iovinian, Jovinian. *See* Seint Jerome.

Iowes, *n., plu.,* jaws.

Ioye, *n.,* joy. *O. F.* joie.

Ioynant, *pres. partic.,* adjoining.

Ioyne, *v.,* join. *O. F.* joindre.

Iuge, *n.,* judge. *O. F.*

Iuge, *v.,* judge. *O. F.* jugier.

Iugement, *n.,* judgment, decision. *O. F.*

Iugge, *v., see* Iuge.

Iulius, Julius Cæsar.

Iuparte, *v.,* imperil, endanger.

Iupartye, *v.,* jeopardy, peril, hazard. *O. F.* jeu parti.

Iust, *adj.,* just, exact, correct. *F.* juste.

Iuste, *v.,* just, tourney. *O. F.* jouster.

Iustes, *n., plu. as sing.,* just, tournament. *O. F.* juste.

Iustyce, Iustyse, *n.,* justice, judgment. *O. F.* justice, justise.

Iuwyse, *n.,* justice, judgment, sentence. *O. F.* juise.

K

Kalendes, *n., plu.,* calends: *so* beginning, *A. S.* calend.

Karf, *v., pret. sing., see* Kerve.

Keep, *n.,* care, heed, notice.

Kembe, *v.,* comb. *A. S.* cemban.

Kempe, *adj.,* shaggy, rough.

Ken, *n.,* kin, kindred. *A. S.* cynn. *See* Kinnes.

Kene, *adj.,* keen, eager, bold. *A. S.* cēne.

Kenne, *v.,* perceive, discern. *A. S.* cennan.

Kepe, *v.,* keep, take care of, regard. *A. S.* cēpan.

Keper, *n.,* keeper.

Kerve, *v.,* carve, cut. *A. S.* ceorfan.

Kerver, *n.,* carver.

Kerving-tolis, *n., plu.,* tools to cut with. —*A. S.* tōl.

Kesse, *v.,* kiss. *A. S.* cyssan.

Kevere, *v.,* cover, recover. *O. F.* covrir.

Keye, *n.,* key. *A. S.* cǣg *f.*

Kidde, *v., pret., see* Kythe.

Kinde, *n.,* nature, kind, race, bent. *A. S.* cynd (*neuter*); gecynd *f.*

Kinde, *adj.,* kind, natural. *A. S.* cynde.

Kindely, Kindeliche (*weak*), *adj.,* natural. *A. S.* cyndelīc.

Kindely, Kindeliche, *adv.,* naturally. *A. S.* cyndelīce.

Kinnes, *n., gen.,* kind's, *A. S.* cynn. *See* Ken.

Kinrede, *n.,* kindred, family. *A. S.* cynrǣden.

Kirtel, *n.,* kirtle. *A. S.* cyrtel.

Kitte, *v., pret. sing.,* cut. *From* Cutte.

Knakkes, *n., plu.,* tricks.

Knarre, *n.,* knotted thickset fellow, sturdy churl.

Knarry, *adj.,* gnarled.

Knave, *n.,* boy, servant-lad. *A. S.* cnafa. **Knave child,** male child.

Knele, *v.,* kneel. *A. S.* cnēowlian.

Knette, *v.,* knit, join. *A. S.* cnyttan.

Knighthede, *n.,* knighthood.

Knitte, *v., see* Knette.

Knobbes, *n., plu.,* knobs.

Knok, *n.,* knock.

Knotte, *n.*, knot, difficulty, gist of a tale. *A. S.* **cnotta.**

Knotteles, *adj.*, without a knot.

Knotty, *adj.*, covered with knots.

Know, *n.*, knee. *A. S.* **cnēow.**

Knyf, *n.*, knife. *A. S.* **cnīf.**

Konninge, *s.*, cunning, skill. *A. S.* **cunnan.**

Kukkow, *n.*, *see* **Cukkow.**

Kunninge, *s.*, *see* **Konninge.**

Kyn, *n.*, *plu.*, kine, cows.

Kynde, *n.*, *see* **Kinde.**

Kyndely, *adj.*, *see* **Kindely.**

Kyte, *n.*, kite: *a bird of the hawk family.* *A. S.* **cȳta.**

Kythe, *v.*, show, make known. *A. S.* **cȳðan.**

L

Laas, *n.*, *see* **Las.**

Lad, *p. p.*, *see* **Lede.**

Lade, *v.*, load, cover. *A. S.* **hladan.**

Ladel, *n.*, ladle. *A. S.* **hlædel.**

Lak, *n.*, want, defect, blame.

Lakke, *v.*, find fault with, disparage, blame.

Lamentacioun, *n.*, lamentation. *F.* **lamentation.**

Lameth, **Lamech** (*Genesis iv and v*).

Lamuel, **Lemuel**, *the King* (*Proverbs xxxi, 1*).

Langage, *n.*, language. *F.*

Languisshe, *v.*, languish, fail. *F.* **languir.**

Lanterne, *n.*, lantern. *F.*

Lapidaire, *n.*, lapidary: *a treatise dealing with precious stones.* *F.*

Lappe, *n.*, flap, fold, edge of a garment, wrapper. *A. S.* **læppa.**

Large, *adj.*, large, wide, free; *adv.*, widely, freely. *O. F.* At thy large, at large.

Largely, *adv.*, fully.

Largesse, *n.*, liberality, bounty. *O. F.*

Larke, *n.*, lark. *A. S.* **lāwerce.**

Las, *n.*, lace, snare, band. *O. F.* **laz.**

Lasse, *adj.*, *compar.*, less. *A. S.* **læssa.**

Lasshe, *n.*, lash.

Lat, *v.*, *imper.*, *see* **Lete.**

Late, *adv.*, lately. *A. S.*

Late, *v.*, let. *A. S.* **lætan.** *See* **Lete.**

Lathe, *n.*, barn. *O. N.* **hlaða.**

Latis, *n.*, lattice. *F.* **lattis.**

Latoun, *n.*, latten: *a brasslike alloy.* *O. F.* **laton.**

Laude, *n.*, praise, honor. *O. F.*

Laudomia, **Laodamia.**

Launce, *v.*, fling oneself, leap, prance. *O. F.* **lancier.**

Launde, *n.*, grassy clearing, glade. *O. F.* **lande.**

Laure, *n.*, laurel-tree. *O. F.*

Laureat, *adj.*, laureate, crowned with laurel. *L.* **laureatus.**

Laurer, *n.*, laurel-tree. *O. F.* **laurier.**

Lauriol, *n.*, spurge-laurel. *F.* **laureole.**

Lavyne, **Lavinia.**

Lawe, *n.*, law. *A. S.* **lagu.**

Laxatyf, *n.*, laxative. *F.* **laxatif.**

Lay, *n.*, song, lay. *O. F.* **lai.**

Lay, *n.*, law, faith, belief. *A. F.* **lei.**

Layser, *n.*, leisure. *O. F.* **leisir.** *See* **Leyser.**

Lazar, *n.*, leper.

Leche, *n.*, physician. *A. S.* **læce.**

Lechecraft, *n.*, art of medicine. *A. S.* **læcecræft.**

Lecherye, *n.*, lechery. *O. F.* **lecherie.**

Lechour, *n.*, lecher. *O. F.* **lecheor.**

Lede, *v.*, lead. *A. S.* **lædan.**

Ledere, *n.*, leader.

Leed, *n.*, lead. *A. S.* **lēad.**

Leef, *adj.*, lief, dear. *A. S.* **lēof.**

Leef, *n.*, leaf. *A. S.* **lēaf.**

Leef, *v.*, *imper.*, *see* **Leve.**

Leek, *n.*, leek. *A. S.* **lēac.**

Leen, *v.*, *imper*, *see* **Lene.**

Lees, *n.*, deceit, fraud.

Lees, *v.*, *pret. sing.*, *see* **Lese.**

Leeste, *adj.*, *superl.*, least. *A. S.* **læsest.**

Leet, *v.*, *pret. sing.*, *see* **Lete.**

Legende, *n.*, legend. *O. F.*

Lekes, *n.*, *plu.*, *see* **Leek.**

Lemes, *n., plu.,* flames. *A. S.* lēoma.

Lene, *adj.,* lean, thin. *A. S.* hlǽne.

Lene, *v.,* lend, give. *A. S.* lǽnan.

Lenger, *adj., compar.,* longer. *A. S.* lengra.

Lenger, *adv., compar.,* longer.

Lengest, *adv., superl.,* longest.

Lengthe, *n.,* length. *A. S.* lengð *f.*

Lente, *n.,* Lent. *A. S.* lencten.

Leoun, *n.,* lion. *F.* lion.

Lepart, *n.,* leopard. *O. F.* liepart.

Lepe, *v.,* leap, run. *A. S.* hlēapan.

Lepe: *a town in Spain.*

Lere, *v.,* teach, learn. *A. S.* lǽran.

Lered, *adj.,* learned. *A. S.* lǽred.

Lerne, *v.,* learn. *A. S.* leornian.

Lese, *n.,* pasture. *A. S.* lǽs *f.*

Lese, *v.,* lose. *A. S.* lēosan.

Lesinge, *n.,* falsehood, lie. *A. S.* lēasung *f.*

Lesse, *adj., compar., see* **Lasse.**

Lessoun, *n.,* lesson. *F.* leçon.

Lest, *n.,* pleasure, desire, inclination. *A. S.* lyst. *See* **List, Lust.**

Lest, *v., pres. sing., impers.,* pleases; **Leste,** *pres. subj.,* please. *A. S.* lystan. *See* **List, Luste.**

Leste, *adj., superl., see* **Leeste.**

Let, *v., pres. sing.; p. p.; see* **Lette.**

Lete, Lethe.

Lete, *v.,* let, leave, forsake, permit. *A. S.* lǽtan. **Let calle,** cause to be called.

Lette, *n.,* hindrance, delay.

Lette, *v.,* hinder, prevent, thwart. *A. S.* lettan.

Lettow, Lithuania.

Lettre, *n.,* letter. *O. F.* letre.

Letuarie, *n.,* electuary, remedy. *O. F.* letuaire.

Leve, *n.,* leave, permission. *A. S.* lēaf *f.*

Leve, *v.,* leave, forsake, leave off. *A. S.* lǽfan.

Leve, *v.,* believe. *A. S.* lēfan.

Leve, *v.,* allow. *A. S.* lēfan.

Lever, *adj., compar.,* liefer, dearer.

Levest, *adj., superl.,* dearest, most desirable.

Lewed, *adj.,* ignorant, unlearned, rude. *A. S.* lǽwed.

Lewedly, *adv.,* ignorantly, simply.

Lewednesse, *n.,* ignorance, ignorant behavior.

Ley, *v., pret. sing., see* **Lye.**

Leye, *v.,* lay, lay a wager. *A. S.* lecgan.

Leyser, *n., see* **Layser.**

Libertee, *n.,* liberty. *F.* libertē.

Libye, Lybia.

Licentiat, *adj.,* one licensed by the Pope to hear confessions and administer penance in all places, independently of the local authorities. *L. L.*

Liche, *adv.,* alike. *A. S.* gelīce.

Liche-wake, *n.,* watch over a corpse. *A. S.* līc—wacu.

Licour, *n.,* moisture, liquor, juice. *O. F.* licur.

Lief, *adj., see* **Leef.**

Lige, *adj.,* liege. *O. F.* liege.

Ligge, *v.,* lie, récline, remain. *A. S.* licgan.

Lighte, *v.,* to make light, rejoice, to feel light, to illuminate. *A. S.* lihtan.

Lighte, *v.,* alight. *A. S.* lihtan.

Lighter, *adv., compar.,* more readily.

Lightles, *adj.,* deprived of light.

Lightnesse, *n.,* lightness, brightness.

Ligne aloes, *n.,* wood of the aloe. *O. F.* lignaloes.

Ligurge, Lycurgus.

Likerous, *adj.,* lecherous, wanton.

Lilie, *n.,* lily. *A. S.*

Lilting-horn, *n.,* horn to be played for a lilt. —*A. S.* horn.

Lim, *n.,* limb. *A. S.* lim.

Limitour, *n.,* limiter: *a friar licensed to beg for alms within certain bounds.*

Limmes, *n., plu., see* **Lim.**

Linage, *n.,* lineage, race, family. *F.* **lignage.**

Lind, *n.,* lime-tree. *A. S.* **lind.**

Linian, Giovanni di Lignano: *Professor of Canon Law at Bologna in 1363, died in 1383.*

Lippe, *n.,* lip. *A. S.* **lippa.**

Lipse, *v.,* lisp.

Lisse, *n.,* comfort, joy, solace. *A. S.* **liss** *f.*

Lisse, *v.,* alleviate, soothe. *A. S.* **lissian.**

List, *n.,* pleasure, will. *A.S.* **lyst.** *See* **Lest, Lust.**

List, *n.,* ear. *A. S.* **hlyst.**

List, *v., pres. sing., impers.,* pleases. **Liste,** *pret. sing.; subj. A. S.* **lystan.** *See* **Lest. Luste.**

Listes, *n., plu.,* lists, place of tournament.

Litarge, *n.,* litharge: *ointment prepared from protoxide of lead. F.* **litharge.**

Lite, *adj., see* **Lyte.**

Lith, *n.,* limb. *A. S.* **liδ.**

Liveree, *n.,* livery. *F.* **livrée.**

Lodemenage, *n.,* pilotage.

Lode-sterre, *n.,* lodestar, polar star. *A. S.* **lād** *f.*—**steorra.**

Lofte, *n., dat.,* loft, upper room. *Cf. O. N.* **lopt. On lofte,** in the air.

Logge, *n.,* lodge, resting-place. *O. F.* **loge.**

Logging, *n.,* lodging.

Logik, *n.,* logic. *F.* **logique.**

Loke, *v., weak,* lock up.

Loke, *v.,* look, discern. *A. S.* **lōcian.**

Loken, *p. p.,* locked up. *From* **Louke.** *A. S.* **lūcan.**

Loking, *n.,* look, gaze.

Lokkes, *n.,* locks of hair. *A. S.* **locc.**

Lollius: *a name which Chaucer seems to have taken as that of a writer of a Trojan history. No such writer is known to have existed; but perhaps the idea arose from a misunderstanding of the lines in Horace:*

"Troiani belli scriptorem,
maxime Lolli,
Dum tu declamas Romæ,
Præneste relegi."

Lond, *n.,* land. *A. S.*

Longe, *adj.,* long, tall. *A. S.* **lang.**

Longe, *adv.,* long, for a long time. *A. S.* **lange.**

Longe, *v.,* desire, long for. *A. S.* **langian.**

Longe, *v.,* belong, befit, concern.

Loos, *n.,* praise, renown. *O. F.* **los.**

Loos, *adj.,* loose.

Looth, *adj.,* loath, odious. *A. S.* **lāδ.**

Looth, *adv.,* with dislike.

Lordings, *n., plu.,* sirs.

Lordshipe, *n.,* lordship, rank, authority. *A. S.* **hlāfordscipe.**

Lore, *n.,* lore, teaching, instruction. *A. S.* **lār** *f.*

Lore, Loren, Lorn, *p. p., see* **Lese.**

Los, *n.,* loss. *A. S.*

Losenges, *n., plu.,* lozenges: *small diamond-shaped shields. F.* **losange.**

Losengour, *n.,* flatterer. *O. F.* **losengeur.**

Loses, *n., plu., see* **Loos.**

Loth, Lot.

Loth, *adj., see* **Looth.**

Lothest, *adj., superl., see* **Looth.**

Loude, *adv.,* loudly. *A. S.* **hlūde.**

Lough, *v., pret. sing.,* laughed. *From* **Laughe.** *A. S.* **hliehhan.**

Lous, *adj., see* **Loos** *adj.*

Loute, *v.,* bow, stoop, do obeisance. *A. S.* **lūtan.**

Lovedayes, *n., plu.,* days for settling disputes by arbitration.

Loveknotte, *n.,* love-knot. *A. S.* **lufu**—**cnotta.**

Lovere, *n.,* lover.

Lowe, *adj.,* low, humble; *adv.,* low, humbly.

Luce, *n.,* luce, pike. *O. F.* **luz.**

Lucina: *a name of Diana; the moon.*

Lucye, Lucia.

Lufsom, *adj.*, lovely, lovable. *A. S.* lufsum.

Lulle, *v.*, lull, soothe.

Lust, *n.*, pleasure, amusement, desire. *A. S. See* **Lest, List.**

Luste, *v.*, please. *A. S.* lystan. *See* **Lest, List.**

Lustihede, *n.*, delight, enjoyment.

Lustily, *adv.*, gaily, merrily.

Lustinesse, *n.*, pleasure, jollity.

Lusty, *adj.*, pleasant, gay.

Luxurie, *n.*, lechery. *O. F.*

Lyde, Lydia.

Lye, *n.*, lie, falsehood. *A. S.* lyge.

Lye, *v.*, lie, recline, remain. *A. S.* licgan. *See* **Ligge.**

Lye, *v.*, tell lies, lie. *A. S.* leogan.

Lyere, *n.*, liar.

Lyes, *n.*, *plu.*, lees, dregs. *F.* lie.

Lyeys, *formerly* **Layas,** *now* **Ayas,** *in Armenia.*

Lyf, *n.*, life. *A. S.* lif.

Lyfly, *adv.*, in a lifelike way. *A. S.* liflic.

Lyk, *adj.*, like. *A. S.* gelice.

Lyke, *v.*, *impers.*, please. *A. S.* lician.

Lyklihede, *n.*, likelihood.

Lyklinesse, *n.*, probability.

Lykly, *adj.*, likely.

Lykne, *v.*, liken, compare.

Lyknesse, *n.*, parable. *A. S.* gelicnes *f.*

Lyma, Lima: *an error for* **Livia,** *who poisoned her husband Drusus at the instigation of Sejanus.*

Lyme, *v.*, cover with birdlime.

Lymere, *n.*, bitch-hound held in leash. *O. F.* limiere.

Lymote, *possibly* **Elymas** *the sorcerer* (Acts *xiii, 8*).

Lyne, *n.*, line. *A. S.* line.

Lyned, *p. p.*, lined.

Lyoun, *n.*, *see* **Leoun.**

Lystow, *v.*, *pron.*, *second pers. sing.*, *pres. indic.*, *see* **Lye.**

Lytargye, *n.*, lethargy. *O. F.* litargie.

Lyte, Lytel, *adj.*, little, small. *A. S.* lytel.

Lyte, *adv.*, little. *A. S.* lytel.

Lyth, *v.*, *third pers. sing.*, *pres. indic.*, *see* **Lye.**

Lythe, *adj.*, easy, soft. *A. S.* liðe.

Lythe, *v.*, alleviate, cheer. *A. S.* liðian.

Lyve, *n.*, *dat.*, *see* **Lyf.**

Lyves, *n.*, *gen.*, *see* **Lyf.** *As adv.*, in life, living.

M

Maad, *p. p.*, *see* **Make.**

Maat, *adj.*, dejected, exhausted, defeated, checkmate. *O. F.* mat.

Macedo, *the* **Macedonian.**

Macrobie, Macrobius: *Roman writer* (*fl. c. 400 A. D.*), *author of a commentary on the* Somnium Scipionis *from the De Republica of Cicero. In the Somnium Scipionis Scipio Africanus Minor dreams that his grandfather shows him the universe and tells him how it is constituted. Macrobius was generally thought to be the author of the vision as well as of the commentary.*

Madde, *v.*, go mad, be furious.

Magicien, *n.*, magician. *F.*

Magik, Magyk, *n.*, magic. *O. F.* magique.

Maille, *n.*, mail, ringed armor. *F.*

Maister, *n.*, master. *O. F.* maistre.

Maisterful, *adj.*, masterful.

Maister-strete, *n.*, main street. *O. F.* maistre—*A. S.* stræt *f.*

Maistow, *v.*, *pron.*, *second pers. sing.*, *pres. indic.*, mayest thou. *See* **Mowe.**

Maistresse, *n.*, mistress. *O. F.*

Maistrye, *n.*, mastery, great skill, control, superiority. *O. F.* maistrie.

Make, *n.*, mate, equal. *A. S.* maca.

Make, *v.*, make, compose, cause, write. *A. S.* macian.

Makelees, *adj.*, peerless.

Making, s., composition. *A. S.* macian.

Maladye, n., malady. *F.* maladie.

Malapert, adj., forward. *O. F.*

Male, n., bag, wallet. *O. F.*

Malencolye, n., see **Melancolye.**

Malencolyk, adj., melancholy. *See* **Colera.**

Malle, Moll.

Malt, v., pret. sing., melted. *From* Melte. *A. S.* meltan.

Manace, n., menace, threat. *F.* menace.

Manace, v., threaten, *O. F.* menacier.

Maner, n., manor, place to dwell in. *O. F.* manoir.

Maner, n., see **Manere.**

Manere, n., manner, method, way. *A. F.* **Maner,** kind, sort (often used without of following, as in maner wight).

Manes: *shades of the dead. The idea that they are the 'gods of pain' is borrowed from Virgil, Æneid vi, 743.*

Manhede, n., manhood.

Mankynde, n., mankind. *See* **Kynde.**

Manly, adv., in a manly way.

Mannes, n., gen., man's. *A. S.* man.

Mansioun, n., dwelling, (astrologically) the position of a planet (see **Hous**). *O. F.* mansion.

Manslaughtre, n., manslaughter.

Mansuete, adj., courteous. *L.* mansuetus.

Mantel, n., mantle, cloak. *O. F.*

Mantelet, n., short mantle. *F.*

Manye, n., mania. *F.* manie.

Mapul, n., maple. *A. S.* mapul- (trēow).

Marbel, n., marble. *O. F.* marble.

Marbul-stones, n., plu., blocks of marble. *O. F.* marble— *A. S.* stān.

Marchant, n., merchant. *O. F.*

Marcia, Marsyas: *the satyr whom Apollo defeated in a trial of musical skill, and afterwards flayed alive. Chaucer found*

the name in Dante, and took it to be feminine.

Marcial, adj., pertaining to war, warlike. *F.* martial.

Marcian, Martianus Capella: *a satirist of the fifth century A. D. who wrote the* De Nuptiis inter Mercuriam et Philologiam, *a treatise on the Seven Liberal Arts with an allegorical setting.*

Mariage, n., marriage. *F.*

Maried, v., pret., caused to be married. *From* **Marie.** *F.* marier.

Mark, n., mark, image, race. *A. S.* mearc.

Mark, n., mark: *piece of money, of the value of 13s. 4d. A. S.* marc.

Markis, n., marquis. *O. F.*

Markisesse, n., marchioness.

Marte, Mars.

Martir, n., martyr. *A. S.* martyr.

Martirdom, n., martyrdom. *A. S.* martyr—dōm.

Martyre, n., martyrdom. *O. F.* martire.

Mary, n., marrow, pith. *A. S.* mearg.

Mary-bones, n., plu., marrowbones. *A. S.* mearg—bān.

Mase, n., maze, bewilderment.

Mased, p. p., bewildered, stunned.

Masednesse, n., amaze.

Masoneries, n., plu., masonry. *F.* maçonnerie.

Masse, n., mass, liturgy of the Eucharist. *A. S.* mæssc.

Massedayes, n., plu., massdays. *A. S.* mæssedæg.

Massinisse, Masinissa: *King of Numidia.*

Masty, adj., fattened (on mast).

Mat, adj., see **Maat.**

Matere, n., matter, affair, subject. *O. F.*

Maudelayne, (St.) **Magdalen.**

Maugre, Maugree, prep., in spite of. *O. F.* maugré.

Maunciple, n., manciple: *an officer who purchased victuals*

for an inn or college. O. F.
manciple.

May, *n.*, maiden. A. S. **mæg.**

Mayde, Mayden, *n.*, maid,
maiden. A. S. **mægden.**

Maydenhede, *n.*, maidenhood,
virginity.

Mayle, *n.*, *see* Maille.

Mayntene, *v.*, maintain. F.
maintenir.

Mayster-hunte, *n.*, chief huntsman. O. F. maistre—A. S.
hunta.

Maystow, *v.*, *pron.*, *second pers.
sing.*, *pres. indic.*, mayest thou.
See Mowe.

Mede, *n.*, mead, meadow. A. S.
mæd *f.*

Mede, *n.*, meed, reward, bribe.
A. S. **mēd** *f.*

Medle, *v.*, mingle, mix. O. F.
medler.

Medlee, *adj.*, medley, of a
mixed color. O. F.

Meel, *n.*, meal. A. S. **mæl.**

Meel-tyde, *n.*, meal-time. A. S.
mæl—**tīd** *f.*

Meeth, *n.*, *see* Meth.

Megera, Megæra: *one of the
Furies.*

Meke, *adj.*, meek.

Mekely, *adv.*, meekly.

Meknesse, *n.*, meekness.

Melancolious, *adj.*, melancholy.
O. F. melancolieus. *See* Melancolye.

Melancolye, *n.*, melancholy. O.
F. melancolie. *See* Colera.

Melodye, *n.*, melody. O. F.
melodie.

Membre, *n.*, limb, member. F.

Memoire, Memorie, *n.*, memory, remembrance, consciousness. O. F.

Mencioun, *n.*, mention. O. F.
mention.

Mene, *adj.*, mean, middle, in-
termediate. O. F. meiien.

Mene, *n.*, means, intermediary,
middle course, way. O. F.
meiien.

Mene, *v.*, mean, say, signify.
A. S. **mænan.**

Mennes, *n.*, *plu.*, *gen.*, men's.
A. S. man.

Menstralcyes, *n.*, *plu.*, min-
strelsies. A. F. menestralsie.

Mente, *v.*, *pret. see* Mene.

Mercenarie, *n.*, hireling. L.
mercenarius.

Mercenrike, *the kingdom of
Mercia.*

Merciable, *adj.*, merciful. O. F.

Mercy, *n.*, mercy. O. F. merci.
Graunt mercy, *see* Graunt.

Mere, *n.*, mare. A. S. **mēre.**

Meriely, *adv.*, merrily.

Merlioun, *n.*, merlin, small hawk.
O. F. esmerillon.

Mermayde, *n.*, mermaid. A. S.
mere—mægden.

Mervaille, Mervayle, Merveille,
n., marvel. O. F. merveille.

Merveillous, *adj.*, marvelous. O.
F. merveillos.

Merye, *adj.*, merry, gay, glad.
A. S. mirige.

Meryte, *n.*, merit, desert. O. F.

Meschaunce, *n.*, mischance, misfortune. O. F. mescheance.
With meschaunce, with bad
luck (*often as a curse:* bad
luck take him!)

Meschief, *n.*, mischief, misfortune, trouble. O. F.

Message, *n.*, message, errand;
messenger. O. F.

Messager, *n.*, messenger. O. F.
messagier.

Messagerye, *n.*, the sending of
messages. O. F. messagerie.

Messe-dayes, *n.*, *see* Massedayes.

Messenus, Misenus: *companion
and trumpeter to Æneas.*

Meste, *adj.*, *superl.*, most. A.
S. **mæst.**

Mester, *n.*, *see* Mister.

Mesurable, *adj.*, moderate. O.F.

Mesure, *n.*, moderation, measure. O. F.

Met, *v.*, *third. pers. sing.*, *pres.
indic.*, *see* Mete.

Mete, *adj.*, meet, fitting, suitable, equal. A. S. **mæte.**

Mete, *n.*, meat, food. A. S. mete.

Mete, v., meet. *A. S.* **mētan.**

Mete, v., dream. *A. S.* **mǣtan.**

Meth, n., mead: *the drink. A. S.* **meodu;** *O. N.* **miǫðr.**

Meting, s., dream. *See* **Mete.** The kinges meting Pharao, the dream of King Pharaoh.

Mette, v., *pret. see* **Mete.**

Meve, v., move, stir. *O. F.* **movoir.**

Mewe, n., mew: *coop used for fattening fowls or for hawks while molting. F.* **mue.**

Mewet, *adj.*, mute. *O. F.* **muët.**

Meynee, n., household, retinue, company. *O. F.* **meisnee.**

Michelmesse, Michaelmas: *feast of St. Michael, the 29th of September.*

Middelburgh, Middelburg *in Holland.*

Might, n., might, power. *A. S.* **miht.**

Mighte, v., *pret., see* **Mowe.**

Mille, n., mill. *A. S.* **mylen.**

Millere, n., miller.

Minde, n., remembrance, memory, mind. *A. S.* **gemynd** *f.*

Ministres, n., *plu.*, officers. *F.* **ministre.**

Minne, v., *imper. sing.*, remember, mention. *A. S.* **gemynnan.**

Minstralcye, n., minstrelsy. *See* **Menstralcyes.**

Mirour, n., mirror. *O. F.*

Mirre, n., myrrh. *O. F.*

Mirthe, n., mirth, pleasure, joy. *A. S.* **myrhð** *f.*

Mirtheles, *adj.*, without mirth, sad.

Mis, *adj., adv.*, wrong, amiss.

Misacounted, *p. p.*, miscounted.

Misaunter, n., misadventure, misfortune. *O. F.* **mesaventure.**

Misboden, *p. p.*, offered to do evil, insulted. *A. S.* **misbēodan.**

Miscarie, v., go amiss. *O. F.* **mes—carier.**

Mischaunce, n., *see* **Meschaunce.**

Misdeme, v., misjudge. *A. S.* **mis—dēman.**

Misericorde, n., mercy, pity. *O. F.*

Miserie, n., misery. *O. F.*

Misfille, v., *pret.*, went amiss. *From* **Misfalle.** *A. S.* **mis— feallan.**

Misforyaf, v., *pret. sing.*, misgave. *From* **Misforyive.** *See* **Yive.**

Mishappe, v., happen ill, meet with misfortune.

Mislyved, *p. p.*, of ill life. *A. S.* **mis—libban.**

Mis-sat, v., *pret. sing.*, was not where it should be, misbecame. *From* **Mis-sitte.** *See* **Sitte.**

Misse, v., miss, fail, lack. *A. S.* **missan.**

Mistake, v., transgress, trespass, commit an error. *O. N.* **mistaka.**

Mister, n., trade, handicraft, occupation. *O. F.* **mester.** *See* **Mester. What mister men,** what sort of men *(of what trade).*

Mistriste, v., mistrust.

Miswent, *p. p.*, gone amiss. *From* **Miswende.** *A. S.* **mis— wendan.**

Miteyn, n., mitten, glove. *F.* **mitaine.**

Mo, *adj., compar.*, more, others. *A. S.* **mā.**

Mo, *adv., compar.*, more, longer. *A. S.* **mā.**

Moche, Mochel, *adj.*, much, great. *A. S.* **mycel.** *See* **Muchel.**

Mochel, *adv.*, much.

Mochel, n., size.

Moder, n., mother. *A. S.* **mōdor.**

Moeble, n., movable goods, personal property. *O. F.*

Moever, n., mover.

Moiste, *adj.*, moist, supple. *O. F. See* **Moyste.**

Molte, *p. p.*, molten, melted. *From* **Melte.** *A. S.* **meltan.**

Monche, v., munch.

Mone, n., moon. *A. S.* **mōna.**

Mone, n., moan, complaint.

Monesteo, Mnestheus.

Moneye, *n.*, money. *O. F.* moneie.

Monstre, *n.*, monster. *F.*

Month, *n.*, month. *A. S.* mōnaŏ.

Mooder, *n.*, see Moder.

Moorninge, *s.*, mourning, plaint. *A. S.* murnan.

Moot, *n.*, *plu.*, notes on a horn. *O. F.* mōt.

Moot, *v.*, *pres. sing.*, may, must, shall. *A. S.* mōt.

Moralitee, *n.*, morality, moral. *F.* moralité.

Mordre, *n.*, murder. *A. S.* morŏor; *O. F.* murdre.

Mordre, *v.*, murder. *A. S.* myrŏrian; *cf. M. E. n.* mordre.

Mordrer, *n.*, murderer. *Cf. M. E. n.* mordre; *A. F.* mordreour.

More, *adj.*, *compar.*, greater, larger, more. *A. S.* māra.

More, *adv.*, more, further.

More, *n.*, root. *A. S.* moru.

Mormal, *n.*, sore, ulcer. *O. F.* mortmal.

Morne, *n.*, morning. *A. S.* morgen. Morne-milk, morning milk.

Morter, *n.*, mortar, night-light. *A. S.* mortere.

Mortreux, *n.*, pottage, thick soup. *O. F.*

Morwe, Morwen, *n.*, morning, morrow. *A. S.* morgen.

Morweninge, *n.*, morning.

Morwe-song, *n.*, morning-song. *A. S.* morgen—song.

Morwe-tyde, *n.*, morning hour. *A. S.* morgen—tīd *f.*

Mosel, *n.*, muzzle. *O. F.* musel.

Moste, *v.*, *pret.*, see Moot.

Moste, *adv.*, *superl.*, greatest. *A. S.* mǣst. See Mo.

Mot, *n.*, atom, particle. *A. S.*

Mottelee, *n.*, motley, motley array.

Motthes, *n.*, *plu.*, moths. *A. S.* moþþe.

Mountance, Mountaunce, *n.*, amount, value, quantity. *O. F.* montance.

Mous, *n.*, mouse. *A. S.* mūs.

Moustre, *n.*, pattern. *O. F.*

Mowe, *n.*, grimace. *O. F.* moe.

Mowe, *v.*, be able, may. *A. S.* magan.

Moyste, *adj.*, moist, fresh. *O. F.* moiste. See Moiste.

Muchel, *adj.*, much, great. *A. S.* mycel. See Moche, Mochel.

Muchel, *adv.*, greatly.

Multiplicacioun, *n.*, multiplication, multiplying: *the art of alchemy. F.* multiplication.

Multiplying, *s.*, increase. *F.* multiplier.

Murmour, *n.*, murmur. *F.* murmure.

Murthe, *n.*, see Mirthe.

Murye, *adj.*, see Merye.

Muse, *v.*, consider, gaze. *O. F.* muser.

Musyke, *n.*, music. *F.* musique.

Muwe, *n.*, see Mewe.

Muwe, *v.*, change. *O. F.* muer.

Myle, *n.*, mile. *A. S.* mīl *f.*

Myn, *pron.*, mine. *A. S.* mīn.

Mynde, *n.*, see Minde.

Myne, *v.*, undermine, mine. *F.* miner.

Mynos, Minos.

Myre, *n.*, mire. *O. N.* mȳrr *f.*

Myrie, *adj.*, see Merye.

Myrra, Myrrha: *daughter of the King of Cyprus, who was changed into a myrrh-tree, Ovid,* Metam., *x, 298.*

Myselven, *pron.*, myself.

Myte, *n.*, mite, thing of no value. *O. F.* mite.

Myte, *n.*, mite: *insect. A. S.* mite.

N

Nabugodonosor, Nebuchadnezzar.

Nacheveth, ne — acheveth, achieves not. —*O. F.* achever.

Naciouns, *n.*, *plu.*, nations. *F.* nation.

Naille, *v.*, nail. *A. S.* nǣglan.

Nakednesse, *n.*, nakedness.

Nakers, *n.*, *plu.*, kettle-drums. *O. F.* nacre.

Name, *n.,* name, reputation, fame. *A. S.* **nama.**

Namely, *adv.,* especially.

Namo, na—mo, *adv.,* no more. *See* **Mo.**

Namore, *adv.,* no more. *See* **More.**

Napoplexye, ne—apoplexye, nor apoplexy. —*F.* apoplexie.

Narette, ne—arette, *see* **Arette.**

Narwe, *adj.,* narrow, close. *A. S.* **nearu.**

Narwe, *adv.,* narrowly, closely. *A. S.* **nearwe.**

Nas, ne—was.

Nassayeth, ne—assayeth, attempts not. —*O. F.* essaier.

Nat, *adv.,* not.

Natal, *adj.,* one who presides over nativities. *L.* **natalis.**

Nath, ne—hath.

Nathelees, *adv.,* nevertheless.

Nativitee, *n.,* nativity, birth. *O. F.* nativité.

Naturel, *adj.,* natural. *O. F.*

Natyf, *adj.,* native. *O. F.* natif.

Navele, *n.,* navel. *A. S.* **nafela.**

Navye, *n.,* navy. *O. F.* navie.

Naxe, ne—axe, *see* **Axe.**

Nay, *adv.,* nay, no. *O. N.* **nei.** Hit is **no nay,** there is no denying it.

Nayl, *n.,* nail. *A. S.* **nægl.**

Ne, *adv., conj.,* not, nor. *A. S.* **ne. Ne ... ne,** neither ... nor.

Nece, *n.,* niece. *O. F.* niéce.

Necessitee, *n.,* necessity. *O. F.* necessité.

Necgligence, *n.,* negligence. *O. F.* negligence.

Nede, *n.,* need, extremity, peril. *A. S.* **nēd** *f.*

Nede, *adv.,* necessarily.

Nedelees, *adv.,* needless.

Nedely, *adv.,* of necessity, necessarily.

Nedes, *adv.,* of necessity, necessarily, needs.

Nedes-cost, *adv.,* of necessity.

Neer, *adv., compar.,* nearer, (*as positive*) near. *A. S.* **nēar.**

Neet, *n., plu.,* neat, cattle. *A. S.* **nēat.**

Negh, Neigh, *adv.,* nearly, almost. *A. S.* **nēah.**

Neighe, *v.,* draw near.

Neighebour, *n.,* neighbour. *A. S.* nēahgebūr.

Nekke, *n.,* neck. *A. S.* **hnecca.**

Nekke-boon, *n.,* neck-bone. *A. S.* hnecca—bān.

Nempne, *v.,* name, tell. *A. S.* nemnan.

Ner, *adv., compar., see* **Neer.**

Nercotikes, *n., plu.,* narcotics. *F.* narcotique.

Nere, ne—were.

Nerf, *n.,* sinew. *O. F.*

Nevene, *v.,* name. *O. N.* nefna.

Nevere, *adv.,* never. *A. S.* næfre.

Nevere-a-del, *adv.,* not a bit.

Nevere-mo, *adv.,* never oftener, never, never again.

Nevere-the-lasse, *adv.,* nevertheless.

Nevew, *n.,* nephew, grandson. *A. F.* nevu.

Newe, *adj.,* new, fresh. *A. S.* nēowe.

Newe, *adv.,* newly, freshly. *A. S.* nīwe.

Newe, *v.,* renew. *A. S.* nīwian.

Nexte, *adj., superl.,* nearest, next, last. *A. S.* nēhst.

Ney, *adv., see* **Neigh.**

Ncyghcbores, *n., plu., see* **Neighebour.**

Nigard, *n.,* miser, niggard.

Nighte, *v.,* grow dark, become night.

Nightertale, *n.,* night-time.

Nil, Nille, *v., first pers. sing., pres. indic.,* will not, shall not. *A. S.* nyllan.

Nis, ne—is.

Niste, *v., pret., see* **Noot.**

Nisus doughter: Scylla, *who was changed into a lark. See* Ovid, Metam. *viii, 9–151.*

Noble, *n.,* noble: *gold coin worth 6s. 8d.*

Noblesse, *n.,* nobleness, nobility. *O. F.* noblece.

Nobleye, *n.,* nobility, dignity. *O. F.* nobleie.

Nof, *conj.*, *prep.*, nor of.

Noght, *adv.*, not, by no means. *A. S.* nāwiht.

Noght, *n.*, nothing. *A. S.* nā-wiht.

Nolde, *v.*, *pret.*, *see* Nil.

Nombre, *n.*, number. *O. F.*

Nombred, *p. p.*, *see* Noumbre.

Nome, *p. p.*, taken. *From* Nime. *A. S.* niman. *Cf.* Y-nome.

Non, *pron.*, *see* Noon.

Nones, nonce. For the nones, for the occasion. *M. E.* for then anes; *A. S.* for ðām ānes.

Nonne, *n.*, nun. *A. S.* nunne.

Noon, *pron.*, none, no. *A. S.* nān.

Noot, *v.*, *first pers. sing.*, *pres. indic.*, know not. *A. S.* nāt.

Norice, *n.*, nurse. *O. F.*

Norished, *p. p.*, nourished, brought up. *O. F.* norir.

Norissing, *n.*, nutriment.

Northfolk, Norfolk.

Northren, *adj.*, northern. *A. S.* norþerne.

Nose-thirles, *n.*, *plu.*, nostrils. *A. S.* nosþyrl.

Noskinnes, *for* Noneskinnes, of no kind.

Nost, Nostow, *v.*, *second pers. sing.*, *pres. indic.*, knowest not, knowest thou not. *See* Noot.

Not, *v.*, *see* Noot.

Notabilitee, *n.*, notable fact. *O. F.* notabilité.

Notable, *adj.*, notorious, remarkable. *F.*

Note, *n.*, musical note, tune. *F.*

Not-heed, *n.*, head with hair cropped short.

Nother, *conj.*, neither.

Nothing, *adv.*, in no respect.

Nouchis, *n.*, *plu.*, jewelled ornaments. *O. F.* nouche.

Nought, *adv.*, *see* Noght.

Noumbre, *n.*, *see* Nombre.

Noumbre, *v.*, number, count. *O. F.* nombrer.

Nouthe, *adv.*, now then, now. *A. S.* nū ðā.

Novelrye, *n.*, novelty. *O. F.* novelerie.

Noveltee, *n.*, novelty. *O. F.* noveltê.

Nowher, *adv.*, nowhere. *A. S.* nāhwǣr.

Noyous, *adj.*, troublesome. *O. F.* enuius.

Noyse, *n.*, noise. *O. F.*

Ny, *adv.*, nigh, nearly. *See* Negh, Neigh.

Nyce, *adj.*, foolish, ignorant, finicky. *O. F.* nice.

Nycely, *adv.*, foolishly.

Nycete, Nycetee, *n.*, folly, simplicity, scrupulousness. *O. F.* nicetê.

Nyne, *adj.*, nine. *A. S.* nigon.

Nynthe, *adj.*, ninth.

O

O, *adj.*, one. *A. S.* ān. *See* On, Oo, Oon.

Obeisant, *adj.*, obedient. *O. F.* obéissant.

Obeisaunce, *n.*, obedience. *O. F.* obéissance.

Observaunce, *n.*, respect, homage, ceremony. *O. F.* observance.

Obstinat, *adj.*, obstinate. *L.* obstinatus.

Octovien, Octavian.

Of, *prep.*, of, off; *adv.*, off, away. *A. S.* of.

Of-caste, *v.*, cast off. *A. S.* of—*O. N.* kasta.

Offende, *v.*, assail, injure. *O. F.* offendre.

Offensioun, *n.*, offense, damage. *O. F.* offension.

Offertorie, *n.*, offertory. *L.* offertorium.

Officere, *n.*, officer. *F.* officier.

Of-newe, *adv.*, newly, again, lately. *A. S.* of—niwe.

Of-spring, *n.*, offspring. *A. S.*

Of-taken, *p. p.*, taken off, taken away. *A. S.* of—tacan.

Ofte, *adv.*, often. *A. S.* oft.

Of-thowed, *p. p.*, thawed away.

Oght, *n.*, aught, anything; *adv.*, aught, at all. *A. S.* āwiht.

Oghte, *v.*, *pret.*, *impers.*, *see* Owe.

Oille, *n.*, oil. *O. F.*

Oise: *a river which flows into the Seine from the north not far below Paris.*

Oistre, *n.*, oyster. *O. F.*

Old, *adj.*, old. *A. S.* eald.

Oliver: *the friend of Roland in the* Chanson de Roland.

Olyve, *n.*, olive-tree. *O. F.* olive.

Omeer, Homer.

On, *adj., see* Oon.

Ones, *adv.*, once, of one, united. *A. S.* ānes.

On-lofte, *adv.*, aloft, up in the air.

On-lyve, *adv.*, alive. *A. S.* on life. *See* A-lyve.

Oo, *adj., see* O.

Ook, *n.*, oak. *A. S.* āc.

Oon, *adj.*, one. *A. S.* ān. *See* O, On, Oo. Oon the faireste, one of the fairest. Evere in oon, ever alike. Oon and oon, one by one. After oon, after one standard. Many oon, many a one.

Ooth, *n.*, oath. *A. S.* āð.

Opie, *n.*, opium. *L.* opium.

Opinioun, *n.*, opinion. *O. F.* opinion.

Opposit, *n.*, opposite point. *O. F.*

Or, *conj., prep.*, ere, before. *A. S.* ær. *See* Er.

Oratorie, *n.*, oratory: *room for prayers. L.* oratorium.

Ordenaunce, *n.*, ordinance, provision, plan. *O. F.* ordenance.

Ordeyne, *v.*, determine. *O. F.* ordener. Ordeynè, *p. p.*, regulated.

Ordinaunce, *n., see* Ordenaunce.

Ordre, *n.*, order, law, religious order. *O. F.* Ordres foure, the four orders: *Augustinian Dominican, Franciscan, and Carmelite Friars*

Orewelle, Orwell: *the name of an English port in Chaucer's day, now Harwich.*

Orgon, *n.*, organ. *L.* organum.

Orient, *n.*, east. *F.*

Original, *n.*, cause. *O. F.*

Orion, Arion: *the harper, see Ovid,* Fasti, *ii, 79–118.*

Orisonte, *n.*, horizon. *O. F.* orizonte.

Orisoun, *n.*, prayer. *O. F.* orison.

Orloge, *n.*, clock. *F.* horloge.

Ost, *n.*, host, army. *O. F.*

Otes, *n., plu.*, oats. *A. S.* āte.

Other, *conj.*, either, or.

Oughte, *v., pret. impers., see* Owe.

Oule, *n.*, owl. *A. S.* ūle.

Ounces, *n., plu.*, small portions. *O. F.* unce.

Ounded, *p. p.*, wavy. *F.* ondé.

Oundy, *adj.*, wavy. *F.* ondé.

Oure, *pron.*, ours. *A. S.* ūre.

Out of, *prep.*, without.

Out-breste, *v.*, burst out. *See* Breste.

Out-bringe, *v.*, bring out, utter. *A. S.* ūt—bringan.

Out-caughte, *v., pret.*, caught out, drew out. *See* Cacche.

Out-drawe, *p. p.*, drawn out. *A. S.* ūt—dragan.

Oute, *adv.*, out. *A. S.* ūte.

Outerly, *adv.*, utterly.

Outfleyinge, *s.*, flying out. *See* Flee.

Out-hees, *n.*, hue and cry, outcry. *A. S.* ūt—hǣs.

Outher, *conj.*, either, or.

Outraye, *v.*, be outrageous, incur disgrace, lose temper. *O. F.* outreier.

Outrely, *adv., see* Outerly.

Out-rood, *v., pret. sing.*, rode out. *See* Ryde.

Out-ryder, *n.*, rider abroad: *an officer of a monastery, whose duty it was to look after the outlying manors belonging to it.*

Out-springe, *v.*, spring abroad, come to light. *A. S.* ūt—springan.

Out-sterte, *v., pret. plu.*, started out. *See* Sterte.

Out-wende, *v.*, come out, proceed. *See* Wende.

Over-al, *adv.*, everywhere.

Over-goon, *v.*, pass away. *See* Goon.

Over-loked, *p. p.,* looked over, perused. *See* **Loke.**

Over-raughte, *v., pret.,* reached over: *so* urged on. *See* **Reche.**

Over-riden, *p. p.,* ridden over. *See* **Ryde.**

Over-shake, *p. p.,* caused to pass away, shaken off. *A. S.* ofer—scacan.

Overshote, *p. p.,* overrun the scent. *From* **Overshete.** *A. S.* ofer—scēotan.

Over-sprat, *v., pres. sing.,* see **Oversprede.**

Oversprede, *v.,* spread over, cover. *A. S.* ofer—sprǣdan.

Overt, *adj.,* open. *O. F.*

Overthwart, Overthwert, *adv.,* across. *A. S.* ofer—*O. N.* þvert.

Ovyde, Ovid.

Owe, *v.,* own, owe, possess; ought; (*refl.*) be incumbent. **Oghte, Oughte,** *pret., impers.,* be necessary, was necessary. *A. S.* āgan.

Owene, *adj.,* own. *A. S.* agen (*p. p.*).

Owher, *adv.,* anywhere. *A. S.* āhwǣr.

Owle, *n., see* **Oule.**

Oxe, *n.,* ox. *A. S.* oxa.

Oxenford, Oxford.

Oxe-stalle, *n.,* ox-stall. *A. S.* oxa—steall.

Oynement, *n.,* ointment. *O. F.* oignement.

Oynons, *n., plu.,* onions. *F.* oignon.

P

Paas, *n., see* **Pas.**

Pace, *v.,* pass, go, surpass. *O. F.* passer. *See* **Passe.**

Pacience, *n.,* patience. *O. F.*

Pacient, *adj.,* patient. *O. F.*

Pacient, *n.,* patient. *O. F.*

Paillet, *n.,* pallet. *F.*

Paine, *n., see* **Peyne.**

Paire, *n.,* pair. *O. F.* pair.

Palatye, Palathia: *in Asia Minor.*

Pale, *n.,* perpendicular stripe. *F.* pal.

Palestral, *adj.,* athletic.

Paleys, *n.,* palace. *O. F.* paleis.

Palfrey, *n.,* palfrey, horse. *O. F.* palefrei.

Palladion, Palladium: *an image of Pallas Athena, particularly that at Troy.*

Pan, *n.,* brain-pan, skull. *A. S.* panne.

Paniers, *n., plu.,* panniers, baskets for bread. *F.* panier.

Papir, *n.,* paper. *A. F.*

Par amour, *see* **Paramour.**

Par cas, by chance. *See* **Cas.**

Paradys, *n.,* paradise. *F.* paradis.

Paramour, by way of secular love, for love, with devotion.

Paraunter, Paraventure, peradventure, perhaps.

Pardee, *interj., a common oath. O. F.* par dé.

Pardieux, *interj., see* **Pardee.**

Pardoneer, *n.,* pardoner, seller of indulgences. *O. F.* pardonier.

Pardoun, *n.,* pardon. *O. F.* pardun.

Parfey, *interj.,* by my faith. *A. F.* par fei.

Parfit, *adj.,* perfect. *O. F.*

Parfitly, *adv.,* perfectly.

Parfourne, *v.,* perform, fulfill. *O. F.* parfournir.

Parisshe, *n.,* parish. *O. F.* paroisse.

Parisshens, *n., plu.,* parishioners. *O. F.* paroissien.

Parlement, *n.,* deliberation, parliament. *O. F.*

Parnaso, Parnassus.

Parodie, *n.,* period, duration. *O. F.* periode.

Part, *n.,* part, party, side. *O. F.*

Parte, *v.,* participate in, share, depart. *O. F.* partir.

Particuler, *adj.,* special. *F.* particulier.

Partrich, *n.,* partridge. *O. F.* perdriz.

Party, *adj.,* partly. *O. F.* parti.

Partye, *n.,* portion, part, side, taker of a side. *O. F.* partie.

Parvys, *n.*, church-porch. *F.* parvis.

Pas, *n.*, pace, step, distance. *F.*

Passant, *pres. partic.*, *as adj.*, surpassing. *F.*

Passe, *v.*, surpass, exceed, pass. *See* Pace.

Passioun, *n.*, passion, suffering. *F.* passion.

Patente, *n.*, patent, a letter of privilege: *so-called because open to inspection.*

Patriarkes, *n.*, *plu.*, patriarchs. *O. F.* patriarke.

Patron, *n.*, patron, pattern. *F.*

Paunche, *n.*, paunch. *O. F.* panche.

Pawmes, *n.*, *plu.*, palms. *F.* paume.

Pay, *n.*, pleasure. *O. F.* paie.

Paye, *v.*, pay, satisfy. *O. F.* paier.

Payen, *adj.*, pagan. *O. F.* paien.

Payre, *n.*, *see* Paire.

Pece, *n.*, piece. *O. F.*

Pecok, *n.*, peacock. *A. S.* pāwa—coc.

Peer, *n.*, peer, equal. *O. F.* per. *See* Pere.

Pees, *n.*, peace. *O. F.* pais.

Peire, *n.*, *see* Paire.

Pekke, *v.*, peck, pick.

Pel, *n.*, peel, small castle. *O. F.* pel.

Pelet, *n.*, pellet, stone cannon-ball. *F.* pelote.

Pemond, Piedmont.

Penalopee, Penelope.

Penaunce, *n.*, penance, suffering. *O. F.* penance.

Pencel, *n.*, pencil, brush. *O. F.* pincel.

Pencel, *n.*, small banner. *O. F.* penoncel.

Penneus, Peneus.

Penoun, *n.*, pennon: *small flag borne at the end of a lance.* *O. F.* penon.

Pens, *n.*, *plu.*, pence.

Peple, *n.*, people. *O. F.* pueple.

Peraventure, *adv.*, *see* Paraunter, Paraventure.

Perce, *v.*, pierce. *O. F.* percier.

Perchaunce, *adv.*, by chance. *O. F.* per—cheance.

Perche, *n.*, perch (*for birds*). *O. F.*

Pere, *n.*, peer, equal. *O. F.* per. *See* Peer.

Perle, *n.*, pearl. *F.*

Permutacioun, *n.*, change. *O. F.* permutacion.

Perotheus, Pirithous.

Perpetuelly, *adv.*, perpetually.

Perre, Perrie, Perrye, *n.*, jewellry. *O. F.* pierrie.

Pers, *n.*, stuff of a sky-blue color. *O. F.*

Perseveraunce, *n.*, endurance, constancy. *O. F.* perseverance.

Persone, Persoune, *n.*, person, figure, parson. *O. F.* persone.

Persuasioun, *n.*, persuasion, belief. *F.* persuasion.

Pertourbe, *v.*, perturb. *O. F.* pertourber.

Pervers, *adj.*, perverse. *F.*

Peter, *interj.*, by St. Peter!

Peyne, *n.*, pain, grief, trouble. *O. F.* peine. Dyen in the peyne, to die by torture.

Peyne, *v.*, take pains, endeavor. *O. F.* pener.

Peynte, *v.*, paint. *O. F.* peindre.

Peyntour, *n.*, painter. *O. F.* peintor.

Peyre, *n.*, *see* Paire.

Pharao, Pharo, Pharoah.

Pheton, Phæthon.

Phillis, Phyllis.

Philosophre, *n.*, philosopher. *F.* philosophe.

Philosophye, *n.*, philosophy. *O. F.* filosofie.

Phisicien, *n.*, physician. *O. F.* physicien.

Phisik, *n.*, physic, medicine. *O. F.* phisique.

Phisiologus: *a Latin collection of allegorical accounts of various animals.*

Phitonesses, *n.*, *plu.*, pythonesses, witches. *O. F.* phitonise.

Pietee, *n.*, pity. *O. F.* piete.

Pietous, *adj.*, piteous, sad. *O. F.* pietos. *See* Pitous.

Pigges, *n.*, *gen.*, pig's.

Pighte, *v.*, *pret.*, pitched.

Piled, *p. p.*, deprived of hair, bare, thin (beard). *A. S.* pylian.

Pileer, Piler, *n.*, pillar, column. *O. F.* piler.

Pilour, *n.*, robber, pillager. *O. F.* pilleur.

Pilwe, *n.*, pillow. *A. S.* pyle.

Pilwe-beer, *n.*, pillow-case.

Pinacles, *n.*, *plu.*, pinnacles. *O. F.*

Pinche, *v.*, find fault with, plait. *O. F.* (pincier).

Piper, *n.*, suitable for pipes.

Piramus, Pyramus.

Pirous, Pyroeis: *a horse in the chariot of the sun.*

Pirrus, Pyrrhus.

Pistel, *n.*, epistle, message. *A. S.* pistol.

Pitaunce, *n.*, pittance. *O. F.* pitance.

Pite, Pitee, *n.*, pity. *O. F.*

Pitous, *adj.*, piteous, compassionate. *O. F.* pitos. See **Pietous.**

Pitously, *adv.*, piteously, sadly.

Plane, *n.*, plane. *O. F.* plasne.

Planete, *n.*, planet. *O. F.*

Plante, *n.*, slip, cutting. *A. S.*

Plat, *adj.*, flat, certain; *adv.*, flat, bluntly. *F.* plat.

Platly, *adv.*, flatly, plainly.

Playn, *adj.*, *see* **Pleyn.**

Pleding, *s.*, pleading.

Plee, *n.*, plea, pleading. *O. F.* plait.

Plentee, *n.*, plenitude, fulness. *O. F.* plenté.

Plentevous, *adj.*, plenteous. *O. F.*

Plesaunce, *n.*, pleasure, pleasant thing, delight. *O. F.* plaisance.

Plesaunt, *adj.*, pleasant, agreeable. *O. F.* pleisant.

Plese, *v.*, please. *O. F.* plaisir.

Plete, *v.*, plead, argue. *O. F.* plaitier.

Pleting, *s.*, pleading, argument.

Pley, *n.*, play, sport. *A. S.* plega.

Pleye, *v.*, play, amuse oneself. *A. S.* plegian.

Pleyinge, *s.*, amusement, sport. *A. S.* plegian.

Pleyn, *adj.*, full, complete; *adv.*, fully. *F.* plein.

Pleyn, *adj.*, plain, clear; *adv.*, plainly, clearly. *O. F.* plain.

Pleyne, *v.*, complain, lament. *F.* plaindre.

Pleynly, *adv.*, plainly, openly; fully.

Pleynte of Kynde: *the* De Planctu Naturæ *by Alanus de Insulis.* *O. F.* plainte. See **Aleyn.**

Plighte, *v.*, *pret.*, plucked, pulled. *A. S.* plyccan.

Plighte, *v.*, *pret.*, plighted, pledged. *A. S.* plihtan.

Plukke, *v.*, pluck, pull. *A. S.* pluccian.

Plye, *v.*, ply, bend. *O. F.* plier.

Plyght, *p. p.*, plighted. See **Plighte.**

Plyt, *n.*, plight, condition, mishap. *O. F.* ploit.

Plyte, *v.*, fold.

Poete, *n.*, poet. *O. F.* poëte.

Poetrye, *n.*, poetry. *O. F.* poëtrie.

Point devys, with great neatness, exactly.

Pokkes, *n.*, *plu.*, pocks, pustules. *A. S.* poc.

Polcat, *n.*, polecat. —*A. S.* cat.

Policye, *n.*, public business. *O. F.* policie.

Polite, *see* **Polyte.**

Polixena, Polixene, Polyxena: *daughter of Priam.*

Pollax, *n.*, pole-axe.

Polynestor, Polymnestor.

Polyte, Polites.

Pomel, *n.*, round part, top. *O. F.* pomel.

Pomely, *adj.*, dappled. *O. F.* pomelé.

Pompe, *n.*, pomp. *F.* pompe.

Pompee, Pompey.

Popet, *n.*, puppet, doll. *O. F.* poupette.

Popinjay, *n.*, popinjay. *O. F.* papegai.

Popler, *n.,* poplar-tree. *O. F.* **poplier.**

Poraille, *n.,* poor people. *O. F.* **povraille.**

Port, *n.,* carriage, behavior, bearing. *F.* **port.**

Portreiture, *n.,* drawing, picture. *O. F.* **portraiture.**

Portreye, *v.,* portray, depict. *O. F.* **portraire.**

Pose, *v.,* suppose, put the case. *F.* **poser.**

Positif, *adj.,* positive, fixed. *O. F.*

Possibilitee, *n.,* possibility. *F.* **possibilité.**

Potage, *n.,* broth. *F.*

Potente, *n.,* staff, crutch.

Pothecarie, *n.,* apothecary. *O. F.* **apotecaire.**

Pouche, *n.,* pouch, pocket. *O. F.* **poche.**

Poudre, *n.,* powder, dust. *O. F.* **poldre.**

Poudre-marchant, *n., a kind of spice. O. F.* **poldre—marchant.**

Poun, *n.,* pawn (*at chess*). *O. F.* **paon.**

Pound, *n., plu.,* pounds. *A. S.* **pund.**

Poupe, *v.,* blow, puff.

Poure, *v.,* pore, gaze steadily.

Pous, *n.,* pulse. *O. F.*

Poverte, *n.,* poverty. *O. F.*

Povertee, *n.,* poverty. *O. F.* **poverté.**

Povre, *adj.,* poor. *O. F.*

Povreliche, *adj.,* poorly, in poverty.

Povrely, *adv.,* in poor array.

Povrest, *adj., superl.,* poorest. *See* **Povre.**

Poynaunt, *adj.,* pungent. *O. F.* **poignant.**

Poynt, *n.,* point, aim. *O. F.* **point.**

Poynte, *v.,* describe. *O. F.* **pointier.**

Practisour, *n.,* practitioner.

Praunce, *v.,* prance, run about.

Prayere, *n.,* prayer. *O. F.* **preiere.**

Preche, *v.,* preach. *O. F.* **prechier.**

Precious, *adj.,* precious, prudish, dainty. *O. F.* **precios.**

Predestinee, *n.,* predestination. *F.*

Predicacioun, *n.,* preaching, sermon. *O. F.* **predicaciun.**

Preef, *n.,* proof. *O. F.* **prueve.**

Prees, *n.,* press, throng. *O. F.* **presse.** *See* **Press.**

Preest, *n.,* priest. *A. S.* **prēost.**

Preise, *v.,* praise, esteem. *O. F.* **preisier.**

Prelat, *n.,* prelate. *O. F.*

Prescience, *n.,* foreknowledge. *F.*

Present, *adv.,* immediately. *O. F.*

Preson, *n.,* prison. *O. F.*

Press, *n.,* throng, press, mould. *O. F.* **presse.** *See* **Prees. On presse,** in a suppressed state.

Prest, *n., see* **Preest.**

Prest, *adj.,* ready, prepared, prompt. *O. F.*

Presumpcioun, *n.,* presumption. *O. F.* **presomption.**

Pretende, *v.,* attempt to reach, seek (after). *F.* **prétendre.**

Preve, *n.,* proof, experience. *O. F.* **prueve.** *See* **Preef.**

Preve, *v.,* prove, test, approve, show. *O. F.* **prover.**

Prevetee, *n.,* secret place, recess. *O. F.* **priveté.** *See* **Privetee.**

Prevy, *adj.,* privy, secret. *O. F.* **privé.** *See* **Privee.**

Preye, *n.,* prey. *A. F.* **preie.**

Preye, *v.,* pray, beseech. *O. F.* **preier.**

Preyere, *n., see* **Prayere.**

Preyse, *v., see* **Preise.**

Priamus, Priam.

Priapus: *the god of fruitfulness; for the episode see Ovid,* Fasti, *i, 415.*

Pricasour, *n.,* a hard rider.

Prike, *v.,* spur, incite, urge, ride. *A. S.* **prician.**

Priking, *s.,* hard riding.

Prikke, *n.,* point, stab. *A. S.* **pricca.**

Princesse, *n.*, princess. *F.*

Prioresse, *n.*, prioress. *O. F.*

Pris, *n.*, *see* Prys.

Prisoun, *n.*, prison. *F.* prison.

Privee, *adj.*, secret, private, intimate. *O. F.* privé. *See* Prevy.

Privee, *n.*, privy.

Prively, *adv.*, secretly.

Privetee, *n.*, privacy, secrets, private affairs. *O. F.* priveté. *See* Prevetee.

Procede, *v.*, proceed. *F.* procéder.

Proces, *n.*, process, course. *O. F.*

Profre, *v.*, proffer, offer. *A. F.*

Proheme, *n.*, proem, prologue. *O. F.*

Proignè, Procne.

Prolixitee, *n.*, prolixity. *F.* prolixité.

Prologe, *n.*, prologue. *O. F.*

Pronounce, *v.*, announce, pronounce. *O. F.* prononcier.

Prophesye, *n.*, prophecy. *O. F.* profecie.

Propre, *adj.*, proper, own, comely. *O. F.*

Proprely, *adv.*, fitly, properly.

Propretee, *n.*, peculiarity, specialty, property. *O. F.* propreté.

Proserpyne, Proserpine.

Proteccioun, *n.*, protection. *O. F.* protection.

Protestacioun, *n.*, protest. *F.* protestation.

Proverbe, *n.*, proverb. *O. F.*

Prow, *n.*, profit, advantage. *O. F.* prou.

Prowesse, *n.*, prowess, valor. *O. F.* proece.

Pruce, Pruyse, Prussia, Prussian.

Pryamus, Priam.

Pryde, *n.*, pride. *A. S.* prȳte.

Prydeles, *adj.*, without pride.

Pryme, *n.*, prime (*of day*): six to nine a. m. *A. S.* prim; *O. F.* prime. Half way pryme: *half-past seven.*

Prymer, *n.*, primer. *O. F.* primier.

Prys, *n.*, price, value, praise, esteem, glory. *O. F.* pris.

Pryvee, *adj.*, *see* Privee.

Pseustis: *unidentified, but perhaps Thespis of Attica whose plays were acted at Athens* (*Skeat*).

Publiced, Publisshed, *p. p.*, proclaimed, published. *O. F.* publier.

Puella: *a figure in geomancy representing a constellation. This figure was dedicated to Venus; perhaps confused with* Puer, *which was dedicated to Mars. See* Rubeus.

Pull, *n.*, a bout at wrestling, a throw.

Pulle, *v.*, pull, pluck. *A. S.* pullian. Pulle a finch, pluck (cheat) a novice (*slang*).

Pulpet, *n.*, pulpit. *L.* pulpitum.

Pultrye, *n.*, poultry. *O. F.* pouletrie.

Punyce, *v.*, punish. *F.* punir.

Purchace, *v.*, procure, win. *A. F.* purchacer.

Purchas, *n.*, proceeds of begging, gain. *O. F.*

Purchasing, *n.*, conveyancing, acquisition of property.

Purchasour, *n.*, conveyancer. *A. F.*

Pure, *adj.*, very, pure, utter; *adv.*, purely. *O. F.* pur.

Purfiled, *p. p.*, ornamented, trimmed. *O. F.* porfiler.

Purgatorie, *n.*, purgatory. *A. F.*

Purpos, *n.*, purpose. *O. F.*

Purpose, *v.*, purpose, propose. *O. F.* purposer.

Purpre, *adj.*, purple. *A. S.* purpure; *O. F.* purpre.

Purs, *n.*, purse. *A. S.*

Pursevauntes, *n.*, *plu.*, pursuivants. *O. F.* pursivant.

Purtreye, *v.*, *see* Portreye.

Purtreyour, *n.*, draughtsman, painter, drawer.

Purveyaunce, *n.*, providence, prescience, provision. *O. F.* purveance.

Purveye, *v.*, provide, take precautions. *A. F.* purveier.

Put, *n.*, pit. *A. S.* pyt.

Putte, v., put, lay, suppose.

Pye, n., magpie. O. F. **pie.**

Pye, n., pie.

Pyk, n., pike (*fish*). A. S. **pīc.**

Pyke, v., peek, pry.

Pykepurs, n., pickpurse. —A. S. **purs.**

Pyne, n., pain, torment. A. S. **pīn** f.

Pyne, v., torture. A. S. **pīnian.**

Pype, n., pipe. A. S. **pīpe.**

Pype, v., play the pipe, pipe.

Pypers, n., plu., pipers. A. S. **pīpere.**

Q

Quaille, n., quail. O. F.

Qualm, n., pestilence, plague, foreboding. A. S. **cwealm.**

Quantite, n., quantity, size, vastness. O. F.

Quappe, v., heave, toss, palpitate.

Quayles, n., plu., see **Quaille.**

Queinte, adj., see **Queynte.**

Quelle, v., kill, strike. A. S. **cwellan.**

Queme, v., please. A. S. **cwēman.**

Quenche, v., quench, extinguish, put a stop to. A. S. (ā)-**cwencan.**

Quene, n., queen. A. S. **cwēn** f.

Querne, n., quern, hand-mill. A. S. **cweorn** f.

Questioun, n., dispute, discussion. O. F. **question.**

Queynt, p. p.; **Queynte,** v., pret.; see **Quenche.**

Queynte, adj., artful, ingeniously wrought, elaborate, elegant; adv., artfully. O. F. **queinte.**

Queynteliche, adv., curiously, cunningly.

Quiete, n., quiet, repose. O. F.

Quik, adj., alive. A. S. **cwic.**

Quike, v., quicken, revive. A. S. **cwician.**

Quiknesse, n., liveliness.

Quiryne: Romulus.

Quisshin, n., cushion. O. F. **coissin.**

Quit, p. p., see **Quyte.**

Quitly, adv., freely, wholly.

Quod, v., pret. sing., said, quoth. A. S. **cweðan.**

Quook, v., pret. sing., trembled, quaked. From **Quake.** A. S. **cwacian.**

Quyte, v., requite, reward, pay, release, free. O. F. **quiter.**

R

Rad, p. p.; **Radde,** v., pret.; see **Rede.**

Raft, p. p.; **Rafte,** v., pret.; see **Reve.**

Rage, n., passion, madness, fierce blast. O. F.

Rage, v., romp, toy wantonly. O. F. **ragier.**

Ragerye, n., passion, wantonness. O. F. **ragerie.**

Rakel, adj., rash, hasty.

Rakelnesse, n., rashness.

Rakle, v., behave rashly.

Ram, n., ram (*as a prize at a wrestling-match*); Aries (*first sign of the zodiac*). A. S. See **Aries.**

Rancour, n., ill-feeling, malice. O. F. **rancor.**

Ransake, v., ransack, search thoroughly.

Rape, n., haste. O. N. **hrap.**

Rascaille, n., mob. A. F.

Rasour, n., razor. O. F. **rasor.**

Rathe, adv., soon, early. A. S. **hræð.**

Rather, adv., sooner, more willingly, rather. A. S. **hraðor.**

Rattes, n., plu., rats. A. S. **ræt.**

Raughte, v., pret., see **Reche.**

Raunsoun n., ransom. O. F. **rançon.**

Rave, v., be mad, speak madly. O. F. **raver.**

Raven, n., raven; Corvus (*the constellation*). A. S. **hræfn.**

Ravisedest, v., second pers. sing., pret. indic., see **Ravisshe.**

Ravisshe, v., ravish, snatch away. F. **ravir.**

Ravyne, n., ravening, ravin, prey, theft. O. F. **ravine.**

Rayed, *p. p.*, striped. *O. F.* raié.

Rayne, *v., see* Reyne.

Razis, Rhasis: *a Spanish Arabian physician of the tenth century.*

Real, *adj.*, royal, regal. *O. F.*

Realme, *n.*, realm, kingdom. *O. F.* reialme.

Rebel, *adj.*, rebellious. *O. F.* rebelle.

Rebelling, *s.*, rebellion. *F.* rebeller.

Recche, *v.*, reck, care, heed. *A. S.* rēcan, rĕccan.

Recche, *v.*, interpret, expound. *A. S.* reccan, reccean.

Recchelees, *adj.*, reckless, careless.

Receyve, *v.*, receive. *O. F.* receivre.

Rechased, *p. p.*, headed back, chased back. *F.* rechasser.

Reche, *v.*, reach, give, touch, proceed. *A. S.* rǣcan.

Recomaunde, *v.*, recommend. *F.* recommander.

Recomforte, *v., see* Reconforte.

Recompensacioun, *n.*, recompense. *O. F.* récompensation.

Reconforte, *v.*, comfort again, encourage. *O. F.* reconforter.

Recorde, *v.*, witness, remember, call to mind. *O. F.* recorder.

Recours, *n.*, recourse, resort. *F.*

Recreaunt, *adj.*, recreant, cowardly. *O. F.* recreant.

Red, *p. p.;* Rede, *v., pret.; see* Rede.

Rede, *v.*, read, advise, study, interpret. *A. S.* rǣdan.

Rede, *n., dat., see* Reed.

Redely, *adv.*, soon, readily, truly.

Redempcioun, *n.*, ransom. *F.* rédemption.

Reder, *n.*, reader. *A. S.* rǣdere.

Redily, *adv., see* Redely.

Redouting, *s.*, reverence.

Redresse, *v.*, redress, set right, make amends, rise again. *O. F.* redresser.

Redy, *adj.*, ready, at hand. *A. S.* rǣde.

Reed, *n.*, reed, musical instrument made of reed. *A. S.* hrēod.

Reed, *n.*, counsel, advice, plan, remedy. *A. S.* rǣd.

Reed, *adj.*, red. *A. S.* rēad.

Rees, *n.*, race, great haste. *A. S.* rǣs.

Reflexioun, *n.*, reflection, thought. *O. F.* réflexion.

Refresshe, *v.*, refresh, recreate. *O. F.* refreschier.

Refreyde, *v.*, grow cold. *O. F.* refreidier.

Refreyn, *n.*, refrain. *O. F.* refrein.

Refus, *adj.*, refused, rejected. *O. F.* refuser.

Regioun, *n.*, region, realm. *A. F.* regiun.

Registre, *n.*, register, story. *O. F.*

Regne, *n.*, kingdom, dominion, realm. *O. F.*

Regne, *v.*, reign, prevail. *O. F.* regner.

Reherce, *v.*, rehearse, enumerate, repeat. *O. F.* rehercer.

Rehersing, *s.*, rehearsal. *See* Reherce.

Reighte, *v., pret., see* Reche.

Reines, *n., plu.*, rain-storms. *A. S.* regn.

Reioyse, *v.*, rejoice, make glad. *O. F.* resjoïr.

Rekene, *v.*, reckon, count. *A. S.* gerecenian.

Rekeninge, *s.*, reckoning, account. *See* Rekene.

Rekke, *v.*, care, reck. *A. S.* rēcan; rĕccan. *See* Recche.

Rekne, *v., see* Rekene.

Relayes, *n., plu.*, fresh sets of hounds, reserve packs. *O. F.* relais.

Relesse, *v.*, release, forgive. *O. F.* relesser.

Releve, *v.*, raise up, relieve. *O. F.* relever.

Religioun, *n.*, religion. *A. F.* religiun.

Religious, *adj.*, belonging to a religious order. *O. F.*

Relik, *n.*, relic. *F.* relique.

Reme, *n.*, realm. *O. F.* reaume.

Remede, *n.*, remedy. *O. F.*

Remedie, Remedye, *n.*, remedy. *O. F.* remedie.

Remembre, *v.*, remember, remind. *O. F.* remembrer.

Remenant, *n.*, remainder, rest. *O. F.*

Remorde, *v.*, cause remorse, vex, plague. *O. F.* remordre.

Remors, *n.*, remorse. *O. F.*

Remuable, *adj.*, changeable, variable. *O. F.*

Renges, *n.*, *plu.*, ranks. *O. F.* renge.

Renne, *v.*, run, be current, spread, continue. *A. S.* irnan.

Renoun, *n.*, renown, fame. *A. F.*

Renovelaunces, *n.*, *plu.*, renewals. *O. F.* renovelance.

Rente, *n.*, income, payment. *O. F.*

Repaire, *v.*, go back, return, find a home. *O. F.* repairer.

Reparaciouns, *n.*, *plu.*, reparations, making up. *O. F.* reparacion.

Repeled, *p. p.*, repealed. *From* Repele. *O. F.* rapeler.

Repentaunce, *n.*, repentance. *F.* repentance.

Repentaunt, *adj.*, repentant. *F.* repentant.

Repeyre, *v.*, *see* Repaire.

Repleccioun, *n.*, repletion. *O. F.* repletion.

Repleet, *adj.*, replete, full. *O. F.*

Replicacioun, *n.*, reply, repartee. *O. F.* replicacion.

Reportour, *n.*, reporter. *O. F.* reporteur.

Reprevable, *adj.*, reprehensible. *O. F.* reprouvable.

Repreve, *n.*, reproof, shame, reproach. *A. F.* repreove.

Repreve, *v.*, reprove, reproach. *O. F.* reprover.

Reputacioun, *n.*, repute, reputation. *L.* reputatio.

Requere, *v.*, require, demand, seek. *O. F.* requerre.

Requeste, *n.*, request. *O. F.*

Rescous, *n.*, rescue, help. *O. F.* rescous.

Rese, *v.*, shake. *A. S.* ræsan.

Resonable, *adj.*, reasonable. *O. F.*

Resoun, *n.*, reason, right. *O. F.* reson.

Resoune, *v.*, resound. *O. F.* resoner.

Respect, *n.*, regard. *L.* respectus. To respect, in respect.

Resport, *n.*, regard. *O. F.*

Respyt, *n.*, respite, delay. *O. F.* respit.

Reste, *n.*, rest, repose. *A. S.* ræst *f.*

Restelees, *adj.*, restless.

Restreyne, *v.*, restrain. *O. F.* restreindre.

Ret, *v.*, *third pers. sing., pres. indic., see* Rede.

Retenue, *n.*, retinue. *O. F.*

Rethor, *n.*, orator. *L.* rhetor.

Rethoryke, *n.*, rhetoric. *O. F.* rethorique.

Retourne, *v.*, return. *O. F.* retourner.

Retourninge, *s.*, return. *O. F.*, retourner.

Reule, *n.*, rule. *O. F.*

Reule, *v.*, rule. *O. F.* reuler.

Reve, *n.*, reeve, steward, bailiff: *appointed by a landowner to superintend his estates. A. S.* gcrēfa.

Reve, *v.*, rob, plunder, take away, bereave. *A. S.* rēafian.

Revelacioun, *n.*, revelation. *F.* révélation.

Revelour, *n.*, reveller.

Reverence, *n.*, reverence, respect, honor. *F.*

Revers, *n.*, reverse, contrary. *O. F.*

Revoke, *v.*, recall. *O. F.* revoquier.

Reward, *n.*, regard, attention. *O. F.*

Rewe, *n.*, row, line. *A. S.* ræw *f.*

Rewe, *v.*, pity, have pity. *A. S.* hrēowan.

Rewfulleste, *adj.*, *superl.*, most rueful.

Rewfully, *adv.*, ruefully, sadly.

Rewthe, *n.*, *see* **Routhe**.

Rewthelees, *adj.*, ruthless, unpitying.

Reyes, *n.*, *plu.*, round dances.

Reyn, *n.*, rain. *A. S.* **regn**.

Reyne, *v.*, rain. *A. S.* **regnian**.

Reyne, *n.*, rein. *O. F.* **resne**.

Reynes, **Rennes**.

Reyse, *v.*, raise. *O. N.* **reisa**.

Reysed, *p. p.*, gone on a military expedition.

Riban, *n.*, ribbon. *O. F.*

Ribaudye, *n.*, ribaldry. *O. F.* **ribaudie**.

Riche, *adj.*, rich. *A. S.* **rīce**; *cf. O. F.* **riche**.

Richesse, *n.*, riches, wealth. *O. F.*

Riden, *v.*, *pret. plu.*; *p. p.*; *see* **Ryde**.

Rightful, *adj.*, perfect.

Rightwisnesse, *n.*, righteousness. *A. S.* **rihtwīsnes** *f.*

Rinde, *n.*, rind, bark, hard skin. *A. S.* **rind** *f.*

Ringe, *v.*, ring, make resound. *A. S.* **hringan**.

Ripheo, **Riphæus**.

Risshe, *n.*, rush. *A. S.* **risce**. **Al dere y-nough a risshe**, quite expensive enough at the price of a rush: *i. e.*, *a rush would be too much to pay for it.*

Rist, *v.*, *third pers. sing.*, *pres. indic.*, *see* **Ryse**.

Roche, *n.*, rock. *O. F. See* **Rokke**.

Rochel, Rochelle: *a town in France.*

Rode, *n.*, rood, cross. *A. S.* **rōd** *f.*

Rode-beem, *n.*, rood-beam. *A. S.* **rod** *f.*—**bēam**.

Rody, *adj.*, ruddy. *A. S.* **rudig**.

Roghte, *v.*, *pret.*, *see* **Recche**.

Rokes, *n.*, *plu.*, rooks. *A. S.* **hrōc**.

Rokke, *n.*, rock. *O. F.* **roke**. *See* **Roche**.

Rolle, *n.*, roll. *O. F.*

Romain, Roman.

Romaunce, *n.*, romance. *O. F.* **romans**.

Romayn, Roman.

Rome, *v.*, roam, wander.

Ron, *v.*, *pret. sing.*, *see* **Reyne**.

Rong, *v.*, *pret. sing.*, *see* **Ringe**.

Ronne, *v.*, *pret.*; *p. p.*; *see* **Renne**.

Roo, *n.*, roe. *A. S.* **rā**.

Roos, *v.*, *pret. sing.*, *see* **Ryse**.

Roost, *n.*, roast. *O. F.* **rost**.

Rore, *n.*, uproar.

Rore, *v.*, roar, resound. *A. S.* **rārian**.

Roste, *v.*, roast. *O. F.* **rostir**.

Rote, *n.*, root, principle, source. *O. N.* **rōt**.

Rote, *n.*, rote. **By rote**, by heart.

Rote, *n.*, stringed musical instrument. *O. F.*

Roughte, *v.*, *pret.*, *see* **Recche**.

Rouke, *v.*, cower, huddle.

Rouncivale: *the hospital of the Blessed Mary of Rouncyvalle in London.*

Rouncy, *n.*, hackney, nag. *O. F.* **ronci**.

Rounde, *adv.*, round, fully.

Roundel, *n.*; roundel, roundelay, small circle. *O. F.* **rondel**.

Roune, *v.*, whisper. *A. S.* **rūnian**.

Route, *n.*, company, troop. *O. F.*

Route, *v.*, roar, murmur, snore. *A. S.* **hrūtan**.

Routhe, *n.*, pity, ruth, compassion.

Routhelees, *adj.*, ruthless, pitiless.

Rowe, *n.*, *see* **Rewe**.

Rowe, *adv.*, roughly, angrily. *A. S.* **rūh**.

Rowland, Roland: *the hero of the* Chanson de Roland.

Rowne, *v.*, *see* **Roune**.

Rowthe, *n.*, *see* **Routhe**.

Royalliche, *adv.*, royally.

Royaltee, *n.*, royalty. *O. F.* **roialté**.

Rubbe, *v.*, rub out.

Rubee, *n.*, ruby. *O. F.* **rubi**.

Rubeus: *a figure in geomancy representing a constellation. It was dedicated to Mars. See* **Puella**.

Ruce, Russia.

Ruddok, *n.*, robin. *A. S.* rudduc.

Rudeliche, *adv.*, rudely.

Rudenesse, *n.*, rusticity, boorishness.

Rufus: *a Greek physician of Ephesus of the second century A. D.*

Ruggy, *adj.*, rough.

Rumbel, *n.*, rumble, rumor.

Rused, *v., pret.*, made a detour, escaped. *O. F.* ruser.

Ruyne, *n.*, ruin. *O. F.*

Ryde, *v.*, ride, go on expeditions. *A. S.* rīdan.

Rym, *n.*, rime, tale in verse. *A. S.* rīm.

Ryme, *v.*, put into rime. *A. S.* rīman.

Ryot, *n.*, riotous living. *O. F.* riot.

Ryotour, *n.*, roisterer. *A. F.* riotour.

Rype, *adj.*, ripe, mature. *A. S.* ripe.

Ryse, *v.*, rise. *A. S.* rīsan.

Ryte, *n.*, rite, ceremony. *L.* ritus.

Ryve, *v.*, pierce, tear. *O. N.* rīfa.

S

Sacrifyse, *n.*, sacrifice. *O. F.* sacrifise.

Sad, *n.*, stable, firm, sober, fixed, grave. *A. S.* sæd.

Sadel, *n.*, saddle. *A. S.* sadol.

Sadel-bowe, *n.*, saddle-bow: *the pieces forming the front of a saddle.* *A. S.* sadelboga.

Sadly, *adv.*, firmly, steadfastly.

Sadnesse, *n.*, staidness, soberness. *A. S.* sædness *f.*

Saffron, *v.*, tinge with saffron, color. *F.* safraner.

Salomon, Solomon.

Saluces, Saluzzo.

Salue, *v.*, greet, salute. *F.* saluer.

Saluinge, *s.*, salutation. *F.* saluer.

Saluwe, *v., see* Salue.

Salve, *n.*, salve, cure. *A. S.* sealf *f.;* sealfe.

Samit, *n.*, samite: *a kind of heavy silk stuff.* *O. F.*

Sampson, Sampsoun, Samson.

Sangwin, *n.*, stuff of a blood-red color.

Sangwyn, *adj.*, very ruddy, blood-red, dominated by the blood. *O. F.* sanguin. *See* Colera.

Santippe, Xanthippus.

Sarge, *n.*, serge. *O. F.*

Sarpedoun, Sarpedon.

Satalye, Attalia *in Asia Minor, now Adalia.*

Sate, *v., pret. subj., see* Sitte.

Saturne, Saturnus, Saturn.

Saturnyn, *adj.*, belonging to Saturn.

Sauf, *adj.*, safe. *O. F.*

Sauf, *prep.*, save, except. *O. F.*

Saufly, *adv.*, safely, with safety.

Saugh, *v.*, saw, looked. *From* See. *A. S.* sēon.

Sautrye, *n.*, psaltery. *O. F.* psalterie.

Savacioun, *n.*, salvation, safety, protection. *O. F.* sauvacion.

Save-garde, *n.*, safe-conduct. *O. F.* sauvegarde.

Saveour, *n.*, savior. *O. F.* saveor.

Savoure, *v.*, taste, have relish for. *O. F.* savorer.

Sawcefleem, *adj.*, covered with pimples. *O. F.* sausefleme.

Sawe, *n.*, saying, speech. *A. S.* sagu.

Sawe, Say, *v., pret.*, saw. *From* See. *A. S.* sēon.

Sayle, *v.*, sail. *A. S.* seglian.

Sayling, *adj.* (*from pres. partic.*), sailing, used in ships. *A. S.* segling.

Scabbe, *n.*, scab.

Scalle, *n.*, scabby disease of the skin. *O. N.* skalle (?)

Scalled, *adj.*, scabby. *See* Scalle.

Scape, *v.*, escape. *O. F.* escaper.

Scariot, Iscariot.

Scarlet, *adj.*, scarlet. *O. F.* escarlate.

Scarlet, *n.*, scarlet stuff. *O. F.* escarlate.

Scarmuche, Scarmyche, *n.*, skirmish, *O. F.* escarmuche.

Scarsly, *adv.*, scarcely, parsimoniously.

Scathe, *n.*, harm, misfortune.
O. N. skaðe.

Scipio, Scipioun, Scipio Africanus Minor. *See* Macrobie.

Scithia, Scythia.

Sclaundre, *n.*, slander. *O. F.* esclandre.

Sclendre, *adj.*, slender.

Scogan: *probably* Henry Scogan, *tutor of the two sons of Henry IV.*

Scole, *n.*, school, manner, discipline. *A. S.* scōlu.

Scoler, *n.*, scholar. *A. S.* scolere; *O. F.* escoler.

Scoleward: to scoleward, toward school.

Scoleye, *v.*, attend school.

Scorne, *v.*, scorn, treat with rudeness, jest at. *O. F.* escorner.

Scorpioun, *the sign of* Scorpio.

Scrippe, *n.*, scrip, bag. *L. L.* scrippum; *O. F.* escrepe.

Scrit, *n.*, writing, deed. *O. F.* escrit.

Scrivenish, *adv.*, like a scrivener.

Scriveyn, *n.*, scribe. *O. F.* escrivain.

Seche, *v.*, seek. *A. S.* sēcan. *See* Seke.

Secree, *adj.*, secret, trusty. *O. F.* secrê.

Secrely, *adv.*, secretly.

Secte, *n.*, sect, company, faith. *F.*

See, *n.*, sea. *A. S.* sǣ. Drye see, dry sea: *perhaps the desert of Gobi. Cf.* Carrenar. Grete see, great sea: *the Mediterranean.*

See, *n.*, seat. *O. F.*

Seed, *n.*, seed. *A. S.* sǣd.

Seed-foul, *n.*, bird living on seeds. *A. S.* sǣd—fugol.

Seek, *adj.*, sick, ill. *A. S.* sēoc. *See* Syk.

Seel, *n.*, seal. *O. F.*

Seestow, *v.*, *pron.*, *second pers. sing.*, *pres. indic.*, seest thou. *From* See. *A. S.* sēon.

Seet, *v.*, *pret. sing.*, *see* Sitte.

Seetes, *n.*, *plu.*, seats.

Sege, *n.*, seat, siege. *A. F.*

Segge, *v.*, *pres. plu.*, *see* Seye.

Seigh, *v.*, *pret. sing.*, saw. *From* See. *A. S.* sēon.

Seint, *adj.*, saint, holy. *O. F.*

Seint, *n.*, saint. *O. F.*

Seint Beneit, Saint Benedict: *founder of the Benedictine order of monks; died c. 544.*

Seinte Loy, Saint Eloi: (*588–659*) *goldsmith and master of the mint, artist and courtier; he once refused to swear an oath.*

Seint Iame, Saint James; *the shine of* St. James (*Santiago*) *at Compostella.*

Seint Ierome, Saint Jerome: (*c. 340–420*) *author of the treatise* Adversus Jovinianum *defending celibacy.*

Seint Ioce, Saint Josse: *confused by the Wife of Bathe with Sir Joce in the* Testament *of Jean de Meun. Sir Joce cared* "*not a prune for his wife's love.*"

Seint Iulian, Saint Julian: *who provides his votaries with good lodgings and other accommodations.*

Seint Maure, Saint Maur: *a disciple of St. Benedict.*

Seint Ronyon, Saint Ronan.

Seint Thomas, Saint Thomas à Becket: *murdered at Canterbury in 1170.*

Seistow, *v.*, *pron.*, *second pers. sing.*, *pres. indic.*, *see* Seye.

Seith, *v.*, *third pers. sing.*, *pres. indic.*, *see* Seye.

Seke, *v.*, seek, search. *A. S.* sēcan. *See* Seche.

Selde, *adj.*, *plu.*, few; *adv.*, seldom.

Self, *adj.*, self-same, same. *A. S.*

Selly, *n.*, wonderful. *A. S.* sellic.

Selve, *adj.*, *see* Self.

Sely, *adj.*, happy, good, innocent, poor. *A. S.* sǣlig.

Seme, *v.*, seem, appear. *O. N.* sǿma.

Semely, *adj.*, seemly, comely; *adv.*, becomingly.

Semicope, *n.,* half-cope, short cope. *L.* semi—*L. L.* capa.

Seming, *s.,* seeming, appearance.

Semyramus, Semiramus.

Sendal, *n.,* thin silk. *O. F.*

Sene, *adj.,* visible, manifest. *A. S.* gesēne. *See* Y-sene.

Sene, *v., gerund.,* see. *From* See. *A. S.* sēon.

Senek, Seneca.

Sent, *v., third pers. sing., pres. indic.,* sends. *From* Sende. *A. S.* sendan.

Sentement, *n.,* feeling, fancy. *O. F.*

Sentence, *n.,* sense, meaning, judgment. *O. F.*

Sepulture, *n.,* mode of burial, burial, tomb. *O. F.*

Serapion: *an Arabian physician of the eleventh century.*

Sergeaunt of the Lawe, sergeant-at-law: *member of a superior order of barristers.* *O. F.* sergent. *A. S.* lagu.

Sermon, *n., see* Sermoun.

Sermone, *v.,* preach, speak. *O. F.* sermoner.

Sermoun, *n.,* discourse, sermon, talk. *A. F.* sermun.

Servage, *n.,* servitude, thraldom. *O. F.*

Servaunt, *n.,* servant. *O. F.* servant.

Servisable, *adj.,* serviceable, willing to serve, useful. *O. F.*

Servitute, *n.,* servitude. *O. F.*

Servyse, *n.,* service, religious service, musical performance. *O. F.* servise.

Sese, *v.,* seize. *O. F.* seisir.

Seson, Sesoun, *n.,* season. *O. F.* seson.

Sessiouns, *n., plu.,* sessions. *F.* session.

Sestow, *v., pron., second pers. sing., pres. indic.,* seest thou. *From* See. *A. S.* sēon.

Sete, *v., pret. sing., subj.;* **Sete, Seten,** *v., pret. plu.;* **Seten,** *p. p.; see* Sitte.

Sethe, *v.,* seethe, boil. *A. S.* sēoðan.

Sette, *v.,* set, place. *A. S.* settan.

Seur, *adv.,* surely. *O. F.*

Seurtee, *n.,* surety, security. *O. F.* seürtee.

Sewe, *v.,* follow, pursue. *A. F.* suire.

Sexte, *ord. num.,* sixth. *A. S.* sixta.

Sey, *v., pret. sing.,* saw. *From* See. *A. S.* sēon.

Seye, *v.,* say. *A. S.* secgan.

Seyl, *n.,* sail. *A. S.* segl.

Seyn, *p. p.,* seen. *From* See. *A. S.* sēon.

Seyn, *v., infin.; pres. plu.; see* Seye.

Seynd, *p. p.,* singed. *From* Senge. *A. S.* sengan.

Seyne, *gerund., see* Seye.

Seynt, *adj.; n.; see* Seint.

Seynt Gyle, Saint Giles: St. Ægidius.

Seynt Iohan, Saint John. "Seynt Iohan on a riche hil" *is a punning reference to John of Richmond (John of Gaunt).*

Seynt Valentyn, Saint Valentine.

Seys, Ceyx.

Shadwe, *n.,* shadow, shade. *A. S.* sceadu.

Shadwed, *p. p.,* shadowed. *A. S.* sceadwian.

Shake, *p. p.,* shaken. *A. S.* scacan.

Shal, *v., first and third pers. sing., pres. indic.,* shall. *A. S.* sculan.

Shale, *n.,* shell. *A. S.* scealu.

Shalmyes, *n., plu.,* shawms, reed pipes. *O. F.* chalemie.

Shaltow, *v., second pers. sing., pres. indic.,* shalt thou. *See* Shal.

Shame, *n.,* shame. *A. S.* sceamu.

Shamfast, *adj.,* modest, shy. *A. S.* scamfæst.

Shamfastnesse, *n.,* modesty.

Shap, *n.,* shape, form. *A. S.* gesceap.

Shape, *v.,* plan, devise, prepare. *A. S.* scieppan.

Shaply, *adj.,* shapely, fit, likely.

Sharpe, *adv.,* sharply.

Sheef, *n.,* sheaf. *A. S.* scēaf.

Sheeld, *n., see* **Sheld.**

Sheep, *n.,* sheep. *A. S.* **scēp.**

Sheld, *n.,* shield; shield: *French crown (worth 3s. 4d.) A. S.* **sceld.**

Shelde, *v., see* **Shilde.**

Shende, *v.,* disgrace, harm, destroy. *A. S.* **scendan.**

Shene, *adj.,* bright, fair, beautiful. *A. S.* **scēne.**

Shepherde, *n.,* shepherd. *A. S.* **scēaphyrde.**

Shepne, *n.,* stable, shed. *A. S.* **scypen.**

Shere, *n.,* shears, pair of shears. *A. S.* **sceara.**

Sherte, *n.,* shirt. *A. S.* **scyrte.**

Shete, *n.,* sheet. *A. S.* **scēte.**

Sheter, *n.,* shooter, fit for shooting.

Shethe, *n.,* sheath. *A. S.* **scǣþ** *f.*

Shette, *v.,* shut, enclose. *A. S.* **scyttan.**

Sheves, *n., plu., see* **Sheef.**

Shewe, *v.,* show, appear. *A. S.* **scēawian.**

Shilde, *v.,* shield, defend. *A. S.* **scyldan.**

Shine, *n.,* shin. *A. S.* **scinu.**

Shipman, *n.,* sailor, seaman. *A. S.* **scipmann.**

Shippes, *n., plu.,* ships. *A. S.* **scip.**

Shire, *n.,* shire. *A. S.* **scīr** *f.*

Shirreve, *n.,* sheriff. *A. S.* **scīrgerēfa.**

Shivere, *v.,* shiver, break.

Sho, *n., see* **Shoo.**

Shode, *n.,* crown of the head. *A. S.* **scēada.**

Sholde, *v., pret., see* **Shal.**

Sholder-boon, *n.,* shoulder-blade-bone. *A. S.* **sculdor—bān.**

Shon, *v., pret. sing., see* **Shyne.**

Shonde, *n.,* shame, disgrace. *A. S.* **sceand** *f.*

Shoo, *n.,* shoe. *A. S.* **scēoh.**

Shoof, *v., pret. sing.,* shoved, pushed. *From* **Shove.** *A. S.* **scūfan.**

Shoon, *v., pret. sing., see* **Shyne.**

Shoop, *v., pret. sing., see* **Shape.**

Shorte, *v.,* shorten. *A. S.* **scortian.**

Shortly, *adv.,* briefly. *A. S.* **sceortlīce.**

Short-sholdred, *adj.,* short in the upper arm.

Shottes, *n., plu.,* shots. *A. S.* **scot.**

Shour, *n.,* shower, onset, conflict. *A. S.* **scūr.**

Showting, *n.,* shouting.

Shrewe, *n.,* scoundrel, accursed wretch, ill-tempered person. *A. S.* **scrēawa.**

Shrewe, *v.,* beshrew, curse.

Shrewed, *adj.,* accursed, evil, wicked.

Shrewednesse, *n.,* wickedness, evil, cursedness.

Shright; *p. p.;* **Shrighte,** *v., pret.;* shrieked. *From* **Shrike.** *Cf.* **Shryked.**

Shrinke, *v.,* shrink, draw (in). *A. S.* **scrincan.**

Shryked, *v., pret.,* shrieked. *From* **Shrike.** *Cf.* **Shrighte.**

Shul, Shullen, *v., pres.,* shall; **Shulde,** *v., pret.,* should. *See* **Shal.**

Shuldres, *n., plu.,* shoulders. *A. S.* **sculdor.**

Shyne, *v.,* shine. *A. S.* **scīnan.**

Sicamour, *n.,* sycamore. *L.* **sycomorus.**

Sight, Sighte, *n.,* sight. *A. S.* **gesiht** *f.*

Sighte, *v., pret., see* **Syke.**

Signe, *n.,* sign. *F.*

Signet, *n.,* signet-ring. *O. F.*

Signifer: *the zodiac.*

Signifiaunce, *n.,* significance. *O. F.* **signifiance.**

Significavit: *the beginning of a writ of excommunication.*

Signifyed, *v., pret.,* signified, meant. *F.* **signifier.**

Sik, *adj., see* **Syk.**

Siker, *adj.,* sure; *adv.,* surely, securely. *A. S.* **sicor.**

Sikerer, *adj., compar.,* more sure. *See* **Siker.**

Sikerly, *adv.,* certainly, surely.

Sikernesse, *n.,* security, safety, confidence.

Sikly, *adv.,* ill, hardly, with ill will.

Siknesse, *n.,* sickness, illness. *A. S.* sēocness *f.*

Silla, Scylla: *who for love of Minos cut off her father's hair upon which his life depended, and who was therefore transformed into a bird. See Ovid,* Metam., *viii, 8.*

Sillable, *n.,* syllable. *O. F.* sillabe.

Silver-brighte, *adj., plu.,* bright as silver.

Simon Magus: *a sorcerer of Samaria* (Acts *viii, 9–24*).

Sin, *conj., adv.,* since. *A. S.* siððan. *Cf.* **Sith, Sithen.**

Sinne, *n.,* sin. *A. S.* synn *f.*

Sinoun, Sinon: *allowed himself to be taken prisoner by the Trojans, and persuaded them to admit to the city the wooden horse which was filled with armed men.*

Sir, Sire, *n.,* sir, master. *O. F.* sire.

Sisoures, *n., plu.,* scissors. *O. F.* cisoires.

Site, *n.,* site, situation. *A. F.*

Sith, *conj.,* since. *A. S.* siððan. *Cf.* **Sin, Sithen.**

Sithen, *conj., adv.,* since. *A. S.* siððan. *Cf.* **Sin, Sith.**

Sitte, *v.,* sit, be situated, dwell, befit, suit. *A. S.* sittan.

Sittingest, *adj., superl.,* most fitting.

Sixte, *ord. num.,* sixth. *A. S.* sixta.

Skarmishe, *n., see* **Scarmuche.**

Skathe, *n., see* **Scathe.**

Skil, *n.,* reason, cause. *O. N.*

Skilful, *adj.,* reasonable.

Skilfully, *adv.,* reasonably.

Skippe, *v.,* skip, jump, dance.

Skye, *n.,* cloud. *O. N.* ský.

Slake, *v.,* slacken, desist, wane. *A. S.* slacian.

Slakke, *adj.,* slow. *A. S.* slæc.

Slawe, Slawen, Slayn, *p. p., see* **Slee.**

Slee, *v.,* slay. *A. S.* slēan.

Sleep, *n.,* sleep. *A. S.* slǣp.

Sleep, *v., pret. sing., see* **Slepe.**

Sleer, *n.,* slayer.

Sleighly, *adv., see* **Sleyly.**

Sleighte, *n.,* sleight, trickery, device, plan.

Slepe, *v.,* sleep. *A. S.* slǣpan.

Slepy, *adj.,* sleepy, sleep-bestowing. *A. S.* slǣpig.

Sleve, *n.,* sleeve. *A. S.* slēf *f.*

Sley, *adj.,* sly, subtle. *O. N.* slǣgr.

Sleyly, *adv.,* slyly, subtly, skillfully.

Sleyn, *p. p., see* **Slee.**

Slinge-stones, *n., plu.,* slingstones. —*A. S.* stān.

Slinke, *v.,* slink, creep. *A. S.* slincan.

Slit, *v., third pers. sing., pres. indic., see* **Slyde.**

Slogardye, *n.,* sluggishness, sloth, indolence.

Slombrestow, *v., pron., second pers. sing., pres. indic.,* slumberest thou. *A. S.* slumerian.

Slomeringe, *s.,* slumber. *A. S.* slomerian.

Slough, *v., pret. sing., see* **Slee.**

Slouthe, *n.,* sloth.

Slow, *v., pret. sing., see* **Slee.**

Slow, *adj.,* slow, slothful, idle. *A. S.* slāw.

Slyde, *v.,* slide, pass. *A. S.* slīdan.

Smal, *adj.,* small; *adv.,* little. *A. S.* smæl.

Smel, *n.,* smell.

Smert, *adj.,* smart, quick, painful. *A. S.* smeart.

Smerte, *adv.,* smartly, sharply.

Smerte, *v.,* smart, sting, feel pain. *A. S.* smeortan.

Smitted, *p. p.,* smutted, besmirched. *A. S.* smittian.

Smok, *n.,* smock. *A. S.* smocc.

Smoke, *n.,* smoke. *A. S.* smoca.

Smoklees, *adj.,* without a smock.

Smothe, *adj.,* smooth; *adv.,* smoothly. *A. S.* smōð.

Smyler, *n.,* smiler.

Smyte, *v.,* smite, strike. *A. S.* smītan.

Snewed, *v., pret. sing.,* snowed. *A. S.* snīwan.

Snibbe, *v.*, snub, reprove, chide.

Snowes, *n.*, *plu.*, snow-storms. *A. S.* snāw.

Snowte, *n.*, snout.

Sobbes, *n.*, *plu.*, sobs.

Sobre, *adj.*, sober, sedate, staid. *O. F.*

Sobrely, *adv.*, soberly, gravely, sadly.

Soch, *adj.*, such. *A. S.* swylc. *See* Swich.

Socour, Socours, *n.*, succor, help. *O. F.* sucurs.

Sodein, *adj.*, prompt, sudden. *O. F.* sodain.

Sodeinly, *adv.*, suddenly.

Softe, *adj.*, soft, mild; *adv.*, softly, gently, tenderly. *A.S.* sŏfte.

Soghte, *v.*, *pret.*, *see* Seke.

Soiorne, *v.*, sojourn, delay, dwell. *O. F.* sojorner.

Solace, *v.*, refresh, comfort. *O. F.* solacier.

Solas, *n.*, solace, amusement, comfort. *O. F.*

Solempne, *adj.*, solemn, festive, grand, important. *O. F.*

Solempnely, *adv.*, pompously, with pomp.

Solempnitee, *n.*, pomp, ceremony. *O. F.* solempnitê.

Soleyn, *adj.*, sole, solitary; unmated.

Solitarie, *adj.*, solitary. *L.* solitarius.

Som, *pron.*, one, a certain one, some one. *A. S.* sum. Al and som, one and all (all and each). Tenthe som, company of ten.

Somdel, *adv.*, somewhat. *A. S.* sum—dæl.

Somer, *n.*, summer. *A. S.* sumor.

Somer-sonne, *n.*, summer sun. *A. S.* sumor—sunne.

Somme, *adj.*, *plu.*, *see* Som.

Somme, *n.*, sum, total. *O. F.* some.

Somnour, *n.*, summoner: *an officer who summoned delinquents before the ecclesiastical courts. O. F.* semoneor.

Somtyme, *adv.*, once, at some time. *A. S.* sum—tīma.

Sond, *n.*, sand. *A. S.*

Sonde, *n.*, message. *A.S.* sand *f.*

Sondry, *adj.*, sundry, various. *A. S.* syndrig.

Sone, *n.*, son. *A. S.* sunu.

Sone, *adv.*, straightway, immediately, soon. *A. S.* sōna.

Sone-in-lawe, *n.*, son-in-law. *A. S.* sunu—in—lagu.

Song, *v.*, *pret. sing.;* Songe, Songen, *pret. plu.;* sang. *From* Singe. *A. S.* singan.

Songe, Songen, *p. p.*, sung. *From* Singe. *A. S.* singan.

Sonne, *n.*, sun. *A. S.* sunne.

Sonnish, *adj.*, sun-like.

Sooth, *adj.*, true. *A. S.* sōð.

Sooth, *n.*, truth. *A. S.* sōð. *See* Sothe.

Soothfastnesse, *n.*, truth.

Soothly, *adv.*, truly. *A. S.* sōð-līce.

Sooty, *adj.*, begrimed with soot. *A. S.* sōtig.

Sop, *n.*, sop: *bread or cake dipped in a liquid.*

Soper, *n.*, supper. *O. F.*

Sophyme, *n.*, a sophism. *O. F.* soffime.

Sore, *n.*, sore, misery, pain. *A. S.* sār.

Sore, *adj.*, sore; *adv.*, sorely. *A. S.* sār.

Sore, *v.*, soar. *O. F.* essorer.

Sorowe, *n.*, *see* Sorwe.

Sort, *n.*, lot, destiny, chance. *O. F.*

Sorwe, *n.*, sorrow, grief. *A. S.* sorh *f.*

Sorweful, *adj.*, sorrowful. *A. S.* sorgful.

Sorwefully, *adv.*, sorrowfully.

Sorwful, *adj.*, *see* Sorweful.

Sory, *adj.*, sorrowful, sad, miserable. *A. S.* sārig.

Sote, *adj.*, sweet. *A. S.* swōt.

Soth, *adj.*, *see* Sooth.

Sothe, *n.*, truth. *A. S.* sōð. *See* Sooth.

Soth-sawe, *n.*, true saying. *A. S.* sōð—sagu.

Sotil, *adj.*, subtle, cunning, thin. *O. F.* soutil.

Souded, *p. p.*, confirmed. *O. F.* souder.

Soughte, *v.*, *pret.*, *see* Seke.

Souke, *v.*, suck. *A. S.* sūcan.

Soule, *n.*, soul. *A. S.* sāwl *f.*

Soulfre, *n.*, sulphur. *A. F.* sulfre.

Soun, *n.*, sound, musical sound. *O. F.* son.

Soune, *v.*, sound, utter, tend (toward), be consonant with, agree with. *O. F.* soner.

Soupe, *v.*, sup. *O. F.* soper.

Souper, *n.*, *see* Soper.

Souple, *n.*, supple, pliant. *O. F.* sople.

Soures, *n.*, *plu.*, sorrels, bucks of the third year. *O. F.* sorel.

Sours, *n.*, source, origin, soaring, swift upward flight. *O. F.* sors.

Soutiltee, *n.*, device. *O. F.* sutiltê.

Soverainetee, Soveraynetee, *n.*, sovereignty, supremacy. *O. F.* sovrainetê.

Sovereyn, *adj.*, sovereign, supreme, chief. *O. F.* sovrain.

Sovereynly, *adv.*, royally, chiefly.

Sowe, *n.*, sow. *A. S.* sugu.

Sowe, *v.*, sew. *A. S.* siowian.

Sowe, *v.*, sow. *A. S.* sāwan.

Sowle, *n.*, *see* Soule.

Sowne, *v.*, *see* Soune.

Space, *n.*, room, space of time, while, opportunity. *O. F.* espace.

Spade, *n.*, spade. *A. S.* spada.

Spak, *v.*, *pret. sing.*, *see* Speke.

Spanne, *n.*, span. *A. S.* spann *f.*

Span-newe, *adj.*, span-new, brand new.

Spare, *v.*, spare, refrain, cease, pass over. *A. S.* sparian.

Sparhauk, *n.*, *see* Sperhawk.

Sparke, *n.*, spark. *A. S.* spearca.

Sparowe, *n.*, *see* Sparwe.

Sparre, *n.*, wooden beam.

Sparth, *n.*, battle-axe. *O. N.* sparða.

Sparwe, *n.*, sparrow. *A. S.* spearwa.

Spayne, Spain.

Spece, *n.*, species, kind. *O. F.* espece.

Speche, *n.*, speech, discourse, talk, address. *A. S.* spǣc *f.*

Specially, *adv.*, especially.

Spede, *v.*, succeed, prosper, hasten. *A. S.* spēdan.

Speed, *n.*, help, success. *A. S.* spēd.

Speke, *v.*, speak. *A. S.* specan.

Spere, *n.*, spear. *A. S.*

Spere, *n.*, sphere. *O. F.* espere.

Sperhauk, *n.*, sparrowhawk. *A. S.* spearhafoc.

Sperred, *p. p.*, barred, fastened. *A. S.* gesparrian.

Spete, *v.*, spit. *A. S.* spittan. *See* Spitte.

Spille, *v.*, destroy, perish, put to confusion, drop. *A. S.* spillan.

Spitte, *v.*, spit. *A. S.* spittan. *See* Spete.

Spones, *n.*, *plu.* spoons. *A. S.* spōn.

Spore, *n.*, spur. *A. S.* spora.

Sporne, *v.*, spurn, kick, tread. *A. S.* spurnan.

Spousaille, *n.*, espousal, wedding. *O. F.* espousailles (*plu.*).

Spouse, *n.*, spouse. *O. F.* epous (*masc.*), epouse (*fem.*).

Sprad, *p. p.*; Spradde, *v.*, *pret.*; *see* Sprede.

Sprede, *v.*, spread, open. *A. S.* sprǣdan.

Spreynd, *p. p.*, *see* Springe (*weak verb*). *Cf.* Y-spreynd.

Springe, *v.*, *strong.*, spring up, rise, grow. *A. S.* springan.

Springe, *v.*, *weak*, sprinkle, scatter. *A. S.* sprengan.

Springes, *n.*, *plu.*, springs, merry dances.

Spronge, *p. p.*, *see* Springe (*strong verb*).

Spyce, *n.*, spice. *O. F.* espice.

Spyced, *p. p.*, spiced, scrupulous.

Spycerye, *n.*, collection of spices,

mixture of spices. *O. F.* espicerie.

Spye, *n.*, spy. *O. F.* espie.

Squerels, *n.*, *plu.*, squirrels. *O. F.* esquireul.

Squyer, *n.*, squire. *O. F.* esquier.

Stable, *n.*, stable. *O. F.*

Stablissed, *p. p.*, established. *O. F.* establir.

Stace, Statius.

Staf, *n.*, staff. *A. S.* stæf.

Stage, *n.*, place, position. *O. F.* estage.

Stak, *v.*, *pret. sing.*, see Stike.

Stal, *n.*, stall. *A. S.* steall.

Stal, *v.*, *pret. sing.*, see Stele.

Stalke, *n.*, stalk, piece of straw.

Stalke, *v.*, creep up, move stealthily, move slowly. *A. S.* stalcian.

Stalle, *n.*, *dat.*, see Stal.

Stampe, *v.*, stamp, crush, strike. *A. S.* stempan.

Stape, *p. p.*, advanced. *A. S.* stapan.

Stare, *n.*, starling. *A. S.* stær.

Starf, *v.*, *pret. sing.*, see Sterve.

Stark, *adj.*, strong. *A. S.* stearc.

Startling, *pres. partic.*, starting, moving suddenly.

Stat, *n.*, estate. *O. F.* estat. See Estaat.

Statut, *n.*, statute. *O. F.* estatut.

Staves, *n.*, *plu.*, see Staf.

Stede, *n.*, place. *A. S.*

Stede, *n.*, steed. *A. S.* stĕda.

Stedfast, *adj.*, steadfast. *A. S.* stedefæst.

Stedfastly, *adv.*, steadfastly.

Stedfastnesse, *n.*, constancy, stability.

Steel, *n.*, steel. *A. S.* stĕl.

Stele, *v.*, steal, go stealthily. *A. S.* stelan.

Stellifye, *v.*, transform into a star or constellation. *O. F.* stellifier.

Steme, *v.*, shine, glow. *A. S.* stĕman.

Stente, *v.*, leave off, cease, stop. *A. S.* styntan. See Stinte.

Stepe, *adj.*, *plu.*, prominent, staring. *A. S.* stĕap.

Stere, *n.*, helm, rudder; helmsman, pilot. *A. S.* stĕora.

Stere, *v.*, steer, rule. *A. S.* stĕeran.

Stere, *v.*, stir, move, excite. *A. S.* styrian.

Steringe, *s.*, stirring, motion. *A. S.* styrian.

Sterlinges, *n.*, *plu.*, sterling coins.

Sterne, *adj.*, stern, violent. *A. S.* styrne.

Sterre, *n.*, star, planet. *A. S.* steorra.

Sterry, *adj.*, starry.

Stert, *n.*, start, moment.

Sterte, *v.*, start, go quickly, rouse. *A. S.* styrtan. See Stirte.

Sterve, *v.*, die. *A. S.* steorfan.

Stevene, *n.*, voice, sound, language, talk. *A. S.* stefn *f.*

Stewe, *n.*, fish-pond. *O. F.* estui.

Stewe, *n.*, small room, brothel. *O. F.* estuve.

Stewe-dore, *n.*, closet-door. *O. F.* estuve—*A. S.* duru.

Steyre, *n.*, stair, staircase. *A. S.* stæger *f.*

Stiborn, *adj.*, stubborn.

Stif, *adj.*, strong. *A. S.* stĭf.

Stike, *v.*, stick, pierce. *A. S.* stician.

Stikke, *n.*, stick, twig. *A. S.* sticca.

Stilbon: *ordinarily* Mercury, *but as Chaucer uses the name it is an error for Chilon mentioned by John of Salisbury.*

Stille, *adj.*, still, mute, silent; *adv.*, still. *A. S.*

Stinte, *v.*, leave off, cease, stop. *A. S.* styntan. See Stente.

Stire, *v.*, see Stere.

Stirte, *v.*, start, go quickly. *A. S.* styrtan. See Sterte.

Stith, *n.*, anvil. *O. N.* steði.

Stiwardes, *n.*, *plu.*, stewards. *A. S.* stĭweard.

Stix, Styx: *a river in the Nether World.*

Stod, *v.*, *pret. sing.*, see Stonde.

Stok, *n.*, stock, stump, post. *A. S.* stocc.

Stoke, *v.*, stab, thrust.

Stomble, *v.*, stumble.

Ston, *n.*, *see* Stoon.

Stonde, *v.*, stand, abide by. *A. S.* standan.

Stongen, *p. p.*, stung. *From* Stinge. *A. S.* stingan. *Cf.* Y-stonge.

Stoon, *n.*, stone, rock, gem. *A. S.* stān.

Stoor, *n.*, store, stock. *O. F.* estor.

Storie, *n.*, history, tale, story. *O. F.* estorie.

Storfen, *v.*, *pret. plu.*, *see* Sterve.

Stot, *n.*, stallion, horse, cob.

Stounde, *n.*, hour, time, while. *A. S.* stund *f.*

Stoundemele, at various times, from time to time. *A. S.* stundmælum.

Stoupe, *v.*, stoop, droop. *A. S.* stūpian.

Stout, *adj.*, strong, bold. *O. F.* estout.

Strake, *v.*, move, proceed.

Stratford atte Bowe, Stratford at Bow: *a Benedictine nunnery in London.*

Straught, *p. p.*, *as adv.*, straight. *See* Strecche.

Straughte, *v.*, *pret.*, *see* Strecche.

Straunge, *adj.*, strange, foreign, difficult, distant. *O. F.* estrange.

Straungely, *adv.*, distantly.

Straw, Iakke: *See* Iakke.

Strecche, *v.*, stretch, reach, extend. *A. S.* streccan.

Stree, *n.*, straw. *A. S.* strēaw.

Streem, *n.*, river, current, stream. *A. S.* strēam.

Streight, *adj.*, straight; *adv.*, straight, straightway. *A. S.* streht.

Streighte, *v.*, *pret.*, *see* Strecche.

Streit, *adj.*, narrow, strict. *A. F.* estreit.

Streit, *adv.*, closely. *O. F.* estreit.

Streite, *p. p. as adj.*, drawn. *Cf.* Strecche.

Streme, *v.*, stream.

Streng, *n.*, string. *A. S.* streng.

Strenger, *adj.*, *compar.*, stronger.

Strengest, *adj.*, *superl.*, strongest.

Strengthe, *n.*, strength, force. *A. S.* strengðu.

Strepe, *v.*, strip. *A. S.* strȳpan.

Strete, *n.*, street, road. *A. S.* strǣt *f.*

Streyne, *v.*, compress, strain, constrain, hold. *O. F.* estreindre.

Streyt, *adv.*, *see* Streight, Streit.

Strike, *n.*, hank.

Strode, Ralph Strode: *a philosopher of Chaucer's time, follower of the doctrines of Albertus Magnus and Aquinas, and opponent of Wycliffe (especially in Wycliffe's doctrine of predestination).*

Strogelest, *v.*, *second person sing.*, *pres. indic.*, *see* Strugle.

Strond, *n.*, strand, shore. *A. S.* strand.

Stroof, *v.*, *pret. sing.*, *see* Stryve.

Strook, *n.*, stroke.

Stroyer, *n.*, destroyer.

Strugle, *v.*, struggle.

Stryf, *n.*, strife. *O. F.* estrif.

Stryve, *v.*, strive. *O. F.* estriver.

Stubbes, *n.*, *plu.*, stubs. *A. S.* stub.

Studie, *n.*, study, meditation. *O. F.* estudie.

Studie, *v.*, study, give heed, deliberate. *O. F.* estudier.

Studye, *n.*, *see* Studie.

Sturdinesse, *n.*, sternness.

Sturdy, *adj.*, stern, cruel, harsh. *O. F.* estourdi.

Style, *n.*, stile. *A. S.* stigel *f.*

Style, *n.*, style, mode of writing. *O. F.* stile.

Subgit, *n.*, subjects. *O. F.* subget.

Substaunce, *n.*, substance, that which is substantial, the thing itself (*cf.* Accident), the majority. *O. F.* substance.

Subtil, *adj.*, subtle, ingenious, skillful. *O. F.*

Subtiltee, *n.*, subtlety, specious reasoning, trick. *O. F.* soutilté.

Successour, *n.*, successor, follower. *O. F.* successor.

Suffisaunce, *n.*, sufficiency, enough, competency. *O. F.*

Suffisaunt, *adj.*, sufficient, able. *O. F.* soufisant.

Suffraunce, *n.*, longsuffering, patience. *O. F.* sufrance.

Suffraunt, *adj.*, patient, tolerant. *A. F.* suffrant.

Suffre, *v.*, suffer, permit. *O. F.* sufrir.

Suffyse, *v.*, suffice, be able. *O. F.* suffire.

Superfluitee, *n.*, superfluity, excess. *O. F.* superfluité.

Supprysed, *p. p.*, surprised. *From* Suppryse. *O. F.* souprendre.

Surcote, *n.*, surcoat, upper coat. *O. F.*

Surgerye, *n.*, surgery. *O. F.* surgerie.

Suspecioun, *n.*, suspicion. *O. F.* suspecion.

Suspect, *n.*, suspicion. *L. L.* suspectus.

Sustene, *v.*, sustain, support, maintain. *O. F.* sustenir.

Suster, *n.*, sister. *A. S.* swuster.

Sustren, *n.*, *plu.*, *see* Suster.

Sute, *n.*, *see* Suyte.

Suwe, *v.*, *see* Sewe.

Suyte, *n.*, suit, array, uniform pattern. *O. F.* siute.

Swal, *v.*, *pret. sing.*, *see* Swelle.

Swalowe, Swalwe, *n.*, swallow. *A. S.* swealwe.

Swappe, *n.*, swoop.

Swappe, *v.*, strike, dash.

Swapte, *v.*, *pret.*, *see* Swappe.

Swartish, *adj.*, darkish, dark.

Swatte, *v.*, *pret.*, *see* Swete.

Swelle, *v.*, swell. *A. S.* swellan.

Swelte, *v.*, die, languish. *A. S.* sweltan.

Swelwe, *v.*, swallow. *A. S.* swelgan.

Swerd, *n.*, sword. *A. S.* sweord.

Swere, *v.*, swear. *A. S.* swerian.

Swete, *adj.*, sweet. *A. S.* swēte.

Swete, *v.*, sweat. *A. S.* swǣtan.

Swetnesse, *n.*, sweetness. *A. S.* swētness *f.*

Sweven, *n.*, dream. *A. S.* swefen.

Sweynte, *p. p.* *as adj.*, tired out, exhausted, slothful. *From* Swenche. *A. S.* swencan.

Swich, *adj.*, such. *A. S.* swilc. **Swiche sevene,** seven times as many.

Swink, *n.*, labor, toil. *A. S.* (ge)swinc.

Swinke, *v.*, labor, toil. *A. S.* swincan.

Swinker, *n.*, laborer.

Swogh, *n.*, sough, low noise, murmur; swoon, state of collapse.

Swollen, *p. p.*, *see* Swelle.

Swommen, *v.*, *pret. plu.*, swam, were filled with swimming things. *From* Swimme. *A. S.* swimman.

Swonken, *p. p.*, *see* Swinke.

Swoor, *v.*, *pret. sing.*, *see* Swere.

Swote, *adj.*, sweet. *A. S.* swōt.

Swote, *adv.*, sweetly. *A. S.* swōte.

Swough, *n.*, *see* Swogh.

Swoune, *v.*, swoon, faint. *A. S.* swōgan.

Swow, *n.*, *see* Swogh.

Swowne, *v.*, *see* Swoune.

Swyn, *n.*, swine, boar. *A. S.* swin.

Swythe, *adv.*, quickly, immediately. *A. S.* swīðe.

Sy, *v.*, *pret. sing.*, saw. *From* See. *A. S.* sēon.

Syde, *n.*, side. *A. S.* sīde.

Sye, *v.*, sink down. *A. S.* sīgan.

Syghes, *n.*, *see* Syk.

Syk, *adj.*, sick. *A. S.* sēoc. *See* Seek.

Syk, *n.*, sigh.

Syke, *v.*, sigh. *A. S.* sīcan.

Sykliche, *adj.*, sickly, ill.

Syre, *n.*, *see* Sire.

Sythe, *n.*, time. *A. S.* sīð. **Ofte sythe,** oftentimes.

T

Tabard, *n.*, a short coat, sometimes sleeveless; the coat of a herald with a coat of arms. *O. F.*

Tabard, *the* Tabard Inn.

Tabernacle, *n.*, tabernacle, shrine. *F.*

Table, *n.*, table, tablet. *F.* Table dormant, permanent side table. Tables, *plu.*, tables, the game of "tables" or backgammon.

Tabreyde, To abreyde, *see* Abreyde.

Tabyde, To abyde, *see* Abyde.

Tacoye, To acoye, *see* Acoye.

Taffraye, To affraye, *see* Affraye.

Taille, *n.*, tally. *F.*

Tak, *v.*, *imper.*, take. *From* Take. *A. S.* tacan.

Takel, *n.*, tackle, archery-gear.

Tale, *n.*, tale, story, enumeration. *A. S.* talu.

Tale, *v.*, tell, talk, speak. *A. S.* talian.

Talent, *n.*, inclination, wish, desire. *O. F.*

Talighte, To alighte, *see* Alighte.

Tantale, Tantalus.

Tapicer, *n.*, upholsterer, maker of carpets. *O. F.* tapicier.

Tapite, *v.*, cover with tapestry. *O. F.* tapissier.

Tappestere, *n.*, female tapster, barmaid. *A. S.* tæppestre.

Tare, *n.*, tare, kind of weed.

Targe, *n.*, target, shield. *O. F.*

Tarraye, To arraye, *see* Arayed.

Tars, Tartarye, Tartary.

Taryinge, *s.*, tarrying, delay. *A. S.* tergan.

Tas, *n.*, heap. *O. F.*

Tassaille, To assaille.

Tassaye, To assaye, *see* Assaye.

Tassoille, To assoille, *see* Assoille.

Tast, *n.*, taste, relish for. *O. F.*

Taverne, *n.*, tavern. *O. F.*

Tecches, *n.*, *plu.*, evil qualities, defects. *O. F.* teche.

Teche, *v.*, teach, instruct, inform. *A. S.* tæcean.

Telle, *v.*, tell, recount, relate, count. *A. S.* tellan.

Tembrace, To embrace.

Teme, *v.*, bring. *A. S.* tēman.

Tempestous, *adj.*, tempestuous. *A. F.*

Temple, *n.*, temple, inn of court. *O. F.*

Tenbrace, To embrace, *see* Enbrace.

Tendre, *adj.*, tender. *O. F.*

Tendrely, *adv.*, tenderly.

Tendyte, To endyte, *see* Endyte.

Tene, *n.*, vexation, grief. *A. S.* tēona.

Tente, *n.*, tent. *O. F.*

Tentifly, *adv.*, attentively, carefully.

Tercel, *adj.*, male. *O. F.*

Tercelet, *n.*, male falcon. *O. F.* tiercelet.

Terciane, *adj.*, tertian, recurring every other day. *O. F.* tierçain.

Tere, *n.*, tear. *A. S.* tēar.

Tere, *v.*, tear. *A. S.* teran.

Tereus: *husband of Procne and Philomela.*

Terme, *n.*, set time, period, set phrase, limit. *O. F.*

Terme-day, *n.*, day appointed. *O. F.* terme—*A. S.* dæg.

Termyne, *v.*, determine, express in set terms. *F.* terminer.

Tertulan, Tertullian: *a Church Father* (*c. 155–c. 222*), *author of treatises on chastity.*

Tery, *adj.*, teary. *A. S.* tēarig.

Tespye, To espye, *see* Espye.

Testif, *adj.*, headstrong. *A. F.*

Tewnes, Tunis.

Thalighte, Thee alighte, *see* Alighte.

Thank, *n.*, expression of thanks. *A. S.* þanc. His thankes, of his free will, willingly.

Thanne, *adv.*, then, than. *A. S.* þanne.

Thapocalips, The Apocalypse.

Thaqueintaunce, The aqueintaunce, *see* Aqueyntaunce.

Thar, *v.*, *pres. sing.*, *impers.*, is

necessary, is needful. *A. S.* þurfan.

Tharivaile, The arivaile, *see* Arivaile.

Tharray, The array, *see* Aray.

Thascry, The ascry, *see* Ascry.

Thassay, The assay, *see* Assay.

Thassege, The assege, *see* Assege.

Thaventayle, The aventayle, *see* Aventaille.

Thavisioun, The avisioun, *see* Avisioun.

The, *pers. pron.*, thee.

Thee, *v.*, prosper, thrive. *A. S.* þēon.

Theef, *n.*, thief, robber. *A. S.* þēof.

Thembassadours, The embassadours, *see* Embassadour.

Then, *conj.*, than. *A. S.* þænne.

Thencens, The encens, *see* Encens.

Thencrees, The encrees, *see* Encrees.

Thende, The ende, *see* Ende.

Thenke, *v.*, think. *A. S.* þencan.

Thenne, *adv.*, then. *See* Thanne.

Thennes, *adv.*, thence, from that place.

Thentente, The entente, *see* Entente.

Thentree, The entree, *see* Entree.

Thenvyous, The envyous, *see* Envyous.

Theodamas, *probably* Thiodamas *in the* Thebaid (*viii, x*).

Theofraste, Theophrastus: *disciple of Aristotle, author of a treatise on marriage, of which a fragment is preserved in Jerome's treatise against Jovinian. See* Seint Ierome.

Ther, *adv.*, there, where, wherefore, wherever. *A. S.* þær.

Ther-aboute, *adv.*, concerned with that, about it, round it. *A. S.* þær—abūtan.

Ther-biforn, *adv.*, beforehand, previously. *A. S.* þær—beforan.

Therfro, *adv.*, therefrom.

Ther-inne, *adv.*, therein. *A. S.* þær—inne.

Ther-oute, *adv.*, out there, outside there. *A. S.* þær—ūte.

Thesiphone, Tisiphone: *a Fury*.

Thewes, *n.*, habit, natural quality, virtue. *A. S.* þēaw.

Thider, *adv.*, thither. *A. S.* þider.

Thiderward, *adv.*, thither.

Thikke, *adj.*, thick. *A. S.* þicce.

Thikke-herd, *adj.*, thick-haired.

Thilke, *pron.*, that same, that. *A. S.* þylc.

Thing, *n.*, thing, fact. *A. S.* þing. Make a thing, draw up a legal document.

Thinke, *v.*, seem. *A. S.* þyncan.

Thinne, *adj.*, thin. *A. S.* þynne.

Thirle, *v.*, pierce. *A. S.* þyrlian.

Tho, *pron.*, *plu.*, those. *A. S.* þā.

Tho, *adv.*, then, at that time. *A. S.* þā.

Thogh, *conj.*, though.

Thoght, *n.*, thought, anxiety. *A. S.* þōht.

Thoghte, *v.*, *pret.*, *see* Thenke, Thinke.

Tholosan, of Toulouse.

Thombe, *n.*, thumb. *A. S.* þūma.

Thonder, *n.*, thunder. *A. S.* þunor.

Thonke, *v.*, thank. *A. S.* þancian.

Thonour, The honour.

Thorgh, *prep.*, through. *A. S.* þurh.

Thorisoun, The orisoun, *see* Orisoun.

Thorp, *n.*, village. *A. S.* þorp.

Thought, *n.*, *see* Thoght.

Thoughte, *v.*, *pret.*, *see* Thenke, Thinke.

Thral, *n.*, thrall, slave, subject. *A. S.* þræl.

Thral, *adj.*, subject.

Thralle, *v.*, subject.

Thraste, *v.*, *pret.*, *see* Threste.

Thredbar, *adj.*, threadbare. *A. S.* þræd—bær.

Threed, *n.*, thread. *A. S.* þrǽd.

Threshfold, *n.*, threshold. *A. S.* þerscwold.

Thresshe, *v.*, thrash. *A. S.* þerscan.

Threste, *v.*, thrust, push. *A. S.* þrǽstan.

Threte, *v.*, threaten. *A. S.* þrēatian.

Thridde, *ord. num.*, third. *A. S.* þridda.

Thrift, *n.*, success, profit, welfare.

Thriftily, *adv.*, profitably, carefully.

Thrifty, *adj.*, profitable.

Thringe,*v.*, press. *A.S.* þringan.

Thriste, *v.*, thrust. *O. N.* þrȳsta *Cf.* Threste.

Throp, *n.*, *see* Thorp.

Throstel, *n.*, throstle, songthrush. *A. S.* þrostle.

Throte, *n.*, throat. *A. S.* þrotu.

Throwe, *n.*, while, period. *A. S.* þrāg *f.*

Throwes, *n.*, *plu.*, throes, torments. *A. S.* þraw.

Thrye, *adv.*, thrice. *A. S.* þriga.

Thryes, *adv.*, thrice.

Thryve, *v.*, thrive.

Thundringe, *n.*, thundering.

Thurfte, *v.*, *pret.*, *see* Thar.

Thurgh, *prep.*, *see* Thorgh.

Thurgh-darted, *p. p.*, transfixed with a dart.

Thurghfare, *n.*, thoroughfare. *A. S.* þurh—faru.

Thurgh-girt, *p. p.*, pierced through.

Thurghoute, *prep.*, throughout. *A. S.* þurh—ūte.

Thurgh-shoten, *p. p.*, shot through. *A.S.* þurh—scēotan.

Thurste, *v.*, thirst. *A. S.* þyrstan.

Thwyte, *v.*, whittle, cut up. *A. S.* þwītan.

Tideus, Tydeus.

Tikelnesse, *n.*, ticklishness, insecurity, uncertainty.

Tikle, *v.*, tickle.

Tipet, *n.*, tippet, cape. *A. S.* tæppet.

Tiptoon, *n.*, *plu.*, tiptoes. —*A. S.* tā.

Tissew, *n.*, tissue. *O. F.* tissu.

Tit, *v.*, *third pers. sing.*, *pres. indic.*, *see* Tyde.

Title, *n.*, title, name, pretence. *O. F.*

To, *adv.*, too. *A. S.*

Toas, Thoas.

To-bete, *v.*, beat severely. *A. S.* tō—bēatan.

To-breke, *v.*, break in pieces. *A. S.* tō—brecan.

To-breste, *v.*, burst in twain, break in pieces. *A. S.* tō—berstan.

To-cleve, *v.*, cleave in twain. *A. S.* tō—clēofan.

To-dasshed, *p. p.*, dashed violently, much bruised.

To-forn, *prep.*, before. *A. S.* tōforan.

Togeder, *adv.*, together. *A. S.* tō-gædere.

To-hange, *v.*, hang thoroughly, put to death by hanging. *A. S.* tō—hangian.

To-hewe, *v.*, hew in twain, cut in pieces. *A. S.* tō—hēawan.

Toke, *v.*, *second pers. sing.*, *pret. indic.*, tookest; *pret. plu.*, took. *From* Take. *A. S.* tacan. *See* Tak.

To-laughe, *v.*, laugh excessively. *A. S.* tō—hliehhan.

Tolle, *v.*, take toll.

Tombesteres, *n.*, *plu.*, female tumblers, dancing girls.

To-melte, *v.*, melt utterly. *A. S.* tō—meltan.

To-morwe, *n.*, to-morrow. *A. S.* tō—morgen.

Tonge, *n.*, tongue, speech. *A. S.* tunge.

Tonged, *adj.*, tongued.

Tonne, *n.*, tun, barrel. *A. S.* tunne.

Tonne-greet, *adj.*, great as a tun. *A. S.* tunne—grēat.

Toon, *n.*, *plu.*, toes. *A. S.* tā.

To-race, *v.*, tear in pieces.

Torche, *n.*, torch. *O. F.*

To-rende, *v.*, rend in twain,

rend in pieces. *A. S.* tō-rendan.

To-rente, *v., pret., see* To-rende.

Torets, *n., plu.*, rings on the collars of dogs. *O. F.* toret.

Torn, *n.*, turn. *A. F.* tourn.

Torne, *v.*, turn. *O. F.* torner.

Torney, *n.*, tourney. *O. F.* tornei.

To-shivered, *p. p.*, broken to pieces.

To-shrede, *v.*, cut into shreds. *A. S.* tō—scrēadian.

To-sterte, *v.*, start asunder, burst. *A. S.* styrtan.

To-swinke, *v.*, labor greatly. *A. S.* tō—swincan.

To-tere, *v.*, tear in pieces, rend. *A. S.* tōteran.

Tough, *adj.*, troublesome, pertinacious, difficult. *A. S.* tōh. Make it tough, be troublesome, be pertinacious.

Tombe, *n.*, tomb. *O. F.*

Toun, *n.*, town. *A. S.* tūn.

Tour, *n.*, tower. *O. F.* tur.

Touret, *n.*, turret. *O. F.* torete.

To-yere, *adv.*, this year. *A. S.* tō—gēar.

Trace, Thrace.

Trad, *v., pret. sing., see* Trede.

Traisoun, *n., see* Tresoun.

Traiterye, *n.*, treachery.

Tramissene, Tremessen: *a Moorish kingdom in Africa.*

Translate, *v.*, translate, change. *F.* translater.

Transmutacioun, *n.*, change. *F.* transmutation.

Transmuwe, *v.*, transform. *F.* transmuer.

Trappe, *n.*, trap, snare, trapdoor. *A. S.* treppe.

Trapped, *p. p.*, furnished with trappings.

Traunce, *n.*, trance. *O. F.* transe.

Traunce, *v.*, tramp about.

Travaile, *n.*, labor, toil. *O. F.* travaille.

Travaile, *v.*, labor. *O. F.* travaillier.

Trays, *n., plu.*, traces. *O. F.* trais.

Trayse, *v.*, betray. *O. F.* trair.

Trayteresse, *n.*, traitress. *O. F.* traitresse.

Traytour, *n.*, traitor. *O. F.* traitor.

Trecherye, *n.*, treachery, trickery. *O. F.* trecherie.

Trede, *v.*, tread. *A. S.* tredan.

Tregetour, *n.*, juggler, magician. *O. F.* tresgeteor.

Tresor, *n.*, treasure. *O. F.*

Tresorere, *n.*, treasurer. *O. F.* tresorier.

Tresorie, *n.*, treasury. *O. F.*

Tresoun, *n.*, treason, treachery. *O. F.* traison.

Tresse, *n.*, plait of hair, tress. *O. F.* trece.

Tretable, *adj.*, tractable, docile. *F.* traitable.

Trete, *v.*, treat, treat of, tell, discourse. *O. F.* traitier.

Tretee, *n.*, treaty. *O. F.* traitiê.

Tretis, *n.*, treaty, treatise, account. *A. F.* tretiz.

Tretys, *adj.*, graceful, well-proportioned. *O. F.* tretis.

Trewe, *adj.*, true, honest. *A. S.* trēowe.

Trewe, *n.*, truce. *A. S.* trēow *f.*

Trewely, Trewly, *adv.*, truly, certainly. *A. S.* trēowlīce.

Treye, *adj.*, three. *O. F.* trei.

Triacle, *n.*, sovereign remedy. *O. F.*

Trist, *n.*, trust.

Triste, *n.*, tryst, station. *O. F.*

Triste, *v.*, trust.

Troden, *v., pret. plu.; p. p.; see* Trede.

Trompe, *n.*, trumpet, trumpeter. *O. F.*

Tronchoun, *n.*, broken shaft of a spear. *O. F.* tronchon.

Trone, *n.*, throne. *O. F.*

Trotula: *this author has not been satisfactorily identified.*

Trouble, *adj.*, troubled, disturbed, anxious. *O. F.*

Trouthe, *n.*, truth, troth. *A. S.* trēowð *f.*

Trowe, *v.*, believe, trust. *A. S.* trēowian.

Troyan, Trojan.
Troyanisshe, Trojan.
Troye, Troy.
Trumpe, v., blow the trumpet. O. F. tromper.
Trussed, p. p., packed. O. F. trousser.
Truwe, n., see Trewe.
Tuel, n., pipe, slender chimney. O. F.
Tukked, p. p., tucked.
Tullius, M. Tullius Cicero.
Turkye, Turkey.
Turneyinge, s., tournament. O. F. torneier.
Turtel, n., turtle-dove. A. S. turtle.
Twelf, adj., twelve. A. S. twelf.
Twelfmonth, n., twelvemonth, year. A. S. twelf—mōnað.
Tweye, adj., two. A. S. twēgen.
Tweyne, adj., twain. A. S. twēgen.
Twigges, n., plu., twigs. A. S. twig.
Twight, p. p., twitched, distraught; Twighte, v., pret., twitched. From Twicche. A. S. twiccian.
Twinkeling, s., twinkling. A. S. twinclian.
Twinne, v., sever, part, separate.
Twyes, adv., twice.
Twyn, n., twine. A. S. twīn.
Twyne, v., twine.
Tyde, n., time, hour. A. S. tīd f.
Tyde, v., befall, happen. A. S. tīdan.
Tydinge, n., tiding, piece of news.
Tygre, n., tiger. O. F. tigre.
Tyme, n., time. A. S. tīma.
Tyraunt, n., tyrant. O. F. tirant.
Tythes, n., plu., tithes. A. S. tēoða.
Tytus, Dictys Cretensis: supposed warrior against Troy and author of a history of the Trojan war, of which the chief extant version is, if genuine, a fourth century Latin translation, the Ephemeris Belli Trojani.

U

Unavysed, p. p., unadvised, unaware. A. S. un—aviser.
Unbodie, v., leave the body.
Unbokele, v., unbuckle. A. S. un—F. bocler.
Unbrent, p. p., unburnt. A. S. un—O. N. brenna.
Unbroyden, p. p., unbraided. A. S. un—bregdan.
Uncommitted, p. p., not entrusted to one. A. S. un—L. committere.
Uncouth, adj., strange, foreign. A. S. uncūð.
Undergrowe, p. p. as adj., of short stature. A. S. under—grōwan.
Undern, n., about nine to ten in the morning. A. S.
Undernethe, prep., underneath.
Understonde, v., understand. A. S. understandan.
Undertake, v., undertake, affirm. A. S. under—tacan.
Undo, v., unfold, reveal, unfasten. A. S. undōn.
Unespyed, p. p., undetected. A. S. un—espier.
Unethe, Unethes, adv., scarcely, with difficulty. A. S. un—ēaðe.
Unfamous, adj., lost to fame, forgotten by fame. A. S. un—L. famosus.
Unfettre, v., unfetter, release.
Unholsom, adj., ailing, weak. A. S. un—hāl—sum.
Unkinde, adj., unnatural, cruel. A. S. un—cynde.
Unkist, adj., unkissed.
Unknowe, p. p., unknown. A. S. un—cnāwan.
Unkonning, adj., unskillful, stupid.
Unkouth, adj., see Uncouth.
Unmanhod, n., unmanly act. A. S. un—man—hād.
Unmerie, adj., sad. A. S. un—mirige.

Unnethe, Unnethes, *adv.*, *see* Unethe.

Unpinne, *v.*, unpin, unfasten.

Unreste, *n.*, unrest, restlessness. *A. S.* un—ræst *f.*

Unright, *n.*, wrong, injury.

Unsad, *adj.*, unsettled, unsteady, fickle. *A. S.* unsæd.

Unsely, *adj.*, unhappy, unfortunate. *A. S.* unsǽlig.

Unshette, *v.*, *pret.*, unlocked; *p. p.*, *as adj.*, not shut. *A. S.* un—scyttan.

Unsittinge, *pres. partic. as adj.*, unfit. *A. S.* un—sittan.

Unswelle, *v.*, decrease in fulness, subside. *A. S.* un—swellan.

Unswete, *adj.*, bitter. *A. S.* un—swēte.

Unteyd, *p. p.*, untied. *A. S.* untīgan.

Unthank, *n.*, want of thanks, the reverse of thanks. *A. S.* unþanc.

Unthrift, *n.*, extravagance, folly.

Unthrifty, *adj.*, profitless.

Untressed, *adj.*, not done up into tresses, unarranged.

Untrewe, *adj.*, untrue, false; *adv.*, untruly. *A. S.* untrēowe.

Untrouthe, *n.*, untruth, deceit, faithlessness. *A. S.* untrēowð *f.*

Unwar, *adj.*, unaware; *adv.*, unexpectedly. *A. S.* unwær.

Unwist, *adj.*, unknown, unwitting.

Unwitingly, *adv.*, unwittingly.

Unwrye, *v.*, uncover, reveal. *A. S.* unwrēon.

Unyolden, *p. p.*, without having yielded. *A. S.* un—gieldan.

Up, *prep.*, on, upon. *A. S.*

Up-born, *p. p.*, upborne, valued. *A. S.* up—beran.

Up-bounde, *p. p.*, bound up. *A. S.* up—bindan.

Up-breyde, *v.*, upbraid, reproach. *A. S.* up—bregdan.

Up-caste, *v.*, cast up, lift up. *A. S.* up—*O. N.* kasta.

Up-haf, *v.*, *pret. sing.*, uplifted.

From Up-heve. *A. S.* up—hebban.

Upright, *adv.*, upright, lying with the face upward. *A. S.* upriht.

Up-rist, *v.*, *third pers. sing.*, *pres. indic.*, rises up. *A. S.* up—rīsan.

Up-rist, *n.*, up-rising.

Upryght, *adv.*, *see* Upright.

Up-so-doun, *adv.*, upside down.

Upsterte, Upstirte, *v.*, *pret.*, started up, arose. *A. S.* up—styrtan.

Up-yaf, *v.*, *pret. sing.*, yielded up, gave. *From* Up-yeve. *A. S.* up—giefan.

Up-yolden, *p. p.*, yielded up. *From* Up-yelde. *A. S.* up—gieldan.

Urne, *n.*, urn. *L.* urna.

Usage, *n.*, usage, custom, habit. *O. F.*

Usaunce, *n.*, custom. *O. F.* usance.

Usure, *n.*, usury. *F.*

Uttereste, *adj.*; uttermost.

V

Vacacioun, *n.*, leisure, spare time. *O. F.* vacation.

Vache, *n.*, cow, beast. *O. F.*

Vache, Sir Philip la Vache: *a distinguished contemporary of Chaucer, — soldier, courtier, Knight of the Garter, keeper of the royal manor and park of Woodstock and of Chiltern, married to Elizabeth Clifford (daughter of Sir Lewis Clifford).*

Valence: Valence *near Lyons, France; or possibly a reference to Valenciennes lace.*

Valerie: *a reference to the Medieval Latin treatise "De non ducenda uxore" which was entitled* Epistola Valerii ad Rufinum.

Valeye, *n.*, valley. *O. F.* valée.

Vanisshinge, *s.*, vanishing. *O. F.* vanir.

Vanitee, *n.*, vanity, folly. *O. F.* vanité.

Variacioun, *n.*, variation, differ-
　ence. *O. F.* **variacion.**
Varie, *v.*, vary, change, shift.
　O. F. **varier.**
Vasselage, *n.*, prowess. *O. F.*
Vavasour, *n.*, sub-vassal, next
　in dignity to a baron. *O. F.*
　vavassour.
Venerye, *n.*, hunting. *O. F.*
　venerie.
Venim, *n.*, venom, poison. *O. F.*
Venimous, *adj.*, venomous, poi-
　sonous. *A. F.*
Venyse, Venice.
Ver, *n.*, the spring. *L.*
Verdit, *n.*, verdict. *O. F.*
Vermine, Vermyne, *n.*, vermin.
　A. F. **vermine** *f.*
Vernicle, *n.*, vernicle: *a small
　copy of the picture of Christ
　which was miraculously im-
　printed upon the handkerchief
　of Saint Veronica. O. F.*
Verray, Verrey, *adj.*, very, true.
　O. F. **verai.**
Verrayly, *adv.*, verily, truly.
Vers, *n.*, verse, line. *A. S.* **fers;**
　O. F. **vers.**
Vertu, *n.*, virtue, power. *A. F.*
Vertuous, *adj.*, virtuous. *O. F.*
Vese, *n.*, rush.
Vesulus, Monte Viso.
Veyl, *n.*, veil. *A. F.*
Veyn, *adj.*, vain, empty. *O. F.*
Veyne, *n.*, vein. *O. F.* **veine.**
Viage, *n.*, voyage, travel, jour-
　ney. *O. F.*
Vicair, *n.*, vicar, deputy. *A. F.*
　vicare.
Vicious, *adj.*, wicked. *O. F.*
Victorie, *n.*, victory. *O. F.*
Vigile, *n.*, vigil, wake. *A. F.*
Vigilies, *n.*, *plu.*, vigils, evening
　meetings on the eve of a
　festival. *L.* **vigilia.**
Vileinye, *n.*, villainy, wrong,
　shameful speech. *O. F.* **vil-
　einie.**
Virgile, Virgilius, Vergil.
Virginitee, *n.*, virginity. *A. F.*
　virginite.
Virgyle, *see* Virgile.
Visitaciouns, *n.*, *plu.*, visits. *A. F.*

Visyte, *v.*, visit. *O. F.* **visiter.**
Vitaille, *n.*, victuals, provisions.
　O. F.
Vois, *n.*, *see* Voys.
Vouche sauf, *v.*, vouchsafe, grant,
　permit. *O. F.* **vochier—sauf.**
Voyde, *v.*, get rid of, expel, de-
　part from. *O. F.* **voidier.**
Voys, *n.*, voice, report. *O. F.*
　vois.
Vulcano, Vulcanus, Vulcan.
Vyce, *n.*, fault, error. *A. F.*
Vyne, *n.*, vine. *O. F.* **vine.**

W

Waast, *n.*, waist.
Wade: *son of Weyland in Teu-
　tonic mythology. Wade and
　his boat are referred to in the
　Merchant's Tale, l. 1424.*
Wade, *v.*, wade, go, pass. *A. S.*
　wadan.
Wafereres, *n.*, *plu.*, makers of
　wafer-cakes, confectioners.
Waite, *v.*, wait, attend, watch.
　O. F. **waitier.**
Wake, *v.*, be awake, lie awake,
　watch, awake. *A. S.* **wacan.**
Wake-pleyes, *n.*, *plu.*, funeral
　games. —*A. S.* **plega.**
Waker, *adj.*, vigilant. *A. S.*
　wacor.
Wakned, *p. p.*, awakened. *A. S.*
　wæcnan.
Wal, *n.*, wall. *A. S.* **wcall.**
Walakye, Wallachia: *part of
　Roumania.*
Walsh-note, *n.*, walnut. *A. S.*
　wealhhnutu.
Walwe, *v.*, wallow, roll. *A. S.*
　wealwian.
Wanhope, *n.*, despair. *A. S.*
　wan—hopa.
Wanie, *v.*, wane. *A. S.* **wanian.**
Wante, *v.*, be wanting, be ab-
　sent, fail, lack. *O. N.* **vanta.**
Wantoun, *adj.*, unrestrained,
　wanton.
Wantownesse, *n.*, wantonness,
　willfulness.
War, *adj.*, prudent, discreet, cau-
　tious. *A. S.* **wær.**
Wardein, *n.*, warden. *O. F.*

Ware, *v.*, beware. *A. S.* warian.

Warente, *v.*, warrant, protect. *O. F.* warantir.

Warisshe, *v.*, cure, recover. *O. F.* warir.

Warly, *adv.*, warily.

Waryce, *v.*, *see* Warisshe.

Wasshe, *v.*, wash. *A. S.* wascan.

Wast, *n.*, waste. *O. F.*

Waste, *adj.*, *plu.*, wasted, partially destroyed. *O. F.* wast.

Wastel-breed, *n.*, cake-bread, bread of the finest quality. *O. F.* wastel—*A. S.* brēad.

Watering, *n.*, watering-place (for horses).

Waterlees, *adj.*, without water. *A. S.* wæterlēas.

Wawe, *n.*, wave.

Waxe, *v.*, wax, grow. *A. S.* weaxan.

Wayk, *adj.*, weak. *O. N.* veikr.

Wayke, *v.*, weaken, lessen.

Wayle, *v.*, wail.

Waymentinge, *s.*, lamentation. *O. F.* waimenter.

Wayte, *v.*, *see* Waite.

Webbe, *n.*, weaver. *A. S.* webba.

Wedde, *n.*, *dat.*, pledge. *A. S.* wedd.

Wede, *n.*, weed, robe. *A. S.* wæde.

Weder, *n.*, weather, storm. *A. S.*

Wedlok, *n.*, wedlock. *A. S.* wed-lāc.

Weel, *adv.*, well. *A. S.* wel. *See* Wel.

Weep, *v.*, *pret. sing.*, *see* Wepe.

Wel, *adv.*, well. *A. S. See* Weel.

Welawey, *interj.*, wellaway! alas!

Welcome, *adj.*, welcome. *A. S.* wilcuma.

Weldy, *adj.*, wieldy, active.

Wele, *n.*, weal, happiness, prosperity. *A. S.* wela.

Welfaringe, *pres. partic. as adj.*, thriving, prosperous. *A. S.* wel—faran.

Welk, *v.*, *pret. sing.*, walked. *From* Walke. *A. S.* wealcan.

Welked, *p. p.*, withered.

Welken, *n.*, welkin, heaven, sky. *A. S.* wolcen.

Welle, *n.*, well, source, spring. *A. S.* wella.

Welle-stremes, *n.*, *plu.*, well-springs. *A. S.* wella—strēam.

Wende, *v.*, go, pass. *A. S.* wendan.

Wene, *n.*, expectation, doubt. *A. S.* wēn *f.*

Wene, *v.*, ween, suppose, consider. *A. S.* wēnan.

Wenged, *adj.*, winged.

Went, *v.*, *third pers. sing.*, *pres. indic.; p. p.; see* Wende.

Wente, *v.*, *pret.*, *see* Wende.

Wente, *n.*, turn, path, passage.

Wepe, *v.*, weep. *A. S.* wēpan.

Wepen, *n.*, weapon. *A. S.* wǣpen.

Wer, *n.*, doubt, distress.

Werbul, *n.*, tune.

Werche, *v.*, work, perform, make. *A. S.* wyrcan.

Were, *n.*, weir. *A. S.* wer.

Were, *v.*, wear. *A. S.* werian.

Were, *v.*, defend. *A. S.* werian.

Werk, *n.*, work, act. *A. S.* werc.

Werke, *v.*, *see* Werche.

Werne, *v.*, refuse, warn off. *A. S.* wyrnan.

Werre, *n.*, war, tumult. *A. S.*

Werreye, *v.*, make war. *A. F.* werreier.

Wers, *adj.*, *adv.*, *compar.*, worse. *A. S.* wyrsa.

Werste, *adj.*, *superl.*, worst. *A. S.* wyrst.

Werte, *n.*, wart. *A. S.* wearte.

Wery, *adj.*, weary. *A. S.* wērig.

Wesh, Wessh, *v.*, *pret. sing.*, *see* Wasshe.

Weste, *v.*, turn to the west, draw near to the west.

Westre, *v.*, go to the west.

Wete, *adj.*, wet. *A. S.* wǣt.

Wex, *n.*, wax. *A. S.* weax.

Wex, *v.*, *pret. sing.*, *see* Waxe.

Wexe, *v.*, *see* Waxe.

Wey, *n.*, way. *A. S.* weg.

Weye, *v.*, weigh. *A. S.* wegan.

Weylaway, Weylawey, *interj.*, *see* Welawey.

Weymentinge, *s.,* *see* **Way-mentinge.**

Weyve, *v.,* waive, neglect, put aside. *O. F.* weiver.

Whan, *adv.,* when. *A. S.* **hwanne.**

Whenne, *adv.,* whence. *A. S.* **hwanon.**

Wher, *adv.,* where. *A. S.* **hwǣr.**

Wher, *contracted form of* **Whether.**

Wher-as, *adv.,* where that, where.

Wherfore, *adv.,* *conj.,* wherefore. *A. S.* **hwǣr—fore.**

Wherin, *adv.,* wherein, in which.

Wher-so, *adv.,* whether, wheresoever.

Wher-through, *adv.,* by means of which.

Wherto, *adv.,* for what purpose, why.

Whete, *n.,* wheat. *A. S.* **hwǣte.**

Whetston, *n.,* whet-stone. *A. S.* **hwetstān.**

Whette, *p. p.,* *plu.,* whetted. *A. S.* **hwettan.**

Whider, *adv.,* whither. *A. S.* **hwider.**

Whippe, *n.,* whip.

Whippeltree, *n.,* cornel-tree or dogwood.

Whistelinge, *s.,* whistling sound. *A. S.* **hwistlian.**

Who-so, *pron.,* whoever.

Whyl, *conj.,* while. *A. S.* **hwīl.**

Whyle, *n.,* while, time. *A. S.* **hwīl** *f.*

Whyles, *n.,* *gen. sing. as adv., see* **Whyle.**

Whylom, *adv.,* once, formerly.

Whyt, *adj.,* white. *A. S.* **hwīt.**

Whyte, *v.,* whiten, grow white.

Whytter, *adj.,* *compar., see* **Whyt.**

Widwe, *n.,* widow. *A. S.* **widuwe.**

Wierdes, *n.,* *plu.,* fates. *A. S.* **wyrd.**

Wight, *n.,* person, creature, man. *A. S.* **wiht.**

Wighte, *n.,* weight. *A. S.* **wiht** *f.* (?)

Wike, *n.,* *see* **Wouke.**

Wikke, *adj.,* evil, wicked, bad.

Wikkedly, *adv.,* wickedly.

Wikkednesse, *n.,* wickedness.

Wil, *n.,* *see* **Wille.**

Wil, *v.,* first and third pers. sing., pres. indic., will. *A. S.* **willan.** *See* **Wol.**

Wilfully, *adv.,* willingly, of free will, purposely.

Wille, *n.,* own accord, will, desire. *A. S.* **will; willa.**

Wilne, *v.,* desire, wish. *A. S.* **wilnian.**

Wilow, *n.,* willow-tree. *A. S.* **welig.**

Wiltow, *v.,* *pron.,* second pres. sing., pres. indic., wilt thou. *See* **Wil.**

Wimpel, *n.,* wimple; *a covering for the head, gathered round it and plaited under the chin. A. S.*

Wind-melle, *n.,* wind-mill. *A. S.* **wind—myln.**

Windowe, *n.,* window. *O. N.* **vindauga.**

Winke, *v.,* wink, shut the eyes, fall asleep. *A. S.* **wincian.**

Winne, *v.,* win, gain, attain to. *A. S.* **winnan.**

Winning, *s.,* gain, profit.

Wirche, *v.,* *see* **Werche.**

Wis, *adv.,* certainly, surely. *A. S.* **wiss.**

Wisly, *adv.,* certainly, surely. *A. S.* **wisslīce.**

Wisse, *v.,* instruct, guide. *A. S.* **wissian.**

Wisshe, *v.,* wish. *A. S.* **wyscan.**

Wist, *p. p.;* **Wiste,** *v.,* pret.; *see* **Wite.**

Wit, *n.,* reason, understanding, intelligence. *A. S.*

Wite, *v.,* know, wit. *A. S.* **witan.**

Withholde, *v.,* retain, shut up. *A. S.* **wið—healdan.**

With-inne, *adv.,* within. *A. S.* **wiðinnan.**

Withoute, Withouten, *adv.,* *prep.,* without. *A. S.* **wiðūtan.**

Withseye, *v.,* contradict, gainsay. *A. S.* **wiðsecgan.**

Witinge, *s.,* knowledge. *See* **Wite.** *A. S.* **witan.**

Wlatsom, *adj.,* loathsome, heinous. *A. S.* **wlǣtta—sum.**

Wo, *n.,* woe. *A. S.* **wā.**

Wode, n., wood. A. S. wudu.

Wode-binde, n., woodbine. A. S. wudubinde.

Wode-craft, n., woodcraft. A. S. wudu—cræft.

Wodnesse, n., see Woodnesse.

Wol, v., first and third pers. sing., pres. indic., will, desire. A. S. willan. See Wil.

Wolde, v., pret., see Wol.

Wolle, n., wool. A. S. wulle.

Woln, v., pres. plu., see Wol.

Wombe, n., belly. A. S. womb f.

Womman, n., woman. A. S. wīfman.

Wommanhede, n., womanhood. A. S. wīfman—hād.

Wommanliche, adj., womanly. A. S. wīfman—līce.

Wommannisshe, adj., plu., wommanish. A. S. wīfman—isc.

Wonder, adj., wonderful; adv., wondrously. A. S. wundor.

Wonderly, adv., wondrously, strangely.

Wondre, v., wonder. A. S. wundrian.

Wone, n., custom, usage. A. S. gewuna.

Wone, v., dwell, inhabit. A. S. wunian.

Woning, s., habitation, house. A. S. wunung.

Wood, adj., mad, raving. A. S. wōd.

Woodly, adv., madly.

Woodnesse, n., madness, rage. A. S. wōdness f.

Wook, v., pret. sing., see Wake.

Woon, n., resource, retreat, shelter, dwelling.

Woot, v., first pers. sing., pres. indic., see Wite.

Worcheth, v., third pers. sing., pres. indic., see Werche.

Worching, s., working, influence. See Worcheth.

Word, n., word. A. S.

Word and ende, beginning and end. A. S. ord. See Ende.

Worm, n., worm, snake. A. S. wurm.

Worm-foul, n., birds which eat worms. A. S. wurm—fugol.

Worship, n., praise, honor, dignity. A. S. weorðscipe.

Worshipe, v., reverence, respect.

Worshipful, adj., respected, worthy of honor.

Wortes, n., plu., herbs. A. S. wyrt.

Worthe, v., become, be. A. S. weorðan.

Worthinesse, n., worth, worthiness.

Wost, v., second pers. sing., pres. indic., see Wite.

Wostow, v., pron., second pers. sing., pres. indic., see Wite.

Wot, v., first pers. sing., pres. indic., see Wite.

Woukc, n., week. A. S. wucu.

Wounde, n., wound, plague. A. S. wund f.

Wowe, v., woo. A. S. wōgian.

Woxen, p. p., see Waxe.

Wrappe, v., wrap, cover.

Wrastling, s., wrestling. A. S. wrastlian.

Wrathe, v., render angry. A. S. gewrāðian.

Wratthe, n., anger, wrath. A. S. wræððo.

Wratthed, p. p., see Wrathe.

Wrecche, n., wretch, sorrowful creature. A. S. wrecca.

Wrecche, adj., wretched.

Wreche, n., vengeance, punishment. A. S. wræc f.

Wree, v., cover, clothe. A. S. wrēon.

Wreeth, n., wreath. A. S. wræð.

Wreke, v., wreak, avenge. A. S. wrecan.

Wreker, n., avenger.

Wreste, v., constrain, force. A. S. wræstan.

Wreye, v., bewray, reveal. A. S. wrēgan.

Wrighte, n., workman. A. S. wyrhta.

Wringe, v., wring, squeeze, force. A. S. wringan.

Writ, v., third pers. sing., pres. indic., see Wryte.

Wroght, *p. p.;* Wroghte, *v., pret., see* Werche.

Wroken, *p. p., see* Wreke.

Wrong, *n.,* wrong. *A. S.* wrang. Had wrong, was wrong.

Wroot, *v., pret. sing., see* Wryte.

Wrooth, *adj.,* wroth, angry. *A. S.* wrāð.

Wrought, *p. p.;* Wroughte, *v., pret., see* Werche.

Wrye, *v.,* cover, clothe, hide. *A. S.* wrēon. *See* Wree.

Wrye, *v.,* turn aside, turn, go. *A. S.* wrigian.

Wryte, *v.,* write. *A. S.* wrītan.

Wryting, *n.,* writing. *A. S.* wrīting.

Wyd, *adj.,* wide. *A. S.* wīd.

Wyde, *adv.,* widely, far. *A. S.* wīde.

Wyf, *n.,* woman, wife. *A. S.* wīf.

Wyfly, *adv.,* womanly, wife-like. *A. S.* wīflīc.

Wyke, *n., see* Wouke.

Wyle, *n.,* wile, plot, guile.

Wyn, *n.,* wine. *A. S.* wīn.

Wyped, *v., pret.,* wiped. *From* Wype. *A. S.* wīpian.

Wyr, *n.,* wire. *A. S.* wīr.

Wys, *adj.,* wise, prudent. *A. S.* wīs. Make it wys, make it a subject for deliberation, hesitate.

Wyse, *n.,* way, manner. *A. S.* wīse.

Wyoly, *adv.,* wisely.

Wyte, *n.,* blame, reproach. *A. S.* wīte.

Wyte, *v.,* blame, reproach. *A. S.* wītan.

Wyve, *v.,* wive, marry. *A. S.* wīfian.

Wyves, *n., gen., see* Wyf.

Y

Yaf, *v., pret. sing., see* Yeve.

Yate, *n.,* gate. *A. S.* geat.

Yave, *v., pret., see* Yeve.

Y-bathed, *p. p.,* bathed. *A. S.* baðian.

Y-been, *p. p.,* been. *See* Ben.

Y-beten, *p. p.,* beaten, forged. *See* Bete.

Y-blent, *p. p.,* blinded. *See* Blende.

Y-blowe, *p. p.,* blown. *A. S.* blāwan.

Y-boren, *p. p.,* born. *See* Bere.

Y-bought, *p. p.,* bought. *See* Beye.

Y-bounden, *p. p.,* bound. *From* Binde. *A. S.* bindan.

Y-brend, Y-brent, *p. p.,* burnt. *See* Brenne.

Y-broght, *p. p.,* brought. *See* Broght.

Y-broken, *p. p.,* broken. *See* Breke.

Y-buried, *p. p.,* buried. *A. S.* byrgan.

Y-caried, *p. p.,* carried. *F.* charrier.

Y-chaped, *p. p.,* furnished with chapes or metal caps (which were placed at the end of the sheath).

Y-cheyned, *p. p.,* chained.

Y-clenched, *p. p.,* clinched, riveted. *A. S.* clencan.

Y-cleped, *p. p.,* called, named. *A. S.* cleopian.

Y-closed, *p. p.,* closed.

Y-clothed, *p. p.,* clothed. *A. S.* claðian.

Y-comen, *p. p.,* come. *See* Com.

Y-corven, *p. p.,* cut. *See* Kerve.

Y-coyned, *p. p.,* coined. *O. F.* coignier.

Y-crammed, *p. p.,* crammed. *A. S.* crammian.

Y-crased, *p. p.,* cracked, broken.

Y-darted, *p. p.,* pierced with a dart.

Ydel, *adj.,* idle, empty, vain. *A. S.* idel.

Ydelly, *adv.,* idly.

Ydelnesse, *n.,* idleness. *A. S.* idelness *f.*

Y-doon, *p. p.,* done. *See* Do.

Y-drawe, *p. p.,* drawn. *See* Drow.

Y-dressed, *p. p.,* dressed, arranged. *See* Dresse.

Y-driven, *p. p.,* driven. *See* Dryve.

Y-dropped, *p. p.,* covered with drops. *A. S.* **dropan.**

Yë, *n.,* eye. *A. S.* **ēage.**

Ye, *adv.,* yea.

Yeddinges, *n., plu.,* songs. *A. S.* **geddung** *f.*

Yede, *v., pret.,* walked, went. *A. S.* **ēode.**

Yeer, *n.,* year. *A. S.* **gēar.**

Yef, *v., imper. sing., see* **Yeve.**

Yelde, *v.,* yield, pay. *A. S.* **gildan.**

Yeldhalle, *n.,* guild-hall. *A. S.* **gield—heall** *f.*

Yelding, *s.,* produce. *A. S.* **gildan.**

Yelleden, *v., pret. plu.,* yelled. *From* **Yelle.** *A. S.* **giellan.**

Yelownesse, *n.,* yellowness.

Yelpe, *v.,* boast, prate. *A. S.* **gilpan.**

Yelt, *v., third pers. sing., pres. indic., see* **Yelde.**

Yelwe, *adj.,* yellow. *A. S.* **geolu.**

Yeman, *n.,* yeoman.

Yemanly, *adv.,* in a yeomanlike manner.

Yën, *n., plu., see* **Yë.**

Yerd, *n.,* yard, garden. *A. S.* **geard.**

Yerde, *n.,* rod, stick. *A. S.* **gerd** *f.*

Yere, *n., dat., see* **Yeer.**

Yerne, *adj.,* eager, brisk, lively. *A. S.* **georn.**

Yerne, *adv.,* eagerly, quickly, soon. *A. S.* **georne.**

Yerne, *v.,* yearn for, desire. *A. S.* **gyrnan.**

Yeve, *v.,* give. *A. S.* **giefan.** *See* **Yive.**

Y-fallen, *p.p.,* fallen. *See* **Falle.**

Y-faren, *p. p.,* gone. *See* **Fare.**

Y-fere, *adv.,* together.

Y-fetered, *p. p.,* fettered. *A. S.* **feterian.**

Y-feyned, *p.p.,* feigned, invented, feigned to be done, pretended. *See* **Feyne.**

Y-finde, *v.,* find. *A. S.* **gefindan.**

Y-folowed, *p. p.,* followed. *See* **Folwe.**

Y-formed, *p. p.,* formed. *F.* **former.**

Y-fostred, *p. p.,* fostered. *See* **Fostre.**

Y-founde, *p. p., see* **Y-finde.**

Y-founded, *p. p.,* founded, based. *F.* **fonder.**

Y-glased, *p. p.,* glazed.

Y-goon, *p. p.,* gone. *See* **Goon.**

Y-graunted, *p. p.,* granted. *See* **Graunte.**

Y-grave, *p. p.,* dug up, cut, engraved, buried. *See* **Grave.**

Y-grounde, *p. p.,* ground, sharpened. *See* **Grint.**

Y-grounded, *p. p.,* grounded.

Y-halowed, *p. p.,* view-hallooed. *O. F.* **halloer.**

Y-hed, *p. p.,* hidden. *See* **Hyde.**

Y-hent, *p. p.,* seized, caught. *See* **Hente.**

Y-here, *v.,* hear. *A. S.* **gehȳran.**

Y-heried, *p. p.,* praised. *A. S.* **geherian.**

Y-hurt, *p. p.,* hurt.

Y-hight, *p. p.,* called. *See* **Hote.**

Y-holde, *p. p.,* held, esteemed, restrained. *See* **Holde.**

Y-iaped, *p. p.,* jested. *See* **Iape.**

Yif, *conj.,* if. *A. S.* **gif.**

Yif, *v., imper. sing., see* **Yive.**

Yifte, *n.,* gift. *A. S.* **gift** *f.*

Yis, yes (*emphatic*). *A. S.* **gise.**

Yit, *adv.,* yet, nevertheless. *A. S.* **giet.**

Yive, *v.,* give. *A. S.* **giefan.** *See* **Yeve.**

Y-kist, *p. p.,* kissed. *A. S.* **cyssan.** *See* **Kesse.**

Y-knowe, *v.,* know, recognize. *A. S.* **gecnāwan.**

Y-korven, *p. p.,* cut. *See* **Kerve.**

Y-lad, *p. p.,* led. *See* **Lede.**

Y-laft, *p. p.,* left. *See* **Leve.**

Y-liche, *adj., plu., see* **Y-lyk.**

Y-liche, *adv.,* alike, similarly. *A. S.* **gelīce.** *See* **Y-lyke.**

Y-lissed, *p. p.,* eased. *See* **Lisse.**

Y-lived, *p. p.,* lived. *A. S.* **libban.**

Y-logged, *p. p.,* lodged. *O. F.* **logier.**

Y-lorn, *p. p.,* lost. *A. S.* **lēosan.**

Y-loved, *p. p.,* loved. *A. S.* **lufian.**

Y-lyk, *adj.*, like, alike. *A. S.* gelic. *See* **Y-liche.**

Y-lyke, *adv.*, alike, equally. *A. S.* gelíce. *See* **Y-liche.**

Y-maad, *p. p.*, made, caused. *See* **Make, Y-maked.**

Ymageries, *n.*, *plu.*, images, carved work. *O. F.* imagerie.

Y-maked, *p. p.*, made. *See* **Make, Y-maad.**

Y-marked, *p. p.*, marked. *A. S.* mearcian.

Y-ment, *p. p.*, intended. *See* **Mene.**

Y-met, *p. p.*, met. *See* **Mete.**

Y-meynd, *p. p.*, mixed, mingled. *From* **Menge.** *A. S.* mengan.

Y-mused, *p. p.*, mused, reflected. *See* **Muse.**

Y-nogh, *adj.*, enough, sufficient; *adv.*, enough, sufficiently. *A. S.* genōh.

Y-nome, *p. p.*, caught, overcome. *From* **Nime.** *A. S.* niman. *See* **Nome.**

Y-norisshed, *p. p.*, educated, nurtured. *O. F.* norir.

Yok, *n.*, yoke. *A. S.* geoc.

Yolden, *p. p.*, see **Yelde.**

Yolle, *v.*, yell, cry out.

Yond, *adv.*, yonder. *A. S.* geond.

Yong, *adj.*, young. *A. S.* geong.

Yore, *adv.*, formerly, of old. *A. S.* gēara.

Youling, *ø.*, howling, loud lamentation.

Youthe, *n.*, youth. *A. S.* geoguð f.

Yow, *pron.*, *dat.*, *accus.*, you. *A. S.* ēow (*dat.*, *accus.*, *of* gē).

Y-payed, *p. p.*, paid. *See* **Paye.**

Ypermistre, Hypermnestra: *Danaus's daughter, saved her husband's life.*

Y-pleyned, *p. p.*, complained. *See* **Pleyne.**

Y-pleynted, *p. p.*, full of complaint.

Ypocras, Hippocrates: *a Greek physician of the fifth century B. C.*

Ypocras, *n.*, a kind of cordial.

Y-prayed, *p. p.*, invited. *See* **Preye.**

Y-preised, *p. p.*, praised. *See* **Preise.**

Y-preved, *p. p.*, proved. *See* **Preve.**

Y-punisshed, *p. p.*, punished. *F.* punir.

Y-raft, *p. p.*, bereft, snatched away. *See* **Reve.**

Yre, *n.*, ire, anger. *F.* ire.

Y-red, *p. p.*, read. *See* **Rede.**

Yren, *n.*, iron. *A. S.* īren.

Y-rent, *p. p.*, torn, taken. *A. S.* rendan.

Y-ronge, *p. p.*, rung. *A. S.* hringan.

Y-ronne, *p. p.*, run, run together. *A. S.* rinnan. *See* **Renne.**

Y-rouned, *p. p.*, whispered. *See* **Roune.**

Y-sayd, *p. p.*, said. *See* **Seye.**

Yse, *n.*, *dat.*, ice. *A. S.* īs.

Y-see, *v.*, see, behold. *A. S.* gesēon.

Y-sene, *adj.*, visible. *A. S.* gesēne. *See* **Sene.**

Y-sent, *p. p.*, sent. *A. S.* sendan.

Y-served, *p. p.*, served. *O. F.* servir.

Y-set, *p. p.*, set, placed. *A. S.* settan.

Y-seye, *p. p.*, see **Y-see.**

Y-seyled, *p. p.*, sailed. *A. S.* seglian.

Y-shapen, *p. p.*, prepared. *See* **Shape.**

Y-shave, *p. p.*, shaven. *A. S.* sceafan.

Y-shette, *p. p.*, *plu.*, shut. *See* **Shette.**

Y-shewed, *p. p.*, shown. *See* **Shewe.**

Y-shorn, *p. p.*, shorn. *From* **Shere.** *A. S.* sceran.

Y-shriven, *p. p.*, shriven. *A. S.* scrīfan.

Ysiphile, Hypsipyle: *loved and deserted by Jason.*

Y-slawe, Y-slayn, *p. p.*, slain. *See* **Slee.**

Y-songe, *p. p.*, sung. *A. S.* singan.

Y-sought, *p. p.*, sought. *See* Seke.

Y-sowen, *p. p.*, sown. *See* Sowe.

Y-sprad, *p. p.*, spread. *See* Sprede. *Cf.* Sprad.

Y-spreynd, *p. p.*, sprinkled. *See* Springe (*weak*). *Cf.* Spreynd.

Y-spronge, *p. p.*, sprung, shot out, divulged. *See* Springe (*strong*). *Cf.* Spronge.

Y-stalled, *p. p.*, installed.

Y-stiked, *p. p.*, stuck, stabbed. *See* Stike.

Y-stonde, *p. p.*, stood, been. *See* Stonde.

Y-stonge, *p. p.*, stung. *See* Stongen.

Y-storve, *p. p.*, dead. *See* Sterve.

Y-suffred, *p. p.*, suffered. *O. F.* sufrir.

Y-sworn, *p. p.*, sworn. *See* swere.

Y-take, *p. p.*, taken. *See* Tak.

Y-taught, *p. p.*, taught. *See* Teche.

Y-thee, *v.*, thrive. *A. S.* geþēon.

Y-thewed, *p. p.*, disposed, mannered.

Y-thonked, *p. p.*, thanked. *See* Thonke.

Y-throwe, *p. p.*, thrown. *A. S.* þrāwan.

Y-tressed, *p. p.*, plaited in tresses.

Y-turned, *p. p.*, turned. *A. S.* turnian.

Yve, *n.*, *see* Erbe.

Yvel, *adj.*, evil, ill. *A. S.* yfel.

Yvel, *adv.*, evilly, ill. *A. S.* yfele.

Yvoire, *n.*, ivory. *O. F.* ivoire.

Y-war, *adj.*, aware. *A. S.* gewær.

Y-warned, *p. p.*, warned. *A. S.* warnian. *See* Werne.

Y-waxen, *p. p.*, grown, become. *See* Waxe.

Y-wedded, *p. p.*, wedded. *A. S.* weddian.

Y-went, *p. p.*, gone. *See* Wende.

Y-wimpled, *p. p.*, provided with a wimple.

Y-wis, *adv.*, certainly, truly. *A. S.* gewis.

Y-wonne, *p. p.*, gained, won. *See* Winne.

Y-writen, *p. p.*, written. *See* Wryte.

Y-wroght, *p. p.*, wrought, made. *See* Werche. *Cf.* Wroght.

Y-wroken, *p. p.*, avenged. *See* Wreke. *Cf.* Wroken.

Y-wryen, *p. p.*, hidden. *See* Wrye.

Y-yive, *p. p.*, given. *See* Yive.

Z

Zanzis, Zeuxis: *a Greek painter of about 420–390 B. C.*

Zeles, *n.*, *plu.*, zeal. *F.* zèle.

Zephirus, Zephyr: *the west wind.*

Canterbury Tales.

wrote this at age of 50 — old enough to see
limitations of his earlier work

got the idea from Decameron

Chaucer's home on road to Canterbury — his
opportunity to observe all classes of people

has painted in brief the whole picture of
England. Abounds in satire
throout.

In the prol. Chaucer's art at its highest —
concentration, much in little.

Chaucer leaned heavily on other writers
yet never imitated other people's,